www.wadsworth.com

www.wadsworth.com is the World Wide Web site for Thomson Wadsworth and is your direct source to dozens of online resources.

At www.wadsworth.com you can find out about supplements, demonstration software, and student resources. You can also send email to many of our authors and preview new publications and exciting new technologies.

www.wadsworth.com
Changing the way the world learns®

Seventh Edition

Evolution and Prehistory

The Human Challenge

WILLIAM A. HAVILAND
University of Vermont

DANA WALRATH
University of Vermont

HARALD E. L. PRINS
Kansas State University

BUNNY McBRIDE
Kansas State University

WADSWORTH
THOMSON LEARNING™

Australia • Canada • Mexico • Singapore • Spain •
United Kingdom • United States

WADSWORTH
THOMSON LEARNING™

Senior Acquisitions Editor: Lin Marshall
Assistant Editor: Nicole Root
Editorial Assistant: Kelly McMahon
Technology Project Manager: Dee Dee Zobian
Marketing Manager: Matthew Wright
Marketing Assistant: Tara Pierson
Advertising Project Manager: Linda Yip
Project Manager, Editorial Production: Catherine Morris
Art Director: Robert Hugel
Print/Media Buyer: Rebecca Cross
Permissions Editor: Kiely Sexton
Production Service: Robin Lockwood Productions
Text Designer: Lisa Buckley
Photo Researchers: Sandra Lord, Sue Howard
Copy Editor: Jennifer Gordon
Illustrator: Carol Zuber-Mallison
Cover Designer: Larry Didona
Cover Image: Large photo: Joseph Van Os/Getty Images. Small photos, clockwise from top left: Manoj Shah/Getty Images, Corbis, Corbis, Tipp Howell/Getty Images, Archivo Iconografico S.A./Corbis, Annie Griffiths Belt/Corbis
Compositor: New England Typographic Service
Text and Cover Printer: Transcontinental Printing/Interglobe

Printed in Canada
2 3 4 5 6 7 08 07 06

Library of Congress Control Number: 2003116264

Student Edition: ISBN 0-534-61016-1

Thomson Wadsworth
10 Davis Drive
Belmont, CA 94002-3098
USA

Asia
Thomson Learning
5 Shenton Way #01-01
UIC Building
Singapore 068808

Australia/New Zealand
Thomson Learning
102 Dodds Street
Southbank, Victoria 3006
Australia

Canada
Nelson
1120 Birchmount Road
Toronto, Ontario M1K 5G4
Canada

Europe/Middle East/Africa
Thomson Learning
High Holborn House
50/51 Bedford Row
London WC1R 4LR
United Kingdom

Latin America
Thomson Learning
Seneca, 53
Colonia Polanco
11560 Mexico D.F.
Mexico

Spain/Portugal
Paraninfo
Calle Magallanes, 25
28015 Madrid, Spain

Dedicated to

Anita de Laguna Haviland
whose efforts have helped sustain
this ever-evolving text for three decades.

About the Authors

Dr. William A. Haviland is Professor Emeritus at the University of Vermont, where he has taught since 1965. He holds a Ph.D. in Anthropology from the University of Pennsylvania and has published widely on archaeological, ethnological, and physical anthropological research carried out in Guatemala, Maine, and Vermont. Haviland is a member of many professional societies, including the American Anthropological Association and the American Association for the Advancement of Science. He has participated in many projects, including "Gender and the Anthropological Curriculum," sponsored by the American Anthropological Association in 1988.

Dr. Haviland, who has always loved teaching and writing for anthropology students was also the technical advisor for the telecourse, Faces of Culture. He has a passionate interest in indigenous rights; he worked with the Maya and Abenaki for years. He continues to work with Native Americans in the northeastern United States, does consulting, and participates in international conferences on urbanization in Mesoamerica. He is also co-editor of the series: *Tikal Reports*.

Dr. Harald Prins is Professor of Anthropology at Kansas State University. Born and raised in the Netherlands, Prins was academically trained in prehistoric archaeology, social anthropology, and comparative history at various universities in the Netherlands and the United States. He has a doctoraal degree from the University of Nijmegen and a Ph.D. from the New School for Social Research. Prins has done extensive fieldwork among indigenous peoples in South and North America. Before joining the faculty at Kansas State University in 1990, he taught at Nijmegen, Bowdoin, and Colby. He typically teaches classes on American Indians (North/South), Anthropological Theory, Ethnohistory, Visual Anthropology, Native Rights, and Introduction to Anthropology. Also professionally trained in filmmaking, Prins has consulted on numerous films, juried documentary film festivals, and served as president of the Society for Visual Anthropology (1999–2001) as well as visual anthropology editor of the journal *American Anthropologist*. His own film work includes co-producing *Our Lives in Our Hands,* a documentary on Mi'kmaq Indians and *Oh, What a Blow That Phantom Gave Me!,* about media ecology pioneer Edmund Carpenter.

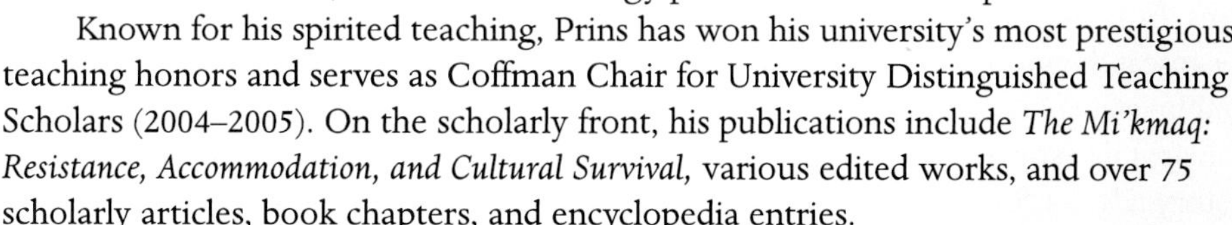

Known for his spirited teaching, Prins has won his university's most prestigious teaching honors and serves as Coffman Chair for University Distinguished Teaching Scholars (2004–2005). On the scholarly front, his publications include *The Mi'kmaq: Resistance, Accommodation, and Cultural Survival,* various edited works, and over 75 scholarly articles, book chapters, and encyclopedia entries.

Committed to balancing teaching and scholarship with native rights advocacy, Dr. Prins played an instrumental role in the successful federal recognition and land claims case of the Aroostook Band of Micmacs and served as expert witness in several Mi'kmaq native rights cases in the U.S. Senate and Canadian courts.

Dr. Dana Walrath is an Assistant Professor of Medicine and a Women's Studies affiliated faculty member at the University of Vermont. She earned a Ph.D. in 1997 from the University of Pennsylvania in medical and biological anthropology. In her doctoral research, Walrath developed novel synthetic techniques and theories for the interpretation of the evolution of human childbirth. Her interests span biocultural aspects of reproduction, genetics, and evolutionary medicine. Her publications have appeared in *Current Anthropology, American Anthropologist,* and *American Journal of Physical Anthropology*. Walrath's work and writings often focus upon the conceptual relationship between evolutionary research and feminism.

Dr. Walrath has received grants and fellowships from the National Science Foundation, Health Resources and Services Administration, the Center for Disease

Control, Foreign Languages Area Studies, the University of Pennsylvania, and the New York Foundation for the Arts. Research sites have ranged from fieldwork at an Aurignacian site in France, to the Marine Biological Laboratory in Woods Hole, Massachusetts, to biomedical settings.

Dr. Walrath's diverse experience includes work in Yemen, Egypt, and Armenia contributing to her research and writing on her Armenian heritage. Before joining the faculty at the University of Vermont in 2000, she taught at the University of Pennsylvania, Temple University, and the Mohamed Ali Othman School in Taiz, Yemen. For the University of Vermont's College of Medicine she has developed an innovative program that brings anthropological perspectives into the study of medicine. She is presently serving on a national committee to develop women's health care learning objectives for medical education sponsored by the Association of Professors of Obstetrics and Gynecology.

Bunny McBride is an award-winning author with a master's degree in Anthropology from Columbia University. Her books include *Women of the Dawn, Molly Spotted Elk: A Penobscot in Paris,* and *Our Lives in Our Hands: Micmac Indian Basketmakers.* Working in close collaboration with Native American communities, she curated museum exhibits based on these books.

From 1978 to 1988, McBride wrote scores of articles for *The Christian Science Monitor* from Africa, Europe, and Asia. She has contributed to many other newspapers and magazines and has written introductions, articles, and chapters in a dozen books, including notable academic titles such as *Sifters: Native American Women's Lives* and *Reading Beyond Words: Contexts for Native History.* She coauthored the *Audubon Society Field Guide to African Wildlife.*

McBride is an adjunct lecturer of anthropology at Kansas State University and has been a regular visiting lecturer at Principia College in Illinois since 1981. She has also taught at the Salt Institute for Documentary Field Studies in Portland, Maine, and given dozens of guest lectures in public and academic venues.

From 1981 to 1991, McBride did historical research and community development work for the Aroostook Band of Micmacs in Maine, contributing to their successful efforts to gain federal status, establish a land base, and revitalize cultural traditions. In 1999 the Maine state legislature gave McBride a special commendation for her research and writing on the history of Native women in the state—an honor initiated by elected tribal representatives in the legislature. Currently, she serves as co-principal investigator for a National Parks Service ethnographic research project, oral history advisor for the Kansas Humanities Council, and board member of the Women's World Summit Foundation, based in Geneva, Switzerland.

Brief Contents

Contents

Features Contents

Anthropologists of Note

Original Studies

Anthropology Applied

Biocultural Connections

Preface

New to the seventh edition are three co-authors. Their involvement reflects two phenomena: the senior author's own retirement from the classroom (but not from anthropology) and the fact that four-field anthropology has grown to the point where no one individual can "do it all." There has been much debate of late about the future of four-field anthropology. In our view, its future will be assured through collaboration among anthropologists with diverse backgrounds, as exemplified in this textbook. Although distinct from one another, our experiences and research interests overlap, and we all share a similar vision of what anthropology is (and should be) about.

PURPOSE

Evolution and Prehistory is designed for introductory anthropology courses at the college level. While focusing on biological anthropology and archaeology, an integrated four-field approach is central to this book. The introductory chapter provides a historic review of anthropology and its four fields to give students a sense of how biological anthropology and archaeology fit within the discipline. In addition, it features a series of Biocultural Connection boxes, to illustrate how cultural and biological processes work together to shape human behavior, beliefs, and biology. A new capstone Epilogue brings this biocultural perspective to global issues relating to human health and disease in the 21st century. In short, with this text students explore the interrelated subjects of biological and cultural evolution and contemporary biological diversity using a holistic anthropological approach.

A textbook that combines archaeology and biological anthropology cannot by itself be an exhaustive introduction to either subdiscipline, but it does provide more of the biological background than one would get in a course in archaeology alone. Alternatively, it provides more of the cultural context than one would get in a course restricted to physical anthropology. The first and most obvious aim of the text, therefore, is to give students a comprehensive introduction to each subfield as it bears on the related topics of the origin of humanity, the origin of culture, and contemporary biological diversity. Drawing from the research and ideas of a number of schools of anthropological thought, this book exposes students to a mix of theoretical perspectives—in biological anthropology and archaeology. Such inclusiveness reflects our conviction that different approaches all reveal important insights about human behavior, biology, and beliefs. To employ the tools of a single approach at the expense of all others is to cut oneself off from significant insights. In the process the student will come to understand the ways human culture and biology are interdependent, with each having an impact on the other.

Most anthropology instructors have two goals for their introductory classes: (1) to provide an overview of principles and processes of anthropology and (2) to plant a seed of awareness about human biological and cultural diversity, past and present, in their students that will continue to grow and to challenge ethnocentrism long past the end of the semester. All seven editions of *Evolution and Prehistory* have tried to support and further these goals.

If most students have little substantive concept of anthropology, they often have less clear—and potentially more destructive—views of the primacy of their own culture and its place in the world. A secondary goal of the text, then, is to persuade our students to understand the true complexity of our evolution and that our presence is *not* the outcome of a process that led inexorably and predictably to where we are today. Indeed, "debunking" is an important function of anthropology; questioning beliefs in the superiority of humans over other forms of life, farming over food foraging, or complex civilizations over cultures based on subsistence farming is something that anthropologists do especially well. Anthropology is, in this sense, a tool to enable students to question their place in the world and their responsibilities to it. This questioning aspect of the discipline is perhaps the most relevant gift we can pass on to our students. If we, as teachers (and textbook authors), do our jobs well, students will gain a wider outlook on the world and a critical perspective on their particular culture. To paraphrase the poet T. S. Eliot: After all our explorations, they will come home and know the place for the first time.

If ever there were a time when students needed anthropological tools to gain a global view of humanity past and present, it is now. Beyond serving as a foundation for anthropology majors, this text is designed to help all students make sense of our increasingly complex and interconnected world, to perceive their particular place in it, and thereby navigate through interrelated biological and cultural networks with knowledge and skill, whatever professional path they take. In short, we see this book as a comprehensive guide for people entering the often bewildering maze of global crossroads in the 21st century.

ORGANIZATION OF THE BOOK

A Unifying Theme

In our own teaching, we have often found that introductory students lack a sense of the bigger picture in their studies of human beings. With this in mind, we present anthropology as the study of humankind's responses to the fundamental challenges of survival. Each chapter is framed by this theme, opening with a Challenge Issue paragraph and photograph and ending with Questions for Reflection tied to that particular challenge.

We emphasize the integration of human culture and biology in every step humans take to meet these challenges. To the traditional anthropological study of the biological evolution of humans as culture-bearing organisms we add new layers of biocultural integration. We include the social history surrounding the development of scientific theories about human biology in the past, providing a framework to think about scientific controversy in the present. We also look at changing views about the capacity for culture in the remarkable behaviors of our closest living biological relatives in the animal world: the nonhuman primates. We believe that the anthropological contextualization of scientific knowledge engages students actively in the process of understanding human biological and cultural evolution as well as contemporary human diversity.

SPECIAL FEATURES OF THE BOOK

Accessible Language

As textbook authors, we aim to transmit and register ideas and information: to induce our readers to look at the unfamiliar as well as to look at the familiar in new ways, and then to urge them to think critically about what they see. This, of course, is easier said than done. A book may be the most content-rich, most handsomely designed, most lavishly illustrated text available on the subject, but if it is not accessible to the student, it is valueless as a teaching tool.

In this text, even the most difficult concepts are presented in prose that is clear, straightforward, and easy for today's first- and second-year students to understand, without feeling that they are being "spoken down to." Where technical terms are necessary, they appear in boldfaced type, are carefully defined in the narrative, and defined again in the running glossary in simple, clear language.

Accessibility involves not only clear writing but also an engaging narrative voice or style. The voice of *Evolution and Prehistory* is distinct among introductory texts in the discipline, for it has been thoroughly internationalized. This means we have avoided the typical "we: they" voice and used a more inclusive one that will resonate with both Western and non-Western students and professors. Moreover, the book highlights the theories and work of anthropologists from all around the world—in the general narrative as well as in special boxed features. In addition, its theories and examples come from throughout the globe.

Photographs, Maps, and Other Illustrations

The accessibility of this text is further enhanced by compelling visuals, including a uniquely large and rich array of four-color photographs, selected to catch the eye and drive home important anthropological points. Many of them are paired or clustered as Visual Counterpoints in order to contrast and compare cultural examples, concepts, and issues across time and around the world.

In addition, this book features a wide variety of line drawings, maps, charts, and tables, many designed exclusively for this edition. As in past editions, we expect these visual tools will effectively illustrate, emphasize, and clarify particular anthropological concepts and prove to be valuable and memorable teaching aids. Maps have been an especially popular aid through each edition of *Evolution and Prehistory,* and the seventh edition builds on this success. Many of the marginal locator maps are new or revised, and several new world maps have been added to provide an overview of important contemporary issues such as pollution, and world population growth. Also of note, we have retained in the front end of the book several contrasting world map projections to illustrate the various messages embedded in cartography. One of the maps (the Robinson projection) locates all of the cultures mentioned in the text.

Original Studies

A special feature of this text is the Original Study that appears in each chapter. Many are new to this edition and others have been updated. These studies consist of selections from ethnographies and other original works by women and men who have done, or are doing, work of anthropological significance. Each study, integrated within the flow of the text, sheds additional light on an important anthropological concept or subject area found in the chapter. Their content is not extraneous or supplemental. The Original Studies bring specific concepts to life through concrete examples. And a number of Original Studies also demonstrate the anthropological tradition of the case study, albeit in abbreviated form.

The idea behind the Original Studies is to coordinate the two halves of the human brain, which have different functions. Whereas the left (dominant) hemisphere is logical and processes verbal inputs in a linear manner, the right hemisphere is creative and less impressed with linear logic. Psychologist James V. McConnell described it as "an analog computer of sorts—a kind of intellectual monitor that not only handles abstractions, but also organizes and stores material in terms of Gestalts [that] include the emotional relevance of the experience." Logical thinking, as well as creative problem solving, occurs when the two sides of the brain cooperate. The implication for textbook writers is obvious: To be truly effective, they must reach both sides of the brain. The Original Studies help to do this by conveying some "feel" for humans and their behavior and how anthropologists actually study them. For example, in Chapter 1 students will read a new Original Study by a North American anthropologist who, in graduate school, met and married a Zulu from South Africa—a personal experience that played a role in her current work with traditional healers and HIV/AIDS patients in her husband's country. In the Epilogue's Original Study they will read a poignant description of the author's comparison of her son's experience with Down syndrome in the United States with what he would have experienced had he been a child in the African country Mali where she was conducting fieldwork on childhood growth. In the United States, cultural recognition of this biological condition provided him simultaneously with a host of medical services and the constraints of a stereotyping label while in Mali he would be free from such limiting categorizations. As with other Original Studies, the striking nature of these experiences drives the discussion of a host of issues deeply relevant to students and anthropology.

Anthropology Applied

A popular carryover from the sixth edition, this boxed feature conveys anthropology's wide-ranging relevance and gives students a glimpse into the variety of careers anthropologists enjoy. New and revised boxes include "The Ethical, Legal, and Social Implications of the Human Genome Project," "Baboon Social Relationships and Primate Conservation," "Paleotourism and the World Heritage List," "Action Archaeology and the Community at El Pilar," and "Picturing Pesticides." In many of the examples carried over from the previous edition, the anthropologist profiled has provided us with updates on their work.

Biocultural Connections

New to the seventh edition, this feature illustrates how cultural and biological processes work together to shape human biology, beliefs, and behavior. It reflects the integrated biocultural approach central to the field of anthropology today. Topics include "The Anthropology of Organ Transplantation," "The Social Impact of Genetics on Reproduction," "Kennewick Man," "Nonhuman Primates and Human Disease," "Evolution and Human Birth," "Paleolithic Prescriptions for the Diseases of Civilization," "Breastfeeding, Fertility, and Beliefs," and "Social Stratification and Diseases of Civilization."

Anthropologists of Note

We have increased the number of profiles in this feature (formerly Biography Boxes) and shifted the coverage to better represent the wide variety of anthropologists in the world. Featuring contemporary scholars as well as important historical figures in the field, these boxes illustrate both the history and evolution of the discipline. New profiles include Berhane Asfaw, Margaret Conkey, Peter Ellison, Kinji Imanishi, Fatimah Jackson, Allan Wilson, and Xinzhi Wu.

Integrated Gender Coverage

Unlike many introductory texts, *Evolution and Prehistory* integrates rather than separates gender coverage. Thus, material on gender related issues is included in *every* chapter. This approach gives the seventh edition a measure of gender-related material that far exceeds the single chapter most introductory textbooks contain.

Why is the gender-related material integrated? Anthropology is itself an integrative discipline. Concepts and issues surrounding gender are almost always too complicated to remove from their context. Moreover, spreading this material through all of the chapters emphasizes how considerations of gender enter into virtually everything people do. Further, integration of gender into the book's "biological" chapters allows students to grasp the analytic distinction between sex and gender, illustrating the subtle influence of gender norms on biological theories about sex difference. Much of the new content for the seventh edition (listed below) relates to gender in some way. These changes generally fall into at least one of three categories: changes in thinking about gender within the discipline; examples that have important ramifications on gender in a particular society or culture; and cross-cultural implications about gender and gender relations. New material includes expanded and updated discussions of gender roles in evolutionary discourse, engendering archaeology, studies of nonhuman primate behavior, female fertility, same-sex marriage, and population control. Through a steady drumbeat of such coverage, this edition avoids ghettoizing gender to a single chapter that is preceded and followed by resounding silence.

Previews and Summaries

An old and effective pedagogical technique is repetition: "Tell 'em what you're going to tell 'em, tell 'em, and then tell 'em what you've told 'em." To do this, each chapter begins with preview questions that set up a framework for studying the contents of the chapter. At the end of the chapter is a summary containing the kernels of the more important ideas presented in the chapter. The summaries provide handy reviews for students without being so long and detailed as to seduce students into thinking they can get by without reading the chapter itself.

Web Links

The Internet continues to be an increasingly important means of communication. The seventh edition draws upon the World Wide Web both as an instructional tool and as a new set of examples of cultural evolution and diversity. Every chapter contains several MediaTrek icons integrated into the text that direct students to the companion Web site for deeper exploration of the topics covered in the narrative. (More on these below.)

Suggested Readings and Bibliography

Each chapter includes an annotated and up-to-date list of suggested readings that will supply the inquisitive student with further information about specific anthropological points that may be of interest. The books suggested are oriented toward both the general reader and the interested student who wishes to explore further the more technical aspects of the subject. In addition, the bibliography at the end of the book contains a listing of more than 500 books, monographs, and articles from scholarly journals and popular magazines on virtually every topic covered in the text that a student might wish to investigate further.

Glossary

The running glossary is designed to catch the student's eye, reinforcing the meaning of each newly introduced term. It is also useful for chapter review, as the student may readily isolate the new terms from those introduced in earlier chapters. A complete glossary is also included at the back of the book. In the glossaries each term is defined in clear, understandable language. As a result, less class time is required for going over terms, leaving instructors free to pursue matters of greater interest.

Length

Careful consideration has been given to the length of this book. On the one hand, it had to be of sufficient length to avoid superficiality or misrepresentation of the discipline by ignoring or otherwise slighting some important aspect of anthropology. On the other hand, it could not be so long as to present more material than could be reasonably dealt with in the space of a single semester, or be prohibitively expensive. The resultant text is comparable in length to introductory texts in the sister disciplines of economics, psychology, and sociology, even though there is more ground to be covered in an introduction to biological anthropology and archaeology.

Special Features beyond the Printed Page

Also, recognizing that contemporary anthropology students welcome, respond to, and even expect instruction materials to include more than printed matter, we have prepared a unique multimedia teaching package for exploring the methods and findings of the discipline. These include the book in hand, as well as an interactive Web site, companion videos, and PowerPoint® program. The text itself reaches beyond the printed word with a rich array of illustrative and thought-provoking visuals, including Visual Counterpoints featuring side-by-side photos to compare and contrast cultural and biological concepts and issues across time and around the world.

The accompanying videos (discussed with the rest of the supplements) show biological anthropology and archaeology in motion and bring action and life into the circle of ideas. The Web Links (also discussed in more detail below) build skills for analysis and research, move the content of the text from standard linear textbook format to a multimedia package, and provide a media database of print and numerous nonprint resources. PowerPoint slides and overhead transparencies bring the ideas and art of the text into the classroom. And, of course, the suggested readings and bibliography continue to show the rich library of anthropological texts students can utilize. The seventh edition thus allows instructors to draw upon a broad set of instructional tools to expand their classrooms. Anthropology has been an archive of human biology, beliefs, and behavior, and it is important that the discipline show the richness and diversity of humanity through the appropriate media.

THE SEVENTH EDITION

The seventh edition is one of the most radical revisions in this book's 20-year lifespan. Every chapter has been thoroughly reconsidered, reworked, and updated, and a new capstone Epilogue has been added. Additions and deletions have been made with an eye toward building on the strengths that have made this text appeal to so many for so long. The writing has been further refined, and the voice of the text "internationalized" to make it more accessible to a wider audience. A host of new photos, charts, tables, illustrations, and maps have been introduced, and every chapter has a new chapter opening photo (tied to the "challenge" theme). The summary is now presented as a series of succinct bulleted points, and we have added several questions for reflection at the end of each chapter. Also, we have increased the number of contemporary texts in the annotated suggested readings list and located many new interactive Internet sites, now labeled as "MediaTreks." Major changes in the seventh edition per chapter include:

Chapter 1: The Essence of Anthropology

The book's opening chapter offers a compelling Original Study, "Fighting HIV/AIDS in Africa: Traditional Healers on the Front Line," written by Suzanne Leclerc-Madlala expressly for this edition. Also new among boxed features is an Anthropologists of Note profile of Yolanda Moses, a Biocultural Connection piece concerning the anthropology of organ transplantation. The Anthropology Applied box on forensic anthropology featuring the work of Clyde Snow has been updated to include the work of Amy Zelson Mundorff who oversaw cataloguing the remains of those who lost their lives in the September 11, 2001, terrorist attack on the World Trade Center in New York City. In a new section titled "Anthropology and Globalization," we offer a cogent overview of one of today's most significant issues. A revised and expanded section on theory includes a discussion on the difference between theory and doctrine, which will be particularly helpful to professors who have students whose religious beliefs do not sit well with the concept of evolution. Our expanded discussion of ethnography and fieldwork now includes a narrative on the challenges anthropologists face in the field. A new illustration representing the four fields incorporates theory and applied anthropology. To enhance the text's four-field foundation, introductory passages on archaeology, linguistics, and especially physical anthropology have been fleshed out. Also, a discussion of medical anthropology has been added.

Chapter 2: Biology and Evolution

We have changed the order of presentation of material in Chapters 2, 3, and 4 to reflect changes in biological anthropology and archaeology. While field methods continue to be a cornerstone of practice in these subfields, new techniques and knowledge in the field of genetics in particular contribute substantially to the discipline of anthropology. Therefore, we have moved our discussion of biology and evolution to Chapter 2 so that students will have this knowledge at their fingertips for all subsequent chapters. We continue to provide clear but simple explanations of evolutionary process at the population, individual, and molecular levels. We integrate cultural and biological approaches through the historical exploration of the genetics revolution in the narrative and new and revised boxed features. A new Biocultural Connection, "The Social Impact of Genetics on Reproduction," featuring the work of cultural anthropologist Rayna Rapp, provides students with concrete examples of the influence of genetics on people's lives. Similarly the revised Anthropology Applied box on the various implications of the Human Genome Project demonstrates the role of biological and cultural anthropologists in this vast scientific endeavor. A new Original Study by biological anthropologist Jonathan Marks illustrates that the relationship between genetic change and major morphological change is far from understood. This Original Study is integrated into our discussion of the alternative classificatory schemes (hominin versus hominid), allowing students to see that the schemes differ depending upon whether classification is based on genetics or morphology. We provide this discussion for two reasons: First, in the popular press students will see both "hominid" (*New York Times*) and "hominin" (*National Geographic*) used. Second, practicing anthropologists such as their professors may prefer one term over the other. By providing this discussion our book is compatible with both classificatory approaches. A simple, elegant table defining the various taxonomic levels accompanies this discussion.

Chapter 3: Living Primates

In our survey of the living primates, we build upon the previous chapter's discussion of alternate taxonomies based on genetics versus morphology among the primates. Unlike previous editions, we employ the traditional grade distinction between prosimians and anthropoid primates (rather than strepsirhine/haplorhine dichotomy) in our survey of diversity among living primates. As in the previous chapter, both taxonomic schemas are presented in the narrative and in tabular form. Through careful streamlining of the narrative and use of figures (a new figure on primate vision, for example), we have been able to expand some content areas without increasing length. The section on primate reproductive biology and the primate life cycle is expanded. Gender issues are featured through the important perspectives contributed by female primatologists and a more balanced focus on both male and female primates in contemporary field studies. A new Original Study written expressly for this book by primatologist Frans de Waal titled "Reconciliation and Its Cultural Modification in Primates" provides an excellent example of how primatologists have reworked older theories—in this case, the emphasis on aggression and male dominance hierarchies. The pioneering contributions of Japanese primatologist Kinji Imanishi and his students to field methods and theory are detailed in a new Anthropologists of Note feature. The practical importance of primatology is emphasized in a new Anthropology Applied box featuring Shirley Strum's work titled "Baboon Social Relationships and Primate Conservation."

Chapter 4: Field Methods in Archaeology and Paleoanthropology

In its new place, this chapter on archaeological and paleoanthropological methods provides a comprehensive introduction to shared excavation and dating techniques as the book shifts its focus to the study of the distant past. A new table summarizes dating methods describing the application and limitations of each method. Genetic techniques, such as the extraction of DNA from fossils, are also described. The growing specialization of bioarchaeology is introduced including a discussion of how gender roles and the status of women in the past can be examined through bioarchaeological analyses. A new Biocultural Connection on the controversy surrounding Kennewick Man has been added.

Chapter 5: Macroevolution and the Early Primates

This chapter's revision concentrates on the general principles of macroevolution while de-emphasizing the details of specific fossil primates. We provide a picture of how paleoanthropologists go about reconstructing evolutionary relationships through the analysis of shared derived characteristics and present the major theoretical models of macroevolution. The Original Study by Steven Jay Gould, "The Unsettling Nature of Variational Change," has been moved into this chapter to emphasize that these alternate models are complementary rather than conflicting. Our discussion of continental drift and geological time (using Sagan's "cosmic calendar") is expanded with a newly designed figure. Because paleoanthropology is a historical science or a science of discovery, we also provide students with an understanding of how reconstructions about the past change with each new discovery. The new Anthropologists of Note box featuring Allan Wilson—the "hybrid scientist" who pioneered merging biochemical and fossil analyses in evolutionary studies—provides an excellent example of how discoveries in the laboratory changed paleoanthropological interpretations. A new Biocultural Connection titled "Nonhuman Primates and Human Disease" also brings this chapter into the present by dealing with cultural aspects of using our closest biological relatives as biomedical research subjects. The spectacular newly discovered fossils from Chad (Toumai) along with those from Kenya (*Orrorin*) conclude this chapter, emphasizing that 5 to 8 million years ago is the critical time period for the divergence of the human lineage from the other apes.

Chapter 6: The First Bipeds

The order of this chapter was reworked to open with the anatomy of bipedalism, the defining derived feature of humans and their ancestors. Several new figures illustrate the anatomical changes associated with bipedalism. A new Original Study by Lee Berger returns to the hominid/hominin terminology debate introduced in Chapter 2 as we explore the Pliocene fossil evidence. The fossils are discussed in chronological order instead of the order of discovery as in the previous edition. The Piltdown forgery is incorporated into the text with an emphasis on how beliefs and biases played a role in the acceptance of the forgery to the exclusion of the Taung specimen. Sex, gender, and the fossil record are discussed both in terms of sex identification in the past and the influence of current gender roles on paleoanthropological theories. A new Biocultural Connection titled "Evolution and Human Birth" discusses the influence of contemporary biomedical birth practices on paleoanthropological theories about the evolution of the human birth pattern.

Chapter 7: *Homo habilis* and Cultural Origins

We introduce Part 3 of the book with Misia Landau's idea that human evolutionary studies simultaneously incorporate scientific and narrative approaches, providing a framework for our discussion of the evolution of the genus *Homo*. She suggests that the evolutionary narrative takes the form of a heroic epic in which evolving humans use their cultural abilities to overcome a series of biological/natural challenges. The issue of establishing the exact relationship between biological change and cultural change is threaded throughout this and subsequent chapters. Hypotheses about human adaptation through behavior are updated and are based more on evidence than derived from hypothetical narratives. A discussion of "lumpers" versus "splitters" is incorporated into the discussion of *Homo habilis* as a valid taxon. This chapter also features a new section titled "Sex, Gender, and the Behavior of Early *Homo*," discussing the issues involved with separating biologically based sex differences and culturally established gender roles when reconstructing behavior of our ancestors. This section connects to the Anthropologists of Note box on Adrienne Zihlman. A new Anthropology Applied box discusses paleotourism at a variety of early hominin sites and the efforts to designate these sites as part of UNESCO'S World Heritage List.

Chapter 8: *Homo erectus* and the Emergence of Hunting and Gathering

While taking a simplified "lumping" approach to the Middle Pleistocene fossil record in this chapter, we also provide an updated table listing species recognized by many working paleoanthropologists. We incorporate the exciting new Dmanisi fossils and also discuss Zhoukoudian more fully. A new Anthropologists of Note featuring Chinese paleoanthropologist Xinzhi Wu reminds students of global differences in scholarly perspectives. We provide a new discussion on the challenges of reconstructing of behavior in the past compared to making anatomical comparisons. A new figure depicts the typical skull shape of *Homo erectus.* The development of language is tied more directly to brain structure in this chapter, and we provide a new figure illustrating language areas of the brain. A new Biocultural Connection titled "Paleolithic Prescriptions for the Diseases of Civilization" introduces students to the perspective of evolutionary medicine.

Chapter 9: Archaic *Homo sapiens* and the Middle Paleolithic

This chapter provides students with an overview of the two major competing theories (recent African origins and multiregional hypothesis) for modern human origins through presenting the data used to support each theory and the history behind their development. As this is one of the major controversies in paleoanthropology, the chapter aims to raise awareness in students of the issues rather than come out in favor of one of these hypotheses. The newest development—the spectacular 160,000-year-old *Homo sapiens idaltu* specimens from Ethiopia—are described along with a new Anthropologist of Note feature on Ethiopian paleoanthropologist Berhane Asfaw. The newly discovered FOXP2 "language gene" is discussed. A figure depicting Neandertal morphology complements a new section titled "Race and Human Evolution" that brings the debates about modern human origins and the relationship between skull shape and cultural behavior into a contemporary context.

Chapter 10: *Homo sapiens* and the Upper Paleolithic

Beginning with the chapter opener, this chapter expands the coverage of the spread of humans to greater Australia and the Americas to balance the traditional emphasis on Europe in discussions of the Upper Paleolithic. New maps clarify and complement the text. Some old figures have been replaced with action photographs and photographs of artifacts. The discussion of entoptic phenomena has been expanded. Gender in the Upper Paleolithic is discussed in terms of interpretation of the Venus figurines as self-representation by Upper Paleolithic female artists. This is complemented by a new Anthropologists of Note box featuring Margaret Conkey and her work incorporating gender and feminist theory into the study of prehistoric art.

Chapter 11: The Neolithic Revolution

A new discussion of differences in the rates of biological and cultural change provides students with a framework for thinking about human health at the Neolithic transition. The discussion of the relationship between fertility and subsistence patterns is updated with an eye to the impacts of cultural practices on human biology of the past, present, and future. A new Biocultural Connection featuring the work of Melvin Konner and Carol Worthman on ovulation and breastfeeding practices among the Ju/'hoansi provides a concrete example of the interaction of cultural practice and human biology relevant to the Neolithic.

Chapter 12: The Emergence of Cities and States

In accordance with the global emphasis of this revision, the archaeological site of Great Zimbabwe was added to the ancient cities and states including a discussion of the false colonial European belief that African people could not be responsible for these ruins. Recent discoveries related to the origins of writing in China and in the Americas (Olmec) are also described. The practical knowledge that can be derived from the archaeological study is emphasized in the narrative and in the new Anthropology Applied feature titled "Action Archaeology and the Community at El Pilar." This box features Anabel Ford's work to establish an international preservation (spanning Belize and Guatemala) and sustainable ecotourism surrounding El Pilar, the Maya site she discovered. Similarly, a new Biocultural Connection illustrates the relationship between poverty and disease that began with the earliest socially stratified societies and continues today.

Chapter 13: Modern Human Diversity

As with other sections of the book, we use a historical approach to provide students with an understanding of human biological variation and particularly to demonstrate why race is not a valid biological category when applied to humans. Previous discussions of the terms *polytypic* and *polymorphic* as applied to the human species are updated and clarified. The work of Linnaeus, Blumenbach, and Samuel Morton is added to the discussion on the intellectual history of the notion of race. The role of physical anthropology in maintaining the false racial typologies of the past is discussed. The term *cline* is introduced as a way to study human variation without the fallacy of racial typologies. A new section on race in the contemporary practice of medicine in the United States discusses how the government's directive to collect health statistics by race can inadvertently result in perpetuation of folk interpretations of biological difference. A new section titled "Race and Human Evolution Revisited" connects this chapter's materials to discussions in Chapters 9 and 10 about the relationship between skull shape and cultural abilities. To close the chapter, we examine the effects of the human-made environment on continued microevolutionary change. A new Anthropology Applied box titled "Picturing Pesticides" on the work of Elizabeth Guillette documenting the effects of pesticides on the neurobehavioral health of children provides an excellent example of the biological effects of cultural actions.

Epilogue: Culture, Disease, and Globalization

This new capstone explores how the anthropological integration of biology and culture provides the keys to understanding the challenges of disease humans must face in the 21st century. A variety of biocultural approaches from medical anthropology are introduced to students including ecological approaches, ethnomedicine, and evolutionary medicine. A new Original Study, excerpted from Katherine Dettwyler's award-winning book *Dancing Skeletons,* illustrates the anthropological distinction between illness and disease through her cross-cultural comparisons of Down syndrome, childhood feeding, and growth. The Epilogue uses the prion diseases kuru and mad cow disease to illustrate how cultural practices and processes on local and global levels contribute to disease. The Anthropology Applied box on emerging infectious diseases (previously in Chapter 13) has been included as it effectively illustrates the interrelationship of culture, disease, and globalization. Two new Anthropologists of Note are featured in the Epilogue: Peter Ellison for his work in reproductive ecology and Fatimah Jackson for her work on human and plant interactions and genetic studies linking individuals from the African burial ground project to their African homelands. The Epilogue closes with an exploration of how structural violence contributes to the distribution of disease globally. This section concentrates on nutrition, population size, and pollution, as health determinants shaped by structural violence. The conclusion focuses on the role that individuals, and anthropologists in particular, can play in addressing the many health challenges of our globalized world.

New Original Studies

Five of the fourteen Original Studies are new to the seventh edition: Chapter 1—"Fighting HIV/AIDS in Africa: Traditional Healers on the Front Line," by Suzanne Leclerc-Madlala; Chapter 2—"Ninety-Eight Percent Alike: What Our Similarity to Apes Tells Us about Our Understanding of Genetics," by Jonathan Marks; Chapter 3—"Reconciliation and Its Cultural Modification in Primates," by Frans deWaal; Chapter 6—"Is It Time to Revise the System of Scientific Naming?" by Lee Berger; Epilogue—"Dancing Skeletons," by Katherine Dettwyler.

New Anthropology Applied

Five of the ten Anthropology Applied boxes are new to the seventh edition: Chapter 1—"Forensic Anthropology"; Chapter 3—"Baboon Social Relationships and Primate Conservation"; Chapter 7—"Paleotourism and the World Heritage List"; Chapter 12—"Action Archaeology and the Community at El Pilar"; Chapter 13—"Picturing Pesticides." Other boxes have been updated and revised.

New Anthropologists of Note

Of the nineteen Anthropologists of Note profiles, eight are new to the seventh edition, reflecting the global diversity of anthropologists and their perspectives: Yolanda Moses, Kinji Imanishi, Allan Wilson, Xinzhi Wu, Berhane Asfaw, Margaret Conkey, Peter Ellison, and Fatimah Jackson.

Biocultural Connections

This new feature alternates with the Anthropologists of Note and Anthropology Applied boxes. Eight completely new Biocultural Connections have been added to this edition. They cover a range of topics, illustrating how cultural and biological processes work together to shape human biology, beliefs, and behavior. Topics covered: Chapter 1—"The Anthropology of Organ Transplantation"; Chapter 2—"The Social Impact of Genetics on Reproduction"; Chapter 4—"Kennewick Man"; Chapter 5—"Nonhuman Primates and Human Disease"; Chapter 6—"Evolution and Human Birth"; Chapter 8—"Paleolithic Prescriptions for the Diseases of Civilization"; Chapter 11—"Breastfeeding, Fertility, and Beliefs"; Chapter 12—"Social Stratification and Diseases of Civilization."

PRINT SUPPLEMENTS

In keeping with the eleventh edition's recognition that the use of many messages requires many media, the selection of ancillaries accompanying *Evolution and Prehistory* should meet most instructors' needs.

A separate Study Guide is provided to aid comprehension of the textbook material. Each chapter begins with concise learning objectives and then offers chapter exercises, review questions, and a glossary review to help students achieve these objectives. This supplement also includes hints on reading anthropology texts and studying for tests.

An Instructor's Manual offers teaching objectives and lecture and class activity suggestions that correspond to each chapter of the textbook. An extensive Test Bank, available in both printed and computerized forms, offers more than 1,200 multiple choice and true/false questions.

MULTIMEDIA SUPPLEMENTS

There are several videos available to accompany the text. *Millennium: Tribal Wisdom and the Modern World,* hosted by anthropologist David Maybury-Lewis, presents a thoughtful exploration of cultures across the world. Many issues are covered, including indigenous rights, definitions of gender and gender roles, and the construction of the self. Instructors can choose from ten 60-minute programs. Qualified adopters may select full-length videos from an extensive library of offerings drawn from excellent education video sources such as Films for the Humanities and Sciences. Also, the CNN Today Anthropology video series is an exclusive series jointly created by Wadsworth and CNN intended for instructors to use as lecture launchers or to illustrate key anthropological concepts.

Acknowledgments

All of us have benefited from the anthropologists with whom we studied at the University of Pennsylvania, the New School for Social Research, City University of New York, Nijmegen University, and Columbia University, not to mention those with whom we have collaborated in research or discussed issues of common interest. They are too numerous to mention here but include colleagues at the various colleges and universities where we have taught. Bill and Dana owe a particular debt to their spouses, Anita de Laguna Haviland and Peter Bingham, not to mention their children, for putting up with their preoccupation with the book. (As spouses, Harald and Bunny's debts on this front balanced each other out.) In addition, Anita has performed valiantly over three decades, doing the typing and later the word processing for previous editions, and also offering valuable ideas, criticism, and encouragement as needed. Without her, this enterprise would have collapsed several editions ago.

As new co-authors, Harald, Dana, and Bunny would like to thank Bill for inviting them to participate in this enterprise, for it brought numerous insights to all of us. Specific thanks, too, to Erin Sawicki who ably kept track of innumerable details in as part of her studies in anthropology. We are grateful to Janet Benson and Donna Roper for their work on the Instructors' Manuals and helpful comments on details within various chapters, and also to M. L. Miranda for his work on the Study Guide and Test Bank. And we extend special thanks to those who wrote or revised special boxed features for the seventh edition.

Thanks are also due the anthropologists who made suggestions for this edition. They include:

Joseph Ball, San Diego State University
Gloria Gozdzik, West Virginia University
S. Homes Hogue, Mississippi State University
Kenneth Kelly, University of South Carolina
Barry Lewis, University of Illinois at Urbana-Champaign
Michael Love, California State University, Northridge
Pamela Stone, Western Michigan University
Suzanne Walker, Southwest Missouri State University

All of their comments were carefully considered; how we have responded to them has been determined by our own perspectives of anthropology, as well as our combined decades of experience with undergraduate students. Therefore, neither they nor any of the other anthropologists mentioned here should be held responsible for any shortcomings in this book. Helpful in seeing this edition through to publication have been our editors at Wadsworth, in particular Lin Marshall. As textbook authors, we feel extremely fortunate to have had an editor who is trained as an anthropologist and brings unusual knowledge, passion, and social insights to her work. We also wish to thank at Wadsworth Publishing Nicole Root, Assistant Editor; Kelly McMahon, Editorial Assistant; Dee Dee Zobian, Technology Product Manager; Matthew Wright, Senior Marketing Manager; Catherine Morris, Project Editor; Eve Howard, Vice President and Editor-in-Chief; Sean Wakely, President; and Susan Badger, CEO. In addition to their help, we had the advantage of working with several freelancers: our able, considerate copyeditor Jennifer Gordon; our diligent, go-the-distance photo researcher Sandra Lord (and her assistant Sue Howard); our illustrator Carol Zuber-Mallison who cheered up many a late night with her humorous email messages and excellent work. We hold special thanks for Robin Lockwood who brought patience, grace, and a keen eye to her coordinating tasks in production service.

William A. Haviland
Dana Walrath
Harald E. L. Prins
Bunny McBride

Putting the World in Perspective

Although all humans that we know about are capable of producing accurate sketches of localities and regions with which they are familiar, CARTOGRAPHY (the craft of mapmaking as we know it today) had its beginnings in 13th century Europe, and its subsequent development is related to the expansion of Europeans to all parts of the globe. From the beginning, there have been two problems with maps: the technical one of how to depict on a two-dimensional, flat surface a three-dimensional spherical object, and the cultural one of whose worldview they reflect. In fact, the two issues are inseparable, for the particular projection one uses inevitably makes a statement about how one views one's own people and their place in the world. Indeed, maps often shape our perception of reality as much as they reflect it.

In cartography, a PROJECTION refers to the system of intersecting lines (of longitude and latitude) by which part or all of the globe is represented on a flat surface. There are more than 100 different projections in use today, ranging from polar perspectives to interrupted "butterflies" to rectangles to heart shapes. Each projection causes distortion in size, shape, or distance in some way or another. A map that shows the shape of land masses correctly will of necessity misrepresent the size. A map that is accurate along the equator will be deceptive at the poles.

Perhaps no projection has had more influence on the way we see the world than that of Gerhardus Mercator, who devised his map in 1569 as a navigational aid for mariners. So well suited was Mercator's map for this purpose that it continues to be used for navigational charts today. At the same time, the Mercator projection became a standard for depicting land masses, something for which it was never intended. Although an accurate navigational tool, the Mercator projection greatly exaggerates the size of land masses in higher latitudes, giving about two-thirds of the map's surface to the northern hemisphere. Thus, the lands occupied by Europeans and European descendants appear far larger than those of other people. For example, North America (19 million square kilometers) appears almost twice the size of Africa (30 million square kilometers), while Europe is shown as equal in size to South America, which actually has nearly twice the land mass of Europe.

A map developed in 1805 by Karl B. Mollweide was one of the earlier equal-area projections of the world. Equal-area projections portray land masses in correct rel-

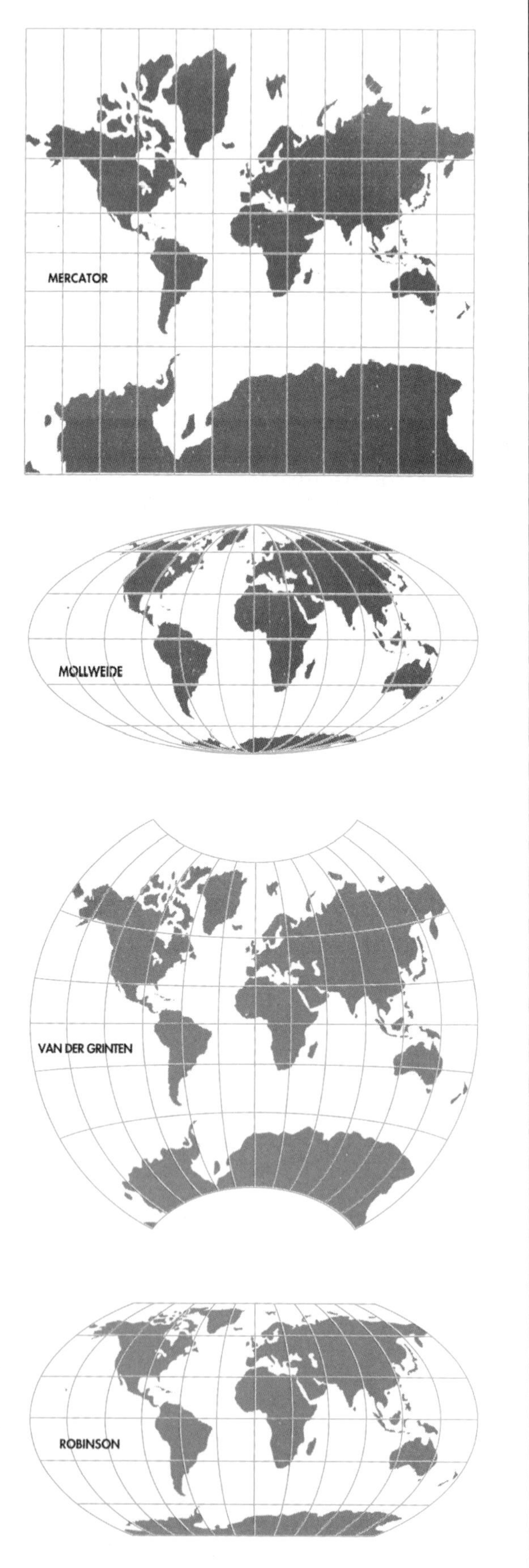

ative size, but, as a result, distort the shape of continents more than other projections. They most often compress and warp lands in the higher latitudes and vertically stretch land masses close to the equator. Other equal-area projections include the Lambert Cylindrical Equal-Area Projection (1772), the Hammer Equal-Area Projection (1892), and the Eckert Equal-Area Projection (1906).

The Van der Grinten Projection (1904) was a compromise aimed at minimizing both the distortions of size in the Mercator and the distortion of shape in equal-area maps such as the Mollweide. Allthough an improvement, the lands of the northern hemisphere are still emphasized at the expense of the southern. For example, in the Van der Grinten, the Commonwealth of Independent States (the former Soviet Union) and Canada are shown at more than twice their relative size.

The Robinson Projection, which was adopted by the National Geographic Society in 1988 to replace the Van der Grinten, is one of the best compromises to date between the distortion of size and shape. Although an improvement over the Van der Grinten, the Robinson projection still depicts lands in the northern latitudes as proportionally larger at the same time that it depicts lands in the lower latitudes (representing most third-world nations) as proportionally smaller. Like European maps before it, the Robinson projection places Europe at the center of the map with the Atlantic Ocean and the Americas to the left, emphasizing the cultural connection between Europe and North America, while neglecting the geographical closeness of northwestern North America to northeast Asia.

The following pages show four maps that each convey quite different "cultural messages." Included among them is the Peters Projection, an equal-area map that has been adopted as the official map of UNESCO (the United Nations Educational, Scientific, and Cultural Organization), and a map made in Japan, showing us how the world looks from the other side.

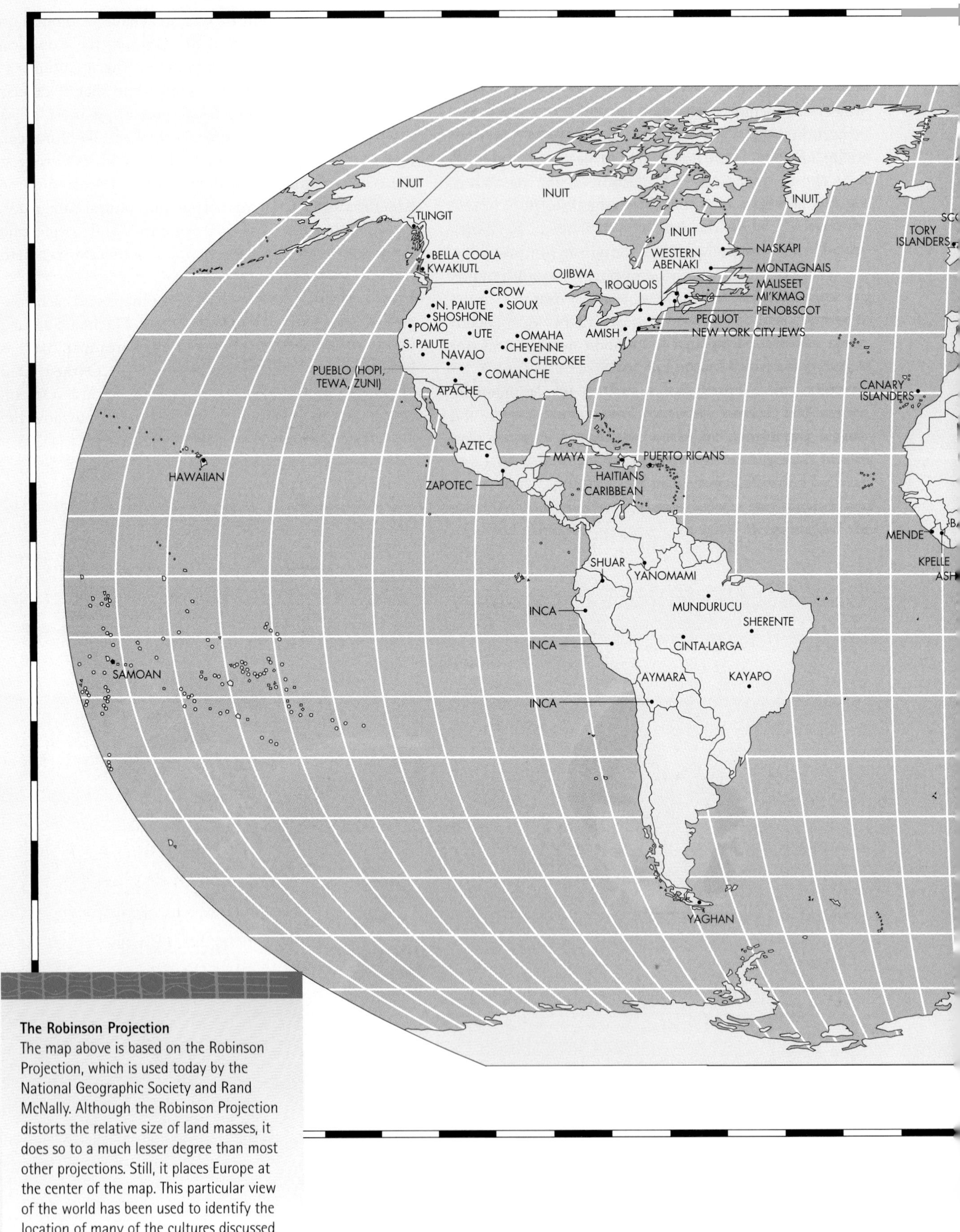

The Robinson Projection
The map above is based on the Robinson Projection, which is used today by the National Geographic Society and Rand McNally. Although the Robinson Projection distorts the relative size of land masses, it does so to a much lesser degree than most other projections. Still, it places Europe at the center of the map. This particular view of the world has been used to identify the location of many of the cultures discussed in this text.

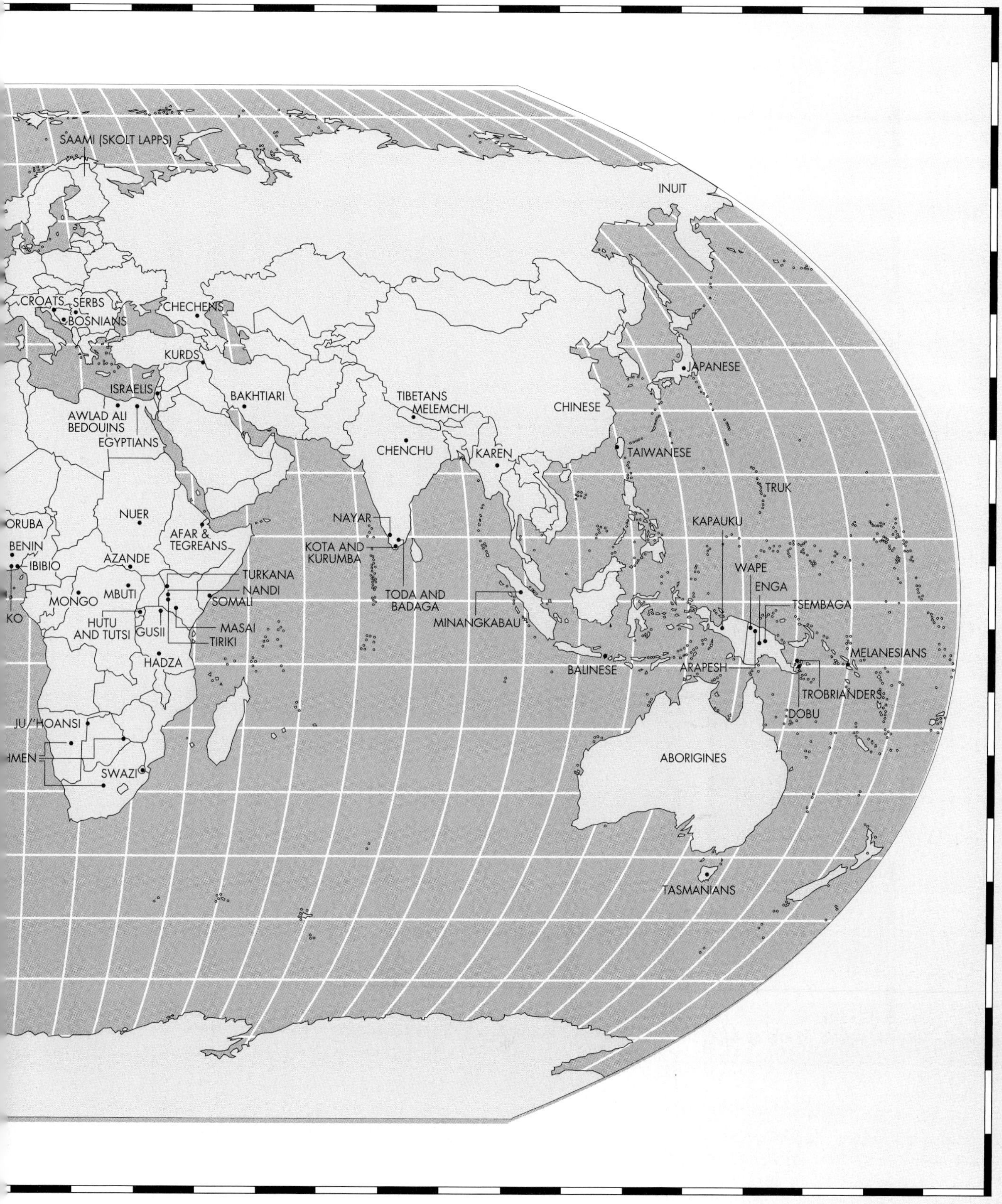

SAAMI (SKOLT LAPPS)
INUIT
CROATS
SERBS
BOSNIANS
CHECHENS
KURDS
JAPANESE
ISRAELIS
BAKHTIARI
TIBETANS
MELEMCHI
CHINESE
AWLAD ALI
BEDOUINS
EGYPTIANS
CHENCHU
KAREN
TAIWANESE
TRUK
ORUBA
NUER
NAYAR
KAPAUKU
AFAR &
TEGREANS
BENIN
KOTA AND
KURUMBA
IBIBIO
AZANDE
WAPE
TURKANA
ENGA
NANDI
MONGO
MBUTI
SOMALI
TODA AND
BADAGA
TSEMBAGA
KO
HUTU
AND TUTSI
GUSII
MASAI
MINANGKABAU
TIRIKI
MELANESIANS
HADZA
BALINESE
ARAPESH
TROBRIANDERS
JU/'HOANSI
DOBU
IMEN
ABORIGINES
SWAZI
TASMANIANS

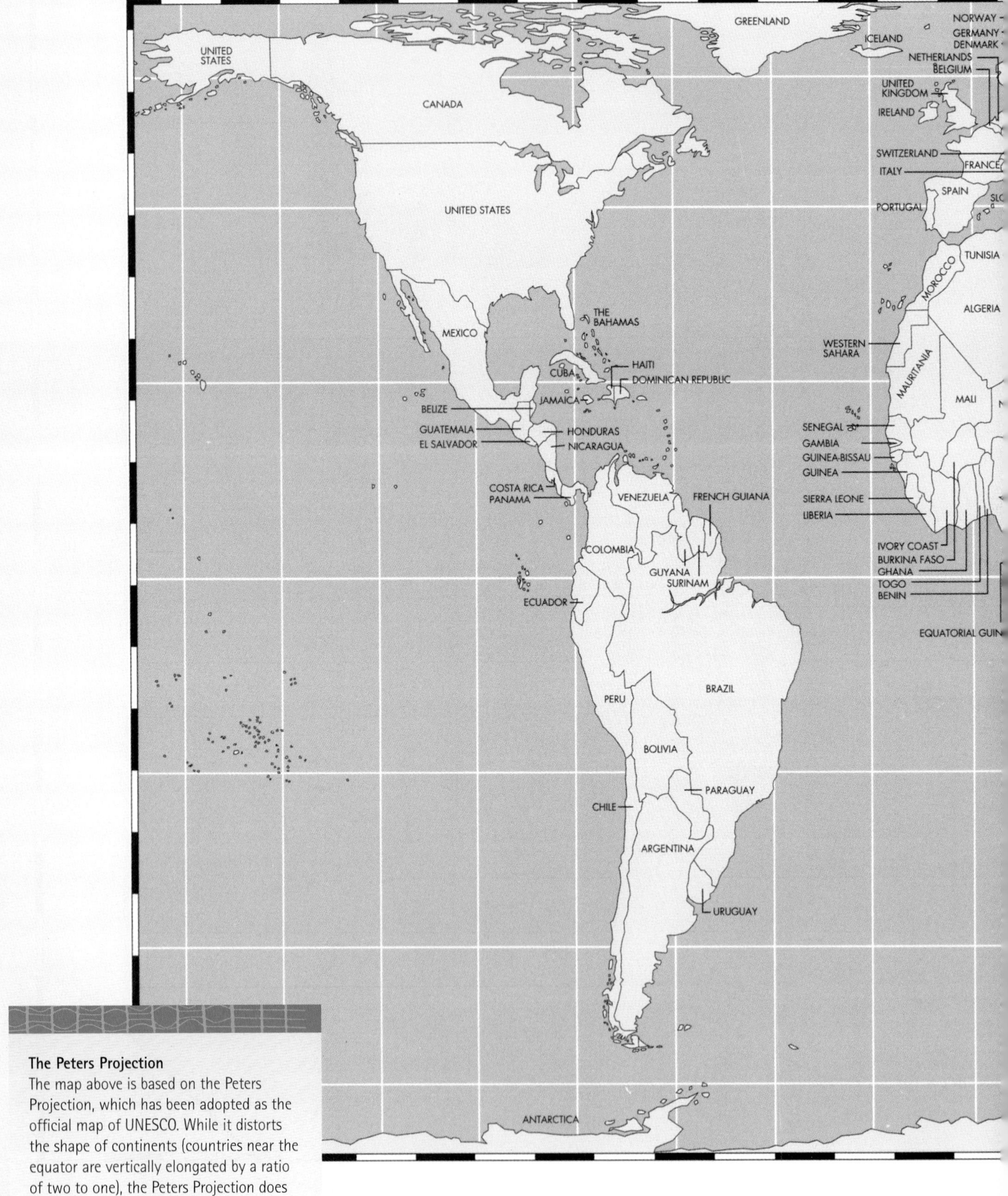

The Peters Projection

The map above is based on the Peters Projection, which has been adopted as the official map of UNESCO. While it distorts the shape of continents (countries near the equator are vertically elongated by a ratio of two to one), the Peters Projection does show all continents according to their correct relative size. Though Europe is still at the center, it is not shown as larger and more extensive than the third world.

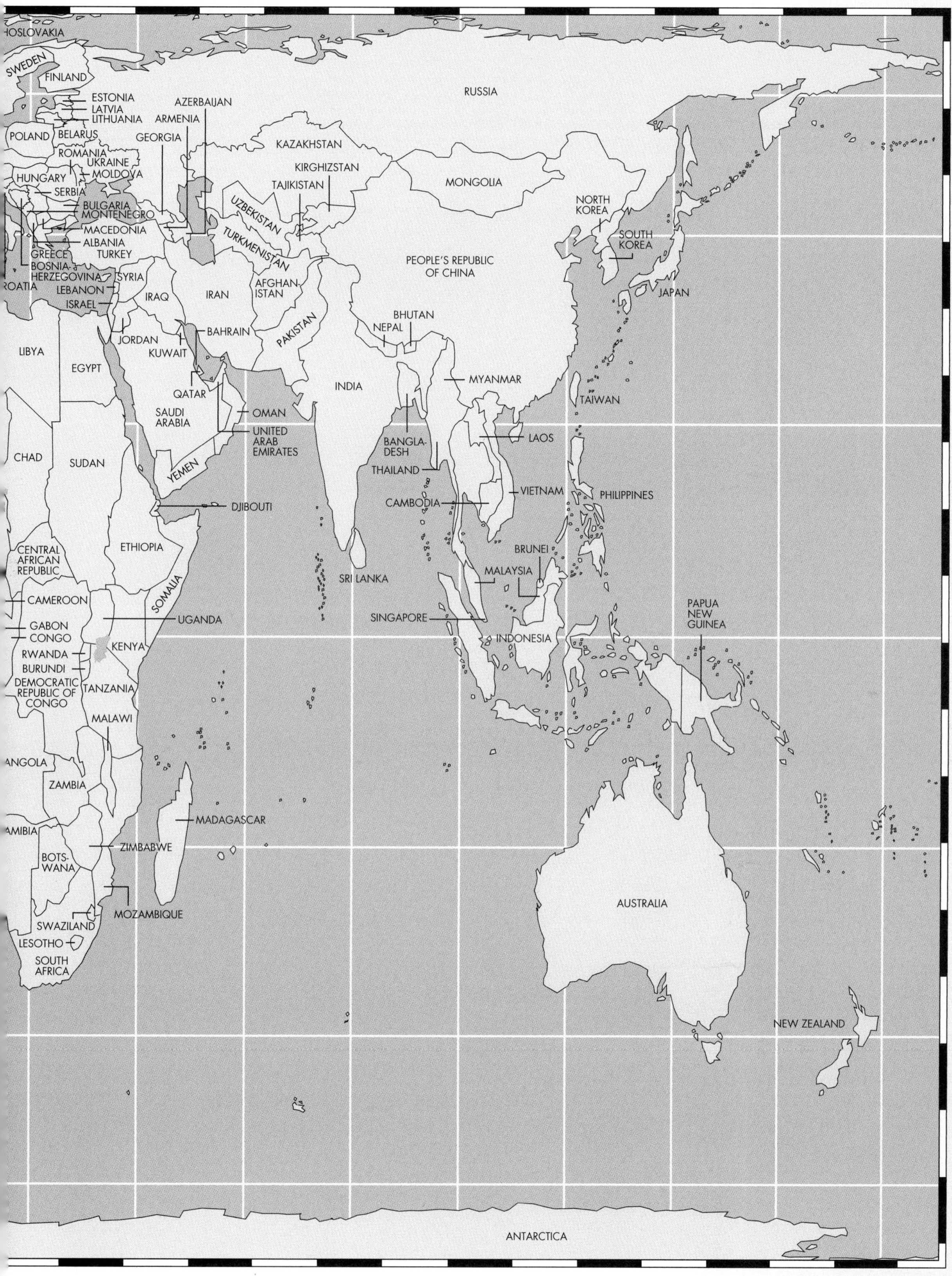

HOSLOVAKIA
SWEDEN
FINLAND
ESTONIA
LATVIA
LITHUANIA
AZERBAIJAN
ARMENIA
RUSSIA
POLAND
BELARUS
GEORGIA
KAZAKHSTAN
ROMANIA
UKRAINE
MOLDOVA
KIRGHIZSTAN
HUNGARY
TAJIKISTAN
MONGOLIA
SERBIA
BULGARIA
MONTENEGRO
UZBEKISTAN
NORTH KOREA
MACEDONIA
ALBANIA
TURKMENISTAN
SOUTH KOREA
GREECE
TURKEY
BOSNIA-HERZEGOVINA
PEOPLE'S REPUBLIC OF CHINA
ROATIA
SYRIA
LEBANON
IRAQ
IRAN
AFGHANISTAN
JAPAN
ISRAEL
BHUTAN
NEPAL
BAHRAIN
PAKISTAN
JORDAN
KUWAIT
LIBYA
EGYPT
MYANMAR
INDIA
QATAR
TAIWAN
SAUDI ARABIA
OMAN
UNITED ARAB EMIRATES
BANGLADESH
LAOS
CHAD
SUDAN
YEMEN
THAILAND
VIETNAM
PHILIPPINES
CAMBODIA
DJIBOUTI
ETHIOPIA
BRUNEI
CENTRAL AFRICAN REPUBLIC
MALAYSIA
SRI LANKA
SOMALIA
CAMEROON
PAPUA NEW GUINEA
UGANDA
SINGAPORE
GABON
CONGO
INDONESIA
KENYA
RWANDA
BURUNDI
DEMOCRATIC REPUBLIC OF CONGO
TANZANIA
MALAWI
ANGOLA
ZAMBIA
MADAGASCAR
AMIBIA
ZIMBABWE
BOTSWANA
AUSTRALIA
MOZAMBIQUE
SWAZILAND
LESOTHO
SOUTH AFRICA
NEW ZEALAND
ANTARCTICA

Japanese Map

Not all maps place Europe at the center of the world, as this Japanese map illustrates. Besides reflecting the importance the Japanese attach to themselves in the world, this map has the virtue of showing the geographic proximity of North America to Asia, a fact easily overlooked when maps place Europe at their center.

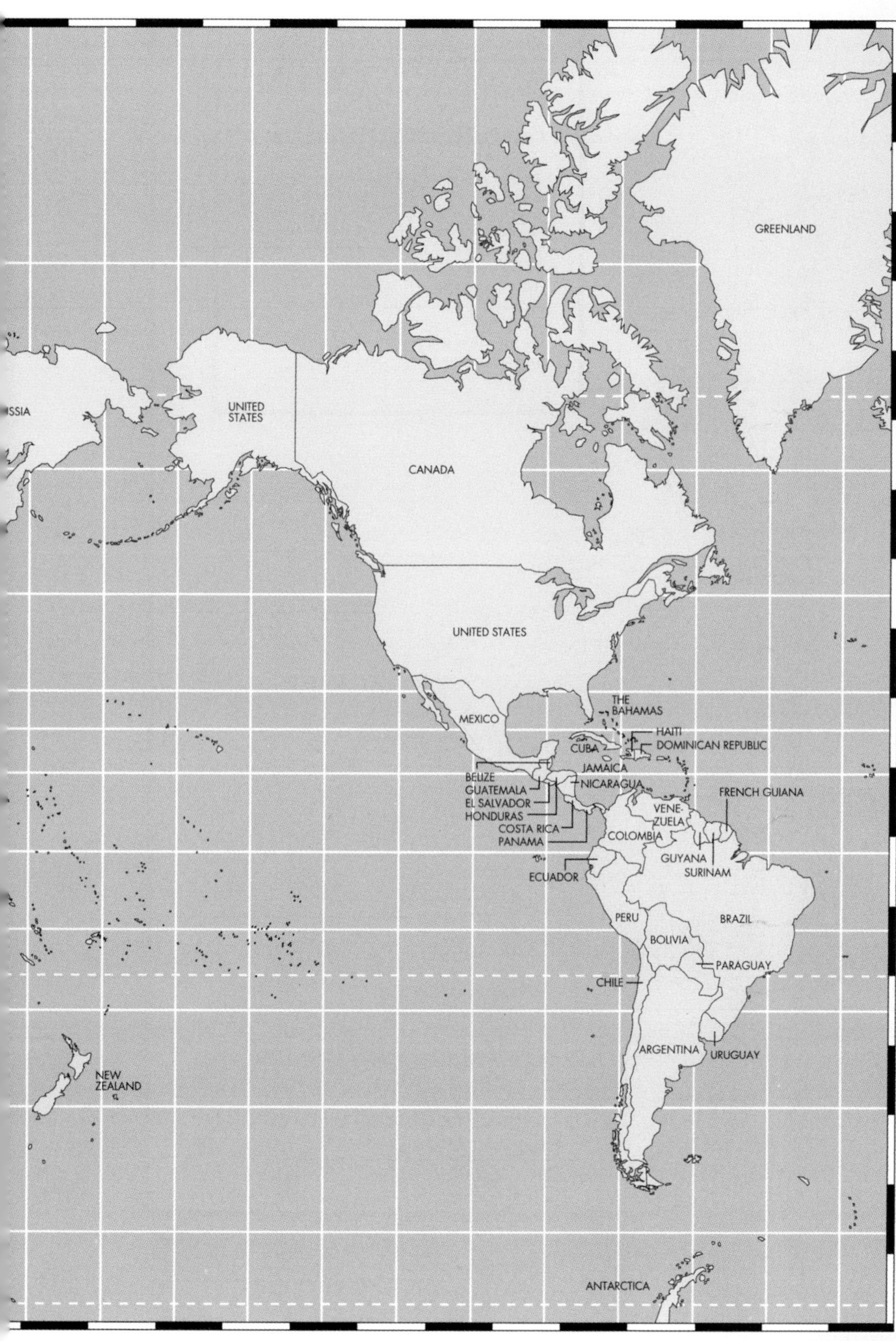

SSIA
UNITED STATES
CANADA
GREENLAND
UNITED STATES
MEXICO
THE BAHAMAS
CUBA
HAITI
DOMINICAN REPUBLIC
JAMAICA
BELIZE
GUATEMALA
EL SALVADOR
HONDURAS
NICARAGUA
COSTA RICA
PANAMA
FRENCH GUIANA
VENE-ZUELA
COLOMBIA
GUYANA
SURINAM
ECUADOR
PERU
BRAZIL
BOLIVIA
PARAGUAY
CHILE
ARGENTINA
URUGUAY
NEW ZEALAND
ANTARCTICA

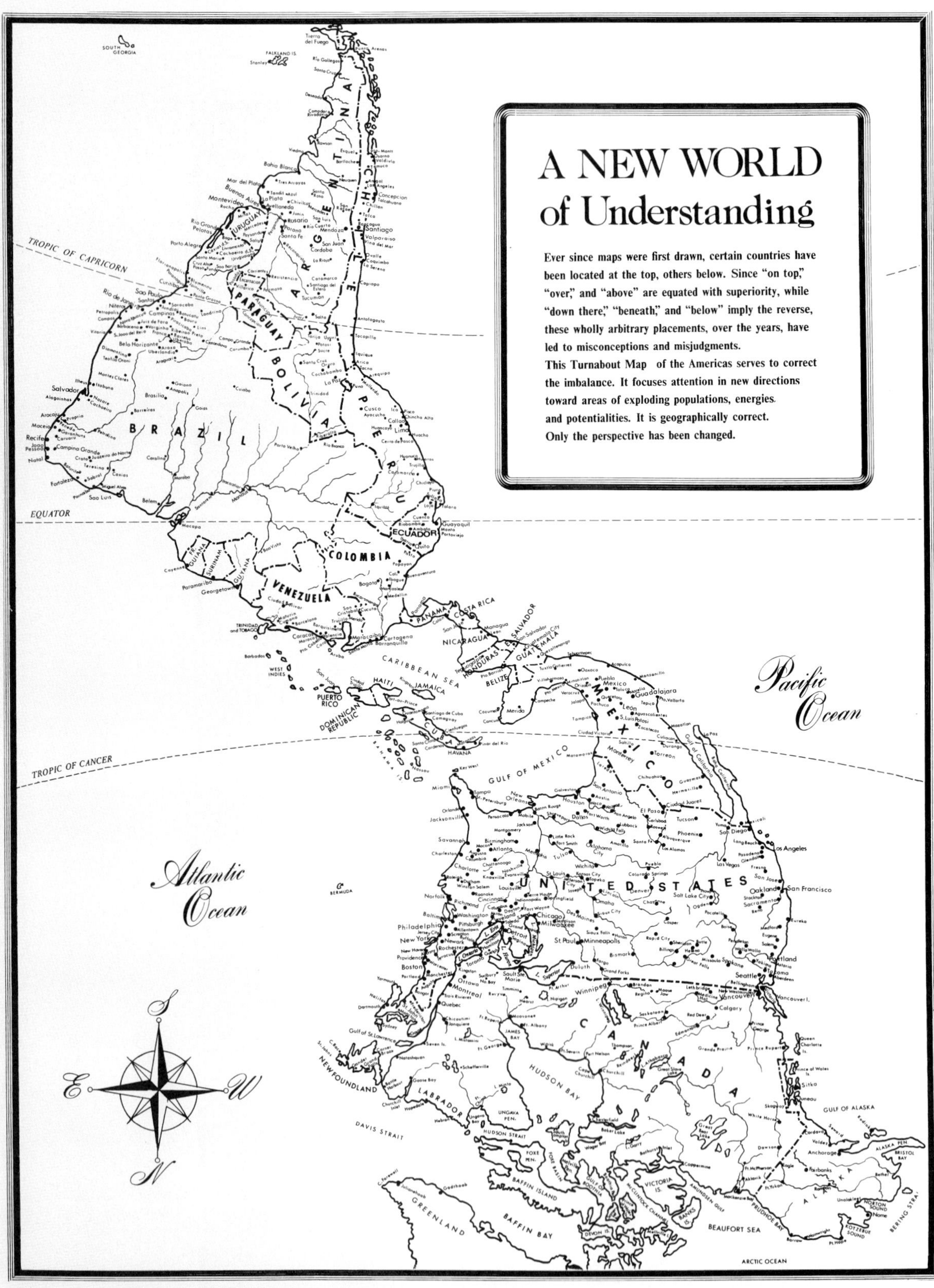

The Turnabout Map

The way maps may reflect (and influence) our thinking is exemplified by the "Turnabout Map," which places the South Pole at the top and the North Pole at the bottom. Words and phrases such as "on top," "over," and "above" tend to be equated by some people with superiority. Turning things upside down may cause us to rethink the way North Americans regard themselves in relation to the people of Central America. © 1982 by Jesse Levine Turnabout Map™—Dist. by Laguna Sales, Inc., 7040 Via Valverde, San Jose, CA 95135

Evolution and Prehistory

The Human Challenge

PART 1

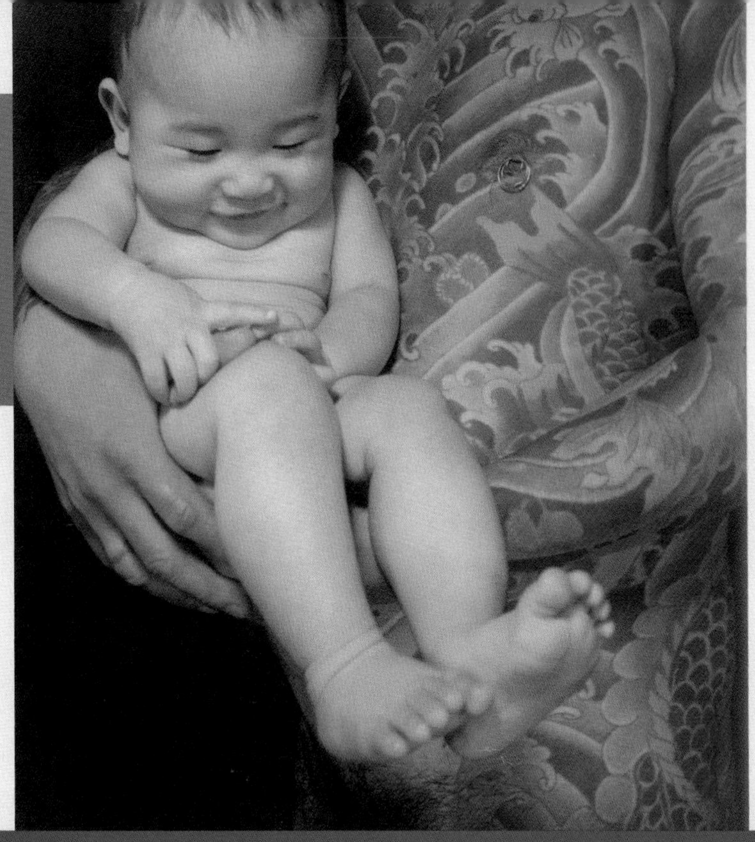

© Sandi Fellman 1984

Anthropology
The Challenge of Knowing Humanity

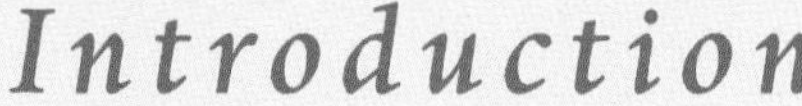

Introduction

Anthropology is the most liberating of all the sciences. Not only has it exposed the fallacies of racial and cultural superiority, but its devotion to the study of all peoples, everywhere and throughout time, has cast more light on human nature than all the reflections of sages or the studies of laboratory scientists. This may sound like the assertion of an overly enthusiastic anthropologist; however, it is a statement made by the philosopher Grace de Laguna in her 1941 presidential address to the Eastern Division of the American Philosophical Association.

The subject matter of anthropology is vast, as we shall see in the first three chapters of this book: It includes everything that has to do with human beings, past and present. Of course, many other disciplines are concerned in one way or another with humans. Some, such as anatomy and physiology, study our species as biological organisms. The social sciences are concerned with the distinctive forms of human relationships, while the humanities examine the achievements in human cultures. Anthropologists are interested in all of these things, too, but they try to deal with them all together, in all places and times. It is this unique, broad, and holistic perspective that equips anthropologists so well to deal with that elusive thing called human nature.

Needless to say, no single anthropologist is able to investigate personally everything that has to do with humanity. For practical purposes, the discipline is divided into various subfields, and individual anthropologists specialize in one or more of these. Whatever their specialization, though, they retain a commitment to a broader, overall perspective on humankind. For example, cultural anthropologists specialize in the study of human ideas, values, and behavior, while physical anthropologists specialize in the study of humans as biological organisms. Yet neither can afford to ignore the work of the other, for human culture and nature are inextricably intertwined, with each affecting the other in important ways. The fact that we are nature-culture beings is evident in the photograph of the famous Japanese tattoo artist Horiyoshi III holding his newborn son. Every one of us comes into the world in a natural state with a biological profile, but over time we acquire cultural identity—etched into our minds and sometimes into our very skin.

Scala/Art Resource, NY

There are countless examples of our species' biocultural connection. For example, in certain parts of Africa and Asia, when humans took up the practice of farming, they altered the natural environment in a way that, by chance, created ideal conditions for the breeding of mosquitoes. As a result, malaria became a serious problem (mosquitoes carry the malarial parasite), and a biological response to this was the spread of certain genes that, in those people living in malarial areas who inherit the gene from one parent, produced a built-in resistance to the disease. Although those who inherit the gene from both parents contract a potentially lethal anemia, such as sickle-cell anemia, those without the gene are vulnerable to malaria. Biology in turn impacts cultural practices, including food choice and folklore. For instance, consider the relationship between fava beans and malaria. Although fava beans contain substances that are potentially toxic to humans, these substances also interfere with the development of the parasite that causes malaria in human red blood cells. In cultures around the Mediterranean Sea where malaria is common, fava beans are incorporated into the diet through foods eaten at the height of the malaria season. The simultaneous toxic effect of fava beans in some genetically susceptible individuals has led to a rich folklore about this simple food, including the ancient Greek belief that fava beans contain the souls of the dead. So it is that we humans have one leg in culture and the other in nature, and in the interplay of both our destinies unfold.

We will begin our study with a survey of the scope of anthropology, marking out its main subfields and showing how they relate to one another and to the other sciences and humanities. The integrated four-field approach introduced in Chapter 1 sets the stage for our exploration of the dynamic interplay between cultural and biological processes fundamental to making humans the kind of creatures that we are today. In Chapter 2, we will turn our attention to the core biological theory of evolution. We will explore the origins of evolutionary theory as well as biological mechanisms at the molecular, individual, and population level. We will conclude Part 1 of the book with a chapter investigating the other living primates, a subgroup of mammals that includes lemurs, lorises, tarsiers, monkeys, apes, and humans. Our exploration of primate biology and behavior offers perspectives on the evolution of our ancestors while providing evidence of the sophistication of our closest living relatives. With these subjects covered, we will have set the stage for an integrated biocultural examination of human evolution, prehistory, and contemporary human variation.

CHAPTER 1

The Essence of Anthropology

© Jodi Cobb/National Geographic Image Collection

©Anup and Manoj Shah

© James L. Stanfield/National Geographic Image Collection

© George H. H. Huey/Corbis

CHALLENGE ISSUE

IT IS A CHALLENGE TO DISCERN ONE'S PLACE IN THE WORLD. Humans are just one of 10 million species. But among these, including 4,000 fellow mammals, we humans are the only ones biologically capable of studying ourselves and the world around us. We do this not only because we are curious, but also because knowledge helps us create and improve our living conditions and make adjustments necessary for survival. Adaptations based on knowledge are essential in every culture, and culture is our species' ticket to survival. Made possible by means of sophisticated communication, human cultures emerged as our ancestors developed the physical capacity for complex language and tool use. The comprehensive study of human development and cultures, past and present, is the business of anthropology.

1 What Is Anthropology?

Anthropology, the study of humankind everywhere, throughout time, seeks to produce reliable knowledge about the things that make people different from one another and the things they all share in common.

2 What Do Anthropologists Do?

Anthropologists do their work within four basic subfields of the discipline. Physical anthropologists focus on humans as biological organisms, tracing the evolutionary development of humankind and looking at biological variations within the species, past and present. Cultural anthropologists are concerned with human cultures, past and present. Meanwhile, archaeologists try to recover information about human cultures—usually from the past and especially those that have left no written records—by studying material objects, skeletal remains, and settlements. Finally, linguists study languages, human communication systems by which cultures are maintained and passed on to succeeding generations. Though each of these four subfields has its own research strategies, they rely upon one another and are united by a common anthropological perspective on the human condition.

3 How Do Anthropologists Do What They Do?

Anthropologists, like other scholars, are concerned with the description and explanation of reality. They formulate and test hypotheses—tentative explanations of observed phenomena—concerning humankind. Their aim is to develop reliable theories—explanations supported by bodies of data—about our species. In order to frame objective hypotheses that are as free of cultural bias as possible, anthropologists typically develop them through "fieldwork," a particular kind of hands-on research that makes them so familiar with the minute details of the situation that they can begin to recognize patterns inherent in the data. It is also through fieldwork that anthropologists test existing hypotheses.

For as long as they have been on earth, people have sought answers to questions about who they are, where they come from, and why they act as they do. Throughout most of human history, though, people relied on myth and folklore for answers, rather than the systematic testing of data obtained through careful observation. Anthropology, over the last 150 years, has emerged as a tradition of scientific inquiry with its own approach to answering these questions. Simply stated, **anthropology** is the study of humankind in all times and places. The anthropologist is concerned primarily with a single species, *Homo sapiens*—the human species, its ancestors, and near relatives. Because anthropologists are members of the species being studied, it can be difficult for them to maintain a scientific detachment toward those they study. This, of course, is part of a larger problem in science where our own cultural ideas and values may impact our approaches to research. In the words of the great German writer-naturalist Goethe: "We see only what we know."

If it's true, as the old saying goes, that we are prone to see what lies behind our eyes rather than what appears before them, can anthropologists who are part of the very humanity they study ever hope to gain truly objective knowledge about people? While concerned about this, anthropologists have found that by maintaining a critical awareness of their assumptions, and constantly testing their conclusions against new sources of data, they can achieve a useful understanding of human thought and behavior. By scientifically approaching how people live and think, anthropologists have learned a great deal about human differences, as well as the many things humans have in common.

MEDIATREK

For information on subdisciplines—such as urban, feminist, and ecological anthropology—plus profiles of theorists, see MediaTrek 1.1 on the companion Web site or CD-ROM.

THE DEVELOPMENT OF ANTHROPOLOGY

Although works of anthropological significance have a considerable antiquity—two examples being cross-cultural accounts of people written by the Greek historian Herodotus about 2,500 years ago and the North African scholar Ibn Khaldun nearly 700 years ago—anthropology as a distinct field of inquiry is a relatively recent product of Western civilization. In the United States, for example, the first course in general anthropology to carry credit in a college or university (at the University of Rochester in New York) was not offered until 1879. If people have always been concerned about themselves and their origins, and those of other people, why then did it take such a long time for a systematic discipline of anthropology to appear?

The answer to this is as complex as human history. In part, it relates to the limits of human technology. Throughout most of history, people have been restricted in their geographical horizons. Without the means of traveling to distant parts of the world, observation of cultures and peoples far from one's own was a difficult—if not impossible—undertaking. Extensive travel was usually the exclusive privilege of a few; the study of foreign peoples and cultures was not likely to flourish until improved modes of transportation and communication could be developed.

This is not to say that people have always been unaware of the existence of others in the world who look and act differently from themselves. The Old and New Testaments of the Bible, for example, are full of references to diverse ancient peoples, among them Babylonians, Egyptians, Greeks, Jews, and Syrians. However, the differences among these people pale by comparison to those between any of the more recent European nations and (for example) traditional indigenous peoples of the Pacific islands, the Amazon rainforest, or Siberia. Using new inventions such as the compass aboard better-equipped sailing ships, it became easier to travel to truly faraway places and meet for the first time such radically different groups. It was the massive encounter with hitherto unknown peoples—which began 500 years ago as Europeans sought to extend their trade and political domination to all parts of the world—that focused attention on human differences in all their amazing variety.

Another significant element that contributed to the emergence of anthropology was that Europeans gradually came to recognize that despite all the differences, they might share a basic "humanity" with people everywhere. Initially, Europeans labeled societies that did not share their fundamental cultural values as "savage" or "barbarian." In the course of time, however, Europeans came to recognize such highly diverse groups as fellow members of one species and therefore relevant to an understanding of what it is to be human and of their collective place in world history. This growing interest in human diversity, coming at a time when there were increasing efforts to explain things in scientific terms of natural laws, cast doubts on the traditional explanations based on authoritative texts such as the Torah, Bible, or Koran and helped set the stage for the birth of anthropology.

anthropology The study of humankind in all times and places.

Although anthropology originated within the historical context of European culture, it has long since gone global. Today, it is an exciting, transnational discipline whose practitioners come from a wide array of societies all around the world. Even societies that have long been studied by European and North American anthropologists—several African and Native American societies, for example—have produced anthropologists who have made and continue to make a mark on the discipline. Their distinct perspectives shed new light not only on their own cultures, but also on those of others. It is noteworthy that in one regard diversity has long been a hallmark of the discipline: From its earliest days both women and men have entered the field. Throughout this text, we will be featuring the work of individual anthropologists, illustrating their diversity, as well as that of their work.

Anthropologists come from many corners of the world and carry out research in a huge variety of cultures all around the globe. Dr. Jayasinhji Jhala hails from the old city of Dhrangadhra in Gujarat, northeast India. A member of the Jhala clan of Rajputs, an aristocratic caste of warriors, he grew up in the royal palace of his father, the maharaja. After earning a bachelor of arts degree in India, he came to the United States and earned a master's degree in visual studies from the Massachusetts Institute of Technology, followed by a Ph.D. in anthropology from Harvard. Currently a professor and director of the programs of Visual Anthropology and the Visual Anthropology Media Laboratory at Temple University, he returns regularly to India with students to film cultural traditions in his own caste-stratified society.

ANTHROPOLOGY AND OTHER ACADEMIC DISCIPLINES

Anthropologists are not the only scholars who study people, but they are uniquely holistic in their approach. They do not think of their findings in isolation from those of other social or natural scientists—psychologists, economists, sociologists, biologists, and so on. Rather, they welcome the contributions researchers from these other disciplines have to make to the common goal of understanding humanity, and they gladly offer their own findings for the benefit of these other disciplines. Anthropologists do not expect, for example, to know as much about the structure of the human eye as anatomists, or as much about the perception of color as psychologists. As synthesizers, however, they are better prepared than any of their fellow scientists to understand how these relate to color-naming practices in different human societies. Because they look for the broad basis of human ideas and practices without limiting themselves to any single social or biological aspect, anthropologists can acquire an especially expansive and inclusive overview of the complex biological and cultural organism that is the human being.

One could say physical anthropology is closely related to the biological sciences just as cultural anthropology is closely related to the other social sciences and the humanities, however it is the integration of these two approaches that characterizes anthropology. The social science to which cultural anthropology has most often been compared is sociology, since both are concerned with describing and explaining the behavior of people within a social context. Sociologists, however, have concentrated heavily on studies of contemporary people living in industrialized North American and European (commonly known as Western) societies, while anthropologists have traditionally focused on non-Western tribal peoples and cultures, past and present. As anthropology developed, its practitioners found that to fully understand the complexities of human ideas, behavior, and biology, all humans, wherever and whenever, must be studied. More than any other feature, this unique cross-cultural and long-term historical perspective distinguishes anthropology from the other social sciences. It guards against the danger that theories of

Anthropologists of Note

Matilda Coxe Stevenson (1849–1915) ▪ Yolanda Moses (1946–)

Smithsonian Institution

Among the founders of North American anthropology were a number of women, whose work was highly influential among 19th-century women's rights advocates. One such pioneering anthropologist was Matilda Coxe Stevenson, who also did fieldwork among the Zuni. In 1885, she founded the Women's Anthropological Society, the first professional association for women scientists. Three years later, hired by the Bureau of American Ethnology, she became one of the first women in the United States to receive a full-time position in science.

AP/Wide World Photos

The tradition of women being active in anthropology continues. In fact, since World War II more than half the presidents of the now 12,000-member American Anthropological Association have been women. In 1996, Dr. Yolanda Moses became the first African American to hold that high office. A specialist on cultural diversity, she has done fieldwork in Alaska, the Caribbean, and East Africa. Since earning her Ph.D. from the University of California, Riverside, in 1976, Dr. Moses has taught at various universities. In 1993, she became president of The City College of New York, followed by three years as president of the American Association of Higher Education. She serves on the boards of numerous international associations and corporations, as well as editorial boards of major academic journals, and she remains tireless in her conviction that anthropologists have a major role to play in educating a wider public about cultural pluralism, notions of race, and diversity in education.

human behavior will be **culture-bound:** that is, based on assumptions about the world and reality that are part of the researcher's own particular culture. It provides a distinctly rich body of comparative data on humankind that can shed light on countless issues, past or present. As a case in point, consider the fact that infants in the United States typically sleep apart from their parents. To most North Americans, this may seem quite normal, but cross-cultural research shows that "co-sleeping," of mother and baby in particular, is the rule. Only in the past two hundred years, generally in Western industrialized societies, has it been considered proper for them to sleep apart. In fact, it amounts to a cultural experiment in child rearing.

Recent studies have shown that this unusual degree of separation of mother and infant in Western societies has important biological and cultural consequences. For one thing, it increases the length of the infant's crying bouts, which may last in excess of 3 hours a day in the child's second and third month. Some mothers incorrectly interpret the cause as a deficiency in breast milk and switch to less healthy bottle formulas, and in extreme cases, the crying may provoke physical abuse, sometimes with lethal effects. But the benefits of co-sleeping go beyond significant reductions in crying: Infants also nurse more often and three times as long per feeding; they receive more stimulation (important for brain development); and they are apparently less susceptible to sudden infant death syndrome ("crib death"). There are benefits to the mother as well: Frequent nursing prevents early ovulation after childbirth, and she gets at least as much sleep as mothers who sleep without their infants.[1]

These benefits may lead one to ask: Why do so many mothers continue to sleep apart from their infants? In North America the cultural values of independence and consumerism come in to play. To begin building unique individual identities, babies are provided with rooms (or at least space) of their own. This room of one's own also provides a place to put all the toys, furniture, and other paraphernalia that signify that the parents are "good" and "caring" (and help keep the consumer economy humming along).

The emphasis anthropology places on studies of traditional, non-Western peoples has often led to findings that run counter to generally accepted opinions derived from Western studies. Thus, anthropologists were the first to demonstrate

> that the world does not divide into the pious and the superstitious; that there are sculptures in jungles and paintings in deserts; that political order is possible without centralized power and principled justice without codified rules; that the norms of reason were not fixed in Greece, the evolution of morality not

culture-bound Theories about the world and reality based on the assumptions and values of one's own culture

[1]Barr, R. G. (1997, October). The crying game. *Natural History,* 47. Also, McKenna, J. J. (2002, September-October). Breastfeeding and bedsharing. *Mothering,* 28–37.

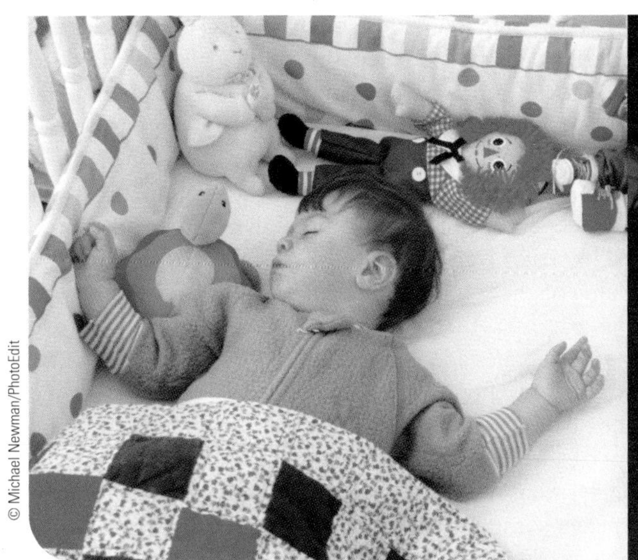

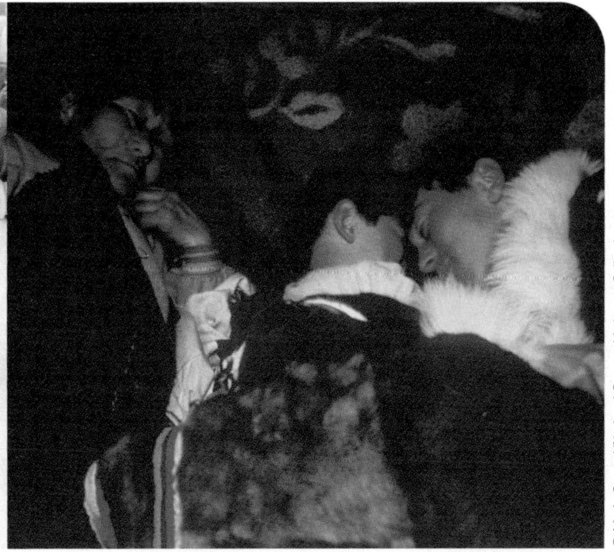

VISUAL COUNTERPOINT Although infants in the United States typically sleep apart from their parents, cross-cultural research shows that co-sleeping, of mother and baby in particular, is the rule. The photo on the right shows a Nenet family sleeping together in their *chum* (reindeer-skin tent). Nenet people are arctic reindeer pastoralists living in Siberia, Russia.

> consummated in England. . . . We have, with no little success, sought to keep the world off balance; pulling out rugs, upsetting tea tables, setting off firecrackers. It has been the office of others to reassure; ours to unsettle.[2]

Although the findings of anthropologists have often challenged the conclusions of sociologists, psychologists, and economists, anthropology is absolutely indispensable to them, as it is the only consistent check against culture-bound assertions. In a sense, anthropology is to these disciplines what the laboratory is to physics and chemistry: an essential testing ground for their theories.

ANTHROPOLOGY AND ITS SUBFIELDS

As noted above, anthropology is traditionally divided into four fields: physical anthropology, archaeology, linguistic anthropology, and cultural anthropology (Figure 1.1). Each is distinct, yet they are all closely related. For example, while linguistic anthropology focuses primarily on the cultural aspects of language, it has deep connections to the evolution of human language and the biological basis of speech and language studied within physical anthropology. As anthropologists, we aim to know how biology and culture do and do not influence each other, certain that understanding what people think and do involves knowing how they are made. Each of anthropology's subfields may take a distinct approach to the study of humans, but all of them gather and analyze data that are essential to explaining similarities and differences among humans, as well as ways that people everywhere have developed and continue to change. Moreover, all of them generate knowledge that has numerous practical applications. In fact, within all four subfields we find individuals who practice **applied anthropology,** which means using anthropological knowledge and methods to solve practical problems. Examples of how anthropology is used in a wide range of problem-solving challenges appear in many chapters of this book in boxes titled Anthropology Applied.

Physical Anthropology

Physical anthropology, also called *biological anthropology,* focuses on humans as biological organisms. Traditionally, biological anthropologists concentrated on human evolution, primatology, growth and development,

[2]Geertz, C. (1984). Distinguished lecture: Anti anti-relativism. *American Anthropologist, 86,* 275.

applied anthropology The use of anthropological knowledge and methods to solve practical problems, often for a specific client.
physical anthropology Also known as biological anthropology. The systematic study of humans as biological organisms.

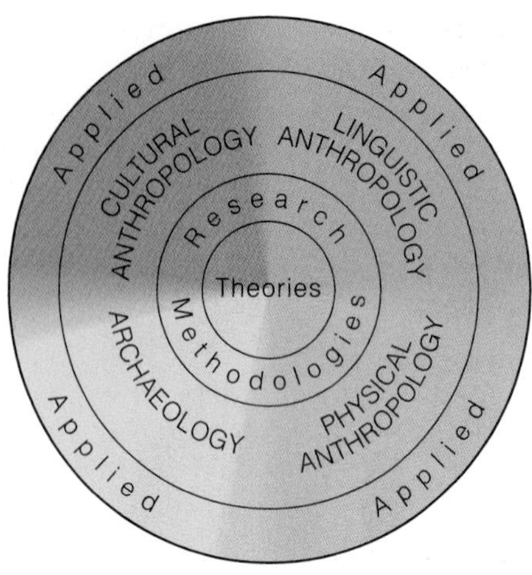

FIGURE 1.1

The four fields of anthropology. Note that the divisions between them are not sharp, indicating that their boundaries overlap. Moreover, each operates on the basis of a common body of knowledge. All four are involved in theory building, developing their own research methodologies, and solving practical problems through applied anthropology.

and human adaptation. Today, **molecular anthropology,** or the anthropological study of genes and genetic relationships, is another vital component of biological anthropology. Comparisons among groups separated by time, geography, or the frequency of a particular gene are critical to biological anthropology. As experts in the anatomy of human bones and tissues, physical anthropologists lend their knowledge about the body to applied areas such as gross anatomy laboratories and to criminal investigations.

Paleoanthropology

Human evolutionary studies focus on the biological changes through time that led to the emergence of our species. Anthropological approaches differ from other evolutionary studies in that the biological basis of human culture is its special emphasis. Whatever other distinctions people may claim for themselves, they are mammals—specifically primates—and, as such, they share a common ancestry with other primates, most specifically apes. Physical anthropologists try to reconstruct the biology and behavior of the human species in order to understand how, when, and why we became the kind of creature we are today. In human evolutionary studies, physical anthropologists, known as **paleoanthropologists,** look back to the earliest primates from 55 million years ago, or even the earliest mammals some 225 million years ago, to reconstruct the complex path of human evolution.

Paleoanthropologists investigating human evolution depend principally upon analysis of the fossilized skeletons of our ancestors. Comparison of the size and shape of these fossils to the bones of living species form the basis of these analyses. Today, biochemical and genetic studies add considerably to this approach. As we will see in later chapters, genetic evidence established the close relationship between humans and ape species—chimpanzees, bonobos, and gorillas. DNA analysis has helped to estimate the origins of the human lineage some 5 to 8 million years ago. Physical anthropology therefore deals with time spans much greater than archaeology or other branches of anthropology.

Primatology

Studying the anatomy and behavior of our closest living relatives helps us understand what is unique about human nature. Therefore, **primatology,** or the study of living and fossil primates is a vital part of physical anthropology. Primates include the Asian and African apes, as well as monkeys, lemurs, lorises, and tarsiers. Biologically, humans are apes—large-bodied, broad-shouldered primates with no tail. Detailed studies of ape behavior in the wild indicate that the sharing of learned behavior is a significant part of the apes' social life. Some primatologists designate the shared, learned behavior of nonhuman apes as culture. For example, tool use and communication systems indicate the elementary basis of language in some ape societies.

Monkeys and apes have long fascinated humans, owing to our many shared anatomical and behavioral characteristics. The study of other primates provides us with important clues as to what life may have been like for our own ancestors.

molecular anthropology A branch of biological anthropology that uses genetic and biochemical techniques to test hypotheses about human evolution, adaptation, and variation.
paleoanthropology The study of the origins and predecessors of the present human species.
primatology The study of living and fossil primates.

Primate studies offer scientifically grounded perspectives on the behavior of our ancestors as well as greater appreciation and respect for the sophistication of our closest living relatives. Considering that the evolution of life on earth is a fascinating story of divergence and differentiation, comparisons of the behavior and biology among living primate groups helps refine our understanding of ongoing evolutionary processes.

Human Growth, Adaptation, and Variation

Another area of research that is of interest to physical anthropologists is the study of human growth and development. Anthropologists examine biological mechanisms of growth as well as the impact of the environment on the growth process. For example, Franz Boas, a pioneer of four-field anthropology of the early 20th century, compared the heights of European immigrants who spent their childhood in "the old country" to the increased heights obtained by their children who grew up in the United States. Today, physical anthropologists study the impacts of disease, pollution, and poverty on growth. Comparisons between human and nonhuman primate growth patterns can provide clues to the evolutionary history of humans. Detailed studies of the hormonal, genetic, and physiological basis of healthy growth in living humans contribute not only to our understanding of the growth patterns of our ancestors but also contribute significantly to the health of children today.

Studies of human adaptation focus on the capacity of humans to adapt, or adjust to their material environment—biologically and culturally. This branch of physical anthropology takes a comparative approach to humans living today in a variety of environments. Humans are remarkable among the primates in that they now inhabit the entire earth. Though cultural adaptations make it possible for humans to live in some environmental extremes, biological adaptations also contribute to survival in extreme cold, heat, and high altitude. Such biological adaptation contributes to present-day human variation.

Although we are all members of a single species, we humans differ from one another in many obvious and not so obvious ways. Our differences include visible traits such as height, body build, and skin color, as well as biochemical factors such as blood type and susceptibility to certain diseases. The physical anthropologist applies all the techniques of modern biology to achieve fuller understanding of human variation and its relationship to the different environments in which people have lived. Research in this branch of anthropology has debunked false notions of racial categories born of widespread misinterpretation of human variation, a subject addressed more fully in upcoming pages. By making systematic comparisons among humans and between humans and other primates, physical anthropologists seek to arrive at scientific conclusions concerning the function and operation of human biology and culture in all times and places.

Physical anthropology has many practical applications, such as forensics. **Forensic anthropology** specializes in the identification of human skeletal remains for legal purposes. Law enforcement authorities call upon forensic anthropologists to identify murder victims, missing persons, or people who have died in disasters, such as plane crashes. From skeletal remains, the forensic anthropologist can establish the age, sex, population affiliation, and stature of the deceased, and often whether the person was right- or left-handed, exhibited any physical abnormalities, or had evidence of trauma (broken bones and the like). In addition, some details of an individual's health and nutritional history can be read from the bones (see Anthropology Applied).

Archaeology

Archaeology is the branch of anthropology that studies material remains in order to describe and explain human behavior. Traditionally, it has focused on the prehistoric human past—the period before writing was invented or introduced. Since material products and traces of human practices, rather than the practices themselves, are all that survive of that past, archaeologists study the tools, pottery, and other enduring features such as hearths and enclosures that remain as the testimony of earlier cultures, some of them as many as 2.5 million years old. Surviving structures and objects, and the way they are situated in or on the ground, reflect aspects of human ideas and behavior. For example, shallow, restricted concentrations of charcoal that include oxidized earth, bone fragments, and charred plant remains, and near which are pieces of fire-cracked rock, pottery, and tools suitable for food preparation, are indicative of cooking and associated food processing. Such remains reveal much about a people's diet and subsistence practices. Moreover, the interpretation of such material remains in conjunction with skeletal remains allows for a complete biocultural reconstruction of human life in the past. Thus the archaeologist is able reach back for

forensic anthropology Field of applied physical anthropology that specializes in the identification of human skeletal remains for legal purposes.
archaeology The study of material remains, usually from the past, to describe and explain human behavior.

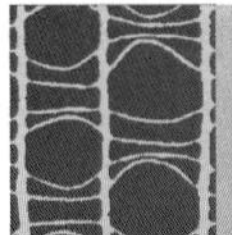

Anthropology Applied: Forensic Anthropology

© Susan Meiselas/Magnum Photos

Physical anthropologists do not just study fossil skulls. Here Clyde Snow holds the skull of a Kurd who was executed by Iraqi security forces. Snow specializes in forensic anthropology, and is widely known for his work identifying victims of state-sponsored terrorism.

Among the best-known forensic anthropologists is Clyde C. Snow. He has been practicing in this field for 40 years, first for the Federal Aviation Administration and more recently as a freelance consultant. In addition to the usual police work, Snow has studied the remains of General George Armstrong Custer and his men from the 1876 battlefield at Little Big Horn, and in 1985, he went to Brazil, where he identified the remains of the notorious Nazi war criminal Josef Mengele.

He was also instrumental in establishing the first forensic team devoted to documenting cases of human rights abuses around the world. This began in 1984 when he went to Argentina at the request of a newly elected civilian government to help with the identification of remains of the *desaparecidos*, or "disappeared ones," the 9,000 or more people who were eliminated by government death squads during seven years of military rule. A year later, he returned to give expert testimony at the trial of nine junta members and to teach Argentineans how to recover, clean, repair, preserve, photograph, x-ray, and analyze bones. Besides providing factual accounts of the fate of victims to their surviving kin and refuting the assertions of "revisionists" that the massacres never happened, the work of Snow and his Argentinean associates was crucial in convicting several military officers of kidnapping, torture, and murder.

Since Snow's pioneering work, forensic anthropologists have become increasingly involved in the investigation of human rights abuses in all parts of the world, from Chile to Guatemala, Haiti, the Philippines, Rwanda, Iraq, Bosnia, and Kosovo. Meanwhile, they continue to do important work for more typical clients. In the United States these clients include the Federal Bureau of Investigation and city, state, and county medical examiners' offices. ■ ■ ■

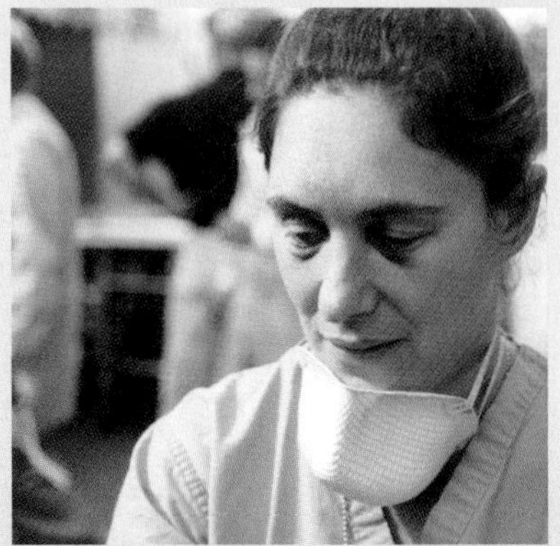

© Rich Press

Amy Zelson Mundorff, a forensic anthropologist for New York City's Office of the Chief Medical Examiner, was injured in the September 11, 2001, terrorist attack on the World Trade Center. Two days later she returned to work to supervise and coordinate the management, treatment, and cataloguing of people who lost their lives in the attack.

clues to human behavior far beyond the mere 5,000 years to which historians are confined by their dependence upon written records.

That said, archaeologists are not limited to the study of prehistoric societies; they may also study those for which historical documents are available to supplement the material remains. In most literate societies, written records are associated with governing elites rather than farmers, fishers, laborers, slaves and other folks at the "grass roots." Thus, although they can tell archaeologists much that might not be known from archaeological evidence alone, it is equally true that archaeological remains can tell historians much about a society that is not apparent from its written documents.

Although most archaeologists concentrate on the human past, some of them study material objects in contemporary settings. One example is the Garbage Project, founded by William Rathje at the University of Arizona in 1973. This carefully controlled study of household waste continues to produce thought-provoking information about contemporary social issues. Among its accomplishments, the project has tested the validity of interview-survey techniques, upon which sociologists, economists, other social scientists and policymakers rely heavily for their data. The tests clearly show a significant difference between what people believe or say they do and what garbage analysis shows they actually do. For example, in 1973, conventional techniques were used to construct and administer a questionnaire to find out

U.S. General Services Administration

Archaeological investigation of the African burial ground in New York City revealed the horror of slavery in North America, showing that even young children were worked so far beyond their ability to endure that their spines were fractured. Biological archaeologist Michael Blakey, who led the research team, notes: "Although *bioarchaeology* and forensics are often confused, when skeletal biologists use the population as the unit of analysis (rather than the individual), and incorporate cultural and historical context (rather than simply ascribing biological characteristics), and report on the lifeways of a past community (rather than on a crime for the police and courts), it is bioarchaeology rather than forensics."[3]

about the rate of alcohol consumption in Tucson. In one part of town, 15 percent of respondent households affirmed consumption of beer, but no household reported consumption of more than eight cans a week. Analysis of garbage from the same area, however, demonstrated that some beer was consumed in over 80 percent of households, and 50 percent discarded more than eight empty cans a week. Another interesting finding of the Garbage Project is that when beef prices reached an all-time high in 1973, so did the amount of beef wasted by households (not just in Tucson but in other parts of the country as well). Although common sense would lead us to suppose just the opposite, high prices and scarcity correlate with more, rather than less, waste. Such findings are important, for they demonstrate that ideas about human behavior based on conventional interview-survey techniques alone can be seriously in error. Likewise, they show what people actually do does not always match what they think they do.

In 1987, the Garbage Project began a program of excavating landfills in different parts of the United States and Canada. From this work came the first reliable data on what materials actually go into landfills and what happens to them there. And once again, common beliefs turned out to be at odds with the actual situation. For example, biodegradable materials such as newspapers take far longer to decay when buried in deep compost landfills than anyone had previously expected. This kind of information is a vital step toward solving waste-disposal problems. (Details about the Garbage Project's past and present work can be seen on its Web site: *http://info-center.ccit.arizona.edu/~bara/report.htm.)*

Linguistic Anthropology

Perhaps the most distinctive feature of the human species is language. Studies have shown that the sounds and gestures made by some other animals—especially by apes—may serve functions comparable to those of human language; yet no other animal has developed a system of symbolic communication as richly complex as that of humans. Ultimately, language is what allows people to preserve and transmit their culture from generation to generation.

The branch of anthropology that studies human languages is called **linguistic anthropology.** Linguists may deal with the description of a language (the way a sentence is formed or a verb conjugated), the history of languages (the way languages develop and change with the passage of time), or with the relation between language and culture. All three approaches yield valuable information about how people communicate and how they understand the world around them. The everyday language of English-speaking North Americans, for example, includes a number of slang words, such as *dough, greenback, dust, loot, bucks, change,* and *bread,* to identify what an indigenous inhabitant of Papua New Guinea would recognize only as "money." Such phenomena help identify things that are considered of special importance to a culture. Through the study of language in its social setting, the anthropologist is able to understand how people perceive themselves and the world around them.

Anthropological linguists also make a significant contribution to our understanding of the human past. By working out the genealogical relationships among languages and examining the distributions of those languages, they may estimate how long the speakers of those languages have lived where they do. By identifying those words in related languages that have survived from an ancient ancestral tongue, they can also suggest both where, and how, the speakers of the ancestral language lived.

linguistic anthropology The study of human languages.

[3]Blakey, M. Personal communication, October 29, 2003.

Cultural Anthropology

Cultural anthropology (sometimes referred to as *socio-cultural anthropology*) is the study of customary patterns in human behavior, thought, and feelings. It focuses on humans as culture-producing and culture-reproducing creatures. Thus, in order to understand the work of the cultural anthropologist, we must clarify what we mean by "culture." The concept is discussed in detail in Chapter 14, but for our purposes here, we may think of culture as the often unconscious standards by which societies—structured groups of people—operate. These standards are socially learned rather than acquired through biological inheritance. Since they determine, or at least guide, the normal day-to-day behavior, thought, and emotional patterns of the members of a society, human activities, ideas, and feelings are above all culturally acquired and influenced. The manifestations of culture may vary considerably from place to place, but no person is "more cultured" in the anthropological sense than any other.

Cultural anthropology has two main components: ethnography and ethnology. An **ethnography** is a detailed description of a particular culture primarily based on **fieldwork,** which is the term anthropologists use for on-location research. Because the hallmark of fieldwork is a combination of social participation and personal observation within the community being studied, as well as interviews and discussion with individual members of the cultural group in question, the ethnographic method is commonly referred to as **participant observation.** Ethnographies provide the basic information used to make systematic comparisons between different cultures all across the world. Known as **ethnology,** such cross-cultural research allows anthropologists to develop anthropological theories that help explain why certain important differences or similarities occur between groups.

cultural anthropology The study of customary patterns in human behavior, thought, and feelings. It focuses on humans as culture-producing and culture-reproducing creatures.
ethnography A detailed description of a particular culture primarily based on fieldwork.
fieldwork The term anthropologists use for on-location research.
participant observation In ethnography, the technique of learning a people's culture through social participation and personal observation within the community being studied, as well as interviews and discussion with individual members of the group over an extended period of time.
ethnology The study and analysis of different cultures from a comparative or historical point of view, utilizing ethnographic accounts and developing anthropological theories that help explain why certain important differences or similarities occur among groups.
holistic perspective A fundamental principle of anthropology, that the various parts of culture must be viewed in the broadest possible context in order to understand their interconnections and interdependence.
informants Members of a society being studied who provide information that helps the ethnographer make sense of what is being said and done.

Ethnography

Through participant observation—eating a people's food, sleeping under their roofs, speaking their language, and personally experiencing their habits and customs—the ethnographer seeks to understand their way of life to a far greater extent than any nonparticipant researcher ever could. One learns a culture best by learning how to speak and behave acceptably in the society in which one is doing fieldwork. Being a participant observer does not mean that the anthropologist must join in a people's battles in order to study a culture in which warfare is prominent; but by living among a warlike people, the ethnographer should be able to understand how warfare fits into the overall cultural framework. He or she must be a careful observer to gain an in-depth overview of a culture without placing undue emphasis on one of its parts at the expense of another. Only by discovering how all aspects of a culture—its social, political, economic, and religious practices and institutions—relate to one another can the ethnographer begin to understand the cultural system. Anthropologists refer to this as the **holistic perspective,** and it is one of the fundamental principles of anthropology. Robert Gordon, an anthropologist from Namibia, speaks of it this way: "Whereas the sociologist or the political scientist might examine the beauty of a flower petal by petal, the anthropologist is the person that stands on the top of the mountain and looks at the beauty of the field. In other words, we try and go for the wider perspective."[4]

MEDIATREK
For a Smithsonian Institution virtual tour of Alice Fletcher's fieldwork among Sioux Indian women in the 1880s, see MediaTrek 1.2 on the companion Web site or CD-ROM.

An ethnographer's most essential tools are notebooks, pen/pencil, camera, tape recorder, and, increasingly, a laptop computer. Most important of all, he or she needs flexible social skills. When participating in an unfamiliar culture, the ethnographer does not just blunder about blindly but enlists the assistance of **informants**—members of the society being studied, who provide information that helps the researcher make sense of activities taking place. Just as parents guide a child

[4]Gordon, R. (1981, December). [Interview for Coast Telecourses Inc.]. Los Angeles.

© Rhoda Sidney/PhotoEdit

© Laura Dwight/PhotoEdit

© Bruce Broce

Sociologists conduct structured interviews and administer questionnaires to *respondents*, while psychologists experiment with *subjects*. Anthropologists, by contrast, learn from *informants*. The researcher in the third photo is Dutch anthropologist Harald Prins, co-author of this book. Doing fieldwork among the Plains Apache Indians in Oklahoma, he is using a camera to document an oral history project with tribal chief Alfred Chalepah.

toward proper behavior, so do informants help the anthropologist in the field unravel the "mysteries" of what at first seems to be a strange culture, full of puzzling things.

So basic is ethnographic fieldwork to cultural anthropology that British anthropologist C. G. Seligman once asserted, "Field research in anthropology is what the blood of the martyrs is to the church."[5] Certainly anthropological fieldwork often involves at least a measure of strain and pain, for it requires the researcher to step out of his or her cultural comfort zone into a world that is unfamiliar and sometimes unsettling. Anthropologists in the field are likely to face a host of challenges—physical, social, mental, political, and ethical. They may have to deal with the physical challenge of adjusting to food, climate, and hygiene conditions that are vastly different from what they are accustomed to. Socially, they are likely to encounter the challenge of not being accepted or trusted and of being unable to communicate until they learn the local language. Typically, anthropologists in the field struggle with such mental challenges as loneliness, feeling like a perpetual outsider, being socially clumsy and clueless in their new cultural setting, and having to be alert around the clock because anything that is happening or being said may be significant to their research. Political challenges include the possibility of unwittingly letting oneself be used by factions within the community, or being viewed with suspicion by government authorities who may suspect the anthropologist is a spy. And there are ethical dilemmas galore: what to do if faced with a cultural practice one finds troubling, such as female circumcision; how to deal with demands for food supplies and/or medicine; the temptation to use deception to gain vital information; and so on.

On the positive side, the ethnographic endeavor often leads to tangible and meaningful personal, professional and social rewards, ranging from lasting friendships to vital knowledge and insights concerning the human condition that make positive contributions to people's lives. Something of the meaning of anthropological fieldwork—its usefulness and its impact on researcher and subject—is conveyed in the following Original Study by Suzanne Leclerc-Madlala, an anthropologist who left her familiar New England surroundings 20 years ago to do AIDS research among Zulu-speaking people in South Africa. Her research interest has changed the course of her own life, not to mention the lives of individuals who have AIDS/HIV and the type of treatment they receive.

[5]Lewis, I. M. (1976). *Social anthropology in perspective* (p. 27). Harmondsworth, England: Penguin.

Original Study

Fighting HIV/AIDS in Africa: Traditional Healers on the Front Line

In the 1980s, as a North American anthropology graduate student at George Washington University in St. Louis, I met and married a Zulu-speaking student from South Africa. It was the height of apartheid, and upon moving to that country I was classified as "honorary black" and forced to live in a segregated township with my husband. The AIDS epidemic was in its infancy, but it was clear from the start that an anthropological understanding of how people

[CONTINUED]

[CONTINUED]

perceive and engage with this disease would be crucial for developing interventions. I wanted to learn all that I could to make a difference, and this culminated in earning a Ph.D. from the University of Natal on the cultural construction of AIDS among the Zulu. The HIV/AIDS pandemic in Africa became my professional passion.

Faced with overwhelming global health-care needs, the World Health Organization passed a series of resolutions in the 1970s promoting collaboration between traditional and modern medicine. Such moves held a special relevance for Africa where traditional healers typically outnumber practitioners of modern medicine by a ratio of 100 to 1 or more. Given Africa's disproportionate burden of disease, supporting partnership efforts with traditional healers makes sense. But what sounds sensible today was once considered absurd, even heretical. For centuries Westerners generally viewed traditional healing as a whole lot of primitive mumbo jumbo practiced by witchdoctors with demonic powers who perpetuated superstition. Yet, its practice survived. Today, as the African continent grapples with an HIV/AIDS epidemic of crisis proportion, millions of sick people who are either too poor or too distant to access modern health care are proving that traditional healers are an invaluable resource in the fight against AIDS.

Of the world's estimated 40 million people currently infected by HIV, 70 percent live in sub-Saharan Africa, and the vast majority of children left orphaned by AIDS are African. From the 1980s onward, as Africa became synonymous with the rapid spread of HIV/AIDS, a number of prevention programs involved traditional healers. My initial research in South Africa's KwaZulu-Natal province—where it is estimated that 36 percent of the population is HIV infected—revealed that traditional Zulu healers were regularly consulted for the treatment of sexually transmitted diseases (STD). I found that such diseases, along with HIV/AIDS, were usually attributed to transgressions of taboos related to birth, pregnancy, marriage, and death. Moreover, these diseases were often understood within a framework of pollution and contagion, and like most serious illnesses, ultimately believed to have their causal roots in witchcraft.

In the course of my research, I investigated a pioneer program in STD and HIV education for traditional healers in the province. The program aimed to provide basic biomedical knowledge about the various modes of disease transmission, the means available for prevention, the diagnosing of symptoms, the keeping of records, and the making of patient referrals to local clinics and hospitals. Interviews with the healers showed that many maintained a deep suspicion of modern medicine. They perceived AIDS education as a one-way street intended to press them into formal health structures and convince them of the superiority of modern medicine. Yet, today, few of the 6,000-plus KwaZulu-Natal healers who have been trained in AIDS education say they would opt for less collaboration; most want to have more.

© Kerry Cullinan

Medical anthropologist Suzanne Leclerc-Madlala visits with "Doctor" Koloko in KwaZulu-Natal, South Africa. This Zulu traditional healer proudly displays her official AIDS training certificate.

Treatments by Zulu healers for HIV/AIDS often take the form of infusions of bitter herbs to "cleanse" the body, strengthen the blood, and remove misfortune and "pollution." Some treatments provide effective relief from common ailments associated with AIDS such as itchy skin rashes, oral thrush, persistent diarrhea, and general debility. Indigenous plants such as *unwele (Sutherlandia frutescens)* and African potato *(Hypoxis hemerocallidea)* are well-known traditional medicines that have proven immuno-boosting properties. Both have recently become available in modern pharmacies packaged in tablet form. With modern anti-retroviral treatments still well beyond the reach of most South Africans, indigenous medicines that can delay or alleviate some of the suffering caused by AIDS are proving to be valuable and popular treatments.

Knowledge about potentially infectious bodily fluids has led healers to change some of their practices. Where porcupine quills where once used to give a type of indigenous injection, patients are now advised to bring their own sewing needles to consultations. Patients provide their own individual razor blades for making incisions on their skin, where previously healers reused the same razor on many clients. Some healers claim they have given up the practice of biting clients' skin to remove foreign objects from the body. It is not uncommon today, especially in urban centers like Durban, to find healers proudly displaying AIDS training certificates in their inner-city "surgeries" where they don white jackets and wear protective latex gloves.

Politics and controversy have dogged South Africa's official response to HIV/AIDS. But back home in the waddle-and-daub, animal-skin-draped herbariums and divining huts of traditional healers, the politics of AIDS holds little relevance. Here the sick and dying are coming in droves to be treated by healers who have been part and parcel of community life (and death) since time immemorial. In many cases traditional healers have transformed their homes into hospices for AIDS patients. Turned away from

[CONTINUED]

provincial hospitals unable to cope with the rising tide of AIDS, the sick are returning home to die. Because of the strong stigma that still plagues the disease, those with AIDS symptoms are often abandoned or sometimes chased away from their homes by family members. They seek refuge with healers who provide them with comfort in their final days. Healers' homes are also becoming orphanages as healers respond to what has been called the "third wave" of AIDS destruction: the growing legions of orphaned children.

The practice of traditional healing in Africa is adapting to the changing face of health and illness in the context of HIV/AIDS. But those who are suffering go to traditional healers not only in search of relief for physical symptoms. They go to learn about the ultimate cause of their disease—something other than the immediate cause of a sexually transmitted "germ" or "virus." They go to find answers to the "why me and not him" questions, the "why now" and "why this." As with most traditional healing systems worldwide, healing among the Zulu and most all African ethnic groups cannot be separated from the spiritual concerns of the individual and the cosmological beliefs of the community at large. Traditional healers help to restore a sense of balance between the individual and the community, on one hand, and between the individual and the cosmos, or ancestors, on the other hand. They provide health care that is personalized, culturally appropriate, holistic, and tailored to meet the needs and expectations of the patient. In many ways it is a far more satisfactory form of healing than that offered by modern medicine.

Traditional healing in Africa is flourishing in the era of AIDS, and understanding why this is so requires a shift in the conceptual framework by which we understand, explain, and interpret health. Anthropological methods and its comparative and holistic perspective can facilitate, like no other discipline, the type of understanding that is urgently needed to address the AIDS crisis. *(By Suzanne Leclerc-Madlala. Adapted in part from Leclerc-Madlala, S. (2002). Bodies and politics: Healing rituals in the democratic South Africa. In V. Faure (Ed.), Les cahiers de 'l'IFAS, No. 2. Johannesburg: The French Institute.)*

The popular image of ethnographic fieldwork is that it occurs among people who live in far-off, isolated places. To be sure, much ethnographic work has been done in the remote villages of Africa or South America, the islands of the Pacific Ocean, the deserts of Australia, and so on. During the heyday of colonialism (1880s–1940s) many European anthropologists did indeed focus on the study of traditional cultures in the colonies overseas. Meanwhile, their North American colleagues were engaged primarily in fieldwork on Indian reservations, documenting endangered Native American cultures. That said, anthropologists have recognized from the start that a generalized understanding of human ideas and behavior depends upon knowledge of all cultures and peoples, including those in the industrialized West. During the years of the Great Depression and World War II, for example, many anthropologists in the United States worked in settings ranging from factories to whole communities.

The conditions and priorities of fieldwork altered dramatically after World War II (1939–1945) in response to changes in the world political order. By the 1960s, European colonial powers had lost almost all of their overseas territorial possessions. A significant number of anthropologists turned their attention to South and Central America, while others focused on changes in the newly independent countries in Africa and Asia. However, as political unrest made fieldwork increasingly difficult in many parts of the world, many anthropologists zeroed in on important cross-cultural issues that needed to be dealt with inside Europe and North America. Many of these issues, which remain focal points to this day, involve immigrants and refugees who come from places where anthropologists have conducted research. Some anthropologists have gone beyond studying such groups to playing a role in helping them adjust to their new circumstances—an example of applied anthropology. Simultaneously, anthropologists are using the same research techniques that served them so well in the study of non-Western peoples to research such diverse subjects as religious cults, street gangs, schools, corporate bureaucracies, health-care delivery systems, and how people deal with consumer complaints in Western cultures.

Although it has much to offer, anthropological study within one's own society may present special problems. Sir Edmund Leach, a major figure in British anthropology, once put it this way:

> Surprising though it may seem, fieldwork in a cultural context of which you already have intimate firsthand experience seems to be much more difficult than fieldwork which is approached from the naïve viewpoint of a total stranger. When anthropologists study facets of their own society their vision seems to become distorted by prejudices which derive from private rather than public experience.[6]

For this reason, the most successful anthropological studies of societies to which the researchers

---

[6]Leach, E. (1982). *Social anthropology* (p. 124). Glasgow, Scotland: Fontana Paperbacks.

themselves belong are usually those carried out by individuals who first worked in some other culture. The more one learns of other cultures, the more one gains a different perspective on one's own.

Ethnology

Although ethnographic fieldwork is basic to cultural anthropology, it is not the sole occupation of the cultural anthropologist. Largely descriptive in nature, ethnography provides the basic data needed for ethnology—the branch of cultural anthropology that makes cross-cultural comparisons and develops theories that explain why certain important differences or similarities occur between groups.

Intriguing insights into one's own beliefs and practices may come from cross-cultural comparisons. Consider, for example, a comparison between industrialized peoples and traditional food foragers (people who rely on wild plant and animal resources for subsistence) concerning the amount of time spent on domestic chores. In the United States, there is a widespread belief that the ever-increasing output of household appliances has resulted in a steady reduction in housework, with a consequent increase in leisure time. Thus, consumer appliances have become important indicators of a high standard of living.

Anthropological research among food foragers, however, has shown that they work far less at household tasks, and indeed less at all subsistence pursuits, than do people in industrialized societies. Aboriginal Australian women, for example, traditionally devote an average of 20 hours per week to collecting and preparing food, as well as other domestic chores. By contrast, women in the rural United States in the 1920s, without the benefit of labor-saving appliances, devoted approximately 52 hours a week to their housework. One might suppose that this has changed over the decades since, yet some 50 years later, urban U.S. women who were not working for wages outside their homes were putting 55 hours a week into their housework—this despite all their "labor-saving" dishwashers, washing machines, clothes dryers, vacuum cleaners, food processors, and microwave ovens.[7]

Considering such cross-cultural comparisons, one may think of ethnology as the study of alternative ways of doing things. But more than that, by making systematic comparisons, ethnologists seek to arrive at scientific conclusions concerning the function and operation of culture in all times and places.

[7]Bodley, J. H. (1985). *Anthropology and contemporary human problems* (2nd ed., p. 69). Palo Alto, CA: Mayfield.

medical anthropology A specialization in anthropology that brings theoretical and applied approaches from cultural and biological anthropology to the study of human health and disease.

Medical Anthropology

In part due to the growing importance of global health organizations, which face a wide cross-cultural array of healing traditions and practices, medical anthropology has emerged as a significant specialization within the discipline of anthropology. In the past, medical anthropologists were individuals trained as physicians and ethnographers who investigated health beliefs and practices of people in exotic places while also providing them with "Western" medicine. Medical anthropologists during this early period translated local experiences of sickness into the scientific language of Western biomedicine. Following a re-evaluation of this ethnocentric approach in the 1970s, medical anthropology emerged as a unified discipline that incorporated theories and practices of anthropology. Today, **medical anthropology** is defined as a specialization that brings theoretical and applied approaches from cultural and biological anthropology to the study of human health and disease. Medical anthropologists study medical systems as cultural systems similar to any other social institution. They use cross-cultural and scientific models drawn from biological anthropology to understand and improve human health. They have also turned their attention toward biomedicine, contributing a wide-ranging perspective to the social and cultural aspects of health care in their own societies. Their work sheds light on the connections between human health and political and economic forces, both globally and locally. Many of the Biocultural Connections featured throughout this text present the work of medical anthropologists.

ANTHROPOLOGY AND SCIENCE

The foremost concern of all anthropologists is the detailed and comprehensive study of humankind in all its rich diversity. Some people refer to anthropology as a social or behavioral science. Others speak of it as a natural science or as one of the humanities. Can the work of the anthropologist properly be labeled "scientific"? What exactly do we mean by the term *science?*

Science, a carefully honed way of producing objective knowledge, aims to reveal and explain the underlying logic, the structural processes, that make the world "tick." It is a creative endeavor that seeks testable explanations for observed phenomena, ideally in terms of the workings of hidden but universal and unchanging principles, or laws. Two basic ingredients are essential for

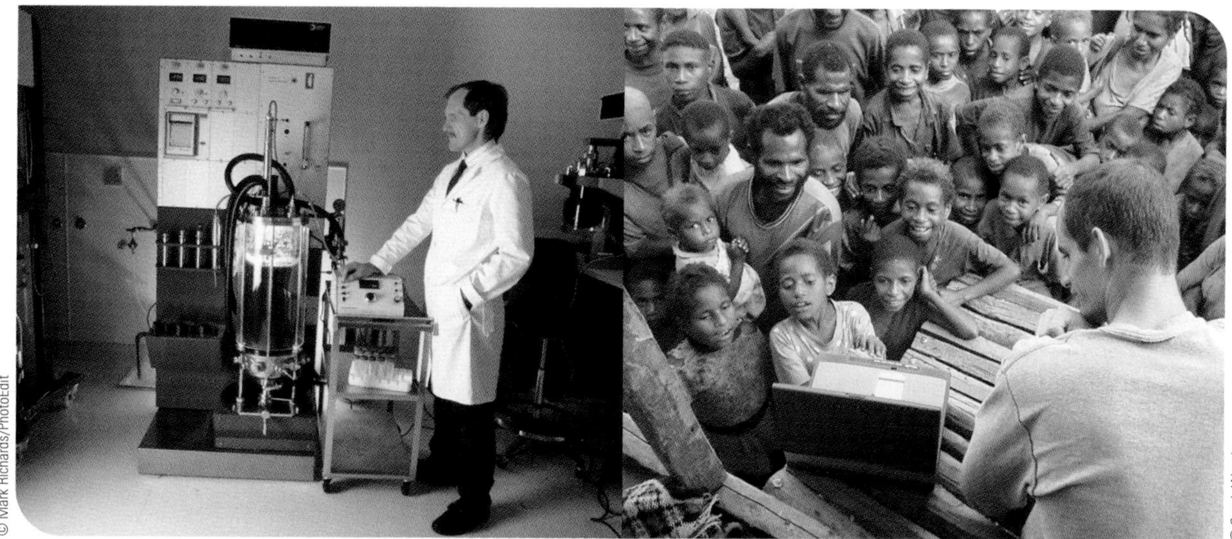

© Mark Richards/PhotoEdit

© Sarah Wesch

VISUAL COUNTERPOINT To many people, a scientist is someone who works in a laboratory, carrying out experiments with the aid of specialized equipment. Contrary to the stereotypical image, not all scientists work in laboratories, nor is experimentation the only technique they use. On the right, villagers in Papua New Guinea watch themselves on a video shown by anthropologist Michael Wesch.

this: imagination and skepticism. Imagination, though capable of leading us astray, is required to help us recognize unexpected ways phenomena might be ordered and think of old things in new ways. Without it, there can be no science. Skepticism is what allows us to distinguish **fact** (an observation verified by several skilled observers) from fancy, to test our speculations, and to prevent our imaginations from running away with us.

In their search for explanations, scientists do not assume that things are always as they appear on the surface. After all, what could be more obvious than that the earth is a stable entity, around which the sun travels every day? And yet, it isn't so.

Like other scientists, anthropologists often begin their research with a **hypothesis** (a tentative explanation or hunch) about the possible relationships between certain observed facts or reported events. By gathering various kinds of data that seem to ground such suggested explanations on evidence, anthropologists come up with **theories**—explanations for natural or cultural phenomena, supported by a reliable body of data. In their effort to demonstrate linkages between known facts or events, anthropologists may discover unexpected facts, events, or relationships. In other words, an important function of theory is that it guides us in our explorations and may result in new knowledge. Equally important, the newly discovered facts may provide evidence that certain explanations, however popular or firmly believed to be true, are unfounded. When the evidence is lacking or fails to support the suggested explanations, anthropologists are forced to drop promising hypotheses or attractive hunches. Moreover, no scientific theory, no matter how widely accepted by the international community of scholars, is beyond challenge. Like other scientists, anthropologists do not view any theory as the final truth. Rather, they measure its validity and soundness by varying degrees of probability; what is considered to be "true" is what is most probable. But while anthropologists cannot claim anything as proven absolutely true, they can and do provide evidence that assumptions widely thought to have been true are unfounded or contrary to the observed facts of reality. Thus a theory, contrary to widespread misuse of the term, is much more than mere speculation; it is a closely examined and critically checked out explanation of observed reality.

In this respect, it is important to distinguish between scientific theories—which are always open to future challenges born of new evidence or insights—and doctrine. A **doctrine,** or dogma, is an assertion of opinion or belief formally handed down by an authority as true and indisputable. Examples of such authority can be found in all religious movements, from the Iroquois Indians and their longhouse tradition in northeast America to Buddhists in Tibet, Orthodox Jews in Israel, Sunni Muslims in Egypt, Roman Catholics in Italy, and so on. For instance, Judaism, Christianity, and Islam each

fact An observation verified by several observers skilled in the necessary techniques of observation.
hypothesis A tentative explanation of the relation between certain phenomena.
theory In science, an explanation of natural phenomena, supported by a reliable body of data.
doctrine An assertion of opinion or belief formally handed down by authority as true and indisputable.

hold as sacred certain ancient writings. Respectively known as the Torah, Bible, and Koran, these holy texts are believed to contain divine wisdom and eternal truths. All three speak of the origin of the human species in a way very similar to that found in the Bible's first chapter, Genesis: *God created the world in seven days, and on day six He created the first human beings, Adam and Eve, in the Garden of Eden.* But while these religions share a creationist doctrine, there are also significant differences among them. Moreover, within each of these religions, major divisions have emerged over doctrine. For instance, not all Christians subscribe to the doctrine of the Virgin Mary's Immaculate Conception. Those who accept this doctrine do so on the basis of religious authority, conceding that this sacred story is contrary to human biology. Such doctrines cannot be tested or proved one way or another: They are accepted as matters of faith.

In contrast to religious doctrine, however, scientific theory depends on demonstrable evidence and testing before an explanation can be accepted as "true." So it is that, as our knowledge expands, the odds in favor of some theories over others are generally increased, even though old "truths" sometimes must be discarded as alternative theories are shown to be more probable.

By way of illustration, we may compare two competing theories that sought to explain the fact of biological evolution: those of Jean Baptiste Lamarck (1744–1829) and Charles R. Darwin (1809–1882). While Lamarck theorized that evolution took place through inheritance of acquired characteristics, Darwin claimed that it was the result of natural selection. Lamarck's theory was laid to rest in the late 1800s due to experiments conducted by August Weismann and other scientists. Breeding twenty generations of mice, Weismann cut off the tails in each generation, only to find them still present in the 21st. By contrast, countless attempts to falsify Darwin's theory have failed to do so. Moreover, as our knowledge of genetics, geology, and paleontology has increased, our understanding of how natural selection works has advanced accordingly. Thus, while Lamarck's theory to account for biological change over time had to be abandoned, evidence has increased the probability that Darwin's is correct.

Difficulties of the Scientific Approach

Straightforward though the scientific approach may seem, there are serious difficulties in its application in anthropology. For instance, once a hypothesis has been proposed, the person who suggested it is strongly motivated to verify it, and this can cause one to unwittingly overlook negative evidence and unanticipated findings. This is a familiar problem in science in general. In the words of paleontologist Stephen Jay Gould, "The greatest impediment to scientific innovation is usually a conceptual lock, not a factual lock."[8] The anthropological perspective highlights an additional difficulty: In order to arrive at useful theories concerning human behavior and its evolution, one must begin with hypotheses that are as objective and as little culture-bound as possible. And here lies a major—some people would say insurmountable—problem: It is difficult for someone who has grown up in one culture to frame hypotheses about others that are not culture-bound.

As one example of this sort of problem, we may look at attempts by archaeologists to understand the nature of settlement in the Classic period of Maya civilization. This civilization flourished between 1,750 and 1,100 years ago in what is now northern Guatemala, Belize, and neighboring portions of Mexico and Honduras. Today much of this region is covered by a dense tropical forest that is thinly inhabited by villagers, who sustain themselves through slash-and-burn farming. (After cutting and burning the natural vegetation, crops are grown for two years or so before fertility is exhausted, and a new field must be cleared.) Yet in these now sparsely populated forests there are numerous archaeological sites, featuring towering temples as tall as modern 20-story buildings, plus other sorts of monumental architecture and carved stone monuments.

Because of their cultural bias against tropical forests as places to prosper, and against slash-and-burn farming as a means of raising sufficient food, North American and European archaeologists were puzzled. How could the Maya have maintained large, permanent settlements on the basis of slash-and-burn farming? At first, the answer seemed self-evident—they couldn't; therefore, the great archaeological sites must have been ceremonial centers inhabited by few, if any, people. Periodically a rural peasantry, living scattered in small hamlets over the countryside, must have gathered in these places for rituals or to provide labor for their construction and maintenance.

This was the generally accepted scholarly view until 1960. That year a group of young University of Pennsylvania archaeologists working at Tikal, one of the largest of all Maya sites in Guatemala, dared to ask some simple, unbiased questions: Did anyone live at this particular site on a permanent basis; if so, how many, and how were they supported? Throwing preconceived notions overboard and working intensively over the next decade, the archaeologists established that Tikal had actually been inhabited on a permanent basis

[8] Gould, S. J. (1989). *Wonderful life* (p. 226). New York: Norton.

Anthropologists of Note

Franz Boas (1858–1942) ▪ Fredric Ward Putnam (1839–1915) ▪ John Wesley Powell (1834–1902)

© Bettman/Corbis

In North America, anthropology among the social sciences has a unique character, owing in large part to the natural science (rather than social science) background of the three men pictured here. **Boas**, educated in physics, was not the first to teach anthropology in the United States, but it was he and his students, with their insistence on scientific rigor, who made such courses a common part of college and university curricula.

The Granger Collection

Putnam, a zoologist specializing in the study of birds and fishes, and permanent secretary of the American Association for the Advancement of Science, made a decision in 1875 to devote himself to the promotion of anthropology. It was through his efforts that many of the great anthropology museums were established: the Phoebe Hearst Museum at the University of California, the Peabody Museum at Harvard University, and the Field Museum in Chicago. Putnam also founded the anthropology department of the American Museum of Natural History in New York.

Culver Pictures

Powell was a geologist and founder of the United States Geological Survey, but he also carried out ethnographic and linguistic research. (His classification of Indian languages north of Mexico is still consulted by scholars today.) In 1879, he founded the Bureau of American Ethnology (ultimately absorbed by the Smithsonian Institution), thereby establishing anthropology within the U.S. government.

by tens of thousands of people! The society was supported by intensive forms of agriculture more productive than slash-and-burn alone. This work at Tikal proved wrong the older, culture-bound hypotheses and paved the way for an improved understanding of Classic Maya civilization.

When anthropologists do research in different cultures, they make an effort to be as objective as possible. To accomplish that goal, they recognize the importance of trying to frame their research strategies in ways that avoid culture-boundedness. In so doing, they rely heavily on a technique that has proved successful in other natural science disciplines. As did the archaeologists working at Tikal, they immerse themselves in the data to the fullest extent possible. In the process, anthropologists become so thoroughly familiar with even the smallest details that they can begin to recognize underlying patterns in the data, many of which might easily have been overlooked. Recognition of such patterns enables the anthropologist to frame meaningful hypotheses, which then may be subjected to further testing in the field.

Unlike many other social scientists, the anthropologist usually does not go into the field armed with prefigured questionnaires; rather, he or she recognizes that there are probably all sorts of things that can be found out only by maintaining as open a mind as one can. As fieldwork proceeds, anthropologists sort their complex observations into a meaningful whole, sometimes by formulating and testing limited or low-level hypotheses, but just as often by making use of intuition and playing hunches. What is important is that the results are constantly checked for consistency, for if the parts fail to fit together in a manner that is internally consistent, then the anthropologist knows that a mistake may have been made and that further inquiry is necessary.

Two studies of a village in Peru illustrate the contrast between anthropological and other social science approaches. One was carried out by a sociologist who, after conducting a survey by questionnaire, concluded

© Anita Haviland

Tikal, one of the largest of all Maya sites in Guatemala was at its height between 1,450 and 1,150 years ago.

that people in the village invariably worked together on one another's privately owned plots of land. By contrast, a cultural anthropologist who lived in the village for over a year (including the brief period when the sociologist did his study) observed that particular practice only once. The anthropologist's sustained fieldwork showed that although a belief in labor exchange relations was important for the people's understanding of themselves, it was not a regular economic practice.[9] This is not to say that all sociological research is bad and all anthropological research is good. The point is that relying exclusively on questionnaire surveys is a risky business, no matter who does it. That is because questionnaires all too easily embody the concepts and categories of the researcher, who is an outsider, rather than those of the subjects themselves. Even where this is not a problem, questionnaire surveys alone are not good ways of identifying causal relationships. They tend to concentrate on what is measurable, answerable, and acceptable as a question, rather than probing the less obvious and more complex, qualitative aspects of society. Moreover, for a host of reasons—fear, prudence, wishful thinking, ignorance, exhaustion, hostility, hope of benefit—people may give partial, false, or self-serving information.[10] Keeping culture-bound ideas out of research methods, as illustrated through the example of standardized questionnaires, is an important point in all of anthropology's subfields.

Another issue in scientific anthropology is the matter of validity. In the natural sciences, replication of observations and/or experiments is a major means of establishing the reliability of a researcher's conclusions. Thus, one can see for oneself if one's colleague has "gotten it right." In anthropology, validation is uniquely challenging because observational access is often limited. Access to a particular research site can be constrained by a number of factors. Difficulty of getting there and obtaining necessary permits, insufficient funding, and the fact that social, political, and environmental conditions often change mean that what could be observed in a certain context at one particular time cannot be at others, and so on. Thus, one researcher cannot easily confirm the reliability or completeness of another's account. For this reason, an anthropologist bears a special responsibility for accurate reporting. In the final research report, she or he must be clear about several basic things: Why was a particular location selected as a research site? What were the research objectives? What were the local conditions during fieldwork? Which local individuals provided the key information and major insights? How were the data collected and recorded? Without such background information, it is difficult for others to judge the validity of the account and the soundness of the researcher's conclusions.

[9]Chambers, R. (1983). *Rural development: Putting the last first* (p. 51). New York: Longman.

[10]Sanjek, R. (1990). On ethnographic validity. In R. Sanjek (Ed.), *Fieldnotes* (p. 395). Ithaca, NY: Cornell University Press.

ANTHROPOLOGY'S COMPARATIVE METHOD

The end product of anthropological research, if properly carried out, is a coherent statement about culture or human nature that provides an explanatory framework for understanding the ideas and actions of the people who have been studied. And this, in turn, is what permits the anthropologist to frame broader hypotheses about human beliefs, behavior, and biology. Plausible though such hypotheses may be, however, the consideration of a single society is generally insufficient for their testing. Without some basis for comparison, the hypothesis grounded in a single case may be no more than a particular historical coincidence. On the other hand, a single case may be enough to cast doubt on, if not refute, a theory that had previously been held to be valid. For example, the discovery in 1948 that aborigines living in Australia's northern Arnhem Land put in an average workday of less than 6 hours, while living well above a level of bare sufficiency, was enough to call into question the widely accepted notion that food-foraging peoples are so preoccupied with finding scarce food that they lack time for any of life's more pleasurable activities. The observations made in the Arnhem Land study have since been confirmed many times over in various parts of the world.

Hypothetical explanations of cultural and biological phenomena may be tested by the comparison of archaeological, biological, linguistic, historical, and/or ethnographic data for several societies found in a particular region. Carefully controlled comparison provides a broader basis for drawing general conclusions about humans than does the study of a single culture or population. The anthropologist who undertakes such a comparison may be more confident that events or features believed to be related really are related, at least within the area under investigation; however, an explanation that is valid in one area is not necessarily so in another.

Ideally, theories in anthropology are generated from worldwide comparisons. The cross-cultural researcher examines a global sample of societies in order to discover whether or not hypotheses proposed to explain cultural

Biocultural Connection

The Anthropology of Organ Transplantation

In 1954, the first organ transplant occurred in Boston when surgeons removed a kidney from one identical twin to place it inside his sick brother. Though some transplants rely upon living donors, routine organ transplantation depends largely upon the availability of organs obtained from individuals who have died.

From an anthropological perspective, the meanings of death and the body vary cross-culturally. While death could be said to represent a particular biological state, social agreement about this state's significance is of paramount importance. Anthropologist Margaret Lock has explored differences between Japanese and North American acceptance of the biological state of "brain death" and how it affects the practice of organ transplants.

Brain death relies upon the absence of measurable electrical currents in the brain and the inability to breathe without technological assistance. The brain-dead individual, though attached to machines, still seems alive with a beating heart and pink cheeks. North Americans find brain death acceptable, in part, because personhood and individuality are culturally located in the brain. North American comfort with brain death has allowed for the "gift of life" through organ donation and subsequent transplantation.

By contrast, in Japan, the concept of brain death is hotly contested and organ transplants are rarely performed. The Japanese do not incorporate a mind-body split into their models of themselves and locate personhood throughout the body rather than in the brain. They resist accepting a warm pink body as a corpse from which organs can be "harvested." Further, organs cannot be transformed into "gifts" because anonymous donation is not compatible with Japanese social patterns of reciprocal exchange.

Organ transplantation carries far greater social meaning than the purely biological movement of an organ from one individual to another. Cultural and biological processes are tightly woven into every aspect of this new social practice. *(Based on Lock, M. (2001).* Twice dead: Organ transplants and the reinvention of death. *Berkeley: University of California Press.)*

phenomena or biological variation are universally applicable. Ideally the sample is selected at random, thereby enhancing the probability that the theoretical conclusions will be valid. However, the greater the number of societies being compared, the less likely it is that the investigator will have a detailed understanding of all the societies encompassed by the study. Therefore, the cross-cultural researcher depends upon data gathered by other scholars as well as his or her own. A key resource for this is the Human Relations Area Files, a vast cross-cultural catalogue discussed in detail in Chapter 14. This resource provides cross-cultural data on a variety of cultural and biological characteristics. Similarly, archaeologists and biological anthropologists rely on artifacts and skeletal collections housed in museums, as well as published descriptions of these collections.

ANTHROPOLOGY AND THE HUMANITIES

Although the sciences and humanities are often thought to be mutually exclusive approaches to learning, they share methods for critical thinking, mental creativity, and deepening knowledge about the substance of reality.[11] In anthropology, both come together, which is why, for example, anthropological research in the United States is funded not only by such "hard science" agencies as the National Science Foundation but also by such organizations as the National Endowment for the Humanities. To paraphrase Roy Rappaport, a past president of the American Anthropological Association:[12]

> The combination of scientific and humanistic approaches is and always has been a source of tension. It has been crucial to anthropology because it truly reflects the condition of a species that lives and can only live in terms of meanings that it must construct in a world devoid of intrinsic meaning, yet subject to natural law. Without the continued grounding in careful observation that scientific aspects of our tradition provide, our interpretive efforts may float off into literary criticism and speculation. But without the interpretive tradition, the scientific tradition that grounds us will never get off the ground.

[11] Shearer, R. R., & Gould, S. J. (1999). Of two minds and one nature. *Science, 286,* 1093.

[12] Rappaport, R. A. (1994). Commentary, *Anthropology Newsletter,* 35, 76.

The humanistic side of anthropology is perhaps most immediately evident in its concern with other cultures' languages, values, achievements in the arts and literature (including oral literature among peoples who lack writing), and how they make sense of their lives. Beyond this, anthropologists remain committed to the proposition that one cannot fully understand another culture by simply observing it; as the term *participant observation* implies, one must *experience* it as well. Thus, ethnographers spend prolonged periods of time living with the people they study, sharing their joys and suffering, their hardships, including sickness and, sometimes, premature death. They are not so naïve as to believe that they can be, or even should be, dispassionate about the people whose trials and tribulations they share. As Robin Fox put it, "our hearts, as well as our brains, should be with our men and women."[13]

The humanistic side of anthropology is evident as well in its emphasis on qualitative—in contrast to quantitative—research. This is not to say that anthropologists are unaware of the value of quantification and statistical procedures; they do make use of them for various purposes. Nevertheless, reducing people and the things they do and think to numbers may have a certain "dehumanizing" effect (it is easier to ignore the concerns of "impersonal numbers" than it is those of flesh-and-blood humans) and keep us from dealing with important issues less susceptible to abstract calculation. For all these reasons, anthropologists tend to place less emphasis on statistical data than do other social scientists.

Given their intense involvement with other peoples, it should come as no surprise that anthropologists have amassed considerable information about human failure and success, weakness and greatness—the real stuff of the humanities. Small wonder, too, that above all anthropologists steer clear of a "cold" impersonal scientific approach that would blind them to the fact that human societies are made up of individuals with rich assortments of emotions and aspirations that demand respect. Anthropology has sometimes been called the most humane of the sciences and the most scientific of the humanities—a designation that most anthropologists accept with considerable pride.

MEDIATREK

To learn more about the American Anthropological Association, including its code of ethics, see MediaTrek1.3 on the companion Web site or CD-ROM.

[13]Fox, R. (1968). *Encounter with anthropology* (p. 290). New York: Dell.

QUESTIONS OF ETHICS

The kinds of research carried out by anthropologists, and the settings within which they work, raise a number of important moral questions about the potential uses and abuses of our knowledge. Who will utilize our findings and for what purposes? Who, if anyone, will profit from them? For example, in the case of research on an ethnic or religious minority whose values or lifeways may be at odds with dominant mainstream society, will governmental or corporate interests use anthropological data to suppress that group? And what of traditional communities around the world? Who is to decide what changes should, or should not, be introduced for community "betterment"? And who defines what constitutes betterment—the community, its national government, or an international agency like the World Health Organization? Then there is the problem of privacy. Anthropologists deal with matters that are private and sensitive, including things that individuals would prefer not to have generally known about them. How does one write about such important but delicate issues and at the same time protect the privacy of informants? Not surprisingly, because of these and other questions, there has been much discussion among anthropologists over the past three decades on the subject of ethics.

Anthropologists recognize that they have special obligations to three sets of people: those whom they study, those who fund the research, and those in the profession who expect us to publish our findings so that they may be used to further our collective knowledge. Because fieldwork requires a relationship of trust between fieldworker and informants, the anthropologist's first responsibility clearly is to his or her informants and their community. Everything possible must be done to protect their physical, social, and psychological welfare and to honor their dignity and privacy. In other words, *do no harm*. Although early ethnographers often provided colonial administrators with the kind of information needed to control the "natives," they have long since ceased to be comfortable with such work and regard as basic a people's right to maintain their own culture.

ANTHROPOLOGY AND GLOBALIZATION

Anthropology has been shaped by a holistic perspective and a long-term commitment to understanding the human species in all its variety. This given, it is better equipped than any other scientific discipline to grapple with an issue that has overriding importance for all of us

© Joyce Choo/Corbis

© Henry S. Hamlin

VISUAL COUNTERPOINT A major feature of globalization is the communications revolution. Cell phones are used by a vast array of people all around the world, from urban bankers engaged in international investments, to semi-nomadic Khampa herders who may never venture beyond their native region of highland Tibet.

at the beginning of the 21st century: **globalization.** The term refers to worldwide interconnectedness, evidenced in global movements of natural resources, trade goods, human labor, finance capital, information, and infectious diseases. Although worldwide travel, trade relations, and information flow have existed for several centuries, the pace and magnitude of these long-distance exchanges has picked up enormously in recent decades; the Internet, in particular, has greatly expanded information exchange capacities.

The powerful forces driving globalization are technological improvements, lower transport and communication costs, faster knowledge transfers, and increased trade and financial integration among countries. Touching almost everybody's life on the planet, globalization is about economics as much as politics, and it changes human relations and ideas as well as our natural environments. Even geographically remote countries are quickly becoming more interdependent through globalization. For these reasons, globalization has been defined as "the intensification of worldwide social relations which link distant localities in such a way that local happenings are shaped by events occurring many miles away and vice versa."[14]

Doing research in all corners of the world, anthropologists are confronted with the impact of globalization on human communities wherever they are located. As participant observers, they describe and try to explain how individuals and organizations respond to the massive changes confronting them. Anthropologists may also find out how local responses sometimes change the global flows directed at them.

Dramatically increasing every year, globalization can be a two-edged sword. It generates economic growth and prosperity, but it also undermines long-established institutions. Generally, globalization has brought significant gains to higher-educated groups in wealthier countries, while doing little to boost developing countries and actually contributing to the erosion of traditional cultures. Upheavals born of globalization are key causes for rising levels of ethnic and religious conflict throughout the world.

Obviously, since all of us now live in a "global village," we can no longer afford the luxury of ignoring our neighbors no matter how distant they still may seem to most of us. Based on 150 years of cross-cultural research throughout the world, anthropologists have accumulated vitally important knowledge about our species in all its amazing variety. In this age of globalization, anthropology may not only provide humanity with useful insights concerning diversity,

globalization Worldwide interconnectedness, evidenced in global movements of natural resources, trade goods, human labor, finance capital, information, and infectious diseases.

[14]Giddens, A. (1990). *The consequences of modernity* (p. 64). Stanford, CA: Stanford University Press.

but it may also assist us in avoiding or overcoming significant problems born of that diversity. In countless social arenas, from schools to businesses to hospitals, anthropologists have done cross-cultural research that makes it possible for educators, businesspeople, and doctors to do their work more effectively. (For example, the brief Biocultural Connection box in this chapter is an important alert for surgeons who carry out organ transplants for patients outside of their cultural niche.)

The wide-ranging relevance of anthropological knowledge for the contemporary world may be illustrated by three quite different examples. In the United States today, discrimination based on notions of race continues to be a serious issue affecting economic, political, and social relations. What anthropology has shown, however, is the fallacy of racial categories themselves. Far from being the biological reality it is supposed to be, the concept of race emerged in the 18th century as a device for justifying European dominance over Africans, American Indians, and other "people of color." In fact, differences of skin color are simply surface adaptations to differing amounts of ultraviolet radiation and have nothing to do with physical or mental capabilities. Nor does its variance correspond to other biological characteristics; a German, for example, may have more in common with a "black" person from Congo than with someone from Greece, Italy, or even Germany itself, depending on what genetically based characteristics other than skin color are considered. Indeed, geneticists find far more biological variation *within* any given human population than *between* them. In short, human "races" are divisive categories based on prejudice, false ideas of differences, and erroneous notions of the superiority of one's own group. The sooner everyone recognizes that the categories lack scientific merit, the better off we will all be.[15] Given the importance of this issue, biological variation will be discussed further in Chapter 13.

A second example involves the issue of same-sex marriage. In 1989, Denmark became the first country to enact a comprehensive set of legal protections for same-sex couples, known as the Registered Partnership Act. At this writing, more than a half-dozen other countries have passed similar laws, variously named, and numerous countries around the world are considering legislation that would provide people in homosexual unions some of the benefits and protections afforded by marriage. In 2001 the Netherlands went a step farther and legalized same-sex marriage. In 2003, Belgium did the

[15]Haviland, W. A. (2000). *Human evolution and prehistory* (5th ed., pp. 348–368). Fort Worth, TX: Harcourt Brace.

© Gordon Gahan/National Geographic Image Collection

Wartenberg/Pictures Press/Corbis

These boys—one from an East African cattle-herding family, the other from northern Europe—share the genetically based ability to digest milk, something that sets them apart from the majority of the world's inhabitants. Because genetic traits are inherited independently, humans cannot be classified into races having any biological validity.

These people are protesting Vermont's "civil union" legislation, which gave legal status to same-sex unions in 2000.

Alden Pellett/The Image Works

same, followed by the Canadian provinces of Ontario and British Columbia. In the United States, Vermont legalized "civil unions" between same-sex couples in 2000, providing *some* of the benefits and protections of heterosexual marriages. In 2003 the Massachusetts Supreme Judicial Court ruled that same-sex marriage was a constitutional right in that state.[16] Those opposed to same-sex unions often argue that marriage has always been between one man and one woman and that only heterosexual relations are "normal." Yet, as we will see in upcoming chapters, neither assertion is true. Anthropologists have documented same-sex marriages in many human societies in various parts of the world, where they are regarded as acceptable under appropriate circumstances. As for homosexual behavior, it is quite common in the animal world, including among humans.[17] The key difference between people and other animals is that human societies specify when, where, how, and with whom it is appropriate or normal (just as they do for heterosexual behavior).

A final example relates to the common confusion of *nation* with *state*. The distinction is important: States are politically organized territories that are internationally recognized, whereas nations are socially organized bodies of people, who share ethnicity—a common origin, language, and cultural heritage. For example, the homeland of the Kurds, known as Kurdistan, is divided between several states, primarily Turkey, Iraq, and Iran. The modern boundaries between these three states were drawn up after World War I and the collapse of the Turkish Ottoman Empire. With the Turks defeated by Britain and her allies, much of the old empire was carved up in 1918. With little regard for the region's ethnic groups or nations such as the Kurds, who had long struggled for self-rule, arbitrary lines were drawn right through Kurdistan, and new political boundaries were imposed. In the process, new countries were created and internationally recognized as independent states.

Similar processes have taken place throughout the world, especially in Asia and Africa, often making the political condition in these countries inherently unstable. As we will see in Chapters 23 and 27, states and nations rarely coincide, nations being split between different states and states typically being controlled by members of one nation who commonly use their control to gain access to the land, resources, and labor of other nationalities. Rarely is the consent of the other nationals obtained, nor are their interests given much (if any) consideration by those who control the government. As a consequence, oppressed nationals often resort to force to defend their land, resources, and even their very identities, feeling they have no other options. Most of the armed conflicts in the world today are of this sort and are not the mere acts of "tribalism" or "terrorism," as commonly asserted.

In numerous ways, our ignorance about other peoples and their ways is a cause of serious problems. In the

---

[16]Merin, Y. (2002). *Equality for same-sex couples: The legal recognition of gay partnerships in Europe and the United States.* Chicago: University of Chicago Press. "Court says same-sex marriage is a right." *San Francisco Chronicle.* Feb. 5, 2004. Up-to-date overviews and breaking news on the global status of same-sex marriage is posted on the Internet by the Partners Task Force for Gay & Lesbian Couples at *www.buddybuddy.com.*

[17]Kirkpatrick, R. C. (2000). The evolution of human homosexual behavior. *Current Anthropology, 41,* 384.

© Patrick Barth/Getty Images

Violence triggered by the Kurd struggle for self-determination in Iraq and neighboring countries exemplifies the problem of multinational states in which members of a more powerful nationality or ethnic group tries to control those of another through brutal force.

words of Edwin Reischauer, U.S. ambassador to Japan from 1961 to 1966, "Education is not moving rapidly enough in the right directions to produce the knowledge about the outside world and attitudes toward other peoples that may be essential for human survival."[18] His comment is all the more true today, and anthropology is part of the answer. It offers a way of looking at and understanding the world's peoples—insights that are nothing less than basic skills for survival in this age of globalization.

[18]Quoted in Haviland, W. A. (1997). Cleansing young minds, or what should we be doing in introductory anthropology? In C. P. Kottack, J. J. White, R. H. Furlow, & P. C. Rice (Eds.), *The teaching of anthropology; problems, issues and decisions* (p. 35). Mountain View, CA: Mayfield.

Chapter Summary

- Throughout human history, people have needed to know who they are, where they came from, and why they believe and behave as they do. Traditionally, myths and legends provided the answers to these fundamental questions. Anthropology, as it has emerged over the last 150 years, offers a more scientific approach to answering the questions people ask about themselves and others.
- Anthropology is the study of humankind. In employing a scientific approach, anthropologists seek to produce a reasonably objective understanding of both human diversity and those things all humans have in common.
- Anthropology contains four major subfields: physical anthropology, archaeology, linguistic anthropology, and cultural anthropology. Physical anthropology focuses on humans as biological organisms. Particular emphasis is given by physical anthropologists to tracing the evolutionary development of the human animal and studying biological variation within the species today. Forensics is an example of applied physical anthropology. Archaeologists study material objects, usually from past cultures, to explain human behavior. Linguists, who study human languages, may deal with the description of a language, with the history of languages, or how languages are used in particular social settings. Cultural anthropologists study humans in terms of their cultures, the often-unconscious standards by which social groups operate. Medical anthropology is a growing specialization.
- Within all of anthropology's subfields, one can find applied anthropologists who utilize the discipline's unique research methodology toward solving practical problems.
- Some cultural anthropologists are ethnographers, who do a particular kind of hands-on fieldwork known as participant observation. They produce a detailed record of a specific culture in writing (and/or visual imagery) known as an ethnography. Other cultural anthropologists are also ethnologists, who study and analyze cultures from a comparative or historical point of view, utilizing ethnographic accounts. Often, they focus on a particular aspect of culture, such as religious or economic practices.
- Unique among the modern sciences, anthropology has long been concerned specifically with traditional tribal societies outside Europe. Today, anthropology stands out among the social and natural sciences for its holistic approach, which aims to formulate theoretically valid explanations of human diversity based on detailed studies of all aspects of human biology, behavior, and beliefs in all known societies, past and present.
- Anthropologists are concerned with the objective and systematic study of humankind. The anthropologist employs the methods of other scientists by developing hypotheses, or assumed explanations, using other data to test these hypotheses, and ultimately arriving at theories—explanations supported by reliable bodies of data. The comparative method is key to all branches of anthropology. Anthropologists make broad comparisons between peoples and cultures past and present, related species, and fossil groups.
- In anthropology, the humanities, social sciences, and natural sciences come together into a genuinely human science. Anthropology's link with the humanities can be seen in its concern with people's beliefs, values, languages, arts, and literature—oral as well as written—but above all in its attempt to convey the experience of living in different cultures. As both science and humanity, anthropology has essential insights to offer the modern world, particularly in this era of globalization when understanding our neighbors in the global village has become a matter of survival for all.

Questions for Reflection

1. Considering the challenge of discerning one's place in the world, what insights have you gained in this chapter that help with this challenge?

2. From the holistic anthropological perspective, humans have one leg in culture and the other in nature, and in the interaction between them our destiny unfolds. Think of examples from your life that illustrate this idea.

3. Globalization can be described as a two-edged sword. How does it foster growth and destruction simultaneously?

4. The textbook definitions of *state* and *nation* are based on scientific distinctions between both organizational types. However, this distinction is sometimes lost in everyday language. Consider, for instance, the names *United States of America* and the *United Nations.*

5. The Biocultural Connection in this chapter contrasts different cultural perspectives on "brain death," while the Original Study featured a discussion about traditional Zulu healers and their role in dealing with AIDS victims. What do these two accounts suggest about the role of applied anthropology in dealing with cross-cultural health issues across the world?

Key Terms

Anthropology	Fieldwork
Culture-bound	Participant observation
Applied anthropology	Ethnology
Physical anthropology	Holistic perspective
Molecular anthropology	Informants
Paleoanthropology	Medical Anthropology
Primatology	Fact
Forensic anthropology	Hypothesis
Archaeology	Theory
Linguistic anthropology	Doctrine
Cultural anthropology	Globalization
Ethnography	

Multimedia Review Tools

Companion Web Site

Visit **http://www.wadsworth.com/anthropology_d/** and click on the companion Web site for this textbook to access a wide range of material to aid your study of anthropology. Among the options for self-study in each chapter are learning objectives, flash cards, Internet activities, Web links, InfoTrac College Edition exercises, and practice tests that can be scored and emailed to your instructor.

CD-ROM

The *Doing Anthropology Today* CD-ROM supplied with your textbook provides unique and valuable information designed to enhance your learning experience. This interactive multimedia resource includes video clips, interviews with renowned anthropologists, map and timeline exercises, chapter study quizzes, and much more. *Doing Anthropology Today* will not only help you in achieving your grade goals, but it will also make your learning experience fun and exciting!

Suggested Readings

Bernard, H. R. (2002). *Research methods in anthropology: Qualitative and quantitative approaches* (3rd ed.). Walnut Creek, CA: Altamira Press.

Written in a conversational style and rich with examples, this extremely useful and accessible book has twenty chapters divided into three sections: preparing for fieldwork, data collection, and data analysis. It touches on all the basics, from literature search and research design to interviewing, fieldnote management, multivariate analysis, ethics, and much more.

Bonvillain, N. (2000). *Language, culture, and communication: The meaning of messages* (3rd ed.). Upper Saddle River, NJ: Prentice-Hall.

An up-to-date text on language and communication in a cultural context.

Erickson, P. A., & Murphy, L. D. (2003). *A history of anthropological theory* (2nd ed.). Peterborough, Ontario: Broadview Press.

A clear and concise survey that spans from antiquity to the modern era, effectively drawing the lines between the old and the new. This edition features several new and expanded sections on topics including feminist anthropology, globalization, and medical anthropology.

Fagan, B. M. (1999). *Archeology: A brief introduction* (7th ed.). New York: Longman.

This primer offers an overview of archaeological theory and methodology, from field survey techniques to excavation to analysis of materials.

Jones, S., Martin R., & Pilbeam, D. (Eds.). (1992). *Cambridge encyclopedia of human evolution.* New York: Cambridge University Press.

This comprehensive introduction to the human species covers the gamut from genetics, primatology, and the fossil evidence to a detailed exploration of contemporary human ecology, demography, and disease. Each topic covered, written by an expert in the field, provides a comprehensive summary of this area of biological anthropology. Over seventy scholars from throughout the world contributed to this encyclopedia.

Peacock, J. L. (2002). *The anthropological lens: Harsh light, soft focus.* (2nd ed.). New York: Cambridge University Press.

This lively and innovative book gives the reader a good understanding of the diversity of activities undertaken by cultural anthropologists, while at the same time identifying the unifying themes that hold the discipline together. Additions to the second edition include such topics as globalization, gender, and postmodernism.

CHAPTER 2

Biology and Evolution

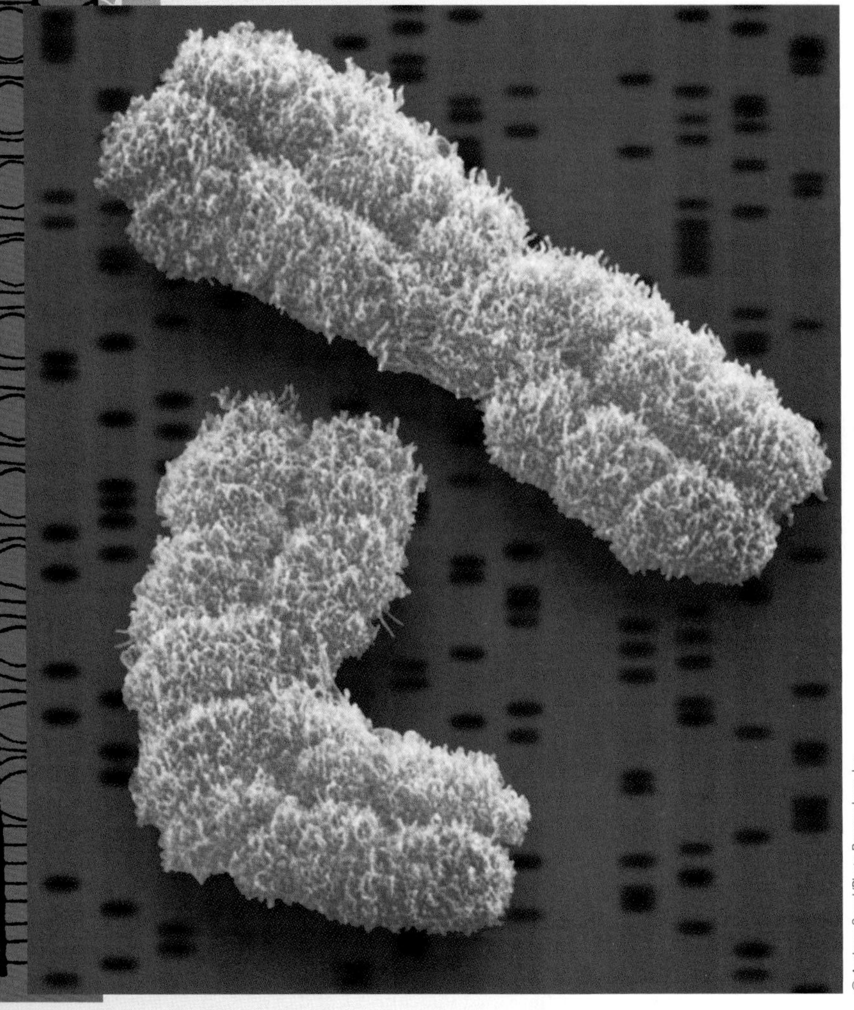

© Andrew Syred/Photo Researchers, Inc.

CHALLENGE ISSUE

BIOLOGY AND ITS CENTRAL THEORY, EVOLUTION, ARE VITAL FOR MEETING THE CHALLENGE OF KNOWING OURSELVES AS CULTURE-BEARING ORGANISMS. While human culture represents one of the most complex manifestations of life on earth, from a scientific standpoint, the evolution of humans is not a story of progressive improvement. Variations on the same genetic processes are shared across all organisms. The evolution of each species involves a unique history combining random events and adaptation to the local environment.

1 What Is Evolution?

Although all living creatures ultimately share a common ancestry, they have come to differ from one another through the process of evolution. Biological evolution refers to genetic change over successive generations. The process of change is characterized by descent with modification, as descendant populations come to differ from ancestral ones. As a population's genetic variation changes from one generation to another, genetic change is reflected in visible differences between organisms.

2 What Are the Forces Responsible for Evolution?

Four evolutionary forces—mutation, genetic drift, gene flow, and natural selection—account for change in the genetic composition of populations. Random mutations introduce new genetic variation into individual organisms. Gene flow (the introduction of new gene variants from other populations), genetic drift (random changes in frequencies of gene variants in a population), and natural selection shape genetic variation at the population level. Natural selection is the mechanism of evolution that results in adaptive change, favoring individuals with genetic variants relatively better adapted to local environment conditions.

3 What Is the Molecular Basis of Evolution?

Molecular biologists have begun to unravel the genetic basis of evolutionary change. DNA (deoxyribonucleic acid) molecules store genetic information in the chromosomes of a cell. Genes, specific portions of DNA molecules, direct the synthesis of the protein molecules that make up all living organisms.

A common part of the mythology of all peoples is a story explaining the appearance of humans on earth. The accounts of creation recorded in the Bible's Book of Genesis, for example, explain human origins. A vastly different example, serving the same function, is the traditional belief of the Nez Perce, a people native to eastern Oregon and Idaho. For the Nez Perce, humanity is the creation of Coyote, a trickster-transformer inhabiting the earth before humans. Coyote chased the giant beaver monster, Wishpoosh, over the earth leaving a trail to form the Columbia River. When Coyote caught Wishpoosh, he killed him and dragged his body to the riverbank. Ella Clark, the North American scholar who collected and published over one hundred stories from the oral traditions of Native Americans of the Pacific Northwest in 1953, retells the story as follows:

> With his sharp knife Coyote cut up the big body of the monster.
>
> "From your body, mighty Wishpoosh," he said, "I will make a new race of people. They will live near the shores of Big River and along the streams which flow into it."
>
> From the lower part of the animal's body, Coyote made people who were to live along the river. "You shall live near the mouth of Big River and shall be traders."
>
> "You shall live along the coast," he said to others. "You shall live in villages facing the ocean and shall get your food by spearing salmon and digging clams. You shall always be short and fat and have weak legs."
>
> From the legs of the beaver monster he made the Klickitat Indians. "You shall live along the rivers that flow down from the big white mountain north of Big River. You shall be swift of foot and keen of wit. You shall be famous runners and great horsemen."
>
> From the arms of the monster he made the Cayuse Indians. "You shall be powerful with bow and arrows and with war clubs."
>
> From the ribs he made the Yakima Indians. "You shall live near the new Yakima River, east of the mountains. You shall be the helpers and the protectors of all the poor people."
>
> From the head he created the Nez Perce Indians. "You shall live in the valleys of the Kookooskia and Wallowa rivers. You shall be men of brains, great in council and in speech making. You shall also be skillful horsemen and brave warriors."
>
> Then Coyote gathered up the hair and blood and waste. He hurled them far eastward, over the big mountains. "You shall be the Snake River Indians," said Coyote. "You shall be people of blood and violence. You shall be buffalo hunters and shall wander far and wide."[1]

Creation stories depict the relationship between humans and the rest of the natural world, sometimes reflecting a deep connection among people, other animals, and the earth. In the traditional Nez Perce creation story, groups of people derive from specific body parts—each possessing a special relationship with a particular animal. By contrast, the story of creation depicted in the Bible's Book of Genesis emphasizes human uniqueness and the concept of time. Creation is depicted as a series of actions occurring over the course of six days. God's final act of creation is to fashion the first human from the earth in his own image before the seventh day of rest.

The theory of **evolution,** the organizing principle of biology, like creation stories, accounts for the diversity of life on earth. However, evolution differs from other creation stories in that it explains the diversity of life in a consistent scientific language, using testable ideas (hypotheses). For example, contemporary scientists make comparisons among living organisms to test hypotheses drawn from the theory of evolution. Evolution also differs from the traditional Judeo-Christian creation story in that it situates humans firmly within the natural world. Though the scientific theory of evolution treats humans as natural biological organisms, at the same time, historical and cultural processes also shape evolutionary theory and hypotheses. The forces and mechanisms of evolution, accounting for the creation of humans and other species, are the subject of this chapter.

THE CLASSIFICATION OF LIVING THINGS

Before defining evolution and exploring the biological mechanisms at genetic and population levels, we will examine how this theory developed. The origins of the contemporary discipline of biology and its organizing

evolution Descent with modification.

[1] Clark, E. E. (1966). *Indian legends of the Pacific Northwest* (p. 174). Berkeley: University of California Press. Reprinted by permission.

An unforeseen consequence of the exploitation of foreign lands by European explorers beginning with Columbus (here at the court of Spain) was a change in the approach to the natural world. New life forms challenged the previously held notion of fixed, unchanging life on earth.

principle of evolution can be found in the cultural changes in Europe related to changing technology during the European Age of Discovery. The great mass of biological data gathered through European exploration and exploitation of foreign lands, as well as the invention of instruments such as the microscope to study the previously invisible interior of cells, led to a new appreciation of the diversity of life on earth.

Before this time, Europeans organized living things and inanimate objects alike into a ladder or hierarchy known as the Great Chain of Being—an approach to nature first developed by Aristotle in ancient Greece over 2,000 years ago. The categories were based upon visible similarities, and one member of each category was considered its "primate" (from the Latin primus), meaning the first or best of the group. For example, the primate of rocks was the diamond, and the primate of birds was the eagle, and so forth. Humans were at the very top of the ladder, just below the angels.

In response to discoveries around the globe and in the inner workings of organisms, Swedish naturalist Carl von Linné developed the *Systema Naturae* or system of nature, in the 18th century, to classify all living things. This compendium reflected a new understanding for the place of humanity among the animals. Von Linné noted the similarity among humans, monkeys, and apes, classifying them together as primates. But instead of being the first or the best of the animals on earth, primates are just one of several kinds of **mammal,** animals with fur who nurse their young. Besides humans, **primates** also include lemurs, lorises, tarsiers, monkeys, and apes.

Following the traditions of scholars from the period, von Linné used the classical languages of Greek and Latin in his naming system. Also, he changed his own name to Carolus Linnaeus, a Latinization of his original name. On the basis of internal and external visual similarities, Linnaeus classified living things into a series of categories that are progressively more inclusive. **Species** are the smallest working units in biological classificatory systems. Species are defined as reproductively isolated populations or group of populations capable of interbreeding to produce fertile offspring. Species are subdivisions of larger, more inclusive groups, called **genera** (singular, **genus**). Humans, for example, are classified in the genus *Homo* and species *sapiens.* This binomial nomenclature, or two-part naming system, mirrors the naming patterns in many European societies where individuals possess two names—one personal and the other reflecting their membership in a larger group of related organisms. Linnaeus based his classificatory system on the following criteria:

1. *Body structure:* A Guernsey cow and a Holstein cow are the same species because they have identical body structure. A cow and a horse do not.
2. *Body function:* Cows and horses give birth to live young. Although they are different species, they are closer than either cows or horses are to chickens, which lay eggs and have no mammary glands.
3. *Sequence of bodily growth:* At the time of birth—or hatching out of the egg—young cows and chickens resemble their parents in their body plan. They are therefore more closely related to each other than either one is to the frog, whose tadpoles undergo a series of changes before attaining the basic adult form.

Modern **taxonomy,** or the science of classification (from the Greek for naming divisions), while retaining the structure of the Linnaean system, is based on more

mammals The class of vertebrate animals distinguished by bodies covered with fur, self-regulating temperature, and in females milk-producing mammary glands.
primates The group of mammals that includes lemurs, lorises, tarsiers, monkeys, apes, and humans.
species The smallest working unit in the system of classification. Among living organisms, species are populations or groups of populations capable of interbreeding and producing fertile viable offspring.
genus, genera (pl.) In the system of plant and animal classification, a group of like species.
taxonomy The science of classification.

VISUAL COUNTERPOINT The wings of birds and butterflies exemplify analogy. Both are used for flight and share similar appearance due to their common function. However, the course of their development and their structure differs.

than body structure, function, and growth. Today, scientists also compare protein structure and genetic material to construct the relationship among living things. Such molecular comparisons can even be aimed at parasites, bacteria, and viruses, allowing scientists to classify or trace the origins of particular diseases, such as the recent outbreak of SARS (sudden acute respiratory syndrome) or HIV (human immunodeficiency virus).

In addition, cross-species comparisons identify anatomical features of similar function as **analogies,** while anatomical features that have evolved from a common ancestral feature are called **homologies.** For example, the hand of a human and the wing of a bat evolved from the forelimb of a common ancestor, though they have acquired different functions: The human hand and bat wing are homologous structures. During their early embryonic development, homologous structures arise in a similar fashion and pass through similar stages before differentiating. The wings of birds and butterflies look similar and have a similar function (flying): These are analogous, but not homologous, structures because the butterfly wing does not develop from its forelimb.

analogies In biology, structures possessed by different organisms that are superficially similar due to similar function; without sharing a common developmental pathway or structure.

homologies In biology, structures possessed by two different organisms that arise in similar fashion and pass through similar stages during embryonic development though they may possess different functions.

hominoid The taxonomic division superfamily within the cattarrhine primates that includes gibbons, siamangs, orangutans, gorillas, chimpanzees, bonobos, and humans.

Through careful comparison and analysis of organisms, Linnaeus and his successors have grouped species into genera and also into even larger groups such as families, orders, classes, phyla, and kingdoms. Each taxonomic level is distinguished by characteristics shared by all the organisms in the group. Table 2.1 presents the main categories of contemporary taxonomy applied to the classification of the human species, with a few of the more important distinguishing features noted for each category.

Taxonomies are human ways of organizing the natural world. Because taxonomies reflect scientists' understanding of the evolutionary relationships among living things, these classificatory systems are continually under construction. With new scientific discoveries, taxonomic categories have to be redrawn, and scientists often differ in their acceptance of a particular category. The classification of humans contains a prime example of a taxonomy under construction.

Humans are placed in the **hominoid** superfamily with chimpanzees, gorillas, orangutans, and gibbons, due to physical similarities such as broad shoulder, absent tail, and long arms. Human characteristics such as bipedalism (walking on two legs) and culture led scientists to think that all the other apes were more closely related to one another than any of them were to humans. Thus, humans and their ancestors were classi-

© Cleo Freelana Photos/Photo Edit

© Colin Milkins, Oxford Scientific Films/Animals, Animals

VISUAL COUNTERPOINT An example of homology: Fish have gills but humans do not. Gill structures do develop in the human embryo but then are modified to serve other purposes. From the rudimentary, gill-like structures are built such things as the jaw, bones of the inner ear, thymus, and parathyroid glands.

© AP/World Wide Photos

Molecular study of the virus that causes SARS allowed scientists to trace its origins and classify it as closely related to the virus causing the common cold.

fied in the **hominid** family to distinguish them from the other apes. As will be discussed in more detail in later chapters, genetic and fossil studies have shown that humans are more closely related to African apes (chimps, bonobos, and gorillas) than they are to orangutans and gibbons. Some scientists then proposed that African apes should be included in the hominid family, with humans and their ancestors distinguished from the other African hominoids at the taxonomic level of subfamily, as **hominins.**

Although all scientists today agree about the close relationship among humans, chimpanzees, bonobos, and gorillas, they differ as to whether they use the term *hominid* or *hominin* to describe the taxonomic grouping of humans and their ancestors. Museum displays and the popular press tend to retain the old term *hominid,* emphasizing the visible differences between humans and the other African apes. Those using *hominin* are emphasizing the importance of genetics in establishing relationships among species. These word choices are more than name games: They reflect theoretical relationships among closely related species.

hominid African hominoid family that includes two subfamilies: the Paninae (chimps, bonobos, and gorillas) and the Homininae (humans and their ancestors). Some scientists use *hominid* to mean only humans and their ancestors. Others, recognizing the close relationship of humans, chimps, bonobos, and gorillas, use this term to refer to all of the African hominoid groups.

hominin The taxonomic subfamily or tribe within the primates that includes humans and our ancestors.

TABLE 2.1 CLASSIFICATION OF HUMANS

Taxonomic Category	Category to Which Humans Belong	Biological Features Used to Define and Place Humans in this Category
Kingdom	Animalia	Humans are animals. We do not make our own food (as plants do) but depend upon intake of living food.
Phylum	Chordata	Humans are chordates. We have a **notochord** (a rodlike structure of cartilage) and nerve chord running along the back of the body as well as gill slits in the embryonic stage of our life cycle.
Subphylum*	Vertebrata	Humans are vertebrates possessing an internal backbone, with a segmented spinal column.
Class	Mammalia	Humans are mammals, warm-blooded animals covered with fur, possessing mammary glands for nourishing their young after birth.
Order	Primates	Humans are primates, a kind of mammal with a generalized anatomy, relatively large brains, and grasping hands and feet.
Suborder	Anthropoidea	Humans are anthropoids, social, daylight-active primates.
Superfamily	Hominoid	Humans are hominoids with broad flexible shoulders and no tail. Chimps, bonobos, gorillas, orangutans, gibbons, and siamangs are also hominoids.
Family	Hominid	Humans are hominids. We are hominoids from Africa, genetically more closely related to chimps, bonobos, and gorillas than to hominoids from Asia. Before this genetic relationship was established, hominid referred to humans and their ancestors only. Some scientists still use hominid in this way.
Subfamily or tribe	Hominin	Humans are hominins, ground-dwelling hominids who move on two legs or bipedally. Chimps, bonobos, gorillas, and their ancestors are classified separately at this taxonomic level because they are not bipedal.
Genus Species	*Homo* *sapiens*	Humans possess large brains and rely on cultural adaptations to survive. Ancestral fossils are placed in this genus and species depending upon details of the skull shape and interpretations of their cultural capabilities. Genus and species names are always italicized.

*Most categories can be expanded or narrowed by adding the prefix "sub" or "super." A family could thus be part of a superfamily and in turn contain two or more subfamilies.

THE DISCOVERY OF EVOLUTION

As Linnaeus and his contemporaries went about their business of classification, species were considered fixed entities. However, naturalists became increasingly aware of continuities between different forms of life, and they began to develop a notion of change in species over time. At the same time, earth-moving for construction and mining, which came with the onset of industrialization in Europe, brought to light all sorts of fossils, or preserved skeletal remains, of past life forms.

notochord A rodlike structure of cartilage that, in vertebrates, is replaced by the vertebral column.

At first, the fossilized remains of elephants and giant saber-toothed tigers in Europe were interpreted according to religious doctrine. For example, the early 19th-century scientific theory of "catastrophism" invoked natural events like the Great Flood of the Book

The large-scale movement of earth in 19th-century Europe, due to mining and construction of railroad lines, unearthed fossils such as mastodons. Such discoveries indicated that life forms of the past were not the same as the present and that change had occurred.

of Genesis to account for the disappearance of these species in European lands. With industrialization, however, the ideas of progress and change became ever more prominent in European thought. In hindsight, it seems inevitable that someone would hit upon the idea of evolution. So it was that, by the start of the 19th century, many naturalists had come to accept the idea that life had evolved, even though they were not clear about how it happened. It remained for Charles Darwin (1809–1882) to formulate a theory that has withstood the test of time.

Grandson of Erasmus Darwin (a physician, scientist, poet, and originator of a theory of evolution himself), Charles Darwin began the study of medicine at the University of Edinburgh, Scotland. Finding himself unfit for this profession, he then went to Christ's College, Cambridge, to study theology. Upon completion of his studies there, he took the position of naturalist and companion to Captain Fitzroy on the *H.M.S. Beagle,* which was about to embark on an expedition to various poorly mapped parts of the world. The voyage lasted for almost five years, taking Darwin along the coasts of South America, to the Galapagos Islands, across the Pacific to Australia, and then across the Indian and Atlantic oceans to South America before returning to England in 1836. Observing the tremendous diversity of living creatures as well as the astounding fossils of extinct animals, Darwin began to note that species varied according to the environments they inhabited. The observations he made on this voyage, his readings of Sir Charles Lyell's *Principles of Geology* (1830), and the arguments he had with the orthodox and dogmatic Fitzroy all contributed to the ideas culminating in Darwin's most famous book, *On the Origin of Species.* This book, published in 1859, described a theory of evolution accounting for change within species and for the emergence of new species in purely naturalistic terms.

It took Darwin over twenty years to develop his theory, adding observations from English farm life and intellectual thought to the ideas he began to develop on the *Beagle.* He paid particular attention to domesticated animals and farmers' practice of breeding their stock to select for specific traits. Darwin's theoretical breakthrough derived partly from an essay by economist Thomas Malthus (1766–1834), which warned of the potential consequences of increased human population. Malthus observed that animal populations, unlike human populations, remained stable, due to a large proportion of animal offspring not surviving to maturity.

MEDIATREK

To explore the wildlife along the route of the *Beagle* through an interactive Web site and access an archive of scholarly articles on Darwin's life and evolutionary theory, see MediaTrek 2.1 on the companion Web site or CD-ROM.

Darwin combined his observations into the theory of **natural selection** as follows: All species display a range of variation, and all have the ability to expand beyond their means of subsistence. It follows that, in their "struggle for existence," organisms with variations that help them to survive in a particular environment will reproduce with greater success than those without them. Thus, as generation succeeds generation, nature selects the most advantageous variations, and species evolve. So obvious did the idea seem in hindsight that Thomas Henry Huxley, known as "Darwin's bulldog" for his fierce support of Darwin's theory in 19th-century public debates, once remarked, "How extremely stupid of me not to have thought of that."[2]

As often happens in the history of science, Darwin was not alone in authoring the theory of natural selection. A Welshman, Alfred Russel Wallace, independently came up with the same idea at the same time while on a voyage to the Malay archipelago in Southeast Asia to collect specimens for European zoos and museums. According to his autobiography, a theory of evolution came to Wallace while he was in a feverish delirium from malaria. He shared excitedly his idea with other scientists in England, including Darwin whose own

[2]Quoted in Durant, J. C. (2000, April 23). Everybody into the gene pool. *New York Times Book Review,* p. 11.

natural selection The evolutionary process through which factors in the environment exert pressure, favoring some individuals over others to produce the next generation.

theory was yet unpublished. The two scientists jointly presented their findings.

However straightforward the idea of evolution by natural selection idea may appear, the theory was (and has continued to be) a source of considerable controversy. The most contentious question of human origins was avoided by Darwin who limited his commentary in the original work to a single sentence near the end: "much light will be thrown on the origin of man and his history." The feisty Thomas Henry Huxley, however, took up the subject of human origins explicitly through comparative anatomy of apes and humans and an examination of the fossils in his book, *On Man's Place in Nature,* published in 1863.

While global exploration, comparative anatomy, fossil discoveries, and the geologic concept of large time scales spanning millions of years led to the development of the theory of evolution in the 19th century, two problems plagued Darwin's theory throughout his career. First, how did variation arise in the first place? Second, what was the mechanism of heredity by which variable traits could be passed from one generation to the next? Ironically, some of the information Darwin needed, the basic laws of heredity, were available by 1866, through the experimental work of Gregor Mendel (1822–1884), an obscure monk, working in the monastery gardens in Brno, a city in the southeast of today's Czech Republic.

Mendel, who was raised on a farm in Moravia, possessed two particular talents: a flair for mathematics and a passion for gardening. As with all farmers of his time, Mendel had an intuitive understanding of biological inheritance. He went a step farther, though, in that he recognized the need for a more systematic understanding. Thus, at age 34, he began careful breeding experiments in the monastery garden, starting with pea plants.

Over 8 years, Mendel planted over 30,000 plants, controlling their pollination, observing the results, and figuring out the mathematics behind it all. This allowed him to predict the outcome of hybridization, or breeding that combined distinct varieties of the same species, over successive generations, in terms of basic laws of heredity. Though his findings were published in 1866 in a respected scientific journal, no one seemed to recognize the importance of Mendel's work during his lifetime. Interestingly, a copy of this journal was found in Darwin's own library with the pages still uncut (journals were printed on long continuous sheets of paper and then folded into pages to be cut by the reader), an indication that the journal had never been read. In 1900, cell biology had advanced to the point where rediscovery of Mendel's laws was inevitable, and in that year three European botanists, working independently of one another, rediscovered not only the laws but also Mendel's original paper. With this rediscovery, the science of genetics began. Still, it would be another 53 years before the molecular mechanisms of heredity, and the discrete units of inheritance, would be discovered. Today, a comprehensive understanding of heredity, molecular genetics, and population genetics support Darwinian evolutionary theory.

> ***genes*** Portions of DNA molecules that direct the synthesis of specific proteins.
> ***law of segregation*** The Mendelian principle that variants of genes for a particular trait retain their separate identities through the generations.
> ***law of independent assortment*** The Mendelian principle that genes controlling different traits are inherited independently of one another.

HEREDITY

In order to understand how evolution works, one has to have some understanding of the mechanics of heredity, because heritable variation constitutes the raw material for evolution. Our knowledge of the mechanisms of heredity is fairly recent; most of the fruitful research into the molecular level of inheritance has taken place in the past five decades. Although some aspects remain puzzling, the outlines by now are reasonably clear.

The Transmission of Genes

Biologists call the actual units of heredity **genes,** a term that comes from the Greek word for "birth," coined at the turn of the 20th century. Mendel had deduced the presence and activity of genes by experimenting with garden peas to determine how various traits are passed from one generation to the next. Specifically, he discovered that inheritance was *particulate,* rather than *blending,* as Darwin and many others thought. That is, the units controlling the expression of visible traits retain their separate identities over the generations rather than blending into a combination of parental traits in offspring. This was the basis of Mendel's first **law of segregation,** which states that genes keep their individuality and are passed on to the next generation, unaltered. Another of his laws—that of **independent assortment**—states that different traits (under the control of distinct genes) are inherited independently of one another.

Mendel's laws were abstract formulations based on statistical frequencies of observed characteristics such as color and texture in generations of plants. His inferences about the mechanisms of inheritance were confirmed through the discovery of the cellular and molecular basis of inheritance in the first half of the 20th century.

When **chromosomes,** the cellular structures containing the genetic information, were discovered at the start of the 20th century, they provided a visible vehicle for separate transmission of traits proposed in Mendel's law of independent assortment.

It was not until 1953 that James Watson and Francis Crick found that genes are actually portions of molecules of deoxyribonucleic acid (**DNA**)—long strands of which form the chromosomes. DNA is a complex molecule with an unusual shape, rather like two strands of a rope twisted around each another with ladder-like steps between the two strands. Alternating sugar and phosphate molecules form the backbone of these strands connected to each other by four base pairs: adenine, thymine, guanine, and cytosine (usually written as A, T, G, and C). The connections are between complementary bases: A with T and G with C (Figure 2.1). This confers upon genes the unique property of being able to replicate or make exact copies of themselves. This happens as a single strand attracts the appropriate bases available within a cell—A to T, T to A, C to G, and G to C—and forms a new strand. This new strand, by the same process, is an exact copy of the original. As long as no errors are made in this replication process, cells within organisms can divide to form daughter cells that are exact genetic copies of the parent cell.

The chemical bases of DNA constitute a recipe for making proteins. As science writer Matt Ridley puts it,

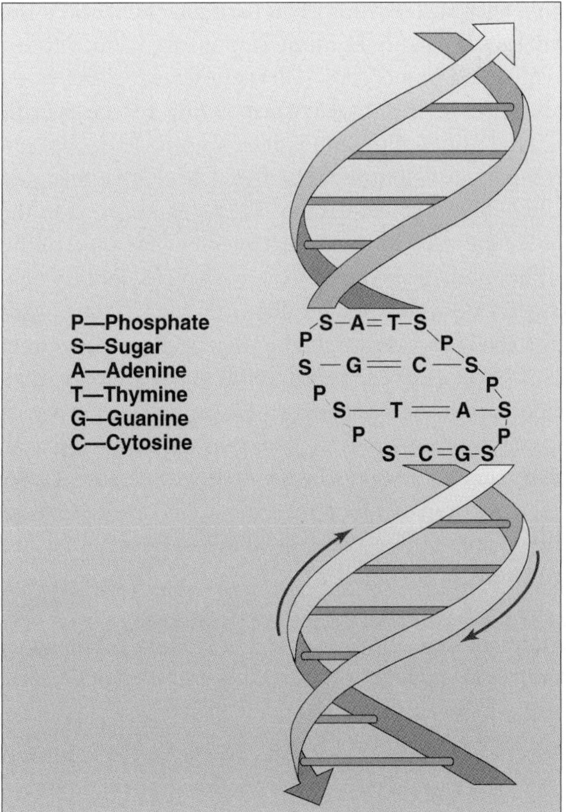

FIGURE 2.1

This diagrammatic representation of a portion of deoxyribonucleic acid (DNA) illustrates its twisted ladder-like structure. Alternating sugar and phosphate groups form the structural sides of the ladder. The connecting "rungs" are formed by pairings between complementary bases—adenine with thymine and cytosine with guanine.

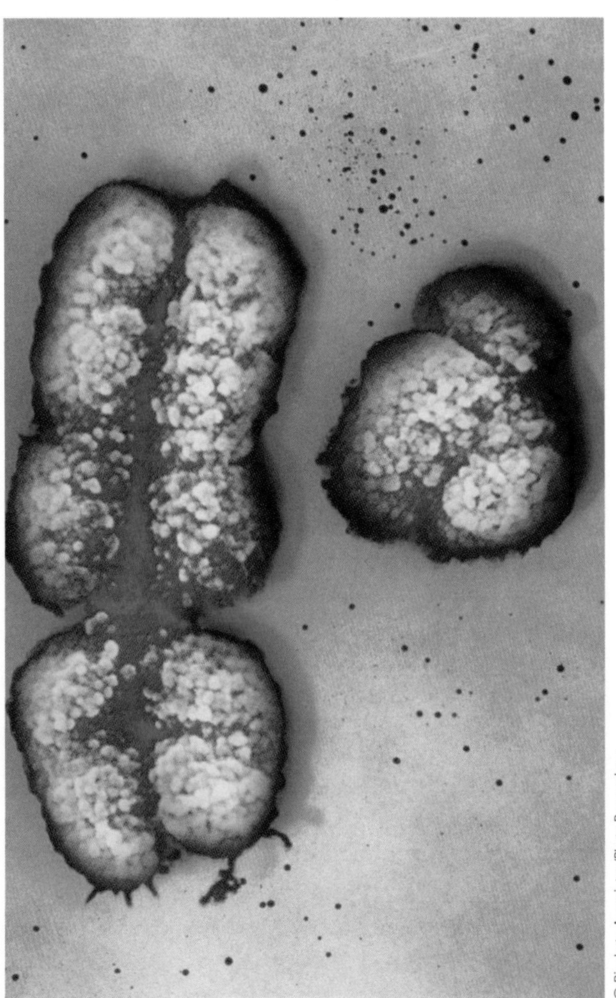

In addition to the twenty-two pairs of somatic or body chromosomes, humans possess one pair of sex chromosomes. Pictured here is the pair found in the normal male phenotype: a larger X chromosome (left) and smaller Y. The female phenotype is determined by the presence of two X chromosomes. Offspring inherit an X chromosome from their mothers but either an X or a Y from their fathers, resulting in approximately equal numbers of male and female offspring in subsequent generations. Though the Y chromosome is critical for differentiation into a male phenotype, compared to other chromosomes the Y is tiny and carries little genetic information.

chromosomes In the cell nucleus, the structures visible during cellular division containing long strands of DNA combined with a protein.

DNA Deoxyribonucleic acid. The genetic material consisting of a complex molecule whose base structure directs the synthesis of proteins.

"Proteins . . . do almost every chemical, structural, and regulatory thing that is done in the body: they generate energy, fight infection, digest food, form hair, carry oxygen, and so on and on."[3] Almost everything in the body is made *of* or *by* proteins.

How is the DNA recipe converted into a protein? Through a series of intervening steps, each three-base sequence of a gene, called a **codon,** specifies production of a particular amino acid, strings of which build proteins. Because DNA cannot leave the cell's nucleus (Figure 2.2), the directions for a specific protein are first converted into ribonucleic acid or **RNA** in a process called **transcription.** RNA differs from DNA in the structure of its sugar phosphate backbone and in the presence of the base uracil rather than thymine. Next the RNA travels to the **ribosomes,** the cellular structure (see Figure 2.2) where **translation** of the directions found in the codons into proteins occurs. For example, the sequence of CGA specifies the amino acid arginine, GCG alanine, CAG glutamine, and so on. There are twenty amino acids, which are strung together in different amounts and sequences to produce an almost infinite number of different proteins. This is the so-called **genetic code,** and it is the same for every living thing, whether it be a worm or a human being. Some simple living things without nucleated cells, such as the retrovirus that causes AIDS, contain their genetic information only as RNA.

Genes

A gene is a portion of the DNA molecule containing a sequence of base pairs that directs the production of a particular protein. Thus, when we speak of the gene for a human blood type in the A-B-O system, we are referring

Since the discovery of the structure of DNA in 1953, this molecule has come to have profound social and biological meaning. This photograph appeared in the prestigious journal *Nature* in its April 2003 issue, commemorating DNA's 50th birthday with the following caption: "Tribal totem: The DNA double helix serves as a unifying symbol and provides a collective identity for many different areas of science."[4]

to the portion of a DNA molecule that is 1,062 "letters" long—a medium-sized gene—that specifies production of an **enzyme,** a particular kind of protein that initiates and directs a chemical reaction. This particular enzyme causes molecules involved in immune responses to attach to the surface of red blood cells. Alternate forms of genes, or **alleles** exist, in this case corresponding to the specific blood type (the A allele and B allele). Genes, then, are not really separate structures, as had once been imagined, but locations, like dots on a map. These genes provide the recipe for the many proteins that keep us alive and healthy.

The human **genome**—the complete sequence of human DNA—contains 3 billion chemical bases, with about 30,000 functioning genes. This is a mere three times as many genes as in the fruit fly. How this seemingly modest difference in numbers of genes can produce so much complexity in humans is suggested by the following analogy: A combination lock with two wheels can display almost a hundred combinations, but a similar lock with six wheels—"only" three times as many—can generate just under 1 million.[5] Those 30,000 human genes account for only 1 to 1.5 percent of the entire genome. Our DNA, "like daytime television, is nine-tenths junk."[6] The genes themselves are split by long stretches of this "junk" DNA. The 1,062 bases of the A-B-O blood group gene, for exam-

[3]Ridley, M. (1999). *Genome: The autobiography of a species in 23 chapters* (p. 40). New York: HarperCollins

[4]Strasser, B. J. (2003). Who cares about the double helix? Collective memory links the past to the future in science as well as history. *Nature, 422,* 803–804.

[5]Solomon, R. (2001, February 20). Genome's riddle. *New York Times,* p. D3.

[6]Lowenstein, J. M. (1992). Genetic surprises. *Discover, 13*(12), 86.

codon Three-base sequence of a gene that specifies a particular amino acid for inclusion in a protein.
RNA Ribonucleic acid; similar to DNA but with uracil substituted for the base thymine. Transcribes and carries instructions from DNA from the nucleus to the ribosomes where it directs protein synthesis.
transcription Process of conversion of instructions from DNA into RNA.
ribosomes Structures in the cell where translation occurs.
translation Process of conversion of RNA instructions into proteins.
genetic code The sequence of three bases (a codon) that specifies the sequence of amino acids in protein synthesis.
enzyme Protein that initiates and directs chemical reactions.
alleles Alternate forms of a single gene.
genome The complete structure sequence of DNA for a species.

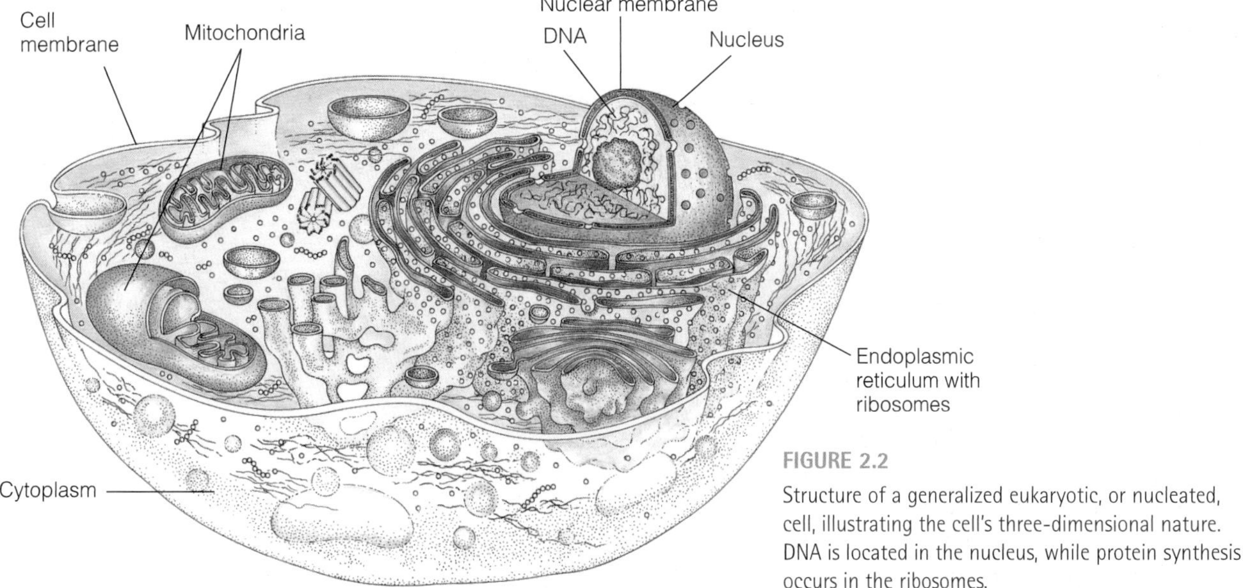

FIGURE 2.2
Structure of a generalized eukaryotic, or nucleated, cell, illustrating the cell's three-dimensional nature. DNA is located in the nucleus, while protein synthesis occurs in the ribosomes.

ple, are interrupted by five such stretches. In the course of producing proteins, junk DNA is metaphorically snipped out and left on the cutting room floor.

Some of this seemingly useless, noncoding DNA was inserted by retroviruses. Retroviruses are some of the most diverse and widespread infectious entities of vertebrates, responsible for AIDS, hepatitis, anemias, and some neurological disorders.[7] Other junk DNA consists of decaying hulks of once-useful but now functionless genes; damaged genes that have been "turned off." As cells divide and reproduce, junk DNA, like known genes, is also replicated. In the replication process mistakes are made fairly frequently, adding or subtracting repeats of the four bases: A, C, G, and T. This happens with sufficient speed and differently in every individual. As these "mistakes" accumulate over time, each person develops his or her unique DNA fingerprint.

Cell Division

In order to grow and maintain good health, the body cells of an organism must divide and produce new cells. Cell division is initiated when the chromosomes replicate, forming a second pair that duplicates the original pair of chromosomes in the nucleus. To do this, the DNA metaphorically "unzips" between the base pairs—adenine from thymine and guanine from cytosine—following which each base on each now-single strand attracts its complementary base, reconstituting the second half of the double helix. Each new pair is surrounded by a membrane and becomes the nucleus that directs the activities of a new cell. This kind of cell division is called **mitosis,** and it produces new cells that have exactly the same number of chromosome pairs, and hence genes, as did the parent cell.

Like most animals, humans reproduce sexually. One reason sex is so "popular," from an evolutionary perspective, is that it provides opportunity for genetic variation. All animals contain two copies of each chromosome, having inherited one from each parent. In humans this involves twenty-three pairs of chromosomes. Sexual reproduction can bring beneficial alleles together, purge the genome of harmful ones, and allow beneficial alleles to spread without being held back by the baggage of disadvantageous variants of other genes. Without sexual reproduction, we would lack genetic diversity, without which we would be more open to attack by various microbes. Nor would we be able to adapt to changing environments.

When new individuals are produced through sexual reproduction, the process involves the merging of two cells, one from each parent. If two regular body cells, each containing twenty-three pairs of chromosomes, were to merge, the result would be a new individual with forty-six pairs of chromosomes; such an individual surely could not survive. But this increase in chromosome number does not occur, because the sex cells that join to form a new individual are the product of a different kind of cell division, called **meiosis.**

mitosis A kind of cell division that produces new cells having exactly the same number of chromosome pairs, and hence copies of genes, as the parent cell.
meiosis A kind of cell division that produces the sex cells, each of which has half the number of chromosomes found in other cells of the organisms.

[7] Amábile-Cuevas, C. F., & Chicurel, M. E. (1993). Horizontal gene transfer. *American Scientist, 81,* 338.

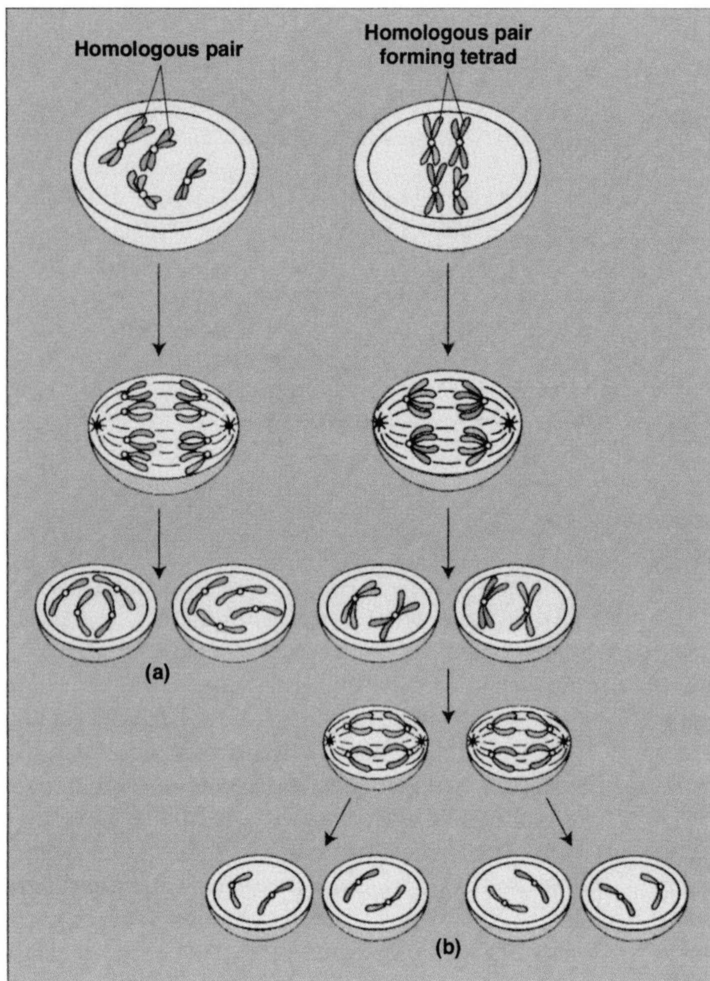

FIGURE 2.3

In cell division both mitosis (a) and meiosis (b) create new cells. However, in mitosis new cells are exact copies of the parent cell, whereas in meiosis "daughter" cells contain half of the parental number of chromosomes. Chromosomes in yellow orginally came from one parent, those in blue from the other.

Although meiosis begins like mitosis, with the replication and doubling of the original genes in chromosomes, it proceeds to divide that number into four new cells rather than two (Figure 2.3). Thus each new cell has only half the number of chromosomes with their genes found in the parent cell. Human eggs and sperm, for example, have only twenty-three single chromosomes (half of a pair), whereas body cells have twenty-three pairs, or forty-six chromosomes.

The process of meiotic division has important implications for genetics. Because paired chromosomes are separated, two different types of new cells will be formed; two of the four new cells will have one-half of a pair of chromosomes, and the other two will have the second half of the original chromosome pair. At the same time, corresponding portions of one chromosome may "cross over" to the other one, somewhat scrambling the genetic material compared to the original chromosomes. Sometimes, the original pair is **homozygous,** possessing identical alleles for a specific gene. For example, if in both chromosomes of the original pair the gene for A-B-O blood type is represented by the allele for type A blood, then all new cells will have the "A" allele. But if the original pair is **heterozygous,** with the "A" allele on one chromosome and the allele for type B blood on the other, then half of the new cells will contain only the "B" allele; the offspring have a 50-50 chance of getting either one. It is impossible to predict any single individual's **genotype,** or genetic composition, but (as Mendel originally discovered) statistical probabilities can be established.

homozygous Refers to a chromosome pair that bears identical alleles for a single gene.
heterozygous Refers to a chromosome pair that bears different alleles for a single gene.
genotype The alleles possessed for a particular trait.

Biocultural Connection

The Social Impact of Genetics on Reproduction

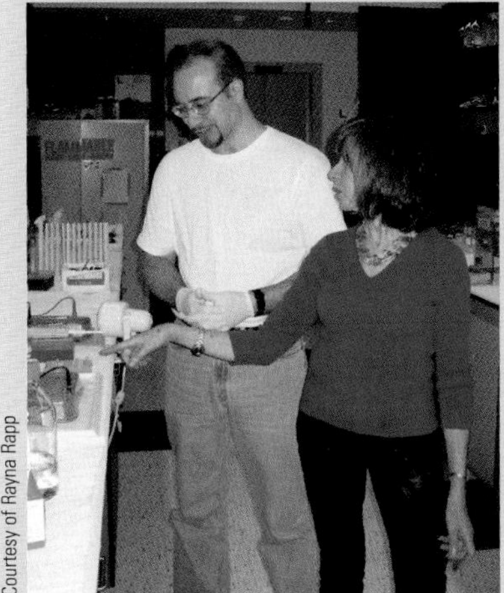
Courtesy of Rayna Rapp

While pregnancy and childbirth have been traditional subjects for cultural anthropological study, the genetics revolution has raised new questions for the biocultural study of reproduction. At first glance, the genetics revolution has simply expanded biological knowledge. Individuals today, compared to a hundred years ago, can now see their own genetic makeup even to the level of base pair sequence. A deeper look illustrates that this new biological knowledge has the capacity to profoundly transform cultures. In many cultures, the social experience of pregnancy and childbirth has changed dramatically as a result of the genetic revolution. New reproductive technologies allow for the genetic assessment of fertilized eggs and embryos (the earliest stage of animal development), with far-reaching social consequences. These new reproductive technologies have also become the object of anthropological study as cultural anthropologists study the social impact of biological knowledge. Over the past twenty years, anthropologist Rayna Rapp has studied the social impact of prenatal (before birth) genetic testing in America. Her work illustrates how biological knowledge is generated and interpreted by humans every step of the way.

Prenatal genetic testing is conducted most frequently through amniocentesis, a technique developed in the 1960s through which fluid, containing cells from the developing embryo, is drawn from the womb of a pregnant woman. The chromosomes and specific genes are then analyzed for abnormalities. Rapp traces the development of amniocentesis from an experimental procedure to one routinely used in pregnancy in America. For example, today pregnant women over the age of 35 routinely undergo this test because certain genetic conditions are associated with older maternal age. Trisomy 21 or Down's syndrome, in which individuals have an extra 21st chromosome, can be easily identified through amniocentesis. Through ethnographic study Rapp shows that a biological fact (such as an extra 21st chromosome) present "potential parents" with new reproductive choices. She also illustrates how genetic testing may lead to the labeling of disabled people as undesirable. Rapp's anthropological investigation of the social impact of amniocentesis illustrates the complex interplay between biological knowledge and cultural practices.

What happens when a child inherits the allele for type O blood from one parent and that for type A from the other? Will the child have blood of type A, O, or some mixture of the two? Many of these questions were answered by Mendel's original experiments.

Mendel discovered that certain alleles are able to mask the presence of others; one allele is dominant, whereas the other is recessive. Actually, it is the traits that are dominant or recessive, rather than the alleles themselves; geneticists merely speak of dominant and recessive alleles for the sake of convenience. Thus, one might speak of the allele for type A blood as being dominant to the one for type O. An individual whose blood type genes are heterozygous, with one "A" and one "O" allele, will have type A blood. In other words, the heterozygous condition (AO) will show exactly the same physical characteristic, or **phenotype,** as the homozygous (AA), even though the two have a somewhat different genetic composition, or genotype. Only the homozygous recessive genotype (OO) will show the phenotype of Type O blood.

The **dominance** of one allele does not mean that the **recessive** one is lost or in some way blended. A type A heterozygous parent (AO) will produce sex cells containing both "A" and "O" alleles. (This is an example of Mendel's

phenotype The observable or testable appearance of an organism that may or may not reflect a particular genotype due to the variable expression of dominant and recessive alleles.
dominance The ability of one allele for a trait to mask the presence of another allele.
recessive An allele for a trait whose expression is masked by the presence of a dominant allele.

law of segregation, that alleles retain their separate identities.) Recessive alleles can be handed down for generations before they are matched with another recessive in the process of sexual reproduction and show up in the phenotype. The presence of the dominant allele simply masks the expression of the recessive allele.

All of the traits Mendel studied in garden peas showed this dominant-recessive relationship, and so for some years it was believed that this was the only relationship possible. Later studies, however, have indicated that patterns of inheritance are not always so simple. In some cases, neither allele is dominant; they are both co-dominant. An example of co-dominance in human heredity can be seen also in the inheritance of blood types. Type A is produced by one allele; type B by another. A heterozygous individual will have a phenotype of AB, because neither allele can dominate the other.

The inheritance of blood types points out another complexity of heredity. Although each of us has at most two alleles for any given gene, the number of *possible* alleles is by no means limited to two. Certain traits have three or more allelic forms. Only one allele can appear on each of the two homologous chromosomes, so each individual is limited to two genetic alleles.

Over one hundred alleles exist for **hemoglobin,** the blood protein that carries oxygen. Expression of normal versus sickle hemoglobin in a heterozygous individual represents an example of incomplete dominance. The sickle abnormality is caused by a change in a single base pair in the DNA of the hemoglobin gene. The resulting mutant allele codes for an amino acid substitution in the hemoglobin protein that leads red blood cells to take on a characteristic sickle shape. In homozygous individuals with two sickle-hemoglobin alleles, collapse and clumping of the abnormal red cells blocks the capillaries and creates tissue damage—causing the symptoms of sickle-cell disease. Afflicted individuals commonly die before reaching adulthood. The homozygous dominant condition (Hb^AHb^A; normal hemoglobin is known as hemoglobin A, not to be confused with blood type A) produces only normal molecules of hemoglobin whereas the heterozygous condition (Hb^AHb^S) produces 50 percent normal and 50 percent abnormal hemoglobin. Except under low-oxygen or other stressful conditions, such individuals suffer no ill effects. As we shall discuss later in this chapter, the heterozygous condition can actually improve individuals' resilience to malaria relative to the "normal" homozygous condition.

hemoglobin The protein that carries oxygen in the red blood cells.
polygenetic inheritance When two or more genes contribute to the phenotypic expression of single character.

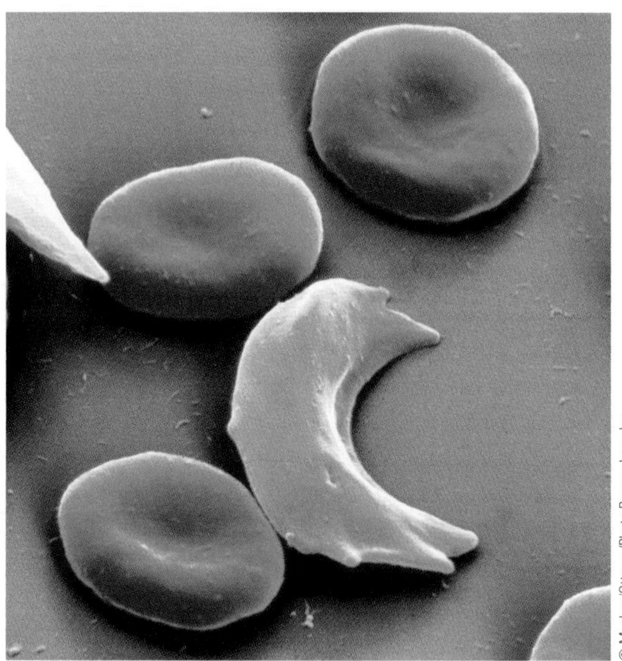

Sickle-cell anemia is caused by abnormal hemoglobin, called hemoglobin S. Those afflicted by the disease are homozygous for the allele S, and all their red blood cells "sickle." Co-dominance is observable with the sickle and normal alleles. Heterozygotes make 50 percent normal hemoglobin and 50 percent sickle hemoglobin. Shown here is a sickle hemoglobin red blood cell among normal red blood cells.

MEDIATREK
To learn how the genetics revolution is changing the practice of medicine, take a great tutorial in genetics, and read the story of the hunt for a cure for the genetic disease cystic fibrosis through gene therapy, see MediaTrek 2.2 on the companion Web site or CD-ROM.

Polygenetic Inheritance

So far, we have spoken as if the traits of organisms are determined by just one gene. However, multiple genes control most physical traits such as height, skin color, or liability to disease. In such cases, we speak of **polygenetic inheritance,** where the respective alleles of two or more genes influence phenotype. Because so many genes are involved, each of which may have alternative alleles, it is difficult to unravel the genetic underpinnings of any continuous trait. For this reason, characteristics subject to polygenetic inheritance exhibit a continuous range of variation in their phenotype expression and illustrate difficulties inherent with reconciling visible traits with their underlying genetic bases. As biological anthropologist Jonathan Marks demonstrates in the following Original Study, tracing the relationship between genetics and continuous traits is a mystery still to be unraveled.

Original Study

Ninety-Eight Percent Alike: What Our Similarity to Apes Tells Us about Our Understanding of Genetics

It's not too hard to tell Jane Goodall from a chimpanzee. Goodall is the one with long legs and short arms, a prominent forehead, and whites in her eyes. She's the one with a significant amount of hair only on her head, not all over her body. She's the one who walks, talks, and wears clothing.

A few decades ago, however, the nascent field of molecular genetics recognized an apparent paradox: However easy it may be to tell Jane Goodall from a chimpanzee on the basis of physical characteristics, it is considerably harder to tell them apart according to their genes.

More recently, geneticists have been able to determine with precision that humans and chimpanzees are over 98 percent identical genetically, and that figure has become one of the most well-known factoids in the popular scientific literature. It has been invoked to argue that we are simply a third kind of chimpanzee, together with the common chimp and the rarer bonobo; to claim human rights for nonhuman apes; and to explain the roots of male aggression.

Using the figure in those ways, however, ignores the context necessary to make sense of it. Actually, our amazing genetic similarity to chimpanzees is a scientific fact constructed from two rather more mundane facts: our familiarity with the apes, and our unfamiliarity with genetic comparisons.

To begin with, it is unfair to juxtapose the differences between the bodies of people and apes with the similarities in their genes. After all, we have been comparing the bodies of humans and chimpanzees for 300 years, and we have been comparing DNA sequences for less than 20 years.

Now that we are familiar with chimpanzees, we quickly see how different they look from us. But when the chimpanzee was a novelty, in the 18th century, scholars were struck by the overwhelming similarity of human and ape bodies. And why not? Bone for bone, muscle for muscle, organ for organ, the bodies of humans and apes differ only in subtle ways. And yet, it is impossible to say just how physically similar they are. Forty percent? Sixty percent? Ninety-eight percent? Three-dimensional beings that develop over

© Richard H. Marks

their lifetimes don't lend themselves to a simple scale of similarity.

Genetics brings something different to the comparison. A DNA sequence is a one-dimensional entity, a long series of A, G, C, and T subunits. Align two sequences from different species and you can simply tabulate their similarities; if they match 98 out of 100 times, then the species are 98 percent genetically identical.

But is that more or less than their bodies match? We have no easy way to tell, for making sense of the question "How similar are a human and a chimp?" requires a frame of reference. In other words, we should be asking: "How similar are a human and a chimp, compared to what?" Let's try and answer the question. How similar are a human and a chimp, compared to, say, a sea urchin? The human and chimpanzee have limbs, skeletons, bilateral symmetry, a central nervous system; each bone, muscle, and organ matches. For all intents and purposes, the human and chimpanzee aren't 98 percent identical, they're 100 percent identical.

On the other hand, when we compare the DNA of humans and chimps, what does the percentage of similarity mean? We conceptualize it on a linear scale, on which 100 percent is perfectly identical, and 0 percent is totally different. But the structure of DNA gives the scale a statistical idiosyncrasy.

Because DNA is a linear array of those four bases—A, G, C, and T—only four possibilities exist at any specific point in a DNA sequence. The laws of chance tell us that two random sequences from species that have no ancestry in common will match at about one in every four sites.

Thus, even two unrelated DNA sequences will be 25 percent identical, not 0 percent identical. (You can, of course, generate sequences more different than that, but greater differences would not occur randomly.) The most different two DNA sequences can be, then, is 75 percent different.

Now consider that all multicellular life on earth is related. A human, a chimpanzee, and the banana the chimpanzee is eating share a remote common ancestry, but a common ancestry nevertheless. Therefore, if we compare any particular DNA sequence in a human and a banana, the sequence would have to be more than 25 percent identical. For the sake of argument, let's say 35 percent. In other words, your DNA is over one-third the same as a banana's. Yet, of course, there are few ways other than genetically in which a human could be shown to be one-third identical to a banana.

[CONTINUED]

That context may help us to assess the 98 percent DNA similarity of humans and chimpanzees. The fact that our DNA is 98 percent identical to that of a chimp is not a transcendent statement about our natures, but merely a decontextualized and culturally interpreted datum.

Moreover, the genetic comparison is misleading because it ignores qualitative differences among genomes. Genetic evolution involves much more than simply replacing one base with another. Thus, even among such close relatives as human and chimpanzee, we find that the chimp's genome is estimated to be about 10 percent larger than the human's; that one human chromosome contains a fusion of two small chimpanzee chromosomes; and that the tips of each chimpanzee chromosome contain a DNA sequence that is not present in humans.

In other words, the pattern we encounter genetically is actually quite close to the pattern we encounter anatomically. In spite of the shock the figure of 98 percent may give us, humans are obviously identifiably different from, as well as very similar to, chimpanzees. The apparent paradox is simply a result of how mundane the apes have become, and how exotic DNA still is. *(By Jonathan Marks. (2000). 98% alike (what our similarity to apes tells us about our understanding of genetics).* The Chronicle of Higher Education, *May 12, B7.)*

POPULATION GENETICS

At the level of the individual, the study of genetics shows how traits are transmitted from parent to offspring, enabling a prediction about the chances that any given individual will display some phenotypic characteristic. At the level of the group, the study of genetics takes on additional significance, revealing mechanisms that support evolutionary interpretations of the diversity of life.

A key concept in genetics is that of the **population,** or a group of individuals within which breeding takes place. It is within populations that natural selection takes place, as some members contribute a disproportionate share of the next generation. Over generations, the relative proportions of alleles in a population changes (biological evolution) according to the varying reproductive success of individuals within that population. By definition, individuals with more reproductive success are better adapted to their environment.

The Stability of the Population

In theory, the characteristics of any given population should remain stable. For example, generation after generation, the bullfrogs in a farm pond, look much alike, have the same calls, and exhibit the same behavior when breeding. The **gene pool** of the population—the genetic variants available to that population—appears to remain stable over time.

Although some alleles may be dominant to others, recessive alleles are not just lost or destroyed. Statistically, an individual who is heterozygous for a particular gene with one dominant (A) and one recessive allele (a) has a 50 percent chance of passing on the dominant allele, and a 50 percent chance of passing on the recessive allele. Even if another dominant allele masks the presence of the recessive allele in the next generation, the recessive allele nonetheless will continue to be a part of the gene pool.

Because alleles are not "lost" in the process of reproduction, the frequency of the different alleles within a population should remain exactly the same from one generation to the next in the absence of evolution. The **Hardy-Weinberg principle** was named for the English mathematician G. H. Hardy (1877–1947) and the German obstetrician W. Weinberg (1862–1937) who worked it out in 1908. The principle algebraically demonstrates that the percentage of individuals homozygous for the dominant allele, homozygous for the recessive allele, and heterozygous will remain the same from one generation to the next provided that certain specified conditions are met. These conditions include that mating is entirely random; that the population is sufficiently large for statistical averages to express themselves; that no new variants will be introduced into the population's gene pool; and that all individuals are equally successful at surviving and reproducing. The last four conditions are equivalent to the absence of evolution. Geographical, physiological, or social factors may favor mating between certain individuals over others. Thus, changes in the gene pools of populations, without which there could be no evolution, can and do take place.

population In biology, a group of similar individuals that can and do interbreed.
gene pool All the genetic variants possessed by members of a population.
Hardy-Weinberg principle Demonstrates algebraically that the percentage of individuals that are homozygous for the dominant allele, homozygous for the recessive allele, and heterozygous should remain constant from one generation to the next, provided that certain specified conditions are met.

EVOLUTIONARY FORCES

Mutation

The ultimate source of evolutionary change is **mutation** of genes. For sexually reproducing species like humans, the only mutations of any *evolutionary* consequence are those occurring in sex cells, since these constitute our link to future generations. However, mutations may arise whenever copying mistakes are made during cell division. This may involve a change in a single base of a DNA sequence, or at the other extreme, relocation of large segments of DNA, including entire chromosomes. As you read this page, the DNA in each cell of your body is being damaged.[8] Fortunately, DNA repair enzymes constantly scan DNA for mistakes, slicing out damaged segments and patching up gaps. These repair mechanisms prevent diseases like cancer and ensure that we get a faithful copy of our parental inheritance. Genes controlling DNA repair therefore form a critical part of any species' genetic makeup. Because no species has perfect DNA repair, new mutations arise continuously, so that all species continue to evolve. Although usually harmful to individuals, random mutations are positive in an evolutionary sense, providing the ultimate source of new genetic variation.

Geneticists have calculated the rate at which various types of mutant genes appear. In human populations, they run from a low of about five mutations per million sex cells formed, in the case of a gene abnormality that leads to the absence of an iris in the eye, to a high of about a hundred per million, in the case of a gene involved in a form of muscular dystrophy. The average is about thirty mutants per million. Environmental factors may increase the rate at which mutations occur. These include certain dyes, antibiotics, and chemicals used in the preservation of food. Radiation, whether of industrial or solar origin, represents another important cause of mutations. There is even evidence that stress can increase mutation rates, increasing the diversity necessary for selection if successful adaptation is to occur.[9]

In humans, as in all multicellular animals, the very nature of genetic material ensures that mutations will occur. For instance, the fact that genes are split by stretches of junk DNA increases the chances that a simple editing mistake in the process of copying DNA will cause mutations. To cite one example, no fewer than fifty segments of junk DNA fragment the gene for collagen—the main structural protein of the skin, bones, and teeth. One result of this seemingly inefficient situation is that it becomes possible to shuffle the gene segments themselves like a deck of cards, putting together new proteins with new functions. Also, humans have longer strings of repetitious DNA within and between genes than do other primates, which may contribute to our higher mutation rate. Although individuals may suffer as a result, mutations also confer versatility at the population level, making it possible for an evolving

Mutagens—such as pollutants, preservatives, cigarette smoke, radiation, and even some medicines—threaten people in industrial societies. While the mutations from these environmental hazards are generally negative, mutation is overall a positive force in evolutionary terms as the ultimate source of all new genetic variation. The positive side of mutation is fictionalized in the special talents of the X-Men.

mutation Chance alteration of genetic material that produces new variation.

[8] Culotta, E., & Koshland, D. E., Jr. (1994). DNA repair works its way to the top. *Science, 266,* 1,926.

[9] Chicurel, M. (2001). Can organisms speed their own evolution? *Science, 292,* 1,824–1,827.

species to adapt more quickly to environmental changes. Another source of genetic remodeling from within is the movement of whole DNA sequences from one locality or chromosome to another. This may disrupt the function of other genes or, in the case of so-called jumping genes, carry important functional messages of their own. In humans, about 1 in every 700 mutations is caused by "jumping genes." It is important to realize that mutations occur randomly and thus do not arise out of need for some new adaptation.

Genetic Drift

Over the course of their lifetime, each individual is subject to a number of random events affecting their survival. For example, an individual squirrel in good health and possessed of a number of advantageous traits may be killed in a forest fire; a genetically well-adapted baby cougar may not live longer than a day if its mother gets caught in an avalanche, whereas the weaker offspring of a mother that does not die may survive. In a large population, such accidents of nature are unimportant; the accidents that preserve individuals with certain alleles will be balanced out by the accidents that destroy them. However, in small populations, such averaging out may not be possible. Because human populations today are so large, we might suppose that human beings are unaffected by chance events. Although it is true that a rock slide that kills five campers whose home community has a total population of 100,000 is not statistically significant, a rock slide that kills five hunters from a small group of food foragers could significantly alter frequencies of alleles in the local gene pool. The group size of food foragers (people who hunt, fish, and gather other wild foods for subsistence) varies between about twenty-five and fifty.

These random events ultimately result in changes in frequencies of gene variants in a population, defined as the evolutionary force of **genetic drift.** The effects of genetic drift are most powerful in small populations. A particular kind of genetic drift, known as **founder's effect,** may occur when an existing population splits up into two or more new ones, especially if one of these new populations is founded by a particularly small number of individuals. In such cases, it is unlikely that the gene frequencies of the smaller population will be representative of those of the larger one. Isolated island populations may possess limited variability due to founder's effect. For example, in 1790, nine British sailors from the *H.M.S. Bounty,* six Tahitian men, and eight or nine Tahitian women settled on Pitcairn Island in the South Pacific. These individuals possessed only a small fraction of the total genetic variation in either England or Tahiti. After a conflict between the Tahitians and the Englishmen, the population was further reduced to one British man, Alexander Smith, the women, and some children. Thus today's population descended from a small number of individuals with a very narrow gene pool. The narrow gene pool results in high frequency of some genetic traits. Genetic drift is likely to have been an important factor in human evolution, because until 10,000 years ago all humans were food foragers who probably lived in relatively small, self-contained populations.

The 1998 Casitas Volcano mudslide in Nicaragua, triggered by the rains of Hurricane Mitch, buried a village, killing over 1,200 people. This is one kind of accident that can produce chance alterations of allele frequency in human gene pools.

genetic drift Chance fluctuations of allele frequencies in the gene pool of a population.

founder's effect A particular form of genetic drift deriving from a small founding population not possessing all the alleles present in the original population.

© Corbis Sygma

American Museum of Natural History

VISUAL COUNTERPOINT Peculiarities in the teeth of the British have attracted attention. In Pitcairn Islanders, an irregularity of the tooth enamel was brought by a founding member from England. Today it appears in high frequency due to one type of genetic drift known as founder's effect.

Gene Flow

Another factor that brings change to the gene pool of a population is **gene flow,** or the introduction of new alleles from nearby populations through interbreeding. Migration of individuals or groups into the territory occupied by others may also lead to gene flow. Geographical factors affect gene flow. For example, when a river that once separated two populations of small mammals changes course, two populations once separated from each other can now interbreed freely. Alleles that may have been present in only one population will now be present in both. Among humans, social factors such as mating rules, intergroup conflict, and our ability to travel great distances affect gene flow. For example, the last 500 years have seen the introduction of alleles into Central and South American populations from both the Spanish colonists and the Africans whom Europeans imported as slaves. The result has been an increase in the range of phenotypic variation. In evolutionary terms gene flow is important because it keeps populations from developing into separate species.

© Bob Daemmrich/The Image Works

New alleles are introduced into populations through gene flow. For specific single genetic traits, diversity increases as migrating people bring their genes with them. Because gene flow has been important throughout our evolutionary history, most human variation is within rather than among populations.

Natural Selection

Although the factors discussed above may produce change in a population, that change would not necessarily make the population better adapted to its biological and social

gene flow The introduction of alleles from the gene pool of one population into that of another.

The Ethical, Legal, and Social Implications of the Human Genome Project

The Human Genome Project, the massive effort to sequence the entire human genetic code, is leading to a massive geneticization of health-care practices in the U.S. and in turn to the way people think about themselves. Anthropologists have brought their unique biocultural perspective to the study of the societal effects of knowledge generated from the new genetics—particularly its ethical, legal, and social implications (ELSI). Anthropologists are uniquely poised to examine how social factors such as gender, class, and ethnicity influence the use of clinical genetic services; the understanding and interpretation of genetic information; and the development of public policy about these new genetic technologies.

In addition, anthropologists contribute to ELSI research surrounding the study of human genetic variation. The working draft of the human genome, completed in time for the 50th anniversary of the discovery of the DNA double helix, does not capture the enormous variation present at the genetic level due to multiple alleles, or alternate forms, that are found for many genes. Anthropologists are contributing to a more complete understanding of this variation through their examination of worldwide genetic diversity so that North Americans are not the only humans represented in the Human Genome Project. Ethical issues have been raised by global genetic investigation, such as whether scientists or the people own the patent rights to beneficial genes discovered through such investigations.

A global understanding of genetic diversity raises additional ELSI questions. For instance, how can genetic diversity be examined without falling into the trap of grouping such differences by race? As anthropologists have shown, the concept of race has no validity as a biological concept when applied to humans (see Chapter 13). However, in health care, the field where practical applications of genetic knowledge are most promising, race is often mistakenly considered a biological feature rather than a social feature of an individual. As individual and population variation for specific genes is understood, anthropologists will play an important role in assuring that this information does not lead to the construction of false biological categories. In this way, social determinants of health and disease will not be mistaken for biological difference. ■ ■ ■

environment. Genetic drift, for example, often produces strange characteristics that have no survival value; mutant genes may be either helpful or harmful to survival, or simply neutral. Natural selection, however, accounts for *adaptive* evolutionary change. **Adaptation** is a series of beneficial adjustments to the environment. As we will explore throughout this textbook, humans can adapt to their environment through culture as well as biology. When biological adaptation occurs at a genetic level natural selection is at work.

Natural selection refers to the evolutionary process through which genetic variation at the population level is shaped to fit local environmental conditions. In other words, instead of a completely random selection of individuals whose traits will be passed on to the next generation, there is selection by the forces of nature. In the process, the frequency of genetic variants for harmful or nonadaptive traits within the population is reduced while the frequency of genetic variants for adaptive traits is increased.

In popular writing, natural selection is often thought of as "survival of the fittest," a phrase coined by British philosopher Herbert Spencer. The phrase implies that the physically weak, being unfit, are eliminated from the population by disease, predation, or starvation. Obviously, the survival of the fittest has some bearing on natural selection. But there are many cases in which individuals survive, and even do quite well, but do not reproduce. They may be incapable of attracting mates, or they may be sterile, or they may produce offspring that do not survive after birth. For example, among the Uganda Kob, a kind of antelope native to eastern Africa, males that are unable to attract females form bachelor herds in which they live out their lives. As members of a herd, they are reasonably well protected against predators, and so they may survive to relatively old ages. They do not, however, pass on their genes to succeeding generations.

adaptation A series of beneficial adjustments to the environment.

MEDIATREK

To find out all the latest research about the Human Genome Project, including its program on ethical, legal, and social issues, see MediaTrek 2.3 on the companion Web site or CD-ROM.

Change in the frequency with which certain genetic variants appear in a population is generally a very slow process. For example, the present frequency of the sickle-cell allele is 0.05 in the entire U.S. population. A 5-percent reduction per generation (about 25 years) would take about 2,000 years to reach a frequency of 0.01, assuming complete selection against those homozygous for the allele. Yet given the great time span

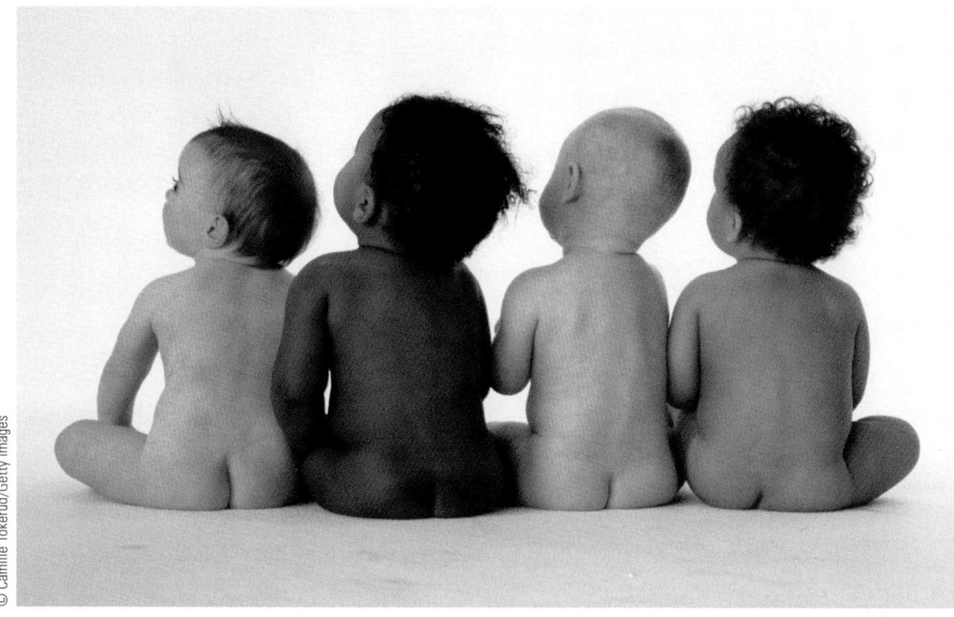

Across the globe, newborn babies weigh on average between 5 and 8 pounds. Stabilizing selection seems to be operating here to keep infant size well matched to the size of the human birth canal for successful childbirth.

involved—life on earth has existed for 3 to 4 billion years—even such small and slow changes will have a significant cumulative impact on both the genotypes and phenotypes of any population. The Anthropology Applied feature explains that the social impact of genetics is sometimes quite rapid, as people face the challenges posed by the scientific study of the human genome.

Natural selection may also promote stability, rather than change. **Stabilizing selection** occurs in populations that are already well adapted or where change would be disadvantageous. In cases where change is disadvantageous, natural selection will favor the retention of allele frequencies more or less as they are. However, the evolutionary history of most forms of life is not one of constant change, proceeding as a steady, stately progression over vast periods of time; rather, it is one of prolonged periods of relative stability or gradual change punctuated by shorter periods of more rapid change (or extinction) when altered conditions require new adaptations or when a new mutation produces an opportunity to adapt to some other available environment. According to the fossil record, most species survive somewhere between 3 and 5 million years.[10]

Discussions of the action of natural selection typically focus on anatomical or structural changes, such as the evolutionary change in the types of teeth found in primates; ample evidence (fossilized teeth, for example) exists to interpret such changes. By extrapolation, biologists assume that the same mechanisms work on behavioral traits as well. It seems reasonable that individuals in a group of vervet monkeys capable of warning one another of the presence of predators would have a significant survival advantage over those without this capability. However, such situations have constituted an enigma for evolutionary biologists who typically see individuals as "survival machines," acting always selfishly in their own interest. By giving an alarm call, an individual calls attention to itself, thereby becoming an obvious target for the predator. How, then, could the kind of **altruism,** or concern for the welfare of others, evolve in which individuals place themselves at risk for the good of the group? One biologist's simple solution substitutes money for reproductive fitness to illustrate one way in which such cooperative behavior may come about:

> You are given a choice. Either you can receive $10 and keep it all or you can receive $10 million if you give $6 million to your next door neighbor. Which would you do? Guessing that most selfish people would be happy with a net gain of $4 million, I consider the second option to be a form of selfish behavior in which a neighbor gains an incidental benefit. I have termed such selfish behavior benevolent.[11]

[10]Thomson, K. S. (1997). Natural selection and evolution's smoking gun. *American Scientist, 85,* 516.

[11]Nunney, L. (1998). Are we selfish, are we nice, or are we nice because we are selfish? *Science, 281,* 1,619.

stabilizing selection Natural selection acting to promote stability, rather than change, in a population's gene pool.
altruism Acts of selflessness or self-sacrificing behavior.

VISUAL COUNTERPOINT Adaptation to a specific climate can be seen in the difference in the size of the ears of the arctic and desert rabbits. The arctic species has shorter ears to conserve heat in cold environmental conditions. The desert rabbit has long ears to radiate heat and keep the body cool in a hot desert environment with little shade.

Natural selection of beneficial social traits was probably an important influence on human evolution, since in the primates some degree of cooperative social behavior became important for food-getting, defense, and mate attraction. Indeed, anthropologist Christopher Boehm argues that, "If human nature were merely selfish, vigilant punishment of deviants would be expected, whereas the elaborate prosocial prescriptions that favor altruism would come as a surprise."[12]

As a consequence of the process of natural selection, populations generally become well adapted to their environments. Anyone who has ever looked carefully at the plants and animals that survive in the deserts of the western United States can cite many instances of adaptation. For example, members of the cactus family have extensive root networks close to the surface of the soil, enabling them to soak up the slightest bit of moisture; they are able to store large quantities of water whenever it is available; they are shaped so as to expose the smallest possible surface to the dry air and are generally leafless as adults, thereby preventing water loss through evaporation; and a covering of spines discourages animals from chewing into the juicy flesh of the plant.

Desert animals are also adapted to their environment. The kangaroo rat can survive without drinking water; many reptiles live in burrows where the temperature is lower; most animals are nocturnal or active only in the cool of the night.

Many of the creation stories traditionally offered to explain observable cases of adaptation rely heavily on the purposeful acts of a supreme being as described earlier. The "Just So" stories of Rudyard Kipling such as "How the Leopard Got His Spots," or the elephant his trunk, are literary caricatures of this approach. Ironically, because specific examples of adaptation can be difficult to prove at times, scientists will sometimes suggest that their colleagues' adaptive scenarios are "Just So" stories.

The adaptability of organic structures and functions, no matter how much a source of wonder and fascination, nevertheless falls short of perfection. This is so because natural selection can only work with what the existing store of genetic variation provides; it cannot create something entirely new. In the words of one evolutionary biologist, evolution is a process of tinkering, rather than design. Often tinkering involves balancing beneficial and harmful effects of a specific allele as the case of sickle-cell anemia illustrates.

[12]Boehm, C. (2000). The evolution of moral communities. *School of American Research, 2000 Annual Report, 7.*

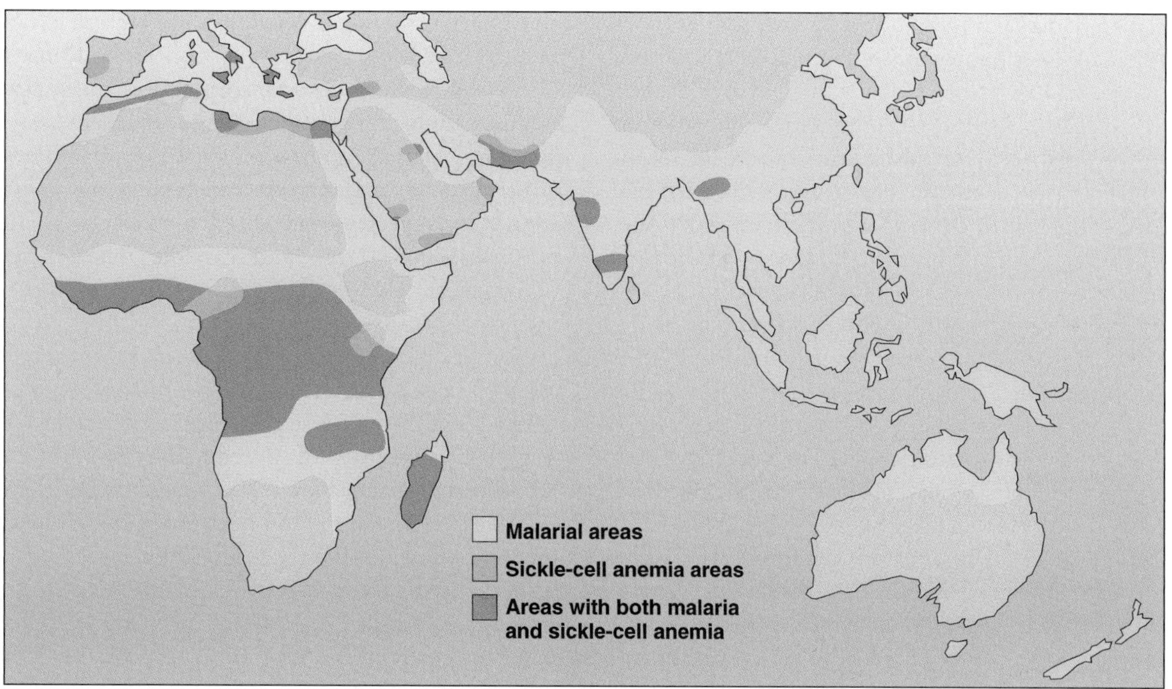

FIGURE 2.4
The allele that, in homozygotes, causes sickle-cell anemia makes heterozygotes resistant to falciparum malaria. Thus, the allele is most common in populations native to regions where this strain of malaria is common.

The Case of Sickle-Cell Anemia

Among human beings, a particularly well-studied case of an adaptation paid for by the misery of many individuals brings us back to the case of **sickle-cell anemia.** This disorder first came to the attention of geneticists when it was observed that most North Americans who suffer from it are of African ancestry. Investigation traced the abnormality to populations that live in a clearly defined belt throughout central Africa (although brought to North America from West Africa, the condition also exists in some non-African populations, as will be noted below).

Geneticists were curious to know why such a harmful hereditary disability persisted in these populations. According to the theory of natural selection, any alleles that are harmful will tend to disappear from the group, because the individuals who are homozygous for the abnormality generally die—are "selected out"—before they are able to reproduce. Why, then, had this seemingly harmful condition remained in populations from central Africa?

sickle-cell anemia An inherited form of anemia caused by a mutation in the hemoglobin protein that causes the red blood cells to assume a sickle shape.

The answer to this mystery began to emerge when it was noticed that the areas with high rates of sickle-cell anemia are also areas in which falciparum malaria is common (Figure 2.4). This severe form of malaria causes high fevers that significantly interfere with the reproductive abilities of those who do not actually die from the disease. Moreover, it was discovered that the same hemoglobin abnormalities are found in people living in parts of the Arabian Peninsula, Greece, Algeria, Syria and India, all regions where falciparum malaria is (or was) common.

Further research established that the abnormal hemoglobin was associated with an increased ability to survive the effects of the malarial parasite; it seems that the effects of the abnormal hemoglobin in limited amounts were less injurious than the effects of the malarial parasite. Thus, selection favored heterozygous individuals (Hb^AHb^S). The loss of alleles for abnormal hemoglobin caused by the death of those homozygous for it (from sickle-cell anemia) was balanced out by the loss of alleles for normal hemoglobin, as those homozygous for it experienced reproductive failure.

This example also points out how adaptations tend to be specific; the abnormal hemoglobin was an adaptation to the particular parts of the world in which the malarial parasite flourished. When Africans adapted to that region came to North America, where in recent times falciparum malaria is almost never seen, what had been an adaptive characteristic became an injurious one. Where there is no malaria to attack those with normal hemoglobin, the abnormal hemoglobin becomes comparatively disadvantageous. Although the rates of sickle-cell trait are still relatively high among African Americans—about 9 percent show the sickling trait—this represents a significant decline from the approximately 22 percent who are estimated to have shown the trait when the first slaves were brought from Africa. A further decline over the next several generations is to be expected, as selection pressure continues to work against the frequency of the sickle-cell allele.

This example also illustrates the important role culture may play even with respect to biological adaptation. In Africa, falciparum malaria was not a significant problem until humans abandoned food foraging for farming a few thousand years ago. In order to farm, people had to clear areas of the natural forest cover. In the forest, decaying vegetation on the forest floor had imparted an absorbent quality to the ground so that the heavy rainfall of the region rapidly soaked into the soil. But once stripped of its natural vegetation, the soil lost this quality.

Furthermore, the forest canopy was no longer there to break the force of the rainfall, and so the impact of the heavy rains tended to compact the soil further. The result was that stagnant puddles commonly formed after rains, providing the perfect breeding environment for the type of mosquito that is the host to the malarial parasite. These mosquitoes then began to flourish and transmit the malarial parasite to humans. Thus, humans unwittingly created the kind of environment that made a hitherto disadvantageous trait, the abnormal hemoglobin associated with sickle-cell anemia, advantageous.

Although it is true that all living organisms have many adaptive characteristics, it is not true that all characteristics are adaptive. All male mammals, for example, possess nipples, even though they serve no useful purpose. To female mammals, however, nipples are essential to reproductive success, which is why males have them. The two sexes are not separate entities, shaped independently by natural selection but are variants upon a single body plan, elaborated in later embryology. Precursors of mammary glands are built in all mammalian fetuses, enlarging later in the development of females, but remaining small and without function in males.

Nor is it true that current utility is a reliable guide to historical origin or future use. For one thing, nonadaptive characters may be co-opted for later utility following origins as developmental consequences of changing patterns in embryonic and postnatal growth. The unusually large size of a kiwi's egg, for example, enhances the survivability of kiwi chicks, in that they are particularly large and capable when hatched. Nevertheless, kiwi eggs probably did not evolve such large size because it is adaptive. Kiwis evolved from large, moa-sized ancestors, and in birds, egg size reduces at a slower rate than does body size. Therefore, the outsized eggs of kiwi birds seem to be no more than a developmental byproduct of a reduction in body size.[13] Similarly, an existing adaptation may come under strong selective pressure for some new purpose, as did insect wings. These did not arise so that insects might fly, but rather as structures that were used to "row," and later skim, across the surface of the water.[14] Later, the larger ones by chance proved useful for purposes of flight. In both these cases, what we see is natural selection operating as "a creative scavenger, taking what is available and putting it to new use."[15]

As primatologist Frans de Waal notes, "Evolution is a magnificent idea that has won over essentially every-

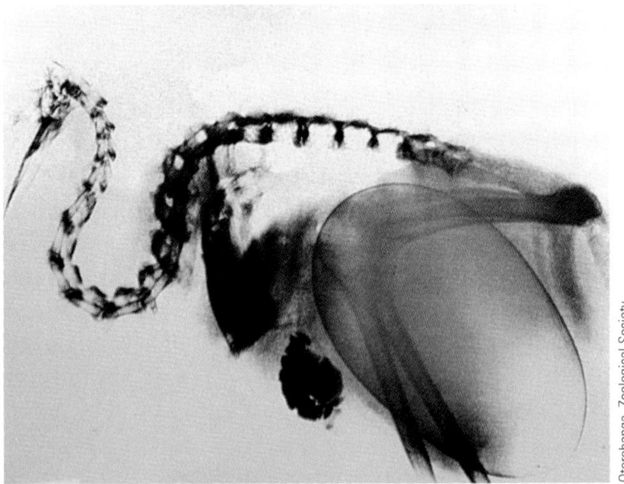

Otorohanga Zoological Society

This x-ray showing the unusually large size of a kiwi's egg illustrates that evolution does not proceed by preplanned design but rather by a process of tinkering with preexisting body forms.

[13]Gould, S. J. (1991). *Bully for brontosaurus* (pp. 109–123). New York: Norton.

[14]Kaiser, J. (1994). A new theory of insect wing origins takes off. *Science, 266,* 363.

[15]Doist, R. (1997). Molecular evolution and scientific inquiry, misperceived. *American Scientist, 85,* 475.

one in the world willing to listen to scientific arguments."[16] We will return to the topic in Chapter 5, as we look at how the primates evolved to produce the many species in the world today. First, however, we will survey the living primates (in Chapter 3) in order to understand the kinds of animals they are, what they have in common, and what distinguishes the various forms.

[16]de Waal, F. (2001). Sing the song of evolution. *Natural History, 110*(8), 77.

Chapter Summary

- In the 18th century, Carl von Linné (Linnaeus) devised a system to classify the great variety of living things then known. On the basis of similarities in body structure, body function, and sequence of bodily growth, he grouped organisms into small groups, or species. Modern taxonomy still uses his basic system but now looks at such characteristics as chemical reactions of blood, protein structure, and the makeup of the genetic material itself. Although Linnaeus regarded species as fixed and unchangeable, this idea was challenged by the finding of fossils, the idea of progress, and the many continuities among different species.
- Evolution may be defined as descent with modification, which occurs as genetic variants in the gene pool of a population change in frequency. Genes, the units of heredity, are segments of molecules of DNA (deoxyribonucleic acid), and the entire sequence of DNA is known as the genome. DNA is a complex molecule resembling two strands of rope twisted around each other with ladder-like rungs connecting the two strands. The sequence of bases along the DNA molecule directs the production of proteins. Proteins, in turn, constitute specific identifiable traits such as blood type. Just about everything in the human body is made of or by proteins, and human DNA provides the instructions for the thousands of proteins that keep us alive and healthy. DNA molecules have the unique property of being able to produce exact copies of themselves. As long as no errors are made in the process of replication, new daughter cells will be exact genetic copies of the parent cell.
- DNA molecules are located on chromosomes, structures found in the nucleus of each cell. Each kind of organism has a characteristic number of chromosomes, which are usually found in pairs in sexually reproducing organisms. Humans have twenty-three pairs. Different versions or alternate forms of a gene for a given trait are called alleles.
- Mitosis, one kind of cell division that results in new cells, begins when the chromosomes (hence the genes) replicate, forming a duplicate of the original pair of chromosomes in the nucleus. Meiosis is related to sexual reproduction; it begins with the replication of original chromosomes, but these are divided into four cells, in humans each containing twenty-three single chromosomes. The normal human number of twenty-three pairs of chromosomes is re-established when an egg and sperm unite in the fertilization process.
- Gregor Mendel discovered the particulate nature of heredity and that some dominant alleles are able to mask the presence of recessive alleles. The allele for type A blood in humans, for example, is dominant to the allele for type O blood. Alleles that are both expressed when present are termed *co-dominant.* For example, an individual with the alleles for type A and type B blood has the AB blood type. Phenotype refers to the physical characteristics of an organism, whereas genotype refers to its genetic composition. Two organisms may have different genotypes but the same phenotype. An individual with type A blood phenotype may possess either the AO or the AA genotype.
- A population is a group of interbreeding individuals. While natural selection works upon individuals, evolution occurs at the population level as changes occur in allele frequency. The total number of different alleles of genes available to a population is called its gene pool. The frequency with which certain alleles occur in the same gene pool theoretically remains the same from one generation to another; this is known as the Hardy-Weinberg principle. Nonetheless, change does take place in gene pools as a result of natural selection and other factors.
- Four evolutionary forces—mutation, genetic drift, gene flow, and natural selection—affect the genetic structures of populations. The ultimate source of genetic variation is mutation, changes in DNA that may be helpful or harmful to the organism. Although mutations are inevitable given the nature of cellular chemistry, environmental factors—such as heat, chemicals, or radiation—can increase the mutation rate. The effect of random events on the gene pool of a small population is called genetic drift. Genetic drift may have been an important factor in human evolution because until 10,000 years ago humans lived in small isolated populations. Gene flow, the introduction of new variants of genes from nearby populations, distributes new variation to all populations and serves to prevent speciation.
- Natural selection is the evolutionary force involved in adaptive change. It reduces the frequency of alleles for harmful or maladaptive traits within a population and increases the frequency of alleles for adaptive traits. A well-studied example of adaptation through natural selection in humans is inheritance of the trait for sickling red blood cells. The sickle-cell trait, caused by the inheritance of an abnormal form of hemoglobin, is an adaptation to life in regions in which malaria is common. In these regions, the sickle-cell trait plays

a beneficial role, but in other parts of the world, the sickling trait is no longer advantageous, while the associated sickle-cell anemia remains injurious. Geneticists predict that as malaria is brought under control, within several generations, there will be a decline in the number of individuals who carry the allele responsible for sickle-cell anemia.

Questions for Reflection

1. Why are biology and its central theory, evolution, vital for meeting the challenge of knowing ourselves as culture-bearing organisms?
2. Creation myths and evolutionary theories for human origins share a number of features but differ in critical ways. Is it possible for spiritual and scientific models of human origins to coexist? How?
3. Anniversaries and other rituals provide opportunities to reflect about personal and cultural meaning. Use the 2003 celebration of the 50th anniversary of discovery of the DNA double helix to reflect on the geneticization of society.
4. The four evolutionary forces—mutation, genetic drift, gene flow, and natural selection—all exert effects on biological variation. Some are at work in individuals while others function at the population level. Compare and contrast these evolutionary forces, outlining their contributions to biological variation.
5. The frequency of the sickle-cell allele in populations provides the classic example of adaptation on a genetic level. Describe the adaptive benefits of this deadly allele. Are mutations good or bad?

Key Terms

Evolution
Mammals
Primates
Species
Genus, genera (plural)
Taxonomy
Analogies
Homologies
Hominoid
Hominid
Hominin
Notochord
Natural selection
Genes
Law of segregation
Law of independent assortment
Chromosomes
DNA
Codon
RNA
Transcription
Ribosomes
Translation
Genetic code
Enzyme
Alleles
Genome
Mitosis
Meiosis
Homozygous
Heterozygous
Genotype
Phenotype
Dominance
Recessive
Hemoglobin
Polygenetic inheritance
Population
Gene pool
Hardy-Weinberg principle
Mutation
Genetic drift
Founder's effect
Gene flow
Adaptation
Stabilizing selection
Altruism
Sickle-cell anemia

Multimedia Review Tools

Companion Web Site

Visit **http://www.wadsworth.com/anthropology_d/** and click on the companion Web site for this textbook to access a wide range of material to aid your study of anthropology. Among the options for self-study in each chapter are learning objectives, flash cards, Internet activities, Web links, InfoTrac College Edition exercises, and practice tests that can be scored and emailed to your instructor.

CD-ROM

The *Doing Anthropology Today* CD-ROM supplied with your textbook provides unique and valuable information designed to enhance your learning experience. This interactive multimedia resource includes video clips, interviews with renowned anthropologists, map and timeline exercises, chapter study quizzes, and much more. *Doing Anthropology Today* will not only help you in achieving your grade goals, but it will also make your learning experience fun and exciting!

Suggested Readings

Berra, T. M. (1990). *Evolution and the myth of creationism.* Stanford, CA: Stanford University Press.

Written by a zoologist, this book is a basic guide to the facts in the debate over evolution. It is not an attack on religion but a successful effort to assist in understanding the scientific basis for evolution.

Gould, S. J. (1996). *Full house: The spread of excellence from Plato to Darwin.* New York: Harmony.

In this highly readable book, Gould explodes the misconception that evolution is inherently progressive. In the process, he shows how trends should be read as changes in variation within systems.

Rapp, R. (1999). *Testing the woman, testing the fetus: The social impact of amniocentesis in America.* New York: Routledge.

This beautifully written, meticulously researched book provides an in-depth historical and sophisticated cultural analysis, as well as a deeply felt personal account of the geneticization of reproduction in America. It demonstrates the importance of cultural analyses of science without ever resorting to an antiscientific stance.

Ridley, M. (1999). *Genome: The autobiography of a species in 23 chapters.* New York: HarperCollins.

Written just as the mapping of the human genome was about to be announced, this book made *The New York Times* best-seller list. The twenty-three chapters discuss DNA on each of the twenty-three human chromosomes. A word of warning, however: The author uncritically accepts some ideas (one example relates to IQ). Still, there's much food for thought here.

Zimmer, C. (2001). *Evolution: The triumph of an idea.* New York: HarperCollins. This is the companion volume to the seven-part television series broadcast by PBS in fall 2001 covering a broad range of topics in modern evolutionary biology in a readable manner. Though it may pay too much attention to the tension between contemporary biblical literalism and the life sciences, it provides a good basic reference.

CHAPTER 3

Living Primates

CHALLENGE ISSUE

OTHER PRIMATES HAVE LONG FASCINATED HUMANS, OWING TO OUR MANY SHARED ANATOMICAL AND BEHAVIORAL CHARACTERISTICS. By studying our closest living relatives, we address the challenge of knowing ourselves. The living primates provide us with important clues about human origins and the biological basis of human behavior.

1 What Is the Place of Humanity among the Other Animals?

Biologists classify humans as belonging to the primate order, a mammalian group that also includes lemurs, lorises, tarsiers, monkeys, and apes. Shared characteristics include similar anatomy, physiology, protein structure, and even the genetic material itself. Among the primates, humans are most closely related to the apes, particularly to chimpanzees, bonobos, and gorillas.

2 What Are the Implications of the Shared Characteristics between Humans and the Other Primates?

A common evolutionary history is responsible for the characteristics shared by humans and other primates. By studying the anatomy, physiology, and molecular structure of the other primates, we can gain a better understanding of what human characteristics we owe to our general primate ancestry and what traits are uniquely ours as humans. Such studies indicate that many of the differences between apes and humans are best understood in terms of a continuum where our biology and behavior differ by degree of expression of shared ape characteristics.

3 Why Do Anthropologists Study the Social Behavior of Monkeys and Apes?

By studying the behavior of monkeys and apes living today—especially those most closely related to us—we may find important clues from which to reconstruct the adaptations and behavior patterns involved in the emergence of our earliest ancestors.

All living creatures, be they great or small, fierce or timid, active or inactive, face a fundamental challenge—that of survival. The diverse life forms on earth attest to the fact that the problem of survival can be solved in many ways. In evolutionary terms, survival means more than continued existence beyond one individual's lifespan. It includes surviving to reproduce subsequent generations. Over the course of countless generations, each species has followed its own unique journey, an evolutionary history including random turns as well as patterned adaptation to the environment. Among living groups, species can be identified by their reproductive isolation. Reconstructing the evolutionary history of species, either from evidence from the past or variation in living groups, is far less precise. According to evolutionary theory, new species are formed as populations diverge from one another. Thus, closely related species resemble one another because they have recent common ancestry—meaning they have shared part of their evolutionary journey together. With each step living creatures can only build on what already exists, making today's diversity a product of tinkering of ancestral body plans, behaviors, and physiology.

In this chapter we will look at the biological equipment possessed by the primates, the group of animals to which humans belong. We shall also sample the diverse flexible behaviors made possible by primate biology. By doing so we will gain a firmer understanding of those characteristics we share with other primates, as well as those that distinguish us from them and make us distinctively human. By studying the biology and behavior of our closest living relatives, we may draw closer to an understanding of how and why humans developed as they did.

THE PRIMATE ORDER

Biologists classify humans within the primate order, a subgroup of the class Mammalia that also includes lemurs, lorises, tarsiers, monkeys, and apes. Humans—together with chimpanzees, bonobos, gorillas, orangutans, gibbons, and siamangs—form the hominoids, colloquially known as apes, a superfamily within the primate order. One could even say that humans are a kind of ape! Though the distinctive biological and cultural capacities of humans are the major focus of this book, studying nonhuman primates is a critical part of our endeavor. Humans have a long evolutionary history as mammals, primates, and hominoids that sets the stage for the beings we are today.

The primate order is only one of several mammalian orders, such as rodents, carnivores, ungulates (hoofed mammals), and so on. As such, primates share a number of features with other mammals. Generally speaking, mammals are intelligent animals, having more in the way of brains than reptiles or other kinds of vertebrates. This increased "brain power," along with the mammalian pattern of growth and development, forms the biological basis of the flexible behavior patterns typical of mammals. In most species, the young are born live, the egg being retained within the womb of the female until the embryo achieves an advanced state of growth. Once born, the young receive milk from their mothers' mammary glands, the structure from which the class Mammalia gets its name. During this period of infant dependency, young mammals are able to learn some of the things they will need for survival as adults.

Relative to other members of the animal kingdom, mammals are highly active. This activity is made possible by a relatively constant body temperature, an efficient respiratory system featuring a separation between the nasal and mouth cavities (allowing them to breathe while they eat), a diaphragm to assist in drawing in and letting out breath, and an efficient four-chambered heart that prevents mixing of oxygenated and deoxygenated blood. It is facilitated as well by a skeleton in which the limbs are positioned beneath the body, rather than out at the sides, for easy flexible movement. The bones of the limbs have joints constructed to permit growth in the young while simultaneously providing strong, hard joint surfaces that will stand up to the stresses of sustained activity.

The skeleton of most mammals is simplified or streamlined, compared to that of most reptiles, in that it has fewer bones. For example, the lower jaw consists of a single bone, rather than several. The teeth, however, are another matter. Instead of the identical, pointed, peglike teeth of reptiles, mammals have specialized teeth for particular purposes: incisors for nipping, gnawing, and cutting; canines for ripping, tearing, killing, and fighting; premolars that may either slice and tear or crush and grind (depending on the kind of animal); and molars for crushing and grinding (Figure 3.1). This enables mammals to eat a wide variety of food—an advantage to them, since they require more food than reptiles to sustain their high activity level. But they pay a price: reptiles have unlimited tooth replacement throughout their lives, whereas mammals are limited to two sets. The first set serves the immature animal, and is replaced by the "permanent" or adult dentition. The specializations of mammalian teeth allow species and evolutionary relationships to be identified through dental comparisons.

Two classificatory systems exist for dividing the primate order into two suborders. The older system, dating back to the time of Linnaeus, divides primates into two

Providing milk to young via the mammary glands distinguishes mammals from other animals. Nursing young individuals is an important part of the general mammalian tendency to invest high amounts of energy into rearing relatively few young at a time. The pattern in reptiles is to lay many eggs that hatch independently, with the young fending for themselves.

groups: the **Prosimii** (from the Latin for "before monkeys"), which includes lemurs, lorises, and tarsiers, and the **Anthropoidea** (from the Greek for "humanlike"), which includes monkeys, apes, and humans. This division was based on the overall similarity of the body plans within each group, a phenomenon biologists refer to as a **grade.** The prosimians have also been called the "lower primates" because they resemble the earliest fossil primates. In Asia and Africa, all prosimians are **nocturnal** (nighttime active) **arboreal** (tree-dwelling) creatures—again, like the fossil primates. The isolated but large island of Madagascar, off the coast of Africa, however, is home to a variety of **diurnal** (daytime active) ground-dwelling prosimians. In the rest of the world, the daytime active primates are all anthropoids. This group is sometimes called the "higher primates" due to appearing later in evolutionary history and to a lingering belief that the group including humans was more "evolved." But from a contemporary biological perspective, no species is more evolved than any other. On the whole, prosimians are cat-sized or smaller, although some larger forms existed in the past. The prosimians also retain certain features common among nonprimate mammals, such as claws and moist, naked skin on their noses, not retained by the anthropoids.

The anthropoid suborder is further divided into two infraorders; the **Platyrrhini,** or New World monkeys; and

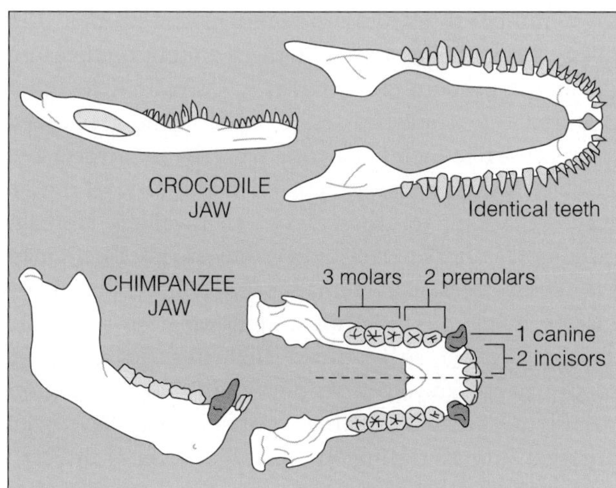

FIGURE 3.1

The crocodile jaw, like all reptiles, contains a series of identical teeth. If a tooth breaks or falls out, a new tooth will emerge in its place. Mammals, by contrast, possess precise numbers of specialized teeth, each with a particular shape characteristic of the group, as indicated on the chimpanzee jaw: Incisors in front are shown in blue, canines behind in red, followed by two premolars and three molars in yellow (the last being the "wisdom teeth" in humans).

Prosimii A suborder of the primates that includes lemurs, lorises, and tarsiers.
Anthropoidea A suborder of the primates that includes New World monkeys, Old World monkeys, and apes (including humans).
grade A general level of biological organization seen among a group of species, useful for constructing evolutionary relationships.
nocturnal Active at night and at rest during the day.
arboreal Living in the trees.
diurnal Active during the day and at rest at night.
Platyrrhini An anthropoid infraorder that includes New World monkeys.

© Dani/Jeske/Animals Animals

© David Harring/OSF/Animals Animals

VISUAL COUNTERPOINT The island of Madagascar is home to many species of diurnal ground-dwelling lemurs whose skeletons resemble the earliest arboreal nocturnal fossil forms. Elsewhere, lorises, the primates most closely related to lemurs, remained arboreal and nocturnal due to competition from monkeys and apes.

the **Catarrhini,** consisting of the superfamilies Cercopithecoidea (Old World monkeys) and Hominoidea (apes). Although the terms *New World* and *Old World* reflect a Eurocentric vision of history (whereby the Americas were considered new only to European explorers and not to the indigenous people and animals already living there), these terms have evolutionary and geological relevance with respect to primates as we will see in Chapter 5. Old World monkeys and apes, including humans, have a 40-million-year shared evolutionary history in Africa distinct from the course taken by anthropoid primates in the tropical Americas. "Old World" in this context represents the evolutionary origins of anthropoid primates rather than a political or historical focus on Europe.

The genetic discoveries discussed in Chapter 2 led to the proposal of a new, primate taxonomy (see Table 3.1). A close genetic relationship was discovered between the tarsiers—animals resembling lemurs and lorises in their outward appearance and behavior, as nocturnal tree dwellers—and monkeys and apes.[1] The taxonomic scheme reflecting this genetic relationship places lemurs and lorises in the suborder **Strepsirhini** (from the Greek for "turned nose"). Tarsiers are placed with monkeys and apes in the suborder **Haplorhini** (from the Greek for "simple nose"). Although this classificatory scheme accurately reflects genetic relationships, it is still useful to make comparisons between "grades" or general levels of organization reflected in the older prosimian and anthropoid classification.

[1]Goodman, M., Bailey, W. J., Hayasaka, K., Stanhope, M. J., Slightom J., & Czelusniak, J. (1994). Molecular evidence on primate phylogeny from DNA sequences. *American Journal of Physical Anthropology, 94*, 7.

Catarrhini An anthropoid infraorder that includes Old World monkeys, apes, and humans.
Strepsirhini In the alternate primate taxonomy, the suborder that includes the lemurs and lorises without the tarsiers.
Haplorhini In the alternate primate taxonomy, the suborder that includes tarsiers, monkeys, apes, and humans.

PRIMATE CHARACTERISTICS

The living primates are a varied group of animals sharing a number of features. We humans, for example, can grasp, throw things, and see in three dimensions because of shared primate characteristics. Compared to other mammals, primates possess a relatively unspecialized anatomy while their behavioral patterns are diverse and flexible. Many primate characteristics are useful in one way or another to arboreal, or tree-dwelling, animals, although (as any squirrel knows) they are not essential to life in the trees. For animals preying upon the many insects living on the fruit and flowers of trees and shrubs, however, such primate characteristics as manipulative hands and keen vision would have been enormously adaptive. The earliest primates may have been arboreal animals relying on visual predation of insects.

The Primate Brain

By far the most outstanding characteristic of primate evolution has been the enlargement of the brain among members of the order. Primate brains tend to be large, relative to their body size, and very complex. Because larger mammals tend to have proportionally larger

TABLE 3.1 TWO ALTERNATE TAXONOMIES FOR THE PRIMATE ORDER: DIFFERING IN PLACEMENT OF TARSIERS

Suborder	Infraorder	Superfamily (family)	Location
I.			
Prosimii (lower primates)	Lemuriformes	Lemuroidea (lemurs, indriids, and aye-ayes)	Madagascar
	Lorisiformes	Lorisoidea (lorises) Tarsioidea (tarsiers)	Asia and Africa Asia
Anthropoidea (higher primates)	Platyrrhini (New World monkeys)	Ceboidea	Tropical Americas
	Catarrhini	Cercopithecoidea (Old World monkeys) Hominoidea (Apes and humans)	Africa and Asia Africa and Asia (humans worldwide)
II.			
Strepsirhini	Lemuriformes	Lemuroidea (lemurs, indriids, and aye-ayes)	Madagascar
	Lorisiformes	Lorisoidea (lorises)	Asia and Africa
Haplorhini	Tarsiiformes	Tarsioidea (tarsiers)	Asia
	Platyrrhini (New World monkeys)	Ceboidea	Tropical Americas
	Catarrhini	Cercopithecoidea (Old World monkeys) Hominoidea (Apes and humans)	Africa and Asia Africa and Asia (humans worldwide)

brains, comparisons across species must take the ratio of brain size to body size into account. The cerebral hemispheres (the areas of conscious thought) have enlarged dramatically and, in catarrhines, completely cover the cerebellum, which is the part of the brain that coordinates the muscles and maintains body equilibrium.

One of the main outcomes of the dominance of the cerebral hemispheres over the cerebellum in primates is the flexibility seen in their behavior. Rather than relying on reflexes controlled by the cerebellum, primates constantly react to a variety of features in the environment. Messages from the hands and feet, eyes and ears, as well as from the sensors of balance, movement, heat, touch, and pain, are simultaneously relayed to the cerebral cortex. Obviously the cortex had to develop considerably in order to receive, analyze, and coordinate these impressions and transmit the appropriate response back down to the motor nerves. The enlarged, responsive cerebral

Grasping hands and three-dimensional vision enables primates like these South American monkeys to effectively lead active lives in the trees. Visual predation of insects may have been an important part of the primate adaptive pattern.

cortex provides the biological basis for more complex cerebration, or thought underlying the flexible behavior patterns found in all primates, including humans.

The reasons for this important change in the anatomy of the brain are many, but it likely began as the earliest primates, along with many other mammals, began to carry out their activities in the daylight hours. Prior to 65 million years ago, mammals seem to have been nocturnal in their habits, but with the extinction of the dinosaurs, inconspicuous, nighttime activity was no longer the key to survival. With the change to diurnal or daytime activity, the sense of vision took on greater importance, and so visual acuity was favored by natural selection. Unlike reptile vision, where the information-processing neurons are in the retina, mammalian vision is processed in the brain, permitting integration with information received by hearing and smelling.

If the evolution of visual acuity led to larger brains, it is likely that the primates' insect predation in an arboreal setting also played a role in enlargement of the brain. This would have required great agility and muscular coordination, favoring development of the brain centers. Thus it is of interest that much of the higher mental faculties are apparently developed in an area alongside the motor centers of the brain.[2]

Another related hypothesis that may help account for primate brain enlargement involves the use of the hand as a tactile organ to replace the teeth and jaws or snout. The hands assumed some of the grasping, tearing, and dividing functions of the snout, again requiring development of the brain centers for more complete coordination.

Primate Sense Organs

The primates' adaptation to arboreal life involved changes in the form and function of their sensory organs. The sense of smell was vital for the earliest nocturnal, ground-dwelling mammals. Smell enables animals to operate at night, to sniff out their food, and to detect silent predators. Moving slowly through the trees at night, ancestral primates relied on their noses to guide them to food. For active diurnal arboreal life, good vision is a better guide than smell in judging the location of the next branch or tasty morsel. Accordingly, the sense of smell declined in primates, while vision became highly developed.

Traveling through trees demands judgments concerning depth, direction, distance, and the relationships of objects hanging in space, such as vines or branches. Monkeys, apes, and humans achieved this through binocular stereoscopic vision. The ability to see the world in the three dimensions of height, width, and depth requires **binocular vision** with two eyes set next to each other allowing the visual fields of the two eyes to overlap. Three-dimensional **stereoscopic vision** results from nerve fibers traveling from each eye to both sides of the brain allowing nerve cells to integrate the images derived from each eye. Many primates also possess color vision, enhancing depth perception as well as food recognition. Enhanced vision also relates to the individualized appearance and expressiveness of the primate face so vital to primate social behaviors.

Visual acuity, however, varies throughout the primate order both in terms of color and spatial percep-

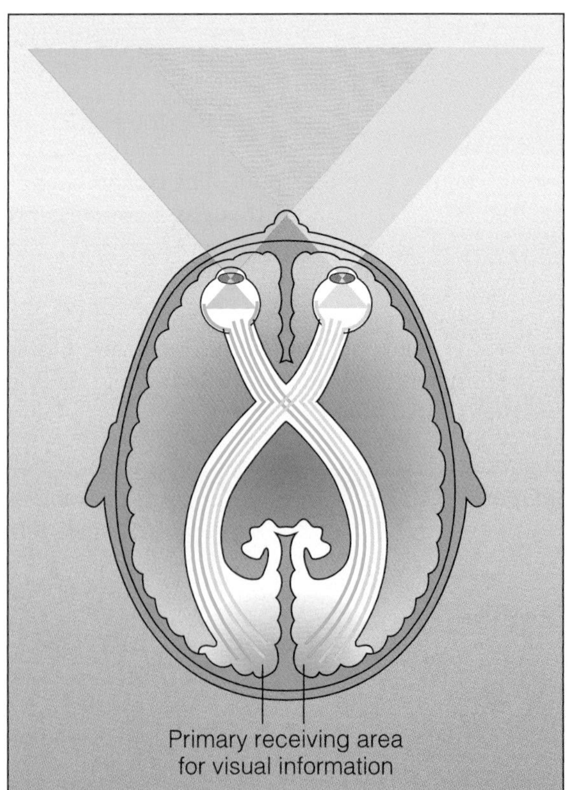

FIGURE 3.2

Anthropoid primates possess binocular stereoscopic vision. Binocular vision refers to overlapping visual fields due to forward-facing eyes. Three-dimensional or stereoscopic vision comes from binocular vision and the transmission of information from each eye to both sides of the brain.

[2]Romer, A. S. (1945). *Vertebrate paleontology* (p. 103). Chicago: University of Chicago Press.

binocular vision Vision with increased depth perception from two eyes set next to each other allowing their visual fields to overlap.
stereoscopic vision Complete three-dimensional vision from binocular vision plus connections from each eye to both sides of the brain allowing nerve cells to integrate the images derived from each eye.

tion. Prosimians, most of whom are nocturnal, lack color vision. The eyes of lemurs and lorises (but not tarsiers) are capable of reflecting light off the back of the retina, the surface where nerve fibers gather images in the back of the eye to intensify the limited light available in the forest at night. In addition, prosimian vision is binocular without the benefits of stereoscopy. Their eyes look out from either side of their muzzle or snout with some overlap of visual fields, but their nerve fibers do not cross from each eye to both halves of the brain. By contrast, monkeys, apes, and humans possess both color and stereoscopic vision. Color vision markedly improves the diet of these primates compared to most other mammals—promoting the identification of food by allowing anthropoid primates to choose ripe fruits or tender immature leaves due to their red rather than green coloration. In addition, anthropoid primates possess a unique structure called the **fovea centralis,** or central pit in the retina of each eye. Like a camera lens, this feature enables the animal to focus on a particular object for acutely clear perception, without sacrificing visual contact with the object's surroundings.

The primates' emphasis on visual acuity came at the expense of their sense of smell. Smells are processed in the forebrain, a part of the brain which projects into the snout of animals depending upon smells. A large protruding snout however, may interfere with stereoscopic vision. But smell is an expendable sense to tree-dwelling animals in search of insects; they no longer needed to live a "nose-to-the-ground" existence, sniffing close to the ground in search of food. The anthropoids especially have the least-developed sense of smell of all

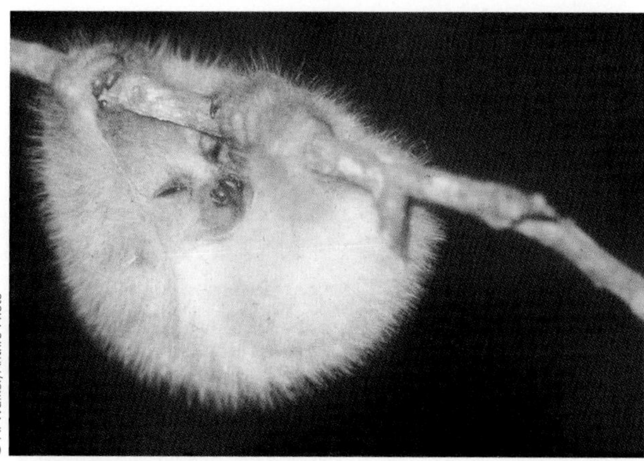

© A. Walker/Anthro-Photo

Over the course of evolutionary history, later-appearing species in the primate order came to rely more on the sense of vision compared to smell. Prosimians, who were the earliest group of primates to appear, still rely on smell, marking their territory and communicating through "smelly" messages left for others with a squirt from glands located on their wrists. Though prosimians appeared before the anthropoids in primate evolution, and retain many ancestral features such as their dependence on smell, they are no less evolved.

land animals. Though humans can smell fear, distinguish perfumes, and even smell the presence of water underground, like other anthropoids, our brains have come to emphasize vision rather than smell. Prosimians, by contrast, still rely on smell, possessing numerous scent glands for marking objects in their territories.

Arboreal primates also possess an acute sense of touch. An effective feeling and grasping mechanism helps prevent them from falling and tumbling while speeding through the trees. The early mammals from which primates evolved possessed tiny touch sensitive hairs at the tips of their hands and feet. In primates, sensitive pads backed up by nails on the tips of the animals' fingers and toes replaced these hairs. This sensitive tissue is also found on the underside of the tails of New World monkeys who use their grasping tails like an extra limb.

Primate Dentition

The varied diet available to arboreal or tree-dwelling primates—shoots, leaves, insects, and fruits—did not require specializations of the teeth seen in other mammals. In most primates (humans included), on each side of each jaw, in front, are two straight-edged, chisel-like broad teeth called incisors (Figure 3.3). Behind the incisors is a canine, which in many mammals is large, flaring, and fanglike and is used for defense as well as for tearing and shredding food. In humans, canine tooth size is relatively small, although it has an oversized root, suggestive of larger canines some time back in our ancestry. Behind the canines are the premolars and molars (the "cheek teeth") for grinding and chewing food. Molars erupt through the gums while a young primate is maturing (6-year molars, 12-year molars, and wisdom teeth in humans). Thus the functions of grasping, cutting, and grinding were served by different kinds of teeth. The exact number of premolars and molars and the shape of individual teeth differ between primate groups (see Table 3.2).

The evolutionary trend for primate dentition has been toward a reduction in the number and size of the teeth. The ancestral **dental formula** or pattern of tooth type and number in mammals consisted of three incisors,

fovea centralis A shallow pit in the retina of the eye that enables an animal to focus on an object while maintaining visual contact with its surroundings.
dental formula The number of each tooth type (incisors, canines, premolars, and molars) on one half of each jaw. Unlike other mammals, primates possess equal numbers on their upper and lower jaws so the dental formula for the species is a single series of numbers.

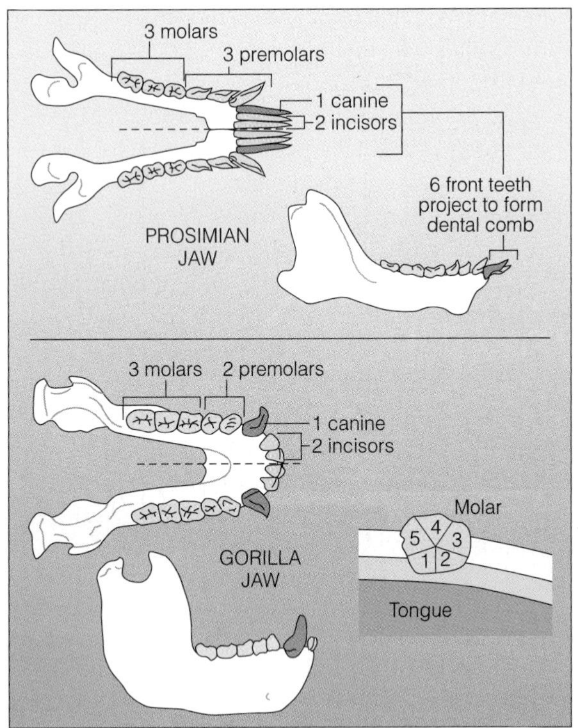

FIGURE 3.3

Because the exact number and shape of the teeth differs between primate groups, teeth are frequently used to identify evolutionary relationships and group membership. Prosimians (top), with a dental formula of 2-1-3-3, possess two incisors, one canine, three premolars, and three molars on each side of their upper and lower jaws. Also, lower canines and incisors project forward, forming a "dental comb," which they use for grooming. A dental formula of 2-1-2-3, typical of Old World monkeys and apes, can be seen in the gorilla jaw (bottom). Note the large projecting canines. On one of the molars, the cusps are numbered to illustrate the Y5 pattern found in all hominoids.

one canine, five premolars, and three molars (expressed as 3-1-5-3) on each side of the jaw, top and bottom, for a total of forty-eight teeth. In the early stages of primate evolution, one incisor and one premolar were lost on each side of each jaw, resulting in a dental pattern of 2-1-4-3 in the early fossil primates. This change differentiated the primates, from other mammals.

Over the millennia, as the first and second premolars became smaller and eventually disappeared altogether; the third and fourth premolars grew larger and added a second pointed projection, or cusp, thus becoming "bicuspid." In humans, all eight premolars are bicuspid, but in other Old World anthropoids, the lower first premolar is not. Instead, it is a specialized, single-cusped tooth with a sharp edge to act with the upper canine as a shearing mechanism. The molars, meanwhile, evolved from a three-cusp pattern to one with four and even five (in apes and humans) cusps. This kind of molar economically combined the functions of grasping, cutting, and grinding in one tooth.

The evolutionary trend for human dentition has generally been toward economy, with fewer, smaller, more efficient teeth doing more work. Thus our own thirty-two teeth (a 2-1-2-3 dental formula shared with the Old World monkeys and apes) are fewer in number than those of some and more generalized than those of most primates. However, this trend does not indicate that species with more teeth are less evolved, only that their evolutionary history followed different trends.

The canines of most primates develop into long, daggerlike teeth that enable them to rip open tough husks of fruit and other foods. Among many species,

© I. DeVore/Anthro-Photo

Columbia/The Kobal Collection

VISUAL COUNTERPOINT Though the massive canine teeth of some male anthropoids such as this baboon are serious weapons, they are used more often to communicate rather than to draw blood. Raising his lip to "flash" his canines to young members of the group will get them in line right away. Over the course of human evolution, overall canine size and sexual dimorphism of the canines reduced. Nevertheless, we associate projecting canines with drawing blood.

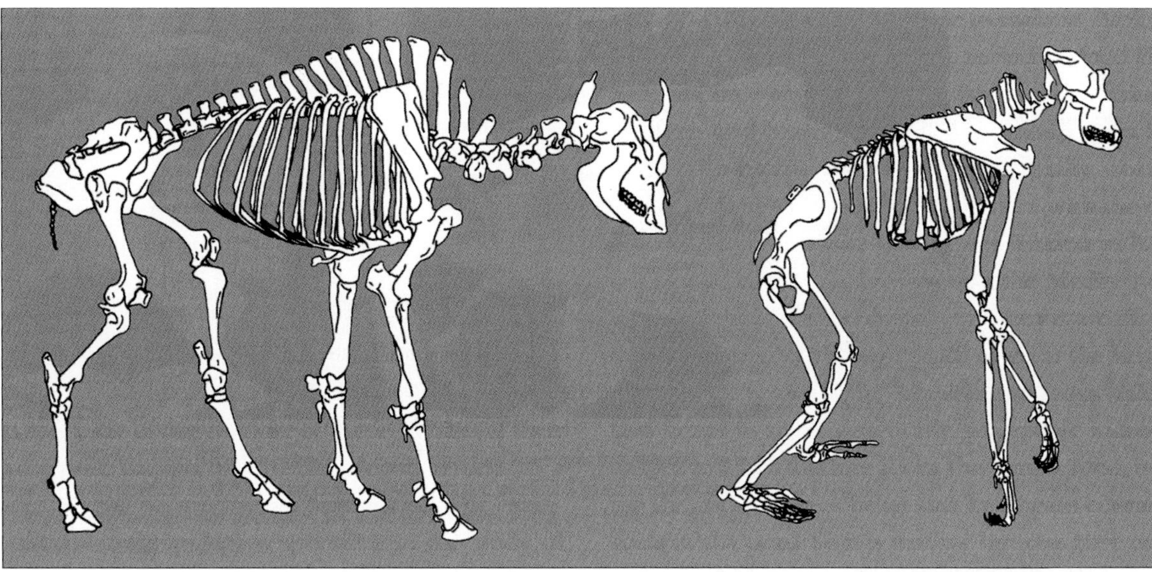

FIGURE 3.4

All primates possess the same ancestral vertebrate limb pattern as seen in reptiles and amphibians, consisting of a single upper long bone, two lower long bones, and five radiating digits, as seen in this gorilla (right) skeleton. Other mammals such as bison (left) have a modified version of this pattern. In the course of evolution they have lost all but two of their digits. The second long bone in the lower portion of the limb is reduced. Note also the joining of the skull and vertebral column in these skeletons. In the bison (as in most mammals) the skull projects forward from the vertebral column, but in the semi-erect gorilla, the vertebral column is further beneath the skull.

sexual dimorphism, or differences between the sexes in the shape or size of a feature, is present in canine teeth with males possessing larger canine teeth. These large canines are used frequently for social communication. All an adult male gorilla or baboon needs to do to get a youngster to be submissive is to raise his upper lip to display his large sharp canines.

The Primate Skeleton

The skeleton gives animals with internal backbones, or **vertebrates,** their basic shape or silhouette, supports the soft tissues, and helps protect vital internal organs. In primates, for example, the skull protects the brain and the eyes. A number of factors are responsible for the shape of the primate skull as compared with those of most other mammals: changes in dentition, changes in the sensory organs of sight and smell, and increased brain size. The primate braincase, or **cranium,** tends to be high and vaulted. A solid partition exists in anthropoid primates between the eye and the temple, affording maximum protection to the eyes from the contraction of the chewing muscles positioned directly next to the eyes.

The **foramen magnum** (the large opening at the base of the skull through which the spinal cord passes and connects to the brain) is an important clue to evolutionary relationships. In most mammals, as in dogs and horses, this opening faces directly backward, with the skull projecting forward from the vertebral column. In humans, by contrast, the vertebral column joins the skull toward the center of its base, thereby placing the skull in a balanced position as required for habitual upright posture. Other primates, though they frequently cling, sit, or hang with their bodies upright, are not as fully committed to such posture as humans, and so their foramen magnum is not as far forward.

In anthropoid primates, the snout or muzzle portion of the skull reduced as the acuity of the sense of smell declined. The smaller snout offers less interference with stereoscopic vision; it also enables the eyes to take a frontal position. As a result, primates have flatter faces than some other mammals.

Below the primate skull and the neck is the **clavicle,** or collarbone, a bone found in ancestral mammals, though lost in mammals such as cats. The size of the clavicle is reduced in quadrupedal primates like monkeys who possess a narrow sturdy body plan. In the apes,

sexual dimorphism Within a single species, differences in the shape or size of a feature for males and females in body features not directly related to reproduction such as body size or canine tooth shape and size.
vertebrates Animals with a backbone including fish, amphibians, reptiles, birds, and mammals.
cranium The braincase of the skull.
foramen magnum A large opening in the skull through which the spinal cord passes and connects to the brain.
clavicle The collarbone connecting the sternum (breastbone) with the scapula (shoulder blade).

TABLE 3.2 PRIMATE ANATOMICAL VARIATION AND SPECIALIZATION

Primate Group	Skull and Face	Dental Formula and Specializations	Locomotor Pattern and Morphology	Tail and Other Skeletal Specializations
Earliest fossil primates	Eye not fully surrounded by bone	2-1-4-3		
Prosimians	Complete ring of bone surrounding eye Upper lip bound down to the gum Long snout	2-1-3-3 Dental comb for grooming	Hind leg dominance for vertical clinging and leaping	Tail present
Anthropoids	Forward facing eyes fully enclosed in bone Free upper lip Shorter snout			
New World monkeys		2-1-3-3	Quadrupedal	Prehensile (grasping) tail
Old World monkeys		2-1-2-3 Four-cusped molars	Quadrupedal	Tail present
Apes		2-1-2-3 Y5 molars on lower jaw	Suspensory hanging apparatus	No tail

by contrast, it is broad, orienting the arms at the side rather than at the front of the body and forming part of the **suspensory hanging apparatus** of this group (Table 3.2). The clavicle also supports the **scapula** (shoulder blade) and allows for the muscle development that is required for flexible, yet powerful, arm movement—allowing large-bodied apes to hang suspended below the tree branches and to **brachiate** or swing from tree to tree.

The limbs of the primate skeleton follow the same basic ancestral plan seen in the earliest vertebrates.

suspensory hanging apparatus The broad powerful shoulder joints and muscles found in all the hominoids allowing these large-bodied primates to hang suspended below the tree branches.
scapula The shoulder blade.
brachiate To use the arms to move from branch to branch, with the body hanging suspended beneath the arms.
prehensile Having the ability to grasp.
opposable Able to bring the thumb or big toe in contact with the tips of the other digits on the same hand or foot in order to grasp objects.

Other animals possess limbs specialized to optimize a particular behavior such as speed. In each primate arm or leg, the upper portion of the limb has a single long bone, the lower portion two long bones, and then hands or feet with five radiating digits. Their grasping feet and hands have sensitive pads at the tips of their digits, backed up (except in some prosimians) by flattened nails. This unique combination of pad and nail provides the animal with an excellent **prehensile** (grasping) device for use when moving from branch to branch. The structural characteristics of the primate foot and hand make grasping possible; the digits are extremely flexible, the big toe is fully **opposable** to the other digits in all but humans and their immediate ancestors, and the thumb is opposable to the other digits to varying degrees.

The retention of the flexible vertebrate limb pattern in primates was a valuable asset to evolving humans. It was, in part, having hands capable of grasping that enabled our own ancestors to manufacture and use tools and to embark on the evolutionary pathway that led to the revolutionary ability to adapt through culture.

© Jeff Greenberg/Photo Researchers, Inc.

© D. Chivers/Anthro-Photo

VISUAL COUNTERPOINT
All apes and humans possess widely spaced flexible shoulder joints for hanging suspended below the branches or swinging from branch to branch. Gibbons are the masters of this form of locomotion called brachiation (from the Latin for "arm motion"). Monkeys, by contrast, are quadrupeds with narrow bodies and rigid shoulder joints for stability. Monkey bars should really be called "ape bars."

© Reuters/Getty Images

Humans are able to grasp and throw things as they do because of characteristics of their hands and shoulders inherited from ape ancestors.

Reproduction and Care of Young

Most mammals mate only during specified breeding seasons occurring once or twice a year, but many primate species are able to breed at any time during the course of the year. Generally, the male primate is ready to engage in sexual activity whenever females are in **estrus,** a period of sexual receptivity corresponding with the time of **ovulation,** or at the time when an egg is released from the ovaries into the womb. In some primate species such as chimpanzees, female estrus and sexual receptivity are signaled to males through swelling of the genitalia. In other primate species such as humans and bonobos, ovulation is concealed, and females are sexually active without synchronization with ovulation.

The average adult female monkey or ape spends most of her adult life either pregnant or nursing her young, times at which she is not sexually receptive. Apes generally nurse each of their young for about 4 years. After her infant is weaned, she will come into estrus periodically, until she becomes pregnant again. Many

estrus In some primate females, the time of sexual receptivity during which ovulation is visibly displayed.
ovulation Moment when an egg released from the ovaries into the womb is receptive for fertilization.

© Michael K. Nichols/National Geographic Image Collection

© Bromhall/Animals Animals

VISUAL COUNTERPOINT This gelada (left), an Old World monkey, who spends much of her day sitting on the ground and feeding, signals ovulation through swelling of glands on her chest. Chimpanzees (right) display their fertility through swelling of the genitalia at the time of ovulation. Animals with such displays are sexually receptive only during their times of fertility.

human societies modify the succession of pregnancy and lactation by a variety of cultural means.

Among primates, as among some other mammals, females generally give birth to one infant at a time. Natural selection may have favored single births among primate tree dwellers because the primate infant, which has a highly developed grasping ability (the grasping reflex can also be seen in human infants), must be transported about by its mother, and more than one clinging infant would seriously encumber her as she moved about the trees. Only among the smaller nocturnal prosimians, the primates closest to the ancestral condition, are multiple births common. Among the anthropoids, only the true marmoset has a pattern of habitual twinning. Other species like humans will twin occasionally. In marmosets, both parents share infant care, with fathers doing most of the carrying.

Primates follow a pattern of bearing few young, but devoting more time and effort to the care of each individual offspring. Compared to other mammals such as mice, which pass from birth to adulthood in a matter of weeks, primates spend a great deal of time growing up. As a general rule, the more closely related to humans the species is, the longer the period of infant and childhood dependency. For example, a lemur is dependent upon its mother for only a few months after birth, while an ape is dependent for 4 or 5 years. A chimpanzee infant cannot survive if its mother dies before it reaches the age of 4 at the very least. During the juvenile period, young primates are still dependent upon the larger social group rather than on their mothers alone, using this period for learning and refining a variety of behaviors. If a juvenile primate's mother dies, he or she will be "adopted" by an older male or female member of the social group.

The long interval between births, particularly among the apes results in small population sizes in our closest relatives. A female chimpanzee, for example, does not reach sexual maturity until about the age of 10, and once she produces her first live offspring, there is a period of 5 or 6 (on average 5.6) years before she will bear another. Thus, assuming that none of her offspring die before adulthood, a female chimpanzee must survive for at least 20 or 21 years just to maintain the size of chimpanzee populations at existing levels. In fact, chimpanzee infants and juveniles do die from time to time, and not all females live full reproductive lives. This is one reason why apes are far less abundant in the world today than are monkeys.

A long slow period of growth and development, particularly among the hominoids, also provides opportunities. Born without built-in responses dictating specific behavior in complex situations, the young monkey or ape, like the young human, learns how to strategically interact with others, and even manipulate them for his or her own benefit—by trial and error, observation, imitation, and practice (Figure 3.5). Young primates make mistakes along the way, learning to modify their behavior based on the reactions of other members of the group. Each member of the community has a unique physical appearance and personality. Youngsters

VISUAL COUNTERPOINT

A long period of infant and childhood dependency is characteristic of primates, particularly the apes. Interestingly, ape mothers tend to nurse their young for up to 4 or 5 years. The contemporary practice of bottle-feeding infants in the United States and Europe is a massive departure from the ape pattern. While the health benefits of breastfeeding for mothers (such as lowered breast cancer rates) and children (strengthened immune systems) are clearly documented, cultural norms have not supported a widespread return to this practice. Across the globe, however, women nurse their children on average for about 3 years.

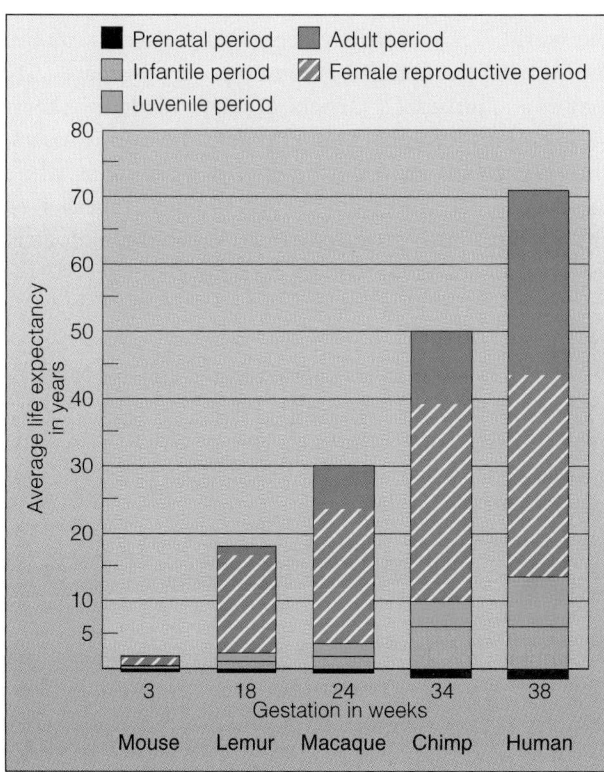

FIGURE 3.5

A long life cycle, including a long period of childhood dependency, is characteristic of the primates. In biological terms, infancy ends when young mammals are weaned, and adulthood is defined as sexual maturation. In many species, such as mice, animals become sexually mature as soon as they are weaned. Among primates, a juvenile period for social learning occurs between infancy and adulthood. For humans, the biological definitions of infancy and adulthood are modified according to cultural norms.

learn to match their interactive behaviors according to each individual's social position and temperament. Anatomical features common to all monkeys and apes—such as a free upper lip (unlike lemurs and cats for example)—allow for varied facial expression, contributing to communication between individuals.

Establishing Evolutionary Relationships through Genetics

Molecular evidence has confirmed the close relationship between humans and other primates while also contributing new evidence for refining evolutionary relationships inferred from visible appearance alone. Scientific methods involving genetic comparisons range from scanning species' entire genomes to comparisons of the precise sequences of base pairs in DNA or amino acids in proteins. For example, the scientific understanding of the evolutionary relationship of the tarsiers to the rest of the primates changed due to the molecular evidence. Most relevant to human evolution, however, are the evolutionary relationships established among the hominoids from the molecular evidence described in Chapter 2. On the basis of tests with blood proteins and DNA, it has been shown that the bonobo, chimpanzee, and gorilla are most close to humans; next comes the orangutan, then the smaller apes (gibbons and siamangs), Old World monkeys, New World monkeys, tarsiers, and then finally the lemurs and lorises. Measurements of genetic affinity confirm these findings, providing further evidence of humanity's close kinship to the great apes, especially those of Africa (Figure 3.6).

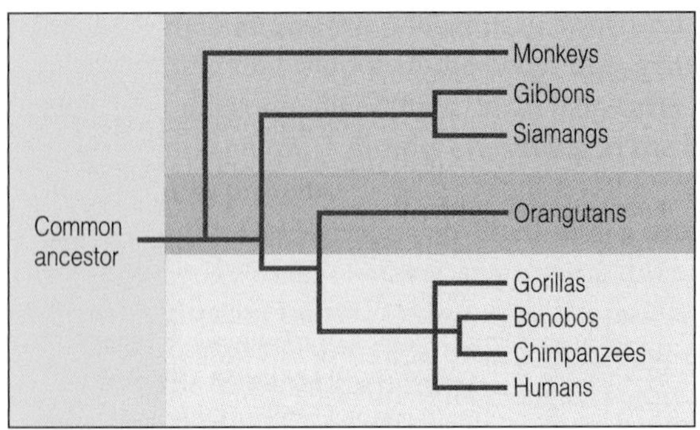

FIGURE 3.6
Based on molecular similarities and differences, a relationship can be established among various catarrhine primates. Present thinking is that the split between the human and African ape lineages took place between 5 and 8 million years ago.

The modern classification of humans places the two species of genus *Pan* (bonobos and chimpanzees) and gorillas together with humans in the family Hominidae. Although the traditional classification of primates placed all great apes (bonobo, chimpanzee, gorilla, and orangutan) together in the pongid family and humans alone as hominids, molecular evidence has demonstrated that this way of grouping apes and humans violates taxonomic principles. Because the way we classify is supposed to reflect evolutionary relationships, recent classifications restrict the Pongidae to orangutans, placing bonobos, chimps, and gorillas with humans in the Hominidae, as a reflection of their closer relation to one another than to orangutans. Taxonomic separation of humans and the other African apes then occurs at the level of a subfamily or tribe into the categories Homininae (humans and their ancestors) and Paninae (chimps, bonobos, and gorillas and their ancestors).

While scientists increasingly use the term *hominin,* the next discovery of a million-year-old skeleton of an ancestral human will certainly be described in the newspaper as a "major find for hominid evolution." Many textbooks retain this terminology for that reason. In this book, by contrast, we shall use *hominin* because it is more reflective of evolutionary relationships, as revealed by both the fossil and molecular evidence.

Though the DNA sequence of humans and African apes is 98 percent identical, the organization of DNA into chromosomes differs between humans and the other great apes. Bonobos and chimps, like gorillas and orangutans, have an extra pair of chromosomes compared to humans in which two medium-sized chromosomes have fused together to form Chromosome 2 (the second largest of the human chromosomes). Of the other pairs, eighteen are virtually identical between humans and the genus *Pan,* whereas the remaining ones have been reshuffled. Overall, the differences are fewer than those between gibbons (with 22 pairs of chromosomes) and siamangs (25 pairs of chromosomes), closely related species that, in captivity, have produced live hybrid offspring. Although some studies of molecular similarities have suggested a closer relationship between *Pan* and humans than either has to gorillas, others disagree, and the safest course at the moment is to regard all three hominid genera as having an equal degree of relationship (the two species of genus *Pan* are, of course, more closely related to each other than either is to gorillas or humans).[3]

To sum up, what becomes apparent when humans are compared to other primates is how many of the characteristics we think of as distinctly human are no such thing; rather, they are variants of typical primate traits. The fact is, we humans look the way we do *because* we are primates, and the differences between us and others of this order—especially the apes—are more differences of degree than kind.

MODERN PRIMATES

Except for a few species of Old World monkeys who live in temperate climates and humans who inhabit the entire globe, the modern primates inhabit warm areas of the world. We will briefly explore the diversity of the five natural groupings of contemporary primates: (1) lemurs and lorises, (2) tarsiers, (3) New World monkeys, (4) Old World monkeys, and (5) apes. Lemurs, lorisers, and tarsiers are grouped together as prosimians while monkeys, apes, and humans are grouped together as anthropoids. Each group's distinctive habitat, biological features, and behavior will be examined.

MEDIATREK
To see and hear living primates; learn about primate behavior, biology, and conservation; and see classic videos from primate field research such as "Chimpanzee Conflict" and "Chimpanzee Food Sharing," see MediaTrek 3.1 on the companion Web site or CD-ROM.

Prosimians

Prosimians are the living primates whose anatomy and behavior most closely resembles the ancestral primate condition. They include lemurs, lorises, and tarsiers.

Lemurs and Lorises

Although lemurs are restricted to the island of Madagascar (off the east coast of Africa), lorises range from Africa to southern and eastern Asia. Only on Madagascar, where there was no competition from

[3]Rogers, J. (1994). Levels of the genealogical hierarchy and the problem of hominid phylogeny. *American Journal of Physical Anthropology, 94,* 81.

© S. Blaffer Hrdy/Anthro-Photo

Prosimians, with their hind limbs longer than their front limbs, move from tree to tree by vertical clinging and leaping. First they hang onto the trunk of one tree in an upright position, with their long legs curled up tightly like springs and their heads twisted to look in the direction they are moving. They propel themselves into the air, do a "180," and land facing the trunk on their tree of choice.

anthropoid primates until humans arrived, are lemurs diurnal, or active during the day; lorises, by contrast, are all nocturnal and arboreal.

All these animals are small, with none larger than a good-sized dog. In general body outline, they resemble rodents and insectivores, with short pointed snouts, large pointed ears, and big eyes. In the anatomy of the upper lip and snout, lemurs and lorises resemble nonprimate mammals, in that the upper lip is bound down to the gum, and the naked skin on the nose around the nostrils is moist and split. They also have long tails, with that of a ring-tail lemur somewhat like the tail of a raccoon.

Lemurs and lorises have characteristically primate "hands," although they use them in pairs, rather than one at a time. Sensitive pads and flattened nails are located at the tips of the fingers and toes, although they retain a claw on their second toe, sometimes called a "toilet claw," which they use for scratching and grooming. Lemurs and lorises possess another unique structure for grooming: a dental comb made up of the lower incisors and canines, which projects forward from the jaw, that can be run through their fur. Behind the incisors and canines, lemurs and lorises have three premolars and molars, resulting in a dental formula of 2-1-3-3. The hind legs of lemurs and lorises are longer than their front legs, and when they move on all fours, the forelimbs are in a "palms-down" position. With their distinctive mix of characteristics, lemurs and lorises appear to occupy a place between the anthropoid primates and insectivores, the mammalian order that includes moles and shrews. Though lemurs and lorises have retained a number of characteristics typical of the earliest fossil primates and the insectivores from which primates evolved, it would be incorrect to think of them as "less evolved."

Tarsiers

Outwardly, tarsiers resemble the lemurs and lorises. Molecular evidence, however, indicates a closer relationship to the monkeys, apes, and humans. The head, eyes, and ears of these kitten-sized arboreal creatures are huge

© Michael Dick/Animals Animals

With their large eyes, tarsiers are well adapted for nocturnal life. If humans possessed eyes proportionally the same size as tarsiers relative to the size of our faces, our eyes would be approximately the size of oranges. In their nocturnal habit and outward appearance, tarsiers resemble the lemurs and lorises. Genetically, however, they are more closely related to monkeys and apes, causing scientists to rework the suborder divisions in primate taxonomy to reflect this evolutionary relationship.

in proportion to the body. They have the remarkable ability to turn their heads 180 degrees, so they can see where they have been as well as where they are going. The digits end in platelike, adhesive discs. Tarsiers are named for the elongated tarsal, or foot bone, that provides leverage for jumps of 6 feet or more. Tarsiers are mainly nocturnal insect eaters. In the structure of the nose and lips, and the part of the brain governing vision, tarsiers resemble monkeys.

Anthropoids: Monkeys, Apes, and Humans

Monkeys, apes, and humans resemble one another more than any of these groups resemble lemurs, lorises, and tarsiers. New World and Old World species are separated from one another at the classificatory level of infraorder: the Platyrrhini (New World monkeys) and Catarrhini (Old World monkeys, apes, and humans). Humans are remarkably like monkeys, but even more like apes, in their appearance.

© J. Pickering/Anthro-Photo

A grasping or prehensile tail is a characteristic unique to the New World monkeys. The naked skin on the undersides of their tails resembles the sensitive skin found at the tips of our fingers and is even covered with whorls like fingerprints. This sensory skin allows New World monkeys to use their tails as a fifth limb.

New World Monkeys

New World monkeys live in tropical forests of South and Central America. They are characterized by flat noses with widely separated, outward-flaring nostrils, from which comes their name of platyrrhine (from the Greek for "flat nosed") monkeys. All are arboreal, possessing long, prehensile or grasping tails, which they use as a fifth limb. These features and a 2-1-3-3 dental formula (three, rather than two, premolars on each side of each jaw) distinguish them from the Old World monkeys, apes, and humans. Platyrrhines walk on all fours with their palms down and scamper along tree branches in search of fruit, which they eat sitting upright. Although New World monkeys spend much of their time in the trees, they rarely hang suspended below the branches or swing from limb to limb by their arms and have not developed the extremely long forelimbs and broad shoulders characteristic of the apes.

Old World Monkeys

Old World, or catarrhine (from the Greek for "sharp nosed"), primates are characterized by noses with closely spaced, downward-pointing nostrils. The Old World monkeys, divided from the apes at the taxonomic level of superfamily, possess a 2-1-2-3 dental formula (two, rather than three, premolars on each side of each jaw) and nonprehensile tails. They may be either arboreal or terrestrial, using quadrupedal pattern of locomotion on the ground or in the trees in a palms-down position. Their body plan is narrow with hind limbs and forelimbs of equal length, a reduced clavicle (collar bone), and relatively fixed and sturdy shoulder, elbow, and wrist joints. The arboreal species include the guereza monkey, the Asiatic langur, and the strange-looking proboscis monkey. Some are equally at home on the ground and in the trees, such as the macaques, of which some nineteen species range from tropical Africa and Asia to Gibraltar on the southern coast of Spain to Japan.

Several species of baboons are largely terrestrial, living in the savannahs, deserts, and highlands of Africa. They have long, fierce faces and eat a diet consisting of leaves, seeds, insects, and lizards. They live in large, well-organized troops comprised of related females and adult males that have transferred out of other troops.

© Mickey Gibson/Animals Animals

Illustration from Curious George by H. A. Rey. Reprinted by permission of Houghton Mifflin Company.

VISUAL COUNTERPOINT Because they share many anatomical and behavioral features due to their common evolutionary history, apes and Old World monkeys are frequently confused with each other. The "Barbary Ape," an Old World monkey from Gibraltar, is not an ape at all. Curious George, the cute "little monkey" from children's literature, is really an ape. The easiest feature to distinguish monkeys from apes is the presence or absence of a tail.

Because baboons have abandoned trees (except for sleeping and refuge) and live in environments like that in which humans may have originated, they are of great interest to paleoanthropologists.

Small and Great Apes

The other apes (the hominoid superfamily) are the closest living relatives we humans have in the animal world. Apes are large wide-bodied primates with no tails. As described earlier in this chapter, apes possess a shoulder anatomy specialized for hanging suspended below tree branches. All apes possess this suspensory hanging apparatus, though only small lithe gibbons and talented gymnasts swing from branch to branch in the pattern known as brachiation. At the opposite extreme are gorillas, which climb trees, using their prehensile hands and feet to grip the trunk and branches. Their swinging is limited to leaning outward as they reach for fruit, clasping a limb for support. Most of their time is spent on the ground. All apes except humans and the ancestral hominins possess arms that are longer than their legs.

In moving on the ground, the African apes "knuckle-walk" on the backs of their hands, resting their weight on the middle joints of the fingers. They stand erect when reaching for fruit, looking over tall grass, or in any activity where they find an erect position advantageous. The semierect position is natural in apes when on the ground because the curvature of their vertebral column places their center of gravity, which is high in their bodies, in front of their hip joint. Thus, they are both "top heavy" and "front heavy." Though apes can walk on two legs or bipedally for short periods of time, the structure of the ape pelvis is not well suited to support the weight of the torso and limbs for more than several minutes.

Gibbons and siamangs, the small apes that are native to Southeast Asia and Malaya, have compact, slim bodies with extraordinarily long arms compared to their short legs, and stand about 3 feet high. Although their usual form of locomotion is brachiation, they can run erect, holding their arms out for balance. Gibbon and siamang males and females are similar in size, living in family groups of two parents and offspring.

Orangutans are found in Borneo and Sumatra. They are somewhat taller than gibbons and siamangs and are much heavier, with the bulk characteristic of the great apes. In the closeness of the eyes and facial prominence, an orangutan looks very humanlike. The people of Sumatra gave orangutans their name, "man of the forest," using the Malay term *oran,* which means "man." On the ground, orangutans walk with their forelimbs in a fists-sideways or a palms-down position. They are, however, more arboreal than the African apes. Although sociable by nature, the orangutans of upland Borneo spend most of their time alone (except in the case of females with young), as they have to forage over a wide area to obtain sufficient food. By contrast, fruits and insects are sufficiently abundant in the swamps of Sumatra to sustain groups of adults and

© PA/Topham/The Image Works

© Peter Drowne/Color-Pic, Inc.

VISUAL COUNTERPOINT While the other hominoids can walk bipedally for brief periods of time when they need their arms free for carrying something, they cannot sustain bipedal locomotion for more than 50 to 100 yards. Hominoid anatomy is better adapted to knuckle-walking and hanging in the trees.

permit coordinated group travel. Thus, gregariousness is a function of habitat productivity.[4]

Gorillas, found in equatorial Africa, are the largest of the apes; an adult male can weigh over 450 pounds with females about half that size. The body is covered with a thick coat of glossy black hair, and

© Michael K. Nichols/National Geographic Image Collection

Though known for their chest-beating displays to protect the members of their troop, adult male "silverback" gorillas are the gentle giants of the forest. As vegetarians, gorillas must spend all day eating enough plants to sustain their massive bodies. Male gorillas, like male orangutans, approach twice the size of the females of their species. Humans and chimpanzees are less sexually dimorphic.

mature males have a silvery gray upper back. There is a strikingly human look about the face, and like humans, gorillas focus on things in their field of vision by directing the eyes rather than moving the head. Gorillas are mostly ground dwellers, but the lighter females and young may sleep in trees in carefully constructed nests. Because of their weight, adult males are limited to raising and lowering themselves among the tree branches when searching for fruit. Gorillas knuckle-walk, using all four limbs with the fingers of the hand flexed, placing the knuckles instead of the palm of the hand on the ground. They will stand erect to reach for fruit, to see something more easily, or to threaten perceived sources of danger with their famous chest-beating displays. Although gorillas are gentle and tolerant, bluffing is an important part of their behavioral repertoire.

Chimpanzees and bonobos are two closely related species of the same genus (*Pan*), bonobos being the least well known and restricted in their distribution to the rainforests of the Democratic Republic of Congo. The common chimpanzee, by contrast, is widely distributed in the forested portions of sub-Saharan Africa. They are probably the best known of the apes and have long been favorites in zoos and circuses. Although thought of as particularly quick and clever, all four great apes are of equal intelligence, despite some differences in cognitive styles. More arboreal than gorillas, but less so than orangutans, chimpanzees and bonobos forage on the

---

[4]Normile, D. (1998). Habitat seen as playing larger role in shaping behavior. *Science, 279,* 1,454.

The genus *Pan* contains two distinct species: *P. troglodytes* or the common chimpanzee and *P. paniscus* (pictured here) or bonobos. In the past, bonobos were known as pygmy chimpanzees not because they are smaller than the common chimps but due to prejudices linking African people to the apes.

ground much of the day, knuckle-walking like gorillas. At sunset, they return to the trees, where they build their nests. Those of chimps are more dispersed than those of bonobos, who prefer to build their nests close to one another.

THE SOCIAL BEHAVIOR OF PRIMATES

In addition to the physical resemblance between human beings and other catarrhine primates, a striking similarity in social behavior also exists. These primates spend more time reaching adulthood compared to many other mammals. During their lengthy growth and development, young primates learn the behaviors of their social group. Primatologists' observations of catarrhines in their natural habitats over the past decades have shown that social organization, learning, and communication among our primate relatives have many similarities to humans, differing in degree, rather than in kind.

The full range of primate behavior is beyond the scope of this book. We shall focus upon the behavior of those species most closely related to humans: bonobos, chimpanzees, and gorillas.

The Group

Primates are social animals, living and traveling in groups that vary in size from species to species. Among chimps and bonobos, the largest social organizational unit is the **community,** composed of fifty or more individuals who collectively inhabit a large geographical area. Rarely, however, are all these animals together at one time. Instead, they are usually found ranging singly or in small subgroups consisting of adult males together, females with their young, or males and females together with young. In the course of their travels, subgroups may join forces and forage together, but sooner or later these subgroups break up again into smaller units. When they do, some individuals split off and others

community A unit of primate social organization composed of fifty or more individuals who inhabit a large geographical area together.

join, so that the new subunits may be different in their composition from the ones that initially came together.

The gorilla group is a "family" of five to twenty individuals led by a mature, silver-backed male and including younger (black-backed) males, females, the young, and occasionally other silverbacks. Subordinate males, however, are usually prevented by the dominant male from mating with the group's females. Thus, young silverbacks often leave their **natal group,** or the community they have known since birth, to start their own social group by winning outside females. If the dominant male is weakening with age, however, one of his sons may remain with the group to succeed to his father's position. Alternatively, an outside male may take over the group. Unlike chimpanzees, gorillas rarely fight over food, territory, or sex, but will fight fiercely to maintain the integrity of the group.

In many primate species, including humans, adolescence is a time during which individuals change the relationships they have had with their natal group. Among primates this change takes the form of migration to new social groups. In many species, females constitute the core of the social system. For example, offspring tend to remain with the group to which their mother, rather than their father, belongs. Among gorillas, male adolescents leave their natal groups more frequently than females. However, adolescent female chimpanzees and bonobos are frequently the ones to migrate. In two Tanzanian chimpanzee communities studied, about half of females may leave the community they have known since birth to join another group.[5] When in estrus, other females may also temporarily leave their group to mate with males of another group. Among bonobos, adolescent females appear to always transfer to another group, where they promptly establish bonds with females of their new group. While biological factors such as the hormonal influences on sexual maturity play a role in adolescent migration, the variation across species, and within the chimpanzees in dispersal patterns, indicate that this variation may also derive from the learned social traditions of the group.

Relationships among individuals within the ape community are relatively harmonious. In the past, primatologists believed that male **dominance hierarchies,** in which some animals outrank and could dominate others, formed the basis of primate social structures. They noted that physical strength and size play a role in determining an animal's rank. By this measure males generally outrank females. However, the gender-biased culture of the human primatologist contributed disproportionately to this theory, with its emphasis on domination through superior size and strength. Male dominance hierarchies seemed "natural" to the early primatologists who often came from human social systems organized according to similar principles. With the benefit of detailed field studies over the last 30 years, many of which were pioneered by female primatologists like Jane Goodall (see Anthropologists of Note), the nuances of primate social behavior and the importance of female primates has been documented. High-ranking (alpha) females may dominate low-ranking males. In groups such as bonobos, females dominate overall. While strength and size contribute to an animal's rank, other important factors include the rank of its mother and effectiveness at creating alliances with other individuals. For males, drive or motivation to achieve high status also influences rank. For example, in the community studied by Goodall, one male chimp hit upon the idea of incorporating noisy kerosene cans into his charging displays, thereby intimidating all the other males.[6] As a result, he rose from relatively low status to the number one (alpha) position.

Among bonobos, female–female bonds play an important role in determining rank. Further, the strength of the bond between mother and son may interfere with the ranking among males. Not only do bonobo males defer to females in feeding, but alpha females have been observed chasing high-ranking males. Alpha males even yield to low-ranking females, and groups of females form alliances in which they may cooperatively attack males, to the point of inflicting blood-drawing injuries.[7] Thus, instead of the male dominance characteristic of chimps, one sees female dominance. Chimpanzees show relatively stronger bonds between males.

Western primatologists' focus on social rank and attack behavior may be a legacy of the militaristic, competitive nature of the societies in which evolutionary theory originated. To a certain degree, natural selection relies upon a struggle between living creatures rather

[5]Moore, J. (1998). Comment. *Current Anthropology, 39,* 412.

[6]Goodall, J. (1986). *The chimpanzees of Gombe: Patterns of behavior* (p. 424). Cambridge, MA: Belknap Press.

[7]de Waal, F., Kano, T., & Parish, A. R. (1998). Comments. *Current Anthropology, 39,* 408, 410, 413.

natal group The group or the community an animal has inhabited since birth.
dominance hierarchies An observed ranking system in primate societies ordering individuals from high (alpha) to low standing corresponding to predictable behavioral interactions including domination.

than peaceful coexistence. By contrast, noted Japanese primatologist Kinji Imanishi (see Anthropologists of Note) developed a harmonious theory of evolution and initiated field studies of bonobos that have demonstrated the importance of social cooperation rather than competition. As the work of Dutch primatologist Frans de Waal illustrates in the following Original Study, reconciliation after an attack may be even more important from an evolutionary perspective than the actual attacks.

Original Study

Reconciliation and Its Cultural Modification in Primates

Despite the continuing popularity of the struggle-for-life metaphor, it is increasingly recognized that there are drawbacks to open competition, hence that there are sound evolutionary reasons for curbing it. The dependency of social animals on group life and cooperation makes aggression a socially costly strategy. The basic dilemma facing many animals, including humans, is that they sometimes cannot win a fight without losing a friend.

This photo shows what may happen after a conflict—in this case between two female bonobos. About 10 minutes after their fight, the two females approach each other, with one clinging to the other and both rubbing their clitorises and genital swellings together in a pattern known as genito-genital rubbing, or GG-rubbing. This sexual contact, typical of bonobos, constitutes a so-called reconciliation. Chimpanzees, which are closely related to bonobos (and to us: bonobos and chimpanzees are our closest animal relatives), usually reconcile in a less sexual fashion, with an embrace and mouth-to-mouth kiss.

© Amy Parish/Anthro-Photo

Two adult female bonobos engage in so-called GG-rubbing, a sexual form of reconciliation typical of this species.

There is now evidence for reconciliation in more than twenty-five different primate species, not just in apes but also in many monkeys. The same sorts of studies have been conducted on human children in the schoolyard, and of course children show reconciliation as well. Researchers have even found reconciliation in dolphins, spotted hyenas, and some other nonprimates. Reconciliation seems widespread: a common mechanism found whenever relationships need to be maintained despite occasional conflict.[a, b]

The definition of reconciliation used in animal research is a friendly reunion between former opponents not long after a conflict. This is somewhat different from definitions in the dictionary, primarily because we look for an empirical definition that is useful in observational studies—in our case, the stipulation that the reunion happen not long after the conflict. There is no intrinsic reason that a reconciliation could not occur after hours or days, or, in the case of humans, generations.

Let me describe two interesting elaborations on the mechanism of reconciliation. One is *mediation.* Chimpanzees are the only animals to use mediators in conflict resolution. In order to be able to mediate conflict, one needs to understand relationships outside of oneself, which may be the reason why other animals fail to show this aspect of conflict resolution. For example, if two male chimpanzees have been involved in a fight, even on a very large island as where I did my studies, they can easily avoid each other, but instead they will sit opposite from each other, not too far apart, and avoid eye contact. They can sit like this for a long time. In this situation, a third party, such as an older female, may move in and try to solve the issue. The female will approach one of the males and groom him for a

[CONTINUED]

[CONTINUED]

brief while. She then gets up and walks slowly to the other male, and the first male walks right behind her.

We have seen situations in which, if the first male failed to follow, the female turned around to grab his arm and make him follow. So the process of getting the two males in proximity seems intentional on the part of the female. She then begins grooming the other male, and the first male grooms her. Before long, the female disappears from the scene, and the males continue grooming: She has in effect brought the two parties together.

There exists a limited anthropological literature on the role of conflict resolution, a process absolutely crucial for the maintenance of the human social fabric in the same way that it is crucial for our primate relatives. In human society, mediation is often done by high-ranking or senior members of the community, sometimes culminating in feasts in which the restoration of harmony is celebrated.[c]

The second elaboration on the reconciliation concept is that it is not purely instinctive, not even in our animal relatives. It is a learned social skill subject to what primatologists now increasingly call "culture" (meaning that the behavior is subject to learning from others as opposed to genetic transmission.[d] To test the learnability of reconciliation, I conducted an experiment with young rhesus and stumptail monkeys. Not nearly as conciliatory as stumptail monkeys, rhesus monkeys have the reputation of being rather aggressive and despotic. Stumptails are considered more laid-back and tolerant. We housed members of the two species together for 5 months. By the end of this period, they were a fully integrated group: They slept, played and groomed together. After 5 months, we separated them again, and measured the effect of their time together on conciliatory behavior.

The research controls—rhesus monkeys who had lived with one another, without any stumptails—showed absolutely no change in the tendency to reconcile. Stumptails showed a high rate of reconciliation, which was also expected, because they also do so if living together. The most interesting group was the experimental rhesus monkeys, those who had lived with stumptails. These monkeys started out at the same low level of reconciliation as the rhesus controls, but after they had lived with the stumptails, and after we have segregated them again so that they were now housed only with other rhesus monkeys who had gone through the same experience, these rhesus monkeys reconciled as much as stumptails do. This means that we created a "new and improved" rhesus monkey, one that made up with its opponents far more easily than a regular rhesus monkey.[e]

This was in effect an experiment on social culture: We changed the culture of a group of rhesus monkeys and made it more similar to that of stumptail monkeys by exposing them to the practices of this other species. This experiment also shows that there exists a great deal of flexibility in primate behavior. We humans come from a long lineage of primates with great social sophistication and a well-developed potential for behavioral modification and learning from others. (*By Frans B. M. de Waal, Living Links, Yerkes National Primate Research Center, Emory University*)

[a] de Waal, F. B. M. (2000). Primates—A natural heritage of conflict resolution. *Science, 28,* 586–590.

[b] Aureli, F., & de Waal, F. B. M. (2000). *Natural conflict resolution.* Berkeley: University of California Press.

[c] Reviewed by Frye, D. P. (2000). Conflict management in cross-cultural perspective. In F. Aureli & F. B. M. de Waal, *Natural conflict resolution* (pp. 334–351). Berkeley: University of California Press.

[d] See de Waal, F. B. M. (2001). *The ape and the sushi master.* New York: Basic Books, for a discussion of the animal culture concept

[e] de Waal, F. B. M., & Johanowicz, D. L. (1993). Modification of reconciliation behavior through social experience: An experiment with two macaque species. *Child Development, 64,* 897–908.

Individual Interaction and Bonding

One of the most notable primate activities is **grooming,** the ritual cleaning of another animal's coat to remove parasites, shreds of grass, or other matter. The grooming animal deftly parts the hair of the one being groomed and removes any foreign object, often eating it. Interestingly, different chimp communities have different styles of grooming. In one East African group, for example, the two chimps groom each other face to face, with one hand, while clasping their partner's free hand. In another group 90 miles distant, the hand clasp is unknown. In East Africa, all communities incorporate leaves in their grooming, but in West Africa they do not. However hygienic it may be, grooming is also an important gesture of friendliness, submission, appeasement, or closeness. Embracing, touching, and jumping up and down are forms of greeting behavior among chimpanzees. Touching is also a form of reassurance.

grooming The ritual cleaning of another animal's coat to remove parasites and other matter.

Gorillas, though gentle and tolerant, are also aloof and independent, and individual interaction among adults tends to be quite restrained. Friendship or closeness between adults and infants is more evident. Among bonobos, chimpanzees, and gorillas, as among most other primates, the mother-infant bond is the strongest and most long-lasting in the group. It may endure for many years—commonly for the lifetime of the mother. Gorilla infants share their mothers' nests but have also been seen sharing nests with mature, childless females. Bonobo, chimpanzee, and gorilla males are attentive to

© Anita de Laguna Haviland

© Anita de Laguna Haviland

VISUAL COUNTERPOINT
Grooming is an important activity among all catarrhine primates, as shown here. Such activity is important for strengthening bonds between individual members of the group.

juveniles and may share in parental responsibilities. Bonobo males seem most involved with their young and even carry infants on occasion, including those from different groups. Moreover, a male bonobo's interest in a youngster does not elicit the nervous reaction from the mother that it does among chimps. The latter may relate to the occasional infanticide on the part of chimpanzee males, a behavior never observed among bonobos.

Sexual Behavior

Among the African apes, as with humans, no fixed breeding season exists. In chimps, sexual activity—initiated by either the male or the female—occurs frequently during estrus, the period when the female is receptive to impregnation. In chimpanzees, estrus is signaled by vivid swelling of the skin around the genitals. Bonobo females, by contrast, conceal their time of ovulation by appearing as if they are fertile at all times due their constantly swollen genitals and interest in sex. Gorillas appear to show less interest in sex compared to either the chimp or bonobos.

By human standards, chimps' sexual behavior is promiscuous. Twelve to fourteen males have been observed to have as many as fifty copulations in one day with a single female in estrus. For the most part, females mate with males of their own group. Dominant males try to monopolize females in full estrus, although cooperation from the female is usually required for this to succeed. In addition, an individual female and a lower ranking male sometimes form a temporary bond, leaving the group together for a few "private" days during the female's fertile period. Interestingly, the relationship between reproductive success and social rank differs for males and females. In the chimpanzee community studied by Goodall, about half the infants were sired by low- or mid-level males. Although for females high rank is linked with successful reproduction, social success—achieving alpha male status does not translate neatly into the evolutionary currency of reproductive success.

© Zig Leszczynski/Animals Animals

Primate infants are treated with interest and special consideration by all members of the group. Often they are allowed to behave in ways not tolerated from adults.

Anthropologists of Note

Jane Goodall (1934–) ▪ Kinji Imanishi (1902–1992)

© Irven DeVore/Anthro-Photo

In July 1960 Jane Goodall arrived with her mother at the Gombe Chimpanzee Reserve on the shores of Lake Tanganyika in Tanzania. The first of three women Kenyan anthropologist Louis Leakey sent out to study great apes in the wild (the others were Dian Fossey and Birute Galdikas, who were to study gorillas and orangutans, respectively), her task was to begin a long-term study of chimpanzees. Little did she realize that, more than 40 years later, she would still be at it.

Born in London, Jane grew up and was schooled in Bournemouth, England. As a child, she dreamt of going to live in Africa, so when an invitation arrived to visit a friend in Kenya, she jumped at the opportunity. While in Kenya, she met Leakey, who gave her a job as an assistant secretary. Before long, she was on her way to Gombe. Within a year, the outside world began to hear the most extraordinary things about this pioneering woman: tales of tool-making apes, cooperative hunts by chimpanzees, and what seemed like exotic chimpanzee rain dances. By the mid-1960s, her work had earned her a Ph.D. from Cambridge University, and Gombe was on its way to becoming one of the most dynamic field stations for the study of animal behavior anywhere in the world.

Although Goodall is still very much involved with her chimpanzees, she spends a good deal of time these days lecturing, writing, and overseeing the work of others. She also is heavily committed to primate conservation, and no one is more dedicated to efforts to halt the illegal trafficking in captive chimps nor a more eloquent champion of humane treatment of captive chimpanzees.

Courtesy Bunataro Imanishi

Kinji Imanishi, a naturalist, explorer, and mountain climber, profoundly influenced primatology in Japan and throughout the world. Like all Japanese scholars, he was fully aware of Western methods and theories but developed a radically different approach to the scientific study of the natural world. He dates his transformation to a youthful encounter with a grasshopper: "I was walking along a path in a valley, and there was a grasshopper on a leaf in a shrubbery. Until that moment I had happily caught insects, killed them with chloroform, impaled them on pins, and looked up their names, but I realized I knew nothing at all about how this grasshopper lived in the wild."[a] In his most important work, *The World of Living Things*, first published in 1941, Imanishi developed a comprehensive theory about the natural world rooted in Japanese cultural beliefs and practices.

Imanishi's work challenged Western evolutionary theory in several ways. First, Imanishi's theory, like Japanese culture, does not emphasize differences between humans and other animals. Second, rather than focusing on the biology of individual organisms, Imanishi suggested that naturalists examine "specia" (a species society) to which individuals belong as the unit of analysis. Rather than focusing on time, Imanishi emphasized space in his approach to the natural world. He highlighted the harmony of all living things rather than conflict and competition among individual organisms. Imanishi's research techniques, now standard worldwide, developed directly from his theories: long-term field study of primates in their natural societies using methods from ethnography.

Imanishi and his students conducted pioneering field studies of African apes, and Japanese and Tibetan macaques, long before Louis Leakey sent the first Western primatologists into the field. Japanese primatologists were the first to document the importance of kinship, the complexity of primate societies, patterns of social learning, and the unique character of each primate social group. Because of the work by Imanishi and his students, we now think about the distinct cultures of primate societies.

[a] Heita, K. (1999). Imanishi's world view. *Journal of Japanese Trade and Industry, 18*(2), 15.

Although mating behavior among bonobos resembles that of chimps, important differences exist. Bonobo sexuality goes far beyond male–female mating, and a majority of their sexual activity has nothing to do with reproduction. Bonobos have been observed having sex in virtually all combinations of ages and sex.[8] This sexual behavior, both hetero- and homosexual, has important social functions. While chimps often settle disputes by aggressive behavior, bonobos often do so through sexual behavior. The variety is remarkable, including sporadic oral sex, tongue-kissing, and massage of another's genitals. Male bonobos may mount each other or, standing back to back, one will rub his scrotum against another's. Bonobo males have also been observed "penis fencing," as two males hang from a branch facing each other while rubbing their erect penises together as if crossing swords. Genito-genital contact between females, accompanying the resolution of social conflicts (described in de Waal's

[8] de Waal, F. (2001). *The ape and the sushi master* (pp. 131–132). New York: Basic Books.

Original Study) is also very common. The constant swelling of the external genitalia of bonobo females described above may have played a role in the elaboration of bonobo sexuality. The constant swelling, in effect, conceals the females' ovulation, or moment when an egg released into the womb is receptive for fertilization. Animals with visible ovulation, such as chimpanzees, limit sexual encounters to times when fertilization can occur. As in humans, concealed ovulation in bonobos may play a role in the social separation of sexual activity from the biological task of reproduction.

In gorilla families, the dominant silverback has exclusive breeding rights with the females, although he may allow a young silverback occasional access to a low-ranking female. In one group studied in Rwanda, in which there was more than one adult male, a single male fathered all but one of ten juveniles.[9] So it is that a young silverback must leave "home," luring partners away from other established groups, in order to have reproductive success.

Although the vast majority of primate species are not **monogamous** in their mating habits, many smaller species of New World monkeys, a few island-dwelling populations of leaf-eating Old World monkeys, and all of the smaller apes (gibbons and siamangs) appear to mate for life with a single individual of the opposite sex. None of these species is closely related to human beings, nor do monogamous species ever display the degree of sexual dimorphism—anatomical differences between males and females—that is characteristic of our closest primate relatives, or that was characteristic of our own ancient ancestors. Evolutionary biologists propose that sexual dimorphism (for example, larger male size in the apes, beautiful feathers as in peacocks) relates to competition between males for access to females. The variation in ape reproductive behavior suggests that social processes contribute to reproductive success as much as variation in a biological feature such as body size.

Play

Frequent play activity among primate infants and juveniles is a means of learning about the environment, learning about social skills, and testing a variety of behaviors. Chimpanzee infants mimic the food-getting activities of adults, "attack" dozing adults, and "harass" adolescents.

Observers have watched young gorillas do somersaults, wrestle, and play various organized games such as jostling for the position on top of a hillside or following and mimicking a single youngster. One juvenile, becoming annoyed at repeated harassment by an infant, picked it up, climbed a tree, and deposited it on a branch from which it was unable to get down on its own, until its mother came to retrieve it.

Communication

Primates, like many animals, vocalize. They have a great range of calls that are often used together with movements of the face or body to convey a message. Observers have not yet established the meaning of all the sounds, but a good number have been distinguished, such as warning calls, threat calls, defense calls, and gathering calls. The behavioral reactions of other animals hearing the call have also been studied. Among bonobos, chimpanzees, and gorillas, vocalizations are emotional rather than propositional. Much of these species' communication takes place by the use of specific gestures and postures. Indeed, a number of these, such as kissing and embracing, are in virtually universal use today among humans, as well as apes.

Primatologists have classified numerous kinds of chimpanzee vocalization and visual communication signals. Facial expressions convey emotional states such as distress, fear, or excitement. Numerous distinct vocalizations or calls have been associated with a variety of sensations. For example, chimps will smack their lips or clack their teeth to express pleasure with sociable body contact. Calls called "pant-hoots" can be differentiated into specific types used for arrival of individuals or inquiring. Together, these facilitate group protection, coordination of group efforts, and social interaction in general. One form of communication appears to be unique to bonobos: the use of trail markers. When foraging, the community breaks up into smaller groups, rejoining again in the evening to nest together. To keep track of each party's whereabouts, those in the lead will, at the intersections of trails or where downed trees obscure trails, deliberately stomp down the vegetation so as to indicate their direction, or rip off large leaves and place them carefully for the same purpose. Thus, they all know where to come together at the end of the day.[10]

Experiments with captive apes, carried out over several decades, reveal that their communicative abilities exceed what they make use of in the wild. In some of

---

[9]Gibbons, A. (2001). Studying humans—and their cousins and parasites. *Science, 292,* 627.

[10]Recer, P. (1998, February 16). Apes shown to communicate in the wild. *Burlington Free Press,* p. 12A.

monogamous Mating for life with a single individual of the opposite sex.

these experiments, bonobos and chimpanzees have been taught to communicate using symbols, as in the case of Kanzi, a bonobo who uses a keyboard. Other chimpanzees, gorillas, and orangutans have been taught American Sign Language. Although this research provoked controversy, it has become evident that apes are capable of understanding language quite well, even using rudimentary grammar. They are able to generate original utterances, ask questions, distinguish naming something from asking for it, develop original ways to tell lies, coordinate their actions, and even spontaneously teach language to others. Even though they cannot literally *speak,* it is now clear that all of the great ape species can develop *language skills* to the level of a 2- to 3-year-old human child.[11] From such knowledge, we may learn something about the origin of human language.

MEDIATREK

To watch Koko the gorilla communicate to humans through sign language and to learn how the Gorilla Foundation is working to protect all of the endangered ape species, see MediaTrek 3.2 on the companion Web site or CD-ROM.

Home Ranges

Primates usually move about within circumscribed areas, or **home ranges,** which are of varying sizes, depending on the size of the group and on ecological factors such as availability of food. Ranges often change seasonally. The number of miles traveled by a group in a day varies. Some areas of a range, known as *core areas,* are used more often than others. Core areas typically contain water, food sources, resting places, and sleeping trees. The ranges of different groups may overlap, as among bonobos, where 65 percent of one community's range may overlap with that of another.[12] By contrast, chimpanzee territories, at least in some regions, are exclusively occupied.

Gorillas do not defend their home ranges against incursions of others of their kind, although they certainly will defend their group if it is in any way threatened. In the lowlands of Central Africa, it is not uncommon to find several families feeding in close proximity to one another.[13] In encounters with other communities, bonobos will defend their immediate space through vocalizations and displays, but rarely through fighting. Usually, they settle down and feed side by side, not infrequently grooming, playing, and engaging in sexual activity between groups as well. Chimpanzees, by contrast, have been observed patrolling their territories to ward off potential trespassers. Moreover, Goodall has recorded the destruction of one chimpanzee community by another invading group. This sort of deadly intercommunity interaction has never been observed among bonobos. Some have interpreted this apparent territorial behavior as an expression of the supposedly violent nature of chimpanzees. However, another interpretation is that the violence that Goodall witnessed was a response to crowding as a consequence of human activity.[14]

Primate Conservation

At present, no fewer than seventy-six species of primates are recognized as being in danger of extinction. Included among them are all of the great apes, as well as such formerly widespread and adaptable species as rhesus macaques. In the wild, these animals are threatened by habitat destruction in the name of economic development, by hunting for food and or recreation, and by trapping for pets and research. Because monkeys and apes are so closely related to humans, they are regarded as essential for biomedical research in which humans cannot be used. Ironically, using live primates to supply laboratories can be a major factor in their local extinction.

Because of their vulnerability, the conservation of primates has become a matter of urgency. Both of the existing approaches to solving this problem apply knowledge gained from studies of free-ranging animals. The first approach is to maintain some populations in the wild, either by establishing preserves where animals are already living or by moving populations to places where suitable habitat exists. In either case, constant monitoring and management are necessary to ensure that sufficient space and resources remain available. The other approach is to maintain breeding colonies in captivity, in which case we must carefully provide the kind of physical and social environment that will encourage psychological and physical well-being, as well as reproductive success. Primates in zoos and laboratories do not successfully reproduce when deprived of such amenities as opportunities for climbing, materials to use for nest building, others with which to socialize, and places for privacy (see Anthropology Applied).

[11]Lestel, D. (1998). How chimpanzees have domesticated humans. *Anthropology Today, 12*(3); Miles, H. L. W. (1993). Language and the orangutan: The "old person" of the forest. In P. Cavalieri & P. Singer (Eds.), *The great ape project* (pp. 45–50). New York: St. Martin's Press.

[12]Parish, A. R. (1998). Comment. *Current Anthropology, 39,* 414.

[13]Parnell, R. (1999). Gorilla exposé. *Natural History, 108*(8), 43.

[14]Power, M. G. (1995). Gombe revisited: Are chimpanzees violent and hierarchical in the "free" state? *General Anthropology, 2*(1), 5–9.

home ranges The geographical areas within which groups of primates usually move.

Anthropology Applied

Baboon Social Relationships and Primate Conservation

As humans encroach on primate habitats, translocation of the primates to a protected area is an excellent strategy for primate conservation. The value of field studies by primatologists for such relocations is illustrated by Shirley Strum's work with three troops of free-ranging baboons in Kenya. The troop she had been studying for 15 years had become a problem, raiding people's crops and garbage on newly established farms. Accordingly it was decided to move this troop and two other local troops—130 animals in all—to more sparsely inhabited country 150 miles away. Knowing their habits, Strum was able to trap, tranquilize, and transport the animals to their new home while preserving the baboons' vital social relationships.

Photo by Ulli Bonnekamp. Courtesy of Dr. Shirley Strum.

Strum's careful work allowed for a smooth transition. With social relations intact, the baboons did not abandon their new homes nor did they block the transfer of new males, with their all-important knowledge of local resources, into the troop. The success of her effort, which had never been tried with baboons, proves that translocation is a realistic technique for saving endangered primate species. As this method is dependent upon available land, preserves must be established to provide habitats for endangered primates. ■ ■ ■

MEDIATREK

To learn how the Bushmeat Project protects endangered primates from being slaughtered for meat and medicine through the development and support of community-based partnerships, see MediaTrek 3.3 on the companion Web site or CD-ROM.

Learning

Observations of monkeys and apes have shown learning abilities remarkably similar to those of humans. Numerous examples of inventive behavior have been observed among Japanese macaques, as well as among apes. One newly discovered example is a technique of food manipulation on the part of captive chimpanzees in the Madrid zoo. It began when a 5-year-old female rubbed apples against a sharp corner of a concrete wall in order to lick the mashed pieces and juice left on the wall. From this youngster, the practice of "smearing" spread to her peers, and within 5 years, most group members were performing the operation frequently and consistently. The innovation has become standardized and durable, having transcended two generations in the group.[15]

Another dramatic example of learning is afforded by the way chimpanzees in West Africa crack open oil-palm nuts. For this they use tools: an anvil stone with a level surface on which to place the nut and a good-sized hammer stone to crack it. Not any stone will do; it must be of the right shape and weight, and the anvil may require leveling by placing smaller stones beneath one or more edges. Nor does random banging away do the job; the nut has to be hit at the right speed and the right trajectory, or else the nut simply flies off into the forest. Last but not least, the apes must avoid mashing their fingers, rather than the nut. According to fieldworkers, the expertise of the chimps far exceeds that of any human who tries cracking these hardest nuts in the world.

Youngsters learn this process by staying near to adults who are cracking nuts, where their mothers share some of the food. This teaches them about the edibility of the nuts, but not how to get at what's edible. This they learn by observing and by "aping" (copying) the adults. At first they play with a nut or stone alone; later they begin to randomly combine objects. They soon learn, however, that placing nuts on anvils and hitting them with a hand or foot gets them nowhere. Only after 3 years of futile efforts do they begin to coordinate all of the multiple actions and objects, but even then it is only after a great deal of practice, by the age of 6 or 7 years, that they become proficient in this task. They do this for over 1,000 days. Evidently, it is *social* motivation that accounts for their perseverance after at least 3 years of failure, with no reward to reinforce their effort. At first, they are motivated by a desire to act like the mother; only later does the desire to feed on the tasty nut-meat take over.[16]

---

[15] Fernandez-Carriba, S., & Loeches, A. (2001). Fruit smearing by captive chimpanzees: A newly observed food-processing behavior. *Current Anthropology, 42,* 143–147.

[16] de Waal, F. (2001). *The ape and the sushi master* (pp. 227–229). New York: Basic Books.

This bonobo figured out by himself how to make stone tools like those our own ancestors made 2.5 million years ago.

Use of Objects as Tools

A **tool** may be defined as an object used to facilitate some task or activity. The nut cracking just discussed is the most complex tool-use task known from the field, involving both hands, two tools, and exact coordination. It is not, however, the only case of tool use among apes in the wild. Chimpanzees, bonobos, and orangutans make and use tools. Here, a distinction must be made between simple *tool use,* as when one pounds something with a convenient stone when a hammer is not available, and *tool making,* which involves deliberate modification of some material for its intended use. Thus, otters that use unmodified stones to crack open clams may be tool users, but they are not toolmakers. Not only do chimpanzees modify objects to make them suitable for particular purposes, but chimps to some extent modify them to regular and set patterns. They also pick up, and even prepare, objects for future use at some other location, and they can use objects as tools to solve new and novel problems. Thus, chimps have been observed using stalks of grass, twigs that they have stripped of leaves, and even sticks up to 3 feet long that they have smoothed down to "fish" for termites. They insert the modified stick into a termite nest, wait a few minutes, pull the stick out, and eat the insects clinging to it, all of which requires considerable dexterity. Chimpanzees are equally deliberate in their nest building. They test the vines and branches to make sure they are usable. If they are not, the animal moves to another site.

> ***tool*** An object used to facilitate some task or activity. Although tool making involves intentional modification of the material of which it is made, tool use may involve objects either modified for some particular purpose or completely unmodified.

Other examples of chimpanzee use of tools involve leaves, used as wipes or as sponges, to get water out of a hollow to drink. Large sticks may serve as clubs or as missiles (as may stones) in aggressive or defensive displays. Twigs are used as toothpicks to clean teeth as well as to extract loose baby teeth. They use these dental tools not just on themselves but on other individuals as well.[17]

In the wild, bonobos have not been observed making and using tools to the extent seen in chimpanzees. However, the use of large leaves as trail markers may be considered a form of tool use. That these animals do have further capabilities is exemplified by a captive bonobo who has figured out how to make tools of stone that are remarkably like the earliest such tools made by our own ancestors.

Medicinal use of plants by chimpanzees, illustrates their selective use of raw materials, a quality related to tool manufacture. Chimps that are ill by outward appearance have been observed to seek out specific plants of the genus *Aspilia.* They will eat the leaves singly without chewing them, letting the leaves soften in their mouths for a long time before swallowing. Primatologists have discovered that the leaves pass through their digestive system whole and relatively

[17] McGrew, W. C. (2000). Dental care in chimps. *Science, 288,* 1,747.

intact having scraped parasites off the intestine walls in the process.

Although gorillas (like bonobos and chimps) build nests, they are the only one of the four great apes that have not been observed to make and use other tools in the wild. The reason for this is probably not that gorillas lack the intelligence or skill to do so; rather, their easy diet of leaves and nettles makes tools of no particular use.

Hunting

Although fruits, other plant foods, and invertebrate animals constitute the bulk of their diet, both chimps and bonobos will kill and eat other animals such as small monkeys, something unusual among primates. Chimpanzee females sometimes hunt, but males do so far more frequently. When on the hunt, they may spend up to 2 hours watching, following, and chasing intended prey. Moreover, in contrast to the usual primate practice of each animal finding its own food, hunting frequently involves teamwork to trap and kill prey particularly when hunting for baboons. Once a potential victim has been partially isolated from its troop, three or more adult chimps will carefully position themselves so as to block off escape routes while another climbs toward the prey for the kill. Following the kill, most of those present get a share of the meat, either by grabbing a piece as chance affords, or by sitting and begging for a piece. Whatever the nutritional value of meat, hunting is not done purely for protein but for social and sexual reasons as well. The giving of meat helps forge alliances between males, and its sharing may be used also to entice a receptive female to have sex. In fact, males are more apt to hunt if a fertile female is present, and fertile females are more successful at begging for meat.

In bonobos, females are more likely to hunt than males. The female hunters regularly share carcasses with other females, but less often with males. Even when the most dominant male throws a tantrum nearby, he may still be denied a share.[18] Not only do females control the spoils of the hunt with one another, they are unusual also in their willingness to share other foods such as fruits.

THE QUESTION OF CULTURE

The more we learn of the behavior of our nearest primate relatives, the more we become aware of the importance to chimps of learned, socially shared practices and knowledge. This raises the question: Do chimpanzees, bonobos, and the other apes have culture? The answer appears to be yes. The detailed study of ape behavior has revealed variation among groups in use of tools and patterns of social engagement that seem to derive from the traditions of the group rather than a biologically determined script. Humans share with the other apes an ability to learn the complex but flexible patterns of behavior particular to a social group during a long period of childhood dependency.

Primate Behavior and Human Evolution

In Western societies there has been an unfortunate tendency to erect what paleontologist Stephen Jay Gould refers to as "golden barriers" that set us apart from the rest of the animal kingdom.[19] It is unfortunate, for it blinds us to the fact that a continuum exists between "us" and "them" (animals). We have already seen that the physical differences between humans and apes are largely differences of degree, rather than kind. It now appears that the same is true with respect to behavior. As primatologist Richard Wrangham once put it,

> Like humans, [chimpanzees] laugh, make up after a quarrel, support each other in times of trouble, medicate themselves with chemical and physical remedies, stop each other from eating poisonous foods, collaborate in the hunt, help each other over physical obstacles, raid neighboring groups, lose their tempers, get excited by dramatic weather, invent ways to show off, have family traditions and group traditions, make tools, devise plans, deceive, play tricks, grieve, and are cruel and are kind.[20]

This is not to say that we are "just" another ape; obviously, "degree" does make a difference. Nevertheless, the continuities between us and our primate kin reflect a common evolutionary heritage; it is just that our later evolution has taken us in a somewhat different direction. But by looking at the range of practices displayed by contemporary apes and other primates, we may find clues to the practices and capabilities possessed by our own ancestors as their evolutionary path diverged from those of the other African apes.

---

[18]Ingmanson, E. J. (1998). Comment. *Current Anthropology, 39,* 409.

[19]Quoted in de Waal, F. (2001). *The ape and the sushi master* (p. 235). New York: Basic Books.

[20]Quoted in Mydens, S. (2001, August 12). He's not hairy, he's my brother. *New York Times,* sec. 4, p. 5.

Chapter Summary

- The modern primates, like most mammals, are intelligent animals whose young are born live and nourished with milk from their mothers. Like other mammals, they maintain constant body temperature and have respiratory and circulatory systems that will sustain high activity levels. Their skeleton and teeth also resemble those of other mammals, although there are differences of detail.
- Two different classificatory systems are used to divide the primate order into two suborders. The first, based on the biological concept of grade or generalized level of organization, divides primates into the prosimians (lemurs, lorises, and tarsiers) and anthropoids (monkeys and apes, including humans). Prosimians are more dependent on the sense of smell than anthropoids, and where competition from anthropoids is present, they are nocturnal arboreal creatures. Nearly all anthropoids are diurnal, exploiting a wide range of habitats and expressing considerable behavioral flexibility and variation. The second taxonomic system recognizes that tarsiers are genetically more closely related to the anthropoid primates even though their outward appearance and nocturnal habits resemble prosimians. This system divides the primate order into the strepsirhines (lemurs and lorises) and the haplorhines (tarsiers, New and Old World monkeys, apes, and humans).
- Primates show a number of characteristics that developed as adaptations to insect predation in the trees. These adaptive characteristics include a generalized set of teeth, suited to insect eating but also a variety of fruits and leaves. These teeth are fewer in number and set in a smaller jaw than in most mammals. Other adaptations that developed in the course of primate evolution include binocular stereoscopic vision, or depth perception, and an intensified sense of touch particularly in the hands. This combination of developments had an effect upon the primate brain, resulting in larger size and greater complexity in later-appearing species. There were also changes in the primate skeleton: in particular, a reduction of the snout, an enlargement of the braincase, and numerous adaptations for upright posture and flexibility of limb movement. In addition, the primate reproductive pattern can be characterized by fewer offspring born to each female and a longer period of infant dependency compared to most mammals.
- The apes are humans' closest relatives. Apes include gibbons, siamangs, orangutans, gorillas, bonobos, and chimpanzees. In their outward appearance, the apes seem to resemble one another more than they do humans, but their genetic structure and biochemistry reveal that bonobos, chimpanzees, and gorillas are closer to humans than to orangutans, gibbons, and siamangs and thus must share a more recent common ancestry.
- The social life of primates is complex. Primates are social animals, and most species live and travel in groups. Frequently individuals transfer to new groups at adolescence. Though male adolescents leave their natal group more frequently in many species including gorillas, female chimpanzees and bonobos are often the ones to migrate. Among bonobos and chimpanzees, sons and daughters will also remain with their mothers for life. In all three species, both males and females can be organized into dominance hierarchies. In the case of females, high rank is associated with enhanced reproductive success. In males however, high rank does not necessarily confer a reproductive advantage.
- A characteristic primate activity is grooming, which is a sign of closeness between individuals. Among gorillas and chimpanzees, sexual interaction between adults of opposite sex generally takes place only when a female is in estrus. In bonobos, however, constant swelling of the female's genitals suggests constant estrus, whether or not she is actually fertile. A consequence of this concealed ovulation in bonobos is a separation of sexual activity from the biological task of reproduction. Among bonobos, sex between both opposite and same-sex individuals serves as a means of reducing tensions, as in the genital rubbing that frequently takes place between females.
- Primates have elaborate systems of communication based on vocalizations and gestures. In addition, bonobos employ trail signs to communicate their whereabouts to others. Usually primates move about within home ranges, rather than defended territories.
- The diet of most primates is made up of a variety of fruits, leaves, and insects, but bonobos and chimpanzees sometimes hunt, kill, and eat animals as well. Among chimps, most hunting is done by males and may require considerable teamwork. By contrast, it is usually bonobo females that hunt. Once a kill is made, the meat is generally shared with other animals.
- Among chimpanzees and the other apes, learned behavior is especially important. From adults, juveniles learn to use a variety of tools and substances for various purposes. Innovations made by one individual may be adopted by other animals, standardized, and passed on to succeeding generations. Because practices are learned, socially shared, and often differ from one group to another, we may speak of chimpanzee culture.

Questions for Reflection

1. How does the study of nonhuman primates help us address the challenge of understanding ourselves?
2. Considering some of the trends seen among the primates, such as increased brain size or reduced tooth number, why can't we say that some primates are more evolved than others? Are humans more evolved than chimpanzees?
3. Two systems exist for dividing the primate order into suborders because of difficulties with classifying tarsiers. Should classification systems be based on genetic relationships or based on the biological concept of grade? Is the continued use

of the older terminology an instance of inertia or a difference in philosophy? How do the issues brought up by the "tarsier problem" translate to the hominoids?

4. Given the variation seen in the specific behaviors of chimp, bonobo, and gorilla groups, is it fair to say that our close relatives possess culture?

5. Many primate species, particularly apes, are endangered today. Though some features of ape biology may be responsible for apes' limited population size, humans, with ever-expanding population sizes, share these same biological features. Besides life cycle biology, what factors are causing endangerment of primates, and how can humans work to prevent the extinction of our closest living relatives?

Key Terms

Prosimii
Anthropoidea
Grade
Nocturnal
Diurnal
Arboreal
Platyrrhini
Catarrhini
Strepsirhini
Haplorhini
Binocular vision
Stereoscopic vision
Fovea centralis
Dental formula
Sexual dimorphism
Vertebrates
Cranium
Foramen magnum
Clavicle
Suspensory hanging apparatus
Scapula
Brachiate
Prehensile
Opposable
Estrus
Ovulation
Community
Natal group
Dominance hierarchies
Grooming
Monogamous
Home ranges
Tool

Multimedia Review Tools

Companion Web Site

Visit **http://www.wadsworth.com/anthropology_d/** and click on the companion Web site for this textbook to access a wide range of material to aid your study of anthropology. Among the options for self-study in each chapter are learning objectives, flash cards, Internet activities, Web links, InfoTrac College Edition exercises, and practice tests that can be scored and emailed to your instructor.

CD-ROM

The *Doing Anthropology Today* CD-ROM supplied with your textbook provides unique and valuable information designed to enhance your learning experience. This interactive multimedia resource includes video clips, interviews with renowned anthropologists, map and timeline exercises, chapter study quizzes, and much more. *Doing Anthropology Today* will not only help you in achieving your grade goals, but it will also make your learning experience fun and exciting!

Suggested Readings

de Waal, F. (2001). *The ape and the sushi master.* New York: Basic Books.

This masterful discussion of the presence of culture among apes removes this concept from an anthropocentric realm and ties it instead to communication and social organization. In an accessible style, Frans de Waal, one of the world's foremost experts on bonobos, demonstrates ape culture while challenging human intellectual theories designed to exclude animals from the "culture club."

Fossey, D. (1983). *Gorillas in the mist.* Burlington, MA. Houghton Mifflin.

The late Dian Fossey is to gorillas what Jane Goodall is to chimpanzees. Fossey devoted years to the study of gorilla behavior in the field. This book is about the first 13 years of her study; as well as being readable and informative, it is well illustrated.

Galdikas, Birute (1995). *Reflections on Eden: My years with the orangutans of Borneo.* New York: Little Brown & Company.

Birute Galdikas is the least well known of the trio of young women sent by Louis Leakey in 1971 to study apes in the wild. Her work with the orangutans of Borneo, however, is magnificent. In this book she presents rich scientific information as well as her personal reflections on a life spent fully integrated with orangutans and the culture of Borneo.

Goodall, J. (1990). *Through a window.* Boston: Houghton Mifflin.

This fascinating book is a personal account of Jane Goodall's experiences over 35 years of studying wild chimpanzees in Tanzania. A pleasure to read and a fount of information on the behavior of these apes, the book is profusely illustrated as well.

Goodall J. (2000). *Reason for hope: A spiritual journey.* New York: Warner Books.

Jane Goodall's most recent book is a memoir linking her monumental life's work with the chimpanzees of Gombe to her inner spiritual convictions. She makes clear her commitment to conferring chimpanzees with the same rights and respect experienced by humans through the exploration of difficult topics such as environmental destruction, animal abuse, and genocide. She expands the concept of humanity while providing us with powerful reasons to maintain hope.

Rowe, N., & Mittermeier, R. A. (1996). *The pictorial guide to the living primates.* East Hampton, NY: Pogonias Press.

Filled with dynamic photographs of primates in nature, this book also provides concise descriptions (including anatomy, taxonomy, diet, social structure, maps, and so on) for 234 species of primates. The book is useful for students and primatologists alike.

PART 2

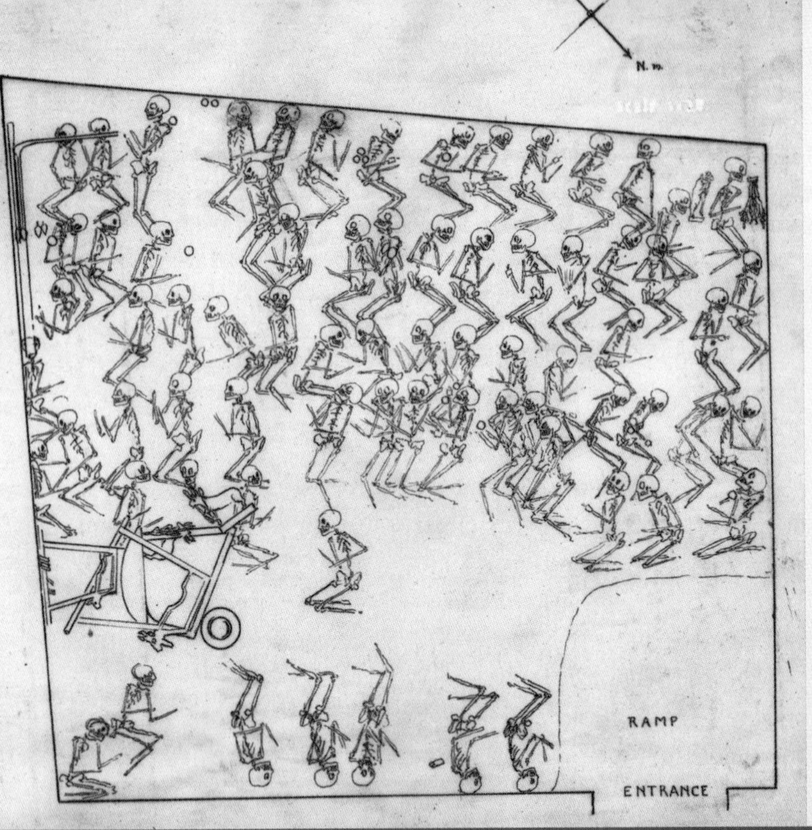

University of Pennsylvania Museum

Evolution

The Challenge of Understanding Human Origins

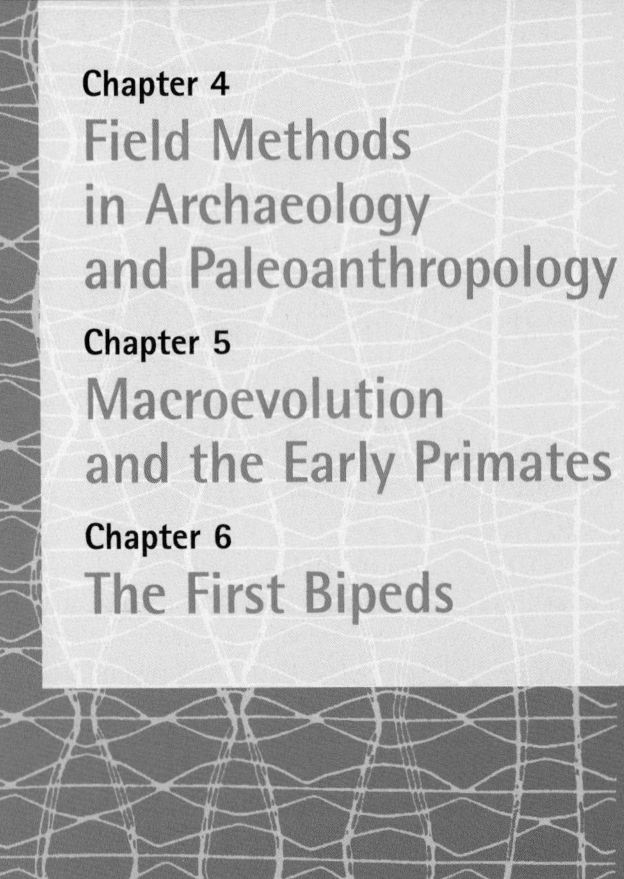

Introduction

The challenge of knowing ourselves is met in part through seeking an understanding of human origins. Although many cultures account for human origins through their creation stories, we begin to examine the scientific account of creation embodied in the theory of evolution. Evolutionary theory seeks to answer the age-old question, where do we come from? It does so by providing a coherent theory to account not only for the origins of humans, but for the origins of other species as well. Through the exploration of the inner workings of molecules and cells, and through observations of the biology and behavior of our closest living relatives—the other primates—scientists have unraveled some of the mechanisms responsible for the evolution of humans.

Fossils reveal that the human evolutionary path led from our primate ancestors living in the tropical forests to a culture-bearing species inhabiting the entire globe. This is not to say that humans represent the pinnacle of evolution. We are understandably fascinated with our own origins, but in the overall scheme of things we are just one small twig among many on the evolutionary tree of life. And as we shall see, there was nothing inevitable about our appearance: We are simply one more primate, successful for the moment as others have been in the past, but with no guarantee that our success will be any more lasting than the successes of others.

With an understanding of human biology and the mechanisms of biological change, we can now begin to focus on the actual reconstruction of human origins through the study of the past. The challenge in human evolutionary studies is to reconstruct a coherent picture of human origins with the fragmentary data available. We begin Chapter 4 with a discussion of the methods used to investigate the past, such as these bodies from the "Great Death-Pit" next to the royal tombs at Ur. This chapter discusses the nature of fossils and archaeological materials, where they are found, how they are unearthed, and the methods used to date and analyze human physical and cultural remains. An appreciation of field methods used in anthropology helps us to understand the value and limitations of the evidence gained.

© Bohan Brecelj/Corbis

In Chapter 5 we look first at macroevolution—a biological mechanism responsible for evolution of groups of species—and then turn our attention to primate evolution. We will explore concepts like continental drift and geological time, as well as trace the primate fossil evidence relating it to the diversity of primate species today. We will travel deep into the past to the earliest primates. We will then concentrate on the fossil hominoids—the apes who inhabited the forests of Asia, Europe, and Africa—focusing particularly on the evidence in Africa, the geographic heart of human evolutionary history.

At some time between 5 and 8 million years ago, African apes diverged into separate lines—leading to chimps, bonobos, gorillas, and to a line of hominoids that walked on two legs (bipedally). Fossil evidence of these earliest bipeds is sketchy, and its interpretation is controversial. Evidence of the genus *Australopithecus,* a varied group of ancestral species that preceded the genus *Homo,* appears around 4 million years ago in the fossil record.

Chapter 6 completes this section of the book with an exploration of the anatomy of bipedalism and the evidence for the biology and behavior of australopithecines as preserved in fossil skeletons, skulls, and teeth; fossilized footprints; and the surrounding environment. *Australopithecus* walked bipedally in a fully human manner but showed essentially apelike behavior patterns, suggesting mental abilities not differing greatly from those of its ancestors a few million years earlier.

We meet the challenge of understanding human origins in Part 2 of this book by exploring the methods used to study our past as well as the evolutionary history of our earliest primate ancestors. Scraps of bones—when combined with detailed understanding of biological processes of change, careful excavation, and analysis techniques—have much to tell us about our origins. These chapters set the stage for the appearance of the genus *Homo* 2.5 million years ago, whose story continues in Part 3.

CHAPTER 4

Field Methods in Archaeology and Paleoanthropology

CHALLENGE ISSUE

THE CHALLENGE OF UNDERSTANDING HUMAN ORIGINS IS MET THROUGH METICULOUS EXCAVATION METHODS AIMED TO UNEARTH HUMAN PHYSICAL AND CULTURAL REMAINS. To excavate the ancient Stone Age site Sima de los Huesos or "Pit of Bones" in Spain, paleoanthropologist Juan Luis Arsuaga and his team spend nearly an hour each day climbing underground through a narrow passage to a small enclosed space, rich with human remains. Here, fossils are excavated with great care and transported back into the laboratory, where the long process of interpretation and analysis begins. The resulting data and analyses answer the challenge of understanding human origins.

1

How Are the Physical and Cultural Remains of Past Humans Investigated?

Archaeologists and paleoanthropologists face a dilemma. The only way to thoroughly investigate our past is to excavate the sites where biological and cultural remains are found. Unfortunately, excavation results in the site's destruction. Thus, every attempt is made to excavate in such a way that the location and context of everything recovered, no matter how small, is precisely recorded. These records help scientists make sense of the data and enhance our knowledge of the past. The success of an excavation also depends upon cooperation and respect between anthropologists who are investigating the past and the living people connected to the sites and remains being studied.

2

Are Human Physical and Cultural Remains Always Found Together?

Archaeological sites are places containing the cultural remains of past human activity. Sites are revealed by the presence of artifacts as well as soil marks, changes in vegetation, and irregularities of the earth's surface. While skeletons of recent peoples are frequently associated with their cultural remains, as we go back in time, the association of physical and cultural remains becomes less likely. Fossils are defined as any surviving trace or impression of an organism from the past. Fossils sometimes accompany archaeological sites, but many of them pre-date the first stone tools or other cultural artifacts. The human cultural practice of burying the dead, starting about 100,000 years ago, changed the nature of the fossil record, providing relatively complete skeletons as well as information about this cultural practice.

3

How Are Archaeological or Fossil Remains Dated?

Calculating the age of physical and cultural remains is an important aspect of interpreting the past. Remains can be dated by noting their stratigraphic position, by measuring the amount of chemicals contained in fossil bones, or through association with other plant, animal, or cultural remains. More precise dating methods rely upon advances in the disciplines of chemistry and physics that use properties such as rates of decay of radioactive elements. These elements may be present in the remains themselves, or in the surrounding soil. By comparing dates and remains across a variety of sites, anthropologists can make inferences about human origins, migrations, and technological developments. Sometimes the development of a new dating technique leads to an entirely new interpretation of physical and cultural remains.

While anthropology's focus is on peoples of all places and times, paleoanthropology and archaeology are the specialties most concerned with our past. These disciplines seek to understand human origins and cultural history across the globe through the study of human physical and cultural remains. While cultural artifacts and fossils represent distinct kinds of data, the fullest interpretations of the human past integrate both of these approaches.

The process of reconstructing the past involves painstaking attention to detail as scientists systematically excavate and analyze fragmentary remains. Scraps of bone, shattered pottery, and scattered campsites speak to the paleoanthropologist and archaeologist who work to place these remains in broad interpretive contexts. These scientists may also make observations on living people and employ a variety of experimental methods in order to validate the theories about human biology and behavior in the past made from fragmentary physical and cultural remains. Furthermore, successful exploration of past humans depends upon cooperation and respect between anthropologists and the living people with ancestral connections to the physical and cultural remains being studied.

Knowledge of the human past is essential if we are to understand what made us distinctively human, as well as how biological and cultural changes have affected the human condition. Indeed, given the radical changes taking place in the world today, an understanding of the nature of change has never been more important.

Most of us are familiar with some kind of archaeological material: the coin dug out of the earth, the fragment of an ancient pot, the spear point used by some ancient hunter. Finding and cataloguing such objects is often thought to be the chief goal of archaeology. While this was true in the 19th and early 20th century, when professional and amateur archaeologists alike appropriated cultural treasures, the situation changed in the mid-20th century. Today, the aim is to use archaeological remains to reconstruct the cultures and worldviews of past human societies. Although it may appear that archaeologists are digging up things, they are really digging up human biology, behavior, and beliefs.

The physical remains of our ancestors, as opposed to the things they left behind, are the concern of paleoanthropologists. Unlike paleontologists, who study all forms of past life from ancient microscopic plants to dinosaurs, paleoanthropologists confine their attention to humans, near humans, and other ancient primates. Just as the finding and cataloguing of objects was once the chief concern of the archaeologist, so the finding and cataloguing of human and other primate fossils was once the chief concern of the paleoanthropologist. But again, a major change in the field occurred in the 1950s. Although recovery, description, and organization of fossil materials are still important, the emphasis has shifted to what fossils can tell us about human biological evolution. It is not so much a case of finding fossils but finding out what the fossils mean.

Often paleoanthropologists and archaeologists work together to reconstruct the biology and culture of our ancestors. For example the first stone tools are interpreted in the context of concurrent changes in brain shape and size. Closer to the present, **bioarchaeology** combines the biological anthropologists' expertise in skeletal biology with archaeological reconstruction of human behavior through fossil analysis. For example, as senior author William Haviland demonstrated more than thirty years ago, social status is reflected in skeletal evidence of differences in diet, sickness, and physical labor among individuals.[1]

In Chapter 1, we surveyed what anthropologists do and why they do it. We also looked briefly at the ethnographic methods used by anthropologists to study the cultures of living peoples. These methods come into play when inferences about past behaviors are made through observations of living groups. However, to study peoples of the past—especially those of the **prehistoric** past, before the existence of written records—other methods are required. The term *prehistoric,* while conjuring up images of cavemen and women, does not imply a lack of history. It means only that a *written* record of history is absent. Since the next two parts of this book are about the prehistoric past, we shall now look at the methods archaeologists and paleoanthropologists use as they study the human past.

METHODS OF DATA RECOVERY

Archaeologists and paleoanthropologists, concentrating on cultural and physical remains respectively, share excavation, dating, and experimental methods. In addition, because biological and cultural aspects of humans are intertwined, archaeologists and paleoanthropologists

bioarchaeology The archaeological study of human remains emphasizing the preservation of cultural and social processes in the skeleton.
prehistoric A conventional term used to refer to the period of time before the appearance of written records. Does not deny the existence of history, merely of *written* history.

[1] Haviland W. (1967). Stature at Tikal, Guatemala: Implications for ancient Maya, demography, and social organization. *American Antiquity,* 32, 316–325.

In rare circumstances, human bodies are so well preserved that they could be mistaken for recent corpses. Such is the case of "Ötzi," the 5,200-year-old "Ice Man," exposed by the melting of an alpine glacier in northern Italy in 1991.

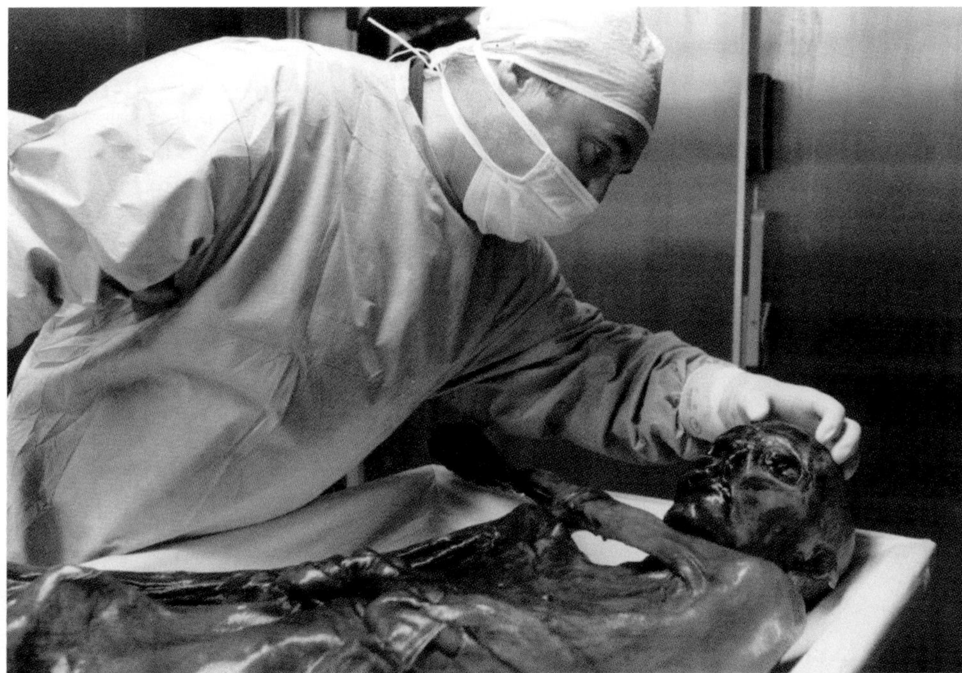

AP/Wide World Photos

work together to reconstruct human culture and biology in the past.

Archaeologists work with **artifacts:** any object fashioned or altered by humans—a flint scraper, a basket, an axe, a pipe, or such things as house ruins or walls. An artifact expresses a facet of human culture. Because it is something that someone made, archaeologists like to say that an artifact is a product or representation of human behavior and beliefs, or, in more technical terms, artifacts are **material culture.**

Just as important as the artifacts themselves is the way they were left in the ground. What people do with the things they have made, how they dispose of them, and how they lose them also reflect important aspects of human culture. Furthermore, the contexts in which the artifacts are found may tell us which objects were contemporary with other objects, which are older, and which are younger.

Without this information, the archaeologist cannot identify, let alone understand, specific cultures of the past. Without context, the archaeologist in effect knows next to nothing! Unfortunately, information is easily lost if the materials have been disturbed, whether by bulldozers or by relic collectors.

While archaeologists work with artifacts, paleoanthropologists work with human or other primate fossils—the remains of past forms of life. And just as the context of an artifact is as important to the archaeologist as the find itself, so is the context of a fossil critical to the paleoanthropologist. Not only does context provide information about which fossils are earlier or later in time than other fossils, but also by noting the association of ancestral human fossils with the remains of other species, the paleoanthropologist may reconstruct the environment of the past.

The Nature of Fossils

Broadly defined, a **fossil** is any trace or impression of an organism that has been preserved in the earth's crust from past geologic time. Fossilization typically involves the hard parts of an organism. Bones, teeth, shells, horns, and the woody tissues of plants are the most successfully fossilized materials. Although the soft parts of an organism are rarely fossilized, the casts or impressions of footprints, brains, and even whole bodies have sometimes been found. Because dead animals quickly attract meat-eating scavengers and bacteria that cause decomposition, they rarely remain long enough to become fossilized. For an organism to become a fossil, it must be covered by some protective substance soon after death.

artifact Any object fashioned or altered by humans.
material culture The durable aspects of culture such as tools, structures, and art.
fossil The remains of plants and animals that lived in the past.

An organism or part of an organism may be preserved in a number of ways. The whole animal may be frozen in ice, like the famous mammoths found in Siberia, safe from the actions of predators, weathering, and bacteria. Or it may be enclosed in a natural resin exuding from evergreen trees, later becoming hardened and fossilized as amber. Specimens of spiders and insects dating back millions of years have been preserved in the Baltic Sea area, which is rich in resin-producing evergreens such as pine, spruce, or fir trees. An organism may be preserved in the bottoms of lakes and sea basins, where the body or body part may be quickly covered with sediment. An entire organism may also be mummified or preserved in tar pits, peat, oil, or asphalt bogs, in which the chemical environment prevents the growth of decay-producing bacteria. Such complete remains, although not common, are often quite spectacular and may be particularly informative. As an example, consider the recovery in 1994 of a young girl's remains in Barrow, Alaska, described in the Original Study.

Original Study

Whispers from the Ice

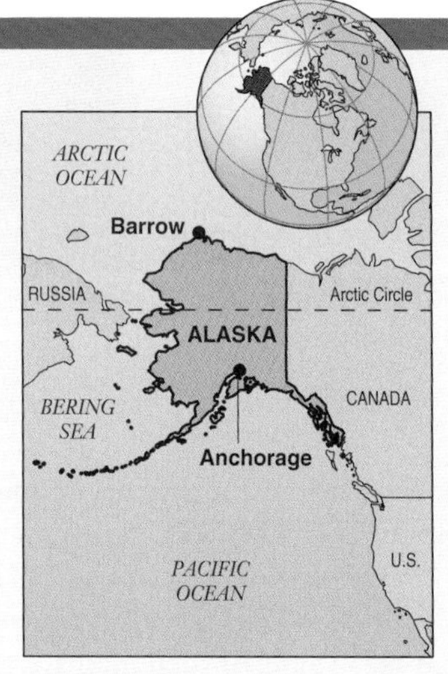

People grew excited when a summer rainstorm softened the bluff known as Ukkuqsi, sloughing off huge chunks of earth containing remains of historic and prehistoric houses, part of the old village that predates the modern community of Barrow. Left protruding from the slope was a human head. Archaeologist Anne Jensen happened to be in Barrow buying strapping tape when the body appeared. Her firm, SJS Archaeological Services, Inc., was closing a field season at nearby Point Franklin, and Jensen offered the team's help in a kind of archaeological triage to remove the body before it eroded completely from the earth. The North Slope Borough hired her and Glenn Sheehan, both associated with Pennsylvania's Bryn Mawr College, to conduct the work. The National Science Foundation, which supported the 3-year Point Franklin project, agreed to fund the autopsy and subsequent analysis of the body and artifacts. The Ukkuqsi excavation quickly became a community event. In remarkably sunny and calm weather, volunteers troweled and picked through the thawing soil, finding trade beads, animal bones, and other items. Teenage boys worked alongside grandmothers. The smell of sea mammal oil, sweet at first then corrupt, mingled with ancient organic odors of decomposed vegetation. One man searched the beach for artifacts that had eroded from the bluff, discovering such treasures as two feather parkas. Elder Silas Negovanna, originally of Wainwright, visited several times, "more or less out of curiosity to see what they have in mind," he says. George Leavitt, who lives in a house on the bluff, stopped by one day while carrying home groceries and suggested a way to spray water to thaw the soil without washing away valuable artifacts. Tour groups added the excavation to their rounds.

"This community has a great interest in archaeology up here just because it's so recent to their experience," says oral historian Karen Brewster, a tall young woman who interviews elders as part of her work with the North Slope Borough's division of Inupiat History, Language, and Culture. "The site's right in town, and everybody was really fascinated by it."

Slowly, as the workers scraped and shoveled, the earth surrendered its historical hoard: carved wooden bowls, ladles, and such clothing as a mitten made from polar bear hide, birdskin parkas, and mukluks. The items spanned prehistoric times, dated in Barrow to before explorers first arrived in 1826.

The work prompted visiting elders to recall when they or their parents lived in traditional sod houses and relied wholly on the land and sea for sustenance. Some remembered sliding down the hill as children, before the sea gnawed away the slope. Others described the site's use as a lookout for whales or ships. For the archaeologists, having elders stand beside them and identify items and historical context is like hearing the past whispering in their ears. Elders often know from experience, or from stories, the answers to the scientists' questions about how items were used or made. "In this instance, usually the only puzzled people are the archaeologists," jokes archaeologist Sheehan.

A modern town of 4,000, Barrow exists in a cultural continuum, where history is not detached or remote but still pulses through contemporary life. People live, hunt, and fish where their ancestors did, but they can also buy fresh vegetables at the store and jet to other places. Elementary school classes include computer and Inupiaq language studies. Caribou skins, still ruddy with blood, and black brant carcasses hang near late-model cars outside homes equipped with television antennas. A man uses power tools to work on his whaling boat. And those who appear from the earth are not just bodies, but relatives. "We're not a people frozen in time," says Jana Harcharek, an Inupiat Eskimo who teaches Inupiaq and nur-

[CONTINUED]

tures her culture among young people. "There will always be that connection between us [and our ancestors]. They're not a separate entity."

The past drew still closer as the archaeologists neared the body. After several days of digging through thawed soil, they used water supplied by the local fire station's tanker truck to melt through permafrost until they reached the remains, about 3 feet below the surface. A shell of clear ice encased the body, which rested in what appeared to be a former meat cellar. With the low-pressure play of water from the tanker, the archaeologists teased the icy casket from the frozen earth, exposing a tiny foot. Only then did they realize they had uncovered a child. "That was kind of sad, because she was about my daughter's size," says archaeologist Jensen.

The girl was curled up beneath a baleen toboggan and part of a covering that Inupiat elder Bertha Leavitt identified as a kayak skin by its stitching. The child, who appeared to be 5 or 6, remained remarkably intact after her dark passage through time. Her face was cloaked by a covering that puzzled some onlookers. It didn't look like human hair, or even fur, but something with a feathery residue. Finally they concluded it was a hood from a feather parka made of bird skins. The rest of her body was delineated muscle that had freeze-dried into a dark brick-red color. Her hands rested on her knees, which were drawn up to her chin. Frost particles coated the bends of her arms and legs.

"We decided we needed to go talk to the elders and see what they wanted, to get some kind of feeling as to whether they wanted to bury her right away, or whether they were willing to allow some studies in a respectful manner—studies that would be of some use to residents of the North Slope," Jensen says. Working with community elders is not a radical idea to Jensen or Sheehan, whose previous work in the Arctic has earned them high regard from local officials who appreciate their sensitivity. The researchers feel obligated not only to follow community wishes, but to invite villagers to sites and to share all information through public presentations. In fact, Jensen is reluctant to discuss findings with the press before the townspeople themselves hear it.

"It seems like it's a matter of simple common courtesy," she says. Such consideration can only help researchers, she points out. "If people don't get along with you, they're not going to talk to you, and they're liable to throw you out on your ear." In the past, scientists were not terribly sensitive about such matters, generally regarding human remains—and sometimes living natives—as artifacts themselves. Once, the girl's body would have been hauled off to the catacombs of some university or museum, and relics would have disappeared into exhibit drawers in what Sheehan describes as "hit-and-run archaeology."

"Grave robbers" is how Inupiat Jana Harcharek refers to early Arctic researchers. "They took human remains and their burial goods. It's pretty gruesome. But, of course, at the time they thought they were doing science a big favor. Thank goodness attitudes have changed."

Today, not only scientists but municipal officials confer with the Barrow Elders Council when local people find skeletons from traditional platform burials out on the tundra, or when bodies appear in the house mounds. The elders appreciate such consultations, says Samuel Simmonds, a tall, dignified man known for his carving. A retired Presbyterian minister, he presided at burial ceremonies of the famous "frozen family," ancient Inupiats discovered in Barrow 13 years ago. "They were part of us, we know that," he says simply, as if the connection between old bones and bodies and living relatives is self-evident. In the case of the newly discovered body, he says, "We were concerned that it was reburied in a respectful manner. They were nice enough to come over and ask us."

The elders also wanted to restrict media attention and prevent photographs of the body except for a few showing her position at the site. They approved a limited autopsy to help answer questions about the body's sex, age, and state of health. She was placed in an orange plastic body bag in a stainless steel morgue with the temperature turned down to below freezing.

With the help of staff at the Indian Health Service Hospital, Jensen sent the girl's still-frozen body to Anchorage's Providence Hospital. There she assisted with an autopsy performed by Dr. Michael Zimmerman of New York City's Mount Sinai Hospital. Zimmerman, an expert on prehistoric frozen bodies, had autopsied Barrow's frozen family in 1982, and was on his way to work on the prehistoric man recently discovered in the Alps.

The findings suggest the girl's life was very hard. She ultimately died of starvation, but also had emphysema caused by a rare congenital disease—the lack of an enzyme that protects the lungs. She probably was sickly and needed extra care all her brief life. The autopsy also found soot in her lungs from the family's sea mammal oil lamps, and she had osteoporosis, which was caused by a diet exclusively of meat from marine mammals.

The girl's stomach was empty, but her intestinal tract contained dirt and animal fur. That remains a

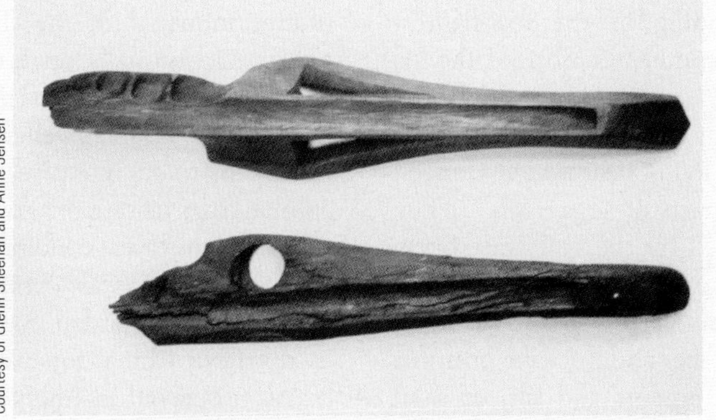

Courtesy of Glenn Sheehan and Anne Jensen

Cultural remains previously stored in far-away museums have been returned to the Inupiat people where they are proudly exhibited at the newly built Inupiat Heritage Center in Barrow, Alaska. In addition to traditional museum displays honoring the past, the center actively promotes the continuation of Inupiat Eskimo cultural traditions through innovations such as the elder-in-residence program.

[CONTINUED]

CONTINUED

mystery and raises questions about the condition of the rest of the family. "It's not likely that she would be hungry and everyone else well fed," Jensen says.

That the girl appears to have been placed deliberately in the cellar provokes further questions about precontact burial practices, which the researchers hope Barrow elders can help answer. Historic accounts indicate the dead often were wrapped in skins and laid out on the tundra on wooden platforms, rather than buried in the frozen earth. But perhaps the entire family was starving and too weak to remove the dead girl from the house, Jensen speculates. "We probably won't ever be able to say, 'This is the way it was,'" she adds. "For that you need a time machine."

The scientific team reported to the elders that radiocarbon dating places the girl's death in about A.D. 1200. If correct—for dating is technically tricky in the Arctic—the date would set the girl's life about 100 years before her people formed settled whaling villages, Sheehan says.

Following the autopsy and the body's return to Barrow in August, one last request by the elders was honored. The little girl, wrapped in her feather parka, was placed in a casket and buried in a small Christian ceremony next to the grave of the other prehistoric bodies. Hundreds of years after her death, an Inupiat daughter was welcomed back into the midst of her community.

The "rescue" of the little girl's body from the raw forces of time and nature means researchers and the Inupiat people will continue to learn still more about the region's culture. Sheehan and Jensen returned to Barrow in winter 1994 to explain their findings to townspeople. "We expect to learn just as much from them," Sheehan said before the trip. A North Slope Cultural Center scheduled for completion in 1996 will store and display artifacts from the dig sites.

Laboratory tests and analysis also will contribute information. The archaeologists hope measurements of heavy metals in the girl's body will allow comparisons with modern-day pollution contaminating the sea mammals that Inupiats eat today. The soot damage in her lungs might offer health implications for Third World people who rely on oil lamps, dung fires, and charcoal for heat and light. Genetic tests could illuminate early population movements of Inupiats. The project also serves as a model for good relations between archaeologists and Native people. "The larger overall message from this work is that scientists and communities don't have to be at odds," Sheehan says. "In fact, there are mutual interests that we all have. Scientists have obligations to communities. And when more scientists realize that, and when more communities hold scientists to those standards, then everybody will be happier." *(Adapted from S. Simpson. (1995, April). Whispers from the ice.* Alaska, *23–28.)*

Cases in which an entire organism of any sort, let alone a human, is preserved are especially rare. Fossils generally consist of such things as scattered teeth and fragments of bones found embedded in rock deposits. Most have been altered in some way in the process of becoming fossilized. **Taphonomy** (from the Greek for "tomb"), the study of the biological and geological processes by which dead organisms become fossils, provides systematic understanding of the fossilization process vital for the scientific interpretations of the fossils themselves.

Fossilization is most apt to occur among marine animals and other creatures living near water. Concentrations of shells and other parts of organisms are covered and completely enclosed by the soft waterborne sediments that eventually harden into shale and limestone in the following fashion: As the remains of organisms accumulate on shallow sea, river, or lake bottoms, they become covered by sediments and silt, or sand. These materials gradually harden, forming a protective shell around the skeleton of the organism. The internal cavities of bones or teeth and other parts of the skeleton fill in with mineral deposits from the sediment immediately surrounding the specimen. Then the external walls of the bone decay and are replaced by calcium carbonate or silica.

taphonomy The study of how bones and other materials come to be preserved in the earth as fossils.

Unless protected in some way, the bones of a land dweller are generally scattered and exposed to the deteriorating influence of the elements, predators, and scavengers. Occasionally, terrestrial animals living near lakes or rivers become fossilized if they happen to die next to or in the water. A land dweller may also become fossilized if it happens to die in a cave, or if some other meat-eating animal drags its remains to a site protected from erosion and decay. In caves, conditions are often excellent for fossilization, as minerals contained in water dripping from the ceiling may harden over bones left on the cave floor. In northern China, for example, many fossils of *Homo erectus* (discussed in Chapter 8) and other animals were found in a cave at a place called Zhoukoudian, in deposits consisting of consolidated clays and rock that had fallen from the cave's limestone ceiling. The cave had been frequented by both humans and predatory animals, which left remains of many a meal there.

Fossils are not always found in the ground. In this picture, paleoanthropologist Donald Johanson searches for fossils in a gully in Ethiopia. The fossils in the foreground were once buried beneath sediments on an ancient lake bottom, but rains in more recent times have eroded the sediments from around them so that they lie exposed on the surface.

Entirely preserved fossil skeletons dated to before the cultural practice of burial about 100,000 years ago are exceedingly rare. The human fossil record from this period consists of more fragmentary remains. The fossil record for many other primates is even poorer, because organic materials decay rapidly in the tropical forests where they lived. The records are much more complete for primates such as evolving humans that lived on the grassy plains, or savannah environments, where conditions were far more favorable to the formation of fossils. This was particularly true in places where ash deposited from volcanic eruptions or waterborne sediments along lakes and streams could quickly cover organisms dying in these environments. Numerous fossils important for our understanding of human evolution have been found near ancient lakes and streams, in Ethiopia, Kenya, and Tanzania in East Africa, often sandwiched between layers of volcanic ash.

SEARCHING FOR ARTIFACTS AND FOSSILS

Where are artifacts and fossils found? Places containing archaeological remains of previous human activity are known as sites. There are many kinds of sites, and sometimes it is difficult to define their boundaries, for remains may be strewn over large areas. Sites are even found underwater. Some examples of sites identified by archaeologists and paleontologists are hunting campsites, from which hunters went out to hunt game; kill sites, in which game was killed and butchered; village sites, in which domestic activities took place; and cemeteries, in which the dead, and sometimes their belongings, were buried.

MEDIATREK

To go underwater and learn about the shipwrecked remains of battleships, steamers, and sailboats, visit the Web site of Florida's Underwater Archaeological Preserves. Each shipwreck site contains a location map and a complete site plan as well as ways to become involved in Florida's underwater archaeology program. Go to MediaTrek 4.1 on the companion Web site or CD-ROM.

While skeletons of recent peoples are frequently associated with their cultural remains, as we go back in time, the association of physical and cultural remains becomes less likely. Physical remains dating from before 2.5 million years ago are found in isolation. This is not proof of the absence of material culture but rather that the earliest forms of material culture were not preserved in the archaeological record. It is likely that the earliest tools were made of organic materials such as the termiting sticks used by chimps described in Chapter 3 that were much less likely to be preserved in the archaeological record. The discovery of early stone tools, however, has sometimes guided paleoanthropologists toward their fossil discoveries. For example, the presence of very crude stone tools in Olduvai Gorge, East Africa, prompted paleoanthropologists Mary and Louis Leakey to search there for human fossils. Their success with this strategy was spectacular (discussed in Chapters 6 and 7).

In addition, some places contain collections of isolated bones from a variety of organisms fossilized together due to the action of predators. For example, in South Africa the fossil remains of early human ancestors have been found in rock fissures, evidently dropped there by predators such as leopards and eagles. Perhaps because many date from more recent periods, archaeological sites may be found just about anywhere. However, the same is not true for fossilized physical remains. One will find fossils only in geological contexts

Sometimes archaeological sites are marked by dramatic ruins, as shown here. This temple stands at the heart of the ancient Maya city of Tikal. Built by piling up rubble and facing it with limestone blocks held together with mortar, it served as the funerary monument of a king, whose body was placed in a tomb beneath the pyramidal base.

where conditions are known to have been right for fossilization.

Site Identification

The first task for the archaeologist is actually finding sites to investigate. Archaeological sites, particularly very old ones, frequently lie buried underground covered by layers of sediment deposited since the site was in use. Most sites are revealed by the presence of artifacts. Chance may play a crucial role in the site's discovery, as in the previously discussed case of the site at Barrow, Alaska. Usually, however, the archaeologist will have to survey a region in order to plot the sites available for excavation. A survey can be made from the ground, but more and more use is made of remote sensing techniques, many of them byproducts of space-age technology. Aerial photographs have been used by archaeologists since the 1920s and are widely used today. Among other things, such photographs were used for the discovery and interpretation of the huge geometric and zoomorphic (from Latin for "animal-shaped") markings on the coastal desert of Peru. More recently, use of high-resolution aerial photographs, including satellite imagery, resulted in the astonishing discovery of over 500 miles of prehistoric roadways connecting sites in the four-corners region of the United States (where Arizona, New Mexico, Colorado, and Utah meet) with other sites in ways that archaeologists had never suspected. This discovery led to a new understanding of prehistoric Pueblo Indian economic, social, and political organization. Evidently, large centers in this region gov-

Some archaeological features are best seen from the air, such as this figure of a hummingbird made in prehistoric times on the Nazca Desert of Peru.

Unusually low water levels revealed these remains of a 1,700-year-old fish weir, for trapping fish, in Maine. Until their discovery, submersion beneath the water preserved the lower portions of wooden stakes.

erned a number of smaller satellite communities, mobilized labor for large public works, and saw to the distribution of goods over substantial distances.

More obvious sites, such as the human-made mounds or "tells" of the Middle East, are easier to spot from the ground, for the country is open. But it is more difficult to locate ruins, even those that are well above ground, where there is a heavy forest cover. Thus, the discovery of archaeological sites is strongly affected by local geography and climate.

Some sites may be spotted by changes in vegetation. For example, the topsoil of ancient storage and refuse pits is often richer in organic matter than that of the surrounding areas, and so it grows distinctive vegetation. At Tikal, an ancient Maya site in Guatemala (Chapter 12), breadnut trees usually grow near the remains of ancient houses, so that archaeologists looking for the remains of houses at this site can use these trees as guideposts. In England, a wooden monument of the Stonehenge type at Darrington, Wiltshire, was discovered from an aerial photograph showing a distinct pattern of vegetation growing where the ancient structure once stood.

On the ground, sites can be spotted by **soil marks,** or stains, showing up on the surface of recently plowed fields. From soil marks, many Bronze Age burial mounds were discovered in northern Hertfordshire and southwestern Cambridgeshire, England. The mounds hardly rose out of the ground, yet each was circled at its core by chalky soil marks. Sometimes the very presence of certain chalky rock is significant.

Documents, maps, and oral history (also known as "ethnohistorical data") are also useful to the archaeologist. Heinrich Schliemann, the famous and controversial 19th-century German amateur archaeologist, was led to the discovery of the ancient city of Troy, after reading the account of the Trojan War in the *Iliad* by the ancient Greek poet Homer. He assumed that the city described by Homer as Ilium was really Troy. Place-names and local lore often are an indication that an archaeological site is to be found in the area. Archaeological surveys therefore often depend upon amateur collectors and local people who are usually familiar with history of the land.

Sometimes natural processes, such as soil erosion or droughts, expose sites or fossils. In eastern North America for example, many prehistoric Indian shell refuse mounds known as shell **middens** have been exposed by erosion along coastlines or river banks. A whole village of stone huts was exposed at Skara Brae in Scotland's Orkney Islands by the action of wind as it blew away sand. And during the long drought of 1853 to 1854, the well-preserved remains of a prehistoric village were exposed when the water level of Lake Zurich, Switzerland, fell dramatically.

soil marks Stains that show up on the surface of recently plowed fields that reveal an archaeological site.
middens A refuse or garbage disposal area in an archaeological site.

MEDIATREK

To learn about the discovery of Ötzi the "Ice Man" and the mystery of his death, visit the Discovery Channel's Web site. Follow filmmakers as they trace the evidence, and cast your vote on the cause of Ötzi's death by going to MediaTrek 4.2 on the companion Web site or CD-ROM.

Newfound sites or fossils may engender considerable controversy. In 1991, the mummified body of a man who lived 5,200 years ago was found in the Tyrolean Alps, where it had been released by glacial melting. Both the Italian and the Austrian governments felt they had legitimate claims on this rare find, and they mounted legal, geographic, and taphonomic arguments for housing the body in their country. These arguments continued as the specimen, just released from the ice, began to thaw. The controversy surrounding "Kennewick Man" the 9,300-year-old skeleton that was dislodged by the Columbia River in Washington in 1996, is discussed in this chapter's Biocultural Connection.

Though natural forces sometimes expose fossils and sites, human physical and cultural remains are more often accidentally discovered in the course of some other human activity. In Chapter 2 we saw how the discovery of fossils of extinct animals in Europe from construction and quarrying played a role in the development of evolutionary theory. Similarly, limestone quarrying at a variety of sites in South Africa early in the 20th century led to the discovery of the earliest human-like fossils from millions of years ago (see Chapter 6). Smaller scale disturbances of earth such as plowing sometimes turn up bones, fragments of pots, and other archaeological objects.

So frequently do construction projects uncover archaeological remains that in many countries, including the United States, construction projects require government approval in order to ensure the identification and protection of archaeological remains. Archaeological surveys in the United States are now routinely

Biocultural Connection

Kennewick Man

"The Ancient One," or the "Kennewick Man," refers to the 9,300-year-old skeletal remains that were found in 1996 below the surface of Lake Wallula, part of the Columbia River, in Kennewick, Washington. This discovery has been the center of increasing controversy since it was made: Who owns these human remains? Who can determine what shall be done with them? This particular conflict involves three major parties.

Because the skeleton was found on a location for which the U.S. Army Corps of Engineers is responsible, this federal agency first took possession of the remains. Appealing to a new federal law, the Native American Graves Protection and Repatriation Act of 1990, a nearby American Indian group named the Confederated Tribes of the Umatilla Indian Reservation (representing the region's Umatilla, Cayuse, and Walla Walla nations) claimed the remains. Because Kennewick Man was found within their ancestral homeland, they argue that they are "culturally affiliated" with the individual they refer to as "The Ancient One." Viewing these human bones as belonging to an ancestor, they wish to return them to the earth in a respectful ceremony.

This claim was challenged in federal court by a group of scientists, including some archaeologists and biological anthropologists. They view these human remains, among the oldest ever discovered in the Western hemisphere, as scientifically precious, with potential to shed light on the earliest population movements in the Americas. By means of DNA analysis, for instance, these scientists expect to determine possible prehistoric linkages between this individual and ancient human remains found elsewhere, including Asia. Moreover, scientific analysis may determine whether there actually exists any biological connection between these remains and currently living Native peoples, including individuals residing on the Umatilla Indian Reservation. Fearing the loss of a unique scientific specimen, they have filed a lawsuit in federal court to prevent reburial before these bones are researched and analyzed. Their legal challenge is not based on "cultural affiliation," which is a very difficult concept when it concerns such ancient human remains, but focuses on the fact that the region's Native peoples cannot prove they are direct lineal descendants. Unless such ties have been objectively established, they argue, Kennewick Man should be released for scientific study.

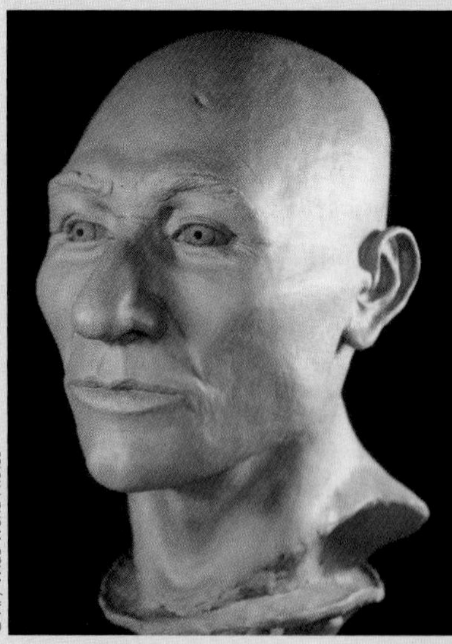

It is unlikely that this complex case will soon be resolved. Conflicting worldviews continue to stir this controversy.

Cultural Resource Management

In June 1979, on a knoll next to a river not far from Lake Champlain, a survey crew working for Peter A. Thomas of the University of Vermont's Consulting Archaeology Program discovered archaeological materials unlike any found before in the region. The following June, Thomas returned to the site with a crew of five in order to excavate a portion of it. What they found were the remains of an 8,000-year-old hunting-and-fishing camp that had been occupied for up to a few months in the spring or fall by perhaps one or two families. From the site they recovered a distinctive tool inventory never recognized before, as well as data related to hunting and fishing subsistence practices, butchery or hide processing, cooking, tool manufacture, and a possible shelter. Because many archaeologists had previously believed the region to be devoid of human occupation 8,000 years ago, recovery of these data was especially important.

What sets this work apart from traditional archaeological research is that it was conducted as part of cultural resource management activities required by state and federal laws to preserve important aspects of the country's prehistoric and historic heritage. In this case, the Vermont Agency of Transportation planned to replace an inadequate highway bridge with a new one. Because the project was partially funded by the U.S. government, steps had to be taken to identify and protect any significant prehistoric or historic resources that might be adversely affected. To do so, the Vermont Agency of Transportation hired Thomas—first to see if such resources existed in the project area, and then to retrieve data from the endangered portions of the one site that was found. As a result, an important contribution was made to our knowledge of the prehistory of northeastern North America.

Since passage of the Historic Preservation Act of 1966, the National Environmental Policy Act of 1969, and the Archaeological and Historical Preservation Act of 1974, the field of cultural resource management has flourished. Today, most archaeological fieldwork in the United States is carried out as cultural resource management. Consequently, many archaeologists are employed by such agencies as the Army Corps of Engineers, the National Park Service, the U.S. Forest Service, and the U.S. Soil and Conservation Service to assist in the preservation, restoration, and salvage of archaeological resources. Archaeologists are also employed by state historic preservation agencies. Finally, they do a considerable amount of consulting work for engineering firms to help them prepare environmental impact statements. Some of these archaeologists, like Thomas, operate out of universities and colleges, while others are on the staffs of independent consulting firms. ■ ■ ■

carried out as part of the environmental review process for federally funded or licensed construction projects (see Anthropology Applied).

Excavation

Before archaeologists or paleoanthropologists plan an excavation, they must ask the question, "Why are we digging?" Then they must consider the amount of time, money, and labor that can be committed to the enterprise. The recovery of archaeological and fossil material long ago ceased to be the province of the enlightened amateur, as it was when any enterprising collector went out to dig for the sake of finding treasures. A modern excavation is carefully planned and rigorously conducted; it should not only shed light on the human past but should also help us to understand cultural and evolutionary processes in general. It also needs to be conducted with sensitivity to the questions of ownership of the materials that are found.

Archaeological Excavation

Once a site likely to contribute to the solution of some important research problem is located, the next step is to plan and carry out excavation. To begin, the land is cleared, and the places to be excavated are plotted as a **grid system.** The surface of the site is divided into squares of equal size, and each square is numbered and marked with stakes. Each object found may then be located precisely in the square from which it came. (Remember, in archaeology, context is everything!) The starting point of a grid system may be a large rock, the edge of a stone wall, or an iron rod sunk into the ground. The starting point is located precisely in three dimensions and is known as the reference or **datum point.** At a large site covering several square miles, the plotting may be done in terms of individual structures, numbered according to the square of a "giant grid" in which they are found (Figure 4.1). In a gridded site, each square is dug separately with great care. Trowels are used to scrape the soil, and screens are used to sift all the loose soils so that even the smallest artifacts, such as flint chips or beads, are recovered.

grid system A system for recording data in three dimensions from an archaeological excavation.
datum point The starting, or reference, point for a grid system.

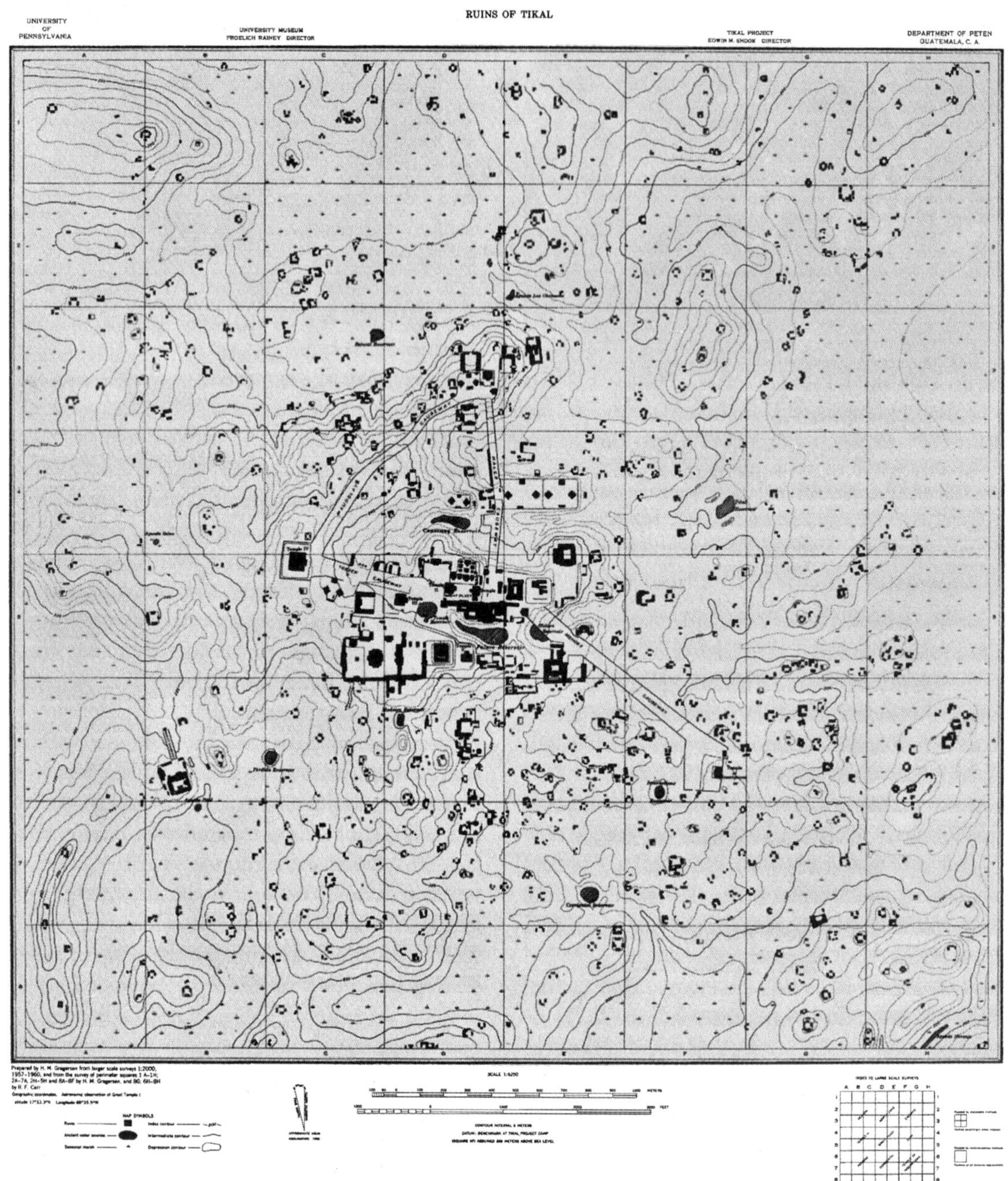

FIGURE 4.1

At large sites covering several square miles, a giant grid is constructed, as shown in this map of the center of the ancient Maya city of Tikal. Each square of the grid is one-quarter of a square kilometer; individual structures are numbered according to the square in which they are found. The temple shown on page 100 can be located near the center of the map, on the east edge of the Great Plaza.

A technique employed when looking for very fine objects, such as fish scales or very small bones, is called **flotation.** Flotation consists of immersing soil in water, causing the particles to separate. Some will float, others will sink to the bottom, and the remains can be easily retrieved. If the site is **stratified**—that is, the remains lie in layers one upon the other—each layer, or stratum, will be dug separately. Each layer, having been laid down during a particular span of time, will contain artifacts deposited at the same time and belonging to the same culture. Culture change can be traced through the order in which artifacts were deposited—deeper layers reveal older artifacts. But, archaeologists Frank Hole and Robert F. Heizer suggest,

flotation An archeological technique employed to recover very tiny objects by immersion of soil samples in water to separate heavy from light particles.
stratified Layered; said of archaeological sites where the remains lie in layers, one upon another.

© William A. Haviland

To recover very small objects easily missed in excavation, archaeologists routinely screen the earth they remove.

Because of difficulties in analyzing stratigraphy, archaeologists must use the greatest caution in drawing conclusions. Almost all interpretations of time, space, and culture contexts depend on stratigraphy. The refinements of laboratory techniques for analysis are wasted if archaeologists cannot specify the stratigraphic position of their artifacts.[2]

[2]Hole, F., & Heizer, R. F. (1969). *An introduction to prehistoric archeology* (p. 113). New York: Holt, Rinehart & Winston.

If no stratification is present, then the archaeologist digs by arbitrary levels. Each square must be dug so that its edges and profiles are straight; walls between squares are often left standing to serve as visual correlates of the grid system.

Excavation of Fossils

Although fossil excavating is similar to archaeological excavation, some key differences exist. The paleoanthropologist must be particularly skilled in the techniques of geology, or have ready access to geological expertise, because a fossil is of little value unless its place in the

© William A. Haviland

This photo shows a section excavated through a building at the ancient Maya site of Tikal and illustrates stratigraphy. Inside the building's base are the remains of walls and floors for earlier buildings. Oldest are the innermost and deepest walls and floors. As time wore on, the Maya periodically demolished upper portions of older buildings, the remains of which were buried beneath new construction.

sequence of rocks that contain it can be determined. In addition, the paleoanthropologist must be able to identify the fossil-laden rocks, their deposition, and other geological details. In order to provide all the necessary expertise, paleoanthropological expeditions these days generally are made up of teams of experts in various fields in addition to physical anthropology. Surgical skill and caution are required to remove a fossil from its burial place without damage. An unusual combination of tools and materials is usually contained in the kit of the paleoanthropologist—pickaxes, dental tools, enamel coating, burlap for bandages, and sculpting plaster.

To remove newly discovered bones, the paleoanthropologist begins uncovering the specimen, using pick and shovel for initial excavation, then small camel-hair brushes and dental picks to remove loose and easily detachable debris surrounding the bones. Once the entire specimen has been uncovered (a process that may take days of back-breaking, patient labor), the bones are covered with shellac and tissue paper to prevent cracking and damage during further excavation and handling.

Both the fossil and the earth immediately surrounding it, or the matrix, are prepared for removal as a single block. The bones and matrix are cut out of the earth (but not removed), and more shellac is applied to the entire block to harden it. The bones are covered with burlap bandages dipped in plaster. Then the entire block is enclosed in more plaster and burlap bandages, perhaps splinted with tree branches, and allowed to dry overnight. After it has hardened, the entire block is carefully removed from the earth, ready for packing and transport to a laboratory. Before leaving the discovery area, the investigator makes a thorough sketch map of the terrain and pinpoints the find on geological maps to aid future investigators.

State of Preservation of Archaeological and Fossil Evidence

The results of excavation depend upon the nature of the remains as much as upon the excavator's digging skills. Inorganic materials such as stone and metal are more resistant to decay than organic ones such as wood and bone. Sometimes the anthropologist discovers an assemblage—a collection of artifacts—made of durable inorganic materials, such as stone tools, and traces of organic ones long since decomposed, such as woodwork (Figure 4.2), textiles, or food.

In addition to climate and local geological conditions, cultural practices also play a role in the state of preservation. For example, the cultural practice of burying the dead, appearing about 100,000 years ago in human evolutionary history, dramatically changed the fossil record (see Chapter 9). From this point on, complete skeletons are preserved together with evidence about burial practices. By contrast, among the early fossils, only a few complete specimens exist. Preservation of an entire fossil skeleton required precise and unusual conditions, such as still water in which a dead organism could be completely covered with sediment. Otherwise, normal processes scattered the bones.

The 1.6 million-year-old adolescent *Homo erectus* boy (see Chapter 8) is the only nearly complete skeleton and skull from early human evolution. Closer to the present, burials yield an abundance of information about past cultures. For example, the ancient Egyptians believed that eternal life could be achieved only if the dead person were buried with his or her worldly possessions. Hence, their tombs are usually filled with a wealth of artifacts even including the skeletons of other humans owned by dynastic rulers. Ancient Egyptian burial practices selec-

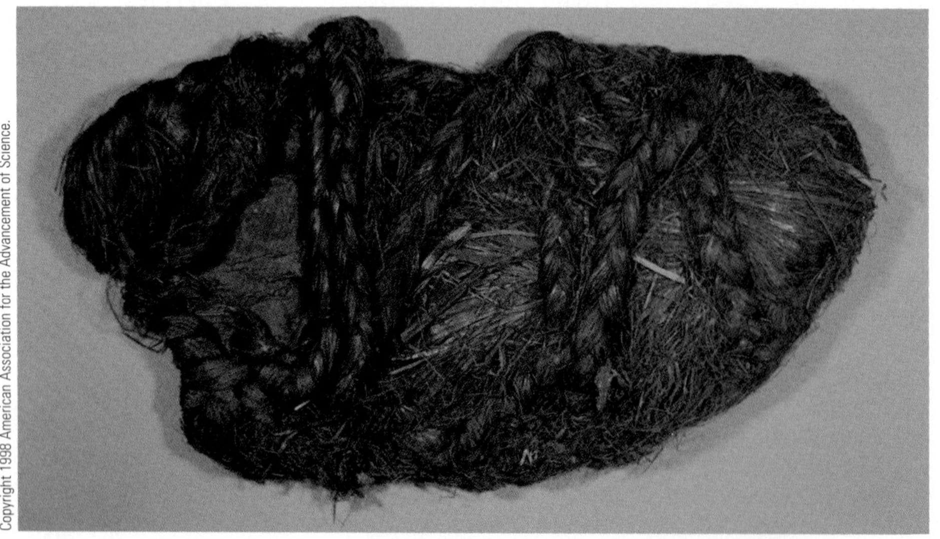

This sandal made of plant fibers is over 8,000 years old, making it North America's oldest known footwear. In most soils, objects made of such materials would have long since decayed. This one survived only because of the dry condition of the cave (Arnold Research Cave in Missouri) in which it was found.

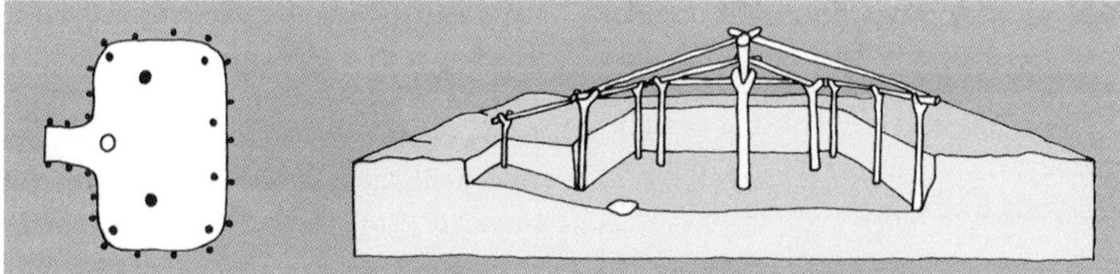

FIGURE 4.2
Although the wooden posts of a house may have long since decayed, their positions may still be marked by discoloration of the soil. The plan shown on the left—of an ancient posthole pattern and depression at Snaketown, Arizona—permits the hypothetical house reconstruction on the right.

tively preserve more information about the elite members of society than the average individual.

MEDIATREK
To learn about everything from virtual excavations in Mesoamerica and Central Asia to the fabulous Egyptian galleries, visit the award-winning Web site of the University of Pennsylvania's Museum of Archaeology and Anthropology by going to MediaTrek 4.3 on the companion Web site or CD-ROM.

In part, our knowledge of ancient Egyptian culture stems not only from their burial practices but from the effects of climate and soil on the state of preservation. Under favorable climatic conditions, even the most perishable objects may survive over vast periods of time. For example, the earliest Egyptian burials consisting of shallow pits in the sand often yield well-preserved corpses. Because these bodies were buried long before mummification was ever practiced, their preservation can only be the result of rapid desiccation, or complete drying out, in the warm desert climate. The elaborate tombs of the rulers of dynastic Egypt often contain wooden furniture, textiles, flowers, and papyri (writing scrolls) barely touched by time, seemingly as fresh looking as they were when deposited in the tomb as long as 5,000 years ago—a consequence of the dryness of the atmosphere.

The dryness of certain caves is also a factor in the preservation of **coprolites,** the scientific term for fossilized human or animal feces. Coprolites provide information on prehistoric diet and health. From the analysis of elements preserved in coprolites such as seeds, insect skeletons, and tiny bones from fish or amphibians, archaeologists and paleoanthropologists can directly determine diet in the past. This information, in turn, can shed light on overall health. Because many sources of food are available only in certain seasons, it is even possible to tell the time of year in which the food was eaten.

Certain climates can obliterate all evidence of organic remains. Maya ruins found in the tropical rain forests of Mesoamerica (the geographical area including southern Mexico and northern Central America) are often in a state of collapse—notwithstanding that many are massive structures of stone—as a result of the pressure exerted upon them by the heavy forest vegetation. The rain and humidity soon destroy almost all traces of woodwork, textiles, or basketry. Fortunately, impressions of these artifacts can sometimes be preserved in plaster, and some objects made of wood or plant fibers are depicted in stone carvings and pottery figurines. Thus, even in the face of complete decay of organic substances, something may still be learned about them.

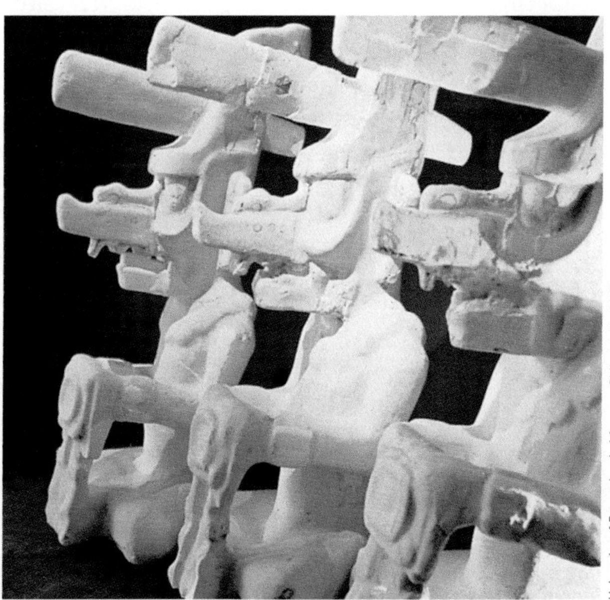

At the Maya site of Tikal, these manikin sceptre figures originally made of wood were recovered from a king's tomb by pouring plaster into a cavity in the soil, left when the original organic material decayed.

coprolites Preserved fecal material providing evidence of the diet and health of past organisms.

Sorting Out the Evidence

It cannot be stressed too strongly that the knowledge that can be derived from physical and cultural remains diminishes dramatically if an accurate and detailed record of the excavations is not kept. As one eminent anthropologist has put it:

> The fundamental premise of excavation is that all digging is destructive, even that done by experts. The archaeologist's primary responsibility, therefore, is to record a site for posterity as it is dug because there are no second chances.[3]

Excavation records include a scale map of all the features, the stratification of each excavated square, a description of the exact location and depth of every artifact or bone unearthed, and photographs and scale drawings of the objects. This is the only way archaeological evidence can later be pieced together so as to arrive at a plausible reconstruction of a culture. Although the archaeologist or paleoanthropologist may be interested only in certain kinds of remains, every aspect of the site must be recorded, whether it is relevant to the particular investigation or not, because such evidence may be useful to others and would otherwise be permanently lost. In sum, archaeological sites are nonrenewable resources. The disturbance of the arrangement of artifacts, even by proper excavation is permanent.

Looting of sites for personal profit can also cause permanent loss—not only of artifacts but of the sites that held them. Looting has long been a threat to the archaeological record. Today, looting has become a high-tech endeavor. Avid collectors and fans of archaeological sites unwittingly aid looting activity through sharing detailed knowledge about site and artifact location over the Internet. The Internet has also provided a market for artifacts.

After photographs and scale drawings are made, the materials recovered from excavation sites are processed in the laboratory. In the case of fossils, the block in which they have been removed from the field is cut open, and the fossil is separated from the matrix. Like the initial removal from the earth, this is a long, painstaking job. This task may be done with hammer and chisel, dental drills, rotary grinders, or pneumatic chisels, and, in the case of very small pieces, with awls and tiny needles under a microscope. Chemicals, such as hydrochloric and hydrofluoric acids, are also used in the separation process to dissolve the surrounding matrix. Often the discovery of new fossils is announced several years following the original excavation.

Once the artifact or fossil has been freed from the surrounding matrix, a variety of other laboratory methods come into play. For example, dental specimens are frequently analyzed under the microscope to determine patterns of tooth wear that may provide clues about diet in the past. Specimens are now regularly scanned using computed tomography (CT scans) to analyze structural

[3]Fagan, B. M. (1995). *People of the earth* (8th ed., p. 19). New York: HarperCollins.

© Andrew Lawler/Science Magazine

© Christophe Calais/ In Visu/ Corbis

VISUAL COUNTERPOINT Looting can occur either before or after artifacts are retrieved through excavation. This ancient Sumerian Tell in Iraq has been so extensively looted that it resembles a moonscape. Similarly, thousands of objects were looted from Iraq's National Archaeology Museum in March 2003 in the chaos brought about by war. In either case, such looting destroys irreplaceable evidence about human cultural history.

Though these 160,000-year-old fossil specimens of two adults and one child were first unearthed in Ethiopia in 1997, their discovery was not announced until 2003. Scientists completed the excavation, reconstructed, and analyzed the remains in the laboratory during the interim.

details of the bone. Imprints or **endocasts** of the insides of skulls are taken to determine the size and shape of ancient brains.

The genetics revolution has carried over even to fossil analyses. Anthropologists extract genetic material from skeletal remains in order to perform DNA comparisons between the specimen, other fossils, and living people. Small fragments of DNA are amplified or copied repeatedly using **polymerase chain reaction (PCR)** technology to provide a sufficient amount of material to perform these analyses. However, unless DNA is preserved in a stable material such as amber, it will decay over time. Therefore, analyses of DNA extracted from specimens earlier than about 50,000 years ago are increasingly unreliable due to the decay of DNA.

Archaeologists, as a rule of thumb, plan on at least 3 hours of laboratory work for each hour of fieldwork. In the lab, artifacts that have been recovered must first be cleaned and catalogued—often a tedious and time-consuming job—before they are ready for analysis. From the shapes of the artifacts as well as from the traces of manufacture and wear, archaeologists can usually determine their function. For example, the Russian archaeologist S. A. Semenov devoted many years to the study of prehistoric technology. In the case of a flint tool used as a scraper, he was able to determine, by examining the wear patterns of the tool under a microscope, that the prehistoric individuals who used it began to scrape from right to left and then scraped from left to right, and in so doing avoided straining the muscles of the hand.[4] From the work of Semenov and others, we now know that right-handed individuals made most stone tools preserved in the archaeological record, a fact that has implications for brain structure (see also Figure 4.3).

Analysis of vegetable and animal remains provides clues about the environment and how human activities

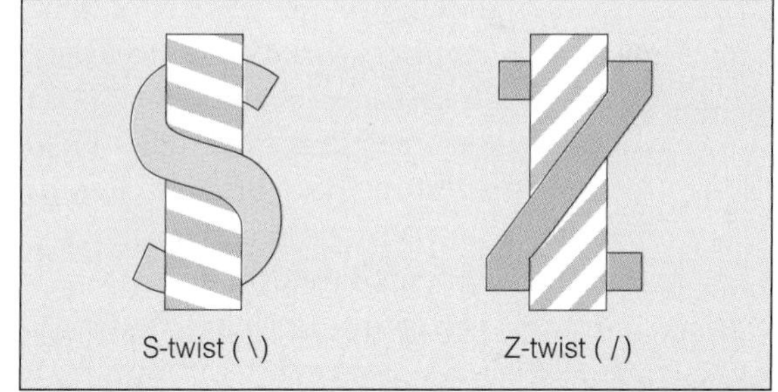

FIGURE 4.3

In northern New England, prehistoric pottery was often decorated by impressing the damp clay with a cord-wrapped stick. Examination of cord impressions reveals that coastal people twisted fibers used to make cordage to the left (Z-twist), while those living inland did the opposite (S-twist). The nonfunctional differences reflect motor habits so deeply ingrained as to seem completely natural to the cordage makers. From this, we may infer two distinctively different populations.

endocast A cast of the inside of a skull; helps determine the size and shape of the brain.

polymerase chain reaction (PCR) A technique for amplifying or creating multiple copies of fragments of DNA so that it can be studied in the laboratory.

[4]Semenov, S. A. (1964). *Prehistoric technology.* New York: Barnes & Noble.

changed with the seasons. For example, we know that the people responsible for Serpent Mound in Ontario, Canada (a mound having the form of a serpent, consisting of burials and discarded shells), were there only in the spring and early summer, when they came to collect shellfish and perform their annual burial rites. Apparently they moved elsewhere at the beginning of summer to pursue other seasonal subsistence activities. Archaeologists have inferred that the mound was unoccupied in winter, because this is the season when deer shed their antlers, yet no deer antlers were found on the site. Nor were duck bones found, and so archaeologists conclude that the mound was also unoccupied in the fall, when ducks stopped on their migratory route southward. Knowledge about living plants and animals in a region thus allow archaeologists to reconstruct patterns of seasonal use.

Bioarchaeology, which seeks to understand past cultures through analysis of skeletal remains, is a growing area within anthropology that exemplifies a biocultural approach. Analysis of human skeletal material provides important insights into ancient peoples' diets, gender roles, social status, and patterns of activity. At the ancient Maya city of Tikal, for example, analysis of human skeletons showed that elite members of society had access to better diets than lower ranking members of society, allowing them to reach their full growth potential. Gender roles in a given society can be assessed through skeletons as well. In fully preserved adult skeletons, the sex of the deceased individual can be determined with a high accuracy, allowing for comparisons of male and female life expectancy, mortality, health status, and differential treatment after death. These analyses provide clues to the social roles of men and women in past societies.

Recently, skeletal analyses have become more difficult to carry out, especially in the United States, as Native American communities request the return of skeletons from archaeological excavations for reburial as required by federal law. Archaeologists find themselves in a quandary over this requirement: As scientists, they know the importance of the information that can be gleaned from studies of human skeletons, but as anthropologists, they are bound to respect the feelings of those whose ancestors the skeletons represent. Currently (as illustrated in the Original Study in this chapter), archaeologists are consulting with representatives of Native American communities to work out procedures agreeable to both parties.

relative dating In archaeology and paleoanthropology, designating an event, object, or fossil as being older or younger than another.
absolute or chronometric dating In archaeology and paleoanthropology, dates for archaeological materials based on solar years, centuries, or other units of absolute time.

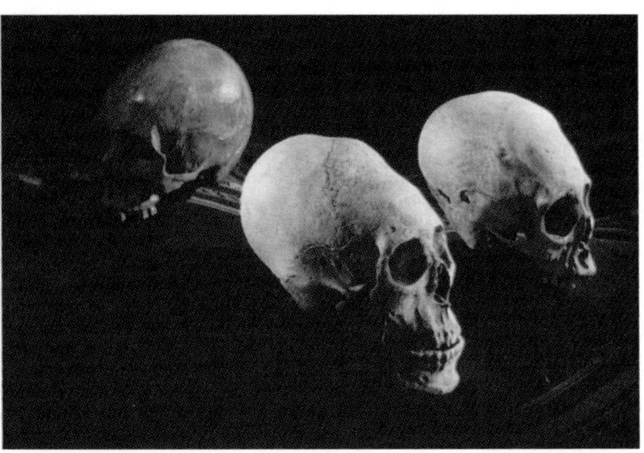

Skulls from peoples of the Tiwanaku Empire who tightly bound the skulls of their children. The shape of the skull distinguished people from various parts of the empire.

Dating the Past

With accurate and detailed records of their excavations in hand, archaeologists and paleoanthropologists are able to deal with a question crucial to their research: the question of age. As we have seen, analysis of physical and cultural remains is dependent on knowledge about the age of the artifacts or specimens. How, then, are the materials retrieved from excavations reliably dated? Because archaeologists and paleoanthropologists deal so often with peoples and events in times far removed from our own, the calendar of historic times is of little use to them. Therefore, they must rely on two kinds of dating: "relative" and "absolute." **Relative dating** consists simply of finding out if an event or object is younger or older than another. Relative dating is useful within a single site, but must be tied to an **"absolute"** or **chronometric** date to make cross-site comparisons. Chronometric (from the Latin for "measuring time") methods provide actual dates based upon solar years. For two reasons, chronometric dates are calculated in "years before the present" rather than by the Gregorian calendar—because the time span for dating the past is so great and to avoid privileging a single (though dominant) calendar.

Many relative and chronometric techniques are available. However many of these techniques are applicable only for certain time spans and in certain environmental contexts (Table 4.1). Bear in mind also that each of the chronometric dating techniques also has a margin of error. Ideally, archaeologists and paleoanthropologists try to utilize as many methods as appropriate, given the materials available to work with and the funds at their disposal. By doing so, they significantly reduce the risk of error. Several of the most frequently employed dating techniques are discussed below.

TABLE 4.1 ABSOLUTE AND RELATIVE DATING METHODS USED BY ARCHAEOLOGISTS AND PALEOANTHROPOLOGISTS

Dating Method	Time Period	Method's Process	Drawbacks
Stratigraphy	Relative only	Based on the law of superposition, which states that lower layers or strata are older than higher layers.	Site specific; natural forces, such as earthquakes, and human activity, such as burials, disturb stratigraphic relationships.
Fluorine analysis	Relative only	Compares the amount of fluorine from surrounding soil absorbed by specimens after deposition.	Site specific.
Faunal and floral series	Relative only	Sequencing remains into relative chronological order based on an evolutionary sequence established in another region with reliable absolute dates. Called palynology when done with pollen grains.	Dependent upon known relationships established elsewhere.
Seriation	Relative only	Sequencing cultural remains into relative chronological order based on stylistic features.	Dependent upon known relationships established elsewhere.
Dendrochronology	About 3,000 years B.P. maximum	Compares tree growth rings preserved in a site with a tree of known age.	Requires ancient trees of known age.
Radiocarbon	Accurate < 50,000 B.P.	Compares the ratio of radioactive ^{14}C (with a half-life of 5,730 years) to stable ^{12}C in organic material.	Increasingly inaccurate when assessing remains from greater than 50,000 years ago.
Potassium argon (K-Ar)	> 200,000 B.P.	Compares the amount of radioactive potassium (^{40}K with a half-life of 1.3 billion years) to stable argon (^{40}Ar).	Requires volcanic ash; requires cross-checking due to contamination from atmospheric argon.
Amino acid racemization	40,000–180,000 B.P.	Compares the change in the number of proteins in a right- vs. left-sided three-dimensional structure.	Amino acids leached out from soil variably cause error.
Thermoluminescence	Possibly up to 200,000 B.P.	Measures the amount of light given off due to radioactivity when sample heated to high temperatures.	Technique developed for recent materials such as Greek pottery; not clear how accurate the dates will be for older remains.
Electron spin resonance	Possibly up to 200,000 B.P.	Measures the resonance of trapped electrons in a magnetic field.	Works with tooth enamel—not yet developed for bone; problems with accuracy.
Fission track	Wide range of times	Measures the tracks left in crystals by uranium as it decays; good cross-check for K-Ar technique.	Useful for dating crystals only.
Paleomagnetic reversals	Wide range of times	Measures orientation of magnetic particles in stones and links them to whether magnetic field of earth pulled toward the north or south during their formation.	Large periods of normal or reversed magnetic orientation require dating by some other method; some smaller events known to interrupt the sequence.
Uranium series	40,000–180,000	Measures the amount of uranium decaying in cave sites.	Large error range.

Some ancient societies devised precise ways of recording dates that archaeologists have been able to correlate with our own calendar. Here is the tomb of an important ruler, Stormy Sky, at the ancient Maya city of Tikal. The glyphs painted on the wall give the date of the burial in the Maya calendar, which is the same as March 18, A.D. 457, in the Gregorian calendar.

Methods of Relative Dating

Of the many relative dating techniques available, **stratigraphy** is probably the most reliable. Stratigraphy is based on the simple principle that the oldest layer, or stratum, was deposited first (it is the deepest) whereas the newest layer was deposited last (in undisturbed situations, it lies at the top). Similarly, archaeological evidence is usually deposited in chronological order. The lowest stratum contains the oldest artifacts and/or fossils, whereas the uppermost stratum contains the most recent ones. Thus, even in the absence of precise dates, one knows the *relative* age of objects in one stratum compared with the ages of those in other strata. Defining the stratigraphy of a given site can be complicated by geological activities such as earthquakes that shift the position of stratigraphic layers.

> ***stratigraphy*** In archaeology and paleoanthropology, the most reliable method of relative dating by means of strata.
> ***fluorine dating*** In archaeology or paleoanthropology, a technique for relative dating based on the fact that the amount of fluorine in bones is proportional to their age.
> ***seriation*** Technique for putting groups of objects into a relative sequence
> ***palynology*** In archaeology and paleoanthropology, a method of relative dating based on changes in fossil pollen over time.

Another method of relative dating is the **fluorine** method. It is based on the fact that the amount of fluorine deposited in bones is proportional to the amount of time they have been in the earth. The oldest bones contain the greatest amount of fluorine and vice versa. The fluorine test is useful in dating bones that cannot be ascribed with certainty to any particular stratum. A shortcoming of this method is that the amount of naturally occurring fluorine is not constant, but varies from region to region making cross-site comparisons of fluorine values invalid. This method was vital for uncovering the infamous Piltdown hoax in which a human skull and orangutan jaw were combined and placed in the earth as false evidence for human evolution (see Chapter 6).

Relative dating can also be done by establishing sequences of plant, animal, or even cultural remains. For these methods, the order of appearance of a succession (or series) of plants, animals, or artifacts provides relative dates for a site based on a series established in another area. An example of **seriation** based on cultural artifacts is the Stone-Bronze-Iron Age series established by prehistorians (see Chapter 12). Within a given region, sites containing artifacts made of iron are generally more recent than sites containing only stone tools. In well-investigated culture areas, series have even been developed for particular styles of pottery.

Similar inferences are made with animal or faunal series. For example, very early North American Indian sites have yielded the remains of mastodons and mammoths—animals now extinct—and on this basis the sites can be dated to a time before these animals died out, roughly 10,000 years ago. For dating some of the earliest African hominin fossils, faunal series have been developed in regions where accurate chronometric dates can be established. These series can then used to establish relative sequences in other regions. Similar series have been established for plants, particularly using grains of pollen. This approach has become known as **palynology.** The kind of pollen found in any geologic stratum depends on the kind of vegetation that existed at the time that stratum was deposited. A site or locality can therefore be dated by determining what kind of pollen was found associated with it. In addition, palynology also helps to reconstruct environments in which prehistoric people lived.

Methods of Chronometric Dating

Chronometric dating methods rely upon advances in the disciplines of chemistry and physics, allowing scientists to calculate the ages of physical and cultural remains. Several methods use naturally occurring radioactive elements that are present either in the remains themselves or in the surrounding soil. One of the most widely used methods of absolute dating is **radiocarbon dating.** This method uses the fact that while they are alive, all organisms absorb radioactive carbon (known as carbon 14 or ^{14}C) as well as ordinary carbon 12 (^{12}C) in proportions identical to those found in the atmosphere. Absorption of ^{14}C ceases at the time of death, and the ratio between the two forms of carbon begins to change as the unstable radioactive element ^{14}C begins to "decay." Each radioactive element decays, or transforms into a stable nonradioactive form, at a specific rate. The amount of time it takes for one-half of the material originally present to decay is expressed as the "half-life." In the case of ^{14}C, it takes 5,730 years for half of the amount of ^{14}C present to decay to stable nitrogen 14. In another 5,730 years (11,460 years total), half of the remaining amount will also decay to nitrogen 14 so that only one-quarter of the original amount of ^{14}C will be present. Thus the age of an organic substance such as charcoal, wood, shell, or bone can be measured through determining the changing proportion of ^{14}C relative to the amount of stable ^{12}C.

Though scientists can measure the amount of radioactive carbon left in even a few milligrams of a given organic substance of a recent specimen, as we get into the more distant past, the amounts of carbon 14 present become so small that it becomes difficult to detect it accurately. The radiocarbon method can adequately date organic materials up to about 50,000 years old, but dates for older material are far less reliable. Of course, one has to be sure that the organic remains were truly contemporaneous with the archaeological materials. For example, charcoal found on a site may have gotten there from a recent forest fire, rather than more ancient activity; or wood used to make something by the people who lived at a site may have been retrieved from some older context.

Because there is always a certain amount of error involved, radiocarbon dates (like all chronometric dating methods) are not as absolute as is sometimes thought. This is why any stated date always has a plus-or-minus ($\pm$) factor attached to it corresponding to one standard deviation above and below the mean value. For example, a date of 5,200 $\pm$ 120 years ago means that there is about a 2 out of 3 chance (or a 67% chance) that the true date falls somewhere between 5,080 and 5,320 radiocarbon years ago. The qualification "radiocarbon years" is used because radiocarbon years are not precisely equivalent to calendar years.

The discovery that radiocarbon years are not precisely equivalent to calendar years was made possible by another method of absolute dating, **dendrochronology.** Originally devised for dating Pueblo Indian sites in the North American Southwest, this method is based on the fact that in the right kind of climate, trees add one (and only one) new growth ring to their trunks every year. The rings vary in thickness, depending upon the amount of rainfall received in a year, so that climatic fluctuation is registered in the growth ring. By taking a sample of wood, such as a beam from a Pueblo Indian house, and by comparing its pattern of rings with those in the trunk of a tree of known age, archaeologists can date the archaeological material. Dendrochronology is applicable only to wooden objects. Furthermore, it can be used only in regions in which trees of great age, such as the giant sequoias and the bristlecone pine, are known to grow. Radiocarbon dating of wood from bristlecone pines dated by dendrochronology allows scientists to correct carbon 14 dates so as to bring them into agreement with calendar dates.

Potassium-argon dating, another commonly used method of absolute dating, is based on a technique similar to that of radiocarbon analysis. Following intense heating, as from a volcanic eruption, radioactive potassium decays at a known rate to form argon—any previously existing argon having been released by the heating of the molten lava. The half-life of radioactive potassium is 1.3 billion years. Deposits that are millions of years old can now be dated by measuring the ratio of potassium to argon in a given rock. Volcanic

radiocarbon dating In archaeology and paleoanthropology, a technique for chronometric dating based on measuring the amount of radioactive carbon (^{14}C) left in organic materials found in archaeological sites.
dendrochronology In archaeology, a method of chronometric dating based on the number of rings of growth found in a tree trunk.
potassium-argon dating In archaeology and paleoanthropology, a technique for chronometric dating that measures the ratio of radioactive potassium to argon in volcanic debris associated with human remains.

© Macduff Everton/Corbis © Royalty-Free/Corbis

VISUAL COUNTERPOINT Through comparing the number of growth rings on tree beams used to build this Pueblo site to trees of known age, this site can be accurately dated. This absolute dating method is called dendrochronology.

debris, such as at Olduvai Gorge and other localities in East Africa, is routinely dated by potassium-argon analysis, indicating when the volcanic eruption occurred. If fossils or artifacts are found sandwiched between layers of volcanic ash, as they are at Olduvai and other sites in East Africa, they can be dated with some precision. As with radiocarbon dates, there are limits to that precision, and potassium-argon dates are always stated with a plus-or-minus margin of error attached. The precision of this method is limited for time periods more recent than about 200,000 years ago.

Though these radiocarbon and potassium-argon methods are extremely valuable, neither technique works well during the time period dating from about 50,000 years ago to about 200,000 years ago. Because this same time period happens to be very important in human evolutionary history, scientists have developed a number of other important methods to obtain accurate dates during this critical period.

One such method, amino acid racemization, is based on the fact that amino acids trapped in organic materials gradually change, or "racemize," after death, from left-handed forms to right-handed forms. Thus, the ratio of left- to right-handed forms should indicate the specimen's age. Unfortunately, in substances like bone, moisture and acids in the soil can leach out the amino acids, thereby introducing a serious source of error. However, ostrich eggshells have proved immune to this problem, the amino acids being so effectively locked up in a tight mineral matrix that they are preserved for thousands of years. Because ostrich eggs were widely used as food, and the shells as containers in Africa and the Middle East, they provide a powerful means of dating sites of the middle part of the Old Stone Age (Paleolithic), between 40,000 and 180,000 years ago.

Electron spin resonance, which measures the number of trapped electrons in bone, and thermoluminescence, which measures the amount of light emitted from a specimen when heated to high temperatures, are two additional methods that have been developed to fill in prehistorical time gaps. Dates derived from these two methods changed the interpretation of key sites in present day Israel vital for reconstructing human origins (see Chapter 9). A few other chronometric techniques rely on the element uranium. Fission track dating, for example, counts radiation damage tracks on mineral crystals. Like amino acid racemization, all these methods have problems: They are complicated and tend to be expensive; many can be carried out only on specific kinds of materials, and some are so new that their reliability is not yet unequivocally established. It is for these reasons that they have not been as widely used as radiocarbon and potassium-argon dating techniques.

Paleomagnetic reversals contribute another interesting dimension to absolute dating methodologies by providing a method to cross-check dates. This method is

In this photo, geologist Carl Swisher orients a rock sample for paleomagnetic dating. This method of dating is based on the fact that the earth's magnetic pole has shifted over time. For example, magnetically charged particles in sediments between 1.8 and 1.6 million years old document a reversal, and fossils found in such sediments can be dated accordingly.

based on the shifting magnetic pole of the earth—the same force that controls the orientation of a compass needle. Today, a compass points to the north because we are in a period defined as the geomagnetic "normal." Over the past several million years, there have been extended periods of time during which the magnetic field of the earth pulled toward the South Pole. Geologists call these periods "geomagnetic reversals." Iron particles in stones will be oriented into positions determined by the dominant magnetic pole at the time of their formation, allowing scientists to derive broad ranges of dates for them. Human evolutionary history contains a geomagnetic reversal starting 5.2 million years ago that ended 3.4 million years ago, followed by a normal period until 2.6 million years ago; then, a second reversal began, lasting until about 700,000 years ago when the present normal period began. This paleomagnetic sequence can be used to date sites to either normal or reversed periods and can be correlated with a variety of other dating methods to cross-check their accuracy.

Establishment of dates for human physical and cultural remains is a vital part of understanding our past. For example, as paleoanthropologists reconstruct human evolutionary history and the movement of the genus *Homo* out of Africa, dates determine the story told by the bones. In the next chapters we will see that many of the theories about human origins are dependent upon dates. Similarly, as archaeologists dig up material culture, interpretations of the movement and interactions of past peoples depend on dating methods to provide a sequence to the cultural remains.

CHANCE AND THE STUDY OF THE PAST

The archaeological and fossil records are imperfect. Chance circumstances of preservation have determined what has and has not survived the ravages of time. Thus, the biology and culture of our ancestors are reconstructed on the basis of incomplete and possibly unrepresentative samples of physical and cultural remains. The problems are further compounded by the role that chance continues to play in the discovery of prehistoric remains. Remains may come to light due to factors ranging from changing sea level, vegetation, or even a local government's decision to build a highway. In addition, past cultural processes have also shaped the archaeological and fossil record. We know more about the past due to the cultural practice of deliberate burial. We know more about the elite segments of past societies because they have left more material culture behind. However, as archaeologists have shifted their focus from gathering treasures to the reconstruction of human behavior, they now reconstruct a more complete picture of past societies. Similarly, paleoanthropologists no longer simply catalogue fossils; they interpret data about our ancestors in order to reconstruct the biological processes responsible for who we are today. The challenge of reconstructing our past will be met by a continual process of reexamination and modification as anthropologists discover new evidence in the earth, among living people, and in the laboratory leading to new understanding of human origins.

Chapter Summary

- Archaeology and physical anthropology are the two branches of anthropology most involved in the study of the human past. Archaeologists study material remains to describe and explain past human cultures; physical anthropologists called paleoanthropologists study fossil remains to understand the processes at work in human biological evolution. Each specialty contributes to the other's objectives, as well as to its own, and the two share many methods of data recovery.
- Artifacts are objects fashioned or altered by humans, such as a flint chip, a pottery vessel, or even a house. A fossil is any trace of an organism of past geological time that has been preserved in the earth's crust. Fossilization typically involves the hard parts of an organism and may involve preservation in bogs or tar pits, immersion in water, or inclusion in rock deposits. Fossilization is most apt to occur among animals and other organisms that live in or near water because of the likelihood that their corpses will be buried and preserved on sea, lake, and river bottoms. On land, conditions in caves or near active volcanic activity may be conducive to fossilization.
- Physical and cultural remains are not always found together. The earliest fossils are not associated with any archaeological remains before the first stone tools about 2.5 million years ago. Material culture, however, likely existed before this time period but was not preserved. The cultural practice of burial of the dead, beginning about 100,000 years ago, improved the fossil record.
- Irregularities of the ground surface, unusual soil discoloration, and unexpected variations in vegetation type and coloring may indicate the location of an archaeological site. Ethnohistorical data—maps, documents, and oral history—may provide further clues to the location of sites. Sometimes both fossils and archaeological remains are discovered accidentally, for example, in plowing, quarrying, or in building construction.
- Once a site or locality has been selected for excavation, the area is divided and carefully marked with a grid system; the starting point of the dig is called the datum point. Each square within the grid is carefully excavated, and any archaeological or fossil remains are recovered through employment of various tools and screens; for very fine objects, the method of flotation is employed. The location of each artifact must be carefully noted. Once excavated, artifacts and fossils undergo further cleaning and preservation in the laboratory with the use of specialized tools and chemicals.
- The durability of archaeological evidence depends upon climate and the nature of the artifacts. Inorganic materials are more resistant to decay than organic ones. However, given a very dry climate, even organic materials may be well preserved. Warm, moist climates as well as thick vegetation act to decompose organic material quickly, and even inorganic material may suffer from the effects of humidity and vegetation growth. The durability of archaeological evidence is also dependent upon the social customs of ancient people.
- Because excavation in fact destroys a site, archaeologists must maintain thorough records in the form of maps, descriptions, scale drawings, and photographs of every aspect of the excavation. All artifacts must be cleaned and classified before being sent to the laboratory for analysis. Often the shape and markings of artifacts can determine their function, and the analysis of vegetable and animal remains may provide information.
- There are two general approaches to dating archaeological and fossil remains. Relative dating methods determine the age of objects relative to one another and include stratigraphy, based on the position of the artifact or fossil in relation to different layers of soil deposits. The fluorine test is based on the determination of the amount of fluorine deposited in the bones. The analysis of series of floral remains (including palynology), faunal deposits, and cultural remains is also widely employed. Methods of absolute or chronometric dating include dendrochronology, based upon tree rings, radiocarbon analysis, which measures the amount of carbon 14 that remains in organic objects, and potassium-argon analysis, which measures the percentage of radioactive potassium that has decayed to argon in volcanic material. Scientists are working to refine other chronometric dating methods for the critical period between 50,000 and 200,000 years ago that cannot be reliably dated by either carbon 14 or potassium-argon dating. These methods are not as widely used, because of difficulty of application, expense, or (as yet) unproven reliability.

Questions for Reflection

1. The field methods described in this chapter help paleoanthropologists and archaeologists meet the challenge of understanding human origins. Through physical and cultural remains, paleoanthropologists and archaeologists attempt to construct behaviors, worldviews, and even the social systems of past peoples. How can bones and things provide clues about the past?
2. The cultural practice of burial of the dead altered the fossil record and provided valuable insight into the beliefs and practices of past cultures. The same is true today. What beliefs are reflected in the traditions for treatment of the dead in your culture?
3. Controversy has surrounded Kennewick Man since this skeleton eroded from the banks of the Columbia River in Washington in 1996. Scientists and Native American people both feel they have a right to these remains. What kinds of evidence support these differing perspectives? How should this controversy be resolved?
4. Why is dating so important for paleoanthropologists and archaeologists? Would an interpretation of physical or cul-

tural remains change depending upon the date assigned to the remains?

5. How have random events as well as deliberate cultural practices shaped both the fossil and archaeological records? Why do we know more about some places and peoples than others?

Key Terms

Bioarchaeology	Endocasts
Prehistoric	Polymerase chain reaction (PCR)
Artifacts	Relative dating
Material culture	Absolute or chronometric dating
Fossil	Stratigraphy
Taphonomy	Fluorine dating
Soil marks	Seriation
Middens	Palynology
Grid system	Radiocarbon dating
Datum point	Dendrochronology
Flotation	Potassium-argon dating
Stratified	
Coprolites	

Multimedia Review Tools

Companion Web Site

Visit **http://www.wadsworth.com/anthropology_d/** and click on the companion Web site for this textbook to access a wide range of material to aid your study of anthropology. Among the options for self-study in each chapter are learning objectives, flash cards, Internet activities, Web links, InfoTrac College Edition exercises, and practice tests that can be scored and emailed to your instructor.

CD-ROM

The *Doing Anthropology Today* CD-ROM supplied with your textbook provides unique and valuable information designed to enhance your learning experience. This interactive multimedia resource includes video clips, interviews with renowned anthropologists, map and timeline exercises, chapter study quizzes, and much more. *Doing Anthropology Today* will not only help you in achieving your grade goals, but it will also make your learning experience fun and exciting!

Suggested Readings

Fagan, B. M., Beck C., & Silberman, N. A. (1998). *The Oxford companion to archaeology.* New York: Oxford University Press.

This encyclopedia of archaeology and prehistory contains 700 entries written in an engaging style by over 300 experts in the field. Topics range from fossils to historical sites conveying the field's critical transition from an amateur to a scientific discipline.

Feder, K. L. (1999). *Frauds, myths, and mysteries* (3rd ed.). Mountain View, CA: Mayfield.

This very readable book is written to enlighten readers about the many pseudo-scientific and even crackpot theories about past cultures that all too often have been presented to the public as "solid" archaeology.

Joukowsky, M. (1980). *A complete field manual of archaeology: Tools and techniques of fieldwork for archaeologists.* Englewood Cliffs, NJ: Prentice-Hall.

This book, encyclopedic in its coverage, explains for the novice and professional alike all of the methods and techniques used by archaeologists in the field.

Sharer, R. J., & Ashmore, W. (2002). *Archaeology: Discovering our past* (3rd ed.). New York: McGraw-Hill.

One of the best presentations of the body of method, technique, and theory that most archaeologists accept as fundamental to their discipline. The authors confine themselves to the operational modes, guiding strategies, and theoretical orientations of anthropological archaeology in a manner well designed to lead the beginner into the discipline.

Shipman, P. (1981). *Life history of a fossil: An introduction to taphonomy and paleoecology.* Cambridge, MA: Harvard University Press.

In order to understand what a fossil has to tell us, one must know how it came to be where the paleoanthropologist found it (taphonomy). In this book, anthropologist-turned-science writer Pat Shipman explains how animal remains are acted upon and altered from death to fossilization.

Thomas, D. H. (1998). *Archaeology* (3rd ed.). Fort Worth, TX: Harcourt Brace.

Some books tell us how to do archaeology, some tell us what archaeologists have found out, but this one tells us why we do archaeology. It does so in a coherent and thorough way, and Thomas' blend of ideas, quotations, biographies, and case studies makes for interesting reading.

CHAPTER 5

Macroevolution and the Early Primates

CHALLENGE ISSUE

MEETING THE CHALLENGE OF UNDERSTANDING HUMAN ORIGINS REQUIRES US TO TRACE THE EVOLUTIONARY HISTORY OF THE ENTIRE PRIMATE ORDER. A comprehensive view of primate evolution brings us also to a consideration of how paleoanthropologists use fragmentary fossil and geologic data to reconstruct extinct groups. This model of a member of the extinct ape genus *Gigantopithecus,* for example, is based on evidence from jaw bones and teeth found in China combined with the anatomy of living species such as the gorilla. The teeth indicate that a vegetarian ape larger than the gorilla lived in East Asia at about the same time that members of the genus *Homo* began to inhabit the region.

The model was created by Hollywood monster maker Bill Munn and anthropologist Russell Ciochon.

1 What Is Macroevolution?

While microevolution refers to changes in the allele frequencies of populations, macroevolution focuses upon the formation of new species (speciation) and on the evolutionary relationships among groups of species. Speciation may proceed in a branching manner, as when reproductive isolation of populations prevents gene flow between them leading to the formation of separate species. Alternatively, in the absence of isolation, a species may evolve without branching in response to environmental changes. The accumulation of small changes from generation to generation may transform an ancestral species into a new one.

2 When and Where Did the First Primates Appear, and What Were They Like?

Fossil evidence indicates that the earliest primates began to develop around 65 million years ago, when the mass extinction of the dinosaurs opened new ecological opportunities for mammals. By 55 million years ago, primates inhabited North America and Eurasia, which at that time were joined together as the "supercontinent" Laurasia and separated from Africa. The earliest primates were small nocturnal insect eaters adapted to life in the trees.

3 When Did the First Monkeys and Apes Appear, and What Were They Like?

By the late Eocene epoch, about 40 million years ago, diurnal anthropoid primates appeared. Many of the Old World anthropoid species became ground dwellers. By the Miocene epoch (beginning 23.5 million years ago), apes were widespread in Asia, Africa, and Europe. While some of these hominoids were relatively small, others were even larger than present-day gorillas. Sometime between 5 and 8 million years ago, a branch of the African hominoid line became bipedal, beginning the evolutionary line that later produced humans.

Today, humans are the only primate to have a global distribution. We inhabit every continent, including areas as inhospitable as the icy Antarctic or the scorching Sahara desert. This extended geographic range reflects the adaptability of *Homo sapiens*. By comparison, our relatives in the hominoid superfamily live in very circumscribed areas of the Old World tropical rainforest. Chimpanzees, bonobos, and gorillas can be found only in portions of Central and West Africa. Orangutans are limited to the treetops on the Southeast Asian islands of Sumatra and Borneo. Gibbons and siamangs swing through the branches of a variety of Southeast Asian forests.

Such comparisons between humans and the other primates feel natural to biologists and anthropologists today, because they accept that modern humans, apes, and monkeys are descended from the same prehistoric ancestors. However, almost a century and a half ago, when Charles Darwin published *Origin of Species* (1859), this notion was so controversial that Darwin limited himself to a single sentence on the subject. Today, anthropologists, as well as the global scientific community in general, accept that human origins are revealed in the evolutionary history of the primates. We now know that much of who we are, as culture-bearing biological organisms, derives from our mammalian primate heritage.

Although many of the primates discussed in this chapter no longer exist, their descendants, which were reviewed in Chapter 3, now live in South and Central America, Africa, Asia, and Gibraltar at the southern tip of Spain. The successful adaptation of the primates largely reflects their intelligence, a characteristic that provides for behavioral flexibility. Other physical traits, such as stereoscopic vision and a grasping hand, have also been instrumental in the success of the primates.

Why do paleoanthropologists attempt to recreate primate evolutionary history from ancient, fragmentary evidence? The study of these ancestral primates gives us a better understanding of the physical forces that caused these early creatures to evolve into today's primates. Ultimately, the study of these ancient ancestors helps us meet the challenge of understanding human origins. It gives us a fuller knowledge of the processes through which an insect-eating, small-brained mammal evolved into a toolmaker, a thinker, a human being.

macroevolution Evolution above the species level.
speciation The process of formation of new species.
isolating mechanisms Factors that separate breeding populations, thereby preventing gene flow, creating divergent subspecies, and ultimately (if maintained) divergent species.
cladogenesis An evolutionary process in which an ancestral population gives rise to two or more descendant populations that differ from each other.

MACROEVOLUTION AND THE PROCESS OF SPECIATION

While microevolution refers to changes in the allele frequencies of populations, **macroevolution** focuses upon the formation of new species (**speciation**) and on the evolutionary relationships among groups of species. To understand how the primates evolved, we must first look at how the evolutionary forces discussed in Chapter 2 led to macroevolutionary change. As noted in that chapter, the term *species* is usually defined as a population or group of populations that is capable of interbreeding and producing fertile, viable offspring. In other words, species are reproductively isolated. The bullfrogs in one farmer's pond are the same species as those in the neighbor's pond, even though the two populations may never actually interbreed; in theory, they are capable of it if they are brought together. This definition, however, is not altogether satisfactory, because in nature isolated populations may be in the process of evolving into different species, and it is hard to tell exactly when they become biologically distinct without conducting breeding experiments.

Certain factors, known as **isolating mechanisms,** can separate breeding populations and lead to the appearance of new species. Because isolation prevents gene flow, changes that affect the gene pool of one population cannot be introduced into the gene pool of the other. Random mutation may introduce new alleles in one of the isolated populations but not in the other. Genetic drift and natural selection may affect the two populations in different ways. Over time, as the two populations come to differ from each other, speciation occurs in a branching fashion known as **cladogenesis** (Figure 5.1) (from the Greek *klados* meaning "branch" or "shoot").

Some isolating mechanisms are geographical—preventing contact, hence gene flow, between members of separated populations. Biological aspects of organisms can also serve as isolating mechanisms. For example, early miscarriage of the hybrid offspring or sterility of the hybrid offspring, as in the case of closely related species such as horses and donkeys (producing sterile mules), serve as mechanisms to keep populations reproductively isolated from one another.

Isolating mechanisms may also be social rather than physical. Speciation due to this mechanism is particularly common among birds. For example, cuckoos (birds that do not build nests of their own but lay their eggs in other birds' nests) attract mates by mimicking the song of the bird species in whose nests they place their eggs. Thus, cuckoos that are physically capable of mating may be isolated due to differences in courtship song behavior, which effectively isolates them from other cuckoos singing different tunes. Though social rules about marriage might be said to impose reproductive isolation among humans, these social barriers have

Although horses and donkeys (two separate species) can mate and produce live offspring (mules, pictured here), sterility of mules maintains the reproductive isolation of the parental species.

no biological counterpart. For humans, no sufficiently absolute or long-lasting barriers to gene flow exist.

Because speciation is a process, it can occur at various rates. Speciation through the process of adaptive change to the environment as proposed in Darwin's *Origin of Species* is generally considered to occur at a slow rate. In this model, speciation may occur as organisms become more adapted to their environments. Sometimes however, speciation can occur quite rapidly. For example, a genetic mutation, such as one involving a key regulatory gene, can lead to the formation of a new body plan. Such genetic accidents may involve material that is broken off, transposed, or transferred from one chromosome to another. Genes that regulate the growth and development of an organism may have a major effect on its adult form. Scientists have discovered certain key genes called **homeobox genes** that are responsible for large-scale effects on the growth and development of the organism. If a new body plan happens to be adaptive, natural selection will maintain this new form during long periods of time rather than promoting change.

Paleontologists Stephen Jay Gould and Niles Eldred proposed that speciation occurs in a pattern of **punctuated equilibria** or the alternation between periods of rapid

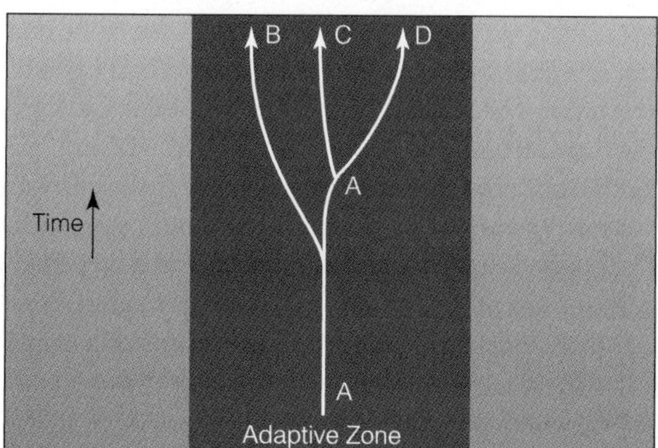

FIGURE 5.1

Cladogenesis occurs as different populations of an ancestral species become reproductively isolated. Through drift and differential selection, the number of descendant species increases.

Sometimes mutations in a single gene can cause reorganization of an organism's body plan. Here the "antennepedia" homeobox gene has caused legs to develop in the place of antennae on the heads of fruitflies.

homeobox gene A gene containing a 180-base-pair segment (the "homeobox") that encodes a protein that regulates DNA expression. Homeobox genes are frequently responsible for major reorganization of body plans in organisms.

punctuated equilibria A model of macroevolutionary change that suggests evolution occurs via long periods of stability or stasis punctuated by periods of rapid change.

© David Bygott/Kybuyu Partners

© Donna Day/Corbis

VISUAL COUNTERPOINT Regulator genes turn other genes on and off, and a mere change in their timing can cause significant evolutionary change. This may have a played a role in differentiating chimps and humans; for example, adult humans retain the flat facial profile of juvenile chimps.

speciation and times of stability. Often, this conception of evolutionary change is contrasted with speciation through adaptation, sometimes known as "Darwinian gradualism." A close look at the genetics and the fossil record indicate that both models of evolutionary change are important. Gould, the champion of the punctuated equilibrium model, describes the importance of the Darwinian approach to change in the following Original Study.

Original Study

The Unsettling Nature of Variational Change

The Darwinian principle of natural selection yields temporal change—evolution in the biological definition—by the twofold process of producing copious and undirected variation within a population and then passing along only a biased (selected) portion of this variation to the next generation. In this manner, the variation within a population at any moment can be converted into differences in mean values (average size, average braininess) among successive populations through time. For this fundamental reason, we call such theories of change *variational* as opposed to the more conventional, and more direct, models of *transformational* change imposed by natural laws that mandate a particular trajectory based on inherent (and therefore predictable) properties of substances and environments. (A ball rolling down an inclined plane does not reach the bottom because selection has favored the differential propagation of moving versus stable elements of its totality but because gravity dictates this result when round balls roll down smooth planes.)

© Gianni Dagli Orti/CORBIS

To illustrate the peculiar properties of variational theories like Darwin's in an obviously caricatured, but not inaccurate, description: Suppose that a population of elephants inhabits Siberia during a warm interval before the advance of an ice sheet. The elephants vary, at random, and in all directions, in their amount of body hair. As the ice advances and local conditions become colder, elephants with more hair will tend to cope better, by the sheer good fortune of their superior adaptation to changing climates—and they will leave more offspring on average. (This differential reproductive success must be conceived as broadly

[CONTINUED]

statistical and not guaranteed in every case: In any generation, the hairiest elephant of all may fall into a crevasse and die.) Because offspring inherit their parents' degree of hairiness, the next generation will contain a higher proportion of more densely clad elephants (who will continue to be favored by natural selection as the climate becomes still colder). This process of increasing hairiness may continue for many generations, leading to the evolution of woolly mammoths.

This little fable can help us understand how peculiar and how contrary to all traditions of Western thought and explanation the Darwinian theory of evolution, and variational theories of historical change in general, must sound to the common ear. All the odd and fascinating properties of Darwinian evolution—the sensible and explainable but quite unpredictable nature of the outcome (dependent upon complex and contingent changes in local environments), the nonprogressive character of the alteration (adaptive only to these unpredictable local circumstances and not inevitably building a "better" elephant in any cosmic or general sense)—flow from the variational basis of natural selection.

Transformational theories work in a much simpler and more direct manner. If I want to go from A to B, I will have so much less conceptual (and actual) trouble if I can postulate a mechanism that will push me there directly than if I must rely upon the selection of "a few good men" from a random cloud of variation about point A, then constitute a new generation around an average point one step closer to B, then generate a new cloud of random variation about this new point, then select "a few good men" once again from this new array—and then repeat this process over and over until I finally reach B.

When one adds the oddity of variational theories in general to our strong cultural and psychological resistance against their application to our own evolutionary origin (as an unpredictable and not necessary progressive little twig on life's luxuriant tree), then we can better understand why Darwin's revolution surpassed all other scientific discoveries in reformatory power and why so many people still fail to understand, and may even resist, its truly liberal content. (I must leave the issue of liberation for another time, but once we recognize that the specification of morals and the search for a meaning to our lives cannot be accomplished by scientific study in any case, then Darwin's variational mechanism will no longer seem threatening and may even become liberating in teaching us to look within ourselves for answers to these questions and to abandon a chimerical search for the purpose of our lives, and for the source of our ethical values, in the external workings of nature.) *(By Stephen Jay Gould. (2000). What does the dreaded "E" word mean anyway?* Natural History, 109*(1), 34-36.)*

Gould also described a fundamental puzzle in the fossil record in his Original Study: The precise moment when variational change led to the formation of a new species—in this case, the woolly mammoth—remained elusive. More recent populations may appear sufficiently changed from ancestral populations to be called different species. The difficulty arises because, given a reasonably good fossil record, one species will appear to grade into the other without any clear break. This gradual directional change over time can occur within a single line, without any evident branching, and is called **anagenesis** (Figure 5.2). Speciation is inferred as organisms take on a different appearance over time.

It may be difficult to determine whether variation preserved in the fossil record presents evidence of separate species. How can we tell whether two sets of fossilized bones represent organisms capable of interbreeding and producing viable fertile offspring? Paleoanthropologists use as many sources of data as possible, checking the proposed evolutionary relationships, in order to approximate an answer to this question. Today, paleoanthropologists use genetic data as well as observations about the biology and behavior of living groups to support theories about speciation in the past. Thus, reconstructing evolutionary relationships draws on much more than bones alone. Fossil finds are always interpreted against the backdrop of scientific discoveries in a variety of disciplines as well as prevailing beliefs and biases. Fortunately the self-correcting nature of scientific

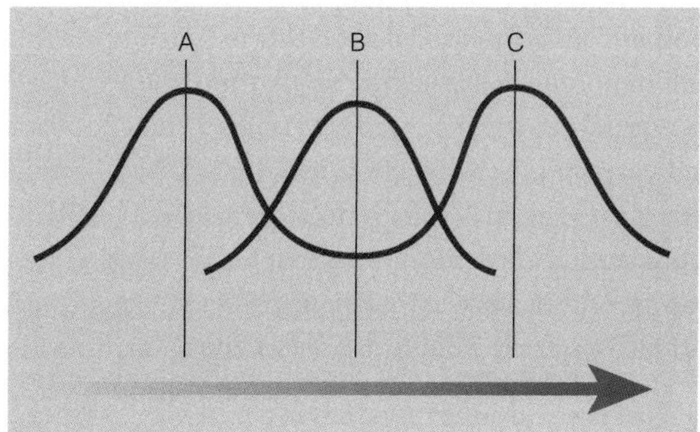

FIGURE 5.2

Anagenesis can occur through a process of variational change that takes place as small differences in traits that (by chance) are advantageous in a particular environment accumulate in a species' gene pool. Over time, this may produce sufficient change to transform an old species into a new one. Genetic drift may also account for anagenesis.

anagenesis A sustained directional shift in a population's average characteristics.

investigation allows evolutionary lines to be redrawn in light of all new discoveries and more compelling explanations.

Constructing Evolutionary Relationships

In addition to designating species in the fossil record, paleoanthropologists and paleontologists construct evolutionary relationships among fossil groups. Scientists pay particular attention to features appearing more recently in evolutionary history that are unique to a line, calling these features **derived.** **Ancestral** characteristics, which are the counterpart to derived traits, are present not only in the particular species at hand but in ancestral forms as well. For example, bilateral symmetry, a body plan in which the right and left sides of the body are mirror images of each other, is an ancestral trait in humans. Because it is a characteristic of all vertebrates including fish, reptiles, birds, and mammals, bilateral symmetry does not contribute to the reconstruction of evolutionary relationships among fossil primates. Instead, paleoanthropologists pay particular attention to recently evolved derived features in order to construct evolutionary relationships among fossil groups. For example, because changes in bones associated with bipedalism are present only in the human line, these derived features can be used to separate humans and their ancestors from other hominoids.

Sorting out evolutionary relationships among fossil species may be complicated by a phenomenon called **convergent evolution,** in which two more distant forms develop greater similarities. The classic examples of convergence involve analogies discussed in Chapter 2 such as the wings of birds and butterflies, which resemble each other because these structures serve similar functions. Convergent evolution occurs when an environment exerts similar pressures on distantly related organisms causing these species to resemble each other. Distinguishing the physical similarities produced by convergent evolution from those resulting from shared ancestry may be difficult, complicating the reconstruction of the evolutionary history of any given species.

Among more closely related groups, convergence of homologous structures can occur as when an identical structure present within several distinct species takes on a similar form in distantly related groups. Among the primates, an example is hind-leg dominance in both lemurs and humans. In most primates, the hind limbs are either shorter or of the same length as the forelimbs. Lemurs and humans are not as closely related to each other as are humans and chimps for example, but both have longer hind limbs related to their patterns of locomotion. Humans are bipedal while lemurs use their long legs to push off and propel them from tree to tree. Hind-leg dominance appeared separately in these two groups and is not indicative of a close evolutionary relationship. Only shared derived features can be used to establish relationships among groups of species.

derived Characteristics that define a group of organisms that did not exist in ancestral populations.
ancestral Characteristics possessed by an organism or group of organisms due to shared ancestry.
convergent evolution A process by which unrelated populations develop similarities to one another.

The Nondirectedness of Macroevolution

Among the lay public, evolution is often seen as leading in a predictable and determined way from one-celled organisms, through various multicelled forms, to humans, who occupy the top rung of a ladder of progress. However, even though one-celled organisms appeared long before multicellular forms, single-celled organisms were not replaced by multicellular descendants. Single-celled organisms exist in greater numbers and diversity than all forms of multicellular life and live in a greater variety of habitats.[1]

As for humans, we are indeed recent arrivals in the world (though not as recent as some new strains of bacteria). Our appearance—like that of any kind of organism—was made possible only as a consequence of a whole string of accidental happenings in the past. To cite but one example, about 65 million years ago the earth's climate changed drastically. Evidence suggests that a meteor or some other sort of extraterrestrial body slammed into earth where the Yucatan Peninsula of Mexico now exists, cooling global temperatures to such an extent as to cause the extinction of the dinosaurs (and numerous other species as well). For 100 million years, dinosaurs dominated most terrestrial environments available for vertebrate animals and would probably have continued to do so were it not for this event. Although mammals appeared at about the same time as reptiles, they existed as small, inconspicuous creatures that an observer from outer space would probably have dismissed as insignificant. But with the demise of the dinosaurs, all sorts of opportunities became available allowing mammals to begin their

[1]Gould, S. J. (1996). *Full house: The spread of excellence from Plato to Darwin* (pp. 176–195). New York: Harmony Books.

© Wolfgang Kaehler/CORBIS © Pete Saloutos/CORBIS

VISUAL COUNTERPOINT The characteristic long legs of prosimians and humans are not the result of a close evolutionary relationship.

great expansion into a variety of species including our own ancestors, the earliest primates. Therefore, an essentially random event—the collision with a comet or asteroid—made our own existence possible. Had it not happened, or had it happened at some other time (before the existence of mammals), we would not be here.[2]

The history of any species is an outcome of many such occurrences. At any point in the chain of events, had any one element been different, the final result would be markedly different. As Gould puts it, "All evolutionary sequences include . . . a fortuitous series of accidents with respect to future evolutionary success. Human brains and bodies did not evolve along a direct and inevitable ladder, but by a circuitous and tortuous route carved by adaptations evolved for different reasons, and fortunately suited to later needs."[3]

CONTINENTAL DRIFT AND GEOLOGICAL TIME

As described in Chapter 4, context and dating are vital for the interpretation of fossils. Because primate evolution extends so far back in time, paleoanthropologists reconstruct primate evolution in conjunction with information about the geological history of the earth. The scale of geological time is not similar to other conceptions of time that most humans use in their daily lives. Few of us deal with hundreds of millions of anything, let alone time, on a regular basis. To understand geological time, astronomer Carl Sagan correlated the geologic time scale for the history of the earth to a single calendar year. In this "cosmic calendar," the earth itself originates on January 1, the first organisms appear approximately 9 months later around September 25, followed by the earliest vertebrates around December 20, mammals on December 25, primates on December 29, hominoids at 12:30 P.M. on New Year's Eve, bipeds at 9:30 P.M., with our species appearing in the last minutes before midnight. In this chapter, we will consider human evolutionary history with the appearance of the mammals in the Mesozoic era, roughly 245 million years ago.

Over such vast amounts of time, the earth itself has changed considerably. During the past 200 million years, the position of the continents has changed through a process called **continental drift** that accounts for the re-arrangement of adjacent land masses through the theory of plate tectonics. According to this theory, the continents, embedded in platelike segments of the earth, move their positions as the edges of the underlying plates are created or destroyed (Figure 5.3). Plate movements are also responsible for geological phenomena such as earthquakes, volcanic activity, and mountain formation. Continental drift is important for understanding the distribution of fossil primate groups whose history we will now explore. The shifting orientation of the earth's continents is also responsible for climatic changes in the environment that affected the course of primate evolutionary history.

continental drift According to the theory of plate tectonics, the movement of continents embedded in underlying plates on the earth's surface in relation to one another over the history of life on earth.

[2]Gould, S. J. (1985). *The flamingo's smile: Reflections in natural history* (p. 409). New York: Norton.

[3]Gould, *The flamingo's smile*, p. 410.

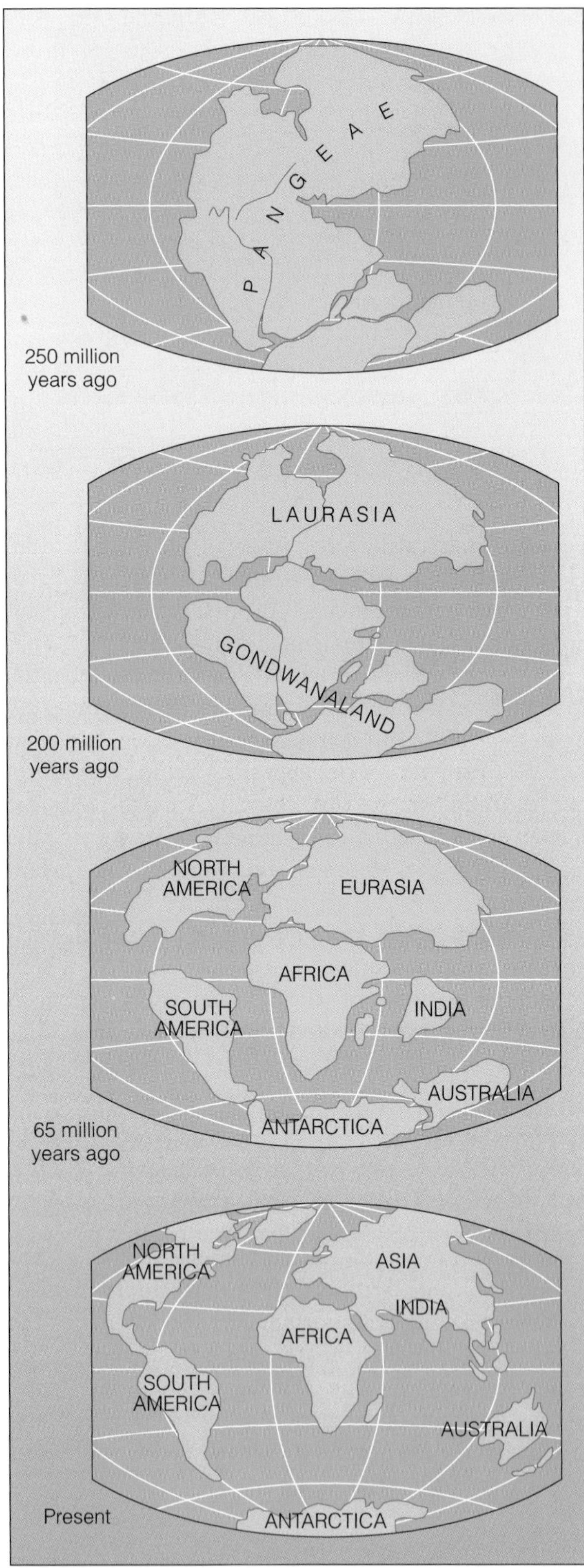

FIGURE 5.3
Continental drift is illustrated by the position of continents during several geological periods. At the end of the Cretaceous period some 65 million years ago, the time of the dinosaurs' extinction, the seas, opened up by continental drift, created isolating barriers between major land masses. During the Miocene epoch, African and Eurasian land masses reconnected.

MEDIATREK
To find out more about plate tectonics and continental drift, try visiting this nifty interactive site created by NASA. To use interactive maps and learn about how these phenomena shape our world and beyond, go to MediaTrek 5.1 on the companion Web site or CD-ROM.

EARLY MAMMALS

By 190 million years ago—the end of what geologists call the Triassic period—true mammals were on the scene. Mammals from the Triassic, Jurassic (190–135 million years ago), and Cretaceous (135–65 million years ago) periods are largely known from hundreds of fossils, especially teeth and jaw parts. Because teeth are the hardest, most durable structures, they often outlast other parts of an animal's skeleton. Fortunately, investigators often are able to infer a good deal about the total animal on the basis of only a few teeth found lying in the earth. For example, as described in Chapter 3, the teeth of mammals are easy to distinguish from those of reptiles. Knowledge of the way the teeth fit together indicates the arrangement of muscles needed to operate the jaws. Reconstruction of the jaw muscles, in turn, indicates how the skull must have been shaped to provide a place for these muscles to attach. The shape of the jaws and details of the teeth also suggest the type of food that these animals consumed. Thus, a mere jawbone fragment with a few teeth contains a great deal of information about the animal from which it came.

An interesting observation about the evolution of the mammals is that the diverse forms with which we are familiar today, including the primates, are the products of an **adaptive radiation,** the rapid increase in number of related species following a change in their environment. This did not begin until after mammals had been present on the earth for over 100 million years. With the mass extinction of many reptiles at the end of the Cretaceous, however, a number of existing **ecological niches,** or functional positions in their habitats, became available to mammals. A species' niche incorporates factors such as diet, activity, terrain, vegetation, predators, prey, and climate.

The story of mammalian evolution starts as early as 280 to 230 million years ago (Figure 5.4). From

adaptive radiation Rapid diversification of an evolving population as it adapts to a variety of available niches
ecological niche A species' way of life considered in the full context of its environment, including other species found in that environment, geology, climate, and so on.

deposits of this period, which geologists call the Permian, we have the remains of reptiles with features pointing in a distinctly mammalian direction. These mammal-like reptiles were slimmer than most other reptiles and were flesh eaters. A series of graded fossils demonstrate trends toward a mammalian pattern such as a reduction in the number of bones, the shifting of limbs underneath the body, the development of a separation between the mouth and nasal cavity, differentiation of the teeth, and so forth.

Eventually these creatures became extinct, but not before some of them developed into true mammals by the Triassic period. During the Jurassic period that followed, dinosaurs and other large reptiles dominated the earth, and mammals remained tiny, inconspicuous creatures occupying a nocturnal niche.

By chance, mammals were **preadapted**—possessing the biological equipment to take advantage of the new opportunities available to them through the mass extinction of the dinosaurs and other reptiles 65 million years ago. As **homeotherms,** mammals possess the ability to maintain a constant body temperature, a trait that appears to have promoted the adaptive radiation of the mammals. Mammals can be active at a wide range of environmental temperatures, whereas reptiles, as **isotherms** who take their body temperature from the surrounding environment, become progressively sluggish as the surrounding temperature drops. Cold global temperatures 65 million years ago appear to be responsible for the mass extinction of the reptiles, while mammals, as homeotherms, were preadapted for this climate change.

The mammalian trait of maintaining constant body temperature however, requires a diet high in calories. Based on evidence from their teeth, scientists know that early mammals ate such foods as insects, worms, and eggs. As animals with nocturnal habits, mammals have well-developed senses of smell and hearing relative to reptiles. Although things cannot be seen as well in the dark as they can in the light, they can be heard and smelled just as well.

The mammalian pattern also differs from reptiles in terms of how they care for their young. Mammals are

MILLIONS OF YEARS AGO	PERIODS	EPOCHS	LIFE FORMS
2		Pleistocene	
		Pliocene	First undoubted hominins
5		Miocene	
23		Oligocene	
34		Eocene	First undoubted monkey-ape ancestors
55		Paleocene	First undoubted primates
65			
	Cretaceous		
135			
	Jurassic		First undoubted mammals
180			
	Triassic		
230			
	Permian		Mammal-like reptiles
280			
	Carboniferous		First reptiles
345			

FIGURE 5.4

This timeline highlights some major milestones in the evolution of those mammals from which humans are descended.

The Kobal Collection/Hammer

Though popular media depict the coexistence of humans and dinosaurs, in reality the extinction of the dinosaurs occurred 65 million years ago while the first bipeds ancestral to humans appeared between 5 and 8 million years ago.

preadapted Possessing characteristics that, by chance, are advantageous in future environmental conditions.
homeotherms Animals maintaining a relatively constant body temperature despite environmental fluctuations
isotherms Animals whose body temperature rises or falls according to the temperature of the surrounding environment.

considered **k-selected** species. This means that they produce relatively few offspring at a time, providing them with considerable parental care. A universal feature of how mammals care for their young is the production of food (milk) via the mammary glands. Reptiles are relatively **r-selected,** which means that they produce many young at a time and invest little effort caring for their young after they are born. Though among mammals some species are relatively more k- or r-selected, the relatively high energy requirements of mammals, entailed by parental investment and the maintenance of a constant body temperature, demand more nutrition than required by reptiles. During their adaptive radiation, the fruits, nuts, and seeds of flowering plants that became more common in the late Cretaceous period provided mammals with high-quality nutrition.

RISE OF THE PRIMATES

Early primates began to emerge during this time of great global change at the start of the Paleocene epoch. The distribution of fossil primates on the earth makes sense only when one understands that the positions of the continents today differ tremendously from what was found in the past (see Figure 5.3). During this period, as noted earlier, North America and Eurasia were connected in the supercontinent called Laurasia. South America, Africa, Antarctica, Australia, and the Indian subcontinent—previously joined together as the supercontinent Gondwanaland—were beginning to separate from one another through continental drift. Africa was separated from Eurasia by a narrow body of water. On land, the dinosaurs had become extinct, and the mammals were undergoing the great adaptive radiation that ultimately led to the development of the diverse forms with which we are familiar today. At the same time, the newly evolved grasses, shrubs, and other flowering plants were undergoing an enormous proliferation. This diversification, along with a milder climate, favored the spread of dense, lush tropical and subtropical forests over much of the earth, including North and South America and much of Eurasia and Africa. With the spread of these huge belts of forest, the stage was set for the movement of some mammals into the trees. Forests would provide our early ancestors with the ecological niches in which they would flourish. Fossil evidence of primatelike mammals from the Paleocene forests has been found in North America and Eurasia. See Figure 5.5 for a full timeline of primate evolution.

Misjudgements and errors of coordination, leading to falls that injured or killed the individuals poorly adapted to arboreal life may have been a part of the initial forays into the trees. Natural selection would favor those that judged depth correctly and gripped the branches strongly. Early primates that took to the trees were probably in some measure preadapted by virtue of behavioral flexibility, better vision, and more dexterous fingers than their contemporaries. Primatologist Matt Cartmill further suggests that primate visual and grasping abilities were also promoted through the activity of hunting for insects by sight. His **visual predation** hypothesis accounts for the observation that other tree-dwelling species and hunting species do not necessarily possess the same combination of visual and manual abilities possessed by the primates. The relatively small size of the early primates allowed them to make use of the smaller branches of trees; larger, heavier competitors, and most predators, could not follow. The move to the smaller branches also gave them access to an abundant food supply; the primates were able to gather insects, leaves, flowers, and fruits directly rather than waiting for them to fall to the ground.

The strong selection in a new environment led to an acceleration in the rate of change of primate charac-

k-selected Reproduction involving the production of relatively few offspring with high parental investment in each.
r-selected Reproduction involving the production of large numbers of offspring with relatively low parental investment in each.
visual predation A hypothesis for the primate origins through adaptation to predation by sight in trees.

The appearance of angiosperm plants provided not only highly nutritious fruits, seeds, and flowers but also a host of habitats for numerous edible insects and worms—just the sorts of foods required by mammals with their high metabolism.

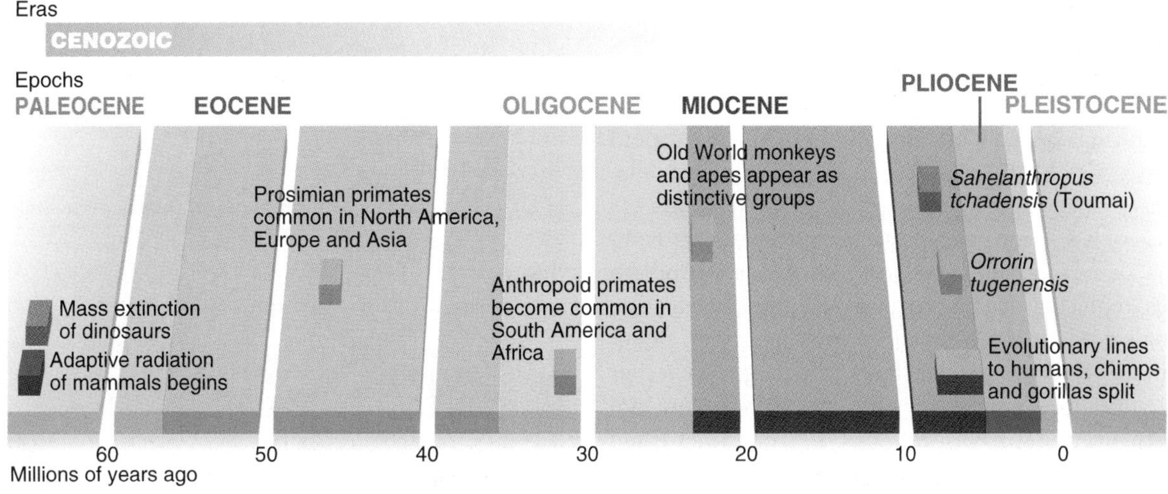

FIGURE 5.5

teristics. Paradoxically, these changes eventually made possible a return to the ground by some primates, including the ancestors of the genus *Homo.*

True Primates

The first well-preserved "true" primates appeared by about 55 million years ago at the start of the Eocene epoch. During this time period, an abrupt warming trend began on earth, causing many older forms of mammals to become extinct, to be replaced by recognizable forerunners of some of today's forms. Among the latter was an adaptive radiation of prosimian primates, of which over fifty fossil genera are known. Fossils of these creatures have been found in Africa, North America, Europe, and Asia, where the warm, wet conditions of the Eocene sustained extensive rainforests. Relative to ancestral primatelike mammals, these early primate families had somewhat enlarged brain cases,

MEDIATREK

To get a complete taxonomic listing of fossil primates as well as an excellent glossary of terms related to primate evolution through a comprehensive primate evolution site, go to MediaTrek 5.2 on the companion Web site or CD-ROM.

The abilities to judge depth correctly and grasp branches strongly are of obvious importance to animals as active in the trees as most primates.

slightly reduced snouts, and a somewhat forward position of the eye orbits, which, though not completely walled in, are surrounded by a complete bony ring called a postorbital bar (Figure 5.6).

During the Eocene, the first signs of anthropoid primates also begin to appear in the fossil record. The earliest evidence is of a tiny species *Eosimias* (Latin for "dawn of the monkeys") represented by fossils from China, dated to about 45 million years ago. The Chinese fossils represent several species of tiny, insect-eating animals and are the smallest primates ever documented.[4] Some scientists have challenged whether these tiny fossils are truly anthropoids as they are reconstructed largely from foot bones rather than skulls or teeth.

Numerous fossils from Fayum, Egypt, show a unique mix of prosimian and anthropoid characteristics. The front teeth resemble those of the Eocene prosimian primates, with the derived dental formula shared by Old World monkeys and apes of two incisors, a canine, two premolars, and three molars on each side of the jaw. The eye orbits have a complete wall, the latter being a feature of anthropoid primates.[5]

Although there is still much to be learned about the Eocene primates, it is clear that they were abundant, diverse, and widespread. Among them were ancestors of today's prosimians and anthropoids.[6] With the end of the Eocene, substantial changes took place among the primates, as among other mammals. In North America, now well isolated from Eurasia, primates became extinct, and elsewhere their range seems to have been reduced considerably. A driving force in all this change was probably climatic change. Through the late Eocene, climates were becoming somewhat cooler and drier, but then temperatures took a sudden dive, triggering the formation of an ice cap over previously forested Antarctica. The result was a marked reduction in the range of suitable environments for primates. At the same time, cold climate led to lower sea levels through the formation of ice caps, perhaps changing opportunities for migration of primates.

Illustration by Nancy J. Perkins, Carnegie Museum of Natural History

The scientists who discovered tiny leg bones, placed in the genus *Eosimias,* suggest these fossils are the earliest anthropoids. Other experts do not feel such claims can be made from leg bones alone. Although its bones suggest overall body form, this reconstruction is otherwise speculative.

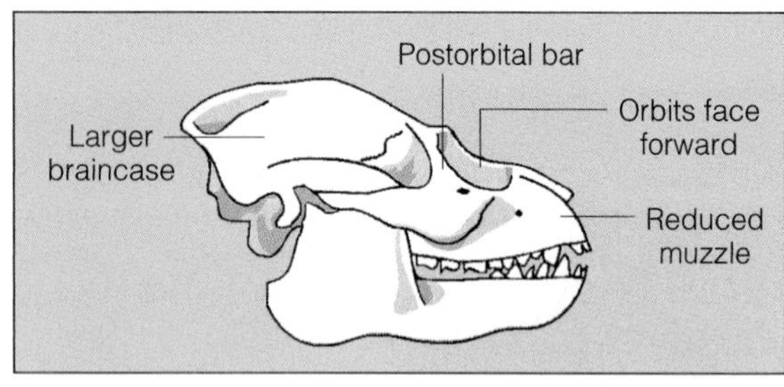

FIGURE 5.6

Ancestral features seen in the Eocene genus *Adapis* are found in prosimians today. Like modern lemurs, it has a postorbital bar, a bony ring around the eye orbit. Note that the orbit is open behind the ring.

Oligocene Anthropoids

During the Oligocene epoch, from about 34 million to 23 million years ago, the anthropoid primates diversified and expanded their range. Fossil evidence from Egypt's Fayum region has yielded sufficient fossils (more than 1,000) to reveal that by 33 million years ago, Old World anthropoid primates existed in consid-

[4]Gebo, D. L., Dagosto, D., Beard, K. C., & Tao, Q. (2001). Middle Eocene primate tarsals from China: Implications for haplorhine evolution. *American Journal of Physical Anthropology,* 116, 83–107.

[5]Simons, E. (1995). Skulls and anterior teeth of *Catopithecus* (Primates: Anthropoidea) from the Eocene and anthropoid origins. *Science, 268,* 1,885–1,888.

[6]Kay, R. F., Ross, C., & Williams, B. A. (1997). Anthropoid origins. *Science,* 275, 803–804.

erable diversity. Moreover, the cast of characters is growing, as new fossils continue to be found in the Fayum, as well as in newly discovered localities in Algeria (North Africa) and Oman (Arabian Peninsula). At present, we have evidence of at least sixty genera included in two families. During the Oligocene, prosimian fossil forms became far less prominent than anthropoids. Only on the large island of Madagascar (off the coast of East Africa), which was devoid of anthropoids until humans arrived, is prosimian diversity still evident. In their isolation, they underwent a further adaptive radiation.

Fossil evidence indicates that these Old World anthropoids were quadrupeds who were diurnal, as evidenced through their smaller orbits (eyes). Many of these Oligocene species possess a mixture of monkey and ape features. Of particular interest is the genus *Aegyptopithecus* (Greek for "Egyptian ape"), an Oligocene anthropoid that has sometimes been called a monkey with an ape's teeth. *Aegyptopithecus* possessed a mosaic of monkey and ape features as well as features shared by both groups. Its lower molars have the five cusps of an ape, and the upper canine and lower first premolar exhibit the sort of shearing surfaces found in monkeys and apes. Its skull possesses eye sockets that are in a forward position and completely protected by a bony wall, as is typical of modern monkeys and apes. The endocast of its skull indicates that it possessed a larger visual cortex than found in prosimians. Relative to its body size, the brain of *Aegyptopithecus* was smaller than that of more recent anthropoids. Still, this primate seems to have had a larger brain than any prosimian, past or present. Possessed of a monkeylike skull and body, and fingers and toes capable of powerful grasping, it evidently moved about in a quadrupedal, monkeylike manner.[7]

The teeth of *Aegyptopithecus* suggest that this species may be closely related to an ancestor of humans and modern apes. Although no bigger than a modern house cat, *Aegyptopithecus* was nonetheless one of the larger Oligocene primates. Differences between males and females include larger body size, more formidable canine teeth, and deeper mandibles (lower jaws) in the males. In modern anthropoids, species with these traits generally live in groups that include several adult females with one or more adult males.

New World Monkeys

The earliest evidence of primates in South America dates from this time. These fossil primates are certainly anthropoid monkeys, with the eyes fully encased in bone and limb bones for quadrupedal locomotion. Scientists hypothesize that these primates came to South America from Africa, because the earliest fossil evidence of anthropoids is from the Old World. Some of the African anthropoids arrived in South America, which at the time was not attached to any other land mass, probably by means of floating masses of vegetation of the sort that originate even today in the great rivers of West and Central Africa. In the Oligocene, the distance between the two continents was far less than it is today; favorable winds and currents could easily have carried "floating islands" of vegetation across within a period that New World

[7]Ankel-Simons, F., Fleagle, J. G., & Chatrath, P. S. (1998). Femoral anatomy of *Aegyptopithecus zeuxis*, an early Oligocene anthropoid. *American Journal of Physical Anthropology, 106*, 421–422.

VISUAL COUNTERPOINT At Egypt's Fayum Depression in the desert west of Cairo, winds and flash floods have uncovered sediments more than 22 million years old, exposing the remains of a tropical rainforest, like the one on the right, that was home to a variety of primates that combine monkeylike and apelike features.

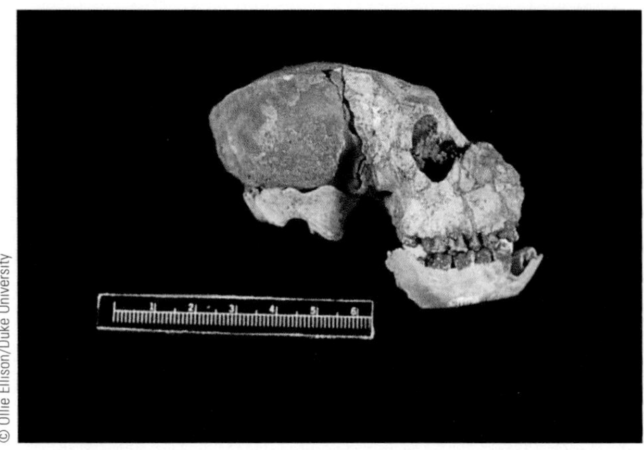

This *Aegyptopithecus* skull dates to the Oligocene epoch. The enclosed eye sockets and dentition mark it as an anthropoid primate, probably ancestral to *Proconsul.*

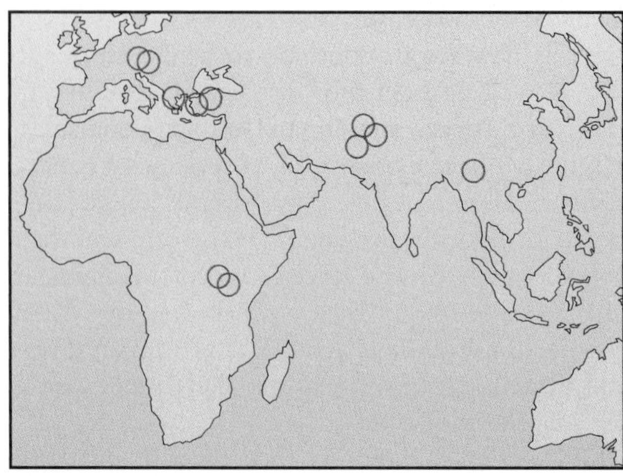

FIGURE 5.7

Fossils of hominoids have been found in East Africa, Europe, and Asia that could be ancestral to large apes and humans.

monkey ancestors could have survived.[8] Nearly all living and fossil New World primates possess the ancestral dental formula (2-1-3-3) of prosimians compared to the derived pattern (2-1-2-3) found in Old World anthropoids.

Miocene Apes

True apes first appeared in the fossil record during the Miocene epoch, 5 to 23 million years ago. It was also during this time period that the African and Eurasian land masses made direct contact. For most of the preceding 100 million years, the Tethys Sea, a continuous body of water that more or less joined what are now the Mediterranean and Black Seas to the Indian Ocean, created a barrier to migration between Africa and Eurasia. Once joined through what is now the Middle East and Gibralter, Old World primate groups such as the apes that got their start in Africa could expand their ranges into Eurasia. Miocene ape fossil remains have been found everywhere from the caves of China, to the forests of France, to eastern Africa where the earliest fossil remains of bipeds have been found.

So varied and ubiquitous were the fossil apes of this period that the Miocene has even been labeled by some as the "golden age of the hominoids" (Figure 5.7). The word *hominoid* comes from the Latin roots *Homo* and *Homin* (meaning "human being") and the suffix *oïdes* ("resembling"). As a group, the hominoids get their name from their resemblance to humans. In addition to the Old World anthropoid dental formula of 2-1-2-3 and Y5 molars, hominoids can be characterized by the derived characteristics of having no tail and having broad flexible shoulder joints (see Chapter 3). The likeness between humans and the other apes bespeaks an important evolutionary relationship which, as explained in the Biocultural Connection box, makes other hominoids vulnerable to human needs in today's world. In the distant past, one of the Miocene apes is the direct ancestor of the human line. Exactly which one is a question still to be resolved.

MEDIATREK

To open the door to information about living and fossil primates as well as the people who study them, visit the Wisconsin Regional Primate Research Center's Primate Info Net by going to MediaTrek 5.3 on the companion Web site or CD-ROM.

An examination of the history of the "contenders" for direct human ancestor among the Miocene apes demonstrates how reconstruction of evolutionary relationships draws on much more than bones alone. Scientists interpret fossil finds by drawing on existing beliefs and knowledge. With new discoveries, interpretations change. The first Miocene ape fossil remains were found in Africa in the 1930s and 1940s by A. T. Hopwood and the renowned paleoanthropologist Louis Leakey. These fossils turned up on one of the many islands in Lake Victoria, the 27,000-square-mile lake where Kenya, Tanzania, and Uganda meet. Impressed with the chimplike appearance of these fossil remains, Hopwood suggested that the new species be named *Proconsul,* combining the Latin root for "before" *(pro)* with the stage name of a chimpanzee who was performing in London at the time. Dated to the early Miocene 17 to 21 million years ago, *Proconsul* has some of the classic hominoid features, lacking a tail and having the characteristic pattern of Y5 grooves in the lower

[8]Houle, A. (1999). The origin of platyrrhines: An evaluation of the Antarctic scenario and the floating island model. *American Journal of Physical Anthropology, 109,* 554–556.

Biocultural Connection

Nonhuman Primates and Human Disease

Biological similarities among humans, apes, and Old world monkeys have led to the extensive use of these nonhuman primate species in biomedical research aimed at preventing or curing disease in humans. A cultural perspective that separates humans from our closest living relatives is necessary for this research to occur. Those who fully support these research efforts state that biomedical research in a limited number of chimpanzees or rhesus macaques lessens human suffering and spares human lives. The successful development of a vaccine for hepatitis B and hepatitis C through testing with chimpanzees, and current work on vaccines for HIV, are often cited as examples of a positive balance between vast human benefits and minimal chimpanzee suffering. Others, such as primatologist Jane Goodall, vehemently disagree with this approach. Goodall emphasizes that cultural processes determine the place of animals within biomedical research. She advocates elimination of the cultural distinction between humans and our closest relatives for purposes of biomedical research.

Courtesy of PETA

Some biomedical research disturbs animals minimally. For example, DNA can be extracted from the hair naturally shed by living primates, allowing for cross-species comparisons of disease genes. To facilitate this process, primate cell repositories have been established for researchers to obtain samples of primate DNA. Other biomedical research is far more invasive to the individual primate. For example, to document the infectious nature of kuru, a disease closely related to Mad Cow disease, the extract from the brains of sick humans was injected into the brains of living chimpanzees. A year and a half later the chimpanzees began to sicken. They had the same classic features of kuru—uncontrollable spasticity, seizures, dementia, and ultimately death.

The biological similarities of humans and other primates leading to such research practices derive from a long shared evolutionary history. By comparison, the cultural rules that allow our closest relatives to be the subjects of biomedical research are relatively short lived. ■ ■ ■

molar teeth. However, the adaptations of the upper body seen in later apes (including humans) were absent. These included a skeletal structure adapted for hanging suspended below tree branches. In other words, *Proconsul* had some apelike features as well as some features of four-footed Old World monkeys (Figure 5.8). This mixture of ape and monkey features makes *Proconsul* a contender for a "missing link" between monkeys and apes but not as a connection between Miocene apes and later-appearing bipeds.

At least seven fossil hominoid groups besides *Proconsul* have been found in East Africa from the early to middle Miocene. But between 14 and 5 million years ago this fossil record thins out. It is not that all the apes suddenly moved from Africa to Eurasia, but rather that the environmental conditions made it less likely that any of the African remains would fossilize. Tropical forests inhabited by chimps and gorillas today make poor conditions for the preservation of bones. As mentioned in Chapter 4, in order to become a fossil, bones must be quickly incorporated into the earth before any rotting or decomposition occurs. In tropical forests, the heat, humidity, and general abundance of life make this unlikely. The bones' organic matrix is consumed by other creatures before it can be fossilized.

Nevertheless, the scarcity of African fossil evidence from this time period fit well with prevailing notions

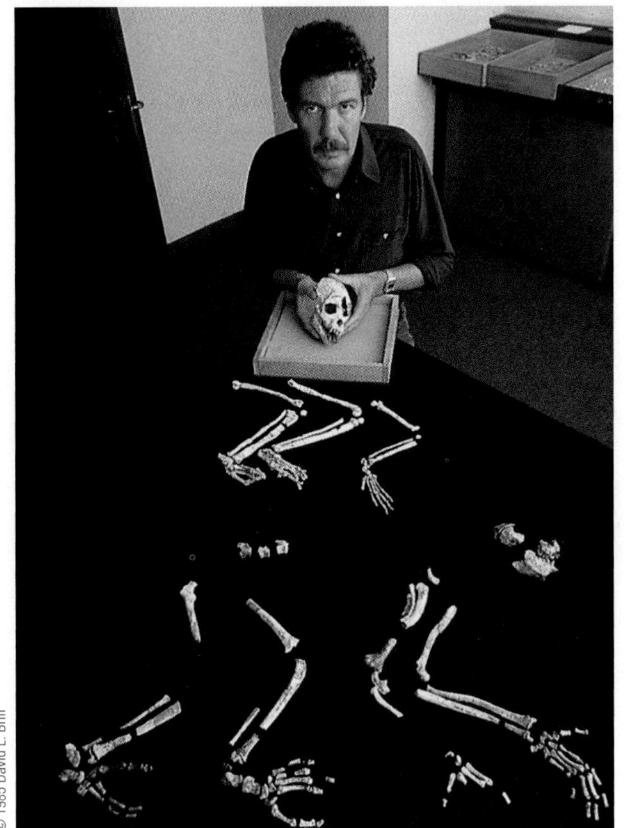
© 1985 David L. Brill

Paleoanthropologist Alan Walker displays bones of *Proconsul*, an unspecialized tree-dwelling, fruit-eating hominoid of the early Miocene.

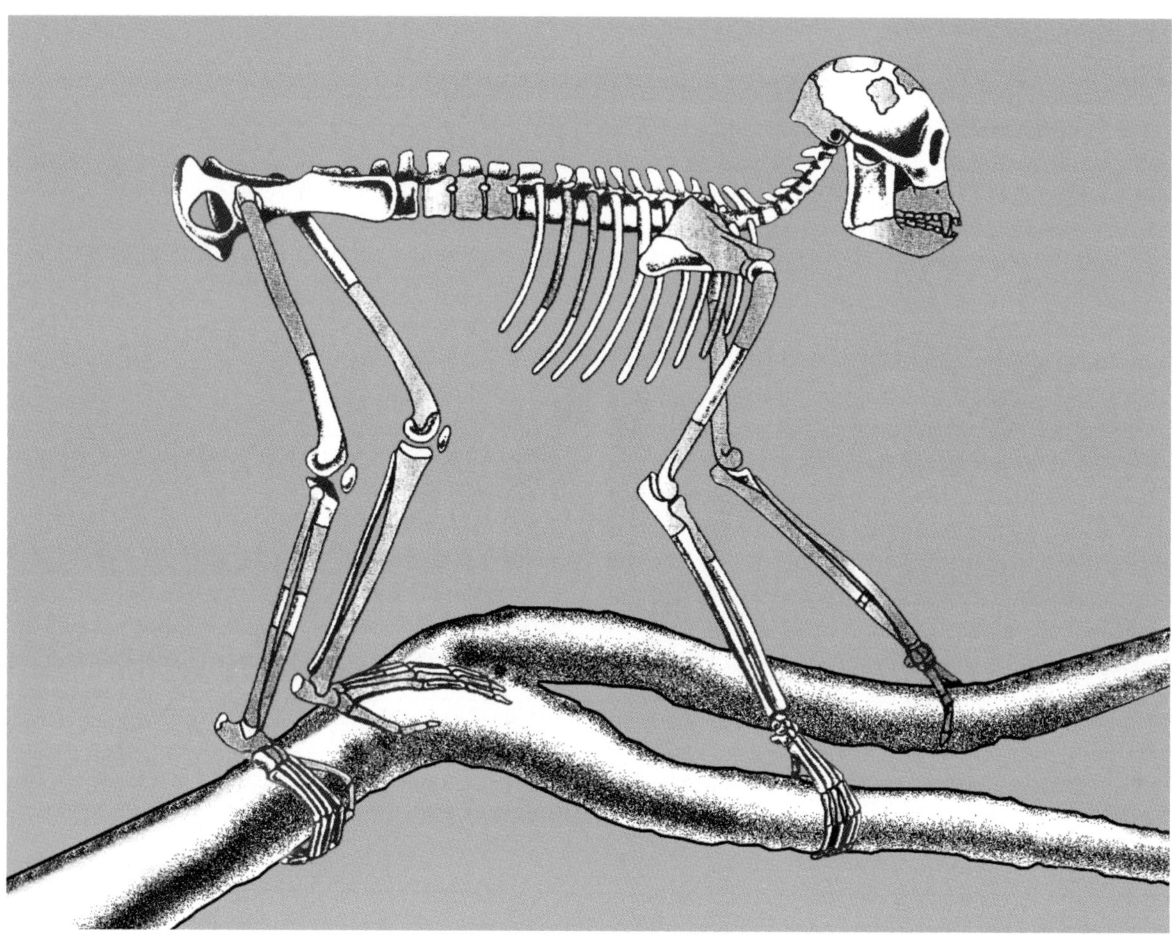

FIGURE 5.8
Reconstructed skeleton of *Proconsul.* Note the apelike absence of tail but monkeylike limb and body proportions. *Proconsul,* however, was capable of greater rotation of forelimbs than monkeys.

about human origins. Two factors conspired to take the focus away from Africa. First, investigators initially did not consider that humans were any more closely related to the African apes than they were to the other intelligent great ape—the Asian orangutan. Chimps, bonobos, gorillas, and orangutans were thought to be more closely related to one another than any of them were to humans. The construction of evolutionary relationships still relied upon visual similarities among species, much as it did in the mid-1700s when Linnaeus developed the taxonomic scheme that grouped humans with other primates. Chimps, bonobos, gorillas, and orangutans all possess the same basic body plan, adapted to hanging by their arms from branches or knuckle-walking on the ground. Humans and their ancestors had an altogether different form of locomotion: walking upright on two legs. On an anatomical basis, it seemed as though the first Miocene ape to become bipedal could have come from any part of the vast Old World range of the Miocene apes.

The second factor at work to pull attention away from African origins was more subtle and embedded not in the bones from the earth but in the subconscious of the scientists of the past. It was hard for these scientists to imagine that humans originated entirely in Africa. As we will see in the next chapter, it took many years for the first bipedal fossils discovered in South Africa in the 1920s to be accepted by the scientific community as a key part of the human line. Instead, human origins were imagined to involve a close link between those who invented the first tools and the people responsible for Western civilization.

During the 1960s, it appeared as though this Miocene human ancestor lived in the Siwaliks, the foothills of the majestic Himalayan mountain range along the northern borders of India and Pakistan, near the ruins of the later Indus Valley civilization. The Himalayas are some of the youngest mountains of the world. They began forming during the Miocene when the Indian subcontinent collided with the rest of Eurasia and have been becoming taller ever since.

In honor of the Hindu religion practiced in the region where the fossils were found, the contender was given the name *Ramapithecus,* after the Indian deity

© Anup and Manoj Shah

Although not identical, the modern ape most like *Sivapithecus* is the orangutan. Chimpanzees and gorillas, like humans, have come to differ more from the ancestral condition than have these Asian apes.

Using this technique, Sarich proposed a sequence of divergence for the living hominoids showing that human, chimp, and gorilla lines split roughly 5 million years ago. He boldly stated that it was impossible to have a separate human line before 7 million years ago "no matter what it looked like." In other words, anything that old would also have to be ancestral to chimps and gorillas as well as humans. Because *Ramapithecus,* even with its humanlike jaws, was dated to between 7 and 12 million years ago, it could no longer be considered a human ancestor.

In the meantime, Pilbeam continued fossil hunting in the Himalayan foothills. Further specimens began to show that *Ramapithecus* was actually a smaller, perhaps female version of *Sivapithecus.*[9] Eventually all the specimens referred to as *Ramapithecus* were "sunk" or absorbed into the *Sivapithecus* group, so that today *Ramapithecus* no longer exists as a valid name for a Miocene ape. Instead of two distinct groups, one of which went on to evolve into humans, they are considered males and females of the sexually dimorphic genus *Sivapithecus.* A spectacular complete specimen found in the Potwar Plateau of Pakistan by Pilbeam showed that *Sivapithecus* was undoubtedly the ancestor of orangutans. This conclusion matched well with the molecular evidence that the separate line to orangutans originated 10 to 12 million years ago.

All of these changes reflect the fact that paleoanthropologists participate in an unusual kind of science. Paleoanthropology, like all paleontology, is a science of discovery. As new fossil discoveries come to light, interpretations inevitably change, making for better understanding of our evolutionary history. Today, discoveries can occur in the laboratory as easily as on the site of an excavation. Molecular studies since the 1970s provide a new line of evidence much the same way that fossils provide new data as they are unearthed. A discovery in the laboratory, like Sarich's molecular clocks, can drastically change the interpretation of the fossil evidence.

MIOCENE APES AND HUMAN ORIGINS

As described above, determining which Miocene apes were directly ancestral to humans is one of the key questions in primate evolution. Molecular evidence directs our attention to Africa between 5 and 8 million years ago (Figure 5.9). Though any fossil discoveries in Africa from this critical time period have the potential to be the "missing link" between humans and the other African ape species, the evidence from this period has until recently been particularly scrappy. Controversy surrounds the interpretation of many of these new fossil finds.

For example, in Chad in the summer of 2002 a team of international researchers led by Michel Brunet of France unearthed a well-preserved skull dated to between 6 and 7 million years ago.[10] Calling their find *Sahelanthropus tchadensis* ("Sahel man of Chad", referring to the Sahel region south of the Sahara Desert), the researchers suggested that this specimen represented the earliest known ancestor of humans, or earliest hominin. Nicknamed "Toumai," from the region's Goran-language word meaning "hope for life" (a name typically given to babies born just before the dry season), this

[9]Pilbeam, D. R. (1987). Rethinking human origins. In R. L. Ciochon & J. G. Fleagle (Eds.), *Primate evolution and human origins* (p. 217). Hawthorne, NY: Aldine de Gruyter.

[10]Brunet, M., et al. (2002). A new hominid from the Upper Miocene of Chad, Central Africa. *Nature, 418,* 145–151.

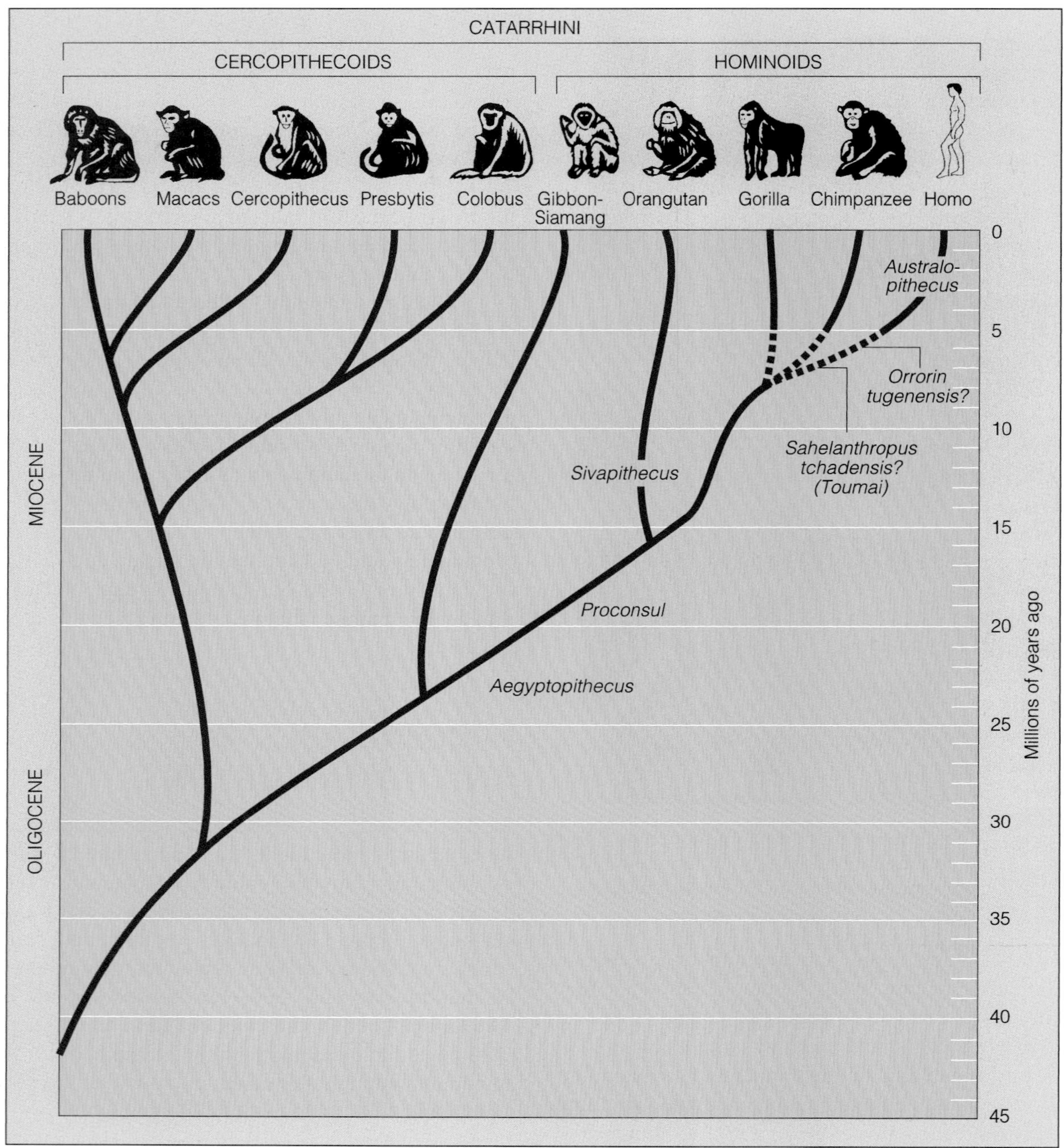

FIGURE 5.9

Although debate continues over details, this chart represents a reasonable reconstruction of evolutionary relationships among the Old World anthropoid primates. (Not shown are extinct evolutionary lines.)

specimen is the only skull from this time period. Considering that bipedalism is the derived characteristic that indicates inclusion in the hominin subfamily, some paleoanthropologists argue that the relationship of this specimen to humans cannot be established from skull bones alone. The research team argues that derived features can be seen in the face of the Toumai specimen, indicating its status as a hominin. Whether or not this specimen proves to be a direct human ancestor, as the only skull from this time period, it is nevertheless a very important find.

In 2001, 6-million-year-old fossils discovered in Kenya by Brigitte Senut and Martin Pickford were also reported as human ancestors.[11] Officially given the species name *Orrorin tugenensis* (*Tugensis* from the

[11] Senut, B., et al. (2001). First hominid from the Miocene (Lukeino formation, Kenya). *C. R. Acad. Sci. Paris, 332,* 137–144.

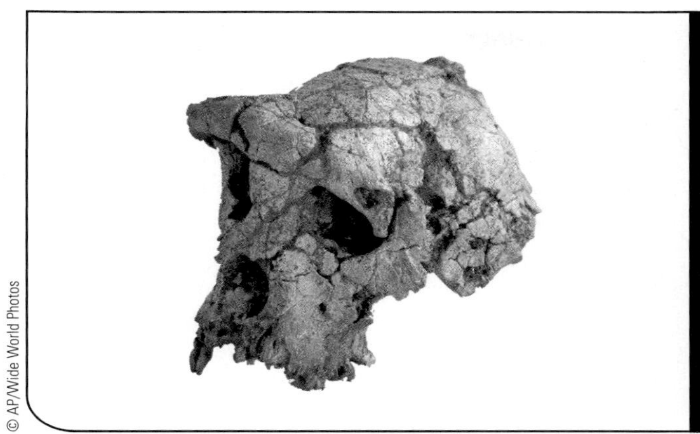
© AP/Wide World Photos

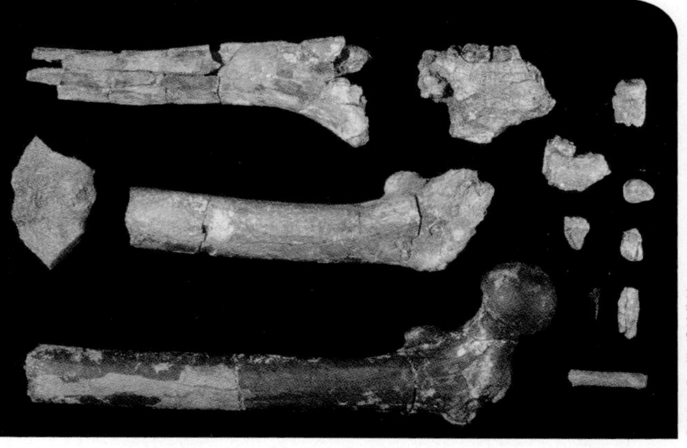
© Marc Deville/GAMMA

VISUAL COUNTERPOINT These recent finds from Chad and Kenya have both been proposed as the earliest hominin. The Toumai specimen is a beautifully preserved skull, though some paleoanthropologists feel that alone, it does not establish bipedalism, the derived trait characteristic of the hominins. The *Orrorin* thigh bones strongly suggest bipedalism in these 6-million-year-old remains.

Tugen hills, *Orrorin* meaning "original man" in the local language) but nicknamed "Millennium Man," these specimens have also been surrounded by controversy. The evidence for *Orrorin* consists of fragmentary thigh bones, a finger bone, some jaw fragments, and teeth. The thigh bones demonstrate possible, but not definite, bipedalism. Unfortunately, the distal or far ends of the thigh bone that would prove this are not fully preserved. The way that paleoanthropologists determine bipedalism from the fossil record will be fully described in the next chapter as we explore the fossil evidence in Africa from 5 to 2.5 million years ago.

Chapter Summary

- Over time, macroevolutionary forces act to produce new species from old ones (speciation). A species is a population or a group of populations that is capable of interbreeding and producing fertile, viable offspring. In cladogenesis or branching evolution, isolating mechanisms serve to separate breeding populations, creating first divergent subspecies and then (if isolation continues) divergent species. Geographical, biological, or social isolating mechanisms block gene flow between groups, contributing to the separate accumulation of genetic mutations in each population. Biological isolating mechanisms include phenomena such as the sterility of hybrid offspring.
- Macroevolution may also proceed through a process of anagenesis whereby natural selection over time favors some variants over others, causing a change in a population's average characteristics. Convergence occurs when two unrelated species come to resemble each other owing to functional similarities.
- Evolution is not a ladder of progress leading in a predictable and determined way to ever-more complex forms. Rather, it has produced, through a series of accidents, a diversity of enormously varied designs that subsequently have been restricted to a lesser number of still less-than-perfect forms.
- Though species can be established through breeding experiments in living groups, paleoanthropologists cannot establish past species with the same degree of objectivity. Instead species are established on the basis of shared derived features observed in the fossil evidence. Ancestral features, by contrast, indicate only shared ancestry. Evolutionary relationships among species can also be established through molecular comparisons.
- The primates arose as part of a great adaptive radiation, a branching of mammalian forms that began more than 100 million years after the appearance of the first mammals. The reason for this late diversification was that most ecological niches that mammals have since occupied were either preempted by the reptiles or were nonexistent until the flowering plants became widespread beginning about 65 million years ago. Geological changes in the orientation and position of the earth's continents affected the global climate, playing a key role in the evolution and distribution of the primates.
- The first primates were arboreal insect eaters, and the characteristics of all primates developed as adaptations to this initial way of life. Although some primates no longer inhabit the trees, it is certain that those adaptations that evolved in response to life in the trees were (by chance) preadaptive to the niche now occupied by the hominins.
- The earliest primates had developed by 55 million years ago in the Paleocene epoch and were small arboreal creatures.

Diverse prosimianlike forms were common in the Eocene across what is now North America and Eurasia. By the late Eocene, perhaps 45 million years ago, small primates combining prosimian and anthropoid features were on the scene.

- In the Miocene epoch, apes proliferated and spread over many parts of the Old World. Among them were apparent ancestors of the large apes and humans. These appeared by 16 million years ago and were widespread even as recently as 8 million years ago. According to the molecular evidence, between 5 and 8 million years ago at least one of these ape populations from Africa became the first hominin. Recent finds—including a well-preserved skull from Chad and some skeletal fragments including thigh bones from Kenya—have been proposed as the earliest hominins, the human subfamily defined by the derived feature bipedalism. Other populations of African Miocene apes remained in the forests, developing into today's bonobo, chimpanzee, and gorilla.

Questions for Reflection

1. How does the study of the evolutionary history of the primates help paleoanthropologists meet the challenge of understanding human origins?
2. Why are shared derived characteristics more important than shared ancestral characteristics in evolutionary reconstructions? Using the Miocene apes and humans think about the ways that conclusions about evolution would change if ancestral rather than derived characteristics were used to figure out evolutionary relationships among species.
3. The biological definition of a species is a population or a group of populations that is capable of interbreeding and producing fertile, viable offspring. Why is this definition of species difficult to apply to the fossil record?
4. The interpretation of fossil material changes with the discovery of new specimens and with discoveries in the laboratory. How has that happened? Can you imagine our understanding of human evolutionary history changing in the future?
5. An understanding of the changing position of the earth's continents through the past several hundred million years is important for the reconstruction of primate evolutionary history. Do you think the evolutionary history of the primates can be understood without knowledge of continental drift?

Key Terms

Macroevolution
Speciation
Isolating mechanisms
Cladogenesis
Homeobox genes
Punctuated equilibria
Anagenesis
Derived
Ancestral
Convergence
Continental drift
Adaptive radiation
Ecological niche
Preadapted
Homeotherms
Isotherms
K-selected
R-selected
Visual predation
Molecular clock

Multimedia Review Tools

Companion Web Site

Visit **http://www.wadsworth.com/anthropology_d/** and click on the companion Web site for this textbook to access a wide range of material to aid your study of anthropology. Among the options for self-study in each chapter are learning objectives, flash cards, Internet activities, Web links, InfoTrac College Edition exercises, and practice tests that can be scored and emailed to your instructor.

CD-ROM

The *Doing Anthropology Today* CD-ROM supplied with your textbook provides unique and valuable information designed to enhance your learning experience. This interactive multimedia resource includes video clips, interviews with renowned anthropologists, map and timeline exercises, chapter study quizzes, and much more. *Doing Anthropology Today* will not only help you in achieving your grade goals, but it will also make your learning experience fun and exciting!

Suggested Readings

Fleagle, J. (1998). *Primate adaptation and evolution.* New York: Academic Press.

This beautifully illustrated book is an excellent introduction to the field of primate evolution, synthesizing the fossil record with primate anatomical and behavioral variation.

Hartwig, W. C. (2002). *The primate fossil record.* New York: Cambridge University Press.

An up-to-date and comprehensive treatment of the discovery and interpretation of primate fossils can be found in this book.

Jones, S., Martin R., & Pilbeam, D. (1992). *Cambridge encyclopedia of human evolution.* New York: Cambridge University Press.

This comprehensive introduction to the human species covers the gamut from genetics, primatology, and the fossil evidence to a detailed exploration of contemporary human ecology, demography, and disease. Over seventy scholars from throughout the world contributed to this encyclopedia.

Mayr, E., & Diamond, J. (2002). *What evolution is.* New York: Basic Books.

Written for a general educated audience, this engaging book provides a comprehensive treatment of evolutionary theory.

CHAPTER 6

The First Bipeds

© Anthro-Photo

CHALLENGE ISSUE

THE FOSSILIZED REMAINS OF THE EARLIEST BIPEDS FROM EASTERN, SOUTHERN, AND CENTRAL AFRICA HELP US MEET THE CHALLENGE OF UNDERSTANDING HUMAN ORIGINS. Clear evidence of bipedalism is preserved in various aspects of the skeleton. Fossilized footprints have even been preserved in volcanic ash at the 3.6 million-year-old Tanzanian site of Laetoli. As shown here, the foot of a living human fits right inside these ancient footprints, which show the characteristic pattern of bipedal walking.

1

What Is the Anatomy of Bipedalism and How Is It Preserved in the Fossil Record?

Bipedalism is the shared derived characteristic used to establish whether a fossilized hominoid is a part of the evolutionary line that produced humans. Evidence for bipedalism is preserved literally from head to toe. Bipedalism can be inferred from the forward position of the large opening in the base of the skull, a series of curves in the spinal column, the basin-shaped structure of the pelvis, the angle of the lower limbs from the hip joint to the knees, and the shape of the foot bones. Thus even fragmentary evidence can prove bipedalism, providing the "right" fragment is preserved. Several groups from between 4 and 7 million years ago have been proposed as the earliest bipeds.

2

Who Were the Australopithecines and What Were They Like?

The fossil record indicates that some time during the early Pliocene, beginning 5 million years ago, the genus *Australopithecus* appeared in Africa. Australopithecines include a diverse group of fully bipedal species still possessing relatively small-sized brains in proportion to their body size. Some of the later-appearing australopithecines, known as "robust" forms, possessed particularly large teeth, jaws, and chewing muscles and represent an evolutionary dead end, disappearing from the fossil record completely by 1 million years ago. One of the other australopithecine species, though it is not clear which one, appears to be a direct ancestor of the genus *Homo.*

3

What Is the Role of Bipedalism in Human Evolutionary History?

Numerous theories stressing adaptation have been proposed to account for the appearance of bipedalism in human evolutionary history. These theories range from the adaptive advantage of free hands to carry young or wield weapons to adaptation to damaging buildup of heat in the brain from direct exposure to the sun in a hot, treeless environment. Bipedalism appeared in human evolutionary history several million years before brain size expanded.

Though genetic evidence established that the human line diverged from those leading to chimpanzees and gorillas between 5 and 8 million years ago, for a long time, the fossil evidence of the early stages of human evolution was both sparse and tenuous. Today, however, several interesting specimens from Africa fill in this important period. Inclusion of any fossil specimen in the human evolutionary line depends upon evidence for bipedalism (also called bipedality), the defining characteristic of the hominin group. The possible human ancestors from Chad and Kenya, dated 6 to 7 million years ago, were described in the last chapter. In this chapter, we will pick up our story with a diverse array of fossil bipeds less than 5 million years old.

Most of the early bipeds are members of the genus ***Australopithecus,*** a name coined for this group of fossils back in 1924 when the first important fossil from Africa proposed to be a human ancestor came to light. This unusual fossil, consisting of a partial skull and natural brain cast of a young individual, was brought to the attention of Professor Raymond Dart of the University of Witwatersrand in Johannesburg, South Africa. The "Taung child," named for the limestone quarry in which it was found, was unlike any creature Dart had ever seen before. Recognizing an intriguing mixture of ape and human characteristics in this unusual fossil, anatomist Dart proposed a new taxonomic category for his discovery—*Australopithecus africanus,* or southern ape of Africa—suggesting that this specimen represented an extinct form that was ancestral to humans.

Although the anatomy of the base of the skull indicated that the Taung child was probably a biped, the scientific community was not ready to accept the notion of a small-brained African ancestor to humans. Dart's original paper describing the Taung child was published in the February 1925 edition of the prestigious journal *Nature.* The next month's issue was filled with venomous critiques rejecting Dart's proposal that this specimen represented an ancestor to humans. Critiques ranged from biased to fussy to sound. Fussy critiques included chastising Dart for incorrectly combining Latin and Greek in the genus and species name he coined. Valid criticisms included questions concerning inferences made about the appearance of an adult of the species based only on the fossilized remains of a young individual. The biggest stumbling block, however, to the acceptance of Dart's proposal lay in the realm of bias. Paleoanthropologists of the early 20th century expected that the ancestor to humans already had a large brain. Moreover, most European scientists expected to find evidence of this large-brained ancestor in Europe or, barring that, Asia.

AP/Wide World Photos

Raymond Dart, who described the first fossil of *Australopithecus* in a paper in the prestigious journal *Nature* in 1924 and correctly diagnosed its bipedal mode of locomotion. It took a number of years for other paleoanthropologists to accept Dart's claim that australopithecines were bipedal and ancestral to humans because scientists of the time had difficulty accepting the notion that human ancestors were small brained bipeds from Africa.

In fact, many scientists of the 1920s even believed that the ancestor to humans had already been found in the Piltdown gravels of Sussex, England, in 1910. The Piltdown specimens consisted of a humanlike skull and an apelike jaw that seemed to fit together though the crucial joints connecting the two were missing. They were discovered along with the bones of some other animal species known to be extinct. Charles Dawson—the amateur archaeologist, paleontologist, and practicing lawyer who found these remains—immodestly named them *Eoanthropus dawsoni,* or "Dawson's dawn man." Until the 1950s the Piltdown remains were widely accepted as representing the missing link between apes and humans rather than as one of the biggest hoaxes in the history of science that we know them to be today.

The reasons for widespread acceptance of Dawson's dawn man were as follows. As Darwin's theory of evolution by natural selection began to gain

Australopithecus The first well-known hominin; lived between 4.4 and 1 million years ago. Characterized by bipedal locomotion, but with an apelike brain; generally includes seven species: *A. afarensis, A. africanus, A. anamensis, A. boisei, A. robustus, A. aethiopicus,* and *A. gahri.*

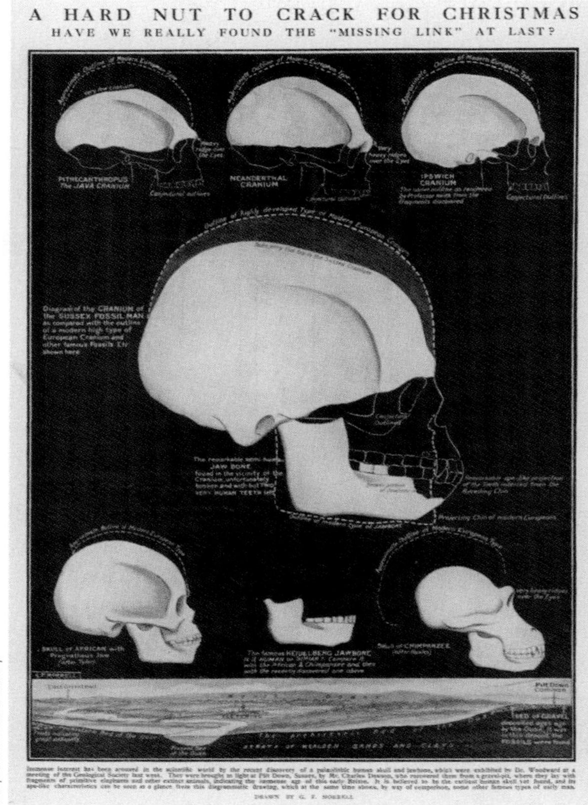

Mary Evans Picture Library

The Piltdown forgery pictured here (center) was widely accepted as ancestral to humans, in large part because it fit with public expectations that the "missing link" would have a large brain and an apelike face.

acceptance, intense interest developed in finding traces of prehistoric human ancestors. Accordingly, predictions were made as to what those ancestors looked like. Darwin himself, on the basis of his knowledge of embryology and the comparative anatomy of living apes and humans, suggested in his 1871 book, *The Descent of Man,* that early humans had, among other things, a large brain and an apelike face and jaw.

Although the tools made by prehistoric peoples were commonly found in Europe, their bones were not. To be sure, a few fossilized skeletons came to light in France and Germany, but they weren't at all like the predicted missing link, nor had any human fossils been discovered in England. Given this state of affairs, the Piltdown finds could not have come at a better time. Here at last was the long-awaited missing link, and it was almost exactly as predicted. Even better, so far as English-speaking scientists were concerned, it was found in English soil!

In the context of the evidence available in the early 1900s, the idea of an ancient human with a large brain and an apelike face became widely accepted as valid.

© The Geological Society/NHMPL

No one knows for certain how many of the "Piltdown Gang," scientists supporting this specimen as the missing link, were actually involved in the forgery. It is likely that Charles Dawson had help from at least one scientist. Sir Arthur Conan Doyle, the author of the Sherlock Holmes detective stories, has also been implicated.

Fortunately, the self-correcting nature of science has prevailed, exposing the Piltdown specimens as a forgery. The discovery of more and more fossils, primarily in South Africa, China, and Java of smaller brained bipeds from the distant past, caused some scientists to question Piltdown. Ultimately, the application of the newly developed fluorine dating method (described in Chapter 4) by Kenneth Oakley and colleagues in 1953 proved that Piltdown was a forgery. The skull, which was indeed human, was approximately 600 years old, while the jaw, which proved to be from an orangutan, was even more recent. Finally, Dart and the Taung child were fully vindicated.

MEDIATREK

Learn more about the most famous hoax in the history of science through a trip to this site about Piltdown man by visiting MediaTrek 6.1 on the companion Web site or CD-ROM.

Today, genetic and fossil evidence both indicate that the human evolutionary line begins with a small-brained bipedal ape from Africa. Since Dart's time, many australopithecine specimens have been discovered. Numerous international expeditions—including researchers from Kenya, Ethiopia, Japan, Belgium, Great Britain, Canada, France, Israel, the Netherlands, South Africa, and the United States—scoured East, South, and Central Africa recovering unprecedented amounts of fossil material. Because this process has resulted in so many fossils, our ideas about early human evolution have had to be constantly revised. Nevertheless, there is widespread agreement over the broad outline, even though debate, often heated, continues over details. What is clear is that the course of human evolution began with a shift toward bipedalism, the shared derived characteristic distinguishing humans and their ancestors (hominins) from the other African apes (hominids). As described in Chapter 2, many scientists continue to restrict the term *hominid* for humans and the other fossil bipeds. The following Original Study by Lee Berger, the director of the paleoanthropology unit at the University of Witwatersrand in South Africa, weighs the issue.

Original Study

Is It Time to Revise the System of Scientific Naming?

A team of researchers led by paleoanthropologist Meave Leakey sparked a controversy among evolutionary scientists and the press alike earlier this year when they announced the discovery of a new genus and species of ape-man. They named their find *Kenyanthropus platyops,* the "flat-faced man of Kenya." Ordinarily, the find itself would be enough to spark a flame of controversy in the heart of any follower of human origins research. But this find also highlighted an ongoing debate within the scientific community over the adoption of a new system for naming, ranking, and classifying organisms. The debate is not confined to ivory tower scientists. The fossil discovery was widely reported. *The New York Times* referred to the new genus as a hominid; *National Geographic* reported on the find as a hominin. *National Geographic* subsequently received several hundred e-mails complaining about the poor editorial work of the staff that had clearly erred by replacing a "d" with an "n." But were they really wrong, and more important, does it really matter?

Linnaean Classification

The taxonomic classification system devised by Linnaeus in 1758 is still used in modified form today. Animals are identified, in descending order, as belonging to a kingdom, phylum, class, order, family, genus, and finally a species. This classification system is based largely on the animal's physical characteristics; things that looked alike were placed together. In the Linnaean system, humans would be categorized first as Animalia; then Chordata because we have a backbone; Mammalia because we have hair and suckle our young; primates because we share with apes, monkeys, and lemurs certain morphological characteristics; Hominidae because, among a few other criteria, we are separated from the other apes by being bipedal; *Homo* being our generic classification as human; and finally *sapiens,* a species name meaning, rightly or wrongly, "wise."

The Linnaean system also recognizes such groupings as superfamilies and subfamilies. In the case of the human lineage, the most often recognized superfamily is the Hominoidea (hominoids), which includes all of the living apes. It is from this point onward that most of the present human origins classification debate begins.

The traditional view has been to recognize three families of hominoid: the Hylobatidae, the Hominidae, and the Pongidae. The Hylobatidae include the so-called lesser apes of Asia, the gibbons, and siamangs. The Hominidae include living humans and typically fossil apes that possess a suite of characteristics such as bipedalism, reduced canine size, and increasing brain size such as the australopithecines. The Pongidae include the remaining African great apes including gorillas, chimpanzees, and the Asian orangutan.

© Kenneth Garrett/National Geographic Image Collection

Lee Berger excavating at the South African site Sterkfontein.

New Molecular Evidence

Modern-day genetic research is providing evidence that morphological distinctions are not necessarily proof of evolutionary relatedness. Recent evidence suggests that humans are in fact more closely related to the chimpanzee and bonobo than either species is to the gorilla. Chimps and humans share something like 98 percent of genes, indicating that we share a common ape ancestor.

Divergence times between the two groups based on a molecular clock suggest that the chimpanzee/human split occurred between 5 and 7 million years ago. In turn, the African apes, including humans, are more closely related to each other than any are to the orangutan.

[CONTINUED]

In recognition of these and other genetic relationships, some argue that we must overhaul the present morphologically based classification system for one that is more representative of our true evolutionary relationships as evinced by our genes.

Reworking the Family Tree

This is where the term *hominin* comes into play. Under the new classification model, hominoids would remain a primate superfamily, as has always been the case. Under this hominoid umbrella would fall orangutans, gorillas, chimps, and humans, all in the family Hominidae.

In recognition of their genetic divergence some 11 to 13 million years ago, the orangutans would be placed in the subfamily Ponginae, and the African apes, including humans, would all be lumped together in the subfamily Homininae. The bipedal apes—all of the fossil species as well as living humans—would fall into the tribe Hominini (thus hominin). All of the fossil genera, such as *Australopithecus*, *Ardipithecus, Kenyanthropus,* and *Homo,* would fall into this tribe.

A few evolutionary biologists want a more extreme classification, which would include humans and chimpanzees within the same genus, the genus *Homo.*

This 3- to 4-million-year-old skull could be another australopithecine or, as its discoverers suggest, a separate genus *Kenyanthropus platyops.*

Old Versus New

So hominid or hominin? Is it just a matter of semantics that only purists should be worried about? *The New York Times'* use of "hominid" and *National Geographic*'s use of "hominin" were both right in the broadest sense. In either the "old" or "new" classification system, hominid works, it just means different things.

In the old system, hominid refers solely to the bipedal ape line. In the new classification system it refers to the broader grouping of all the great apes, which would by definition certainly include the new *Kenyanthropus* fossils.

The use of hominin by *National Geographic* is technically more correct in that it recognizes the relationship of *Kenyanthropus* to the other bipedal apes and distinguishes it from other living and fossil African apes, which are not so closely related to us based on the molecular evidence we have to date.

In the long run, "hominin" is likely to win out against the term "hominid." It is more precise and recognizes the biological reality that moves beyond physical morphology.

Do I like it? Well, I would never try to stand in the way of the advancement of science, but just try saying Hominidae, Homininae, Hominini three times fast in front of a first-year Introduction to Anthropology class, and you will have some sympathy for the scientist who clings to the term "hominid" for a few more years.

So what's in a name? The classification debate is not just a debate for the purist; it cuts to the very core of our understanding of human's place in nature and our evolutionary relationships with our closest living relatives. All hominins are hominids, but not all hominids are hominins. *(By Lee R. Berger for National Geographic News, December 4, 2001)*

THE ANATOMY OF BIPEDALISM

Because comparative anatomy is a key to paleoanthropologists' work, understanding the anatomy of bipedalism—the shared derived characteristic distinguishing humans and their ancestors (hominins) from the other African apes—is important. Bipedalism is associated with anatomical changes literally from head to toe (Figures 6.1 and 6.2). As noted in the Taung child, evidence of bipedalism can even be preserved in the skull. In order for the head to be balanced above the spinal column in an upright posture, the position of the skull is relatively centered above the spinal column. The spinal cord leaves the skull at its base through an opening called the foramen magnum. In a knuckle-walker like a chimp, the foramen magnum is placed more toward the back of the skull while in a biped it is in a more forward position.

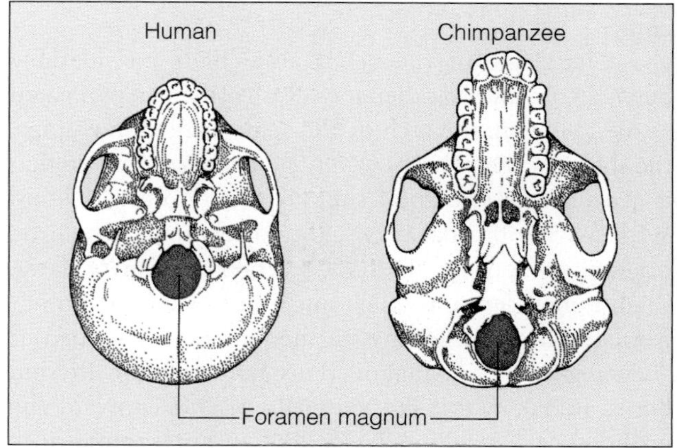

FIGURE 6.1

Bipedalism can be inferred form the position of the foramen magnum, the large opening at the base of the skull. Note its relatively forward position on the human skull (left) compared to the chimp skull.

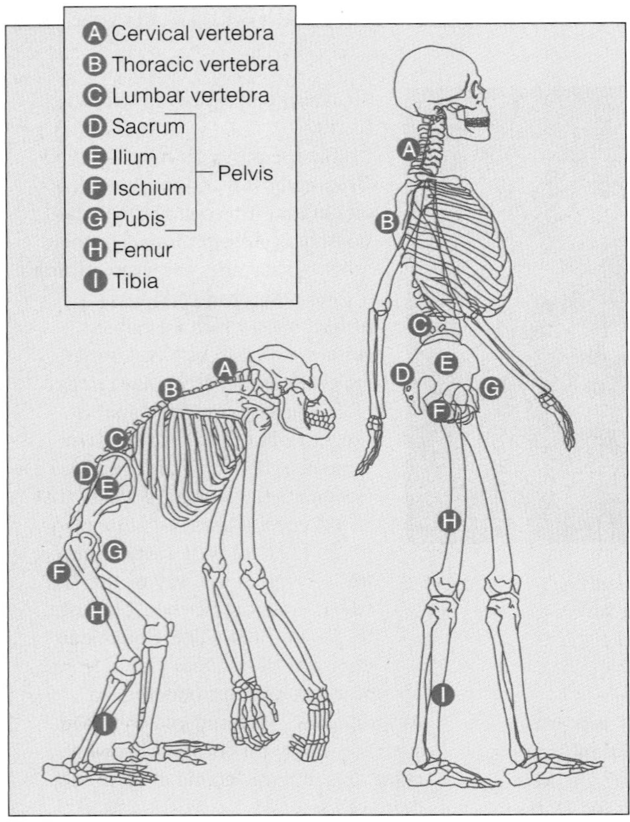

FIGURE 6.2

Working down from the skull of a biped, the spinal column makes a series of convex and concave curves that together maintain the body in an upright posture by positioning the body's center of gravity above the legs rather than forward. The curves correspond to the neck (cervical), chest (thoracic), lower back (lumbar), and pelvic (sacral) regions of the spine, respectively. In a chimp, the shape of the spine follows a single arching curve.

The shape of the pelvis also differs considerably between bipeds and other apes. Rather than an elongated shape following the arch of the spine as seen in chimps, the shape of the pelvis is wider and foreshortened so that it can provide structural support for the upright body. With a wide bipedal pelvis, the lower limbs would be oriented away from the body's center of gravity if the thigh bones (femora) didn't angle in toward each other from the hip to the knee, a phenomenon described as "kneeing-in." This angling does not continue in shin bones (tibia), which are vertically oriented toward the ground. The resulting knee joint is not symmetrical, allowing the thigh and shin bones to meet despite their different orientations. Another characteristic of bipeds is their stable arched feet and the absent opposable big toe. In general, humans and their ancestors possess shorter toes than the other apes. (Figure 6.3).

These anatomical features allow paleoanthropologists to "diagnose" bipedal locomotion even in fragmentary remains such as the top of the shin bone or the base of a skull. In addition, bipedal locomotion can also be established through fossilized footprints, preserving not so much the shape of foot bones but the characteristic stride used by humans and their ancestors. Bipedal locomotion is really a process of alternation between supporting the body's weight on either foot. While the body is supported in a one-legged stance, a biped takes a stride by swinging the other leg forward. The heel of the foot is the first part of the swinging leg to hit the ground. Then as the biped continues to move forward, he or she rolls from the heel toward the toe, pushing or "toeing off" into the next swing phase of the stride. While one leg is moving from heel strike to toe off of the stance phase, the other leg is moving forward through the swing phase of walking (Figure 6.4 on page 150).

The most dramatic confirmation of australopithecines' walking ability comes from Laetoli, Tanzania, where, 3.6 million years ago, three individuals walked across newly fallen volcanic ash. Because it was damp, the ash took the impressions of their feet, and these were sealed beneath subsequent ash falls until discovered by chemist Paul Abell in 1978. The shape of the footprints, the linear distance between the heel strikes and toe off, are all quite human.

The exploration of the fossil record of human evolution throughout this and the next several chapters will entail making anatomical comparisons among various fossil and living groups. Once bipedalism is established in a fossil specimen, paleoanthropologists turn to other features such as the skull or teeth to establish relationships among the various hominins.

THE PLIOCENE FOSSIL EVIDENCE

Since Dart's original find, hundreds of other fossil bipeds have been discovered, first in South Africa and later in Tanzania, Malawi, Kenya, Ethiopia, and Chad (Figure 6.5). As they were discovered, many were placed in variety of different genera and species, but now usually all are considered to belong to the single genus *Australopithecus*. Most anthropologists recognize seven species of the genus (Table 6.1 on page 150). In addition, some other groups of fossil bipeds from the Pliocene epoch (5 million to 1.6 million years ago) have been discovered. We will describe those species and the australopithecines in the order in which they inhabited the earth in this chapter.

As described in the previous chapter, the Miocene epoch was a time of tremendous geological change. The steady movement of geological plates supporting the

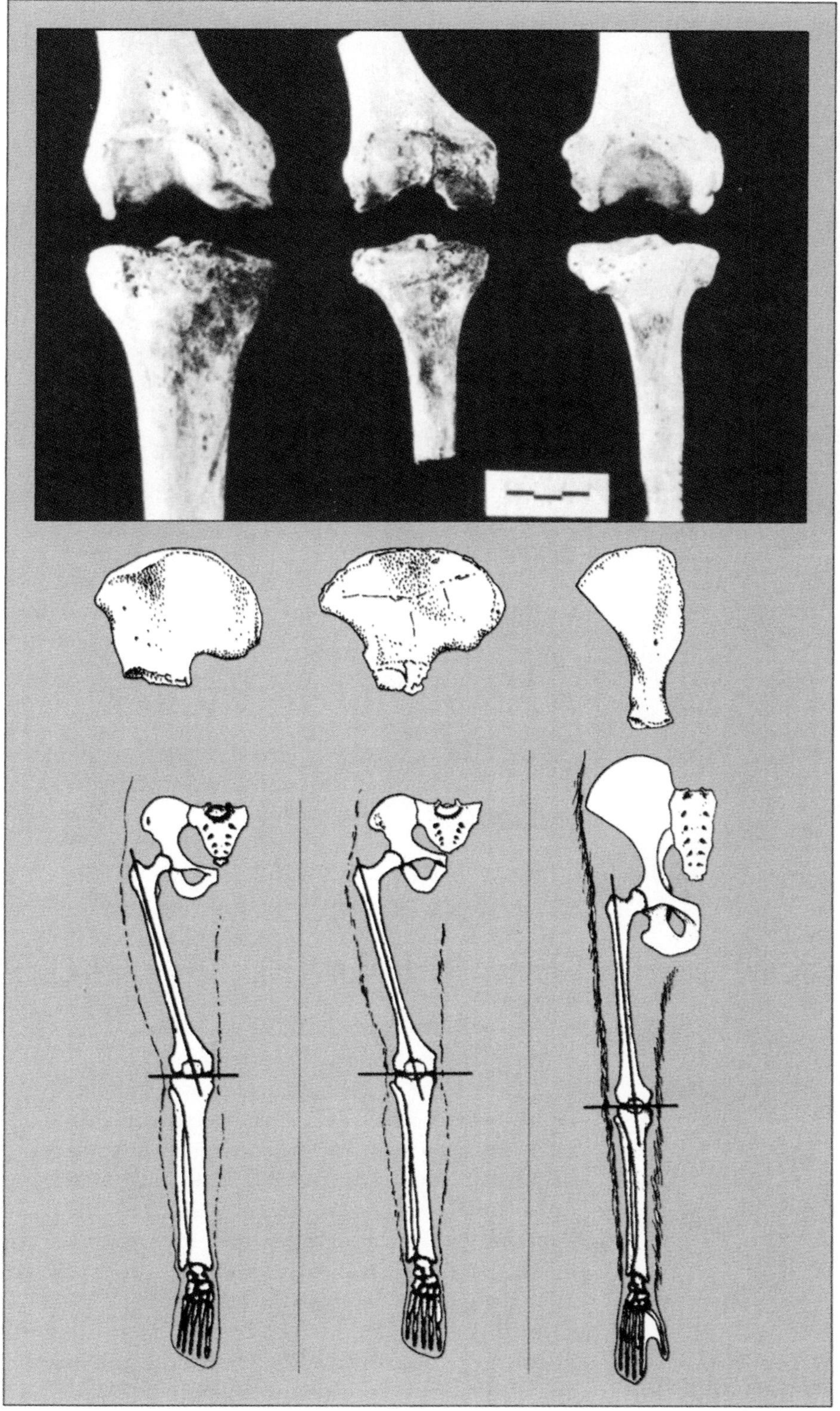

FIGURE 6.3

Examination of the upper hip bones and lower limbs of (from left) *Homo sapiens*, *Australopithecus*, and an ape can be used to determine means of locomotion. The similarities of the human and australopithecine bones are striking and are indicative of bipedal locomotion.

African and Eurasian continents resulted in a collision of the two landmasses at either end of what now is the Mediterranean Sea (see Figure 6.5). This contact allowed for the spread of species between these continents. Associated with this collision is a suite of geological changes that produced the Great Rift Valley system. This system consists of a separation between geological plates, extending from the Middle East through the Red Sea and eastern Africa into southern Africa. Part of rifting involves the steady increase in the elevation of the eastern third of the African continent, which experienced a cooler and drier climate and a transformation of vegetation from

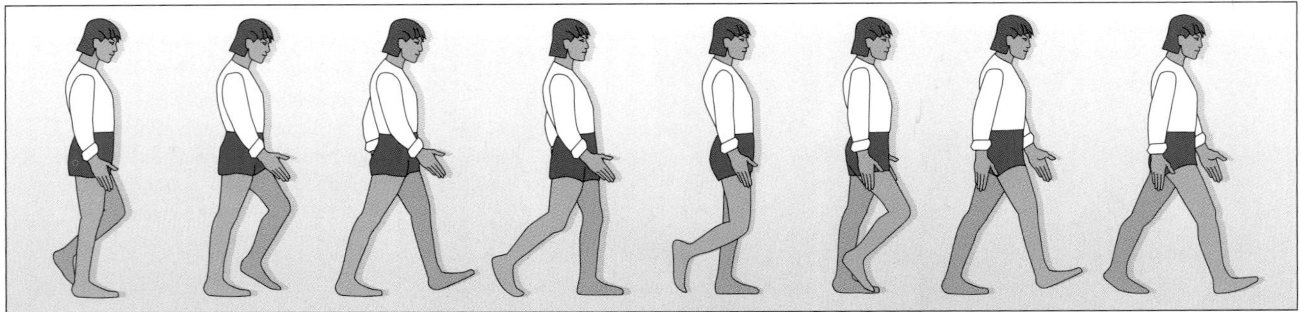

FIGURE 6.4
The bipedal gait in some regards is really "serial monopedalism" or locomotion one foot at a time. Note how the body's weight shifts from one foot to the other as an individual moves through the swing phase to heel strike and toe off.

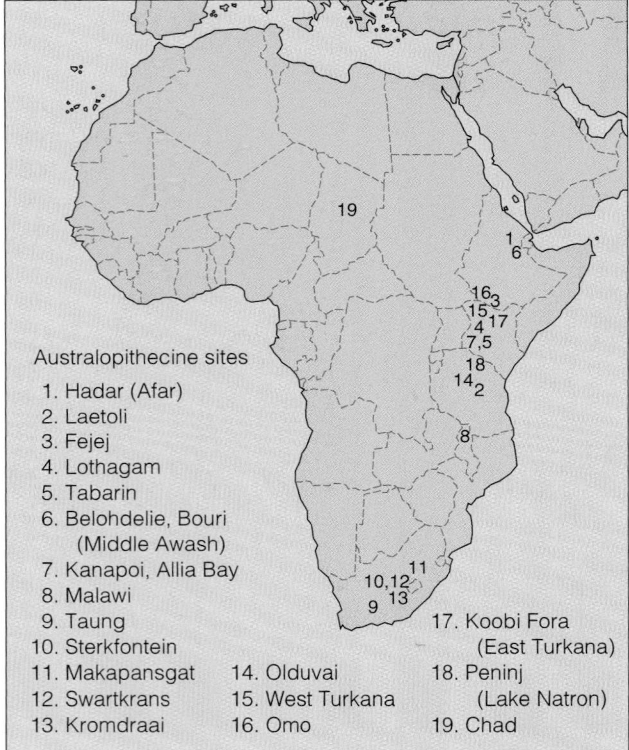

FIGURE 6.5
Australopithecine fossils have been found in South Africa, Malawi, Tanzania, Kenya, Ethiopia, and Chad. In the Miocene the Eurasian and African continents made contact at the eastern and western ends of what now is the Mediterranean Sea.

forest to dry grassy **savannah.** The system also contributed to the volcanic activity in the region, which provides opportunities for accurate dating of fossil specimens. Also in the Miocene, the Indian subcontinent, which had been a solitary landmass for many millions of years, came

savannah Semi arid plains environment as in eastern Africa.
Ardipithecus ramidus One of the earliest hominins that lived in eastern Africa about 5.8 to 4.4 million years ago.

TABLE 6.1 SPECIES OF AUSTRALOPITHECUS

Species	Location
A. anamensis	East Africa
A. afarensis	East Africa
A. africanus	South Africa
A. aethiopicus	East Africa
A. boisei	East Africa/Central Africa
A. gahri	East Africa
A. robustus	South Africa

Note: Paleoanthropologists differ in the number of genera and species they recognize.

into its present position through a collision with Eurasia contributing further to cooler, drier conditions globally. In addition to contributing to global climate change, these geological events also provided excellent opportunities for the discovery of fossil specimens as layers of the earth become exposed through the rifting process.

Geological and climatic changes in human evolutionary history have been frequently incorporated in theories about the evolution of bipedalism with an emphasis on adaptation to the dry savannah environment. As more fossil evidence is discovered from the early Pliocene, we increasingly see that some of the early bipeds may have inhabited a forested environment. For example, in 1994 pieces of several individuals were discovered in 4.4-million-year-old deposits along Ethiopia's Awash River accompanied by fossils of forest animals. Subsequent finds in the same region date between 5.8 and 5.2 million years ago. They are thought to represent early and later varieties of a single species, ***Ardipithecus ramidus.*** The name is fitting for an ultimate human ancestor as *Ardi* means "floor" and *ramid* means "root" in the local Afar language. Unfortunately, the task of freeing the actual fossils from their matrix has proved time-consuming and is not yet complete. Hence a full description of this important material is not yet available.

The development of a rift valley such as the one pictured here is thought to be a precursor to the break up of a continent and is generally associated with volcanic and earthquake activity.

Preliminary indications are that *Ardipithecus*, which was about the size of a modern chimpanzee, though bipedal, was more apelike than any australopithecine in terms of proportions of the limbs and some features of the teeth. The large canines and lower first premolar resemble those of apes, the enamel layer of the molar teeth is thin as it is in African apes and unlike the thick enamel found in humans and other hominins.

Because of this and the presence of several more apelike features, *Ardipithecus* may be a side branch in human evolution.

The *Ardipithecus* finds along with the *Orrorin* and Toumai specimens described in the previous chapter have begun to provide evidence for the time period before australopithecines appeared. So what are we to make of these fossils? Until we have better samples, we will not know for sure. What seems likely on present genetic and fossil evidence is that bipedal hominins evolved from late Miocene apes, becoming distinct by 5 million years ago. It seems that more than one line of biped appeared at this time, but just how many is not known. Australopithecines emerged from this early hominin branching. In turn, one of these species from the middle Pliocene evolved into the genus *Homo*.

Until the *Ardipithecus* specimens were discovered, the earliest bipeds were thought to have lived in a savannah environment. These fossils, however, were found together with other animals and plant remains, indicating a forested environment.

These teeth and jaw fragments are from *Ardipithecus*, a hominin that lived between 5.8 and 4.4 million years ago in Ethiopia.

Anthropologists of Note

Louis S. B. Leakey (1903–1972) ▪ Mary Leakey (1913–1996)

Few figures in the history of paleoanthropology discovered so many key fossils, received so much public acclaim, or stirred up as much controversy as Louis Leakey and his second wife, Mary Leakey. Born in Kenya of missionary parents, Louis received his early education from an English governess and subsequently was sent to England for a university education. He returned to Kenya in the 1920s to begin his career there.

© Melville Bell Grosvenor/National Geographic Society

It was in 1931 that Louis and his research assistant from England, Mary Nicol (whom he married in 1936), began working in their spare time at Olduvai Gorge in Tanzania, searching patiently and persistently for remains of early hominins. It seemed a good place to look, for there were numerous animal fossils, as well as crude stone tools lying scattered on the ground and eroding out of the walls of the gorge. Their patience and persistence were not rewarded until 1959, when Mary found the first hominin fossil. A year later, another skull was found, and Olduvai was on its way to being recognized as one of the most important sources of hominin fossils in all of Africa. While Louis reconstructed, described, and interpreted the fossil material, Mary made the definitive study of the Oldowan tools.

The Leakeys' important discoveries were not limited to those at Olduvai. In the early 1930s, they found the first fossils of Miocene apes in Africa at Rusinga Island in Lake Victoria. Also in the 1930s, Louis found a number of skulls at Kanjera, Kenya, that show a mixture of modern and more primitive features. In 1948, at Fort Ternan, Kenya, the Leakeys found the remains of a late Miocene ape with features that seemed appropriate for a hominin ancestor. After Louis's death, a member of an expedition led by Mary Leakey found the first footprints of *Australopithecus* at Laetoli, Tanzania.

In addition to their own work, Louis Leakey promoted a good deal of important work on the part of others. He made it possible for Jane Goodall to begin her landmark field studies of chimpanzees; later on, he was instrumental in setting up similar studies among gorillas (by Dian Fossey) and orangutans (by Birute Galdikas). Last but not least, the Leakey tradition has been continued by son Richard, his wife, Maeve, and their daughter Louise.

Louis Leakey had a flamboyant personality and a way of making interpretations of fossil materials that frequently did not stand up well to careful scrutiny, but this did not stop him from publicly presenting his views as if they were the gospel truth. It was this aspect of the Leakeys' work that generated controversy. Nonetheless, the Leakeys accomplished and promoted more work that resulted in the accumulation of knowledge about human origins than anyone before them. Anthropology clearly owes them a great deal.

The oldest australopithecine species known so far consists of some jaw and limb bones from Kenya that date to between 4.2 and 3.9 million years ago (see *Australopithecus anamensis* in Table 6.1). Meave and Louise Leakey, daughter-in-law and granddaughter of Louis and Mary Leakey, discovered these fossils and in 1995, decided to place them in a separate species from other known australopithecines. Its name means "ape man of the lake" and it shows particularities in the teeth such as a true "sectorial" premolar tooth shaped to hone the upper canine as seen in apes. As in other australopithecines and humans, the enamel in the molar teeth is thick. The limb bone fragments indicate bipedalism.

Moving closer to the present, the next species defined in the fossil record is *Australopithecus afarensis*. No longer the earliest australopithecine species, it still remains one of the most well known due to the famous "Lucy" specimen and the Laetoli footprints from Tanzania. Lucy consists of bones from almost all parts of a single skeleton discovered in 1974 in the Afar triangle of Ethiopia (hence the name *afarensis*). The Afar region is also famous for the "First Family," a collection of bones from at least thirteen individuals, ranging in age from infancy to adulthood, who died together as a result of some single calamity. At least sixty individuals have been removed from fossil localities in Ethiopia and Tanzania. Specimens from Ethiopia's Afar region are securely dated by potassium argon to between 3.9 and 2.9 million years ago. Material from Laetoli, in Tanzania, is securely dated to 3.6 million years ago. Altogether, *A. afarensis* appears to be a sexually dimorphic bipedal species with estimates of body size and weight ranging between 1.1 and 1.6 meters ($3^{1/2}$–5 feet) and 29 and 45 kilograms (64–100 pounds), respectively.[1]

MEDIATREK

To learn more about our ancestors, as well as the people who discovered them, visit the Institute of Human Origins Web site by going to MediaTrek 6.2 on the companion Web site or CD-ROM.

[1]McHenry, H. M. (1992). Body size and proportions in early hominids. *American Journal of Physical Anthropology, 87*, 407.

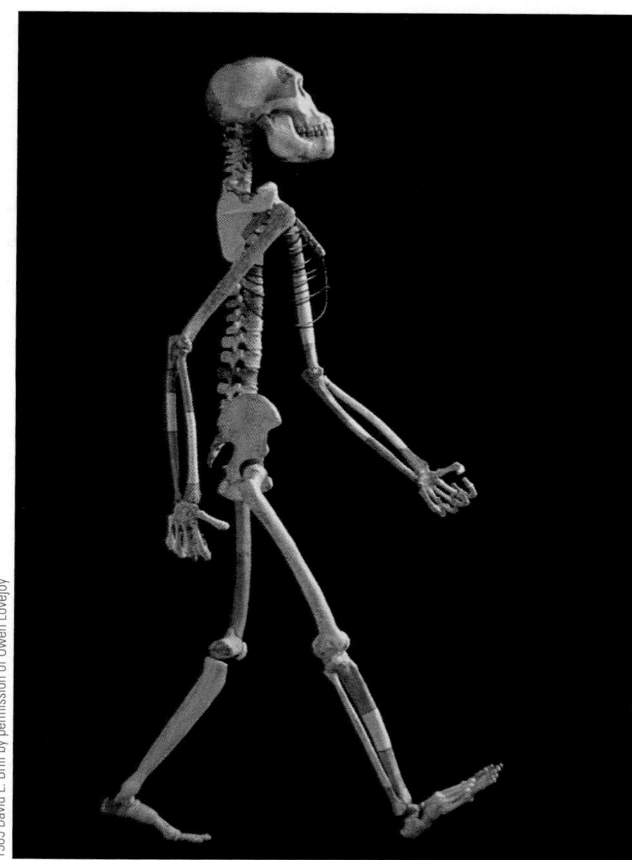

A 40-percent complete australopithecine skeleton "Lucy," named after the Beatles' song "Lucy in the Sky with Diamonds," playing at the time of discovery, indicates these ancestors were bipedal. This adult female was only $3^1/_2$ feet tall, typical of the small size of australopithecines.

If paleoanthropologists are correct in assuming that larger fossil specimens were males and smaller specimens females, males were about $1^1/_2$ times the size of females. In this respect, they were somewhat like the Miocene African apes, with sexual dimorphism greater than one sees in a modern chimpanzee but less than one sees in gorillas and orangutans. Male canine teeth, too, are significantly larger than canine teeth of females, though canine size is reduced compared to that of chimps (Figure 6.6).

The nearly 40-percent complete Lucy specimen has provided invaluable information about the shape of the pelvis and torso of early human ancestors. *A. afarensis'* physical appearance was unusual by human standards: They may be described as looking like an ape from the waist up and like a human from the waist down (Figure 6.7). In addition, a forearm bone from Lucy, which is relatively shorter than that of an ape, suggests that the upper limb was lighter and the center of gravity lower in the body than in apes. Still, the arms of Lucy and other early australopithecines are long in proportion to their legs when compared to the proportions seen in humans. Though fully competent as bipeds, the curvature of the fingers and toes and the somewhat elevated position of the shoulder joint indicate *A. afarensis* was more adapted to tree climbing compared to more recent hominins.

The skull of *A. afarensis* is relatively low, the forehead slopes backward, and the brow ridge that helps give apes such massive-looking foreheads is also present. The lower half of the face is chinless and accented by jaws that are quite large, relative to the size of the skull. The brain is small and apelike, and the general conformation of the skull seems nonhuman. Even the semicircular canal, a part of the ear crucial to maintenance of balance, is apelike. Cranial capacity, commonly used as an index of brain size for *A. afarensis,* averages about 420 cubic centimeters (cc), roughly equivalent to the size of a chimpanzee and about one-third the size of living humans.[2] Intelligence, however, is not indicated by absolute brain size alone but is roughly indicated by the ratio of brain to body size. Unfortunately, with such a wide range of adult weights, it is not clear whether australopithecine brain size was larger than a modern ape's relative to body size.

Much has been written about australopithecine teeth because they are one of the primary means to

[2]Grine, F. E. (1993). Australopithecine taxonomy and phylogeny: Historical background and recent interpretation. In R. L. Ciochon & J. G. Fleagle (Eds.), *The human evolution source book* (pp. 201–202). Englewood Cliffs, NJ: Prentice-Hall.

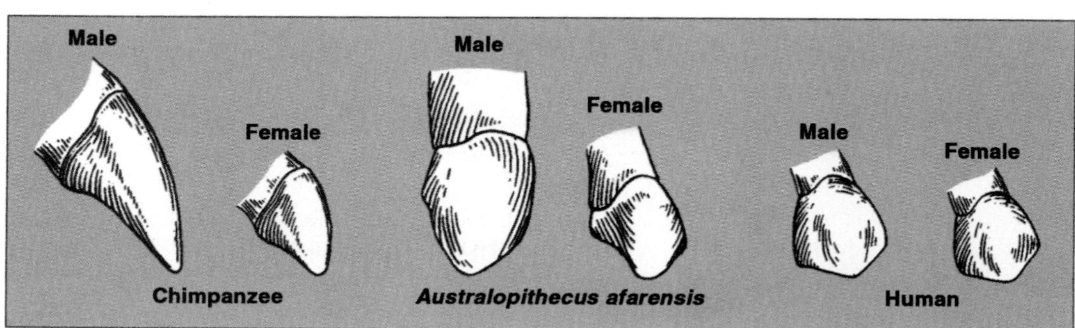

FIGURE 6.6
Sexual dimorphism in canine teeth.

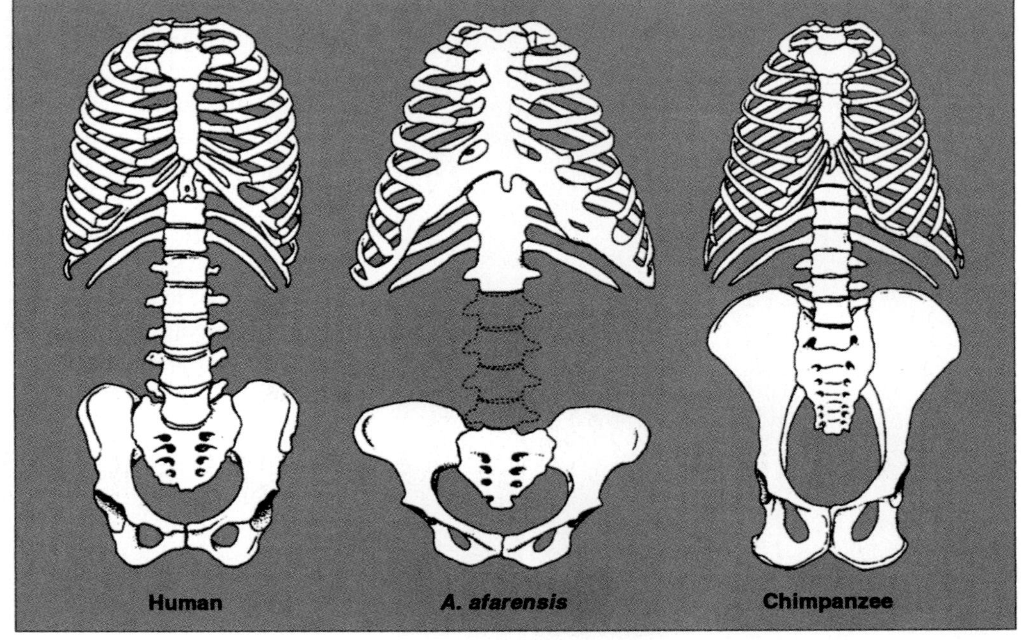

FIGURE 6.7
Trunk skeletons of modern human, *A. afarensis,* and chimpanzee, compared. In its pelvis, the australopithecine resembles the modern human, but its rib cage shows the pyramidal configuration of the ape.

make distinctions between closely related groups. In *A. afarensis,* unlike humans, the teeth are all quite large, particularly the molars. The premolar is no longer fully sectorial as in *A. anamensis,* but most other features of the teeth represent a more ancestral rather than derived condition. For example, the rows of the teeth are more parallel (the ancestral ape condition) compared to the arch seen in the human tooth rows. The canines project slightly and a slight space or gap known as a **diastema** remains between the upper incisors and canines as found in the apes (Figure 6.8).

To further complicate the diversity seen in *A. afarensis,* in 2001 Maeve and Louise Leakey announced the discovery of an almost complete cranium, parts of two upper jaws, and assorted teeth from a site in northern Kenya.[3] Contemporary with early East African *Australopithecus,* The Leakeys see this as a different genus named ***Kenyanthropus platyops*** ("flat-faced man of Kenya"). Unlike contemporary australopithecines, *Kenyanthropus* is said to have a small braincase and small molars set in a large, humanlike, flat face. But again, there is controversy; the Leakeys see the fossils as ancestral to the genus *Homo.* Other paleoanthropologists are not convinced, suggesting that the Leakey's interpretation rests on a questionable reconstruction of badly broken fossil specimens.[4]

South Africa

Throughout the 20th century and into the present, paleoanthropologists have continued to recover australopithecine fossils from a variety of sites in South Africa. Included in this group are numerous fossils found beginning in the 1930s at Sterkfontein and Makapansgat (see Figure 6.5), in addition to Dart's original find from Taung. It is important to note, however, that South African sites, lacking the clear stratigraphy and volcanic ash of East African sites, are much more difficult to date and interpret (Figure 6.9). One unusually complete skull and skeleton has been dated by paleomagnetism to about 3.5 million years ago[5] as was a partial foot skeleton (Figure 6.10) described in 1995.[6] The other South African remains are difficult to date. A faunal series

[3]Leakey, M. G., Spoor, F., Brown, F. H., Gathogo, P. N., Kiare, C., Leakey, L. N., & McDougal, I. (2001). New hominin genus from eastern Africa shows diverse middle Pliocene lineages. *Nature, 410,* 433–440.

diastema A space between the canines and other teeth allowing large projecting canines space within the jaw.
Kenyanthropus platyops A new proposed hominin contemporary with early australopithecines; may not be separate genus.

[4]White, T. D. (2003). Early hominids—diversity or distortion? *Science, 299,* 1,994–1,997.

[5]Clarke, R. J. (1998). First ever discovery of a well preserved skull and associated skeleton of Australopithecus. *South African Journal of Science, 94,* 460–464.

[6]Clarke, R. J., & Tobias, P. V. (1995). Sterkfontein member 2 foot bones of the oldest South African hominid. *Science, 269,* 521–524.

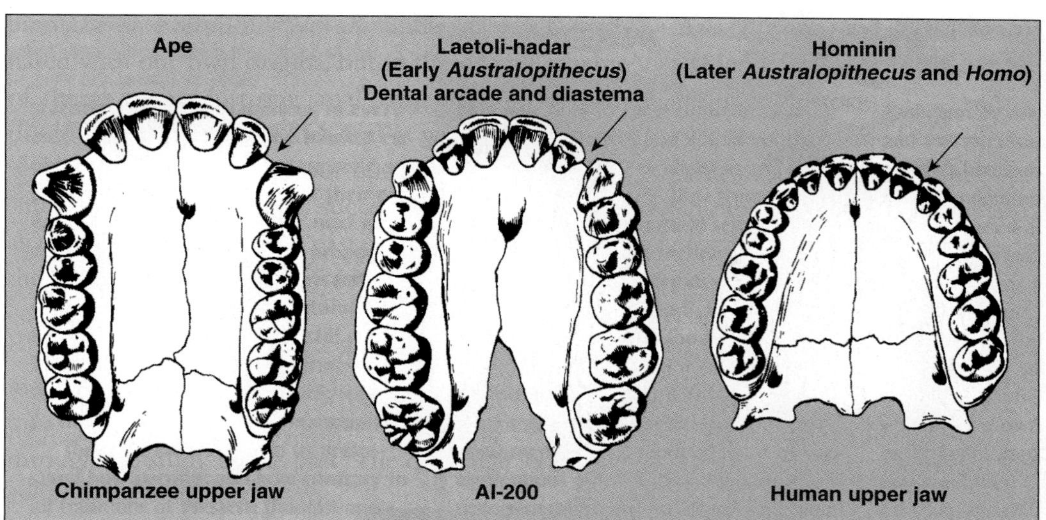

FIGURE 6.8

The upper jaws of an ape, *Australopithecus,* and modern human show important differences in the shape of the dental arch and the spacing between the canines and adjoining teeth. Only in the earliest australopithecines can a diastema (a large gap between the upper canine and incisor) be seen.

established in East Africa places these specimens between 3 and 2.3 million years ago. These specimens are all classified in the australopithecine species named by Dart—*A. africanus,* also known as **gracile australopithecines.**

The reconstruction of australopithecine biology is controversial. Some researchers think they see evidence for some expansion of the brain in *A. africanus,* while others vigorously disagree. Paleoanthropologists also compare the outside appearance of the brain, as revealed by casts of the insides of skulls. Some researchers suggest that cerebral reorganization toward a human condition is present,[7] while others state the

[7]Holloway, R. L., & de LaCoste-Lareymondie, M. C. (1982). Brain endocast asymmetry in pongids and hominids: Some preliminary findings on the paleontology of cerebral dominance. *American Journal of Physical Anthropology, 58,* 101–110.

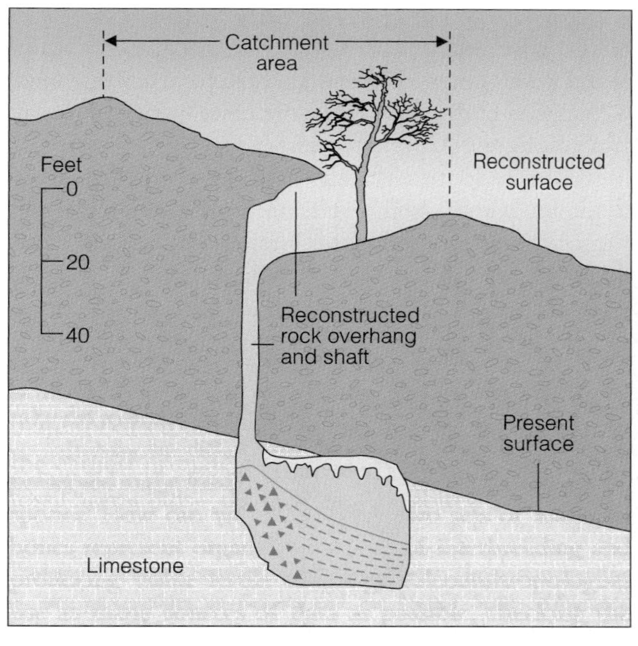

FIGURE 6.9

Many of the fossil sites in South Africa were limestone caverns connected to the surface by a shaft. Over time, dirt, bones, and other matter that fell down the shaft accumulated inside the cavern, becoming fossilized. In the Pliocene, the earth next to the shaft's opening provided a sheltered location for trees that, in turn, may have been used by predators for eating without being bothered by scavengers.

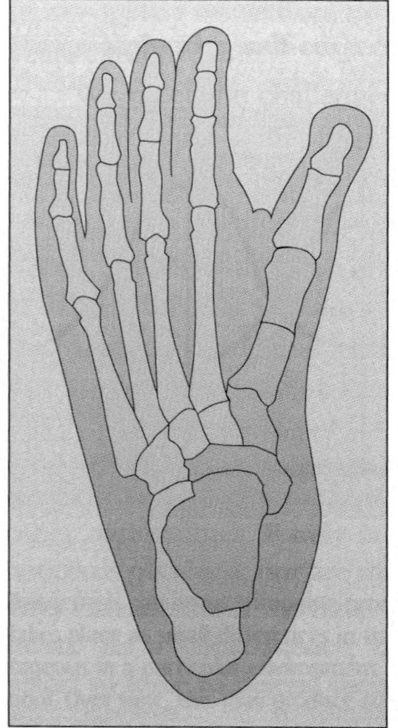

FIGURE 6.10

Drawing of the foot bones of a 3- to 3.5-million-year-old *Australopithecus* from Sterkfontein, South Africa, as they would have been in the complete foot. Note how long and flexible the first toe (at right) is.

gracile australopithecines Members of the genus *Australopithecus* possessing a more lightly built chewing apparatus.

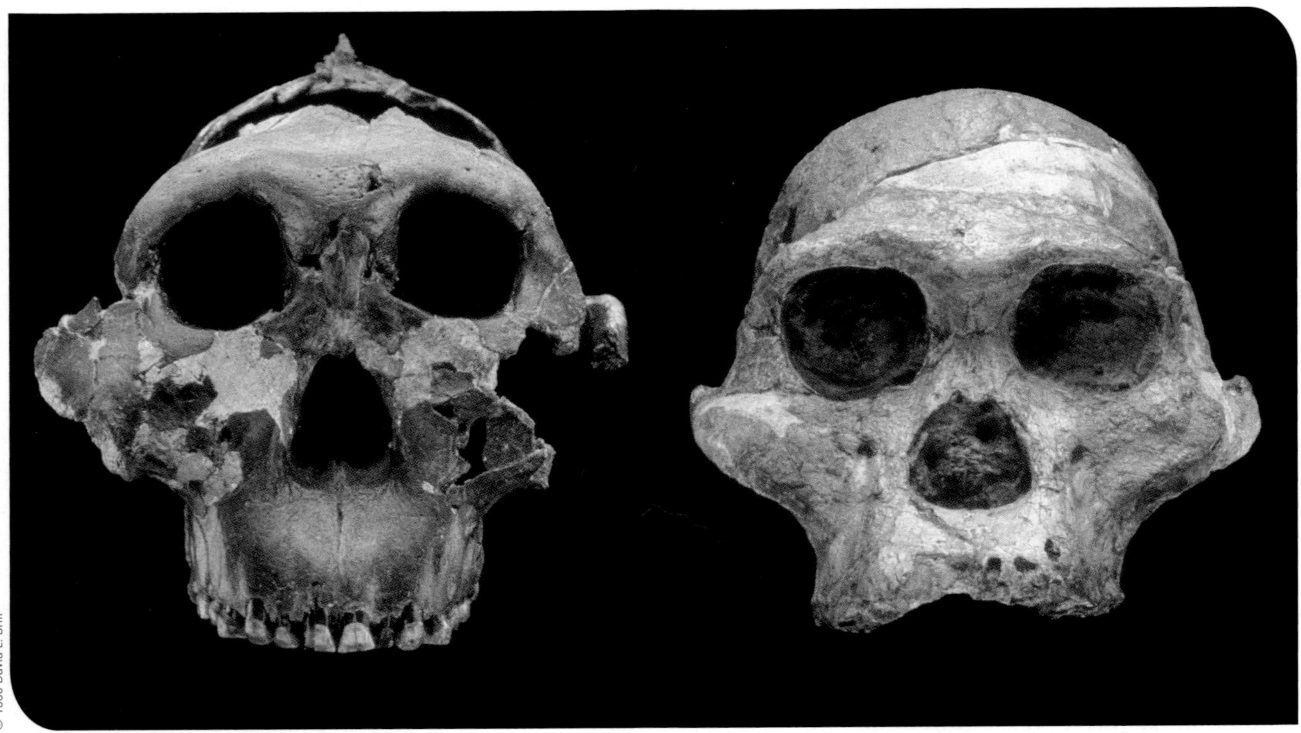

VISUAL COUNTERPOINT The differences between gracile and robust australopithecines are related primarily to their chewing apparatus. Robust species have extremely large cheek teeth, large chewing muscles, and a bony ridge on the top of their skulls for the attachment of large chewing muscles. The front and back teeth of gracile species are balanced in size, and their chewing muscles (reflected in a less massive skull) are more like those seen in the later genus *Homo*.

organization of the brain is more apelike than human.[8] At the moment, the weight of the evidence favors mental capabilities for all gracile australopithecines as being comparable to those of modern great apes (chimps, bonobos, gorillas, orangutans).

Using patterns of tooth eruption in young australopithecines such as Taung, North American paleoanthropologist Alan Mann and colleagues suggested that the developmental pattern of australopithecines was more humanlike than apelike,[9] though some other paleoanthropologists do not agree. A current understanding of genetics and macroevolutionary process indicates that a developmental shift is likely to have accompanied a change in body plan such as the emergence of bipedalism among the African hominoids.

Other South African sites have yielded fossil hominins whose skull and teeth looked quite different from the gracile australopithecines described above. These South African fossils are known as *Australopithecus robustus.* They are notable for having teeth, jaws, and chewing muscles that are massive (robust) relative to the size of the braincase. The gracile forms are slightly smaller on average and lack such robust chewing structures. Over the course of hominin evolution, several distinct groups of **robust australopithecines** have appeared not only in South Africa, but throughout East Africa as well.

Robust Australopithecines

The remains of robust australopithecines were first found at Kromdraai and Swartkrans in South Africa by paleoanthropologists Robert Broom and John Robinson in the 1930s in deposits that, unfortunately, cannot be securely dated. Current thinking puts them anywhere from 1.8 to 1.0 million years ago. Usually referred to as *A. robustus* (see Table 6.1 and Figure 6.5), this species

[8]Falk, D. (1989). Apelike endocast of "ape-man" Taung. *American Journal of Physical Anthropology, 80,* 339.

[9]Mann A., Lampl, M., & Monge, J. (1990). Patterns of ontogeny in human evolution: Evidence from dental development. *Yearbook of Physical Anthropology, 33,* 111–150.

robust australopithecines Slightly larger and more robust than gracile members of genus *Australopithecus,* with large, more powerful jaws and teeth.
sagittal crest A crest running from front to back on the top of the skull along the midline to provide a surface of bone for the attachment of the large chewing muscles.

In 1999, Ethiopian paleoanthropologist Y. Haile Selassie discovered fossil material placed into the new species *Australopithecus gahri.*

possessed characteristic robust chewing apparatus including a **sagittal crest** running from front to back along the top of the skull. This feature provides sufficient area on a relatively small braincase for attachment of the huge temporal muscles required to operate powerful jaws. Because it is present in robust australopithecines and gorillas today, this feature provides an example of convergent evolution.

The first robust australopithecine to be found in East Africa was discovered by Mary Leakey in the summer of 1959, the centennial year of the publication of Darwin's *On the Origin of Species.* She found it in Olduvai Gorge, a fossil-rich area near Ngorongoro Crater, on the Serengeti Plain of Tanzania, East Africa. Olduvai is a huge gash in the earth, about 25 miles long and 300 feet deep, which cuts through Plio-Pleistocene and recent geological strata revealing close to 2 million years of the earth's history.

Mary Leakey's discovery was reconstructed by her husband Louis, who gave it the name *"Zinjanthropus boisei"* (Zinj, an Arabic word for East Africa, boisei for a benefactor). At first, he thought this hominin seemed more humanlike than *Australopithecus* and extremely close to modern humans in evolutionary development

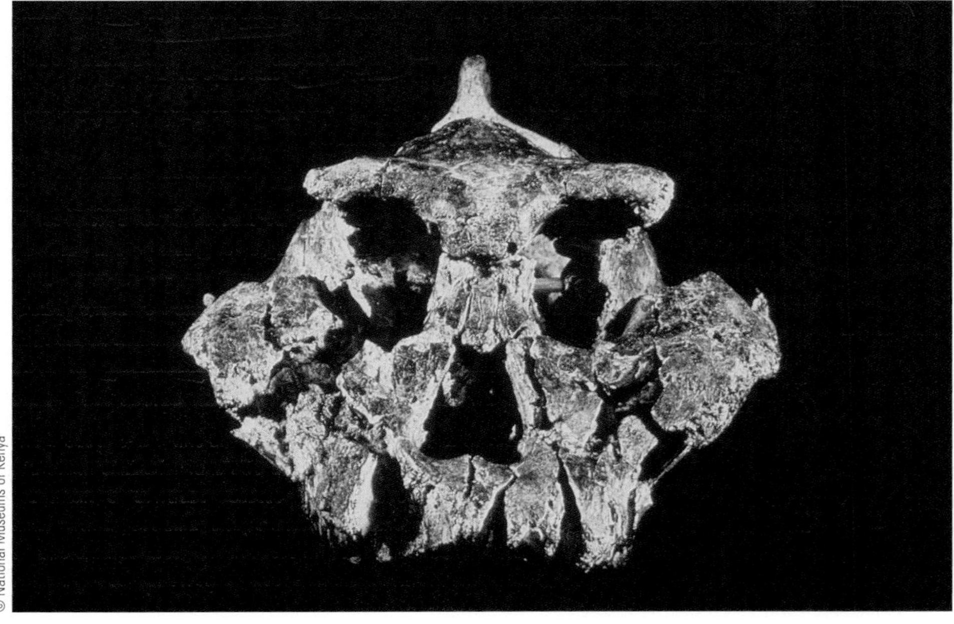

The so-called Black Skull, found West of Lake Turkana, Kenya, is the earliest known robust *Australopithecus.* At 2.5 million years old, it appears ancestral to later robust australopithecines from East Africa.

in part due to the stone tools found in association with this specimen. Further study, however, revealed that *Zinjanthropus,* the remains of which consisted of a skull and a few limb bones, was an East African representative of *Australopithecus.* Although similar in many ways to *A. robustus,* it is now most commonly referred to as *Australopithecus boisei* (see Table 6.1 and Figure 6.5). Potassium-argon dating places this early hominin at about 1.75 million years old. Since the time of Mary Leakey's original find, numerous other fossils of this robust species have been found at Olduvai, as well as north and east of Lake Turkana in Kenya. Although one fossil specimen often referred to as the "Black Skull" (see *A. aethiopicus* Table 6.1 and Figure 6.5) is known to be as much as 2.5 million years old, some date to as recently as 1.3 million years ago.

Like robust australopithecines from South Africa, East African robust forms possessed enormous molars and premolars. Despite a large mandible and palate, the anterior teeth (canines and incisors) were often crowded, owing to the room needed for the massive molars.

The heavy skull, more massive even than seen in the robust forms from South Africa, has a sagittal crest and prominent brow ridges. Cranial capacity ranges from about 500 to 530 cubic centimeters. Body size, too, is somewhat larger; whereas the robust South African robust forms are estimated to have weighed between 32 and 40 kilograms, the East African robusts probably weighed from 34 to 49 kilograms.

Because the earliest robust skull from East Africa (2.5 million years), the so-called Black Skull from Kenya, retains a number of ancestral features shared with earlier East African australopithecines, it is possible that it evolved from *A. afarensis,* giving rise to the later robust East African forms. Whether the South African robust australopithecines represent a southern offshoot of the East African line or convergent evolution from a South African ancestor is so far not settled; arguments can be presented for both interpretations. In either case, what happened was that the later australopithecines developed molars and premolars that are both absolutely and relatively larger than those of earlier australopithecines who possessed front and back teeth more in proportion to those seen in the genus *Homo.*

Larger teeth require more bone to support them, hence the prominent jaws of the robust australopithecines. Larger jaws and heavy chewing activity require more jaw musculature that attaches to the skull. The marked crests seen on skulls of the late australopithecines provide for the attachment of chewing muscles on a skull that has increased very little in size. In effect, robust australopithecines had evolved into highly efficient chewing machines. Clearly, their immense cheek teeth and powerful chewing muscles bespeak the kind of heavy chewing a diet restricted to uncooked plant foods require. This kind of general level of biological organization shared by separate fossil groups as seen in the robust australopithecines is referred to as a grade.

Many anthropologists believe that, by becoming a specialized consumer of plant foods, the late australopithecines avoided competing for the same niche with early *Homo,* with which they were contemporaries. In the course of evolution, the **law of competitive exclusion** dictates that when two closely related species compete for the same niche, one will out-compete the other, bringing about the loser's extinction. That early *Homo* and late *Australopithecus* did not compete for the same niche is suggested by their coexistence for something like 1.5 million years from about 2.5 million to 1 million years ago (see Figure 6.11).

Australopithecines and the Genus *Homo*

A variety of bipeds inhabited Africa about 2.5 million years ago, around the time the first evidence for the genus *Homo* begins to appear. In 1999, another possible species of australopithecine was added into the mix. Found in the Afar region of Ethiopia, these fossils were named *Australopithicus gahri* after the word for "surprise" in the local Afar language. Though the teeth were large, this australopithecine possessed an arched dental arcade and a ratio between front and back teeth more like humans and gracile australopithecines rather than like robust groups. For this reason, some have proposed that *A. gahri* is ancestral to the genus *Homo.* More evidence will be needed to prove whether or not this is true.

The precise relationship among all the australopithecine species (and other hominins) that have been defined during the Pliocene is still somewhat controversial. In this mix, the question of which australopithecine was ancestral to humans remains particularly

law of competitive exclusion When two closely related species compete for the same niche, one will out-compete the other, bringing about the latter's extinction.

MEDIATREK

To use an interactive evolutionary tree and figure out the relationship among the ancestral hominin groups, visit MediaTrek 6.3 on the companion Web site or CD-ROM.

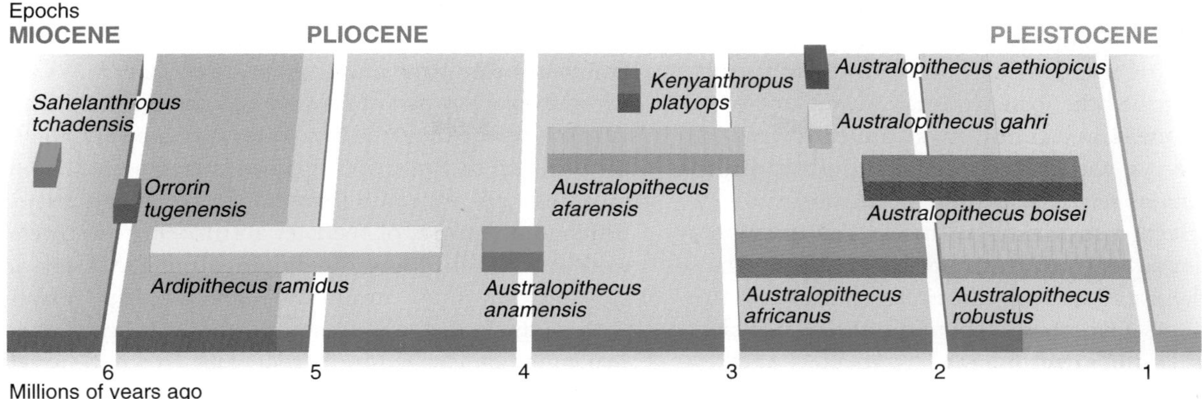

FIGURE 6.11

The earliest hominine fossils and the scientific names by which they have been known, arranged according to when they lived. *A. aethiopicus, A. boisei*, and *A. robustus* are all *Robust Australopithecines; A. afarensis, A. africanus*, and *A. anamensis* are gracile *Australopithecines*. Whether all the different species names are warranted is hotly debated.

controversial. A variety of scenarios have been proposed, each one giving a different australopithecine group the "starring role" as the immediate human ancestor (Figure 6.12). Though paleoanthropologists debate which species is ancestral to humans, they agree that the robust australopithecines, though successful in their time, ultimately represent an evolutionary side branch.

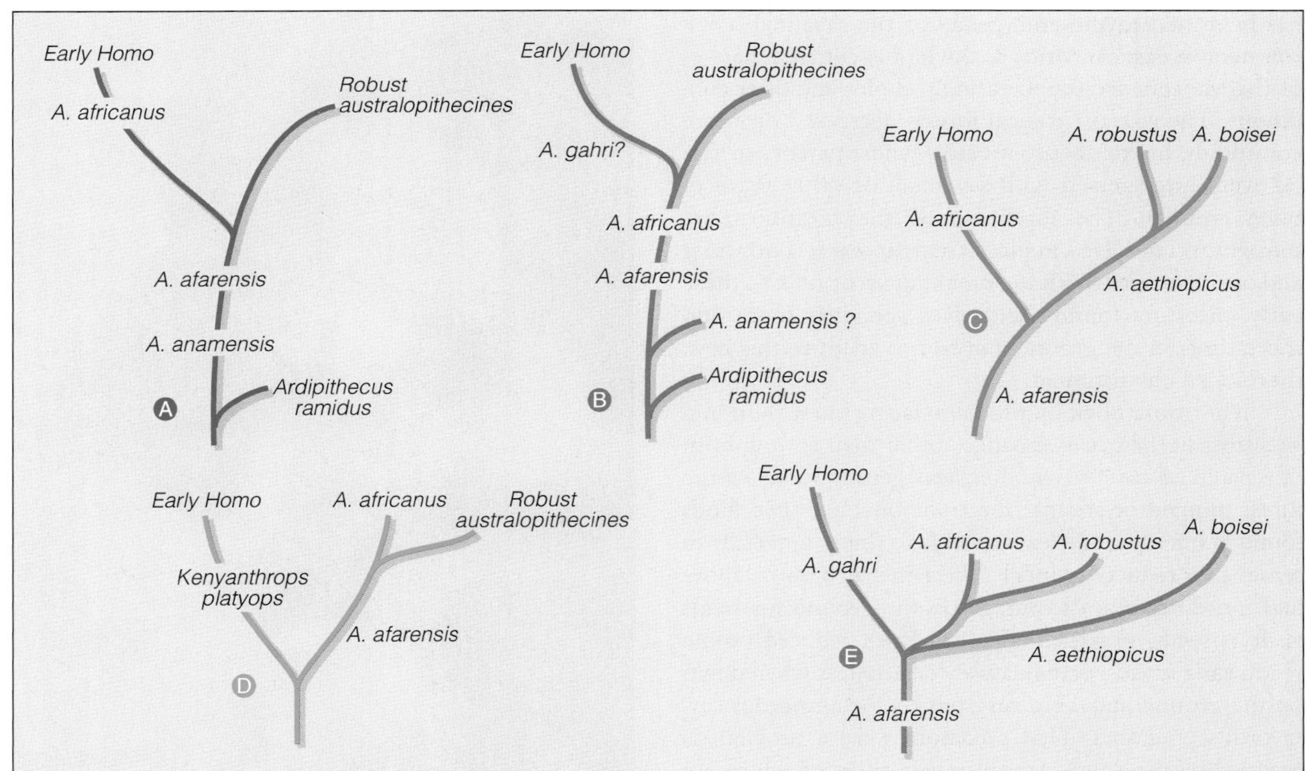

FIGURE 6.12

The relationship among the various australopithecine (and other) Pliocene groups, and the question of which group is ancestral to the genus *Homo*, is debated by anthropologists. Several alternative hypotheses are presented in these diagrams. Most agree, however, that the robust australopithecines represent an evolutionary side branch.

ENVIRONMENT, DIET, AND AUSTRALOPITHECINE ORIGINS

Having described the fossil material, we may now consider *how* evolution transformed an early ape into *Australopithecus*. Generally, such paleoanthropological reconstructions rely heavily on the evolutionary role of natural selection in their hypotheses. The question at hand is not so much *why* did bipedalism appear as *how* did bipedalism allow early hominins to adapt to their environment? Hypotheses about hominin adaptation begin with features evident in the fragmentary fossil evidence. For example, the fossil record indicates that once bipedalism appeared, over the next several million years the shape of the face and teeth shifted from a more ape-like to a humanlike condition. To refine their hypotheses, paleoanthropologists add scientifically reconstructed environmental conditions and inferences made from data gathered on living nonhuman primates and humans to the fossil evidence. In this regard, evolutionary reconstructions involve piecing together a coherent story or narrative about the past. Sometimes these narratives are quite tenuous. But as paleoanthropologists consider their own biases and incorporate new evidence as it is discovered, the narrative changes and its quality improves.

For many years, the human evolutionary narrative has been tied to the emergence of the savannah environment in eastern Africa as the global climate changes of the Miocene led to increasingly cooler and drier conditions. The size of tropical forests decreased or, more commonly, broke up into mosaics where patches of forest were interspersed with savannah or other types of open country. The forebears of the hominins are thought to have lived in places with access to both trees and open country. With the breaking up of forests, these early ancestors found themselves spending more and more time on the ground and had to adapt to this new, more open environment.

The most obvious problem facing these hominin ancestors in their new situation, other than getting from one patch of trees to another, was getting food. As the forest thinned or shrank, the traditional ape-type foods found in trees became less available to them, especially in seasons of reduced rainfall. Therefore, it became more and more necessary to forage on the ground for foods such as seeds, grasses, and roots. With reduced canine teeth, early bipeds were relatively defenseless when down on the ground and were easy targets for numerous carnivorous predators. That predators were a problem is revealed by the South African fossils, most of which are from individuals that were dropped into rock fissures by leopards or, in the case of Dart's original find, by an eagle.

Many investigators have argued that the hands of early bipeds took over the weapon functions of the reduced canine teeth, by enabling them to threaten predators by using wooden objects as clubs and throwing stones. This quality is shared with many of the other hominoids. Recall the male chimpanzee (Chapter 3) who wielded objects as part of his display to obtain alpha status. In australopithecines the use of clubs and throwing stones may have set the stage for the much later manufacture of more efficient weapons from bone, wood, and stone. Although the hands of the later australopithecines were suitable for tool making, no evidence exists that any of them actually made stone tools. Similarly, experiments with captive bonobos have shown that they are capable of making crude chipped stone tools, but they have never been known to do so outside of captivity. Thus, to be able to do something is not necessarily equivalent to doing it. In fact, the earliest known stone tools, dating to about 2.5 million years ago, are about 2 million years more recent than the oldest fossils of *Australopithecus*. However, *Australopithecus* certainly had no less intelligence and dexterity than do modern great apes, all of whom make use of tools when it is to their advantage to do so. Orangutans, bonobos, and chimpanzees have all been observed in the wild making and using simple tools such as those described in Chapter 3. Gorillas seem not to

Photo by Dr. Rose Seveik. Courtesy of The Language Research Center.

In captivity great apes have been known to make stone tools similar to those made by our ancestors 2.5 million years ago.

© John Giustina

Just as chimpanzees use wooden probes to fish for termites, so do orangutans use probes to extract termites, ants, or honey. Such tool use likely goes back to a time preceding the split between Asian and African hominoids, long before the appearance of the earliest bipeds.

do so in the wild only because they developed a diet of leaves and nettles that does not require tools. Most likely, the ability to make and use simple tools is something that goes back to the last common ancestor of the Asian and African apes, before the appearance of the first bipeds.

It is reasonable to suppose, then, that australopithecines were tool users, though not toolmakers. Unfortunately, few tools that they used are likely to have survived for a million and more years, and any that did would be hard to recognize as such. Although we cannot be certain about this, in addition to clubs and missiles for defense, sturdy sticks may have been used to dig edible roots, and convenient stones may have been used (as some chimpanzees do) to crack open nuts. In fact, some animal bones from australopithecine sites in South Africa show microscopic wear patterns suggesting their use to dig edible roots from the ground. We may also allow the possibility that, like chimpanzees, females may have used tools more often to get and process food than males, but the latter may have used tools more often as "weapons."[10]

Humans Stand on Their Own Two Feet

From the broad-shouldered, long-armed, tailless ape body plan, the early hominins became fully bipedal. Their late Miocene forebears seem to have been primates that combined quadrupedal tree climbing with at least some swinging below the branches. On the ground, they were capable of assuming an upright stance, at least on occasion (optional, versus obligatory, bipedalism). Paleoanthropologists generally take the negative aspects of bipedal locomotion into account when considering the advantages of this pattern of locomotion. For example, paleoanthropologists have suggested that bipedalism makes an animal more visible to predators, exposes its soft underbelly or gut, and interferes with the ability to change direction as instantly while running. They also emphasize that bipedalism does not result in particularly fast running; quadrupedal chimpanzees and baboons, for example, are 30 to 34 percent faster than we bipeds. For 100-meter distances, our best athletes today may attain speeds of 34 to 37 kilometers per hour, while the larger African carnivores that bipeds might run from can attain speeds up to 60 to 70 kilometers per hour. The consequences of a serious leg or foot injury are more serious for a biped while a quadruped can do amazingly well on three legs. A biped with only one functional leg is seriously hindered—an easy meal for some carnivore. Because each of these drawbacks would have placed our early hominin ancestors at risk from predators, paleoanthropologists have tended to ask, what made bipedal locomotion worth paying such a high price? Paleoanthropologists have found it hard to imagine bipedalism becoming a viable adaptation in the absence of strong selective pressure in its favor; therefore, a number of theories have been proposed to account for the adaptive advantages of bipedalism.

One once-popular suggestion is that bipedal locomotion allowed males to gather food on the savannah and transport it back to females, who were restricted from doing so by the dependence of their offspring.[11] This explanation is unlikely, however, because female apes, not to mention women among food-foraging

[10]Goodall, J. (1986). *The chimpanzees of Gombe: Patterns of behavior* (pp. 552, 564). Cambridge, MA: Belknap Press.

[11]Lovejoy, C. O. (1981). The origin of man. *Science, 211*, 341–350.

peoples, routinely combine infant care with foraging for food. Indeed, among most food foragers, it is the women who commonly supply the bulk of the food eaten by both sexes. Moreover, the pair bonding (one male attached to one female) presumed by this model is not characteristic of terrestrial primates, nor of those displaying the degree of sexual dimorphism that was characteristic of *Australopithecus.* Nor is it really characteristic of *Homo sapiens.* In a substantial majority of recent human societies, including those in which people forage for their food, some form of polygamy—marriage to two or more individuals at the same time—is not only permitted, but preferred. And even in the supposedly monogamous United States, it is relatively common for an individual to marry (and hence mate with) two or more others (the only require-

Biocultural Connection

Evolution and Human Birth

Because biology and culture have always shaped human experience, it can be a challenge to separate the influences of each of these factors on human practices. For example, in the 1950s, paleoanthropologists developed the theory that human childbirth is particularly difficult compared to birth in other mammals. This theory was based in part on the observation of a "tight fit" between the human mother's birth canal and the baby's head, though several other primates also possess similarly tight fits between the newborn's head or shoulders and the birth canal. Nevertheless, changes in the birth canal associated with bipedalism were held responsible for difficult birth in humans.

At the same historical moment, American childbirth practices were changing. In one generation from the 1920s to the 1950s birth shifted from the home to the hospital. In the process childbirth transformed from something a woman normally accomplished at home, perhaps with the help of a midwife or relatives, into the high-tech delivery of a neonate (the medical term for a newborn) with the assistance of medically trained personnel. During the 1950s women were generally fully anesthetized during the birth process. Paleoanthropological theories mirrored the cultural norms, providing a scientific explanation for the change in American childbirth practices.

As a scientific theory, the idea of difficult human birth stands on shaky ground. No fossil neonates have ever been recovered, and only a handful of complete pelves (the bones forming the birth canal) exist. Instead, scientists must examine the birth process in living humans and nonhuman primates to reconstruct the evolution of the human birth pattern. Cultural beliefs and practices, however, shape every aspect of birth. Cultural factors determine where a birth occurs, the actions of the individuals present, and beliefs about the nature of the experience. When paleoanthropologists of the 1950s and 1960s asserted that human childbirth is more difficult than birth in other mammals, they may have been drawing upon their own North American cultural beliefs that childbirth is dangerous and belongs in a hospital. A quick look at global neonatal mortality statistics indicates that in countries such as The Netherlands and Sweden, healthy well-nourished women give birth successfully outside of hospitals as they did throughout human evolutionary history. In other countries, deaths related to childbirth reflect malnutrition, infectious disease, and the low social status of women, rather than an inherently faulty biology.

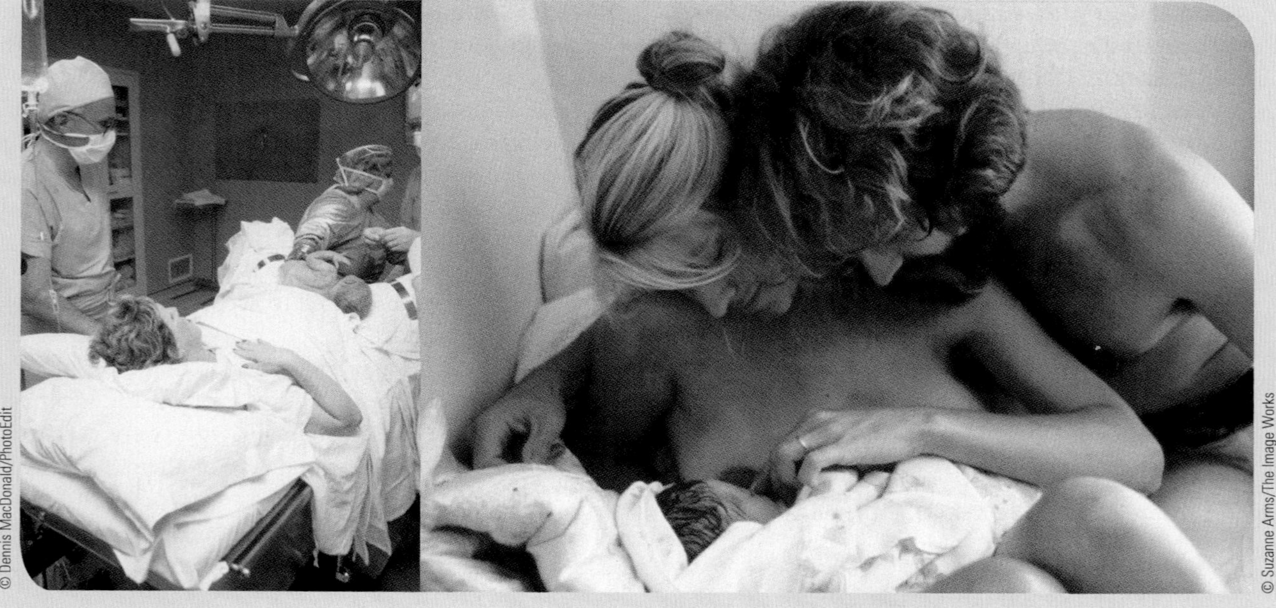

ment is that he or she not be married to them at the same time).

Although we may reject as culture-bound the idea of male "breadwinners" provisioning "stay-at-home moms," it is true that bipedal locomotion does make transport of bulky foods possible. (See the Biocultural Connection for another example of the influence of socially defined roles for males and females and the "hazards model" of bipedalism on theories about the evolution of hominin biology.) Nevertheless, a fully erect biped on the ground—whether male or female—has the ability to gather such foods for transport back to a tree or other place of safety for consumption. The biped does not have to remain out in the open, exposed and vulnerable, to do all of its eating.

Besides making food transport possible, bipedalism could have facilitated the food quest in other ways. With their hands free and body upright, the animals could reach otherwise unobtainable food on thorn trees too flimsy and too spiny to climb. Furthermore, with both hands free, they could gather other small foods twice as fast. And in times of scarcity, their ability to travel far without tiring would help get them between widely distributed sources of food. Distant sources of food and water can be located more easily with the head positioned higher than in a quadrupedal stance.

Still other advantages of bipedalism would have enhanced survivability. With their heads well up above the ground, bipeds are more likely to spot predators before they get too close for safety. Finally, if hominins did get caught away from a safe place of refuge by a predator, manipulative and dexterous hands freed from locomotion provided them with a means of protecting themselves by brandishing and throwing objects at their attackers. But, as the fate of the South African specimens attests, even this strategy was not foolproof.

Food may not have been the only thing transported by early bipeds. As we saw in Chapter 3, infants must be able to cling to their mothers in order to be transported; because the mother is using her forelimbs in locomotion, to either walk or swing by, she can't very well carry her infant. Chimpanzee infants, for example, must cling by themselves to their mother, and even at the age of 4, they make long journeys on their mothers' backs. Injuries caused by falling from the mother are a significant cause of infant mortality among apes. Thus, the ability to carry infants would have made a significant contribution to the survivorship of offspring, and the ancestors of *Australopithecus* would have been capable of doing just this.

Another suggestion—that bipedal locomotion arose as an adaptation for nonterritorial scavenging of meat[12]—is unlikely. Although it is true that a biped is able to travel long distances without tiring, and that a daily supply of dead animal carcasses would have been available to hominins only if they were capable of ranging over vast areas, no evidence exists to indicate that hominins did much in the way of scavenging prior to about 2.5 million years ago. Furthermore, the heavy wear seen on australopithecine teeth is indicative of a diet high in tough, fibrous plant foods. Thus, scavenging was likely an unforeseen by-product of bipedal locomotion, rather than a cause of it.

Yet more recent is the suggestion that our ancestors stood up as a way to cope with heat stress out in the

[12]Lewin, R. (1987). Four legs good, two legs bad. *Science, 235,* 969–971.

Because apes do not normally walk bipedally, they cannot easily hold on to their infants when moving about. The ability to carry infants while walking bipedally probably reduced the risk of fatal falls for the infants of our bipedal ancestors.

open. In addition to bipedalism, one of the most obvious differences between humans and other living hominoids is our relative nakedness. Body hair in humans is generally limited to a fine sparse layer over most of the body with a very dense cover of hair limited primarily to the head. Peter Wheeler, a British physiologist, has suggested that bipedalism and the human pattern of body hair growth are both adaptations to the heat stress of the savannah environment.[13] Building upon the earlier "radiator" theory of North American paleoanthropologist Dean Falk, Wheeler developed this hypothesis through comparative anatomy, experimental studies, and the observation that humans are the only apes to inhabit the savannah environment.

Many other animals, however, inhabit the savannah, and each of them possesses some mechanism for coping with heat stress. Some animals, like many of the carnivores, are active only when the sun is low in the sky, early or late in the day, or when it is absent altogether at night. Some, like antelope, are evolved to tolerate high body temperatures that would kill humans due to overheating of the brain tissue. They accomplish this through cooling their blood in their muzzles through evaporation before it enters the vessels leading to the delicate tissues of the brain.

According to Wheeler, the interesting thing about humans and other primates is that

> We can't uncouple brain temperature from the rest of the body, the way an antelope does, so we've got to prevent any damaging elevations in body temperature. And of course the problem is even more acute for an ape, because in general, the larger and more complex the brain, the more easily it is damaged. So, there were incredible selective pressures on early hominins favoring adaptations that would reduce thermal stress-pressures that may have favored bipedalism.[14]

Though the idea that bipedal posture reduces the amount of heat from solar radiation to which humans are exposed is not completely new, Wheeler has scientifically studied this phenomenon. He took a systematic series of measurements on the exposure of an early hominin like "Lucy" to solar radiation in upright and quadrupedal stances. He found that the bipedal stance reduced exposure to solar radiation by 60 percent, indicating that a biped would require less water to stay cool in a savannah environment compared to a quadruped. Wheeler further suggests that bipedalism made the human body hair pattern possible. Fur can keep out solar radiation as well as retaining heat. A biped, with reduced exposure to the sun everywhere except the head, would benefit from hair loss on the body surface to increase the efficiency of sweating to cool down. On the head, hair serves as a shield, blocking the solar radiation.

An objection to the above scenario might be that when bipedalism developed, savannah was not as extensive in Africa as it is today (Figure 6.13). In both East and South Africa, environments included both closed and open bush and woodlands. Moreover, fossil flora and fauna found with *Ardipithecus* and the possible hominins from the Miocene are typical of a moist, closed, wooded habitat. However, the presence of bipedalism in the fossil record without a savannah environment does not indicate that bipedalism was not adaptive to these conditions. It merely indicates that bipedalism appeared without any particular adaptive benefits at first, likely through a random macromutation. Bipedalism provided a body plan preadapted to the heat stress of the savannah environment.

[13]Quoted in Folger, T. (1993). The naked and bipedal. *Discover, 14*(11), 34–35. Reprinted with permission.

[14]Quoted in Folger.

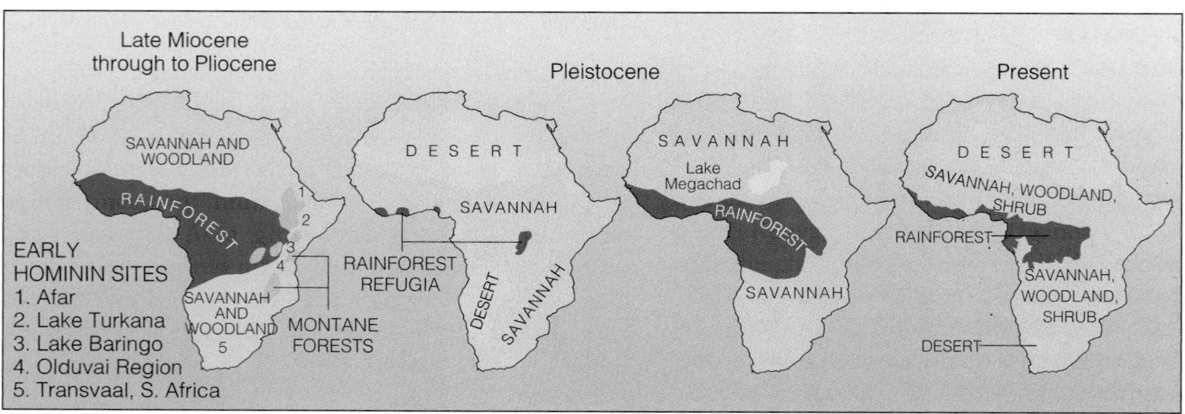

FIGURE 6.13

Since the late Miocene, the vegetation zones of Africa have changed considerably.

In an earlier era of human evolutionary studies, larger brains were thought to have permitted the evolution of bipedalism. Around the mid-20th century, theories for the adaptability of bipedalism involved a feedback loop between tool use, brain expansion, and free hands brought about by bipedalism. We now know not only that bipedality preceded the evolution of larger brains by several million years, but we can also now consider the possibility that bipedalism may have pre-adapted hominins for brain expansion. According to Wheeler,

> The brain is one of the most metabolically active tissues in the body. . . . In the case of humans it accounts for something like 20 percent of total energy consumption. So you've got an organ producing a lot of heat that you've got to dump. Once we'd become bipedal and naked and achieved this ability to dump heat, that may have allowed the expansion of the brain that took place later in human evolution. It didn't cause it, but you can't have a large brain unless you can cool it.[15]

Consistent with Wheeler's hypothesis is the fact that the system for drainage of the blood from the cranium of the earlier australopithecines is significantly different from that of the genus *Homo* (Figure 6.14).

Though paleoanthropologists cannot resolve every detail of the exact course of human evolution from the available data, over time the narrative they reconstruct has improved. Human evolution evidently took place in fits and starts, rather than at a steady pace. Today we know that bipedalism preceded brain expansion by several million years. Bipedalism likely occurred as a sudden shift in body plan while the tempo for the evolution of brain size differed considerably. For example, fragments of an *Australopithecus* skull 3.9 million years old are virtually identical to the corresponding parts of one 3 million years old. Evidently, once a viable bipedal adaptation was achieved, stabilizing selection took over, and there was little change for at least a few million years. Then, 2.5 million years ago, change was again in the works, resulting in the branching out of new forms, including several robust species as well as the first appearance of the genus *Homo*. But again, from about 2.3 million years ago until robust australopithecines became extinct around 1 million years ago, the robust forms underwent

[15]Quoted in Folger.

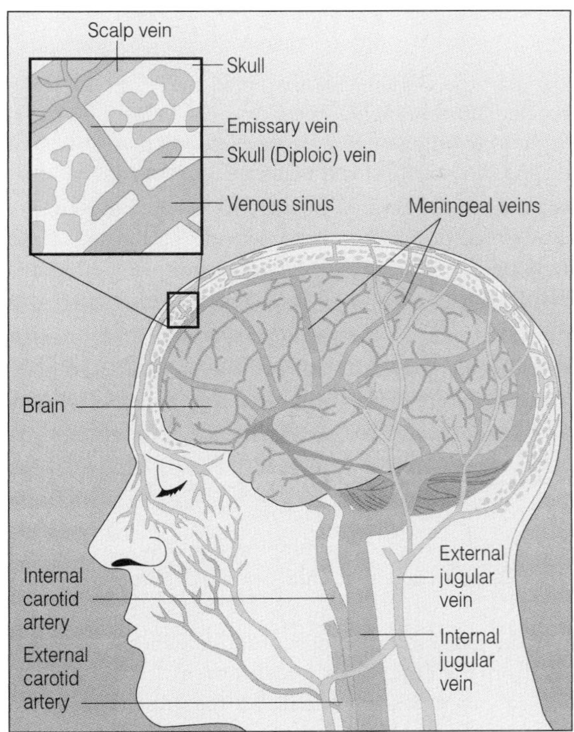

FIGURE 6.14

In humans, blood from the face and scalp, instead of returning directly to the heart, may be directed instead into the braincase, and then to the heart. Already cooled at the surface of the skin, it is able to carry away heat from the brain.

Though human evolutionary history is commonly depicted as a gradual transformation to upright posture and human abilities, we now know that a shift to bipedalism and upright posture occurred suddenly, sometime between 5 and 8 million years ago.

relatively little change.[16] Evidently, the pattern in early hominin evolution has been relatively short periods of marked change with diversification, separated by prolonged periods of relative stasis or stability in the surviving species. In the following chapters, we will trace the next period of change as seen in the steady course of brain expansion beginning with the first appearance of the genus *Homo* 2.5 million years ago until brain size reached its current state.

[16] Wood, B., Wood, C., & Konigsberg, L. (1994). Paranthropus boisei: An example of evolutionary stasis? *American Journal of Physical Anthropology, 95,* 134.

Chapter Summary

- The course of hominin evolution, as revealed by fossil finds, has not been a simple, steady advance in the direction of modern humans. Instead, it began with a shift to bipedal locomotion and the appearance in the early Pliocene of diverse species of this form.
- By 4 million years ago, the bipedal genus *Australopithecus,* which most anthropologists divide into seven species, appeared. Though fully bipedal, the early australopithecines were considerably smaller than the worldwide average size of humans today, and their general appearance was that of an apelike human. The size and outward appearance of their brain suggest a degree of intelligence probably not greatly different from that of contemporary bonobos, chimpanzees, and gorillas. The earliest australopithecines exhibit traits reminiscent of some of the late Miocene apes of Africa.
- Fossils fitting time-wise between early apes and *Australopithecus* suggest the latter arose as part of an early diversification of bipeds. Like most great apes, australopithecines may have made some use of objects as tools, although likely made of materials not easily preserved.
- Later australopithecine species can be divided into two forms or grades corresponding to a general level of biological organization: gracile and robust. These forms differ from each other primarily in the teeth, bones, and muscles related to chewing. Robust australopithecines were more highly specialized for the consumption of plant foods, with large molar teeth, jaws, and chewing muscles. Robust australopithecines, though successful in their time, appear to be an evolutionary dead end, while the genus *Homo* evolved from one of the less specialized australopithecines.
- During the late Miocene and Pliocene, the climate became markedly cooler and drier; many areas that had once been heavily forested became a mosaic of woodland and more open country. These environmental changes are incorporated into theories about the adaptations of early bipeds. These models compare the disadvantages and benefits of bipedalism in an open savannah environment for the earliest hominins.
- Some disadvantages proposed for bipedalism as a means of locomotion are that it makes an animal more visible to predators, exposes its soft underbelly, slows the animal down, and leaves nothing to fall back on when one leg is injured. Advantages for bipedalism include providing hominins with a means of keeping their brains from overheating, of protecting themselves and holding objects while running, of traveling long distances without tiring, and of seeing farther.
- During the Pliocene a trend toward a reduction in the size of the teeth is evident. As teeth became smaller, many of their functions may have been taken over by the hands. Brian size appears relatively stable until the appearance of the genus *Homo* around 2.5 million years ago.

Questions for Reflection

1. How has the fossil evidence from the early Pliocene helped paleoanthropologists meet the challenge of understanding human origins? How have beliefs and biases affected the interpretation of this fossil material?
2. Describe the anatomy of bipedalism, providing examples from head to toe of how bipedalism can be "diagnosed" from a single bone. Do you think evidence from a single bone is enough to determine whether an organism from the past was bipedal?
3. Paleoanthropological theories about bipedalism tend to describe a balance between the advantages and disadvantages of this mode of locomotion. Why do you think these paleoanthropological depictions emphasize this kind of balance sheet? Does evolutionary theory necessarily require a balance between positive and negative factors?
4. Who were the robust australopithecines? What evidence is used to demonstrate that they are an evolutionary dead end?
5. How do paleoanthropologists decide whether a fossil specimen from the distant past is male or female? Do our cultural ideas about males and females in the present affect the interpretation of early hominin behavior?
6. Do you think that australopithecines were tool users? What evidence would you use to support a case for tool use in these early bipeds?

Key Terms

Australopithecus
Savannah
Ardipithecus ramidus
Diastema
Kenyanthropus platyops
Gracile australopithecines
Robust australopithecines
Sagittal crest
Law of competitive exclusion

Multimedia Review Tools

Companion Web Site

Visit **http://www.wadsworth.com/anthropology_d/** and click on the companion Web site for this textbook to access a wide range of material to aid your study of anthropology. Among the options for self-study in each chapter are learning objectives, flash cards, Internet activities, Web links, InfoTrac College Edition exercises, and practice tests that can be scored and emailed to your instructor.

CD-ROM

The *Doing Anthropology Today* CD-ROM supplied with your textbook provides unique and valuable information designed to enhance your learning experience. This interactive multimedia resource includes video clips, interviews with renowned anthropologists, map and timeline exercises, chapter study quizzes, and much more. *Doing Anthropology Today* will not only help you in achieving your grade goals, but it will also make your learning experience fun and exciting!

Suggested Readings

Ciochon, R. L., & Fleagle, J. G. (Eds.). (1993). *The human evolution source book.* Englewood Cliffs, NJ: Prentice-Hall.

In the first four parts of this book, the editors have assembled articles to present data and survey different theories on the evolution and diversification of the earliest hominins. A short editors' introduction to each section places the various articles in context.

Falk, D. (1992). *Braindance.* New York: Henry Holt & Company.

In this book Falk presents her "radiator theory" to account for the lag between the appearance of bipedalism and the increase in the size of the brain over the course of human evolutionary history.

Johanson, D., & Edey, M. (1981). *Lucy: The beginnings of humankind.* New York: Simon & Schuster.

This book tells the story of the discovery of Lucy and the other fossils of *Australopithecus afarensis* and how they have enhanced our understanding of the early stages of human evolution. It reads like a first-rate detective story, while giving an excellent description of australopithecines and an accurate account of how paleoanthropologists analyze their fossils.

Johanson, D., Edgar, B., & Brill, D. (1996). *From Lucy to language.* New York: Simon & Schuster.

This coffee table-sized book includes more than 200 color pictures of major fossil discoveries along with a readable, intelligent discussion of many of the key issues in paleoanthropology.

Larsen, C. S., Matter, R. M., & Gebo, D. L. (1998). *Human origins: The fossil record.* Long Grove, IL: Waveland Press.

This nearly up-to-date volume covers all the major fossils discoveries relevant to the study of human origins beginning with the Miocene apes. It has detailed drawings and clear brief descriptions of each specimen, introducing the reader to the nature of the fossil evidence.

PART 3

AP/Wide World Photos

The Genus Homo

Biocultural Challenges

Introduction

By 2.5 million years ago, long after the appearance of bipedalism separated the human evolutionary line from that of chimpanzees, bonobos, and gorillas, a new kind of evolutionary change was set in motion. The fossil record reveals a gradual increase in brain size, proceeding for the next 2 or so million years. Simultaneously, the archaeological record begins to provide evidence of increased cultural manipulation of the physical world by these early ancestors through their use of stone tools. These new hominins were the first members of the genus *Homo.* With the passage of time, they came to intensify their reliance on cultural adaptation as a rapid and effective way of adjusting to their environments. The evolution of culture also provided humans with a means for self expression. This wall painted 32,000 years ago in Chauvet cave in Southeastern France provides spectacular evidence of the early artistic expression of our ancestors. These Ice Age images of bison, panthers, and rhinoceroses as well as other symbolic figures indicate that humans used culture to comprehend the world around them. While the evolution of culture became critical for human survival, it was intricately tied to underlying biological capacities, specifically the evolution of the human brain. Increasing brain size and specialization of function, as preserved in fossilized skulls, permitted the development of language, planning, new technologies, and artistic expression. With the evolution of a brain that made versatile behavior possible, members of the genus *Homo* became biocultural beings. The challenge for paleoanthropolitists is to simultaneously reconstruct the biology and culture of our ancestors from fossils and archaeological remains.

North American anthropologist Misia Landau has interpreted the story of human evolution as one that follows the narrative form of a heroic epic, like the creation stories of many cultures. The hero, or evolving hominin, is faced with a series of natural challenges that cannot be overcome from a strictly biological standpoint. However, endowed with the gift of intelligence, the heroic evolving hominin can overcome these challenges and become fully human. This story is complicated by differences in the rates of cultural and biological change. Cultural equipment and techniques can change rapidly with innovations occurring during the lifetime of individuals. By contrast, because it depends upon the natural selection of heritable traits, biological change requires many generations. One of the challenges for paleoanthropologists is to try to decipher whether an evident cultural change in the past corresponds to a major biological change such as the formation of a new species. The biological evidence for new species consists of small changes in the shape or size of skulls. When one takes into account the variation present within the species *Homo sapiens* as in the skulls depicted here, one can see why reconciling the relation between differences in skulls and culture change is often a source of debate within paleoanthropology.

The next four chapters discuss how evolving humans developed the ability to invent their own solutions to the problems of survival and how this ingenuity took on increasing importance as the human mechanism for adapting to the environment. We begin, in Chapter 7, with the appearance of the genus *Homo.* Although the earliest members of this genus had far smaller brains than ours, their brains were significantly larger than those of *Australopithecus.*

Over the next nearly 2.5 million years—a period known as the Paleolithic, or Old Stone Age—the evolving genus *Homo* relied increasingly on expanded mental capabilities for survival, as we shall see in Chapters 8, 9, and 10. In the process, hunting came to replace scavenging as the main means by which meat was procured, and other changes in lifeways took place. As a consequence of cultural inventions, the human evolutionary line, originally biologically adapted to tropical environments, was able to adapt to a wide range of environments. By 200,000 years ago, humans had acquired essentially modern sized brains and the cultural ability to survive frigid conditions. Survival under such difficult conditions ranks as no less an achievement than sending the first man to the moon.

CHAPTER 7

Homo habilis and Cultural Origins

© 1999 David L. Brill

CHALLENGE ISSUE

INTEGRATED BIOLOGICAL AND CULTURAL CAPABILITIES ALLOWED THE EARLIEST MEMBERS OF THE GENUS *HOMO* TO FACE THE CHALLENGES OF EXISTENCE. In turn, paleoanthropologists like Sileshi Semaw are faced with the challenge of establishing the relationship between biological change and cultural change throughout human evolutionary history. Semaw, who is from Ethiopia himself, discovered the oldest known human artifacts—stone tools dated to between 2.5 and 2.6 million years ago in Gona, Ethiopia.

1 When, Where, and How Did the Genus *Homo* Develop?

Since the late 1960s, a number of sites in South and East Africa have produced the fossil remains of lightly built bipeds all but indistinguishable from the earlier gracile australopithecines, except that the teeth are smaller and the brain is significantly larger relative to body size. The earliest fossils to exhibit these trends appeared around 2.5 million years ago, along with the earliest evidence of stone tool making. *Homo habilis* or "handy man," was the name given to the first members of the genus as a reflection of their tool-making capacities. The genus *Homo* therefore appears to have developed from one of the smaller-brained bipedal australopithecines in Africa by 2.5 million years ago.

2 When Did Reorganization and Expansion of the Human Brain Begin?

Though a minimal amount of reorganization and expansion of the brain may have occurred in australopithecines, significant changes in the size and structure of the brain did not begin until several million years after the development of bipedal locomotion. Brain expansion began in conjunction with the manufacture of stone tools by 2.5 million years ago. This marks the appearance of the genus *Homo*. Larger-brained *Homo* appears to have occupied a scavenging niche, using stone tools to obtain meat. In contrast, the robust australopithecines, who coexisted with early *Homo* for a million years or so, appear to have relied on a vegetarian diet as indicated by their massive teeth and jaws and tooth wear patterns.

3 What Is the Relationship Between Biological Change and Cultural Change in Early *Homo?*

Paleoanthropologists make species designations in the fossil record according to their interpretation of physical traits such as skull shape and size combined with archaeological evidence. Because the earliest stone tools appear in the archaeological record along with fossil evidence of increased brain size, paleoanthropologists attribute the cultural change—the making of stone tools—to the associated increase in brain size. The fabrication and use of stone tools needed to crack open the bones of animals for marrow or to butcher dead animals required improved eye-hand coordination and a precision grip. These behavioral abilities depended on the capacity to learn. This exquisite ability to learn to coordinate vision and movement depended upon larger, more complex brains.

Louis and Mary Leakey began their search for human origins at Olduvai Gorge, Tanzania, because of the presence of crude stone tools found there. The tools were found in deposits dating back to very early in the Pleistocene epoch, which began almost 2 million years ago. In 1959, when the Leakeys found the bones of the first specimen of robust *Australopithecus boisei* in association with some of these tools, they thought they had found the remains of one of the toolmakers. They later changed their minds, however, and suggested that these tools were not produced by *A. boisei,* nor were the associated bones of the birds, reptiles, antelopes, and pigs the remains of a meal eaten by *A. boisei*. Instead, *A. boisei* may have been a victim of a contemporary who created the tools, ate the animals, and possibly had the *A. boisei* for dessert. The Leakeys and colleagues named that contemporary ***Homo habilis*** (Latin for "handy man"). Of course, we don't really know whether *A. boisei* from Olduvai Gorge met its end in this way, but we do know that cut marks from a stone tool are present on a 2.4-million-year-old hominin mandible from South Africa.[1] This was done, presumably, to remove the mandible, but for what purpose we do not know. In any event, it does lend credibility to the idea of *A. boisei* on occasion being dismembered by *H. habilis.*

EARLY REPRESENTATIVES OF THE GENUS *Homo*

The Leakeys discovered the remains of this second hominin at Olduvai Gorge, *Homo habilis,* in 1960, only a few months after their earlier discovery, and just a few feet below it. The fossil remains consisted of more than one individual, including a few cranial bones, a lower jaw, a clavicle, some finger bones (Figure 7.1), and the nearly complete left foot of an adult (Figure 7.2). Skull and jaw fragments indicated that these specimens represented a larger-brained biped without the specialized chewing apparatus of the robust australopithecines. Subsequent work at Olduvai has unearthed not only more skull fragments but other parts of the skeleton of *H. habilis* as well.

[1]White, T. D., & Toth, N. (2000). Cutmarks on a Plio-Pleistocene hominid from Sterkfontein, South Africa. *American Journal of Physical Anthropology, 111,* 579–584.

Homo habilis Earliest representative of the genus *Homo;* lived between about 2.4 and 1.6 million years ago.

Since the late 1960s, fossils of the genus *Homo* that are essentially contemporaneous with those from Olduvai have been found elsewhere in Africa such as South Africa, Ethiopia, and several sites in Kenya (Figure 7.3). The eastern shores of Lake Turkana, on the border between Kenya and Ethiopia, have been particularly rich with fossils from earliest *Homo*. One of the best of these fossils, known as KNM ER 1470, was discovered by the Leakeys' son Richard. (The letters KNM stand for Kenya National Museum; the ER, for East Rudolf, the former name for Lake Turkana dating back to the colonial era in Kenya.) The deposits in which it was found are about 1.9 million years old; these deposits, like those at Olduvai, also contain crude stone tools. The KNM ER 1470 skull is more modern in appearance than any *Australopithecus* skull and has a cranial capacity of 752 cubic centimeters. However, the large teeth and face of this specimen resemble the earlier australopithecines. From this same site another well-preserved skull from the same time period (KNM ER 1813) possesses a cranial capacity of less than 600 cubic centimeters and the derived characteristics of a smaller, less projecting face and teeth. Generally, specimens attributed to *H. habilis* have cranial capacities greater than 600 cubic centimeters. However, cranial capacity of any individual is also in proportion to its body size. Therefore, many paleoanthropologists interpret KNM ER 1813 and ER 1470 as a female and male of a very sexually dimorphic species, and the small cranial capacity of KNM ER 1813 as a reflection of her small body size.

MEDIATREK

To use an interactive timeline of key discoveries in paleoanthropology and experience the groundbreaking research conducted by the Leakey family and the investigators they have supported for over three decades, go to MediaTrek 7.1 on the companion Web site or CD-ROM.

Other paleoanthropologists do not agree with placing such diverse specimens in the single taxonomic group of *H. habilis.* Instead they feel that the diversity represented in these specimens warrants separating them into several distinct coexisting groups, adding the species *Homo ergaster* and *Homo rudolphensis* to *H. habilis*. Placing specimens into separate species in this manner signifies the biological property of reproductive isolation. The question of how many species of early *Homo* existed illustrates two different taxonomic approaches that paleoanthropologists can take with regard to the fossil record. Fossil names imply specific evolutionary relationships among groups. Some investigators, described as "lumpers," prefer to limit the number of separate species in the fossil record, emphasizing that taxonomic distinctions at the level of biological species

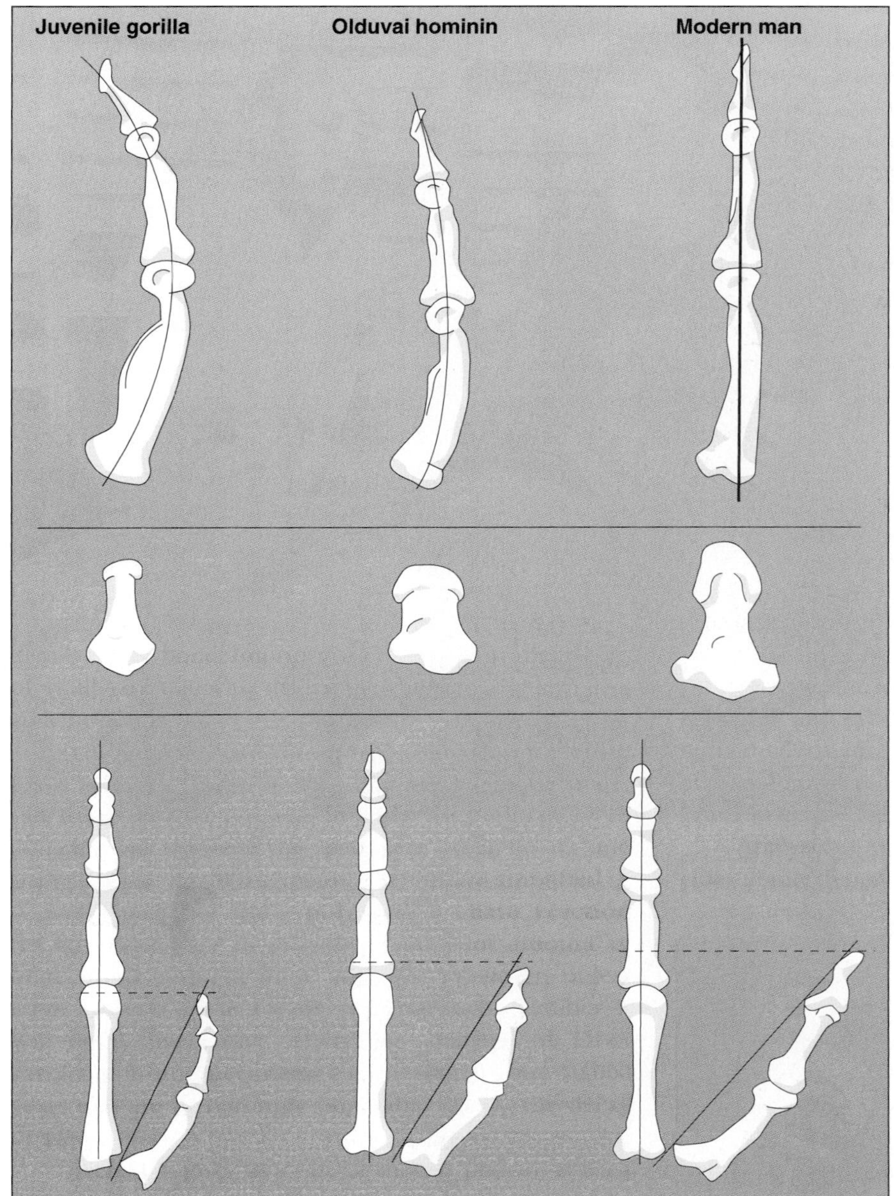

FIGURE 7.1

A comparison of hand bones of a juvenile gorilla, *Homo habilis* from Olduvai, and a modern human highlights important differences in the structure of fingers and thumbs. In the top row are fingers and in the second row are terminal (end) thumb bones. Although terminal finger bones are more human, lower finger bones are more curved and powerful. The bottom row compares thumb length and angle relative to the index finger.

are arbitrary and that variability exists within any group.[2] They tend to "lump" fossil specimens together in inclusive groups, emphasizing the impossibility of proving whether a collection of bones represents a group of organisms capable of interbreeding and producing viable young. "Splitters," by contrast, think in terms of ideal types and interpret differences in the shape of a skull as evidence of distinctive biological species with corresponding cultural capacities. Referring to the variable shape of the bony ridge above the eyebrows, South African paleoanthropologist Philip Tobias has said, "splitters will create a new species at the drop of a brow ridge!"[3]

The association of stone tools with all the early *Homo* finds tends to support a single taxonomic category of *H. habilis*, as does the finding that the range of physical variation within *H. habilis* is not unlike that found in other groups. In other words, fossil species like contemporary humans are best thought of in terms of expressing a range of variation across a variety of characteristics rather than as fixed ideal types.

[2]Miller, J. M. A. (2000). Craniofacial variation in *Homo habilis:* An analysis of the evidence for multiple species. *American Journal of Physical Anthropology, 112,* 122.

[3]Personal communication.

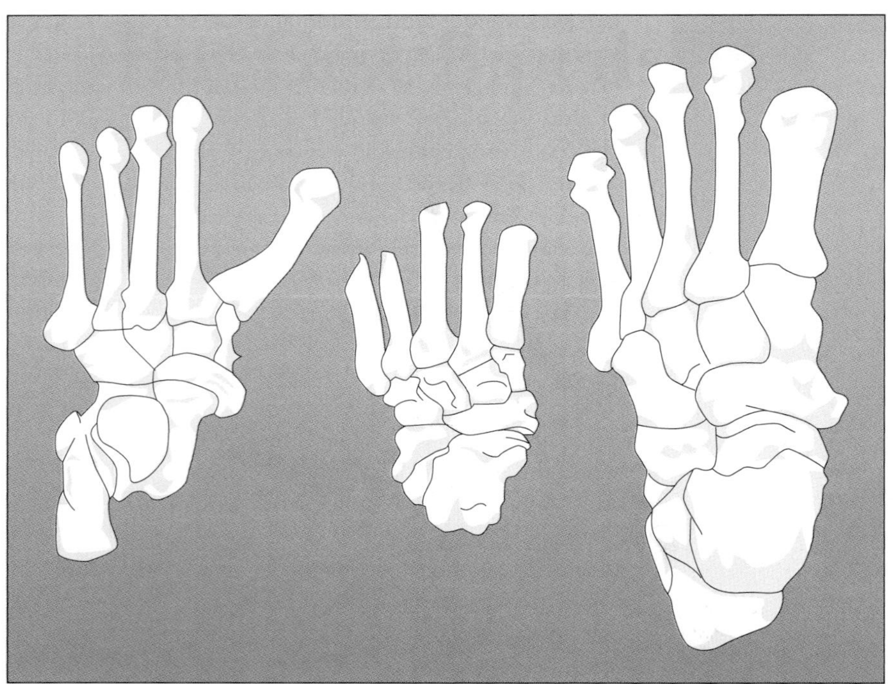

FIGURE 7.2

A partial foot skeleton of *Homo habilis* (center) is compared with the same bones of a chimpanzee (left) and modern human (right). Note how *H. habilis'* bone at the base of the great toe is in line with the others, as in modern humans, making for effective walking but poor grasping.

Differences between *Homo habilis* and *Australopithecus*

By 2.4 million years ago, the evolution of *Homo* was proceeding in a direction different from that of *Australopithecus.* In terms of body size, *H. habilis* differs little from *Australopithecus. H. habilis* had undergone enlargement of the brain far in excess of values predicted on the basis of body size alone. Therefore, *Homo habilis'* mental abilities probably exceeded those of Australopithecus. This means that *H. habilis* likely possessed a marked increase in ability to learn and to process information compared with australopithecines.

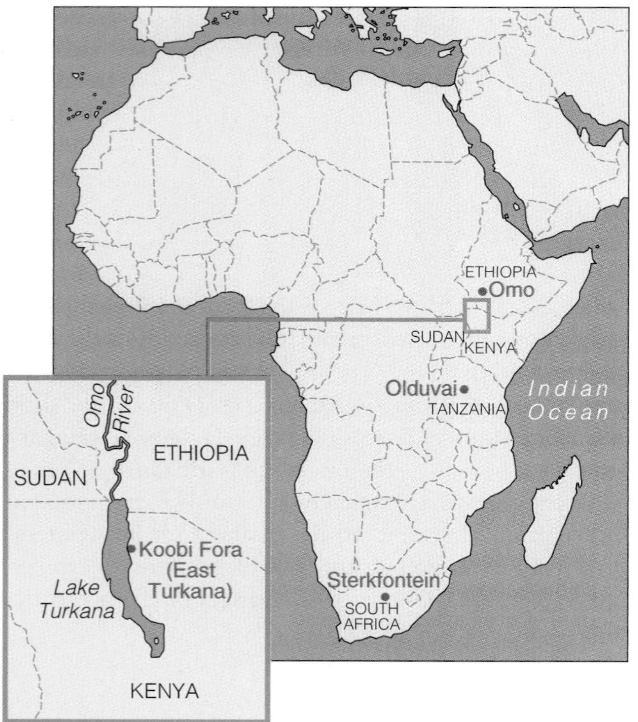

FIGURE 7.3

Imprints or endocasts of the inside of early fossil *Homo* skulls reflect a left cerebral hemisphere shape that has been associated with a language area.[4] In humans, areas of the brain that control speech, language, and movement of the right hand lie in adjacent areas in the left cerebral hemisphere. An asymmetry between the two cerebral hemispheres of the early *Homo* skulls resembles modern humans more than it does apes and is also consistent with evidence from wear and manufacture patterns on tools that these hominins were predominately right-handed. While the fact that the anatomy of their brains resembles humans does not prove that these bipeds possessed language, it does suggest a marked advance in information-processing capacity over that of australopithecines (see the discussion of language in Chapter 8).

Because larger brains generate more heat, it is not surprising to find that *H. habilis'* brain was provided with a heat exchanger of a sort not seen in the earliest

[4]Ambrose, S. H. (2001). Paleolithic technology and human evolution. *Science, 291,* 1,750.

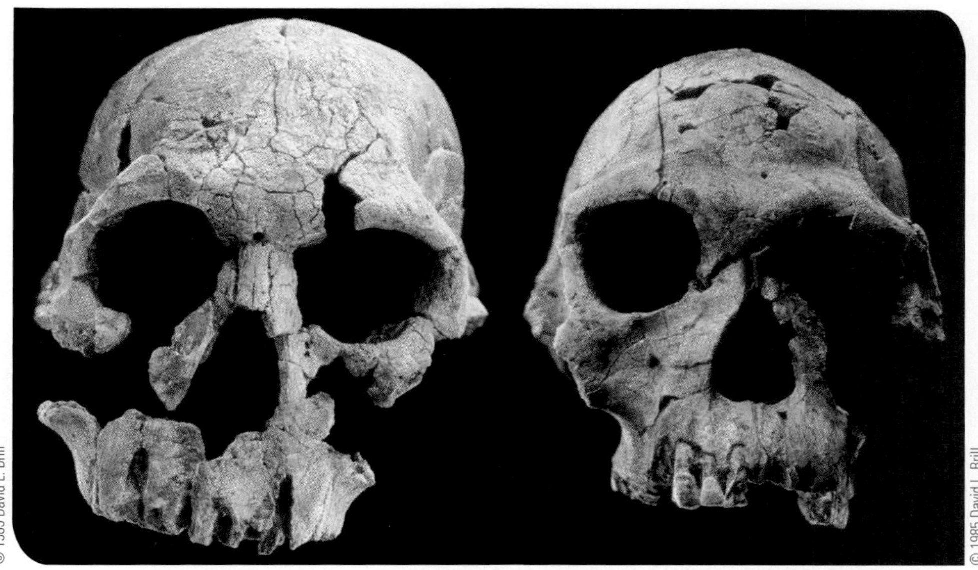

VISUAL COUNTERPOINT The KNM ER 1470 skull (left): One of the most complete skulls of *Homo habilis* is close to 2 million years old and is probably a male; it contrasts with the considerably smaller KNM ER 1813 skull (right), probably a female.

bipeds or in the apes.[5] This heat-exchange system consists of small openings in the braincase through which veins pass, allowing cooled blood from the face and scalp to be directed back to the braincase before returning to the heart to carry off excess heat as described in Chapter 6 (see Figure 6.13). This physiologic mechanism prevents damage to the brain from excessive heat.

Although *H. habilis* had teeth that are large by modern standards—or even by those of a half-million years ago—they are smaller in relation to the size of the skull than those of any australopithecine. Because major brain-size increase and tooth-size reduction are important trends in the evolution of the genus *Homo,* but not of *Australopithecus,* it looks as if *H. habilis* was becoming somewhat more human. Consistent with this are the indications that the brain of *H. habilis* was less apelike and more humanlike in structure. It is probably no accident that the earliest fossils to exhibit these features appear close to the same time as the earliest evidence (to be discussed shortly) for stone tool making and the use of these tools to process meat.

As noted earlier, the australopithecine diet seems to have consisted largely of plant foods, although they likely consumed limited amounts of animal protein as well. The later robust australopithecines from East and South Africa evolved into more specialized "grinding machines" as their jaws became markedly larger (Figure 7.4) for processing plant foods. Robust australopithecine brain size did not change, nor is there firm evidence that they made stone tools. Thus, in the period between 2.5 and 1 million years ago, two kinds of bipeds were headed in very different evolutionary directions: the robust australopithecines, specializing in plant foods and ultimately becoming extinct, and the genus *Homo,* with expanding cranial capacity and a varied diet that included meat.

If none of the robust australopithecines belong in the direct line of human ancestry, what of earlier species of *Australopithecus?* From the standpoint of anatomy alone, it has long been recognized that gracile australopithecines constitute suitable ancestors for the genus *Homo,* and it now seems clear that the body of *H. habilis* had changed little from gracile australopithecines. However, problems with dating the South African gracile specimens make the construction of ancestor and descendent relationships involving these fossils difficult (Figure 7.5). In East Africa, the situation is complicated by the presence of a variety of fossil species. Precisely which of the East African australopithecines gave rise to *H. habilis* and the relationship to the hominins from eastern and southern Africa is vigorously debated. The arguments have become more complex with the discovery of *Kenyanthropus* (Chapter 6), which Maeve Leakey argues excludes all australopithecines from the ancestry of *Homo.* Others see this newly defined genus as a faulty reconstruction of an australopithecine.

[5]Falk, D. (1993). A good brain is hard to cool. *Natural History, 102*(8), 65.

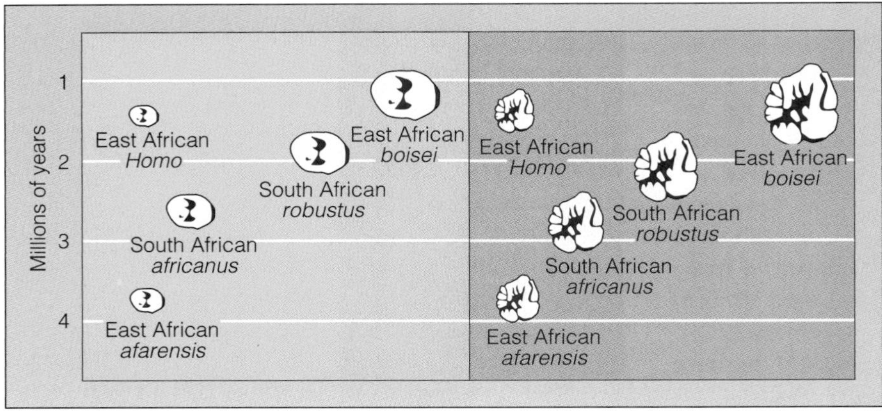

FIGURE 7.4

Premolars (left) and molars (right) of *Australopithecus* and *Homo habilis* compared. Though there is little difference in absolute size between the teeth of early *Australopithecus* (*A. afarensis*) and those of *H. habilis,* the australopithecine teeth are larger relative to the size of the skull. Moreover, the back teeth become even larger in the later robust australopithecines who coexisted with the genus *Homo.*

Most paleoanthropologists see the early East African australopithecines as sufficiently generalized to have given rise to both *Homo* and the robust forms of *Australopithecus,* noting that the earliest robust specimen, the so-called Black Skull, shows some holdovers from the earlier East African forms. This skull's age, 2.5 million years, is too old for any but the very earliest East African australopithecine to have figured in its ancestry. Because the earliest *H. habilis* skull is nearly as old as the Black Skull, it seems the same may be true for it. More information will be needed before we can tell whether the new *A. gahri* specimens or *Kenyanthropus* exclude other australopithecines from the line leading directly to humans. Paleoanthropologists have proposed a number of potential evolutionary relationships between the fossil bipeds that lived during the Pliocene. Evidently, at least a two-way split was underway by 2.5 million years ago (Figure 7.6).

MEDIATREK

To access a comprehensive source of information about human evolutionary history, including excellent descriptions of each of the fossil hominin species, go to MediaTrek 7.2 on the companion Web site or CD-ROM.

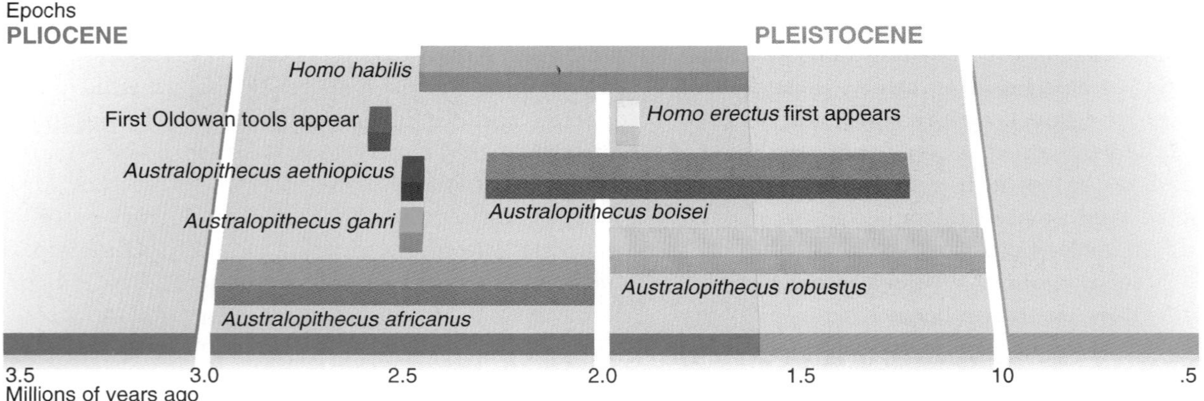

FIGURE 7.5

Homo habilis and other early hominins. When found with fossil hominins, Oldowan tools are always associated with genus *Homo.*

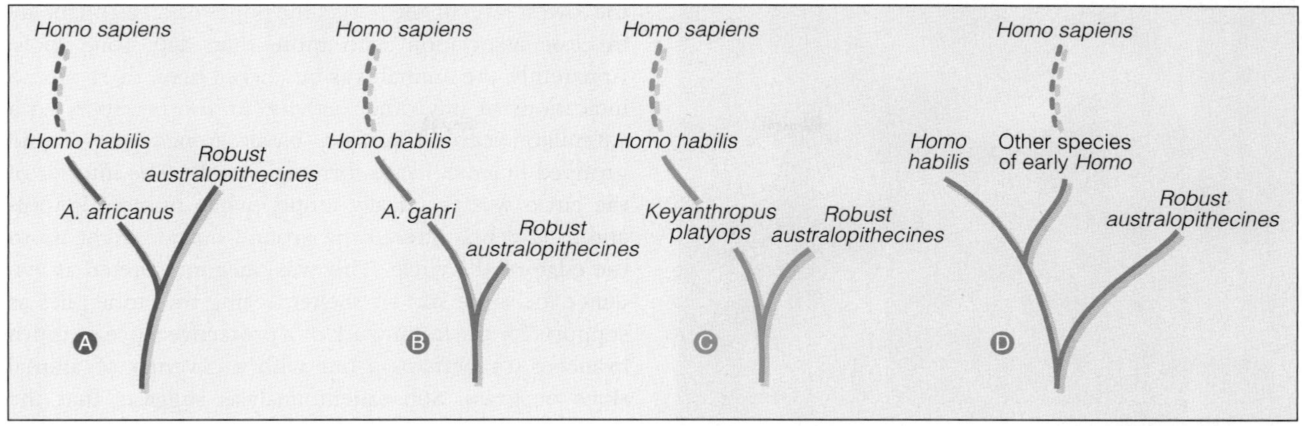

FIGURE 7.6

These diagrams present alternate views of early human evolution. Though the nature of the transition to the genus *Homo* is hotly debated, paleoanthropologists agree that the robust australopithecines represent an evolutionary dead end.

LOWER PALEOLITHIC TOOLS

The earliest stone tools have been found in the vicinity of Lake Turkana in northwest Kenya, in southern Ethiopia, in Olduvai Gorge in Tanzania, and in Hadar in Ethiopia—often in the same geological strata as *Homo habilis* fossils. These earliest *identifiable* tools consist of a number of implements made using a system of manufacture called the **percussion method** (Figure 7.7). Sharp-edged flakes were obtained from a stone (often a large, water-worn pebble) either by using another stone as a hammer (a hammerstone) or by striking the pebble against a large rock (anvil) to remove the flakes. The finished flakes had two sharp edges, effective for cutting and scraping. Microscopic wear patterns show that these flakes were used for cutting meat, reeds, sedges, and grasses and for cutting and scraping wood. Small indentations on their surfaces suggest that the leftover cores were transformed into choppers, for breaking open bones, and they may also have been employed to defend the user. The appearance of these tools marks the beginning of the **Lower Paleolithic,** the first part of the Old Stone Age.

The makers of these early tools were highly skilled, consistently producing many well-formed flakes with few misdirected blows.[6] The apparent objective of the task was to obtain large, sharp-edged flakes from available raw materials with the least effort. Thus, the toolmaker had to have in mind an abstract idea of the tool to be made, as well as a specific set of steps that would accomplish the transformation from raw material to finished product. Furthermore, only certain kinds of stone have the flaking properties that will allow the transformation to take place. The toolmaker must know about these, as well as where such stone can be found. The archaeological record also provides evidence of thinking

percussion method A technique of stone tool manufacture performed by striking the raw material with a hammerstone or by striking raw material against a stone anvil to remove flakes.
Lower Paleolithic The first part of the Old Stone Age; its beginning is marked by the appearance by 2.5 million years ago of Oldowan tools.

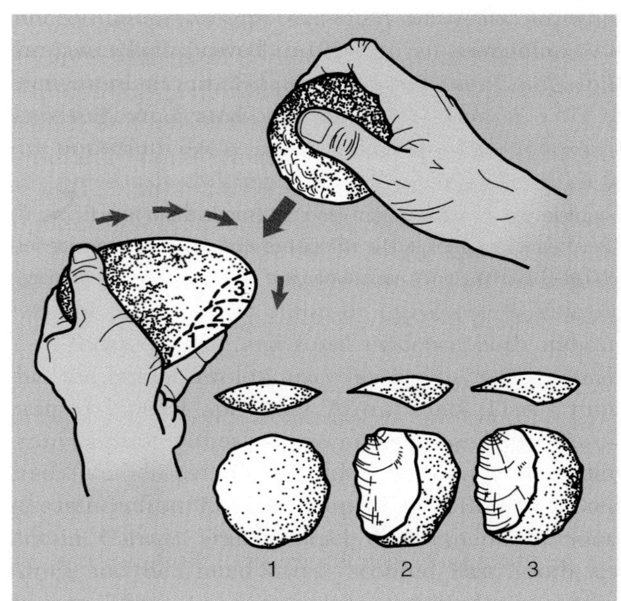

FIGURE 7.7

By 2.5 million years ago, early *Homo* in Africa had invented the percussion method of stone tool manufacture. This technological breakthrough, which is associated with a significant increase in brain size, made possible the butchering of meat from scavenged carcasses.

[6]Ambrose, p. 1,749.

The oldest stone tools, dated to between 2.5 and 2.6 million years ago, were discovered in Gona, Ethiopia, in 1996.

and planning, since tool fabrication required the transport of raw materials over great distances. Such planning for the future undoubtedly was associated with natural selection favoring changes in brain structure.

At Olduvai and Lake Turkana, these tools are close to 2 million years old; the Ethiopian tools are older at 2.5 to 2.6 million years. Before this time, early hominins probably used tools such as heavy sticks to dig up roots or ward off animals, unshaped stones to use as missiles for defense or to crack open nuts, and perhaps simple carrying devices made of knotted plant fibers. These perishable tools, however, are not preserved in the archaeological record.

OLDUVAI GORGE

What is now Olduvai Gorge was once a lake. Almost 2 million years ago, its shores were inhabited not only by numerous wild animals but also by groups of hominins, including robust australopithecines and *H. habilis* as well as (later) *Homo erectus* (Chapter 8). The gorge, therefore, is a rich source of Paleolithic remains as well as a key site providing evidence of human evolutionary change. Among the finds are assemblages of stone tools that are about 2 million years old. These were found little disturbed from when they were left, together with the bones of now-extinct animals that provided food. At one spot, in the lowest level of the gorge, the bones of an elephant lay in close association with more than 200 stone tools. Apparently, the animal was butchered here; there are no indications of any other activity. At another spot, on a 1.8-million-year-old surface, basalt stones were found grouped in small heaps forming a circle. The interior of the circle was practically empty, while numerous tools and food debris littered the ground outside, right up to the edge of the circle. This was once interpreted as evidence for some sort of shelter, seeing the stone piles as supports for the framework of a protective fence of thorn branches, or perhaps a hut with a covering of animal skins or grass. Subsequent analysis suggests that the stones were "stockpiled" ahead of time, to be made into tools as needed, or to be hurled as missiles to hold off carnivorous animals while the hominins scavenged the skin as well as sinew and marrow, the protein and energy-rich tissue inside of long bones from the remaining bones. Many Oldowan archaeological sites therefore appear to be temporary places where animal remains were processed, rather than campsites.

Oldowan Tools

The oldest tools found at Olduvai Gorge belong to the **Oldowan tool tradition** and were also made by the percussion method described above. Crude as they were, Oldowan tools mark an important technological advance for early *Homo;* previously, they depended on found objects requiring little or no modification, such as bones, sticks, or conveniently shaped stones. Oldowan tools made possible new additions to the diet because, without such tools, hominins could eat few animals (only those that could be skinned by tooth or nail); therefore, their diet was limited in terms of animal proteins. The advent of Oldowan tools meant more than merely saving labor and time: They made possible the addition of meat to the diet on a frequent, rather than occasional, basis. Much popular literature has been written about this penchant for meat in early human evolution, often with numerous colorful references to "killer apes." Such references are misleading because no one knows whether these ancestors were very aggressive, as "killer" suggests. Meat can be obtained, after all, by scavenging or by stealing it from other predators. What is significant is that a dentition such as that possessed by *Australopithecus* and *Homo habilis* is poorly suited for meat eating. What is needed if substantial amounts of meat are to be eaten, without teeth like those possessed by carnivorous animals (or even chimpanzees), are sharp tools for butchering.

Oldowan tool tradition The earliest identifiable stone tools.

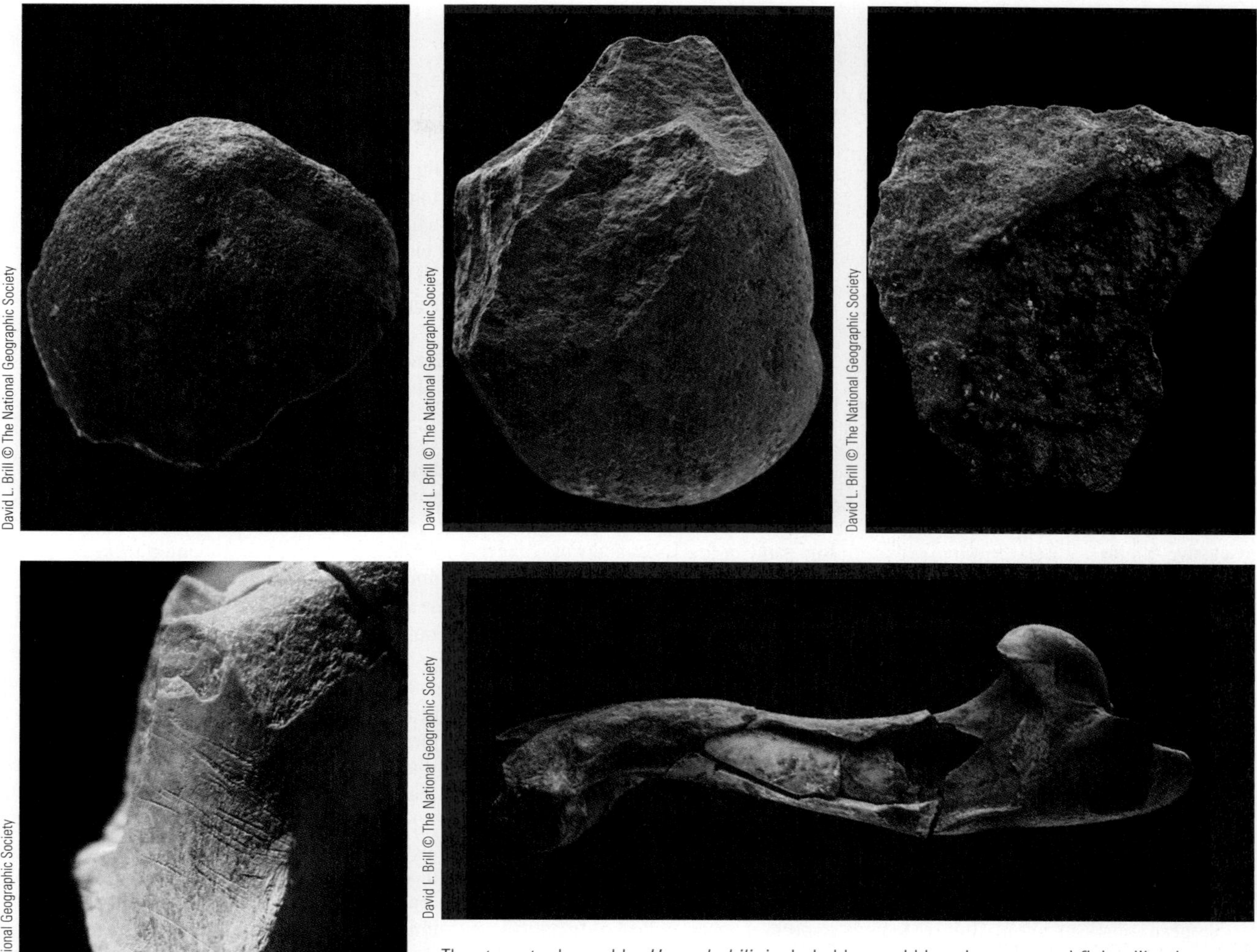

The stone tools used by *Homo habilis* included lava cobbles, choppers, and flakes like those shown here. Most choppers were probably the result of flakes being struck from one cobble by another. These flakes were used to remove meat from bones, leaving cut marks (lower left). The cobbles and choppers were used to break open bones (lower right) to get at the marrow.

Increased consumption of animal flesh on the part of evolving humans was important for human evolution. On the arid savannah, it is hard for a primate with a humanlike digestive system to satisfy its protein requirements from available plant resources. Moreover, failure to do so has serious consequences: growth stunting, malnutrition, starvation, and death. Leaves and legumes (nitrogen-fixing plants, familiar modern examples being beans and peas) provide most readily accessible plant sources of protein. The problem is that these plants are difficult for primates to digest unless they are cooked. The leaves and legumes available contain substances causing the proteins to pass right through the gut without being absorbed.[7]

Chimpanzees have a similar problem when out on the savannah. In such a setting, they spend about a third of their time foraging for insects (ants and termites), eggs, and small vertebrate animals. Such animal foods not only are easily digestible, but they provide high-quality proteins that contain all the essential amino acids, the building blocks of protein. The proteins provided in plant food based on only one species of plant cannot provide this nutritional balance. Only a combination of plants can supply the range of amino acids provided by meat alone. Lacking long, sharp teeth for shearing meat, our earliest ancestors likely solved their "protein problem" in much the same way that chimps on the savannah do today. Even chimpanzees, whose canine teeth are far larger and sharper than ours or those of early *Homo,* frequently have trouble tearing through the skin of other animals.[8] For

[7]Stahl, A. B. (1984). Hominid dietary selection before fire. *Current Anthropology, 25,* 151–168.

[8]Goodall, J. (1986). *The chimpanzees of Gombe: Patterns of behavior* (p. 372). Cambridge, MA: Belknap Press.

Anthropologists of Note

Adrienne Zihlman (1940–)

Up until the 1970s, the study of human evolution, from its very beginnings, was permeated by a deep-seated bias reflecting the privileged status enjoyed by men in Western society. Beyond the obvious labeling of fossils as particular types of "men," irrespective of the sex of the individual represented, it took the form of portraying males as the active players in human evolution. Thus, it was males who were seen as providers and innovators, using their wits to become ever-more effective providers of food and protection for passive females. The latter were seen as spending their time getting pregnant and caring for offspring, while the men were getting ahead by becoming ever smarter. Central to such thinking was the idea of "man the hunter," constantly honing his wits through the pursuit and killing of animals. Thus, hunting by men was seen as the pivotal humanizing activity in evolution.

© r.r. jones

We now know, of course, that such ideas are culture-bound, reflecting the hopes and expectations of late-19th- and early-20th-century European and European American culture. This recognition came in the 1970s and was a direct consequence of the entry of a number of highly capable women into the profession of paleoanthropology. Up until the 1960s, there were few women in any field of physical anthropology, but with the expansion of graduate programs and changing attitudes toward the role of women in society, increasing numbers of women went on to earn a Ph.D. One of these was Adrienne Zihlman, who earned her doctorate at the University of California at Berkeley in 1967. Subsequently, she authored a number of important papers critical of "man the hunter" scenarios. She was not the first to do so; as early as 1971, Sally Linton had published a preliminary paper on "woman the gatherer," but it was Zihlman who from 1976 on especially elaborated on the importance of female activities for human evolution. Others have joined in the effort, including Zihlman's companion in graduate school and later colleague, Nancy Tanner, who collaborated with Zihlman on some of her papers and has produced important works of her own.

The work of Zihlman and her co-workers was crucial in forcing a reexamination of existing "man the hunter" scenarios, out of which came recognition of the importance of scavenging in early human evolution as well as the importance of female gathering and other activities. Although there is still plenty to learn about human evolution, thanks to these women we now know that it was not a case of females being "uplifted" as a consequence of their association with progressively evolving males. Rather, the two sexes evolved together with each making its own important contribution to the process.

efficient utilization of meat, our ancestors needed sharp tools for butchering.

The initial use of tools by early *Homo* may be related to adaptation to an environment that we know was changing since the Miocene from forests to grasslands (see Figure 6.12).[9] The physical changes that adapted hominins for spending increasing amounts of time on the new grassy terrain encouraged tool making.

SEX, GENDER, AND THE BEHAVIOR OF EARLY *Homo*

Paleoanthropological depictions of early *Homo* from the 1960s and 1970s focused on "man the hunter," wielding tools in a savannah teeming with meat, while females stayed at home tending their young. These depictions of our ancestors mirrored the cultural norms of middle-class North Americans and Europeans as well as the scientists who discovered and interpreted the fossil specimens in the 1960s. The best hypothesis-testing traditions of science allowed for reworking of the "man the hunter" hypothesis with each new scientific discovery. The first modification of the "man the hunter" model began with the documentation of the vital role of "woman the gatherer" in provisioning the social group.

In this model, the development of some cooperation in the procurement of foods and a division of labor by sex are seen as prime factors in the success of early *Homo*. Because these evolutionary speculations relate to proposed behavioral differences between males and females in the *distant* past, they are generally attributed to biologically determined sex differences rather than the socially defined category of **gender.** However, the gender roles

[9]Behrensmeyer, A. K., Todd, N. E., Potts, R., & McBrinn, G. E. (1997). Late Pliocene faunal turnover in the Turkana basin, Kenya, and Ethiopia. *Science, 278,* 1,589–1,594.

gender The elaborations and meanings assigned by cultures to the biological differentiation of the sexes.

© The Field Museum

In this artist's reconstruction separate distinct roles are portrayed for male and female hominins. Do the roles depicted here derive from biological differences between the sexes or culturally established gender differences?

internalized by the working paleoanthropologist from his or her own culture may be inadvertently applied to the fossil specimens in these behavioral reconstructions. Paleoanthropologists literally have only fragmentary evidence with which to reconstruct behavior.

Paleoanthropologists' behavioral reconstructions from fragments of bone and stone have relied heavily on observations of living primates, including both human and nonhuman living primates. For example, the observation that food sharing and a division of labor by gender characterize many modern food foragers has been used to support depictions of our male and female ancestors as "hunter" and "gatherer," respectively. However, the division of labor among contemporary food foragers, like all gender relations, reflects both cultural and biological factors. Division of labor by food-foraging societies does not conform to fixed boundaries defined through biologically based sex differences. Instead, it is influenced by cultural and environmental factors. It appears likely that the same principle applied to our human ancestors.

Evidence from chimpanzees and bonobos casts further doubt on the notion of a strict, sex-based division of labor in human evolutionary history. As described in Chapter 3, among chimpanzees, females have been observed to participate in male hunting expeditions. Meat gained from the successful hunt of a smaller mammal is shared within the group whether provided by a male or a female chimpanzee. Among bonobos, females hunt regularly and share meat as well as plant foods with one another. In other words patterns of food sharing and hunting behaviors in these apes are variable, lending credit to the notion that culture plays a role in establishing these behaviors. Similarly, in our evolutionary history it is likely that culture—the shared learned behaviors of each *H. habilis* group—played a role in their food-sharing behaviors rather than strict biological differences between the sexes.

Though increased consumption of scavenged meat on the part of *Homo habilis* may have promoted more food sharing among adults, this remains a hypothesis, as does the notion that a division of labor characterized early *Homo*. The fossil and archaeological records provide evidence only of cut marks on bones, the stone tools that made these marks, along with information about our ancestors' bodies and brains. No evidence exists to establish definitively how procured foods may have been shared. When the evidence is fragmentary, as it is in all paleoanthropological reconstructions of behavior, gaps are all too easily filled in with behaviors that seem "natural" and familiar such as contemporary gender roles. In reconstructing the behavior of our ancestors from the distant past, current paleoanthropologists today pay careful attention to the ways in which contemporary gender norms and other cultural factors inform their models. A return to the evidence with an awareness of its limits will define which inferences can be legitimately made about behaviors in human evolutionary history.

Microscopic examination of tooth and cut marks on fossilized bones reveals that carnivorous animals sometimes got to the bones before tool-wielding hominins and sometimes after.

What do these assemblages of Oldowan tools and broken animal bones have to tell us about the life of early *Homo?* First, they tell us that both *H. habilis* and large carnivorous animals were active at these locations, for in addition to marks on the bones made by slicing, scraping, and chopping with stone tools, there are tooth marks from gnawing. Some of the gnawing marks overlie the butcher marks, indicating that enough flesh remained on the bones after the hominins were done with them to attract other carnivores. In other cases, though, the butcher marks overlie the tooth marks of carnivores, indicating that the animals got there first. This is what we would expect if *H. habilis* were scavenging the kills of other animals, rather than doing its own killing. Consistent with this picture is that whole carcasses are not represented in the fossil record; apparently, only parts were transported away from the original location where they were obtained, again what we could expect if they were "stolen" from the kill of some other animal. The stone tools, too, were made of raw material procured at distances of up to 60 kilometers from where they were used to process the parts of carcasses. Finally, the incredible density of bones at some of the sites and patterns of weathering indicate that the sites were used repeatedly over periods guessed to be on the order of 5 to 15 years.

All of this is quite unlike the behavior of historically known and contemporary food-foraging peoples or hunters, who typically bring whole carcasses back to camp or form camp around a large animal in order to fully process it. After processing, neither meat nor marrow is left as they were at Oldowan sites. The bones themselves are broken up not just to get at the marrow (as at Oldowan sites) but to fabricate tools and other objects of bone (unlike at Oldowan sites). The picture that emerges of our Oldowan forebears, then, is of scavengers, getting their meat from the Lower Paleolithic equivalent of modern-day road kills, taking the spoils of their scavenging to particular places where tools, and the raw materials for making them (often procured from faraway sources), had been stockpiled in advance for the purpose of butchering. At the least, this may have required fabrication of carrying devices such as net bags and use of trail signs of the sort (described in Chapter 3) used by modern bonobos. Thus, the Oldowan sites were not campsites or "home bases" at all. Quite likely, *H. habilis* continued to sleep in trees or rocky cliffs, as do modern small-bodied terrestrial or semi-terrestrial primates, in order to be safe from predators. However, the advanced preparation for meat processing implied by the storing of stone tools, and the raw materials for making tools, attests to considerable foresight and ability to plan ahead.

In addition, microscopic analysis of cut marks on bones has revealed that the earliest members of the genus *Homo* were actually **tertiary scavengers**—that is, third in line to get something from a carcass after a lion or leopard managed to kill some prey. Leopards, for example, generally chew a limb from a zebra it has felled and haul it into the treetops for a relaxed feast. *Homo habilis* might have climbed into the trees to scavenge meat hauled there by a leopard. If the carcass remains on the ground, hyenas grab what they can, followed by vultures who swarm the rotting carcass. By the time a lightly built *H. habilis* could get near the carcass of a dead zebra, only bones remained. Fortunately, these tool-wielding ancestors could break open the shafts of long bones to get at the rich marrow inside.

Tools, Food, and Brain Expansion

As we have seen, by 2.5 million years or so after early hominins became fully bipedal, the size and structure of the brain were beginning to change. Until about 2.5 million years ago, early hominins lived on foods that

tertiary scavenger In a food chain, the third animal group (second to scavenge) to obtain meat from a kill made by a predator.

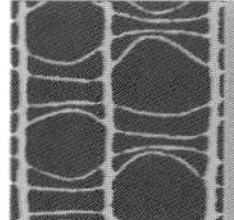

Anthropology Applied

Paleotourism and the World Heritage List

Travel to early hominin sites and to museums where original fossil specimens are housed is an important part of the paleoanthropologist's life. Increasingly, these same destinations are becoming popular with tourists traveling across the globe. Making sites accessible for tourists while protecting the sites for further excavation requires considerable skill and knowledge. The paleoanthropologist's expertise is indispensable for responsible paleotourism. Features such as footpaths for tourists, access roads, and even the numbers of tourists allowed to visit on a given day must be planned carefully so that paleotourism does not damage the sites permanently.

Since 1972, UNESCO's World Heritage List has been an important part of maintaining paleoanthropological sites for responsible tourism while preserving these sites for the global community. The goal of the World Heritage List is "protecting natural and cultural properties of outstanding value against the threat of damage in a rapidly developing world." Individual states apply to UNESCO for site designation, receiving financial and political support for maintaining the sites if approved. The tasks of documenting the value of a fossil hominin site and working to effectively maintain the site for research and tourism fall to the paleoanthropological experts. When designated sites are threatened by natural disaster, war, pollution, or poorly managed tourism, they are placed on a danger list forcing the local governments to institute measures to protect the sites in order to continue receiving UNESCO support.

Each year approximately thirty new World Heritage sites are designated. In 2003 the list had grown to 754 sites: 149 natural preserves, 582 cultural sites, and 23 mixed sites. Hominin fossil and archaeological sites are well represented on the World Heritage List. Sites important for human evolution are generally designated as cultural sites because the knowledge gained from these sites is considered to be of cultural importance to the world community. Occasionally, important fossil remains have been recovered within an area that is designated as a larger natural reserve. For example, Olduvai Gorge—known for *Homo habilis* and robust australopithecine remains as well as Oldowan tools—is within the Ngorongoro Conservation Area of Tanzania, as are the Laetoli footprints mentioned in Chapter 6. The Maasai people have inhabited this region for hundreds of years. Today, this Maasai near Olduvai Gorge reminds us that Paleotourism affects both the present and the past. Responsible tourism at these sites today promotes public education on the subject of human evolution while preserving our common heritage for future generations. It may also benefit local inhabitants such as the Maasai, helping them preserve their culture.

© Tom Brown

could be picked or gathered: plants, fruits, invertebrate animals such as ants and termites, and perhaps even an occasional piece of meat scavenged from kills made by other animals. After 2.5 million years ago, meat became more important in the diet of *Homo,* and scavenging began on a more regular basis. Bone marrow may have been an important part of the diet of *H. habilis* and other early hominins. We know this because the marks of stone tools on the bones of animals that were butchered commonly overlie marks made by the teeth of carnivores. A small amount of marrow is a concentrated source of both protein and fat. Muscle alone, particularly from lean game animals, contains very little fat.

With the appearance of the genus *Homo* and the first archaeological evidence—the tools of the Old Stone Age—human evolution began a course of brain expansion through variational change (see Chapter 5) that continued until about 200,000 years ago. By this point, brain size had approximately tripled and reached the levels of contemporary people. During this time period, the increasing cultural capabilities accompanying larger brains required parallel improvements in diet. The energy demands of nerve tissue, of which the brain is made, are high—higher, in fact, than the demands of other types of tissue in the human body. One can meet these demands on a vegetarian diet, but the overall energy content of a given amount of plant food is generally less than that of the same amount of meat. Thus, the use of meat, marrow in particular, in addition to plant foods ensured the availability of a reliable source of high-quality protein to support a more highly developed brain.

In addition, animals that live on plant foods must spend their time eating large quantities of vegetation. Gorillas, for example, spend all day munching on plants to maintain their large bodies. Meat eaters, by contrast, have no need to eat so much, or so often. Consequently, meat-eating bipeds may have had more leisure time available to explore and manipulate their environment.

VISUAL COUNTERPOINT A power grip (left) utilizes more of the hand while the precision grip (right) relies on the fingers for control, requiring corresponding organizational changes in the brain.

Like lions and leopards, they would have time for activities other than eating.

The archaeological record provides us with a tangible record of our ancestors' cultural abilities that corresponds with the simultaneous biological expansion of the brain. Tool making itself puts a premium on manual dexterity, precision, and fine manipulation. In addition, the patterns of tools and animal bones at Oldowan sites are indicative of changes in the nervous system. The stone used to make cutting and chopping tools came far from sites where tools were used to process parts of carcasses. Also, the high density of bones at some Oldowan sites, and the patterns of seasonal weathering, indicate the sites were repeatedly used over a period of years. Apparently, the Oldowan sites represent places where tools and the raw materials for making them had been stockpiled in advance for the purpose of butchering. This finding attests to the growing importance of foresight and the ability to plan ahead. Beginning with the appearance of *Homo habilis* in Africa 2.5 million years ago, human evolution began a sure course of increasing brain size and increasing cultural development, each presumably acting to promote the other.

Because early *Homo* lacked size and strength to drive off large predators, or to compete directly with other scavengers attracted to kills, they must have had to rely on their wit and cunning for success. It has been observed that monkeys and apes, for example, often use objects such as sticks and stones in their threat displays. The change to an upright bipedal posture—coupled with existing flexibility at the shoulder, arms, and hands—allowed hominins to make threat displays as well as hurl objects with significant momentum, helping them to compete successfully with the largely predatory carnivores that shared their environments.

Homo habilis filled the same niche on the ground that these vultures fill in the air: a nonterritorial scavenger.

© J & B Photos/Animals, Animals

Becoming scavengers put *Homo habilis* in competition with formidable adversaries like hyenas.

One may imagine early *Homo* lurking in the vicinity of a kill, sizing up the situation as the predator ate its fill while hyenas and other scavengers gathered, and devising strategies to outwit them all so as to seize a piece of the carcass. Increased "brain power" would certainly help in this situation conferring a competitive advantage on this individual. An ability to anticipate problems, devise distractions, bluff competitors into temporary retreat, and recognize, the instant it came, an opportunity to rush in and grab what it could of the carcass translates into a much better chance of surviving, reproducing, and proliferating.

One means by which early hominins may have gained access to a reasonably steady supply of carcasses while at the same time minimizing the risks involved is suggested by recent field studies of leopards. How this could have worked and the arguments in favor of it are the subject of the following Original Study.

Original Study

Cat in the Human Cradle

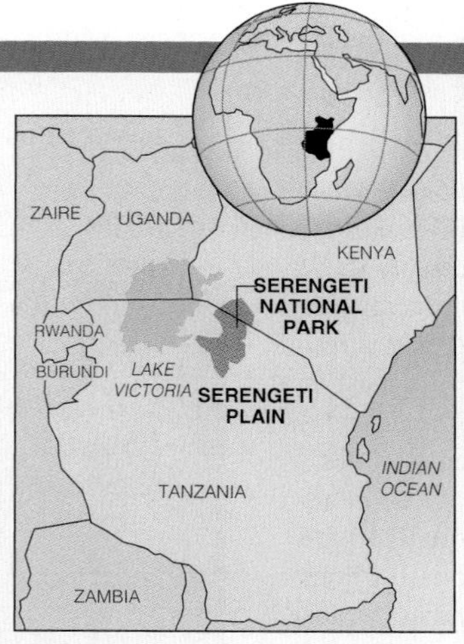

Recent evidence, such as marks on some of the Olduvai bones, indicates that animals the size of wildebeests or larger were killed, eaten, and abandoned by large predators such as lions, hyenas, and saber-toothed cats; hominins may have merely scavenged the leftovers. Several specialists now agree that early hominins obtained at least marrow mainly in this way. The picture with regard to the remains of smaller animals, such as gazelle-sized antelopes, is less certain. Paleoanthropologists Henry Bunn and Ellen Kroll believe that the cut-marked upper limb bones of small, medium-sized, and large animals found at Olduvai Gorge demonstrate that hominins were butchering the meaty limbs with cutting tools. Since modern-day lions and hyenas rapidly and completely consume small prey, leaving little or nothing for potential scavengers, Bunn and Kroll conclude that hominins must have acquired the smaller animals by hunting. But another scholar, Kay Behrensmeyer, suggests that a small group of hominins could have obtained these bones not by hunting, but by driving off timid predators, such as cheetahs or jackals, from their kills.

Since carnivores play a key role in all these scenarios, three years ago I began thinking about studying their behavior and ecology. About the same time, a colleague directed me to a paper on the tree-climbing abilities of early hominins. The authors (anatomists Randall L. Susman, Jack T. Stern, and William L. Jungers) analyzed the limb bones of *Homo habilis* specimens from Olduvai Gorge, as well as those of the early hominin *Australopithecus afarensis* (better known as Lucy). They concluded that early hominins were probably not as efficient as we are at walking on two feet, but they were better than we are at climbing trees and suspending themselves

[CONTINUED]

[CONTINUED]

from branches. At the very least, given their apparent lack of fire, early hominins must have used trees as refuges from large predators and as sleeping sites.

One evening, as I watched a documentary film by Hugh Miles about a female leopard and her cubs in Kenya's Masai Mara Reserve, carnivore behavior and early hominin tree climbing suddenly connected for me. In the film, a pack of hyenas attempt to scavenge an antelope that the mother leopard has killed. At the sight of the hyenas, the leopard grabs the prey in her jaws and carries it up a small tree. This striking behavior sparked my curiosity and sent me to the library the next morning to find out more about leopards.

I learned that the leopard differs from other large African carnivores in a variety of ways. Although it occasionally kills large animals, such as adult wildebeests and topi or young giraffes, the leopard preys primarily on smaller antelopes, such as Thomson's gazelles, impala, and Grant's gazelles, and on the young of both large and small species. Unable to defend its kills on the ground from scavenging by lions and spotted hyenas, both of which often forage in groups, the usually solitary leopard stores each kill in a tree, returning to feed but otherwise frequently abandoning it for varying lengths of time.

Although the leopard may not consume its entire prey immediately, the tree-stored kills are relatively safe from theft. (Even lions, which can climb trees, usually take little notice of this resource.) As a result, a kill can persist in a tree for several days. Also, leopard kills appear to be more predictably located than those of lions and hyenas because leopards tend to maintain a small territorial range for several years and occasionally reuse feeding trees. Finally, leopard kills are usually found in the woodlands near lakes and rivers, the habitat apparently preferred by early hominins.

Such circumstances, I reasoned, might have once provided an ideal feeding opportunity for tree-climbing hominins, particularly *Homo habilis.* By scavenging from the leopard's temporarily abandoned larder, early hominins could have obtained the fleshy and marrow-rich bones of small- to medium-sized prey animals in relative safety.

Fossil evidence shows that ancestors of present-day leopards were contemporaneous with early hominins and shared the same habitats. The antiquity of tree-caching behavior is harder to prove, but it is supported by paleoanthropologist C. K. Brain's excavations of ancient caves in southern Africa's Sterkfontein Valley. In the vertical, shaftlike caves, Brain found the fossil remains of hominins, baboons, and antelopes, and of leopards and other large carnivores. The size of the prey animals and the selection of body parts, as well as puncture marks on some of the cranial bones of hominins and baboons, suggested that many of these fossils were the remains of leopard meals. Brain guessed that they had fallen into the caves from leopard-feeding trees growing out of the mouths of the caves.

Given its similarities to the ancient environments represented at the early archeological sites—extensive grasslands with wooded lakes, rivers, and streams—the Serengeti National Park in northern Tanzania seemed an ideal living laboratory in which to test my hypothesis. I traveled there in July 1987, accompanied by Robert J. Blumenschine, who had conducted an earlier study there on scavenging opportunities provided by lions and hyenas. Along the Wandamu River, a tributary of the Seronera, we were fortunate to find an adult female leopard and her 13-month-old (nearly full-grown) male cub that tolerated our Land Rover. We spent a total of about 50 hours, during the day and at night, observing these leopards at three fresh, tree-stored kills of Thomson's gazelles. The leopards frequently left the carcasses unguarded between feedings. On one occasion, a complete young Thomson's gazelle, killed the previous evening, was abandoned for 9 daylight hours (we found the leopards resting approximately 2 miles away). Without directly confronting these predators, therefore, a creature able to climb trees could have easily carried off the same amount of flesh and marrow as it could obtain from hunting.

While Brain's work in South Africa implicates leopards as predators of early hominins, including the genus *Homo,* some hominins may have also benefited from living near these carnivores. Tree-stored leopard kills could have provided an important resource to early scavenging hominins, and the sharp, broken limb bones from the partly eaten prey could have been used to peel back the hide, expose the flesh of the carcasses, and remove large muscle bundles. This activity may even have given early hominins the initial impetus to make and use tools in the extraction of animal nutrients.

Some paleoanthropologists have argued that scavenging was an unlikely subsistence strategy for early hominins, since large predators require expansive home ranges, and kills by these carnivores are rare in any particular area. They also contend that very little is left over from such kills after the predator is finished and that hominin competition with large carnivores for these leftovers would

This leopard has carried part of a Thomson's gazelle up into a tree to prevent other scavengers from consuming what is left. Such tree-stored carcasses may have been the principal source of meat for *Homo habilis.*

be a dangerous activity. My 1988 observations suggest something quite different. During approximately 2 months in the dry season, I documented 16 kills of small and medium antelopes made by my adult male and female leopards within an approximately 4-by-8-mile area. The majority of these kills, still retaining abundant flesh and marrow, were temporarily abandoned by the leopard for 3 to 8$^1/_2$ hours during a single day.

The tree-stored leopard kills consisted mainly of adult and juvenile Thomson's gazelles. Compared with kills of similar-sized prey made on the ground by Serengeti lions and hyenas, as recorded by Blumenschine, the tree-stored leopard kills lasted longer, offering large quantities of flesh and marrow for 2 or more days. In part this was because they were not subject to many scavengers. The leopard kills were also more predictably located on the landscape than those of lions in the same area. In modern leopard populations, a male maintains a relatively large territory that overlaps with the usually smaller territories of several females. This pattern often means that several tree-stored kills are available simultaneously during a given period of time within a relatively small area.

An obvious question is how leopards would have responded to repeated theft of their tree-stored kills. Would they, perhaps, have abandoned portions of their ranges if such thefts occurred with sufficient regularity? Although I haven't yet tested this, I don't think they would have. According to my observations and those of other researchers, leopards are usually more successful at hunting larger prey, such as gazelles and impala, at night. This gives them the opportunity to consume part of such kills before the arrival of any daytime scavengers. They thus should be able to obtain enough nourishment to warrant remaining in a territory, despite some such losses.

Like modern baboons and chimpanzees, early hominins may have killed some small animals, such as newborn antelopes. But they could have acquired all sizes of animal carcasses without hunting if the prey killed by leopards is taken into account. The wide assortment of animal bones at sites like Olduvai Gorge, which have been attributed to ground-based hunting and scavenging, could instead be attributed to scavenging only, both in trees and on the ground. Leopard kills would then have provided much of the flesh consumed by early hominins, while carcasses abandoned on the ground by other large predators would have yielded primarily bone marrow. Additional flesh may have come from the remains of large kills made by saber-toothed cats or from the carcasses of animals that drowned when herds migrated across ancient lakes.

While we can't observe the behavior of our early ancestors, the present-day interactions between leopards and some other primate species can be instructive. Baboons, for example, often fall victim to leopards while they sleep at night in trees or caves. During the day, however, baboons regularly attack, displace, and according to one account, even kill leopards. In western Tanzania, a park ranger reported that during the day, a group of baboons saw a leopard in a tree with the carcass of an impala. Barking out alarm calls, the adult and adolescent male baboons chased the leopard for about $^3/_{10}$ of a mile.

The females and young baboons stayed with the carcass and began to eat, until the males returned and took possession of the kill.

Similarly, although chimpanzees in western Tanzania are the occasional prey of leopards, there is a report that one day some chimpanzees scavenged what was apparently a tree-stored leopard kill. On a more dramatic occasion, also during the day, a group of chimpanzees was observed noisily surrounding a leopard lair from which an adult leopard was heard growling. A male chimpanzee entered the lair and emerged with a leopard cub, which it and the others killed without reprisal from the adult leopard. This type of shifting day-night, predatory-parasitic relationship may once have existed between leopards and our early hominin ancestors. *(Adapted from J. A. Cavallo. (1990). Cat in the human cradle. Natural History, 54-56, 58-60.)*

The importance of increased consumption of meat for early hominin brain development is suggested by the size of their brains: The cranial capacity of the largely plant-eating *Australopithecus* ranged from 310 to 530 cubic centimeters (cc); that of the earliest known meat eater, *Homo habilis* from East Africa, ranged from 580 to 752 cc; whereas *Homo erectus* (the subject of Chapter 8), who eventually hunted as well as scavenged for meat, possessed a cranial capacity of 775 to 1,225 cc. Many scenarios about behavioral adaptation in early *Homo,* such as the relationship among tools, food, and brain expansion, propose a kind of feedback loop between brain size and behavior. The behaviors made possible by larger brains confer advantages to large-brained individuals, contributing to their increased reproductive success. Over time, large-brained individuals contribute more to successive generations, so that the population evolves to a larger-brained form. Natural selection for increases in learning ability has thus led to the evolution of larger and more complex brains over about 2 million years. Though it preceded increases in brain size by several more million years, bipedalism set the stage for the evolution of large brains and human culture in these behavioral scenarios by opening new opportunities for variational change to occur through this new body plan. Bipedalism freed the hands for activities such as tool making and carrying of resources or infants.

LANGUAGE ORIGINS

The cooperation, planning, and foresight inferred for *H. habilis* suggest the existence of some sort of rudimentary language, as do some features of this species' brain. Modern apes communicate through a combination of calls and gestures. Although most humans rely on spoken language, we also use this gesture-call system. Like the apes, we have inherited this from ancient ancestors that predate the evolutionary split between humans and the other apes. After three decades of experiments by several different researchers with captive apes, there is a growing consensus that all great apes share an ability to develop language skills at least to the level of a 2- to 3-year-old human, though they lack the vocal tract to produce speech.[10] In the wild, the apes display these skills through the use of gestures. Again, because this linguistic potential is shared, it is likely one that the earliest hominins possessed as well. In view of these considerations, the previously noted features of the brain of *H. habilis* that in modern humans are associated with language take on added interest.

Regions of the brain that control speech and language lie adjacent to regions involved in precise hand control. This brings us back to the fact that the manufacture of Oldowan tools requires manual skills that go beyond those of chimpanzees in the wild or even the skills of Kanzi the bonobo who fashioned stone tools in captivity.[11] As previously noted, the Oldowan toolmakers, like modern humans, were overwhelmingly right-handed; in making tools, they gripped the core in the left hand, striking flakes off with the right. Chimpanzees, by contrast, show no overall preference for right-handedness at the population level.[12] Handedness (whether right or left) is associated with lateralization of brain functions; that is, the two hemispheres specialize for different functions rather than duplicating each other. Lateralization, in turn, is associated with language. Thus, tool making appears to have been associated with structural changes in the brain necessary for language development. Therefore, *H. habilis* may have developed at least a rudimentary gestural language. With the hands freed from locomotion, they were certainly more available for communication than are the hands of apes.

With the appearance of the earliest members of the genus *Homo,* human evolutionary history began a phase of gradual increase through variational change in cranial capacity and a corresponding complexity in behavior. In the next chapter, this trajectory continues with the even larger-brained species *Homo erectus* and the spread of human ancestors from Africa to the Eurasian continent.

[10]Miles, H. L. W. (1993). Language and the orangutan: The old person of the forest. In P. Singer (Ed.), *The great ape project* (p. 46). New York: St. Martin's.

[11]Ambrose, p. 1,749.

[12]Ambrose, p. 1,750

Chapter Summary

■ Since 1960, a number of fossils have been found in East Africa at Olduvai Gorge, east of Lake Turkana, and in South Africa at Sterkfontein, among other places; these fossils have been attributed to *Homo habilis,* the earliest representative of the genus *Homo. Homo habilis* is identified by anatomical changes in the face and skull shape along with an increase in brain size. Among them is the well-known KNM ER 1470 skull, which possesses a larger cranial capacity than any *Australopithecus* skull, though its face retains many ancestral features. Another *H. habilis* specimen, KNM ER 1813, also from Lake Turkana, possesses a more derived, humanlike face and skull shape but a smaller cranial capacity. From the neck down, however, the skeleton of *H. habilis* differs little from that of *Australopithecus.* Because it does show a significant increase in brain size and some reorganization of its structure, *H. habilis'* mental abilities likely exceeded those of *Australopithecus.* By 2.5 million years ago, the evolution of *Homo* was proceeding in a direction different from that of *Australopithecus.*

■ The same geological strata that have produced *Homo habilis* have also produced the earliest known stone tools. These Lower Paleolithic artifacts from Olduvai Gorge, Lake Turkana, and sites in Ethiopia are simple in form but required considerable skill and knowledge for their manufacture. These tools are in the Oldowan tool tradition, named after Olduvai Gorge where they were first discovered. The earliest tools, however, come from the Gona, Ethiopia. The Oldowan tradition is characterized by all-purpose generalized flakes and chopping tools. The percussion method of manufacture was used to make them. The simple but effective Oldowan choppers and flakes made possible the addition of scavenged meat to the diet on a regular basis because early *Homo* could use these tools to butcher meat, skin any animal, and break open bones for marrow. Many Oldowan archaeological sites appear to be temporary places where meat was processed, rather than campsites.

■ Some changes in the brain structure of *Homo habilis* seem to have been associated with the changes in diet. Increased consumption of meat, beginning about 2.5 million years ago, made new demands on coordination and behavior by *H. habilis.* Successful procurement of meat through scavenging depended on *H. habilis'* ability to outthink far more powerful predators and scavengers. The competitive advantage of an increased brain size in these situations may have played a role in variational change toward larger cranial capacity.

■ Tool making and use also favored the development of a more complex brain. To make stone tools, one must have in mind at the outset a clear vision of the tool to be made, one must know the precise set of steps necessary to transform the raw material into the tool, and one must be able to recognize the kind of stone that can be successfully worked. Complex eye-hand coordination is also required as well as the fine motor skills of the precision grip.

- The cooperation, planning, and foresight inferred for *Homo habilis* through tool making and scavenging suggest the existence of some sort of rudimentary language, as do some features of this species' brain. Experiments with captive apes favor some sort of gestural language, suggesting that at the very least *H. habilis* possessed these abilities. Evidence of handedness and lateralization of the brain support the notion of increased language abilities in early *Homo* relative to australopithecines.

Questions for Reflection

1. The earliest members of the genus *Homo* drew upon integrated biological and cultural capabilities to face the challenges of existence. Provide examples of how *Homo habilis* increasingly relied on cultural abilities and how these abilities are tied to biological evidence preserved in the fossil record.
2. Paleoanthropologists can be characterized as either "lumpers" or "splitters" depending upon their approach to recognizing species in the fossil record. Which of these approaches do you prefer and why?
3. Paleoanthropologists draw upon a wide variety of sources for reconstructing the behavior of our ancestors. Describe the kinds of evidence used for the reconstruction of behavior in the past. Is this evidence sufficient to define a biological basis for food-sharing behavior in the past?
4. Though language itself does not "fossilize," the archaeological and fossil records provide some evidence of the linguistic capabilities of our ancestors. Using the evidence available for *Homo habilis,* what sort of linguistic abilities do you think this species possessed?
5. In his 1871 book *Descent of Man and Selection in Relation to Sex,* Charles Darwin stated, "Thus man has ultimately become superior to woman. It is indeed fortunate that the law of equal transmission of characters prevails with mammals. Otherwise it is probable that man would have become as superior in mental endowment to woman as the peacock is in ornamental plumage to the peahen." How were the cultural norms of Darwin's time reflected in his statement? Can 21st-century paleoanthropologists speak about differences between the sexes in evolutionary contexts without introducing their own cultural biases?

Key Terms

Homo habilis	Oldowan tool tradition
Percussion method	Gender
Lower Paleolithic	Tertiary scavenger
Marrow	

Multimedia Review Tools

Companion Web Site

Visit **http://www.wadsworth.com/anthropology_d/** and click on the companion Web site for this textbook to access a wide range of material to aid your study of anthropology. Among the options for self-study in each chapter are learning objectives, flash cards, Internet activities, Web links, InfoTrac College Edition exercises, and practice tests that can be scored and emailed to your instructor.

CD-ROM

The *Doing Anthropology Today* CD-ROM supplied with your textbook provides unique and valuable information designed to enhance your learning experience. This interactive multimedia resource includes video clips, interviews with renowned anthropologists, map and timeline exercises, chapter study quizzes, and much more. *Doing Anthropology Today* will not only help you in achieving your grade goals, but it will also make your learning experience fun and exciting!

Suggested Readings

Ciochon, R. L., & Fleagle, J. G. (Eds.). (1993). *The human evolution source book.* Englewood Cliffs, NJ: Prentice-Hall.

This collection of original articles by specialists provides a more detailed look at the different theories on human evolution. It contains classic papers such as the original work proposing the new species *H. habilis* as well as many papers proposing and critiquing models about the behavior of our ancestors.

Corballis, M. C., (2003). *From hand to mouth: The origins of human language.* Princeton, NJ: Princeton University Press.

This book, written by a psychologist, takes the position that facial and manual gestures rather than vocalization are key to the development of language. It brings data from linguistics, molecular genetics, animal behavior, psychology, and neurology to the anthropological question of when human language arose.

Johanson, D., & Shreeve, J. (1989). *Lucy's child: The discovery of a human ancestor.* New York: Avon.

This sequel to *Lucy* is written in the same engaging style. Although it covers some of the same ground with respect to *Australopithecus,* its focus is on *Homo habilis.* Besides giving a good description of this earliest member of the genus *Homo,* it presents one of the best discussions of the issues concerning when (and why) *Homo* appeared.

Tobias, P. V. (1991). *Olduvai Gorge: Volume 4, The skulls, endocasts, and teeth of Homo habilis.* New York: Cambridge University Press.

For a definitive description of the earliest members of the genus *Homo* discovered at Olduvai Gorge, see this well-illustrated volume.

Zihlman, A. (2001). *The human evolution coloring book.* New York: Harper Resources.

Do not be deceived by the title or the book's visual hands-on format. This book provides an authoritative scientific approach to all aspects of the study of human evolution.

CHAPTER 8

Homo erectus and the Emergence of Hunting and Gathering

© Russell L. Ciochon, University of Iowa

CHALLENGE ISSUE

MORE "HUMAN" THAN *HOMO HABILIS*, THOUGH LESS SO THAN *HOMO SAPIENS*, *HOMO ERECTUS* EMERGED ABOUT 1.8 MILLION YEARS AGO BIOLOGICALLY EQUIPPED TO USE CULTURE TO SURVIVE. New stone tool industries provide evidence of *H. erectus'* cultural capabilities. The ability to use fire and plan ahead allowed the genus *Homo* to spread from Africa into the colder regions of Eurasia. When reconstructing the lifeways of these ancestors, the challenge for paleoanthropologists is to limit the influence of their own cultural beliefs and values on hypotheses about biocultural adaptations in the past. One of the most famous *H. erectus* sites—at Zhoukoudian, China, shown here—is a case in point. Does the evidence support the hypothesis that *H. erectus* practiced seasonal hunting and gathering and controlled use of fire here, or is *H. erectus* just another animal whose bones were brought here by carnivores? Discovered in the 1920s, Zhoukoudian is now included on UNESCO's World Heritage List.

1. Who Was *Homo erectus?*

Because the earliest fossils identified as *Homo erectus* come from Africa, this fossil group appears to have descended directly from *Homo habilis. H. erectus* possessed a larger brain than earlier *Homo* that matched their increased cultural capabilities while retaining ancestral features in the face and the shape of the skull. In addition, body size appears to have increased in this species. Populations of *H. erectus* were widespread between about 1.8 million and 400,000 years ago, from Africa and Europe in the west to Indonesia and China in the East.

2. What Were the Cultural Capabilities of *Homo erectus?*

Having a larger brain than its ancestors, *Homo erectus* became increasingly able to adapt to different challenges through the medium of culture. Evidence of *Homo erectus'* cultural capabilities is preserved in the archaeological record through better-made tools, a greater variety of tool types, regional diversification of tool kits, and the controlled use of fire. In addition, cultural abilities can be inferred from the planning required to inhabit some of the colder regions of Eurasia previously uninhabited by any hominins.

3. What Were the Consequences of *Homo erectus'* Improved Abilities to Adapt through Culture?

As culture became more important as the adaptive mechanism of this species, life appears to have become more secure, allowing population size to expand. Evidence of increased reproductive success can be inferred by the spread of *H. erectus* into previously uninhabited regions. Geographical expansion in turn contributed to further culture change, as various populations of *H. erectus* found independent solutions to meet the challenges of existence in newly inhabited regions of the earth. Regional diversification of stone tools indicates that more than one cultural tradition of *H. erectus* existed.

In 1887, long before Darwin's theory of biological evolution had gained wide acceptance, the Dutch physician Eugene Dubois set out to find the "missing link" between humans and apes. The presence of humanlike orangutans in the Dutch East Indies (now Indonesia) led him to start his search there. He joined the colonial service as an army surgeon and set sail. After several years of searching in vain, Dubois found fossilized remains consisting of a skull cap, a few teeth, and a thighbone at Trinil, on the island of Java. Its features seemed to Dubois part ape, part human. The flat skull, for example, with its low forehead and enormous brow ridges, appeared to be like that of an ape; but at about 775 cubic centimeters it possessed a cranial capacity much larger than an ape's, even though small by modern human standards. The femur, or thighbone, was clearly human in shape, and its proportions indicated the creature was a biped. Several years earlier, the German zoologist Ernst Haeckel, who strongly supported Darwin's theory, had proposed that if the "missing link" were ever found that it should be placed in the genus *Pithecanthropus* (from the Greek *pithekos* meaning "ape," *anthropus* meaning "man"). Believing that his specimens represented the missing link and that the thigh bone indicated this creature was bipedal, Dubois named his find *Pithecanthropus erectus,* or "erect ape man."

As with the Taung child, the first australopithecine discovered in the 1920s, many in the scientific community ridiculed and criticized Dubois' claim, suggesting instead that the apelike skull and humanlike femur came from different individuals. Controversy surrounded these specimens throughout Dubois' lifetime. He eventually retreated from the controversy, keeping the fossil specimens stored safely under the floorboards of his dining room. Ultimately, the discovery of more fossils provided evidence to support Dubois' claim fully. In the 1950s, the Trinil skull cap and similar specimens from

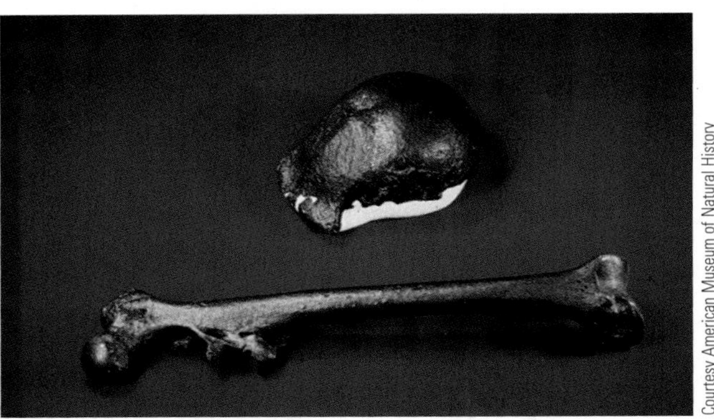

Courtesy American Museum of Natural History

These casts of the skull cap and thighbone of *Homo erectus* were made from the original bones found by Eugene Dubois at Trinil, Java.

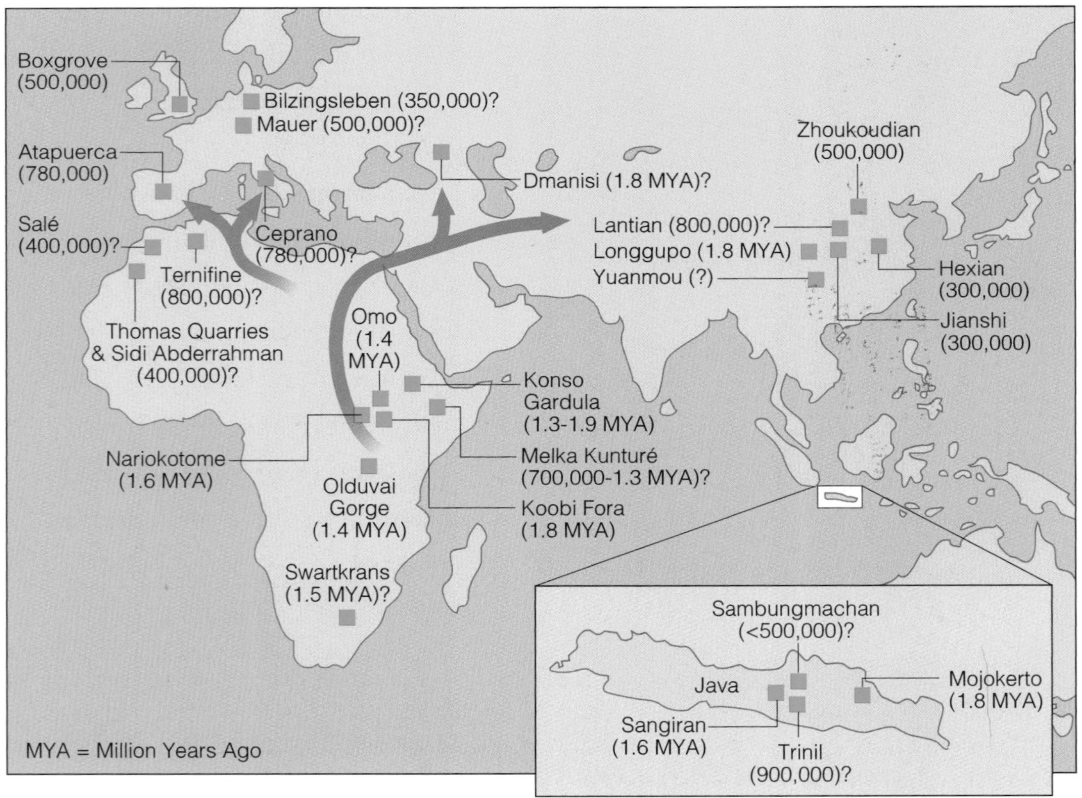

FIGURE 8.1

Sites, with dates, at which *Homo erectus* remains have been found. The arrows indicate the proposed routes by which *Homo* spread from Africa to Eurasia.

Indonesia and China were assigned to the species *Homo erectus* because they were more human than apelike.

Homo erectus FOSSILS

Until about 1.8 million years ago, Africa was the only home to the hominins. It was on this continent that hominins, and the genus *Homo,* originated. It was also in Africa that the first stone tools were invented. But by the time of *Homo erectus,* hominins had begun to spread far beyond their original homeland. Fossils of this species are now known from a number of localities not just in Africa, but in China, western Europe, Georgia (in the Caucasus Mountains), and India, as well as Java (Figure 8.1). Although remains of *H. erectus* have been found in many different places in three continents, "lumpers" emphasize that they are unified by a number of shared characteristics. However, because the fossil evidence also suggests some differences within and among populations of *H. erectus* inhabiting discrete regions of Africa, Asia, and Europe, some paleoanthropologists prefer to split *H. erectus* into several distinct groups, limiting the species *H. erectus* only to the specimens from Asia.

Physical Characteristics of *Homo erectus*

The specific features characteristic of *H. erectus* are best known from the skull. Interestingly many of the *H. erectus* fossils consist of isolated skull caps as in Dubois'original discovery. Cranial capacity in *H. erectus* ranges from 600 to 1,225 cubic centimeters (average about 1,000 cc). Thus cranial capacity overlaps with the nearly 2-million-year-old KNM ER 1470 skull from East Africa (752 cc) and the 1,000 to 2,000 cc range (average 1,300 cc) for modern human skulls (Figure 8.2). The cranium itself has a low vault (height of the dome of the skull top), and the head is long and narrow. When viewed from behind, its width is greater than its height, with its greatest width at the base. The skulls of modern humans when similarly viewed are higher than they are wide, with the widest dimension in the region above the ears. The shape of the inside of *H. erectus'* braincase shows near-modern development of the brain, especially in the speech area. Although some anthropologists argue that the vocal apparatus was not adequate for speech, others argue that asymmetries of the brain suggest the same pattern of right-handedness with left cerebral dominance that, in modern peoples, is correlated with the capacity for language.[1]

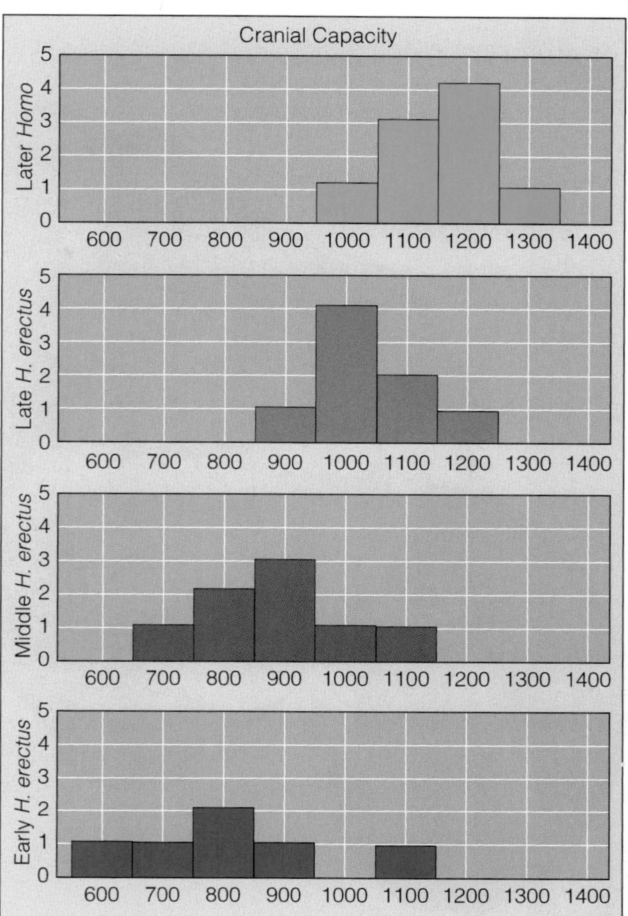

FIGURE 8.2

Cranial capacity in *Homo erectus* increased over time, as illustrated by these bar graphs, shown in cubic centimeters. The cranial capacity of late *Homo erectus* overlaps with the range seen in living humans.

H. erectus possessed massive brow ridges (Figure 8.3). When viewed from above, a marked constriction or "pinching in" of the skull can be seen just behind the massive brow ridges. *H. erectus* also possessed a sloping forehead and a receding chin. Powerful jaws with large teeth, a protruding mouth, and huge neck muscles added to *H. erectus'* generally rugged appearance. Nevertheless, the face, teeth, and jaws of this hominin are smaller than those of *Homo habilis.*

Apart from its skull, the skeleton of *H. erectus* differs only subtly from that of modern humans. Although its bodily proportions are like ours, it was more heavily muscled. Stature seems to have increased from the smaller size typical of the australopithecines and the earliest members of the genus *Homo.* The best evidence for this comes from a remarkably well-preserved skeleton of an adolescent male from Lake Turkana in Kenya. Sexual dimorphism in body size also appears to have decreased in *H. erectus*

[1]Holloway, R. L. (1981). The Indonesian *Homo erectus* brain endocasts revisited. *American Journal of Physical Anthropology, 55,* 521.

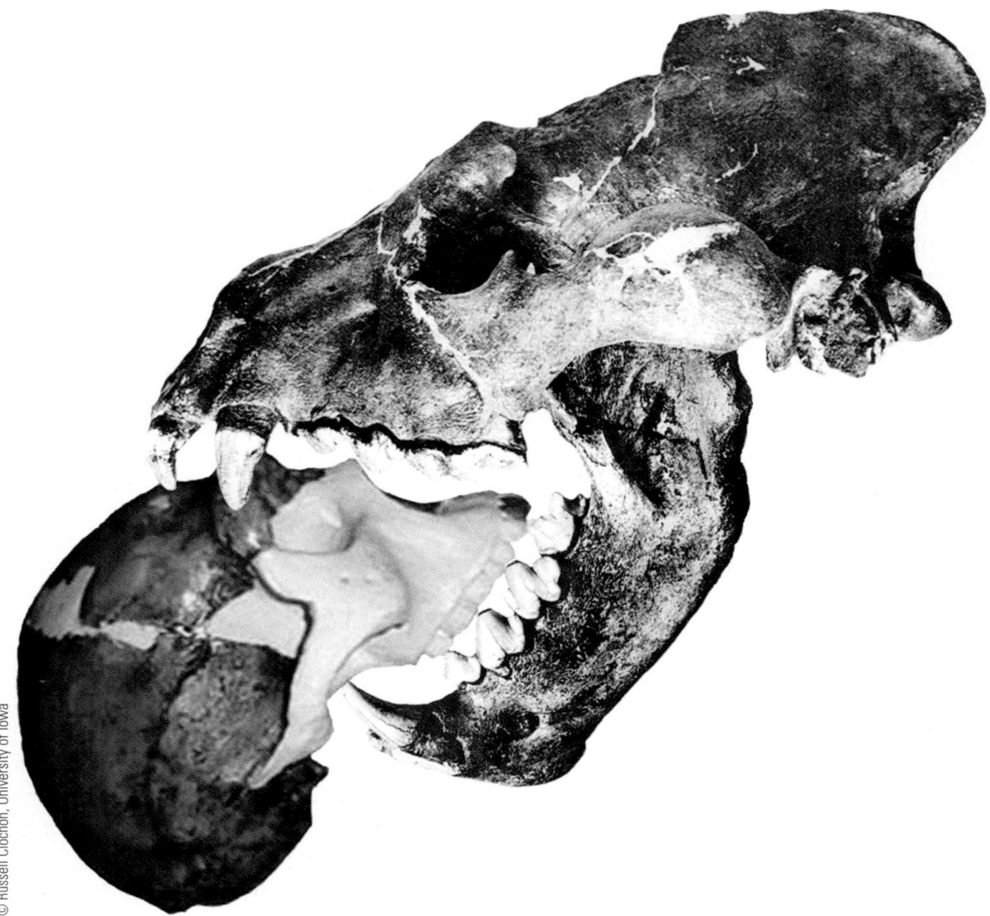

Many of the *Homo erectus* fossils consist of isolated skull caps. This reconstruction suggests that the faces may be missing because they are the isolated remains of individuals who were consumed by the now-extinct giant hyena. This composite shows how the giant hyena could have attacked the face.

compared to earlier hominins. A reduction in sexual dimorphism may be due to the increase in female size as an adaptation to childbirth.

Relationship among *Homo erectus*, *Homo habilis*, and Other Proposed Fossil Groups

The smaller teeth and larger brains of *H. erectus* seem to mark continuation of a trend first seen in *Homo habilis*. Increased body size, reduced sexual dimorphism, and more "human" body form of *H. erectus* are newly derived characteristics. Nonetheless, some skeletal resemblance to *H. habilis* exists, for example, in the long neck and low neck angle of the thighbone, the long low vault and marked constriction of the skull behind the eyes, and smaller brain size in the earliest *H. erectus* fossils. Indeed, as already noted, it is very difficult to distinguish between the earliest *H. erectus* and the latest *H. habilis* fossils (Figure 8.4). Presumably the one form evolved from the other, fairly abruptly, around 1.9 to 1.8 million years ago (Figure 8.5). As described in our earlier discussion of *H. habilis,* some paleoanthropologists prefer to "split" the fossil record from this period into discrete species. Some propose that the species *Homo ergaster* be used for African specimens from this period that others describe as early *H. erectus* (see Table 8.1). Regardless of species designation in the early Pleistocene, it is clear that beginning 1.8 million years ago these larger-brained members of the genus *Homo* lived not only in Africa but also had spread to Europe and Asia. Fossil specimens dating to 1.8 million years old have been recovered from Dmanisi, Georgia, as well as from Mojokerto, Indonesia. Many additional specimens have been found at a variety of sites in Europe and Asia.

Generally speaking, African *H. erectus* skulls are similar to those from Asia; one difference is that their bones aren't quite as thick; another is that some Africans had smaller brow ridges. It may be, too, that individuals living in Asia were shorter and stockier, on the whole, than those living in Africa. However, the detailed anatomical comparisons indicate levels of variation approximating those seen in *H. sapiens.*[2] Consistent with the notion of a single species is the

[2] Rightmire, G. P. (1998). Evidence from facial morphology for similarity of Asian and African representatives of *Homo erectus*. *American Journal of Physical Anthropology, 106,* 61.

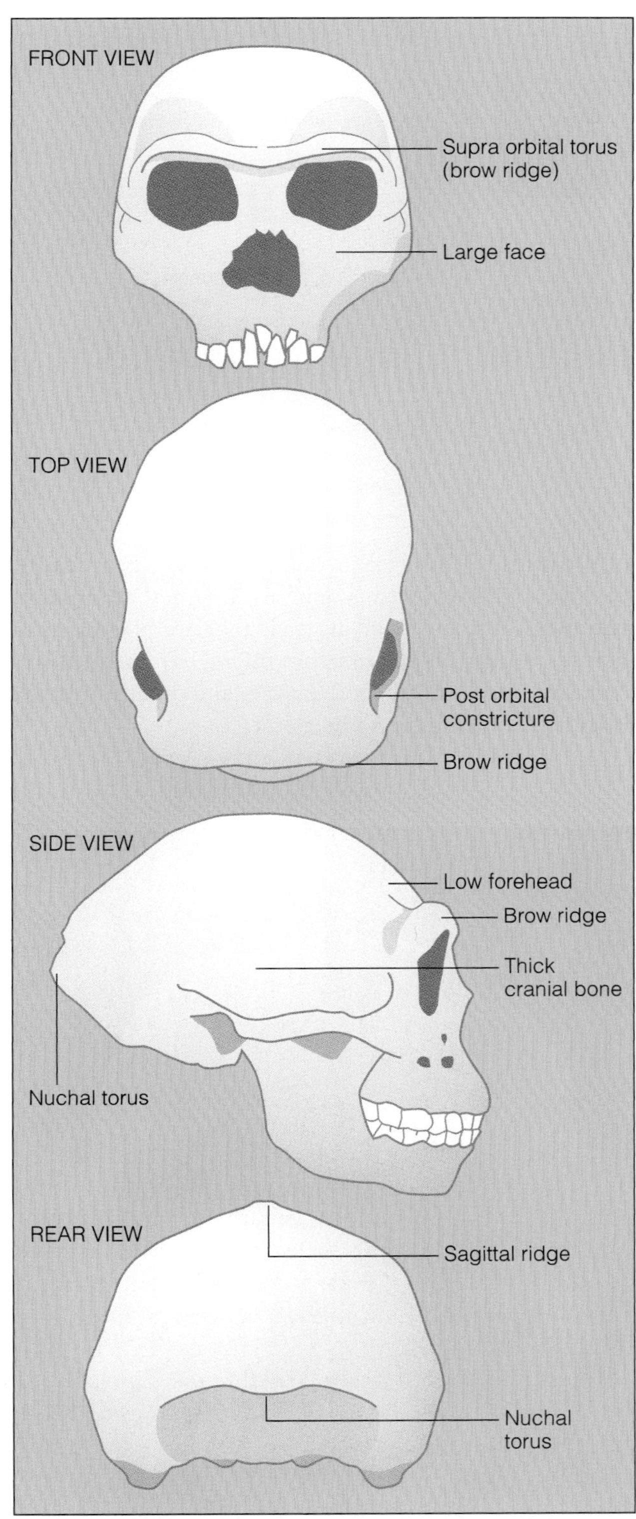

FIGURE 8.3

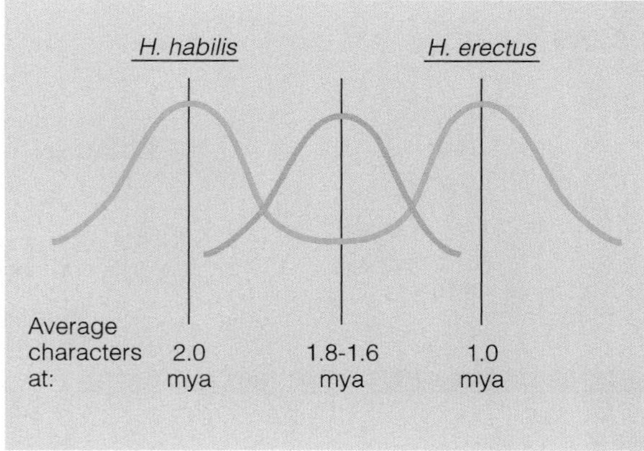

FIGURE 8.4

To understand the evolution of any species, the full range of variation must be considered, not merely typical representatives. The fact that fossils seemingly attributed to *H. habilis* and *H. erectus* coexisted between 1.8 and 1.6 million years ago (mya) need not mean coexistence of two separate species. If one evolved from the other, we would expect that at some point the full range of variation included some individuals that still resembled *H. habilis,* whereas others were increasingly taking on the appearance of *H. erectus.*

observation that 1.8-million-year-old specimens from Dmanisi, in the Caucasus—a region that lies more or less halfway between Africa and Indonesia—show a mix of characteristics seen in African and Asian erectus populations.[3] Overall, it seems that comparisons between African and Asian populations of *Homo erectus* possess levels of variations similar to those seen if modern human populations from the east and the west are compared. As in Asia, the most recent African fossils are more derived in appearance, and the oldest fossils (up to 1.8 million years old) display features reminiscent of the earlier *Homo habilis.* Indeed, distinguishing early *H. erectus* from late *H. habilis* is problematic—precisely what one would expect if the one evolved from the other. We will explore the *H. erectus* finds by region, beginning with the fossil evidence from Africa.

Homo erectus from Africa

Although our samples of *H. erectus* fossils from Asia remain among the best, several important specimens are also known from Africa. Fossils now assigned to this species were discovered there as long ago as 1933, but the better-known finds have been made since 1960, at Olduvai Gorge and at Lake Turkana, Kenya. Among them is the most complete *H. erectus* skeleton ever found, that of a boy who died 1.6 million years ago at about the age of 12. Paleoanthropologists infer the age of this specimen from his teeth (the 12-year molars are

[3]Rosas, A., & Bermudez de Castro, J. M. (1998). On the taxonomic affinities of the Dmanisi mandible (Georgia). *American Journal of Physical Anthropology, 107,* 159.

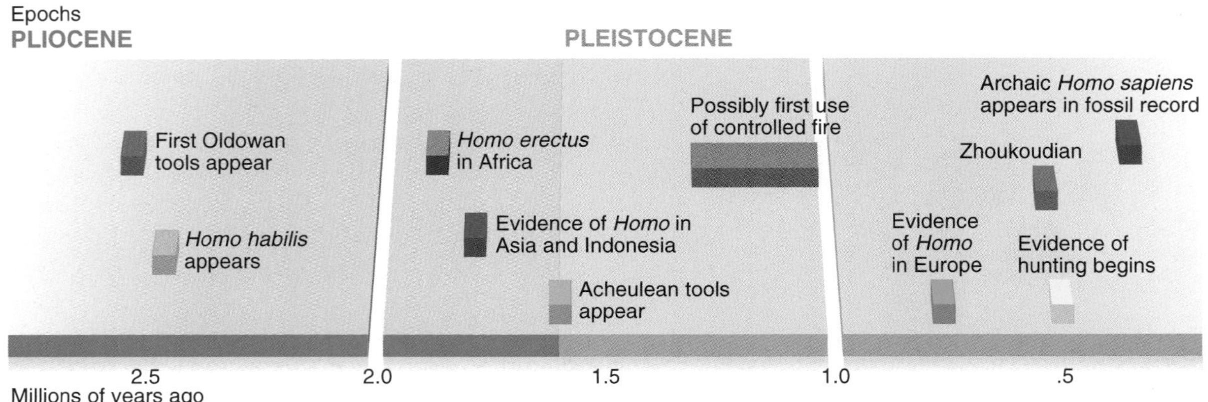

FIGURE 8.5
Timeline of Early and Middle Pleistocene Hominins

fully erupted) and the state of maturity of the bones. With a height of about 5 feet 3 inches at adolescence, this specimen was expected to attain a stature of about 6 feet by adulthood.

Another partial skeleton, this time of an adult, had diseased bones, possibly the result of a massive overdose of vitamin A. This excess could have come from eating the livers of carnivorous animals, for they accumulate vitamin A in their livers at levels that are poisonous to human beings. More probable might have been heavy consumption of bee brood (larvae) and other immature insects, producing the same result.

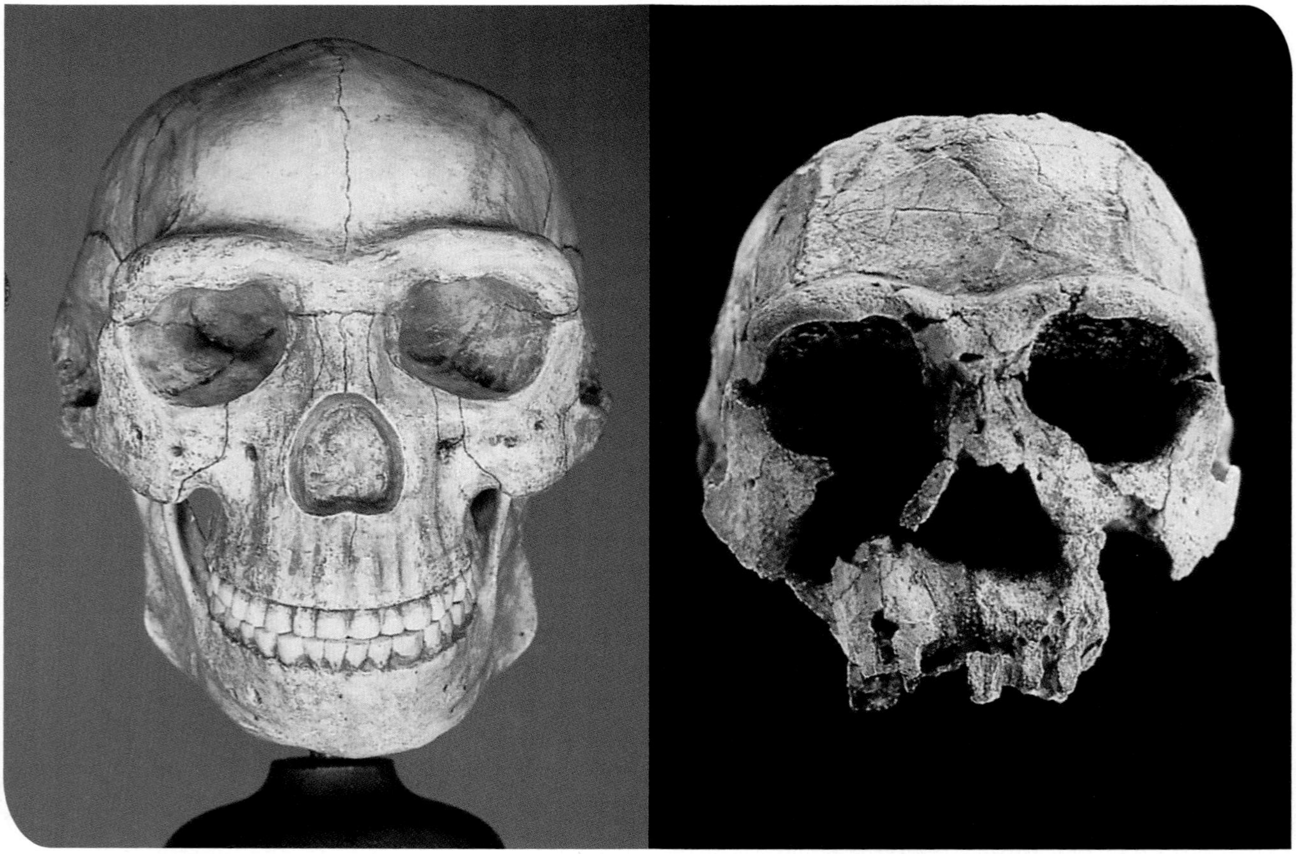

Courtesy Dept. of Library Sciences, American Museum of Natural History

© 1985 David L. Brill

VISUAL COUNTERPOINT This photo of a reconstructed late *H. erectus* skull (left) from Zhoukoudian, China, and the earlier African *H. erectus* skull shown at right illustrate the features common to this species across a broad range of time and space.

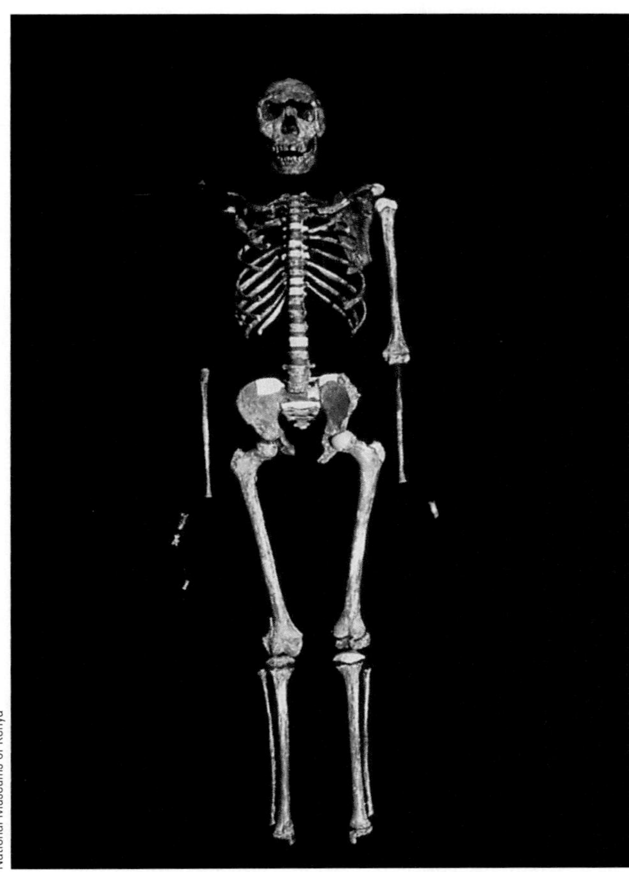

One of the oldest and certainly the most complete *Homo erectus* fossils is the "Nariokotome Boy" from Lake Turkana, Kenya. The remains are those of a tall adolescent boy.

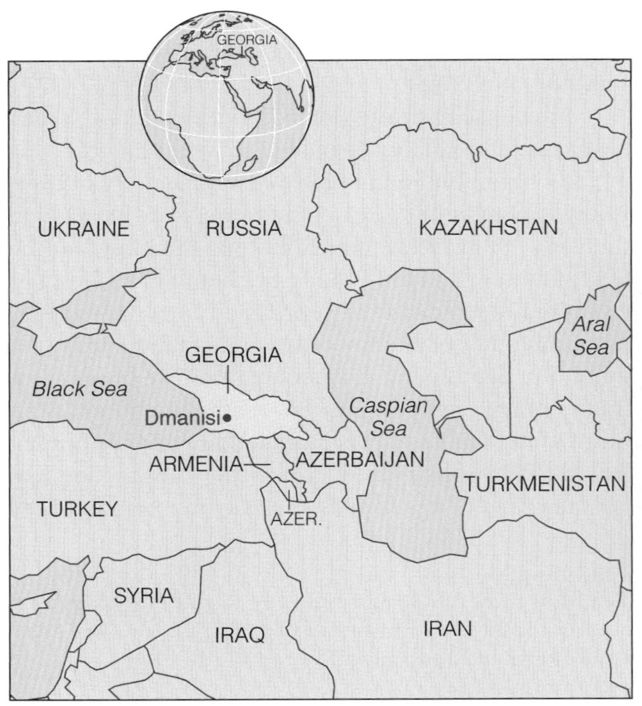

Homo erectus from Eurasia

Evidence of the spread of *H. erectus* from Africa into Eurasia is well preserved at the interesting site of Dmanisi in the Caucasus Mountains of Georgia. Dmanisi was first excavated as an archaeological site because of its importance as a crossroads for the caravan routes of Armenia, Persia, and Byzantium in medieval times. When Oldowan stone tools (see Chapter 7) were found at this site in 1984, the hunt for fossil specimens began here as well. Since then, paleoanthropologists have recovered some remarkable remains that can be accurately dated to 1.8 million years ago through past volcanic activity in the region. In 1999, two well-preserved skulls, one with a partial face, were discovered. Thus the early habitation of this region by members of the genus *Homo* is supported at Dmanisi by archaeological, anatomical, and geological evidence. Because rising sea levels since the Pleistocene make it impossible for paleoanthropologists to document coastal routes for the spread of *Homo* from Africa to Eurasia, the evidence from Georgia constitutes the only direct evidence of the presence of evolving humans between Africa, Europe, and Asia.

Homo erectus from Indonesia

As described in the opening of the chapter, the intellectual community was reluctant to accept Dubois' claim that his Javanese fossils were part of the human line. It was not until the 1930s, particularly when other fossils of *H. erectus* were discovered by German paleoanthropologist G. H. R. von Königswald at Sangiran, Java, that scientists almost without exception agreed that both discoveries were the remains of an entirely new kind of early hominin. Von Königswald found a small skull that fluorine analysis and (later) potassium-argon dating assigned to the Early Pleistocene. This indicated that

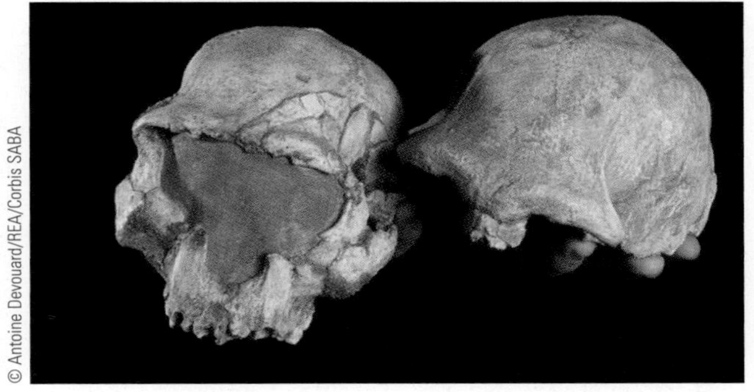

These two skulls of *Homo erectus* from Dmanisi, Georgia, are probably from a male and female. They are about 1.8 million years old, resembling African fossils from the same time period.

TABLE 8.1 ALTERNATE SPECIES DESIGNATIONS FOR *Homo erectus* FOSSILS FROM EURASIA AND AFRICA

Name	Explanation
Homo ergaster	Some paleoanthropologists feel that the large-brained successors to *H. habilis* from Africa and Asia are too different to be placed in the same species. Therefore, they use *H. ergaster* for the African specimens, saving *H. erectus* for the Asian fossils. Some paleoanthropologists place the recent discoveries from Dmanisi into this taxon.
Homo antecessor	This name was coined for the earliest hominin fossils from western Europe discovered in Spain; *antecessor* is Latin for "explorer" or "pioneer."
Homo heidelbergensis	Originally coined for the Mauer jaw (Mauer is not far from Heidelberg, Germany), this name is now used by some as a designation for all European fossils from about 500,000 years ago until the appearance of the Neandertals (Chapter 9).

these fossils were older than the Trinil skull cap found by Dubois, dating to approximately 500,000 to 700,000 years ago. Since 1960, additional fossils have been found in Java, and we now have remains of around forty individuals. A long continuity of *H. erectus* populations in Southeast Asia is indicated, from perhaps as many as 1.8 million to about 500,000 years ago. Interestingly, the teeth and jaws of some of the earliest Javanese fossils are in many ways quite similar to those of *Homo habilis.*[4] When considering the spread of *H. erectus* to Java, it is important to note that in the past, lower sea levels resulted in a continuous land mass between Indonesia and the Asian continent.

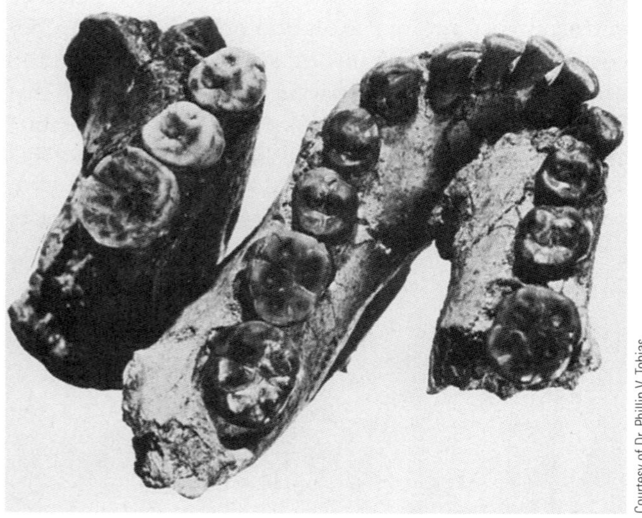

Courtesy of Dr. Phillip V. Tobias

The fragment of the early *Homo erectus* jaw from Java on the left is nearly identical to the jaw of *Homo habilis* from Olduvai Gorge on the right.

Homo erectus from China

In the mid-1920s another group of fossils from Asia, now known as *H. erectus,* was found by Davidson Black, a Canadian anatomist teaching at Peking Union Medical College. Black was led to this site after purchasing a few ancient humanlike teeth offered for their medicinal properties from a Beijing drugstore. He set out for the nearby countryside to discover the "owner" of the teeth and perhaps a species of early human ancestor. At a place called Dragon Bone Hill in Zhoukoudian, 30 miles from Beijing, on the day before closing camp at the end of his first year of excavation, he found one molar tooth. Subsequently, Chinese paleoanthropologist W. C. Pei, who worked closely with Black, found a skull encased in limestone. Between 1929 and 1934, the year of his death from silicosis—a lung disease caused by exposure to silica particles in the cave—Black labored along with Pei and French paleontologist Pierre Teilhard de Chardin in the fossil-rich deposits of Zhoukoudian, uncovering fragment after fragment of the hominin. On the basis of the anatomy of that first molar tooth, Black named these fossils Sinanthropus *pekinensis,* or "Chinese human of Peking" (Beijing) called "Peking Man" for short at the time. They are now recognized as an East Asian representative of *H. erectus.*

After Black's death, Franz Weidenreich, a German anatomist and paleoanthropologist, was sent to China by the Rockefeller Foundation to continue this work (see Anthropologists of Note). As a Jew in Nazi Germany in the early 1930s, Weidenreich had sought refuge in the United States. By 1938, Wiedenreich and his colleagues recovered the remains of more than forty individuals, more than half of them women and children, from the limestone deposits of Zhoukoudian. Most fossils were fragmentary, represented by teeth, jawbones, and incomplete skulls. A spectacular composite specimen has been reconstructed from the most complete remains. World War II (1939–1945) brought a halt to the

[4]Tobias, P. V., & von Königswald, G. H. R. (1964). A comparison between the Olduvai hominines and those of Java and some implications for hominid phylogeny. *Nature, 204,* 515–518.

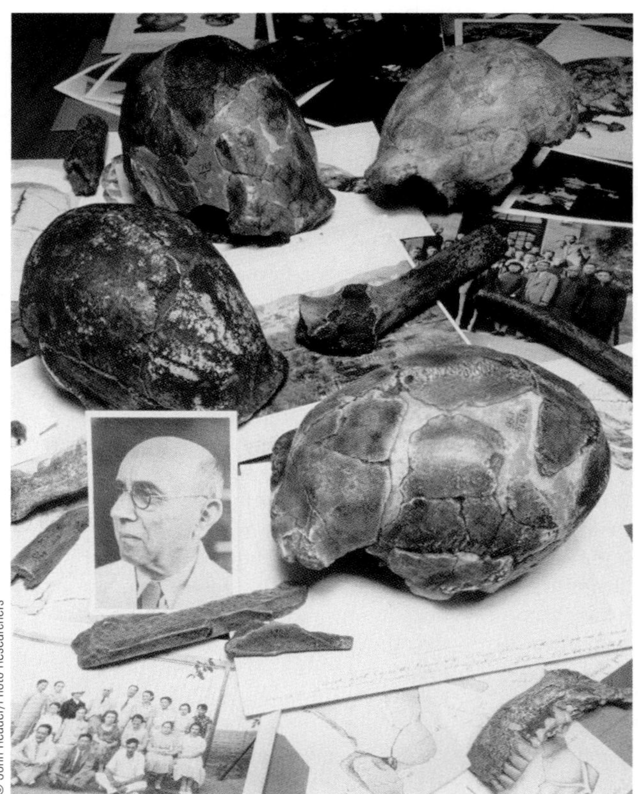

© John Reader/Photo Researchers

The original *Homo erectus* fossils from Zhoukoudian had been packed and shipped to the United States for safe keeping during World War II, but they mysteriously disappeared. Fortunately, excellent casts of the specimens and detailed anatomical descriptions (by Weidenreich) were made before the fossils were lost during the war.

digging, and the original Zhoukoudian specimens were lost during the Japanese occupation of China. The fossils had been carefully packed by Weidenreich and his team and placed with the U.S. Marines, but in the chaos of war, these precious fossils disappeared.

Fortunately, Weidenreich had made superb casts of most of the Zhoukoudian fossil specimens and sent them to the United States before the war. After the war, other specimens of *H. erectus* were discovered in China, at Zhoukoudian and at a number of other localities (see Figure 8.1). The oldest skull is about 700,000 to 800,000 years old and comes from Lantian in central China. Even older is a fragment of a lower jaw from a cave in south-central China (Lunggupo) that is as old as the oldest Indonesian fossils. Like some of their Indonesian contemporaries, this Chinese fossil is reminiscent of African *H. habilis*. In contrast to these ancient remains, the original Zhoukoudian fossils appear to date between 600,000 and 300,000 years ago.

Although the two populations overlap in time, the majority of the Chinese fossils are, on the whole, not quite as old as those from Indonesia. Not surprisingly, Chinese *H. erectus* is less ancestral in appearance. Its average cranial capacity is about 1,000 cubic centimeters, compared to 900 cc for Indonesian *H. erectus* (see Figure 8.2). The smaller teeth and short jaw of the Chinese fossil specimens are further evidence of their more derived status.

Homo erectus from Western Europe

Although the fossil evidence indicates the presence of the genus *Homo* on the Eurasian landmass 1.8 million years ago (at Dmanisi, Georgia), the fossil evidence from western Europe dates to about 800,000 years ago. The evidence from the Grand Dolina site in north-central Spain (see Table 8.1) consists of fragments of four individuals dating to 780,000 years ago. A skull from Ceprano in Italy is thought to be approximately the same age if not older. Again, whether one lumps these specimens into the inclusive but varied species *H. erectus* or into several separate species differs according to the approach taken by paleoanthropologists with regard to the fossil record. Some other fossils attributable to *H. erectus*—such as a robust shinbone from Boxgrove, England, and a large lower jaw from Mauer, Germany—are close to half a million years old. The jaw certainly came from a skull wide at the base, typical of *H. erectus*. As might be expected, these remains are similar to *H. erectus* material from North Africa from the same time period. This observation, and the fact that the earliest evidence of the genus *Homo* in western Europe comes from Spain and Italy, suggests that they arrived there by crossing from northern Africa.[5] At the time, a mere 6 or 7 kilometers separated Gibraltar from Morocco (compared to 13 kilometers today), and islands dotted the straits from Tunisia to Sicily. The only direct land connection between Africa and Eurasia is through the Middle East and into Turkey and the Caucasus. Otherwise *H. erectus* may have come to western Europe by crossing open water. Though evidence (discussed later in this chapter) demonstrates that *H. erectus* was capable of crossing open water by 800,000 years ago, no proof of such a crossing exists in Europe.

MEDIATREK

To learn about the earliest hominins from western Europe, see virtual fossils, and find out about the Sierra de Atapuerca excavation and the place of these recently discovered specimens in human evolutionary history, go to MediaTrek 8.1 on the companion Web site or CD-ROM.

[5] Balter, M. (2001). In search of the first Europeans. *Science, 291*, 1,724.

Anthropologists of Note

Franz Weidenreich (1873–1948) ▪ Xinzhi Wu (1930–)

Franz Weidenreich was born and educated in Germany, where he held professorships in anatomy and anthropology, first at Strassburg and later at Heidelberg and Frankfurt. In 1926, he published his first study of a human fossil, an archaic *Homo sapiens* cranium from Ehringsdorf. His skills as an anatomist and his independent mind are evident in the fact that he was one of the few scientists of his day to absolutely refute the Piltdown forgery when these specimens were first put forward as the "missing link." As the Nazi regime took power in Germany in the 1930s, Weidenreich sought refuge in the United States. In 1935, he was sent by the Rockefeller Foundation to take up the study of fossils of *Homo erectus* at Zhoukoudian, China, following the death of Davidson Black. When the Japanese takeover of China forced Weidenreich to leave, he took with him to the United States several painstakingly prepared casts, as well as detailed notes on the actual fossils. From these he was able to prepare a major monograph that set new standards for paleoanthropological reports. For this alone, anthropology owes him a great debt, for the fossils themselves were among the casualties of World War II.

Unlike many physical anthropologists of his time or ours, Weidenreich had an extensive firsthand knowledge of extant human fossils from Europe, China, and Southeast Asia (he collaborated in the 1930s study of *Homo erectus* and later fossils from Java). What struck him about the fossils in each of these regions was the evident continuity from the earliest to the latest specimens. From this observation, he developed his polycentric theory of human evolution, which received its first clear statement in a 1943 publication. In it, he argued the thesis that hominin populations in distinct regions evolved in the same directions such that regional characteristics are evident while all populations show an increasing cranial capacity. Although some have (mis)understood this as the completely separate but parallel evolution of separate human lines, Weidenreich was quite clear about the continued operation of gene flow in the process of human evolution. Weidenreich's ideas have been taken up by others and developed into the modern multiregional theory of human evolution.

Xinzhi Wu is one of China's foremost paleoanthropological scholars, contributing to the development of the discipline for the past 50 years. As with many other paleoanthropologists, the study of human anatomy has been of vital importance to him. He began his academic career with a degree from Shanghai Medical College followed by teaching in the Department of Human Anatomy at the Medical College in Dalian before beginning graduate studies in paleoanthropology. He is presently a professor at the Chinese Academy of Sciences Institute of Vertebrate Paleontology and Paleoanthroplogy in Beijing and the honorary president of the Chinese Society of Anatomical Sciences. In addition to managing excavations in China and other parts of Asia, Wu has played a major role in the development of theories about modern human origins in cooperation with scholars internationally. He collaborated with Milford Wolpoff of the United States and Alan Thorne of Australia in the development of the theory of mutiregional continuity for modern human origins. This theory (which will be discussed in great detail in Chapter 9) fits well with the Asian fossil evidence proposing an important place for *Homo erectus* in modern human origins. Interestingly it builds upon the model for human origins developed by Franz Weidenreich. According to Wu, early humans from China are as old if not older than humans anyplace else. He suggests that the reason more fossils have been found in Africa recently is that more excavations are occurring there than elsewhere.

Zhoukoudian remains a site of particular importance for Wu, as it documents continuous habitation of early humans and one of the earliest controlled use of fire. Wu has predicted that more important discoveries will still be made at Zhoukoudian as one third of this site has still not been fully excavated. The Chinese government has responded to Wu's suggestions and is presently constructing a 2.4-square-kilometer "Peking Man" exhibition and paleoanthropology research area at Zhoukoudian.

Wu has welcomed many international scholars to China to study the Asian evidence. He also has led efforts to make descriptions of fossil material available in English. Collaborating with American anthropologist Frank Poirier, he published the comprehensive volume, titled *Human Evolution in China,* describing all of the fossil evidence and archaeological sites with great accuracy and detail.

THE CULTURE OF *Homo erectus*

As one might expect given its larger brain, *H. erectus* outstripped its predecessors in cultural ability. In Africa, Europe, and Asia, a refinement of the stone tool-making technology begun by the makers of earlier flake and chopper tools is evident. At some point, fire began to be used for protection, warmth, and cooking, though precisely when is still a matter for debate. Finally, there is indirect evidence that the organizational and planning

Kenneth Garrett/NSG Image Collection

This skull from Ceprano, Italy, is one of the oldest fossils of *H. erectus* from Europe. It may be more than 800,000 years old.

abilities of *H. erectus,* or at least the later ones, were improved over those of their predecessors. Many sites preserve a rich array of archaeological remains without any fossil hominins. Therefore the following discussion will draw on larger geographic areas rather than limiting the discussion only to the specific sites where actual *H. erectus* fossils have been found.

Paleoanthropological reconstructions of the culture and behavior of our ancestors differ considerably from simple interpretations of biological change based on comparative anatomy. Behavioral reconstructions combine evidence about the environment, archaeological evidence of tools, hearths, and shelters, with biological data about brain size and structure. Because the cultural capacity of our ancestors is rooted in biology, paleoanthropologists are faced with the challenge of integrating biology and culture in the interpretation of the fragmentary evidence from the past. However, it is in these reconstructions that paleoanthropologists shift into a narrative mode, telling the "heroic story" of human evolution in which our ancestors increasingly use their cultural capabilities rather than biology to survive. In the following paleoanthropological reconstructions of the culture of *H. erectus,* a curious blend of scientific method and story telling coexist. In this regard, paleoanthropologists are also faced with the challenge of keeping their own cultural beliefs and values out of the paleoanthropological reconstructions.

The Acheulean Tool Tradition

Associated with the remains of *Homo erectus* in Africa, Europe, and Southwest Asia are tools of the **Acheulean tradition.** The signature piece of this tradition first identified in stone tools discovered at Saint Acheul, France, is the hand-axe: a teardrop-shaped tool pointed at one end with a sharp cutting edge all around. The earliest hand-axes, from East Africa are about 1.6 million years old. Those found in Europe are no older than about 500,000 years. At the same time that hand-axes appeared, archaeological sites in Europe became dramatically more common than earlier ones. This suggests an influx of individuals bringing Acheulean technology with them, implying continued gene flow into Europe. Because the spread of the genus *Homo* from Africa into Asia took place before the invention of the hand-axe, it is not surprising to find that different forms of tools were developed in East Asia.

That the Acheulean grew out of the Oldowan tradition is indicated by an examination of the evidence discovered at Olduvai Gorge. In Bed I, the lowest level, chopper tools were found along with remains of *Homo*

Acheulean tradition The tool-making tradition of *Homo erectus* in Africa, Europe, and Southwest Asia in which hand-axes were developed from the earlier Oldowan chopper.

habilis. Above, in lower Bed II, the first crude hand-axes were found intermingled with chopper tools. The more finished-looking Acheulean hand-axes appear in middle Bed II together with *H. erectus* remains.

Early Acheulean tools represent a significant step beyond the generalized cutting, chopping, and scraping tools of the Oldowan tradition. The shapes of Oldowan tools were largely controlled by the original form, size, and mechanical properties of raw materials. The shapes of hand-axes and some other Acheulean tools, by contrast, are more standardized, apparently reflecting arbitrary preconceived designs imposed upon a diverse range of raw materials.[6] Overall, sharper points, more regular cutting edges, and more cutting edge were produced from the same amount of stone.

During this part of the Lower Paleolithic, or Old Stone Age, tool kits began to diversify (Figure 8.6). Besides hand-axes, *H. erectus* used tools that functioned as cleavers (hand-axes with a straight, sharp edge where the point would otherwise be), picks and knives (variants of the hand-axe form), and flake tools (generally smaller tools made by hitting a flint core with a hammerstone, thus knocking off flakes with sharp edges). Many flake tools were by-products of hand-axe and cleaver manufacture. Their sharp edges made them useful "as is," but many were retouched to make points, scrapers, borers, and other sorts of tools. Diversification of tool kits is also indicated by the smaller numbers of hand-axes in northern and eastern Europe where people relied more on simple flaked choppers; a wide variety of unstandardized flakes; and supplementary tools of bone, antler, and wood. In eastern Asia, by contrast, people developed a variety of choppers, scrapers, points, and burins (chisel-like tools) different from those in western Asia, Europe, and Africa. Besides direct percussion, anvil (striking the raw material against a stationary stone) and bipolar percussion (holding the raw material against an

[6]Ambrose, S. H. (2001). Paleolithic technology and human evolution. *Science, 291,* 1,750.

VISUAL COUNTERPOINT To fabricate this Acheulean hand-axe (left) from flint, the toolmaker imposed a standardized arbitrary form on the naturally occurring raw material. The photo on the right shows archaeologist Dr. Alban Defleur, collecting a fine grained stone for flint knapping.

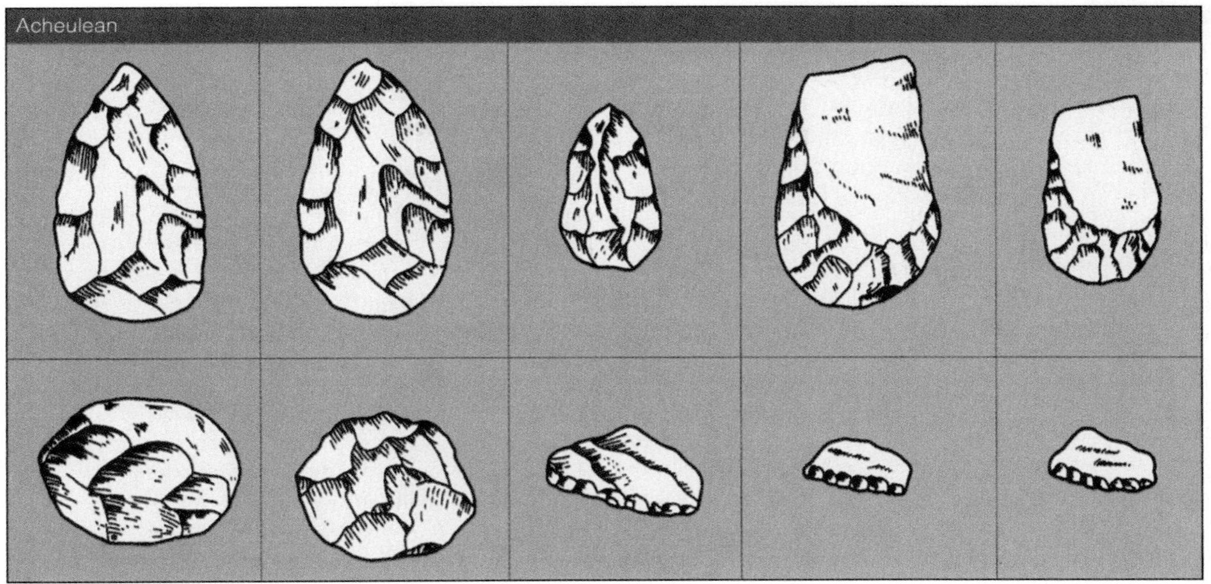

FIGURE 8.6
Ten percent of the shaped tools in a typical Acheulean assemblage are the forms drawn here.

anvil, but striking it at the same time with a hammerstone) methods were used in tool manufacture. Although tens of thousands of stone tools have been found with *H. erectus* remains at Zhoukoudian, stone implements are not at all common in Southeast Asia. Here, favored materials likely were materials that do not preserve well such as bamboo and other local woods, from which excellent knives, scrapers, and so on can be made as described in the following Original Study.

Original Study

Homo erectus and the Use of Bamboo

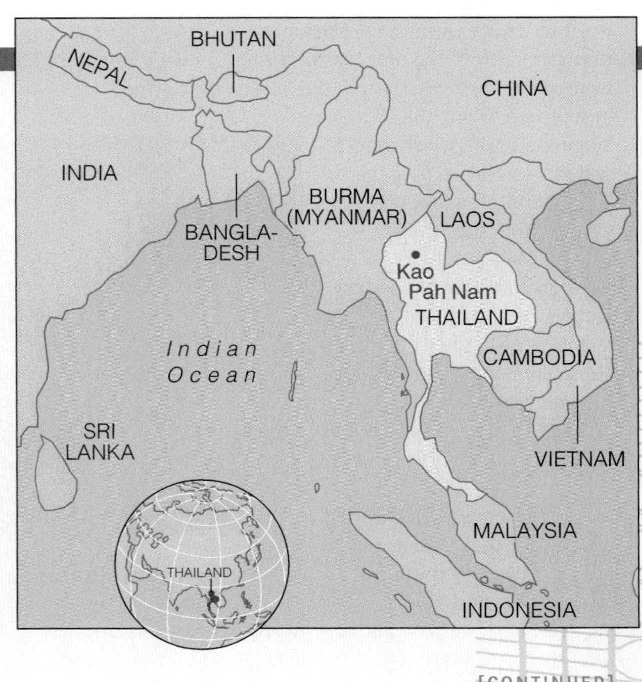

Bamboo provides, I believe, the solution to a puzzle first raised in 1943, when the late archaeologist Hallam Movius of Harvard began to publish his observations on Paleolithic (Old Stone Age) cultures of the Far East. In 1937 and 1938 Movius had investigated a number of archeological localities in India, Southeast Asia, and China. Although most of the archeological "cultures" that he recognized are no longer accepted by modern workers, he made another, more lasting contribution. This was the identification of the "Movius line" (which his colleague Carleton Coon named in his honor): a geographical boundary,

[CONTINUED]

[CONTINUED]

extending through northern India, that separates two long-lasting Paleolithic cultures. West of the line are found collections of tools with a high percentage of symmetrical and consistently proportioned hand-axes (these are called Acheulean tools, after the French site of Saint Acheul). More or less similar tool kits also occur in Mongolia and Siberia, but with few exceptions (which are generally relatively late in time), not in eastern China or Southeast Asia, where more tools known as choppers and chopping tools prevail.

My own research on the Movius line and related questions evolved almost by accident. During the course of my work in Southeast Asia, I excavated many sites, studied a variety of fossil faunal collections, and reviewed the scientific literature dealing with Asia. As part of this research I compared fossil mammals from Asia with those recovered from other parts of the world. In the beginning, my purpose was biostratigraphic—to use the animals to estimate the most likely dates of various sites used by early hominins. On the basis of the associated fauna, for example, I estimate that Kao Pah Nam [a site in Thailand] may be as old as 700,000 years. After years of looking at fossil collections and faunal lists, I realized that something was very strange about the collections from Southeast Asia: There were no fossil horses of Pleistocene age or for a considerable time before that. The only exceptions were a few horse fossils from one place in southern China, the Yuanmou Basin, which was and is a special small grassland habitat in a low, dry valley within the Shan-Yunnan Massif.

To mammalian biostratigraphers this is unusual, since members of the horse family are so common in both the Old and New World that they are a primary means of dating various fossil localities. Fossil horses have been reported from western Burma, but the last one probably lived there some 20 million years ago. Not a single fossil horse turns up later than that in Southeast Asia, although they are known from India to the west and China to the north and every other part of Europe and Asia.

I then began to wonder what other normally common animals might be missing. The answer soon became apparent: camels—even though they too were once widespread throughout the world—and members and relatives of the giraffe family. Pleistocene Southeast Asia was shaping up as a kind of "black hole" for certain fossil mammals! These animals—horses, camels, and giraffids—all dwell in open country. Their absence on the Southeast Asian mainland and islands (all once connected, along with the now inundated Sunda Shelf) is indicative of a forested environment. The mammals that are present—orangutans, tapirs, and gibbons—confirm this conclusion.

The significance of this is that most reconstructions of our evolutionary past have emphasized the influence of savannah grassland habitats, so important in Africa, the cradle of hominin evolution. Many anthropologists theorize that shrinking forests and spreading grasslands encouraged our primarily tree-dwelling ancestors to adapt to ground-dwelling conditions, giving rise to the unique bipedal gait that is the hallmark of hominins. Bipedalism, in turn, freed the hands for tool use and ultimately led to the evolution of a large-brained, cultural animal. Tropical Asia, instead, apparently was where early hominins had to readapt to tropical forest.

© Michael S. Yamashita/CORBIS

In regions where bamboo was readily available for the fabrication of effective tools, the same stone tool industries might not have developed. This contemporary scaffolding demonstrates bamboo's strength and versatility.

In studying the record, I noticed that the forested zone—the zone that lacked open-dwelling mammals—coincided generally with the distribution of the chopper-chopping tools. The latter appeared to be the products of a forest adaptation that, for one reason or another, deemphasized the utilization of standardized stone tools. At least this held for Southeast Asia; what at first I could not explain was the existence of similar tools in northern China, where fossil horses, camels, and giraffids were present. Finally, I came upon the arresting fact that the distribution of naturally occurring bamboo coincided almost directly with the distribution of chopper-chopping tools. The only exceptions that may possibly be of real antiquity—certain hand-axe collections from Kehe and Dingcun, in China, and Chonggok-Ni, in Korea—fall on the northernmost periphery of the distribution of bamboo and probably can be attributed to fluctuation of the boundary.

Today there are, by various estimates, some 1,000 to 1,200 species of bamboo. This giant grass is distributed worldwide, but more than 60 percent of the species are from Asia. Only 16 percent occur in Africa, and those on the Indian subcontinent—to an unknown extent the product of human importation and cultivation—are discontinuous in distribution and low in diversity. By far, the greatest diversity occurs in East and Southeast Asia.

Based on these observations, I hypothesized that the early Asians relied on bamboo for much of their technology. At first I envisioned bamboo simply as a kind of icon representing all nonlithic technology. I now think bamboo specifically must have been an extremely important resource. This was not, in my opinion, because appropriate rock was scarce but because bamboo tools would have been efficient, durable, and highly portable.

There are few useful tools that cannot be constructed from bamboo. Cooking and storage containers, knives, spears, heavy and light projectile points, elaborate traps, rope, fasteners, clothing, and even entire villages can be

[CONTINUED]

manufactured from bamboo. In addition to the stalks, which are a source of raw material for the manufacture of a variety of artifacts, the seeds and shoots of many species can be eaten. In historical times, bamboo has been to Asian civilization what the olive tree was to the Greeks. In the great cities of the Far East, bamboo is still the preferred choice for the scaffolding used in the construction of skyscrapers. This incomparable resource is also highly renewable. One can actually hear some varieties growing, at more than 1 foot per day.

Some may question how bamboo tools would have been sufficient for killing and processing large and medium-size animals. Lethal projectile and stabbing implements can in fact be fashioned from bamboo, but their importance may be exaggerated. Large game accounts for a relatively small proportion of the diet of many modern hunters and gatherers. Furthermore, animals are frequently trapped, collected, killed, and then thrown on a fire and cooked whole prior to using bare hands to dismember the roasted carcass. There are many ethnographic examples among forest peoples of this practice. The only implements that cannot be manufactured from bamboo are axes or choppers suitable for the working of hard woods. More than a few archaeologists have suggested that the stone choppers and resultant "waste" flakes of Asia were created with the objective of using them to manufacture and maintain nonlithic tools. Bamboo can be easily worked with stone flakes resulting from the manufacture of choppers (many choppers may have been a throwaway component in the manufacture of flakes). *(Adapted from G. C. Pope. "Bamboo and Human Evolution," Natural History, 10, 50–54. With permission of Natural History. Copyright 1989 The American Museum of Natural History.)*

Use of Fire

The use of fire provides another sign of *H. erectus'* developing culture and technology. The 700,000-year-old Kao Poh Nam rock shelter in Thailand provides compelling evidence for deliberate controlled use of fire. Here, a roughly circular arrangement of fire-cracked basalt cobbles was discovered in association with artifacts and animal bones. Because basalt rocks are not native to the rock shelter and are quite heavy, they probably had to have been carried in by *H. erectus*. Limestone rocks, more readily available in the shelter, cannot be used for hearths because, when burned, limestone produces quicklime, a caustic substance that causes itching and burning skin rashes.[7] The hearth, located near the rock shelter entrance, away from the deeper recesses favored by animals making dens, is associated with bones, showing clear evidence of cut marks from butchering, as well as burning.

Homo erectus may have been using fire even earlier, based on evidence from Swartkrans in South Africa. Here, in deposits estimated to date between 1.3 and 1 million years ago, bones have been found that had been heated to temperatures far in excess of what one would expect as the result of natural fires. Natural grass fires in the region will not heat bones above 212 degrees Fahrenheit, whereas coals in campfires reach temperatures from 900° to 1200° F. Consequently, bones thrown into controlled fires reach higher temperatures. Furthermore, the burned bones at Swartkrans do not occur in older, deeper deposits. If these fires were natural they would be distributed among all archaeological layers. Because the bones indicate heating to such high temperatures that any meat on them would have been inedible, South African paleoanthropologists Andrew Sillen and C. K. Brain suggest that the Swartkrans fires functioned as protection from predators.[8] Thus, fire may not have been "tamed" initially for cooking or to keep people warm; such uses may have come later.

Whatever the reason for *H. erectus'* original use of fire, it proved invaluable to populations that spread from the tropics into regions with cooler climates. Not only did fire provide warmth, but it may have assisted in the quest for food. In places like central Europe and China, food would have been hard to come by in the long, cold winters when edible plants were unavailable and the large herds of animals dispersed and migrated. One solution could have been to search out the frozen carcasses of animals that had died naturally in the late fall and winter, using long wooden probes to locate them beneath the snow, wooden scoops to dig them out, and fire to thaw them so that they could be butchered and eaten.[9] Furthermore, such fire-assisted scavenging would have made available meat and hides of woolly mammoths, woolly rhinoceroses, and bison, which were probably beyond the ability of *H. erectus* to kill, at least until late in the species' career.

Perhaps it was the use of fire to thaw carcasses that led to the idea of cooking food. Some paleoanthropologists suggest that this behavioral change altered the forces of natural selection, which previously favored

[7]Pope, G. C. (1989). Bamboo and human evolution. *Natural History, 10,* 56.

[8]Sillen, A., & Brain, C. K. (1990). Old flame. *Natural History, 4,* 10.

[9]Gamble, C. (1986). *The Paleolithic settlement of Europe* (p. 387). Cambridge, England: Cambridge University Press.

Geoffrey G. Pope

Archaeologists excavate a hearth at a rock shelter in Kao Poh Nam, Thailand. This hearth testifies to human use of controlled fire 700,000 years ago.

individuals with heavy jaws and large, sharp teeth (food is tougher and needs more chewing when it is uncooked), favoring instead further reduction in tooth size along with supportive facial structure. Alternatively, the reduction of tooth size and supporting structure may have occurred outside the context of adaptation. For example, the genetic changes responsible for increasing brain size may also have caused a reduction in tooth size as a secondary effect. Sometimes it is not possible to infer the reasons for an anatomical change visible in the fossil record. Instead, paleoanthropologists must remain content with making observations such as that, between early and late *H. erectus*, chewing-related structures undergo reduction at a rate markedly above the fossil vertebrate average.[10]

Hypotheses regarding the benefits of certain cultural innovations such as cooking are another matter altogether. Cooking does more than soften food. It detoxifies a number of otherwise poisonous plants; alters digestion-inhibiting substances so that important vitamins, minerals, and proteins can be absorbed while in the gut, rather than just passing through it unused; and makes complex carbohydrates like starch—high-energy foods—digestible. With cooking, the nutritional resources available to humans were substantially increased and made more secure.

In the story of human evolution, the biological consequences of cultural change can sometimes be inferred. For example, the partial predigestion of food by cooking also may have allowed a reduction in the size of the digestive tract. To establish this biological change, paleoanthropologists do not have the benefit of fossilized digestive tracts. Instead they turn to comparative anatomy of the living hominoids. Despite its overall similarity of form to those of apes, the digestive tract of modern humans is substantially smaller. The advantage of this gut reduction is that it draws less energy to operate, thereby competing less with the high energy requirements of a larger brain. Although a mere 2 percent of body weight, the brain accounts for about 20 to

[10]Wolpoff, M. H. (1993). Evolution in *Homo erectus:* The question of stasis. In R. L. Ciochon & J. G. Fleagle (Eds.), *The human evolution source book* (p. 396). Englewood Cliffs, NJ: Prentice-Hall.

25 percent of energy consumed at resting metabolic rate in modern human adults.[11]

Like tools, then, fire gave people more control over their environment. Possibly, *H. erectus* in Southeast Asia used fire, as have more recent populations living there, to keep areas in the forest clear for foot traffic. Certainly, the resistance to burning, which is characteristic of many hardwood trees in this forest today, indicates that fire has long been important in their evolution. Fire may also have been used by *H. erectus,* as it was by subsequent hominins, not just for protection from animals out in the open but to frighten away cave-dwelling predators so that the fire-users might live in the caves themselves. In addition, fire could be used to provide warmth and light in these otherwise cold and dark habitations. Even more, fire modified the natural succession of day and night, perhaps encouraging *H. erectus* to stay up after dark to review the day's events and plan the next day's activities. Though we cannot know whether *H. erectus* enjoyed socializing and planning around campfires at night, we do have evidence at least of some planning behavior. Planning is implied by the existence of populations in temperate climates, where the ability to anticipate the needs of the winter season by preparing in advance to protect against the cold would have been crucial to survival.[12]

OTHER ASPECTS OF *Homo erectus'* CULTURE

With *H. erectus* the first evidence exists of hominin populations living outside the Old World tropics. Presumably, control of fire was a key element in permitting them to move into cooler regions like much of Europe and China. In cold winters, however, a fire is of little use without adequate shelter, and *H. erectus'* increased sophistication in the construction of shelters is suggested by three circular foundations of bone and stone 9 to 13 feet across at a 350,000-year-old site in Bilzingsleben, Germany. These could mark the bases of shelters made of poles and grass similar to those used in recent times by contemporary foragers. In the middle of one foundation, a long mammoth tusk was found that was possibly used as a center post. Adjacent to these possible huts were hearths.

Keeping warm by the hearth is one thing, but keeping warm away from the hearth when procuring food or other necessities is another. Studies of modern humans indicate that they can remain reasonably comfortable down to 50 degrees Fahrenheit with a minimum of clothing as long as they are active; below that temperature, the extremities cool to the point of pain.[13] Thus, the dispersal of early humans into regions where winter temperatures regularly went below 50° F, as they must have in much of China and Europe, was probably not possible without more in the way of clothing than our ancestors had previously worn. Unfortunately, clothing, like many other aspects of material culture, does not fossilize, so we have no direct evidence as to the kind of clothing worn by *H. erectus.* We only know that it must have been more sophisticated than was required in warmer climates.

Controversy surrounds these behavioral constructions suggested for *H. erectus.* The Chinese *H. erectus* site, Zhoukoudian, provides an excellent case in point. Many paleoanthropologists interpret evidence of fires, hackberries, and animal bones as demonstrating hunting, gathering, and humanlike occupation of this cave site by *Homo erectus.* Archaeologist Lewis Binford suggests instead that the fires were natural—that due to the presence of bat guano (feces), a reliable fuel, high temperature and fires occurred naturally. He suggests too that the hackberries were brought into the cave in animal feces and that all the animal remains including those of humans were brought into this cave by carnivores. However, the well-documented use of controlled fire by *H. erectus* 700,000 years ago in Thailand, described above, supports its use at Zhoukoudian as well.

MEDIATREK

To review the evidence for the use of fire and hunting and gathering by *Homo erectus* and learn about the history of the World Heritage site (Dragon Bone Hill) at Zhoukoudian, go to MediaTrek 8.2 on the companion Web site or CD-ROM.

Evidence that *H. erectus* developed the ability to organize in order to hunt large animals is suggested by remains such as those from the 400,000-year-old sites of Ambrona and Torralba, in Spain. At the latter site, in what was an ancient swamp, the remains of several elephants, horses, red deer, wild oxen, and rhinoceroses were found. Their skeletons were dismembered and scattered, rather than in the anatomical order found in

[11]Leigh, S. R., & Park, P. B. (1998). Evolution of human growth prolongation. *American Journal of Physical Anthropology, 107,* 347.

[12]Goodenough, W. H. (1990). Evolution of the human capacity for beliefs. *American Anthropologist, 92,* 601.

[13]Whiting, J. W. M., Sodergem, J. A., & Stigler, S. M. (1982). Winter temperature as a constraint to the migration of preindustrial peoples. *American Anthropologist, 84,* 289.

Biocultural Connection

Paleolithic Prescriptions for the Diseases of Civilization

Though increased life expectancy is often hailed as one of modern civilization's greatest accomplishments, in some ways we in the "developed" world lead far less healthy lifestyles than our ancestors. Throughout most of our evolutionary history, humans led more physically active lives and ate a more varied low-fat diet than we do now. They did not drink or smoke. They spent their days scavenging or hunting for animal protein while gathering vegetable foods with some insects thrown in for good measure. They stayed fit through traveling great distances each day over the savannah and beyond. Today we may survive longer but in old age are beset by chronic disease. Heart disease, diabetes, high blood pressure, and cancer shape the experience of old age in wealthy industrialized nations. The prevalence of these "diseases of civilization" has increased rapidly over the past 50 years. Anthropologists Melvin Konner and Marjorie Shostak and physician Boyd Eaton have suggested that our Paleolithic ancestors have provided a prescription for a cure. They propose that as "stone-agers in a fast lane," people's health will improve by returning to the lifestyle to which their bodies are adapted. Such Paleolithic prescriptions are an example of evolutionary medicine—a branch of medical anthropology that uses evolutionary principles to contribute to human health.

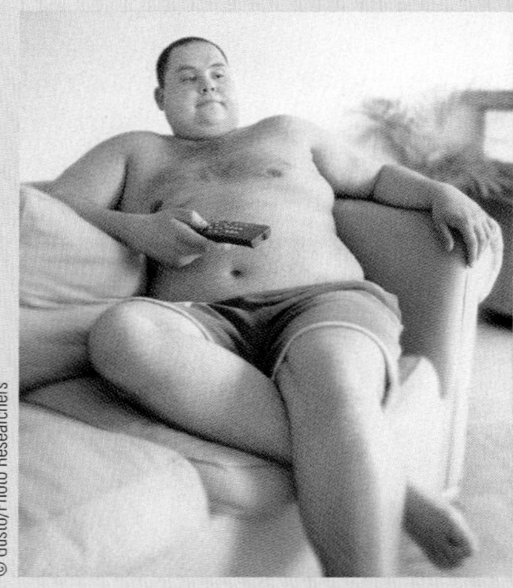
© Gusto/Photo Researchers

Evolutionary medicine bases its prescriptions on the idea that rates of cultural change exceed the rates of biological change. Our food forager physiology was shaped over millions of years, while the cultural changes leading to contemporary lifestyles have occurred rapidly. Anthropologist George Armelagos suggests that the downward trajectory for human health began with the earliest human village settlements some 10,000 years ago. When humans began farming rather than gathering, they often switched to single-crop diets. In addition, settlement into villages led directly to the increase in infectious disease. While the cultural invention of antibiotics has cured many infectious diseases, it also led to the increase in chronic diseases. In many cases, alternative treatments for these conditions stem from evolutionary medicine.

a living organism. This fact cannot be explained as a result of any natural geological process. Therefore, it is clear that these animals did not accidentally get mired in a swamp where they simply died and decayed.[14] In fact, the bones are closely associated with a variety of stone tools—a few thousand of them. Furthermore, there is very little evidence of carnivore activity and none at all for the really big carnivores. Clearly, hominins were involved—not just in butchering the animals but evidently in killing them as well. It appears that the animals were actually driven into the swamp so that they could be easily dispatched. The remains of charcoal and carbon, widely but thinly scattered in the vicinity, raise the possibility that grass fires were used to drive the animals into the swamp. In any event, what we have here is evidence for more than opportunistic scavenging. Not only was *H. erectus* able to hunt, but considerable organizational and communicative skills are implied as well.

Additional evidence for hunting 400,000 years ago was discovered accidentally in 1995 in the course of strip-mining at Schöningen in northern Germany. Here five well-constructed and finely balanced spears made entirely of wood, the longest one measuring more than 7 feet in length, were found. These are sophisticated weapons made by hunters who clearly knew what they were doing. The nearby butchered bones of more than a dozen horses attest to the effectiveness of their weapons.

There is no reason to suppose that *H. erectus* became an accomplished hunter all at once. As described in Chapter 3, coordinated hunting behavior is seen in chimpanzees and bonobos. Presumably, the most ancient members of this species, like *Homo habilis,* and australopithecines before them, got the bulk of their meat through scavenging with occasional hunting of

[14]Freeman, L. G. (1992). *Ambrona and Torralba: New evidence and interpretation.* Paper presented at the 91st Annual Meeting, American Anthropological Association, San Francisco.

FIGURE 8.7

Homo erectus' ability to cross open water is evidenced by the presence of stone tools on the Indonesian island Flores. Even during times of lowered sea level, a deepwater straight separated this island from the rest of Indonesia.

smaller prey. As their cultural capabilities increased, however, they could have devised ways of doing their own killing, rather than waiting for larger animals to die or be killed by other predators. As they became more proficient predators over time, they would have been able to count on a more reliable supply of meat.

Yet other evidence of *H. erectus'* capabilities comes from the island of Flores in Indonesia. This island lies east of a deepwater strait that has acted throughout the Pleistocene as a barrier to the passage of animals to and from Southeast Asia. To get to Flores, even at times of lowered sea levels, required crossing open water: at minimum 25 kilometers from Bali to Sumbawa, with an additional 19 kilometers to Flores (Figure 8.7). That early humans did just this is indicated by the presence of 800,000-year-old stone tools.[15] Precisely how they navigated across the deep, fast-moving water is not known, but at the least it required some sort of substantial raft.

Evidence for a developing symbolic life is suggested by the increased standardization and refinement of Acheulean hand-axes over time. Moreover, at several sites in Europe, deliberately marked objects of stone, bone, and ivory have been found in Acheulean contexts. These include several objects from Bilzingsleben,

At Bilzingsleben, Germany, archaeologists have uncovered an arrangement of stones and bones suggesting pavement of an area, perhaps for group rituals.

Germany—among them a mastodon bone with a series of regular lines that appear to have been deliberately engraved. Though a far cry from the later Upper Paleolithic cave art of France and Spain, these are among the earliest Paleolithic artifacts that have no obvious utility or model in the natural world. Such apparently symbolic artifacts became more common in later phases of the Paleolithic, as more derived forms of the genus *Homo* appeared on the scene. Similarly, the world's oldest known rock carvings are associated with Acheulean tools in a cave in India.[16] Archaeologist Alexander Marshack argues that the use of such symbolic images requires some sort of spoken language, not only to assign meaning to the images but to maintain the tradition they seem to

[15]Gibbons, A. (1998). Ancient island tools suggest *Homo erectus* was a seafarer. *Science, 279,* 1,635.

[16]Bednarik, R. G. (1995). Concept-mediated marking in the Lower Paleolithic. *Current Anthropology, 36,* 610–611.

This 300,000-year-old ox rib from a site in France is one of several from the Lower Paleolithic that exhibit engraved designs.

represent.[17] That such a symbolic tradition did exist is suggested by similar motifs on later Paleolithic artifacts. It is also in late Acheulean contexts on three continents that we have our earliest evidence for the use of red ochre, a pigment that more modern forms of *Homo* employed to color symbolic as well as utilitarian artifacts, to stain the bodies of the dead, to paint the bodies of the living, and (ultimately) to make notations and paint pictures.

THE QUESTION OF LANGUAGE

We do not, of course, know anything definitive about *H. erectus'* linguistic abilities, but the evidence for a developing symbolic life, as well as the need to plan for seasonal changes and to coordinate hunting activities (and cross stretches of open water), implies improving linguistic competence. Stone tools provide another interesting source for evidence of evolving humans' linguistic capabilities. The vast majority of the stone tools preserved in the fossil record were made by right-handed individuals, providing evidence of the specialization and lateralization of the hominin brain. In other primates and most mammals, the right and left sides of the brain duplicate each other's function; therefore these animals use the right and left sides of their bodies equally and interchangeably. In humans, specific regions of the brain are specialized for particular tasks (Figure 8.8). Thus, "handedness" indicates that the kind of brain specialization required for language was well underway.

[17]Marshack, A. (1976). Some implications of the Paleolithic symbolic evidence for the origin of language. *Current Anthropology, 17,* 280.

The vocal tract and brain of *H. erectus* are intermediate between those of *H. sapiens* on the one hand and earlier *Australopithecus* on the other. Another clue is the size of the **hypoglossal canal,** the opening in the skull through which the nerve that controls tongue move-

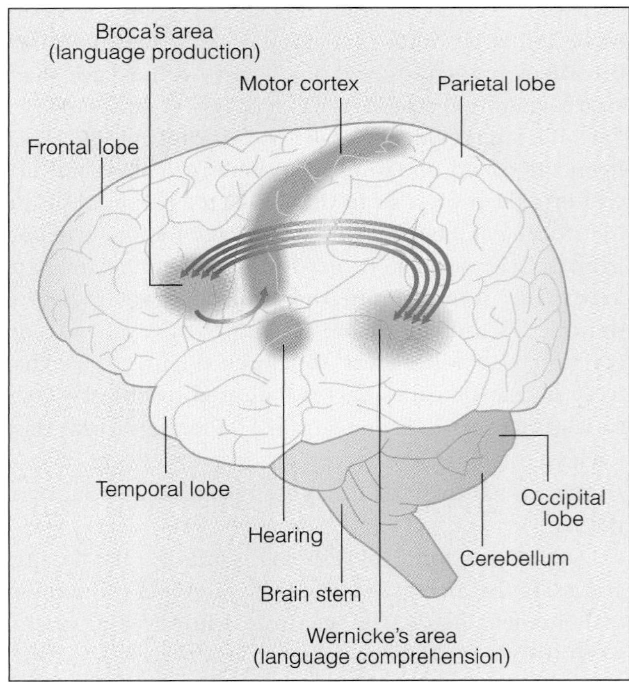

FIGURE 8.8

Language areas in the left side of the brain.

hypoglossal canal The opening in the skull through which the tongue-controlling hypoglossal nerve passes.

ments, so important for spoken language, passes from the skull (Figure 8.9). In contemporary people this is twice the size that it is in any ape. It is in the skulls of late *H. erectus*, about 500,000 years ago, that we first see this characteristic in fossil remains.[18] Possibly, a changeover from reliance on gestural to spoken language was a driving force in these evolutionary changes. The reduction of tooth and jaw size, facilitating the ability to articulate speech sounds may have also played a role.

From an evolutionary standpoint, spoken language could be said to provide some advantages over a gestural one. Individuals do not have to stop whatever they are doing with their hands to "talk" (useful to a species increasingly dependent on tool use), and it is possible to talk in the dark, past opaque objects, or among people whose gaze is concentrated on something else (potential prey, for example).

With *H. erectus,* then, we find a clearer manifestation of the interplay among cultural, physical, and environmental factors than ever before. However slowly, social organization, technology, and communication developed in tandem with an increase in brain size and complexity. In fact, the cranial capacity of late *H. erectus* is 31 percent greater than the mean for early *H. erectus,* a rate of increase more rapid than the average fossil vertebrate rate.[19] As a consequence of these changes, *H. erectus'* resource base was enlarged significantly; the supply of meat could be increased by hunting as well as by scavenging, and the supply of plant foods was increased as cooking allowed the consumption of vegetables that otherwise are toxic or indigestible. This, along with an increased ability to modify the environment in advantageous ways—for example, by using fire to provide warmth—undoubtedly contributed to a population increase and territorial expansion. In all living creatures, any kind of adaptation that enhances reproductive success causes population growth. This growth causes fringe populations to spill over into neighboring regions previously uninhabited by the species. Thus, *Homo erectus* was able to move into areas that had never been inhabited by hominins before—first into the warm, southern regions of Eurasia and ultimately into the cooler regions of China and Europe.

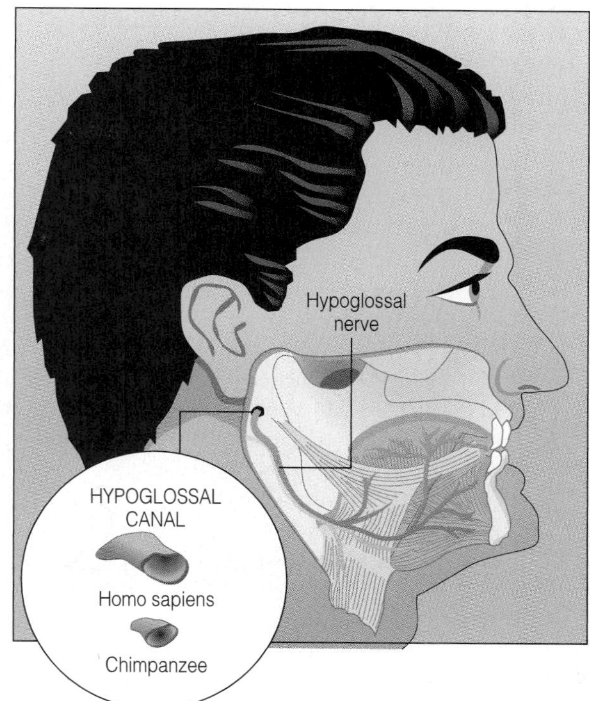

FIGURE 8.9
The size of the hypoglossal canal is much larger in humans than in chimpanzees. The nerve that passes through this canal controls tongue movement, and complex tongue movements are involved in spoken language. All hominins after about 500,000 years ago have an enlarged hypoglossal canal.

[18]Cartmill, M. (1998). The gift of gab. *Discover 19*(11), 64.

[19]Wolpoff, pp. 392, 396.

Chapter Summary

- The remains of *Homo erectus* have been found at sites in Africa, the Caucasus, western Europe, China, and Java. *H. erectus* appears to have evolved in Africa, from *H. habilis,* then spreading to regions outside of Africa. The population size of these early hominins appears to have increased, perhaps due to successful biocultural adaptations. A larger population size may have allowed *H. erectus* to expand into new geographic areas.
- Lumpers place all the larger-brained hominins from about 1.8 million to 400,000 years ago into *Homo erectus.* Splitters divide these representatives of Pleistocene *Homo* into a variety of species by geographic regions, saving the category *H. erectus* for only the Asian specimens.
- The earliest *Homo* erectus specimens from Africa date from about 1.8 to 1.9 million years old. Fossils nearly as old have been recovered from Dmanisi, Georgia, and possibly from Java, Indonesia. The species endured until about 400,000 years ago, by which time cranial capacity reached the range of

today's humans. These late fossils exhibit a mosaic of features characteristic of both *H. erectus* and *H. sapiens.*

- The brain, although small by modern standards, was larger than that of *H. habilis.* The skull was generally low, with maximum breadth near its base, and massive brow ridges. Powerful teeth and jaws added to a generally rugged appearance. From the neck down, the body of *H. erectus* was essentially modern in appearance and much larger than earlier hominins.
- Archaeological evidence indicates that as cranial capacity increased, *H. erectus* relied more upon culture to rise to the challenges of existence compared to earlier hominins. The Oldowan chopper evolved into the Acheulean hand-axe. These tools, the earliest of which are about 1.6 million years old, are teardrop-shaped, with a pointed end and sharp cutting edges. They were remarkably standardized in form over large geographical areas. During Acheulean times, tool cultures began to diversify. Along with hand-axes, tool kits included cleavers, picks, scrapers, and flakes.
- Further signs of *H. erectus'* developing technology were the selection of different stone for different tools and the use of fires to provide protection, warmth, and light; thawing frozen carcasses; and cooking. Cooking was a significant cultural adaptation because it detoxified various substances in plants; cooking also increased the food resources available and allowed reduction in the size of the digestive tract. The large, heavy jaws and teeth characteristic of earlier hominins were unnecessary in *Homo erectus* because cooked food is easier to chew.
- Reduced jaw and tooth size may also correlate with a change from reliance on gestural to spoken language. Some aspects of *H. erectus'* behavior imply improved communicative skills. Planning abilities are inferred from habitation in colder northern climates as well as coordinated hunting of large mammals.

Questions for Reflection

1. When reconstructing the lifeways of ancestral hominins, paleoanthropologists are faced with the challenge of limiting the influence of their own cultural beliefs and values on hypotheses about the biocultural adaptations in the past. In the proposed reconstructions of *Homo erectus'* behavior, how well do paleoanthropologists meet this challenge?
2. What are the advantages and disadvantages of using the single taxonomic category *H. erectus* compared to splitting *H. erectus* into a series of separate species?
3. What are the differences between *H. erectus* and the species of *Homo* that came before (*Homo habilis*) and after (*Homo sapiens*)? Can we tell that these are distinct species?
4. Animals ranging from rabbits to plants have come to occupy new niches without the benefits of culture. How does the spread of *Homo* out of the African continent tell paleoanthropologists anything about this species' cultural capabilities?
5. Though language itself does not "fossilize," the archaeological and fossil records provide some evidence of the linguistic capabilities of our ancestors. Using the evidence available for *Homo erectus,* what sort of linguistic abilities do you think this species possessed?

Key Terms

Acheulean tradition

Hypoglossal canal

Multimedia Review Tools

Companion Web Site

Visit **http://www.wadsworth.com/anthropology_d/** and click on the companion Web site for this textbook to access a wide range of material to aid your study of anthropology. Among the options for self-study in each chapter are learning objectives, flash cards, Internet activities, Web links, InfoTrac College Edition exercises, and practice tests that can be scored and emailed to your instructor.

CD-ROM

The *Doing Anthropology Today* CD-ROM supplied with your textbook provides unique and valuable information designed to enhance your learning experience. This interactive multimedia resource includes video clips, interviews with renowned anthropologists, map and timeline exercises, chapter study quizzes, and much more. *Doing Anthropology Today* will not only help you in achieving your grade goals, but it will also make your learning experience fun and exciting!

Suggested Readings

Delson, E., Tattersal, I., Brooks, A., & Van Couvering, J. (1999) *Encyclopedia of human evolution and prehistory.* New York: Garland Publishing.

Using an A–Z format, this user-friendly encyclopedia includes over 800 entries relating to human evolution and prehistory. It includes excellent diagrams, illustrations, and descriptions of key archaeological sites.

Potts, R. (1997) *Humanity's descent: The consequences of ecological instability.* New York: Avon

Written by the director of the Smithsonian Institution's Human Origins Program, this book suggests that environmental instability was the unifying factor contributing to the acquisition of human language and culture.

Rightmire, G. P. (1990). *The evolution of Homo erectus: Comparative anatomical studies of an extinct human species.* Cambridge, England: Cambridge University Press.

This is the standard work on our current understanding of *Homo erectus.*

Stanford, C. B. (2001). *The hunting apes: Meat eating and the origins of human behavior.* Princeton, NJ: Princeton University Press.

Though updated and less gender biased, this work revisits the old "Man the Hunter" hypothesis, suggesting that human intelligence is linked to the acquisition of meat and food sharing.

Trevathan, W., McKenna, J., & Smith, E. O. (1999). *Evolutionary medicine.* New York: Oxford University Press.

A wealth of "Paleolithic prescriptions" can be found in this edited volume that applies an evolutionary perspective to a variety of contemporary health questions.

Walker, A., & Shipman, P. (1997). *The wisdom of the bones: In search of human origins.* New York: Vintage Books.

This book provides an engaging description of the story of the discovery the most complete *Homo erectus* specimen—the Nariokotome Boy from Lake Turkana, Kenya—as well as placing it within the context of the larger story of human evolution.

CHAPTER 9

Archaic *Homo sapiens* and the Middle Paleolithic

CHALLENGE ISSUE

The challenge for paleoanthropologists studying the Middle Paleolithic (200,000 to 40,000 years ago) is to determine the relationship between biological change and cultural change in fossil groups of this time period. Though possessing modern-sized brains, the skulls of Middle Paleolithic *Homo* retain a number of ancestral features as well as some specialized features typically not seen in modern *Homo sapiens*. In other words, do these features in the shape of the skull indicate biological differences in brain structure sufficient to affect the cultural capabilities of these fossil groups? Some paleoanthropologists consider the Neandertals pictured here as early members of our species, *Homo sapiens*. Others suggest that the Neandertals with their distinctive skulls lie outside of the evolutionary line leading to contemporary people, attributing the state of their cultural abilities to underlying biological difference.

1

Who Was "Archaic" *Homo sapiens?*

"Archaic" *Homo sapiens* is the name used for past members of the human species with essentially modern-sized brains in skulls that still retained a number of ancestral features. Archaic *H. sapiens* descended from *Homo erectus.* The transition took place between about 400,000 and 200,000 years ago as skull size reached modern proportions. Populations of archaic *H. sapiens* are known from Africa and Eurasia.

2

What Was the Culture of Archaic *Homo sapiens* Like?

By 200,000 years ago, when the human brain had reached its modern size, cultures throughout the inhabited globe had become rich and varied compared to those of earlier hominins. The archaeological and fossil records provide evidence of a wide variety of tools for special purposes, objects for purely symbolic purposes, ceremonial activities, and care for the old and disabled.

3

Who Were the Neandertals and What Became of Them?

Much debate surrounds the fate of the Neandertals, members of the genus *Homo* from Southwest Asia and Europe whose remains date from 125,000 to about 30,000 years ago. Some paleoanthropologists state that Neandertals, like other archaic forms, evolved into anatomically modern versions of *Homo sapiens* as different features of "modern" anatomy arising in other regional populations were carried to them through gene flow. In this framework, human populations throughout Africa, Europe, and Asia contributed to the making of modern humans. Other paleoanthropologists contend that anatomically modern humans with superior cultural capabilities appeared first in Africa about 200,000 years ago, replacing existing archaic forms as they spread from Africa to the rest of the world.

As well as being a scholar, the anthropologist attempting to piece together the innumerable parts of the puzzle of human evolution must be a detective, publicist, and creative thinker, for the available evidence is often scant, enigmatic, or full of misleading and even contradictory clues. The quest for the origin of modern humans from more ancient representatives of the genus *Homo* has elements of a detective story, for it contains a number of mysteries concerning the emergence of humanity, none of which has been completely resolved to this day. The mysteries involve the appearance of the first fossils with human-sized brains, the identity of the Neandertals, and the relationship of changes in the shape of the skull to cultural abilities.

THE APPEARANCE OF *Homo sapiens*

At various sites in Africa, Asia, and Europe, a number of hominin fossils—primarily skulls, jaws, and jaw fragments—have been found that seem to date roughly between 400,000 and 200,000 years ago. Most consist of parts of one or a very few individuals, the one exception being a large number of bones and teeth from the Sierra de Atapuerca in northern Spain. Here, sometime between 325,000 and 205,000 years ago,[1] the remains of at least twenty-eight individuals of both sexes, juveniles as well as adults, were deliberately dumped (after defleshing their skulls) by their contemporaries into a deep cave shaft known today as Sima de los Huesos ("Pit of the Bones"). This makes it the best population sample from this time period anywhere in the world (Figure 9.1). As expected of any population, this one displays a significant degree of variation. Cranial capacity, for example, ranges from 1,125 to 1,390 cubic centimeters, overlapping the upper end of the range for *H. erectus* and the average size of *H. sapiens'* range (1,300 cc). Overall, the bones display a mix of features, some typical of *H. erectus,* others of *H. sapiens,* including some incipient Neandertal characteristics. Of interest is the observation that varied as it is, the sample appears to show no more sexual dimorphism than displayed by modern humans.[2]

Other remains from Africa and Europe dating between 400,000 and 200,000 years ago, have sometimes been classified as *H. sapiens*—for example, skulls from Ndutu in Tanzania, Swanscombe (England), and Steinheim (Germany)—and sometimes as *H. erectus,* as in the case of skulls from several African sites as well as Arago (France), Bilzingsleben (Germany), and Petralona (Greece). Yet all have cranial capacities that fit within the range exhibited by the Sima de los Huesos skulls, and all display the same mosaic of *H. erectus* and *H. sapiens* features. Some trends are evident when these skulls are compared to the average shape and size seen in living people and *H. erectus.* For instance, the Swanscombe and Steinheim skulls are large and robust, with their maximum breadth lower on the skull, more prominent brow ridges, larger faces, and bigger teeth. Similarly, the face of the Petralona skull from Greece resembles European Neandertals, while the back of the skull looks like *H. erectus.* Conversely, a skull from Salé in Morocco, which

[1]Parés, J. M., Perez-Gonzalez, A., Weil, A. B., & Arsuaga, J. L. (2000). On the age of hominid fossils at the Sima de los Huesos, Sierra de Atapuerca, Spain: Paleomagnetic evidence. *American Journal of Physical Anthropology, 111,* 451–461.

[2]Lorenzo, C., Carretero, J. M., Arsuaga, J. L., Gracia, A., & Martinez, I. (1998). Intrapopulational body size variation and cranial capacity variation in middle Pleistocene humans: The Sima de los Huesos sample (Sierra de Atapuerca, Spain). *American Journal of Physical Anthropology, 106,* 30.

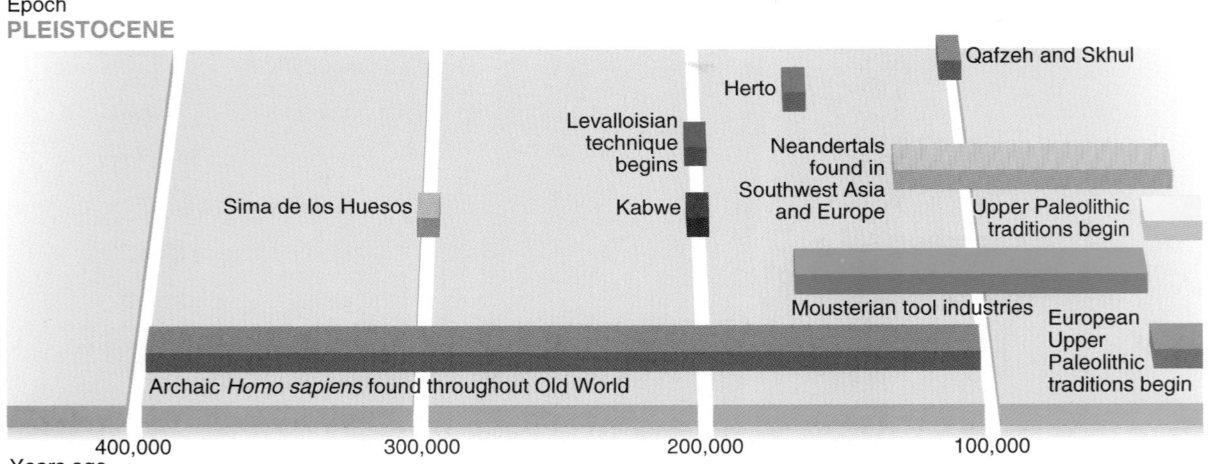

FIGURE 9.1

The fossils from Sima de los Huesos, from the Sierra de Atapuerca, Spain, represent the best collection of hominin fossils from this period. With the well-preserved remains of at least twenty-eight individuals, paleoanthropologists can interpret these fossils in the context of the range of variation seen within this population.

had a rather small brain for *H. sapiens* (930–960 cc), looks surprisingly modern from the back. Finally, various jaws from France and Morocco (in northern Africa) seem to combine features of *H. erectus* with those of the European Neandertals.

A similar situation exists in East Asia, where skulls from several sites in China exhibit the same mix of *H. erectus* and *H. sapiens* characteristics. Lumpers suggest that calling some of these early humans "late *H. erectus*" or "early *H. sapiens*" (or any of the other proposed species names within the genus *Homo*) serves no useful purpose and merely obscures their apparently transitional status. Splitters use a series of discrete names for specimens from this period. These arguments about species names for specimens are more than a name game. Fossil names correspond to a statement about evolutionary relationships among groups. When specimens are given separate species names, it signifies the biological property of reproductive isolation. Given the variability of the human species and the difficulties with proving reproductive isolation in the past, we will refer to all of these hominins from 300,000 to 40,000 years ago as archaic *Homo sapiens*. Despite retaining a number of features of *H. erectus*, the brain size of archaic *H. sapiens* shows a clear increase over that of even late representatives of *H. erectus* (see Figure 8.2).

Levalloisian Technique

With the appearance of hominins transitional between *H. erectus* and *H. sapiens*, the pace of culture change began to accelerate. Although hand-axes and other Acheulean tools were still made, a new method of flake

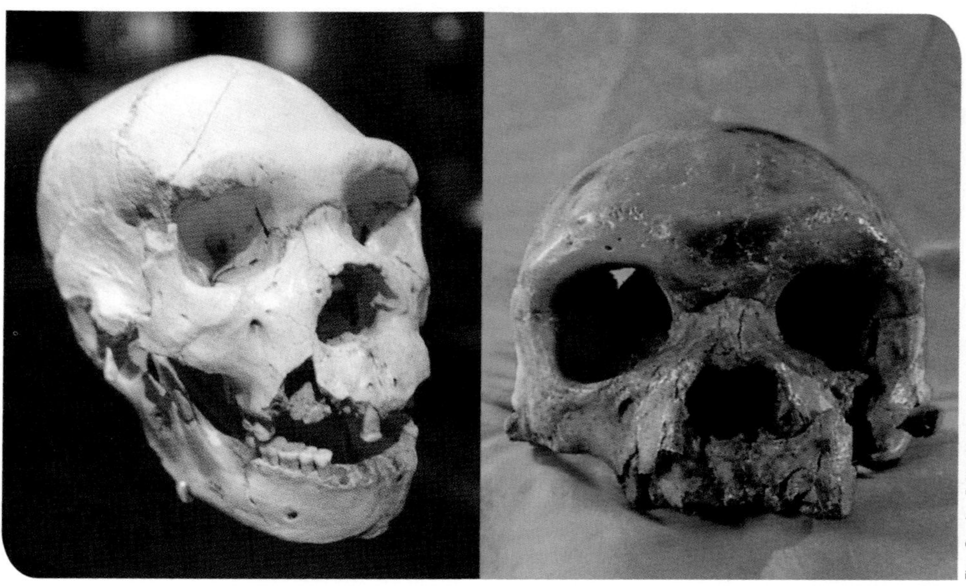

VISUAL COUNTERPOINT
Though from different ends of the Eurasian land mass, these two skulls from the sites of Atapuerca, Spain, and Dali, China, from the Middle Pleistocene resemble each other considerably.

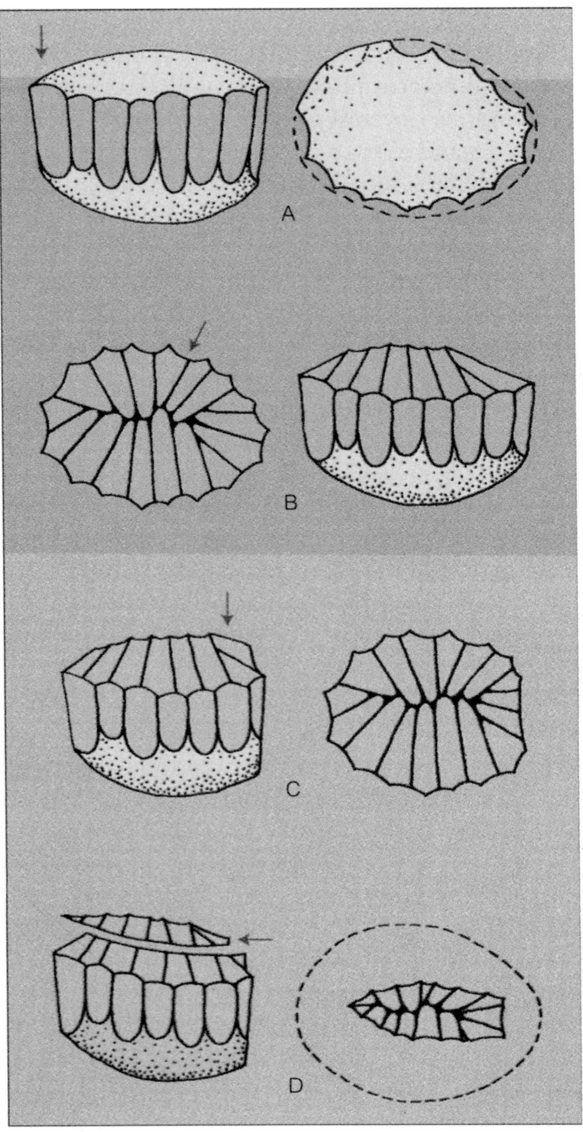

FIGURE 9.2

These drawings show top and side views of the steps in the Levalloisian technique. Drawing A shows the preparatory flaking of the stone core; B, the same of the top surface; C, the striking platform; and D, the final step of detaching a flake of a size and shape predetermined by the preceding steps.

manufacture was invented: the **Levalloisian technique,** so named after the French site where such tools were first excavated. Flake tools produced by this technique have been found widely in Africa, Europe, Southwest Asia, and even China. In China, the technique could represent a case of independent invention, or it could represent the spread of ideas from one part of the inhabited world to another. The Levalloisian technique produces tools by first preparing a core by removal of small flakes over its surface. Following this, a striking platform is set up by a crosswise blow at one end of the core of stone (Figure 9.2). Striking the platform removes three or four long flakes, whose size and shape had been predetermined by the preceding preparation. What is left, besides small waste flakes, is a nodule that looks like a tortoise shell. This method produces a longer edge for the same amount of flint than the previous ones used by evolving humans. The edges are sharper and can be produced in less time.

At about the same time the Levalloisian technique was developed, another technological breakthrough took place. This was the invention of hafting—the fastening of small stone bifaces and flakes to handles of

Levalloisian technique Tool-making technique by which three or four long triangular flakes were detached from a specially prepared core. Developed by hominins transitional from *Homo erectus* to *Homo sapiens.*

The practice of hafting, the fastening of small stone bifaces and flakes to handles of wood, was a major technological advance appearing in the archaeological record at about the same time as the invention of the Levalloisian technique.

wood—to make improved knives and spears. Unlike the older handheld tools made simply by reduction (flaking of stone or working of wood), these new composite tools involved three components: assembly of a handle or shaft, a stone insert, and the materials to bind them. The acquisition and modification of each component involved planned sequences of actions that could be performed at different times and places.

With this new technology, regional stylistic and technological variants are clearly evident, suggesting the emergence of distinct cultural traditions and culture areas. At the same time, proportions of raw materials procured from faraway sources increase; whereas sources of stone for Acheulean tools were rarely more than 12 miles away, Levalloisian tools are found up to 200 miles from the sources of their stone.[3]

Another development, first identified in Africa, was the use of yellow and red pigments of iron oxide, called ocher, becoming especially common by 130,000 years ago.[4] The use of ocher may signal a rise in ritual activity, as may the deliberate deposition of the human remains in the Sima de los Huesos, Atapuerca, already noted. The presence of other animal bones in the same pit with humans raises the possibility that the early humans simply dumped all bones there. Alternatively, the treatment of the dead at Atapuerca may have involved ritual activity that presaged burial of the dead, a practice that became common after 100,000 years ago. The use of red ocher in these ancient burials may be due to its similarity to the color of blood as a powerful symbol of life.

The Neandertals

Of all the remains of *Homo* from the Late Pleistocene, the **Neandertals** are perhaps the most notorious. Neandertals are typically represented as the classic "cave men," frequently depicted as brutes in popular media such as cartoons, films, and even natural history museum displays. One of the most contentious issues in paleoanthropology today concerns whether the Neandertals represent an inferior side branch of human evolution, not surviving after the appearance of "modern" humans. Alternatively, Neandertals could represent one of many archaic forms of *Homo sapiens* whose descendents walk the earth today.

Neandertals were an extremely muscular people living from 125,000 to approximately 30,000 years ago in Europe and southwestern Asia. While having brains of modern size, Neandertals possessed faces distinctively

© Bettmann/CORBIS

The Field Museum, John Weinstein

VISUAL COUNTERPOINT
Perceptions about the capabilities of fossil groups are expressed in visual representations of fleshed out versions of fossil remains. The Neandertal diorama from the 1920s exhibit in the Field Museum of Chicago contains a message about their evolutionary distance from us, while positive cultural attributes are given to "anatomically modern" specimens.

[3]Ambrose, S. H. (2001). Paleolithic technology and human evolution. *Science, 291,* 1,752.

[4]Barham, L. S. (1998). Possible early pigment use in southcentral Africa. *Current Anthropology, 39,* 703–710.

Neandertals Representatives of "archaic" *Homo sapiens* in Europe and western Asia, living from about 125,000 years ago to about 30,000 years ago.

different from those of "modern" humans. Their large noses and teeth projected forward. They had prominent bony brow ridges over their eyes, and on the back of the skull, a bunlike bony mass provided for attachment of powerful neck muscles. These features, not in line with classic forms of Western beauty, may have contributed to the depiction of Neandertals as brutes. Their rude reputation may also derive from the timing of their discovery.

The first Neandertal was found in a cave in the Neander Valley ("thal" pronounced "tal" means "valley" in German) near Düsseldorf, Germany, in 1856, well before scientific theories to account for human evolution had gained acceptance. Darwin published his theory of evolution by natural selection 3 years later in 1859. Although the discovery was of considerable interest, the experts were generally at a loss as to what to make of it. Examination of the fossil skull, a few ribs, and some limb bones revealed that the individual was a human being, but it did not look "normal." Some people believed the bones were those of a sickly and deformed contemporary. Others thought the skeleton belonged to a soldier who had succumbed to "water on the brain" during the Napoleonic Wars. One prominent anatomist thought the remains were those of an idiot suffering from malnutrition, whose violent temper had gotten him into many fights, flattening his forehead and making his brow ridges bumpy.

The idea that Neandertals were somehow deformed or abnormal was given impetus by an analysis of a skeleton found in 1908 near La Chapelle-aux-Saints in France. The analysis mistakenly concluded that the specimen's brain was apelike and that he walked like an ape. Although a team of North American investigators subsequently proved that this French Neandertal specimen was that of an elderly *H. sapiens* who had suffered from malnutrition, severe arthritis, and other deformities, the brutish image has persisted. To many nonanthropologists, the Neandertal has become the quintessential "caveman," portrayed by imaginative cartoonists as a slant-headed, stooped, dim-witted individual clad in animal skins and carrying a big club as he plods across the prehistoric landscape, perhaps dragging behind him an unwilling female or a dead saber tooth tiger. The stereotype has been perpetuated in novels and film. The popular image of Neandertals as brutish and incapable of spoken language, abstract or innovative thinking, or even planning ahead may play a subtle role in the interpretation of the fossil and archaeological evidence.

The evidence indicates that Neandertals were nowhere near as brutish and apelike as originally portrayed, and some scholars began to see them as the archaic *H. sapiens* of Europe and Southwest Asia, ancestral to the more derived, "anatomically modern" populations that held exclusive sway in Europe and Southwest Asia after 30,000 years ago. For example, paleoanthropologist C. Loring Brace of the University of Michigan observes that "classic" Neandertal features (Figure 9.3) are commonly present in 100,000 year old skulls from Denmark and Norway.[5] Nevertheless, Neandertals are somewhat distinctive when compared to more recent populations. Although they held modern-sized brains (average cranial capacity 1,400 cc versus 1,300 cc for modern *H. sapiens*), Neandertal skulls are notable in the projection of their noses and teeth resulting in a protruding appearance of the mid-facial region. The wear patterns on their large front teeth indicate that they may have been heavily used for tasks other than

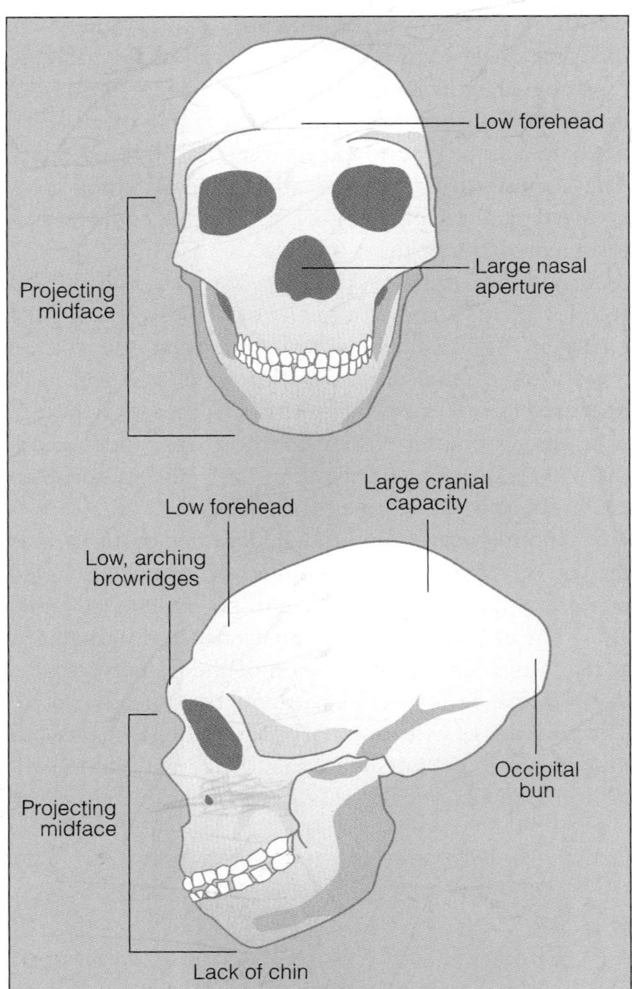

FIGURE 9.3
This figure depicts features of the skull seen in "classic" Neandertals.

[5]Ferrie, H. (1997). An interview with C. Loring Brace. *Current Anthropology, 38,* 861.

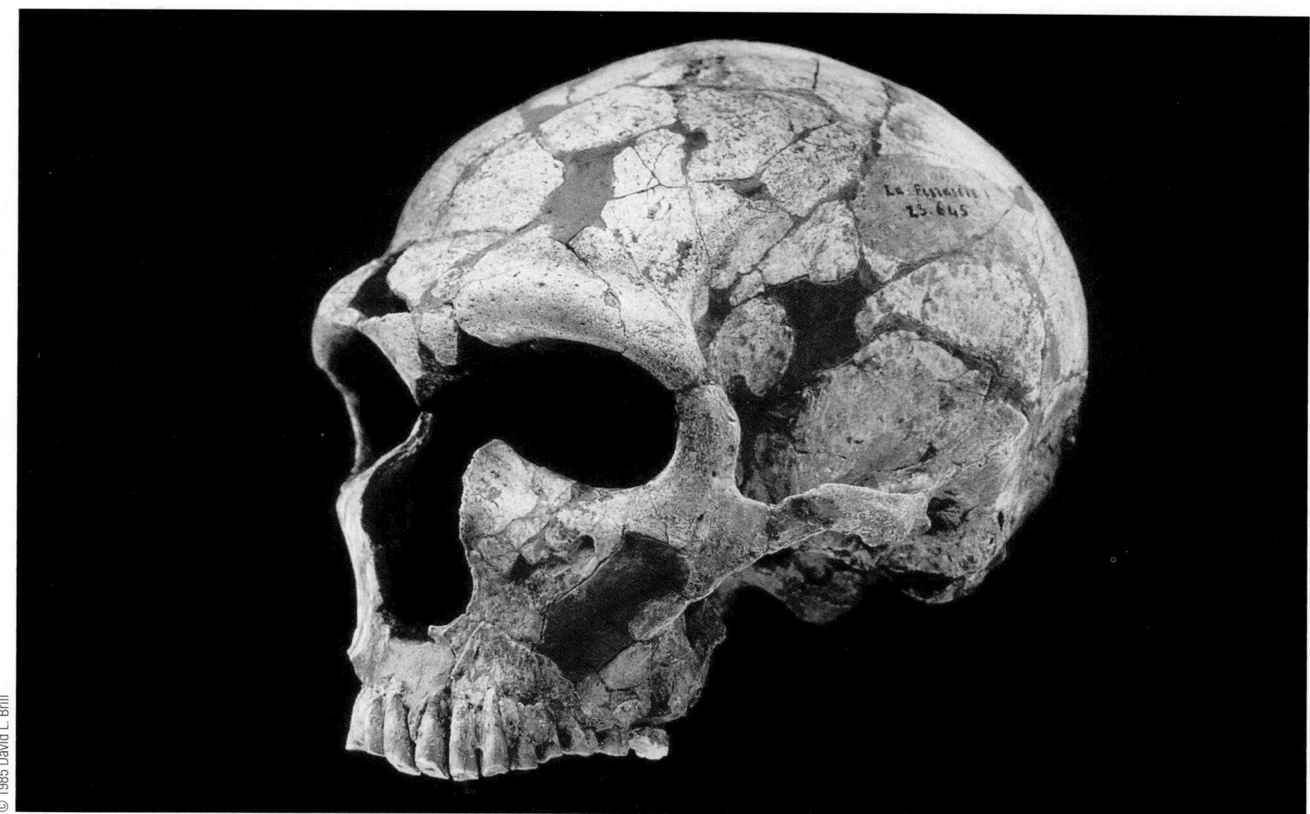

This Neandertal from La Ferrassie in France shows the marked bony ridge above the eyes, the receding forehead, and heavy wear on the front teeth typical of this fossil group.

chewing. In many individuals, front teeth were worn down to the stubs of their roots by 35 to 40 years of age. The large noses of Neandertals probably were necessary to warm, moisten, and clean the dry, dusty frigid air of the glacial climate, preventing damage to the lungs and brain as seen in cold-adapted people of recent times. At the back of the skull, the bunlike bony mass providing attachment for the powerful neck muscles counteracted the weight of a heavy face.

All Neandertal fossils indicate that both sexes were extraordinarily muscular, with extremely robust and dense limb bones. Relative to body mass, the limbs were relatively short (as they are in modern humans native to especially cold climates). Details of the shoulder blades indicate the importance of over-arm and downward thrusting movements. Their arms were exceptionally powerful, and pronounced attachments on their hand bones attest to a remarkably strong grip. Science writer James Shreeve suggests that a healthy Neandertal could lift an average North American football player over his head and throw him through the goalposts.[6] Their massive dense foot and leg bones suggest high levels of strength and endurance, though individuals this robust certainly exist today. Because brain size is related to overall body mass, heavy robust Neandertal bodies account for the large average size of the Neandertal brain.

Throughout the previous chapters increasing brain size was linked to increasing cultural capabilities of evolving hominins. With archaic *H. sapiens* including Neandertals, brain size falls easily within the range for contemporary humans. With these and later fossil groups the challenge for paleoanthropologists is to decide whether changes in the shape of the skull indicate changes in cultural capabilities.

Though the interpretation of Neandertal fossils has changed dramatically compared to when Neandertals were first discovered, they are still surrounded by controversy. Academic debates relating to their fate still rely upon the shape of the Neandertal skeleton and the relationship between the skeleton and human cultural capacities. Those who favor extinction theories emphasize a notion of Neandertal biological difference and cultural inferiority. Those who include Neandertals in our direct ancestry emphasize the sophistication of Neandertal culture, attributing differences in skull shape

[6]Shreeve, J. (1995). *The Neandertal enigma: Solving the mystery of modern human origins* (p. 5). New York: William Morrow.

Paul Jaronski, UM Photo Services

As this face-off between paleoanthropologist Milford Wolpoff and his reconstruction of a Neandertal shows, the latter did not differ all that much from modern humans of European descent.

and body form to regional adaptation to an extremely cold climate and the retention of ancestral traits in an isolated population.

Javanese, African, and Chinese Populations

Other parts of the world were inhabited by variants of archaic *H. sapiens* lacking the extreme mid-facial projection and massive muscle attachments on the back of the skull characteristic of the Neandertals. A number of skulls have been found in Java, Africa, and China that date to roughly the same time period.

The eleven skulls found near the Solo River in Ngandong, Java, are a prime example. Though their dating was not precisely known at the time of their discovery in the 1930s, they were generally considered to be Southeast Asian equivalents of the Neandertals. These skulls indicated modern-sized brains ranging from 1,013 to 1,252 ccs, while retaining features of earlier Javanese *H. erectus.* With time, opinion on the dating of these specimens has changed, with scholars regarding them as considerably earlier than the Neandertals. This opinion focused attention on their resemblance to *H. erectus,* so that when their dating was recently revised (to some time between 53,000 and 27,000 years ago) some concluded that this proved a late survival of *H. erectus* in Asia, contemporary with *H. sapiens* elsewhere. But the Ngandong skulls remain what they always were: representatives of archaic *H. sapiens,* with modern sized brains in otherwise ancient-looking skulls.

Fossils from various parts of Africa, the most famous being a 200,000 year old skull from Kabwe in Zambia, show a similar combination of ancient and modern traits. Finally, equivalent remains have been found at several localities in China.

African and eastern Asian contemporaries of the Neandertals differ from the Neandertals primarily in their lack of mid-facial projection and massive muscle attachments on the back of the skull. Thus, the Neandertals represent an extreme form of archaic *H. sapiens.* Elsewhere, the archaics look like robust ver-

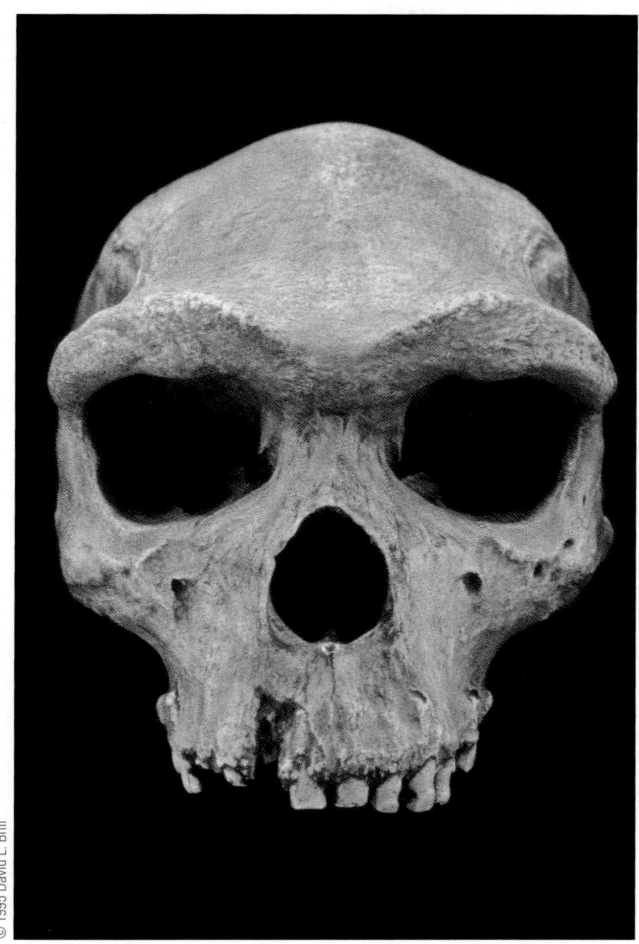

The cranial capacity of this typical archaic *Homo sapiens* from Kabwe in Central Zambia is large, although many ancestral features are evident in the shape of the skull. In the past, the ancestral features in this skull were used to support claims of the primitiveness of African people. Now, paleoanthropologists recognize these features as signs of Kabwe's antiquity.

sions of the early modern populations that lived in the same regions or like somewhat more derived versions of the *H. erectus* populations that preceded them. All had fully modern-sized brains in skulls retaining some ancestral features.

THE CULTURE OF ARCHAIC *Homo sapiens*

Adaptations to the environment by archaic *Homo sapiens* were, of course, both biological and cultural, but the capacity for cultural adaptation was predictably superior to what it had been in earlier members of the genus *Homo*. As the first hominins to possess brains of modern size, archaic *H. sapiens* had, as we would expect, greater cultural capabilities than their ancestors. Such a brain played a role in technological innovations, conceptual thought of considerable sophistication, and, almost surely, communication through spoken language.

Middle Paleolithic

The improved tool-making capabilities of evolving humans are represented by various **Middle Paleolithic** traditions. The **Mousterian** and Mousterianlike tool traditions of Europe, western Asia, and North Africa, dating between about 166,000 and 40,000 years ago, are the best known of these. Comparable traditions are found in China and Japan, where they likely arose independently from local tool-making traditions. All these traditions represent a technological advance over preceding industries. For example, the 16 inches of working edge that an Acheulean flint worker could get from a 2-pound core compares with the 6 feet the Mousterian could get from the same core. Mousterian tools were used by *all* people, Neandertals as well as other members of the genus *Homo* said to possess more "anatomically modern" skulls, in Europe, North Africa, and the Middle East during this time period. At around 35,000 years ago, the Mousterian traditions were replaced by the Upper Paleolithic traditions that will be the subject of the next chapter.

The Mousterian Tradition

The Mousterian tradition is named after the Neandertal cave site of Le Moustier, in southern France. The presence of Acheulean hand-axes at Mousterian sites is one indication that this culture was ultimately rooted in the older Acheulean tradition. Mousterian tools are generally lighter and smaller than those of earlier traditions. Whereas previously only two or three flakes could be obtained from the entire core, Mousterian toolmakers obtained many smaller flakes, which they skillfully retouched and sharpened. Their tool kits also contained a greater variety of types than the earlier ones: hand-axes, flakes, scrapers, borers, notched flakes for shaving wood, and many types of points that could be attached to wooden shafts to make spears. This variety of tools

Middle Paleolithic The middle part of the Old Stone Age characterized by the development of the Levalloisian and Mousterian tradition of tool making.
Mousterian tradition Tool-making tradition of the Neandertals and their contemporaries of Europe, western Asia, and northern Africa, featuring flake tools that are lighter and smaller than earlier Levalloisian flake tools.

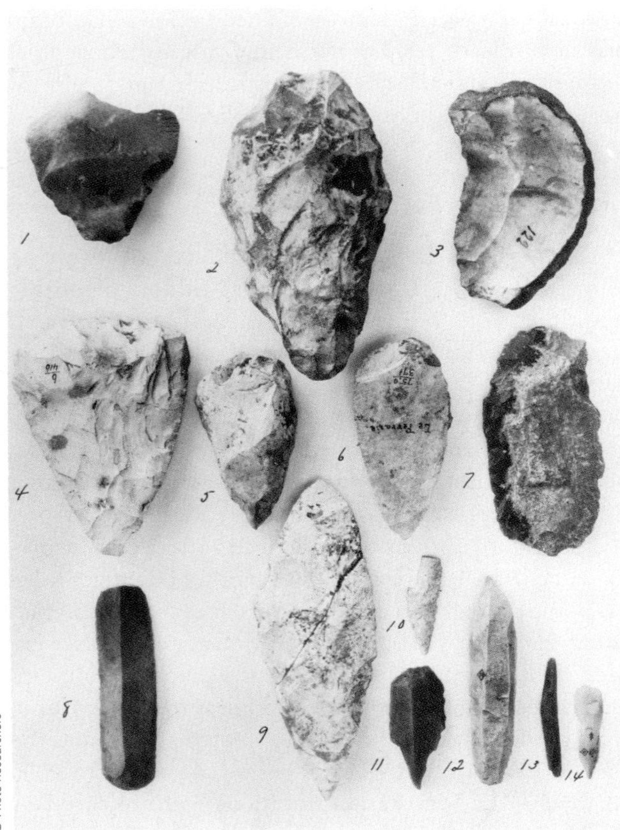

Tools such as 5, 6, and 7 are characteristic of the Mousterian tradition (1-4 are earlier, 8-14 later).

facilitated more effective use of food resources and enhanced the quality of clothing and shelter.

With the Mousterian cultural traditions, for the first time members of the genus *Homo* could cope with the nearly Arctic conditions that became prevalent in Eurasia as the glaciers expanded about 70,000 years ago. People likely came to live in cold climates as a result of a slow but steady population increase during the Pleistocene. Population expansion into previously uninhabited colder regions was made possible through a series of cultural adaptations to cold climate. Under such cold conditions, vegetable foods are only rarely or seasonally available, and meat is the staff of life. In particular, animal fats, rather than carbohydrates, become the chief source of energy. Energy- rich animal fat in the diets of cold-climate meat eaters provides them with the extra energy needed for full-time hunting, as well as keeping the body warm.

That meat was important to the makers of Mousterian tools is indicated by an abundance of associated animal bones, often showing clear cut marks. Frequently, the remains consist almost entirely of very large game—wild cattle (including the European bison known as the aurochs), wild horses, and even mammoths and woolly rhinoceroses. At several sites there is striking evidence that particular species were singled out for the hunt. For example, at one site in the French Pyrenees, well over 90 percent of the faunal assemblage (representing at least 108 animals) consists of large members of the cattle family. These bones accumulated at the foot of a steep riverside escarpment, over which the animals were evidently stampeded. Similar mass hunting techniques are documented at other Mousterian sites. At La Quina in western France, a dense accumulation of wild cattle, horse, and reindeer bones (many with clear cut marks from butchering) occurred at the base of a steep cliff. At another site in the Channel Islands just off the northwest coast of France, dense deposits of mammoth and woolly rhinoceros bones indicate use of a deep coastal ravine for cliff-fall hunting. Clearly, the Neandertals were not mere casual or opportunistic hunters but engaged in a great deal of deliberate and organized hunting of very large and potentially dangerous game.[7] This required careful planning, forethought, and logistical organization.

The importance of hunting to Mousterian peoples may also be reflected in their hunting implements, which are more standardized with respect to size and shape than are household tools. The complexity of the tool kit needed for survival in a cold climate may have played a role in lessening the mobility of the users of all these possessions. That they were less mobile is suggested by the greater depth of deposits at Mousterian sites compared with those from the earlier Lower Paleolithic. Similarly, Mousterian sites provide evidence for long habitation preserving long production sequences, resharpening and discarding of tools, and large-scale butchering and cooking of game. Evidence of efforts to improve living conditions in some caves and rock shelters can be seen with pebble paving, construction of simple walls, and the digging of postholes and artificial pits. This evidence suggests that Mousterian sites were more than mere stopovers in peoples' constant quest for food.

In addition, evidence suggests that Neandertal social organization had developed to the point of being able to care for physically disabled members of the group. For the first time, the remains of old people are well represented in the fossil record. Furthermore, many elderly Neandertal skeletons show evidence of trauma having been treated, with extensive healing of wounds and little or no infection.[8] Particularly dramatic

[7] Mellars, P. (1989). Major issues in the emergence of modern humans. *Current Anthropology, 30,* 356–357.

[8] Conroy, G. C. (1997). *Reconstructing human origins: A modern synthesis* (p. 427). New York: Norton.

examples include the remains of a partially blind man (the eye socket indicates serious injury) with a withered arm discovered in Shanidar Cave in Iraq, an individual found at Krapina in Croatia whose hand may have been surgically amputated, and a man badly crippled by arthritis from La Chapelle, France. The earliest example comes from a 200,000-year-old site in France, where a toothless man was able to survive probably because others in his group processed his food so he could swallow it. Whether this evidence indicates true compassion on the part of these early people is not clear; what is certain is that culture had become more than barely adequate to ensure survival, allowing individuals to provide care for others.

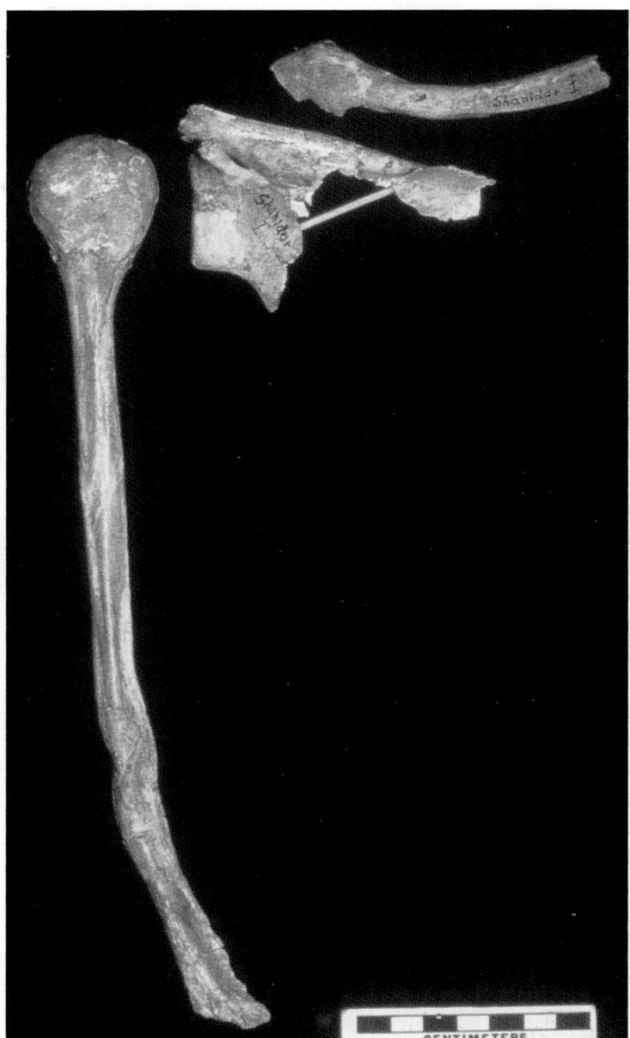

© Erik Trinkaus

The withered humerus (upper arm bone) from the Shanidar Neandertal indicates that this individual survived for quite a long period of time after losing the lower half of the arm. If the individual had died when the lower arm was lost, the humerus would have a normal appearance. Care of the sick and disabled can be inferred from this specimen.

The Symbolic Life of Neandertals

Indications of a rich symbolic life of Neandertals exist. At several sites, there is clear evidence for deliberate burial of the dead. This is one reason for the relative abundance of reasonably complete Neandertal skeletons. To dig a grave large enough to receive an adult body without access to metal shovels suggests how important a social activity this was. Moreover, intentional positioning of dead bodies by evolving humans, whatever the specific reason may have been, nonetheless constitutes evidence of symbolism.[9] To date, at least seventeen sites in Europe, South Africa, and Southwest Asia include Middle Paleolithic burials. To cite but two examples, at Kebara Cave in Israel, around 60,000 years ago, a Neandertal male aged between 25 and 35

[9]Schepartz, L. A. (1993). Language and modern human origins. *Yearbook of Physical Anthropology, 36*, 113.

© Kenneth Garrett/National Geographic Image Collection

The position of the body and the careful removal of the skull indicate that the fossil from Kebara Cave in Israel was deliberately buried there about 60,000 years ago.

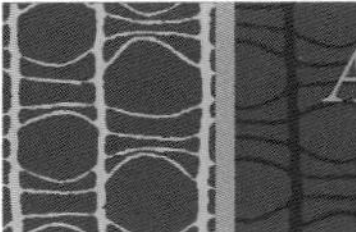

Anthropology Applied: Forensic Archaeology

Although the fields of Paleolithic and forensic archaeology might appear to have little in common, the two do share techniques of data recovery. The difference is that in one case what is recovered is evidence to be used in legal proceedings involving cases of murder, human rights abuses, and the like; in the other, the evidence is used to reconstruct ancient human behavior.

Forensic archaeologists commonly work closely with forensic anthropologists (Chapter 1). The relation between them is rather like that between a forensic pathologist, who examines a corpse to establish time and manner of death, and a crime scene investigator, who searches the site for clues. While the forensic anthropologist deals with the human remains—often only bones and teeth—the forensic archaeologist controls the site, recording the position of all relevant finds and recovering any clues associated with the remains. In Rwanda, for example, a team assembled in 1995 to investigate a mass atrocity for the United Nations included archaeologists from the U.S. National Park Service's Midwest Archaeological Center. They performed the standard archaeological procedures of mapping the site, determining its boundaries, photographing and recording all surface finds, and excavating, photographing, and recording buried skeletons and associated materials in mass graves.[a]

© Brian Concannon

Karen Burns

In another example, Karen Burns of the University of Georgia was part of a team sent to northern Iraq after the 1991 Gulf War to investigate alleged atrocities. On a military base where there had been many executions, she excavated the remains of a man's body found lying on its side facing Mecca, conforming to Islamic practice. Although there was no intact clothing, two threads of polyester used to sew clothing were found along the sides of both legs. Although the threads survived, the clothing, because it was made of natural fiber, had decayed. "Those two threads at each side of the leg just shouted that his family didn't bury him," says Burns.[b] Proper though his position was, no Islamic family would bury their own in a garment sewn with polyester thread; proper ritual would require a simple shroud. ■ ■ ■

[a]Connor, M. (1996). The archaeology of contemporary mass graves. *SAA Bulletin, 14*(4), 6, 31.

[b]Cornwell, T. (1995, November 10). Skeleton staff. *Times Higher Education*, 20.

years was placed in a pit on his back, with his arms folded over his chest and abdomen. Some time later, after complete decay of attaching ligaments, the grave was reopened and the skull removed (a practice that, interestingly, is sometimes seen in burials in the same region roughly 50,000 years later). Another example is from Shanidar Cave in Iraq, where evidence was found of a burial accompanied by what may have been funeral ceremonies. In the back of the cave a Neandertal was buried in a pit. Pollen analysis of the soil around the skeleton indicated that flowers had been placed below the body and in a wreath about the head. Because the key pollen types came from insect-pollinated flowers, few if any of the pollen grains could have found their way into the pit via air currents. The flowers in question consist solely of varieties valued in historic times for their medicinal properties.

Other evidence for symbolic behavior in Mousterian culture comes from the naturally occurring pigments: manganese dioxide and the red and yellow forms of ocher as described above. Recovered chunks of these pigments reveal clear evidence of scraping to produce powder, as well as crayonlike facets from use. Thus, Mousterian peoples were applying color to things. An example of the application of color is the carved and shaped section of a mammoth tooth that was worked by Mousterian people about 50,000 years ago. This object

Courtesy of Professor Ralph Solecki

The Shanidar burial provides evidence of symbolism of the Neandertals. Pollen grains indicate that the corpse was buried with flowers. Among living people, flowers are frequently symbols of rebirth. Because the Shanidar specimens were discovered in the 1960s, they are sometimes referred to as the first "flower children."

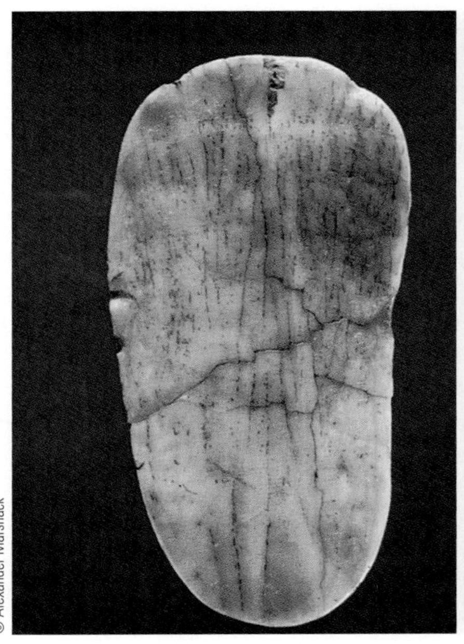

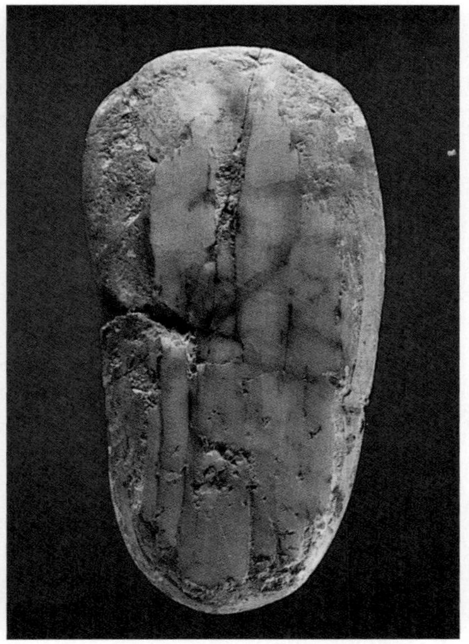

© Alexander Marshack

© Alexander Marshack

This carved symbolic plaque or *churinga* made from a section of a mammoth molar was excavated at the Mousterian site of Tata, Hungary. The edge is rounded and polished from long handling. The plaque has been symbolically smeared with red ocher. The reverse face of the plaque (right) shows the beveling and shaping of the tooth.

and others like it may have been made for cultural symbolic purposes. In addition, it is similar to a number of plaques of bone and ivory made during the later Upper Paleolithic and to the *churingas* made of wood by Australian aborigines and other objects made by various other traditional peoples across the world for ritual purposes. The Mousterian object, which was once smeared with red ocher, has a highly polished face as if from long handling. Microscopic examination reveals that it was never provided with a working edge for any utilitarian purpose. Such objects imply, as archaeologist Alexander Marshack observed, "that the Neandertals did in fact have conceptual models and maps as well as problem-solving capacities comparable to, if not equal to, those found among anatomically modern humans."[10]

Evidence for symbolic activity on the part of Neandertals raises the possibility of the presence and use of musical instruments, such as a proposed bone flute from a Mousterian site in Slovenia in southern Europe. The object consisting of a hollow bone with perforations has sparked controversy. Some see it as nothing more than a cave bear bone that was chewed on by carnivores—hence the perforations. Its discoverer, French archaeologist Marcel Otte, on the other hand, sees it as a flute. Unfortunately, the object is fragmentary; surviving are five holes, four on one side and one on the opposite side. The regular spacing of the four holes, fitting perfectly to the fingers of a human hand, and the location of the fifth hole

[10]Marshack, A. (1989). Evolution of the human capacity: The symbolic evidence. *Yearbook of Physical Anthropology, 32,* 22.

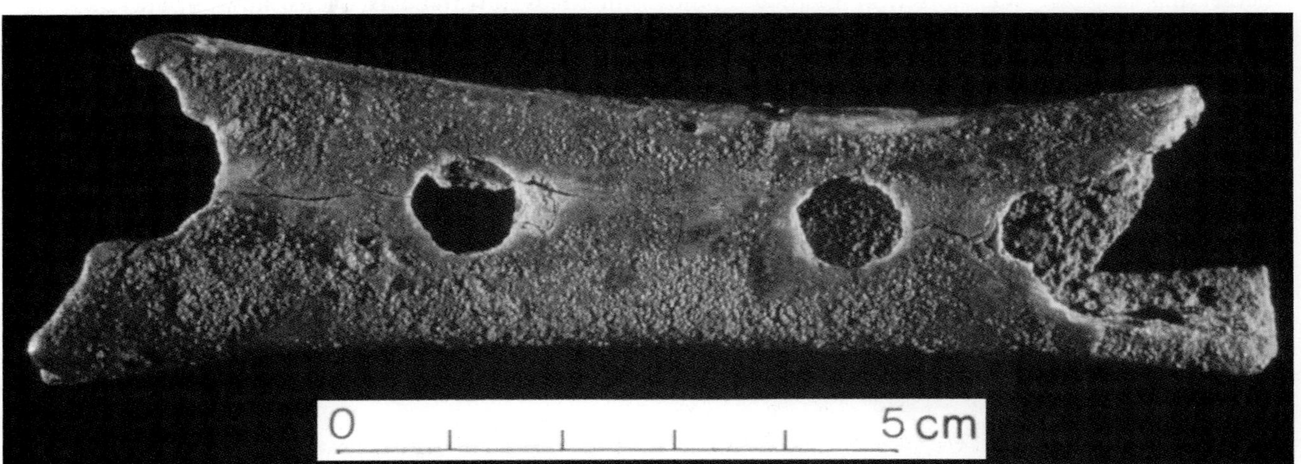

Courtesy of Marcel Otte

The first musical instrument? There is a strong possibility that this object, found in trash left by Neandertals, is all that remains of a flute made of bone.

at the base of the opposite side, at the natural location of the thumb, all lend credence to the flute hypothesis. Furthermore, signs of gnawing by animals are superimposed on traces of human activity.[11] Thus, the object cannot be rejected as a flute. Were it found in an Upper Paleolithic context, it would probably be accepted without argument. However, because its early date indicates it was made by a Neandertal, the interpretation of this object is tied to the larger controversy about Neandertals' cultural abilities and their place in human evolutionary history.

Neandertals: Speech and Language

Among modern humans, the sharing of thoughts and ideas, as well as the transmission of culture from one generation to the next, is dependent upon language. Because the Neandertals had modern-sized brains and a sophisticated Mousterian tool kit, it might be supposed that they had some form of language. As pointed out by paleoanthropologist Stanley Ambrose, the Mousterian tool kit included composite tools involving the assembly of parts in different configurations to produce functionally different tools. He likens this ordered assembly of parts into tools to grammatical language, "because hierarchical assemblies of sounds produce meaningful phrases and sentences, and changing word order changes meaning."[12] Furthermore, "a composite tool may be analogous to a sentence, but explaining how to make one is the equivalent of a recipe or a short story."[13] In addition, the evidence for the manufacture of objects of symbolic significance supports the presence of language in Neandertals. Objects such as the colored section of mammoth tooth already described would seem to have required some form of explanation through language.

While the archaeological evidence supports the symbolic thinking characteristic of language, specific anatomical features can be examined to determine whether this language was spoken or gestural. Some have argued that the Neandertals lacked the physical features necessary for speech. For example, an early 20th-century reconstruction of the angle at the base of the Neandertal skull was said to indicate that the larynx was higher in the throat than it is in modern humans, precluding humanlike speech. This reconstruction is now known to be faulty. Further, the hyoid bone associated with the muscles of speech in the larynx is preserved from a skeleton from the Kebara Cave burial in Israel. Its shape is identical to that of contemporary humans, indicating that the vocal tract was adequate for speech.

With respect to the brain, paleoneurologists, working from endocranial casts, are agreed that Neandertals had the neural development necessary for spoken language. Indeed, they argue that the changes associated with language began even before the appearance of archaic *Homo sapiens,*[14] as described in previous chapters. Consistent is the size of the hypoglossal canal, which in Neandertals is like that of modern humans and unlike that of apes.[15] As discussed in the previous chapter, this feature is apparent in hominin fossils that are at least 400,000 years old and indicates an ability to make the tongue movements necessary for articulate speech. Consistent, too, is an expanded thoracic vertebral canal (the thorax is the upper part of the body), a feature Neandertals share with modern humans but not early *Homo erectus* (or any other primate). This feature suggests the increased breath control required for speech.[16] This control enables production of long phrases or single expirations of breath, punctuated with quick inhalations at meaningful linguistic breaks.

MEDIATREK

To learn about the discovery, lifeways, tool kits, and ritual practices of Neandertals, go to MediaTrek 9.1 on the companion Web site or CD-ROM.

MEDIATREK

To learn more about the Neandertal question, including features about making a documentary television program on this controversial subject, go to MediaTrek 9.2 on the companion Web site or CD-ROM.

Another argument—that a relatively flat base in Neandertal skulls would have prevented speech—has no merit, as some modern adults show as much flattening, yet have no trouble talking. Clearly, when the anatomical evidence is considered in its totality, there seems no compelling reason to deny Neandertals the ability to speak.

The recent discovery of a "language gene" by Svante Pääbo and colleagues at the Max Planck Institute for Evolutionary Anthropology in Leipzig, Germany, adds an interesting new dimension to the question of the evo-

[11]Otte, M. (2000). On the suggested bone flute from Slovenia. *Current Anthropology, 41,* 271.

[12]Ambrose, p. 1,751.

[13]Ambrose, p.1,751.

[14]Schepartz, p. 98.

[15]Cartmill, M. (1998). The gift of gab. *Discover, 19*(11), 62.

[16]MacLarnon, A. M., & Hewitt, G. P. (1999). The evolution of human speech: The role of enhanced breathing control. *American Journal of Physical Anthropology, 109,* 341–363.

lution of language.[17] The form of this gene, called FOXP2 found on chromosome 7 in humans, differs from the versions of the gene found in the chimpanzee, gorilla, orangutan, rhesus macaque, and mouse. Changes in the gene are suggested to control the ability to make fine movements of the mouth and larynx necessary for spoken language. Interestingly, the gene was identified through the analysis of a family in which members spanning several generations have severe language problems. Because some modern members of the human species possess a version of this gene that is nearly incompatible with speech, other researchers argue that such changes in single genes with powerful phenotypic effects do not necessarily correlate with speciation.

CULTURE, SKULLS, AND MODERN HUMAN ORIGINS

For Middle Paleolithic hominins, their cultural adaptive abilities relate to the fact that brain size was comparable to that of people living today. Archaeological evidence indicates sophisticated technology as well as conceptual thought of considerable complexity, matching the increased cranial capacity. During this same time period, individuals with an anatomically "modern" appearance, a brain of the same size but differently shaped skull, began to appear. The earliest specimens with this skull shape appear first in Africa and later in Asia and Europe. Whether the derived features in the skull, a more vertical forehead, diminished brow ridge, and a chin indicate the appearance of a new species with improved cultural capabilities remains a hotly debated question.

The transition from the Middle Paleolithic to the tools of the Upper Paleolithic occurred around 40,000 years ago, some 100,000 years or so after the appearance of the first anatomically "modern" specimens. The Upper Paleolithic is known not only for a veritable explosion of tool industries, but also for clear artistic expression preserved in representative sculptures, paintings, and engravings (see Chapter 10). But the earliest anatomically modern humans used tools of the Middle Paleolithic traditions like the archaic *H. sapiens.*

The relationship between cultural developments of the Upper Paleolithic and underlying biological differences between anatomically modern humans and archaic forms remains one of the most contentious debates in paleoanthropology. The fate of the Neandertals and their cultural abilities are integral to this debate. Whether or not a new kind of human—anatomically modern with correspondingly superior intellectual and creative abilities—is responsible for the cultural explosion of the Upper Paleolithic is a difficult question to resolve. The biological and cultural evidence preserved in fossil and archaeological records, respectively, do not tell a simple story.

On a biological level, the great debate can be distilled to a question of whether one, some, or all populations of the archaic groups played a role in the evolution of modern *H. sapiens.* Those supporting the multiregional hypothesis argue that the fossil evidence suggests a simultaneous local transition from *Homo erectus* to modern *Homo sapiens* throughout the parts of the world inhabited by members of the genus *Homo.* By contrast, those supporting a theory of recent African origins use primarily genetic evidence to argue that all contemporary people are derived from one single population of archaic *H. sapiens* from Africa. This model proposes that the improved cultural capabilities of anatomically modern humans allowed this group to replace other archaic forms as they began to migrate out of Africa some time after 100,000 years ago.

The Multiregional Hypothesis

As several anthropologists have noted, African, Chinese, and Southeast Asian fossils of archaic *Homo sapiens* imply local population continuity from *Homo erectus,* through archaic, to modern *Homo* sapiens,[18] lending strong support to the interpretation that there was genetic continuity in these regions. For example, in China hominin fossils consistently have small forward-facing cheeks and flatter faces than their contemporaries elsewhere, as is still true today. In Southeast Asia and Australia, by contrast, skulls are consistently robust, with huge cheeks and forward projection of the jaws. In this model, gene flow among populations keeps the human species unified throughout the Pleistocene. No speciation events remove ancestral populations such as *Homo erectus* or Neandertals from the line leading to *Homo sapiens.* Although proponents

[17]Lai, C. S. L., et al. (2001). A forkhead-domain gene is mutated in severe speech and language disorder. *Nature, 413,* 519–523; Enard, W., et al. (2002). Molecular evolution of FOXP2, a gene involved in speech and language. *Nature, 418,* 869–872.

[18]Wolpoff, M. H., Wu, X. Z. & Thorne, A. G. (1984). Modern *Homo sapiens* origins: A general theory of hominid evolution involving fossil evidence from East Asia (pp. 411–483). In F. H. Smith & F. Spencer (Eds.), *The origins of modern humans.* New York: Alan R. Liss; Wolpoff, M. H., & Caspari, R. (1997). *Race and human evolution.* New York: Simon & Schuster; Pope, G. C. (1992). Craniofacial evidence for the origin of modern humans in China. *Yearbook of Physical Anthropology, 35,* 291.

© Milford H. Wolpoff

VISUAL COUNTERPOINT Shown on the left is one of the skulls of archaic *H. sapiens* from Ngandong, Java. On the right is the more recent skull from Lake Mungo, Australia. The similarity between the two is obvious, suggesting continuity of populations in the region rather than replacement by "anatomically modern" forms.

of the **multiregional hypothesis** accept the idea of continuity from the earliest European fossils through the Neandertals to living people, many other paleoanthropologists resist the idea that Neandertals were involved in the ancestry of modern Europeans.

The "Eve" or Recent African Origins Hypothesis

The **recent African origins hypothesis** (also called the "Eve" hypothesis) states that anatomically modern humans are descended from one specific population of *H. sapiens,* replacing not just the Neandertals but other populations of archaic *H. sapiens* as our ancestors spread out of their original homeland. This idea did not originate from fossils, but from a relatively new technique that uses mitochondrial DNA (mtDNA) to reconstruct family trees. Unlike nuclear DNA (in the cell nucleus), mtDNA is located in the mitochondria, the cellular structures that produce the energy needed to keep cells alive. Because sperm contribute virtually no mtDNA to the fertilized egg, all of mtDNA is inherited only from one's mother and is not subject to recombination through meiosis and fertilization with each succeeding generation as is nuclear DNA. Therefore, changes in mtDNA over time occur only through mutation. By comparing the mtDNA of living individuals from diverse geographical populations, anthropologists and molecular biologists seek to determine when and where modern *H. sapiens* originated. As widely reported in the popular press (including cover stories in *Newsweek* and *Time*), preliminary results suggest that the mitochondrial DNA of all living humans could be traced back to a "Mitochondrial Eve" who lived in Africa some 200,000 years ago. If so, all other popula-

multiregional hypothesis The model for modern human origins through simultaneous local transition from *Homo erectus* to modern *Homo sapiens* with links among these populations through gene flow.

recent African origins The model for modern human origins in which anatomically modern humans arose in Africa approximately 200,000 years ago, replacing archaic forms in the rest of the world. Also called the "Eve" hypothesis.

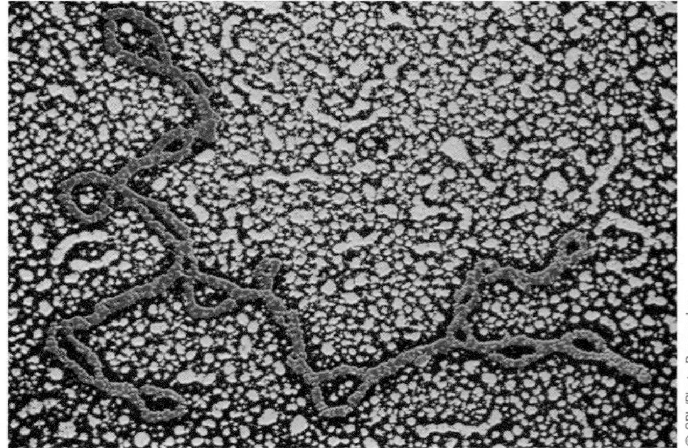

© SPL/Photo Researchers

Because it is inherited maternally, mitochondrial DNA (mtDNA) is not subject to recombination. Therefore, mtDNA can be used to study the accumulation of mutations to establish evolutionary relationships through molecular clocks. However, population size is known to affect the amount of mtDNA variation preserved, as described in this chapter's Original Study.

Anthropologists of Note

Berhane Asfaw (1953–)

Born in Addis Ababa, Ethiopia, in 1953, Berhane Asfaw is a world-renowned paleoanthropologist leading major expeditions in Ethiopia. He is co-leader of the international Middle Awash Research Project, the research team responsible for the discovery of hominin fossils dating from the entire 6-million-year course of human evolutionary history, including *Ardipithecus ramidus, Australopithecus afarensis, Australopithecus gahri, Homo erectus,* and, most recently, the *Homo sapiens idaltu* fossils from Herto, Ethiopia. At the June 2003 press conference, organized by Ethiopia's Minister of Culture, Teshome Toga, Asfaw described the Herto specimens as the oldest "anatomically modern" humans, likening Ethiopia to the "Garden of Eden." This conference marked a shift in the Ethiopian government's stance toward the paleoanthropological research spanning Asfaw's career. Previous discoveries

© 1988 David L. Brill

in the Middle Awash were also very important, but the government did not participate or support this research.

Asfaw entered the discipline of paleoanthropology through a program administered by the Leakey Foundation providing fellowships for Africans to pursue graduate studies in Europe and the United States. Since this program's inception in the late 1970s, the Leakey foundation has awarded sixty-eight fellowships totaling $1.2 million to Kenyans, Ethiopians, and Tanzanians to pursue graduate education in paleoanthropology. Asfaw, mentored by American paleoanthropologist Desmond Clark at the University of California, Berkeley, was among of the earliest fellows in this program. They first met in 1979 when Asfaw was a senior studying geology in Addis Ababa. Asfaw obtained his Ph.D. in 1988 and returned to Ethiopia, where he had few Ethiopian anthropological colleagues and the government had halted fossil exploration. Since that time, Asfaw has recruited and mentored many Ethiopian scholars, including Sileshi Semaw (see Chapter 7), and now has about a dozen on his team. Local scientists can protect the antiquities, keep fossils from disappearing, and marshal government support. Asfaw's leadership in paleoanthropology has played a key role in helping the Ethiopian government to recognize how important prehistory is for the country of Ethiopia.

tions of archaic *H. sapiens,* as well as non-African *H. erectus,* would have to be ruled out of the ancestry of modern humans.

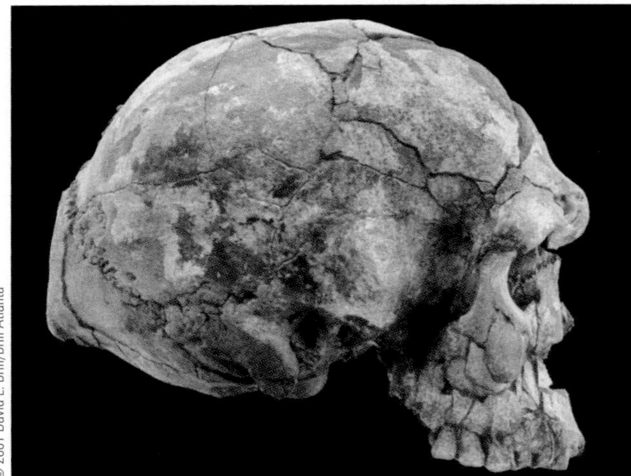
© 2001 David L. Brill/Brill Atlanta

The recently discovered well-preserved specimens from Herto, Ethiopia, provide the best fossil evidence in support of the recent African origins hypothesis. Though these fossils unquestionably possess an "anatomically modern" appearance, they are still relatively robust. In addition, the question of whether the higher skull and forehead indicate superior cultural abilities still remains open.

For many years, the absence of good fossil evidence from Africa to support the recent African origins hypothesis has been a weakness of this theory. In 2003, however, skulls of two adults and one child described as "anatomically modern" discovered in 1997 in Ethiopia in East Africa were reconstructed and dated to 160,000 years ago.[19] The discoverers of these fossils called them *Homo sapiens idaltu* (meaning "elder" in the local Afar language). While conceding that these skulls are robust, they believe that they have conclusively proved the recent African origins hypothesis, relegating Neandertals to a side branch of human evolution with these finds.

MEDIATREK

To see Berhane Asfaw and colleagues' assertion on how the Herto specimens conclusively prove the hypothesis of recent African origins, go to MediaTrek 9.3 on the companion Web site or CD-ROM.

[19]White, T., Asfaw, B., Degusta, D., Gilbert, H., Richards G., Suwa G., Howell, F. C. (2003). Pleistocene *Homo sapiens* from the Middle Awash, Ethiopia. *Nature, 423,* 742–747.

RECONCILING THE EVIDENCE

Though the recent African origins hypothesis is the majority position among Western paleoanthropologists, the theory does not prevail throughout the globe. Chinese paleoanthropologists, for example, favor the multiregional hypothesis because it fits well with the fossil discoveries from Asia and Australia. By contrast, the recent African origins hypothesis depends more upon the interpretation of fossils and cultural remains from Europe, Africa, and the Middle East. The recent African origins hypothesis can be critiqued on several additional grounds. For example, the molecular evidence upon which it is based has come under considerable criticism. Genetic studies indicate that Africa was not the sole source of DNA in "modern" humans.[20] In addition, because both theories proposed African origins for the human line, molecular data could be interpreted as evidence supporting the African origins of the genus *Homo,* rather than the more recent species *Homo sapiens.* Both models place ultimate human origins firmly in Africa. In addition, recent work described in the following Original Study also indicate that population size accounts for the variability of mtDNA globally.

[20]Templeton, A. R. (1995). The "Eve" Hypothesis: A genetic critique and reanalysis. *American Anthropologist, 95*(1), 51–72.

Original Study

African Origin or Ancient Population Size Differences?

The Eve theory depends on genetic evidence indicating an African origin for modern humanity, because . . . the fossil evidence is quite equivocal on this issue. But there is no particular reason to suggest Africa was the place of origin for the current mtDNA [mitochondrial DNA] lineages. The original studies suggesting an African origin were invalid because the computer program used in the analysis was not applied correctly. Then the greater genetic variability in Africans was taken to mean humans evolved there longer: The variation was thought to reflect more mutations and therefore a longer time span for their accumulation. Templeton [a geneticist] has argued that no statistical analysis shows that the genetic variation of Africans actually is greater than that of other populations; but even if it is, there is another, more compelling explanation.

Ancient population sizes expanded first and are larger in Africa than in other regions, which would have the same effect, creating more African variation. Consider what happens in an expanding population. Average family size is greater than two, and all variations have a good chance of being passed on; at least, if they are not selected against, they will probably not get lost by accident. But if a population is decreasing, drift can play a very active role since average family size is less than two. The role of drift is greatly amplified for mtDNA, because for transmission of this molecule the number of female offspring is important. Decreasing populations stand an excellent chance of losing mtDNA lineages.

The notion of a single African "Eve," mother of all humans, living a mere 200,000 years ago captured the public's imagination and the press's attention.

Now, consider a small but stable population, neither increasing nor decreasing. Here, existing variations may each occur in only one individual. If it is a woman, and she has no female offspring, which can happen one-fourth of the time in a stable population, her unique variation is lost, her mtDNA lineage terminated. But in a large stable population with the same amount of genetic variability, it is likely each mtDNA variant is shared by many individuals. The odds are the same against one woman having no female offspring, but it is very unlikely all the women with a certain mtDNA variant will lack female offspring. It is much harder for mtDNA lines to end by accident in large populations.

These comparisons show that prehistoric population demography, how large or small populations were in the past and how much they fluctuated, can affect mtDNA evolution. Small, fluctuating populations will lose many mtDNA lines. The last common ancestor for the remaining mtDNA variations will be more recent because there is less remaining variation. Large or increasing populations will retain more variation. For them, the roots will be deeper, and the last common ancestor will be farther in the past since more variations are retained.

Thus, ancient population size can dictate how long genetic lineages have existed and therefore when they arose. Because ancient population size differences are an alternate explanation that unlinks the origin of genetic lineages from the origin of a population, it seems as though genetic analysis cannot help solve the problem of whether today's variation reflects African origin or ancient population size differences.

However, genetic analysis can indicate ancient population expansions. Henry Harpending and colleagues studied the probability distributions of pairwise mtDNA comparisons within populations for evidence of past population structure and size expansions. They conclude: "Our results show human populations are derived from separate ancestral populations that were relatively isolated from each other before 50,000 years ago." These studies clearly reveal there have been a series of recent, very significant, population expansions. Some of these are without question associated with the development and spread of agricultural revolutions. But others are earlier.

This means population size history by itself can explain the pattern of mtDNA variation. If, as we believe and as the archaeological record seems to show,

- there were more people living in Africa for most of human prehistory, and
- human populations outside of Africa were smaller and fluctuated more because of the changing ice-age environments

we would expect just what we do see—African mtDNA has deeper roots, while in other places the coalescent time is more recent. But this explanation does not mean the populations living out of Africa have a more recent origin, or that they originated in Africa. MtDNA history, in other words, is not population history.

John Relethford and Henry Harpending examined the consequences of the possibility that greater African population size, and not greater time depth for modern humans in Africa, may account for their greater variation.

> Our results support our earlier contention that regional differences in population size can explain the genetic evidence pertaining to modern human origins. Our work thus far has involved examination of the classic genetic markers and craniometrics, but it also has implications for mitochondrial DNA. The greater mtDNA diversity in sub-Saharan African populations could also be a reflection of a larger long-term African population.

Moreover, they write, a unique African ancestry implies there was a bottleneck for the human species, as moderns would be able to trace their ancestry to only a small portion of humanity, as it existed then.

> While this seems at first glance a reasonable notion, it soon becomes apparent that the actual effect of such a [bottleneck] event depends on both the magnitude and duration of a shift in population size. Rogers and Jorde show that given reasonable parameters for our species, the bottleneck would have to be more severe and long-lasting than considered plausible. We have to think of a population of 50 females for 6,000 years, for example.

(By M. H. Wolpoff & R. Caspari. (1997). Race and human evolution *(pp. 305-307). New York: Simon & Schuster.)*

Other assumptions made by DNA analysts are problematic. For example, it is assumed that rates of mutation are steady, when in fact they can be notoriously uneven. Another assumption is that mtDNA is not subject to selection, when in fact variants have been implicated in epilepsy and a disease of the eye.[21] A third is that DNA is seen as traveling exclusively *from* Africa, when it is known that, over the past 10,000 years, there has been plenty of movement of humans into Africa as well. In fact, one study of DNA carried on the Y chromosome (the sex chromosome inherited exclusively in the male line) suggests that some DNA seen on the Y chromosome of some Africans was introduced from Asia, where it originated some 200,000 years ago.[22]

Since 1997, studies of mitochondrial DNA have not been limited to living people. In that year, mtDNA was extracted from the original German Neandertal remains, and two others have since been studied. Because the mtDNA of each of these differs substantially from modern Europeans, many have concluded that there can be no Neandertal ancestry in living humans and that Neandertals must constitute a separate species that went extinct. But as biological anthropologist John Relethford (a specialist in anthropological genetics) points out, these conclusions are premature.[23] For one thing, the average differences are not as great as those seen among living subspecies of the single species of chimpanzee. For another, the differences between populations separated in time by tens of thousands of

[21]Shreeve, p. 121.

[22]Gibbons, A. (1997). Ideas on human origins evolve at anthropology gathering. *Science, 276,* 535–536.

[23]Relethford, J. H. (2001). Absence of regional affinities of Neandertal DNA with living humans does not reject multiregional evolution. *American Journal of Physical Anthropology, 115,* 95–98.

years tell us nothing about differences between populations contemporaneous with each other. More meaningful would be comparison of the DNA from a late Neandertal with an early "anatomically modern" European. Finally, if we are to reject Neandertals in the ancestry of modern Europeans because their DNA cannot be detected in their supposed ancestors, then we must also reject any connection between a 40,000- to 62,000-year-old skeleton from Australia (that everyone agrees is anatomically modern) and more recent native Australians. In this case, an mtDNA sequence present in an ancient human seems to have become extinct, in which case we must allow the same possibility for the Neandertals.[24] In short, it is definitely premature to remove from modern human ancestry all populations of archaic *H. sapiens* save those of Africa. Not even the Neandertals can be excluded.

Though the recent fossil discoveries may provide evidence of the earliest anatomically modern specimens in Africa, they do not resolve the relationship between biological change in the shape of the skull and culture change as preserved in the archaeological record. The changes in the archaeological record and the appearance of anatomically modern skulls are separated by some 100,000 years. The evidence from Southwest Asia is particularly interesting in this regard. Here, at a variety of sites dated to between 50,000 and 100,000 years ago, fossils described as both anatomically modern and Neandertal are present and associated with Mousterian technology.

Nevertheless, recent African origins proponents argue that anatomically modern people coexisted for a time with other archaic populations until the superior cultural capacities of the "moderns" resulted in extinction of the archaic peoples. Especially clear evidence of this is said to exist in Europe, where Neandertals and "moderns" are said to coexist in close proximity between 40,000 and 30,000 years ago. However, defining fossils as either Neandertals or "moderns" illustrates the difficulty with defining a distinct biological species, given the presence of variation found in humans.

If we think in terms of varied populations—as we should[25]—instead of ideal types, we find that features reminiscent of modern humans can be discerned in some of the latest Neandertals. A specimen from Saint Césaire in France, for example, has a higher forehead and chin. A number of other Neandertals, too, show incipient chin development as well as reduced facial protrusion and smaller brow ridges. Conversely, the earliest anatomically modern human skulls from Europe often exhibit features reminiscent of Neandertals (see Chapter 10). Accordingly, we might view the population of this region between 40,000 and 30,000 years ago as a varied one, with some individuals retaining a stronger Neandertal heritage than others, in whom modern characteristics are more prominent (Figure 9.4).

Courtesy of Dana Walrath

French archaeologist Jacques Pelegrin's demonstration of a variety of flint-knapping techniques illustrates the intelligence and thought involved in producing these stone tools.

Further, this mix of "modern" and Neandertal features is so strong in a child's skeleton recently found in Portugal as to lead several specialists to regard it as clear evidence of hybridization, or successful reproduction between the two groups.[26] This, if true, means that the two forms are of a single rather than separate species. In fact, an explanation that accounts for all this evidence is that all of these fossils belong to a single varied population, with some individuals showing more of typical Neandertal features than others. This accords

[24]Gibbons, A. (2001). The riddle of coexistence. *Science, 291,* 1,726.

[25]Gould, S. J. (1996). Full house: *The spread of excellence from Plato to Darwin* (pp. 72–73). New York: Harmony Books.

[26]Holden, C. (1999). Ancient child burial uncovered in Portugal. *Science, 283,* 169.

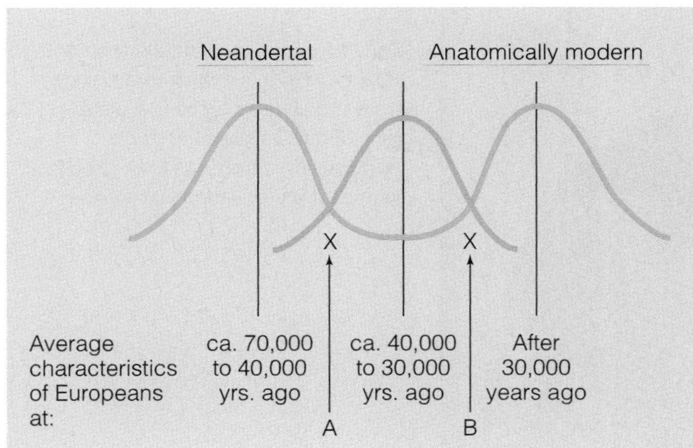

FIGURE 9.4

Graphically portrayed here is a shift in average characteristics of an otherwise varied population over time from Neandertal to more modern features. Between 40,000 and 30,000 years ago, we would expect to find individuals with characteristics such as those of the Saint Césaire "Neandertal" (A) and the almost (but not quite) modern Cro-Magnon (B; this fossil is discussed in Chapter 10).

with archaeological evidence that the intellectual abilities of "late Neandertals" were no different from those of "early moderns."[27]

It is difficult to find evidence for something in the physical or mental makeup of Neandertals that would have prevented them from leading a typical Upper Paleolithic way of life. In fact, the latest Neandertals of Europe developed their own Upper Paleolithic technology comparable to the industries used by anatomically modern *H. sapiens.* No earlier than 36,500 years ago,[28] a new Upper Paleolithic technology, known as the **Aurignacian tradition**—named after Aurignac, France, where tools of this sort were first discovered—appeared in Europe (Figure 9.5).Though commonly considered to have spread from Southwest Asia, a recent re-analysis failed to sustain this idea suggesting instead that the Aurignacian is a distinctively European development.[29] Skeletal remains are rarely associated with Aurignacian tools, although anatomically modern humans are generally considered the makers of these tools. A notable exception to this notion is the central European site of Vindija, Croatia, where Neandertals are associated with an Aurignacian split-bone point.[30] However, some argue that the Upper Paleolithic technology of the Neandertals was a crude imitation of the true technological advancements practiced by anatomically modern humans. In some respects, Neandertals outdid their anatomically modern contemporaries, as in the use of red ocher, a substance less frequently used by Aurignacian peoples than by their late Neandertal neighbors.[31] This cannot be a case of borrowing ideas and techniques from Aurignacians, as these developments clearly predate the Aurignacian.[32]

Neandertals and anatomically modern humans also coexisted in Southwest Asia long before the cultural innovations of the Upper Paleolithic. Here neither the skeletal nor the archaeological evidence supports cultural difference between the fossil groups or absolute biological difference. Although Neandertal skeletons are clearly present at sites such as Kebara and Shanidar caves, skeletons from some older sites have been described as anatomically modern. At the Mount Carmel site of Qafzeh in Israel, for example, 90,000-year-old skeletons are said to show none of the Neandertal hallmarks; although their faces and bodies are large and heavily built by today's standards, they are nonetheless claimed to be within the range of living peoples. Yet, a statistical study comparing a number of measurements among Qafzeh, Upper Paleolithic, and Neandertal skulls found those from Qafzeh to fall in between the anatomically modern and Neandertal norms, though slightly closer to the Neandertals.[33] Nor

[27] d'Errico, F., Zilhão, J., Julien, M., Baffier, D., & Pelegrin, J. (1998). Neandertal acculturation in Western Europe? *Current Anthropology, 39,* 521.

[28] Zilhão, J. (2000). Fate of the Neandertals. *Archaeology, 53*(4), 30.

[29] Clark, G. A. (2002). Neandertal archaeology: Implications for our origins. *American Anthropologist, 104*(1), 50–67.

[30] Karavani, I., & Smith, F. H. (2000). More on the Neanderthal problem: The Vindija case. *Current Anthropology, 41,* 839.

[31] Bednarik, R. G. (1995). Concept-mediated marking in the lower Paleolithic. *Current Anthropology, 36,* 606.

[32] Zilhão, p. 40.

[33] Corruccini, R. S. (1992). Metrical reconsideration of the Skhul IV and IX and Border Cave I crania in the context of modern human origins. *American Journal of Physical Anthropology, 87,* 433–445.

Aurignacian tradition Tool-making tradition in Europe and western Asia at the beginning of the Upper Paleolithic.

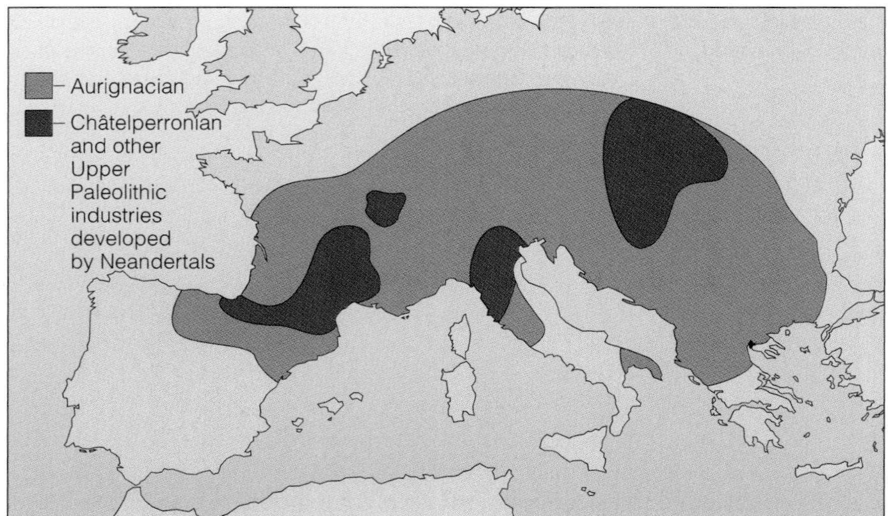

FIGURE 9.5

Between 36,500 and 30,000 years ago, Upper Paleolithic industries developed from the Mousterian by European Neandertals coexisted with the Aurignacian industry, usually associated with anatomically modern humans.

is the dentition functionally distinguishable when Qafzeh and Neandertal are compared.[34]

While skeletons from another Mount Carmel site of the same period called Skhul, are similar to those from Qafzeh, they were also part of a population whose continuous range of variation included individuals with markedly Neandertal characteristics. Furthermore, the idea of two distinctly different but coexisting populations receives no support from the archaeological evidence. Individuals living at Skhul and Qafzeh were making and using the same Mousterian tools as those at Kebara and Shanidar. Thus, there are no indications of biologically distinct groups with different cultural abilities.

Furthermore, the examination of sites continuously inhabited throughout the upper Pleistocene provides no significant evidence for behavioral differences between Middle Paleolithic and early Upper Paleolithic at these sites. For example, the Upper Paleolithic people who used Kebara Cave continued to live in exactly the same way as their Neandertal predecessors: They procured the same foods, processed them in the same way, used similar hearths, and disposed of their trash in the same way. The only evident difference is that the Neandertals did not bank their fires for warmth with small stones or cobbles as did their Upper Paleolithic successors.[35]

Nevertheless, by 28,000 years ago, many of the extreme anatomical features seen in archaic groups like Neandertals seem to disappear from the fossil record in Europe and Southwest Asia. Instead, people with higher foreheads, smoother brow ridges and distinct chins seemed to have Europe more or less to themselves. However, an examination of the full range of individual

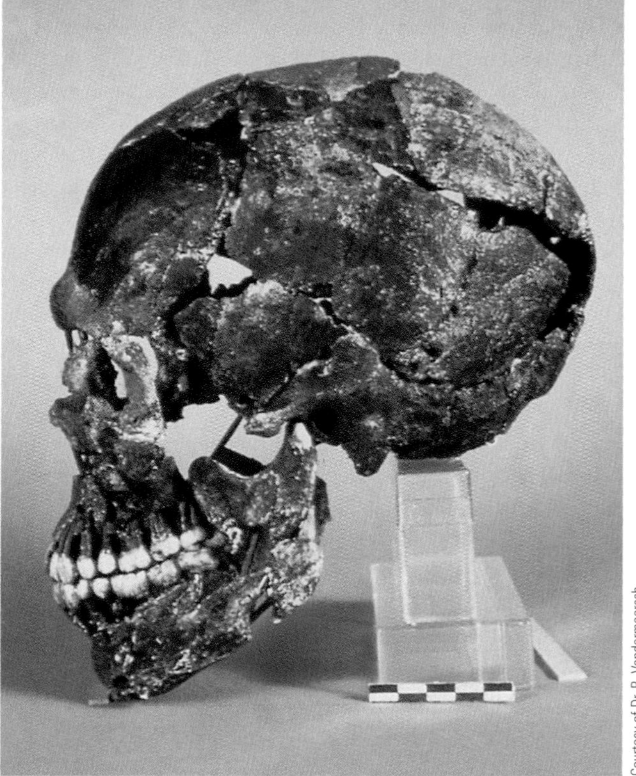

Courtesy of Dr. B. Vandermeersch

This *H. sapiens* skull from Qafzeh, Israel, is 90,000 years old. Though it looks more "modern" than a Neandertal, measurements taken on the skull fall slightly closer to those of the Neandertals than they do to those of more modern-looking Upper Paleolithic people.

[34]Brace, C. L. (2000). *Evolution in an anthropological view* (p. 206). Walnut Creek, CA: Altamira.

[35]Corruccini, p. 436.

human variation across the globe and into the present reveals contemporary humans with skulls not meeting the anatomical definition of "modernity" proposed in the standard evolutionary arguments.[36] Similarly, many Neandertal features can be seen in living people today. As is usual in human populations, contemporary people and Upper Paleolithic people exhibit considerable physical variability.

RACE AND HUMAN EVOLUTION

The Neandertal question can be viewed as more than simply a fascinating discussion about interpreting the fossil evidence. It raises fundamental issues about the relationship between biological and cultural variation. Can a series of biological features indicate particular cultural abilities? As we examined the fossil record throughout this chapter and others, we made inferences about the cultural capabilities of our ancestors based on biological features in combination with archaeological features. The increased brain size of *Homo habilis* around 2.5 million years ago compared to the earlier australopithecines supported the notion that these ancestors were capable of more complex cultural activities, including the manufacture of stone tools. When we get closer to the present, can we make the same kinds of assumptions? Can we say that only the anatomically modern humans with high foreheads and reduced brow ridges and not archaic *Homo sapiens,* even with their modern-sized brains, were capable of making sophisticated tools and representational art? Supporters of the multiregional hypothesis argue that we cannot.[37] They suggest that using a series of biological features to represent a type of human being (Neandertals) with certain cultural capacities (inferior) is like making assumptions about cultural capabilities of living humans based on their appearance. In living people, such an assumption represents a stereotype at best or racist prejudice at worst. Supporters of the recent African origins hypothesis

[36]Wolpoff & Caspari.

[37]Wolpoff & Caspari.

Living people today such as this native Australian do not all meet the definition of anatomical modernity proposed in the recent African origins model. Some paleoanthropologists suggest that this proves that the definition is problematic because all living people are clearly full-fledged members of the species *Homo sapiens.*

counter that because their theory embraces African human origins, it could hardly be considered prejudicial.

While paleoanthropologists all acknowledge African origins for hominins and the genus *Homo*, considerable disagreement exists with regard to the interpretation of the relationship between biological change and culture change as we approach the present. The fossil and archaeological evidence from the Middle Paleolithic does not indicate a simple one-to-one correspondence between cultural innovations and a biological change preserved in the shape of the skull.

Chapter Summary

- At various sites in Africa and Eurasia, a number of fossils have been found that date between about 400,000 and 200,000 years ago, showing a mixture of traits of both *H. erectus* and *H. sapiens*. They are indicative of the transition from the older into the younger species and are called archaic *Homo sapiens*. Their cultures were enriched by development of a new technique of tool manufacture known as the Levalloisian.
- The brains of archaic *H. sapiens* were no different in size and organization than our own, although their skulls retained some ancestral characteristics. With a larger brain, they were able to utilize culture as a means of adaptation to a far greater extent than any of their predecessors; they were capable of complex technology and sophisticated conceptual thought.
- In Europe and Southwest Asia, archaic *H. sapiens* are represented by the Neandertals—a fossil group retaining some ancestral features as well as some specializations that may be related to adaptation to extreme cold. Neandertals appeared around 125,000 years ago. Beginning around 30,000 years ago, classic Neandertals are no longer seen in the fossil record, although some Neandertal traits can be seen in living people today as well as in some of the more recent fossil specimens. Whether or not Neandertals are ancestors to the contemporary people of these regions is hotly debated within paleoanthropology.
- The cultures of archaic *H. sapiens* are known as Middle Paleolithic, and the best known is the Mousterian of Europe, northern Africa, and western Asia. Mousterian tools included hand-axes, flakes, scrapers, borers, wood shavers, and spears. Mousterian flake tools were lighter and smaller than those of the Levalloisian. Mousterian tools increased the availability and quality of food, shelter, and clothing. Archaeological evidence indicates that Mousterian peoples buried their dead, cared for the disabled, and made a variety of objects for purely symbolic purposes.
- According to the multiregional hypothesis, all populations of archaic *H. sapiens* are easily derivable from earlier populations of *H. erectus* from the same regions, and all could be ancestral to more modern populations in the same regions. Gene flow between populations prevented a speciation event in this phase of human evolutionary history. The alternative recent African origins hypothesis suggests that the transition from archaic to anatomically modern *H. sapiens* took place in one specific population, in Africa. From here, people spread to other regions, replacing older populations as they did so.

Questions for Reflection

1. The challenge for paleoanthropologists studying the Middle Paleolithic is to determine the relationship between biological change and cultural change in fossil groups of this time period. Do these features in the shape of the skull indicate biological differences sufficient to impact the cultural capabilities of these fossil groups?
2. What does it mean to be "modern," biologically or culturally? How should we define "human"?
3. Compare and contrast the recent African origins and multiregional hypothesis for the origins of humans. Describe the kinds of data each of these theories use to support their arguments.
4. How do you feel personally about the possibility of having Neandertals as part of your ancestry? How might you relate the Neandertal debates to stereotyping or racism in contemporary society?
5. What is the difference between speech and language? Describe the evidence for each in archaic *H. sapiens*.

Key Terms

Levalloisian technique
Neandertals
Middle Paleolithic
Mousterian tradition
Multiregional hypothesis
Recent African origins
Aurignacian tradition

Multimedia Review Tools

Companion Web Site

Visit **http://www.wadsworth.com/anthropology_d/** and click on the companion Web site for this textbook to access a wide range of material to aid your study of anthropology. Among the options for self-study in each chapter are learning objectives, flash cards, Internet activities, Web links, InfoTrac College Edition exercises, and practice tests that can be scored and emailed to your instructor.

CD-ROM

The *Doing Anthropology Today* CD-ROM supplied with your textbook provides unique and valuable information designed to enhance your learning experience. This interactive multimedia resource includes video clips, interviews with renowned anthropologists, map and timeline exercises, chapter study quizzes, and much more. *Doing Anthropology Today* will not only help you in achieving your grade goals, but it will also make your learning experience fun and exciting!

Suggested Readings

Shreeve, J. (1995). *The Neandertal enigma: Solving the mystery of modern human origins.* New York: William Morrow.

Shreeve is a science writer who has written extensively about human evolution. This book is engagingly written and covers most of the major issues in the Neandertal—modern debate.

Stringer, C. B., & McKie, R. (1996). *African exodus: The origins of modern humanity.* London: Jonathan Cape.

Chris Stringer of the British Museum is a leading champion of the "Out of Africa" or "Eve" recent African origins hypothesis, and in this book one will find a vigorous presentation of his arguments.

Trinkaus, E., & Shipman, P. (1992). *The Neandertals: Changing the image of mankind.* New York: Alfred A. Knopf.

The senior author of this book is a long-time specialist on the Neandertals. Eminently readable, the book chronicles the changing interpretations of these fossils since the first recognized find in 1856. For a good look at what is known about the Neandertals, there is no better place to go than this.

Wolpoff, M., & Caspari, R. (1997). *Race and human evolution.* New York: Simon & Schuster.

One of the problems in evaluating the multiregional and recent African origins hypotheses is that many writers misrepresent the former. That is no problem in this book, written by the leading champions of multiregionalism. The hypothesis is presented and defended in a straightforward and thorough way so that anyone can understand it.

CHAPTER 10

Homo sapiens and the Upper Paleolithic

CHALLENGE ISSUE

The Upper Paleolithic is defined by changes in technology and archaeological evidence of increased human creativity and ingenuity in art and problem solving. The hands and other figures painted on the walls of this cave site in Australia indicate a rich symbolic life. An additional example of the technological capabilities of early Australians can be seen in their ability to arrive on this continent by boat. The earliest habitations of Australia and New Guinea are separated from the eastern islands of Indonesia by a deep ocean trench that never empties of water even during times when sea levels were dramatically lowered by glaciers. Thus, early humans crossed miles of open water, distances that Australian paleoanthropologist Alan Thorne described as "beyond the horizon." The challenge for paleoanthropologists is to determine whether biological change was exclusively responsible for the cultural changes evident in the archaeological record.

1 When Did Anatomically Modern Forms of *Homo sapiens* Appear?

Although 160,000-year-old specimens from Ethiopia have been described as anatomically modern, the answer to this question is quite complex. Anatomical modernity refers to particular characteristics in the shape of the skull. While all humans today are members of a single species, and as such are equally "modern," some contemporary populations do not meet the definition of anatomical modernity used by some paleoanthropologists. To exclude contemporary humans from the species based on the shape of their skulls is an obvious impossibility. By extension this challenges the application of this definition to the fossil record. Still, it is generally agreed that by 30,000 years ago, Upper Paleolithic populations in all parts of the inhabited world show some resemblance to more recent human populations.

2 What Was the Culture of Upper Paleolithic Peoples Like?

Upper Paleolithic cultures generally include a greater diversity of tools than before and a predominance of blade tools. Pressure flaking techniques and the use of burins to fashion implements of bone and antler became widespread. In Europe, large game hunting was improved by the invention of the spear-thrower, or atlatl, while net hunting allowed effective procurement of small game. In Africa the earliest small points appropriate for arrowheads appear during this time period. There was as well an explosion of creativity, represented by impressive works of art discovered in a variety of sites from Africa, Australia, and Eurasia.

3 When and How Did Humans Spread to Australia and the Americas?

Around the time of the Upper Paleolithic humans expanded into new regions, most dramatically Australia and the Americas. Expansion into Australia and New Guinea required crossing a deep, wide ocean channel and was thus dependent upon some sort of watercraft. Spread to the Americas involved successful adaptation to Arctic conditions and movement over land through northeastern Asia to the Americas and/or the use of watercraft over even more extended distances. Anthropologists use archaeological, linguistic, and biological evidence to reconstruct the spread of humans into these new regions.

The remains of ancient people who looked more like contemporary Europeans than Neandertals were first discovered in 1868 at Les Eyzies in France, in a rock shelter together with tools of the **Upper** (late) **Paleolithic.** Consisting of eight skeletons, they are commonly referred to as **Cro-Magnons,** after the rock shelter in which they were found. The name was extended to thirteen other specimens recovered between 1872 and 1902 in the caves of southern coastal France, and since then, to other Upper Paleolithic skeletons discovered in other parts of Europe.

Because Cro-Magnons were found with Upper Paleolithic tools and seemed responsible for the production of impressive works of art, they were seen as particularly clever when compared with the Neandertals. The idea that Neandertals were basically dim-witted fit comfortably with the prevailing stereotype of their supposedly brutish appearance, and their Mousterian tools were interpreted as evidence of cultural inferiority. Hence the idea was born of an anatomically modern people with a superior culture sweeping into Europe and replacing a primitive local population. This idea was not unlike the image Europeans had of themselves regarding their colonial expansion. With the invention of reliable dating techniques in the 20th century, we now know that many Neandertal specimens of Europe and the later Cro-Magnon specimens date from different time periods. Instead, the Middle Paleolithic Mousterian technology is associated with earlier fossil specimens and Upper Paleolithic technology and art with later fossil specimens, both Neandertal and Cro-Magnon.

UPPER PALEOLITHIC PEOPLES: THE FIRST MODERN HUMANS

Much as Neandertals were stereotyped as particularly brutish, the Cro-Magnons of Europe benefited from a stereotypical depiction epitomizing northern European ideals of beauty that went beyond what can be inferred from skeletal remains alone. This image found its way into popular culture, as in a best-selling novel and film from the 1970s, *The Clan of the Cave Bear.* In this book, the heroine is portrayed as a tall, slender, blonde-haired, blue-eyed beauty. But as Upper Paleolithic remains (from various parts of Africa and Asia as well as Europe) have become better understood, it has become clear that the differences from earlier populations have been greatly exaggerated. In the case of Europeans, for example, there is some resemblance between Cro-Magnons and later populations: in braincase shape, high broad forehead, narrow nasal openings, and common presence of chins. But Cro-Magnon faces were on average shorter and broader than those of modern Europeans, their brow ridges were a bit more prominent, and their teeth and jaws were as large as those of Neandertals. Some (a skull from the original Cro-Magnon site, for instance) even display the distinctive "occipital bun" of the Neandertals on the back of the skull.[1] Nor were they particularly tall, as their height of 5 feet 7 or 8 inches (170–175 centimeters) does not fall outside the Neandertal range.

Although the Cro-Magnons and Upper Paleolithic peoples from Africa and Asia are now routinely referred to as "anatomically modern," it is surprisingly difficult to be precise about what we mean by this. We think of people with brains the size of modern people, but this had already been achieved by archaic *H. sapiens.* Average brain size actually peaked in Neandertals at 10 percent larger than the contemporary human average. The reduction to today's average size correlates with a reduction in brawn, as bodies have become less massive overall. Modern faces and jaws are, by and large, less massive as well, but there are exceptions. For example, anthropologists Milford Wolpoff and Rachel Caspari have pointed out that any definition of modernity that excludes Neandertals also excludes substantial numbers of recent and living aboriginal Australians, although they are, quite obviously, a contemporary people. The fact is, no multidimensional diagnosis of "anatomical modernity" can be both exclusive of archaic populations and inclusive of all contemporary humans.[2]

The appearance of modern-sized brains in archaic *H. sapiens* no doubt was related to increased reliance on cultural adaptation. Ultimately, this emphasis on cultural adaptation led to the development of more complex tool kits. Technological improvements may also have reduced the intensity of selective pressures that had previously favored especially massive robust bodies, jaws, and teeth. With new emphasis on elongate tools having greater mechanical advantages, more effective techniques of hafting, a switch from thrusting to throwing spears, and development of net hunting, there was a marked reduction in overall muscularity. In addition, as the environ-

Upper Paleolithic The last part of the Old Stone Age, characterized by the emergence of more modern-looking hominins and an emphasis on the blade technique of tool making.
Cro-Magnons Europeans of the Upper Paleolithic after about 36,000 years ago.

[1] Brace, C. L. (1997). Cro-Magnons "R" us? *Anthropology Newsletter, 38*(8), 1.

[2] Wolpoff, M., & Caspari, R. (1997). *Race and human evolution* (pp. 344–345, 393). New York: Simon & Schuster.

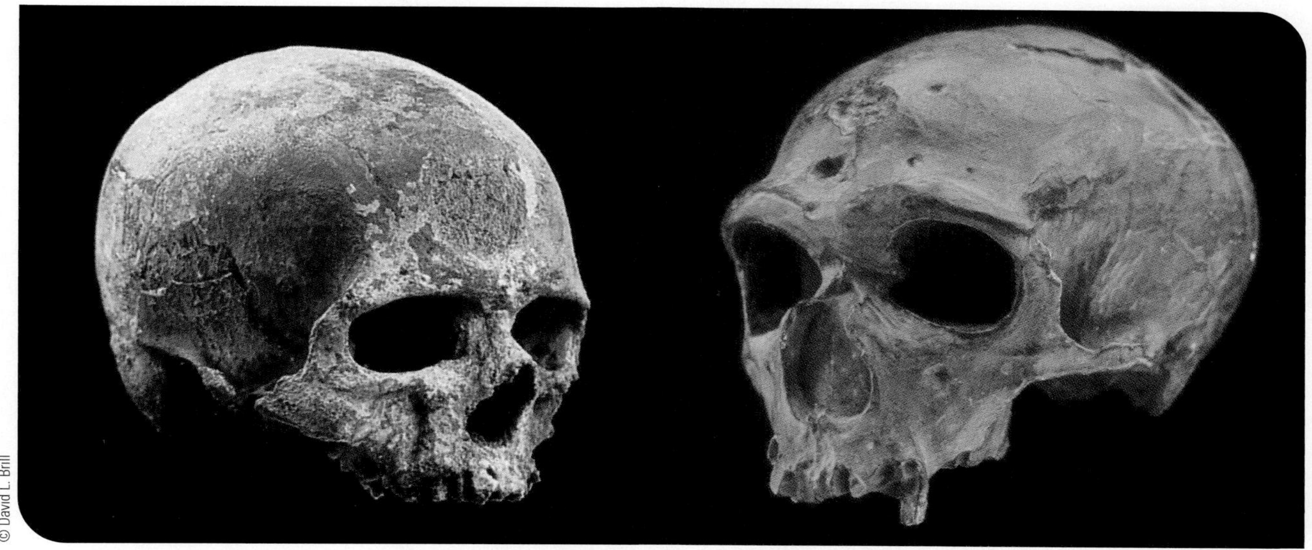

© David L. Brill

© David L. Brill

VISUAL COUNTERPOINT With a high forehead, the Cro-Magnon skull (left) is more like contemporary Europeans than the prominent brow ridge and sloping forehead seen in the Neandertal skull (right). In addition, cultural continuity in diet can be seen between the Cro-Magnon skull and local contemporary French people. The Cro-Magnon skull has evidence of a fungal infection, perhaps from eating tainted mushrooms. Mushrooms are a tremendous delicacy in this region of France to this day.

Jonesfilm/Warner Bros/The Kobal

In the novel and movie *Clan of the Cave Bear*, the "anatomically modern" heroine is depicted as a tall blonde beauty while Neandertals are depicted as dark and sloppy. These images conform both to the stereotypes about Neandertals and aesthetic standards in the western dominant culture.

ment changed from the extreme cold that prevailed in Eurasia during the last Ice Age to milder conditions, selective pressure for short stature as an adaptation to conserve body heat may have also diminished.

Upper Paleolithic Tools

The Upper Paleolithic was a time of great technological innovation. Upper Paleolithic tool kits are known for a predominance of blade tools, with flint flakes at least twice as long as they are wide. The earliest blade tools come from sites in Africa, but these tools do not make up the majority of the tool types until well into the Upper Paleolithic. New techniques of core preparation allowing more intensive production of highly standardized blades permitted the proliferation of this tool type. The toolmaker formed a cylindrical core, struck the blade off near the edge of the core, and repeated this procedure, going around the core in one direction until finishing near its center (Figure 10.1). The procedure is analogous to peeling long leaves off an artichoke. With

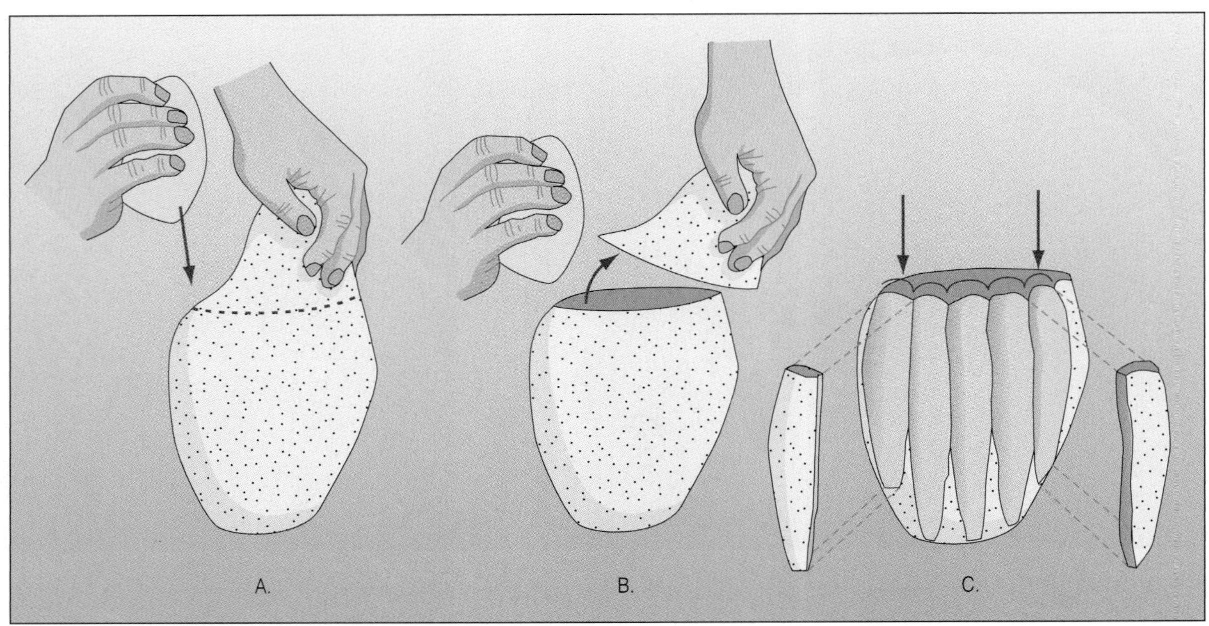

FIGURE 10.1
During the Upper Paleolithic, a new technique was used to manufacture blades. The stone is flaked to create a striking platform; long almost parallel-sided flakes then are struck around the sides, providing sharp-edged blades.

this **blade technique,** an Upper Paleolithic flint knapper could get 75 feet of working edge from a 2-pound core; a Mousterian knapper could get only 6 feet from the same-sized core.

Other efficient techniques of tool manufacture also came into common use at this time. One such method was **pressure flaking,** in which a bone, antler, or wooden tool was used to press rather than strike off small flakes as the final step in stone tool manufacture (Figure 10.2). The advantage of this technique was that the toolmaker had greater control over the final shape of the tool than is possible with percussion flaking alone. The so-called Solutrean laurel leaf bifaces found in Spain and France are examples of this technique. The longest of these tools is 13 inches in length but only about a quarter of an inch thick. Through pressure flaking, tools could be worked with great precision into a variety of final forms, and worn tools could be effectively resharpened over and over until they were too small for further use.

Another common Upper Paleolithic tool was the burin, although it too was invented earlier, in the Middle Paleolithic. **Burins,** with their chisel-like edges, facilitated the working of bone, horn, antler, and ivory into such useful things as fishhooks, harpoons, and eyed needles, all of which made life easier for *H. sapiens,* especially in colder northern regions where the ability to stitch together animal hides was particularly important for warmth. The spear-thrower, also known by its Aztec name atlatl, appeared at this time as well. Atlatls are wooden devices, one end of which is gripped in the hunter's hand, while the other end has a hole or hook, in or against which the end of the spear is placed. It is held so as to effectively extend the length of the hunter's arm, thereby increasing the velocity of the spear when thrown. Using a spear-thrower greatly added to the efficiency of the spear as a hunting tool. With handheld spears, hunters had to get close to their quarry to make

blade technique A technique of stone tool manufacture by which long, parallel-sided flakes are struck off the edges of a specially prepared core.
pressure flaking A technique of stone tool manufacture in which a bone, antler, or wooden tool is used to press, rather than strike off, small flakes from a piece of flint or similar stone.
burins Stone tools with chisel-like edges used for working bone and antler.

FIGURE 10.2
Two methods used for pressure flaking in which a bone, antler, or wooden tool is used to press rather than strike off small flakes.

The techniques of the Upper Paleolithic allowed for the manufacture of a wide variety of tool types. The finely wrought Solutrean bifaces of Europe (shaped like the leaf of a plant) were made using the pressure technique. Tools such as eyed needles and harpoons began to be manufactured out of bone as well.

the kill, and because many of the animals they hunted were large and fierce, this was a dangerous business. The need to approach closely, and the improbability of an instant kill, exposed the spear hunter to considerable risk. But with the spear-thrower, the effective killing distance was increased; experiments demonstrate that the effective killing distance of a spear when used with a spear-thrower is between 18 and 27 meters as opposed to less than a meter without.[3] The use of poison on spear tips, as employed by the Hadza hunters in Tanzania today, shortens this killing distance considerably, but it is not clear from the archaeological record when this innovation began. Also, the invention of tiny

[3]Frayer, D. W. (1981). Body size, weapon use, and natural selection in the European Upper Paleolithic and Mesolithic. *American Anthropologist, 83,* 58.

Spear-throwers allowed individual Upper Paleolithic people to throw spears at animals from a safe distance while still maintaining reasonable speed and accuracy. Contemporary enthusiasts of the Upper Paleolithic are throwing the atlatl at competitions such as this one organized by The World Atlatl Association.

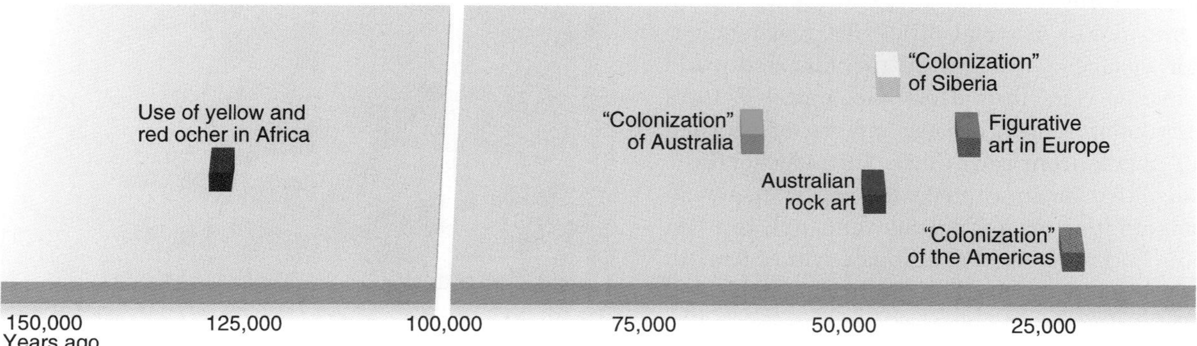

FIGURE 10.3

sharp stone blades for arrow tips shortens kill distances. Although the earliest examples of these "microliths" began during this time period in Africa, this technology was not widespread till the Mesolithic or Middle Stone Age, as will be described in detail in Chapter 11.

Another important innovation, net hunting, appeared some time between 29,000 and 22,000 years ago.[4] Knotted nets, made from the fibers of wild plants such as hemp or nettle, left their impression on the clay floors of huts when people walked on them. These impressions were baked in when the huts later burned, which is how we know that nets existed. Their use accounts for the high number of hare, fox, and other small mammal and bird bones at archaeological sites. Like historically known and contemporary net hunters, such as the Mbuti of the Congo, everyone—men, women, and children—probably participated, frightening animals with loud noises to drive them to where hunters were stationed with their nets. In this way, large amounts of meat could be amassed without requiring great speed or strength on the part of the hunters.

A further improvement of hunting techniques came with the invention of the bow and arrow, which appeared first in Africa, but not until the end of the Upper Paleolithic in Europe. The greatest advantage of the bow is that it increases the distance between hunter and prey; beyond 24 meters, the accuracy and penetration of a spear thrown with a spear-thrower is not very good, whereas even a poor bow will shoot an arrow further, with greater accuracy and penetrating power. A good bow is effective even at nearly 91 meters. Thus, hunters were able to maintain more distance between themselves and dangerous prey, dramatically decreasing their chances of being seriously injured by an animal fighting for its life as well as decreasing the chance of startling an animal and triggering its flight.

Upper Paleolithic peoples not only had better tools but also a greater diversity of types than earlier peoples. The highly developed Upper Paleolithic kit included tools for use during different seasons, and regional variation in tool kits was greater than ever before. Thus, it is really impossible to speak of a single Upper Paleolithic culture even in Europe, a relatively small and isolated region compared to Asia and Africa. For foot nomads, the size of Europe and the rest of the inhabited world for that matter were formidable. Geological features such as mountain ranges, oceans, and glaciers isolated groups of people from each other. To understand the Upper Paleolithic, one must make note of the many different traditions that made it possible for people to adapt ever more specifically to the various environments in which they were living. Just how proficient people had become at securing a livelihood is indicated by bone yards containing thousands of skeletons. At Solutré in France, for example, Upper Paleolithic hunters killed 10,000 horses; at Predmosti in the Czech Republic, they were responsible for the deaths of 1,000 mammoths. The favored big game of European hunters, however, was reindeer, which they killed in even greater numbers.

[4]Pringle, H. (1997). Ice Age communities may be earliest known net hunters. *Science, 277,* 1,203.

UPPER PALEOLITHIC ART

Although the creativity of Upper Paleolithic peoples is evident in the tools and weapons they made, it is nowhere more evident than in their outburst of artistic expression. Some have argued that this was made possible by a newly evolved biological ability to manipulate symbols and make images. However, the modern-sized brains of archaic *H. sapiens* and increasingly compelling evidence of the presence of language or behaviors involving symbolism—such as burials—undercut this notion. Like agriculture, which came later (see the next chapter), the artistic explosion may have been no more than a consequence of innovations made by a people who had the capacity to make them for tens of thousands of years already.

In fact, just as many of the distinctive tools that were commonly used in Upper Paleolithic times first appear in the Middle Paleolithic, so too do objects of art. In Southwest Asia, a crude figurine of volcanic tuff is some 250,000 years old.[5] If carved, the fact that it exists at all indicates that people had the ability to carve all sorts of things from wood, a substance easier to work than volcanic tuff but rarely preserved for long periods of time. Furthermore, ocher "crayons" from Middle Paleolithic contexts in various parts of the world must have been used to decorate or mark. In southern Africa,

[5]Appenzeller, T. (1998). Art: Evolution or revolution? *Science, 282,* 1,452.

Upper Paleolithic artists frequently combined artistic expression with practical function, as in this spear-thrower (atlatl) ornamented by two (headless) ibexes from Enlene cave, France.

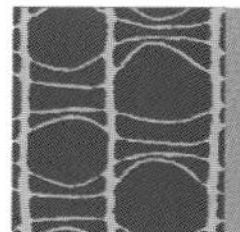

Anthropology Applied: Stone Tools for Modern Surgeons

When anthropologist Irven DeVore of Harvard University was to have some minor melanomas removed from his face, he did not leave it up to the surgeon to supply his own scalpels. Instead, he had graduate student John Shea make a scalpel. Making a blade of obsidian (a naturally occurring volcanic "glass") by the same techniques used by Upper Paleolithic people to make blades, he then hafted this in a wooden handle, using melted pine resin as glue and then lashing it with sinew. After the procedure, the surgeon reported that the obsidian scalpel was superior to metal ones.[a]

DeVore was not the first to undergo surgery in which stone scalpels were used. In 1975, Don Crabtree, then at Idaho State University, prepared the scalpels that his surgeon would use in Crabtree's heart surgery. In 1980, Payson Sheets at the University of Colorado prepared obsidian scalpels that were used successfully in eye surgery. And in 1986, David Pokotylo of the Museum of Anthropology at the University of British Columbia underwent reconstructive surgery on his hand with blades he himself had made (the hafting was done by his museum colleague, Len McFarlane).

The reason for these uses of scalpels modeled on ancient stone tools is that the anthropologists realized that obsidian is superior in almost every way to materials normally used to make scalpels: It is 210 to 1,050 times sharper than surgical steel, 100 to 500 times sharper than a razor blade, and 3 times sharper than a diamond blade (which not only costs much more, but cannot be made with more than 3 mm of cutting edge). Obsidian blades are easier to cut with and do less damage in the process (under a microscope, incisions made with the sharpest steel blades show torn ragged edges and are littered with bits of displaced flesh).[b] As a consequence, the surgeon has better control over what she or he is doing, and the incisions heal faster with less scarring and pain. Because of the superiority of obsidian scalpels, Sheets went so far as to form a corporation in partnership with Boulder, Colorado, eye surgeon Dr. Firmon Hardenbergh. Together, they developed a means of producing cores of uniform size from molten glass, as well as a machine to detach blades from the cores. ■ ■ ■

[a]Shreeve, J. (1995). *The Neandertal enigma: Solving the mystery of modern human origins* (p. 134). New York: William Morrow.

[b]Sheets, P. D. (1987). Dawn of a New Stone Age in eye surgery. In R. J. Sharer & W. Ashmore (Eds.), *Archaeology: Discovering our past* (p. 231). Palo Alto, CA: Mayfield.

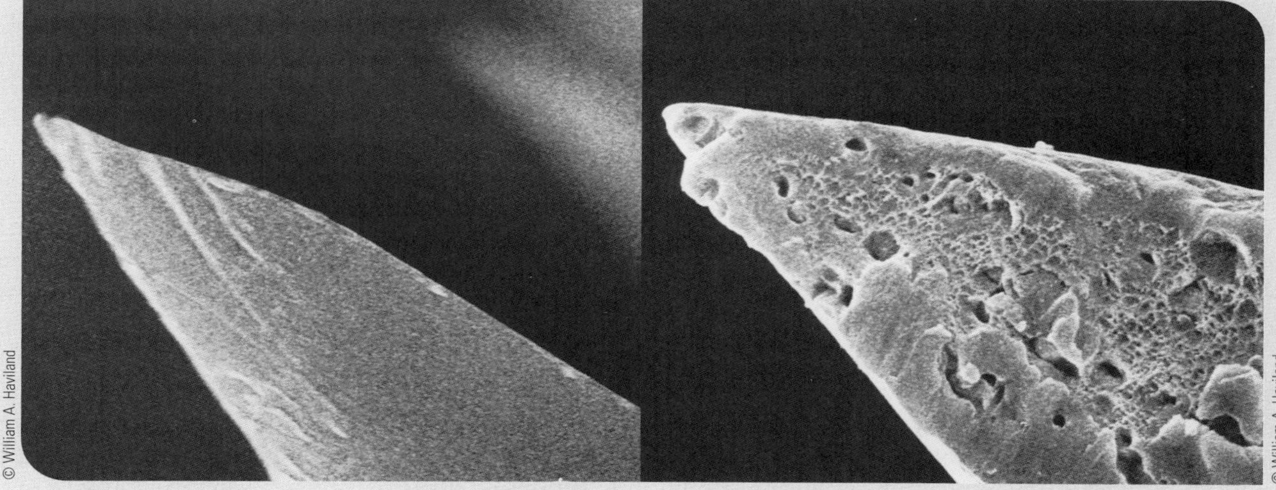

© William A. Haviland

VISUAL COUNTERPOINT These electron micrographs of the tips of an obsidian blade (left) and a modern steel scalpel illustrate the superiority of the obsidian.

for example, regular use of yellow and red ocher goes back 130,000 years, with some evidence as old as 200,000 years.[6] Perhaps pigments were used on people's bodies, as well as objects, as the 50,000-year-old mammoth-tooth *churinga* discussed and illustrated in Chapter 9 might suggest.

That there was music in the lives of Upper Paleolithic peoples is indicated by the presence of bone flutes and whistles in sites, some up to 30,000 years old. But again, such instruments may have their origin in Middle Paleolithic prototypes, such as the probable "Neandertal flute" discussed in Chapter 9. Although we cannot be sure just where and when it happened, some genius discovered that bows could be used not just for killing, but to make music as well. Because the

[6]Barham, L. S. (1998). Possible early pigment use in south-central Africa. *Current Anthropology, 39,* 709.

© Alexander Marshack

Erich Lessing/Art Resources, NY

VISUAL COUNTERPOINT The Venus figurine tradition may have a very long history. Crude though it may be, this piece of tuff (left), carved some 250,000 years ago, looks like a woman if viewed from the right angle. It was found in 1980 on the Golan Heights in the Middle East. Some researchers do not accept this tuff as art, suggesting instead that despite its carved surface, natural forces are primarily responsible for its "female" form. The Venus figurines from the Upper Paleolithic, such as this one, were widespread and highly stylized.

bow and arrow is an Upper Paleolithic invention, the musical bow likely is as well. We do know that the musical bow is the oldest of all stringed instruments, and its invention ultimately made possible the development of all of the stringed instruments with which we are familiar today.

The earliest evidence of figurative pictures goes back 32,000 years in Europe although they do not become common until much later. Pictorial "art" is probably equally old in Africa. Both engravings and paintings are known from many rock shelters and outcrops in southern Africa, where they continued to be made by Bushman peoples into the present. Scenes feature both humans and animals, depicted with extraordinary skill, often in association with geometric and other abstract motifs. People still have the seemingly irresistible urge to add to existing rock paintings, or to create new sites for what we may today call graffiti.

entoptic phenomena Bright pulsating forms that are generated by the central nervous system and seen in states of trance.

Because this rock art tradition continues unbroken into the present, it has been possible to discover what this art means. There is a close connection between the art and shamanism, and many scenes depict visions seen in states of trance. Distortions in the art, usually of human figures, represent sensations felt by individuals in a state of trance, whereas the geometric designs depict illusions that originate in the central nervous system in altered states of consciousness. These **entoptic phenomena** are luminous grids, dots, zigzags, and other designs that seem to shimmer, pulsate, rotate, and expand and are seen as one enters a state of trance (sufferers of migraines experience similar hallucinations). In many recent cultures, geometric designs are used as symbolic expressions of genealogical patterns, records of origins, and maps to achieve rebirth.[7] The animals depicted in this art, often with startling realism, are not the ones most often eaten. Rather, they are powerful beasts like the eland (a large African antelope), and this power is important to shamans—individuals skilled at manipulat-

[7]Schuster, C., & Carpenter, E. (1996). *Patterns that connect: Social symbolism in ancient and tribal art*. New York: Harry N. Abrams.

© Anthony Bannister; Gallo Images/Corbis

In South Africa, rock art, like these paintings from Namibia, depict things seen by dancers while in states of trance. Simple geometric designs such as zigzags, notches, curves, and dots (as on the right hand figure) are common in these paintings.

ing supernatural powers and spirits for human benefit—who try to harness it for their rain-making and other rituals.

Rock art in Australia goes back at least 45,000 years; the earliest examples consist entirely of entoptic motifs. Later art, as seen in the chapter opening photograph, is largely figurative. But the most famous Upper Paleolithic art is that of Europe, largely because most students of prehistoric art are themselves of European background. The earliest of this art took the form of sculpture and engravings often portraying such animals as reindeer, horses, bears, and ibexes. There are also numerous portrayals of voluptuous women with exaggerated sexual and reproductive characteristics. Many appear to be pregnant, and some are shown in birthing postures. These so-called Venus figures have been found at sites from southwestern France to as far east as Siberia. Made of stone, ivory, antler, or baked clay, they differ little in style from place to place, testifying to the sharing of ideas over vast distances. Although some have interpreted the Venuses as objects associated with a fertility cult, others suggest that they may have been exchanged to cement alliances among groups. Art historian LeRoy McDermott has suggested that the Venus figurines are "ordinary women's views of their own bodies" and the earliest examples of self-representation.[8] Paleolithic archaeologist Margaret Conkey (see Anthropologist of Note) opened the door to such interpretations through her work combining gender theory and feminist theory with the science of archaeology.

Most spectacular are the paintings on the walls of 200 or so caves in southern France and northern Spain, the oldest of which date from about 32,000 years ago. Most common are visually accurate portrayals of Ice Age mammals, including bison, bulls, horses, mammoths, and stags, often painted one on top of another.

[8]McDermott, L. (1996). Self-representation in Upper Paleolithic female figurines. *Current Anthropology, 37* ,227–276.

VISUAL COUNTERPOINT
According to art historian LeRoy McDermott, the distortions and exaggerations of the female form visible in the Venus figurines are a result of perspective taken by female artists representing their own bodies.

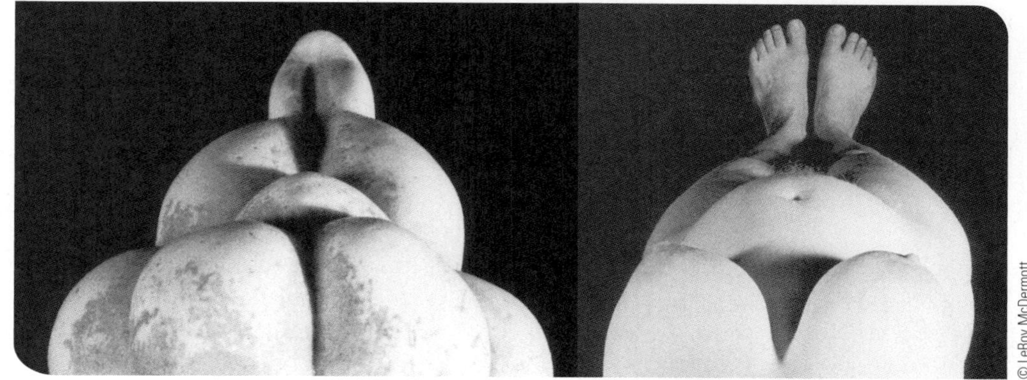

© LeRoy McDermott

Anthropologists of Note

Margaret Conkey (1943–)

Throughout her career, Margaret Conkey has blended the science of archaeology with theoretical perspectives from feminist scholarship and gender studies. Her goal has not been to create a separate "feminist archaeology" but rather to practice archaeology as a feminist. This consists of asking different kinds of research questions as well as challenging the ways that gender affects the practice of archaeology. Conkey attended Mount Holyoke College, graduating in 1965. She is currently professor in the anthropology department at the University of California, Berkeley. She is co-author (with Joan Gero) of the major 1991 work that brought feminist perspectives into archaeology: *Engendering Archaeology.* Recently her work in this field brought her recognition as one of the "Fifty Most Important Women in Science," named by *Discover* magazine.

Courtesy of Theresa Babineau

With a particular interest in the Upper Paleolithic art of Europe, Conkey has spent decades challenging the traditional notion that Paleolithic art was made by male artists as an expression of spiritual beliefs related to hunting activities. She emphasizes that many reconstructions of behavior in the past rely upon contemporary gender norms to fill in blanks left in the archaeological record. In other words, she is interested in the role of gender today in shaping the reconstruction of gender in the past. In the archaeological research she conducts, she is looking for clues about gender in the deep past, evidence that is not shaped by gender stereotypes from the present. For example, she is currently directing a field project called 'between the caves" in the French Midi-Pyrenees. The goal of this large-scale project is to provide a context for the art and material culture of this region's Cro-Magnons through surveying the regions between the caves. With a multidisciplinary, international team, she aims to reconstruct daily life and the environments in which Upper Paleolithic people expressed themselves through art.

Although well represented in other media, humans are not commonly portrayed in cave paintings, nor are scenes or depictions of events at all common. Instead, the animals are often abstracted from nature and rendered two-dimensionally—no small achievement for these early artists. Sometimes the artists made use of bulges and other features of the rock to impart a more three-dimensional feeling. Frequently, the paintings are in hard-to-get-at places while suitable surfaces in more accessible places remain untouched. In some caves, the lamps by which the artists worked have been found; these are spoon-shaped objects of sandstone in which animal fat was burned. Experimentation has shown that such lamps would have provided adequate illumination over several hours.

American Museum of Natural History

Upper Paleolithic artists created images on the walls of caves using light from sandstone lamps for burning animal fat. This lamp was found in Lascaux Cave in France.

MEDIATREK
To get a visual treat featuring cave and rock art from Australia to Africa, some of which dates back to the Paleolithic, go to MediaTrek 10.1 on the companion Web site or CD-ROM.

The techniques used by Upper Paleolithic peoples to create their cave paintings were unraveled a decade ago through the experimental work of Michel Lorblanchet. Interestingly, they turn out to be the same ones used by aboriginal rock painters in Australia. Lorblanchet's experiments are described in the following Original Study by science writer Roger Lewin.

Original Study

Paleolithic Paint Job

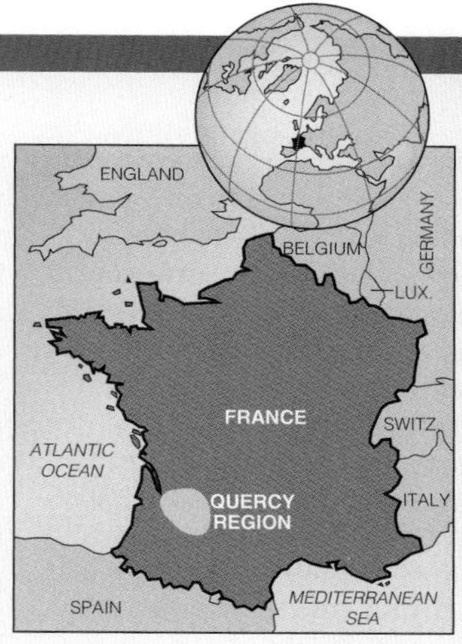

Lorblanchet's recent bid to re-create one of the most important Ice Age images in Europe was an affair of the heart as much as the head. "I tried to abandon my skin of a modern citizen, tried to experience the feeling of the artist, to enter the dialogue between the rock and the man," he explains. Every day for a week in the fall of 1990 he drove the 20 miles from his home in the medieval village of Cajarc into the hills above the river Lot. There, in a small, practically inaccessible cave, he transformed himself into an Upper Paleolithic painter.

And not just any Upper Paleolithic painter, but the one who 18,400 years ago crafted the dotted horses inside the famous cave of Pech Merle.

You can still see the original horses in Pech Merle's vast underground geologic splendor. You enter through a narrow passageway and soon find yourself gazing across a grand cavern to where the painting seems to hang in the gloom. "Outside, the landscape is very different from the one the Upper Paleolithic people saw," says Lorblanchet. "But in here, the landscape is the same as it was more than 18,000 years ago. You see what the Upper Paleolithic people experienced." No matter where you look in this cavern, the eye is drawn back to the panel of horses.

The two horses face away from each other, rumps slightly overlapping, their outlines sketched in black. The animal on the right seems to come alive as it merges with a crook in the edge of the panel, the perfect natural shape for a horse's head. But the impression of naturalism quickly fades as the eye falls on the painting's dark dots. There are more than 200 of them, deliberately distributed within and below the bodies and arcing around the right-hand horse's head and mane. More cryptic still are a smattering of red dots and half-circles and the floating outline of a fish. The surrealism is completed by six disembodied human hands stenciled above and below the animals.

Lorblanchet began thinking about re-creating the horses after a research trip to Australia over a decade ago. Not only is Australia a treasure trove of rock art, but its aboriginal people are still creating it. "In Queensland I learned how people painted by spitting pigment onto the rock," he recalls. "They spat paint and used their hand, a piece of cloth, or a feather as a screen to create different lines and other effects. Elsewhere in Australia people used chewed twigs as paintbrushes, but in Queensland the spitting technique worked best." The rock surfaces there were too uneven for extensive brushwork, he adds—just as they are in Quercy.

This spotted horse in the French cave of Pech Merle was painted by an Upper Paleolithic artist.

When Lorblanchet returned home he looked at the Quercy paintings with a new eye. Sure enough, he began seeing the telltale signs of spit-painting—lines with edges that were sharply demarcated on one side and fuzzy on the other, as if they had been airbrushed—instead of the brushstrokes he and others had assumed were there. Could you produce lines that were crisp on both edges with the same technique, he wondered, and perhaps dots too? Archeologists had long recognized that hand stencils, which are common in prehistoric art, were produced by spitting paint around a hand held to the wall. But no one had thought that entire animal images could be created this way. Before he could test his ideas, however, Lorblanchet had to find a suitable rock face-the original horses were painted on a roughly vertical panel 13 feet across and 6 feet high. With the help of a speleologist, he eventually found a rock face in a remote cave high in the hills and set to work.

Following the aboriginal practices he had witnessed, Lorblanchet first made a light outline sketch of the horses with a charred stick. Then he prepared black pigment for the painting. "My intention had been to use manganese dioxide, as the Pech Merle painter did," says Lorblanchet, referring to one of the minerals ground up for paint by the early artists. "But I was advised that manganese is somewhat toxic, so I used wood charcoal instead." (Charcoal was used as

[CONTINUED]

pigment by Paleolithic painters in other caves, so Lorblanchet felt he could justify his concession to safety.) To turn the charcoal into paint, Lorblanchet ground it with a limestone block, put the powder in his mouth, and diluted it to the right consistency with saliva and water. For red pigment he used ocher from the local iron-rich clay.

He started with the dark mane of the right hand horse. "I spat a series of dots and fused them together to represent tufts of hair," he says, unself-consciously reproducing the spitting action as he talks. "Then I painted the horse's back by blowing the pigment below my hand held so"—he holds his hand flat against the rock with his thumb tucked in to form a straight line—"and used it like a stencil to produce a sharp upper edge and a diffused lower edge. You get an illusion of the animal's rounded flank this way."

He experimented as he went. "You see the angular rump?" he says, pointing to the original painting. "I reproduced that by holding my hand perpendicular to the rock, with my palm slightly bent, and I spat along the edge formed by my hand and the rock." He found he could produce sharp lines, such as those in the tail and in the upper hind leg, by spitting into the gap between parallel hands. The belly demanded more ingenuity; he spat paint into a V-shape formed by his two splayed hands, rubbed it into a curved swath to shape the belly's outline, then finger-painted short protruding lines to suggest the animals' shaggy hair. Neatly outlined dots, he found, could not be made by blowing a thin jet of charcoal onto the wall. He had to spit pigment through a hole made in an animal skin. "I spent seven hours a day for a week," he says. "Puff . . . puff . . . puff. . . . It was exhausting, particularly because there was carbon monoxide in the cave. But you experience something special, painting like that. You feel you are breathing the image onto the rock—projecting your spirit from the deepest part of your body onto the rock surface."

Was that what the Paleolithic painter felt when creating this image? "Yes, I know it doesn't sound very scientific," Lorblanchet says of his highly personal style of investigation, "but the intellectual games of the structuralists haven't got us very far, have they? Studying rock art shouldn't be an intellectual game. It is about understanding humanity. That's why I believe the experimental approach is valid in this case."

(By R. Lewin. (1993). Paleolithic paint job. Discover, *14(7), 67-69.)* Copyright ©1993 The Walt Disney Co. Reprinted with permission of Discover Magazine.

Theories to account for the early European cave art are difficult because they so often depend on conjectural and subjective interpretations. Some have argued that it is art for art's sake; but if that is so, why were animals so often painted over one another, and why were they so often placed in inaccessible places? The latter might suggest that they were for ceremonial purposes and that the caves served as religious sanctuaries. One suggestion is that the animals were drawn to ensure success in the hunt, another that their depiction was seen as a way to promote fertility and increase the size of the herds on which humans depended. In Altamira cave in northern Spain, for example, the art shows a pervasive concern for the sexual reproduction of the bison.[9] In cave art generally, though, the animals painted show little relationship to those most frequently hunted. Furthermore, there are few depictions of animals being hunted or killed, nor are there depictions of animals copulating or with exaggerated sexual parts as there are in the Venus figures. Another suggestion is that rites by which youngsters were initiated into adulthood took place in the painted galleries. In support of this idea, footprints, most of which are small, have been found in the clay floors of several caves, and in one, they even circle a modeled clay bison. The animals painted, so this argument goes, may have had to do with knowledge being transmitted from the elders to the youths. Furthermore, the transmission of information might be implied by countless so-called signs, apparently abstract designs that accompany much Upper Paleolithic art. Some have interpreted these as tallies of animals killed, a reckoning of time according to a lunar calendar, or both.

Musée national de Préhistoire

The dedication of Upper Paleolithic artists to express themselves creatively and perhaps spiritually is exemplified in the engravings in the Combarelles in France. Here the cave is a narrow snakelike passage with low ceilings into which artists crept on hands and knees in order to create hundreds of detailed engravings such as this feline.

These abstract designs, including such ones as the spots on the Pech Merle horses, suggest yet another possibility. For the most part, these are just like the entoptic designs seen by subjects in experiments dealing with altered states of consciousness and that are so consistently present in the rock art of southern Africa.

[9]Halverson, J. (1989). Review of the book *Altimira revisited and other essays on early art. American Antiquity, 54,* 883.

© Randall White

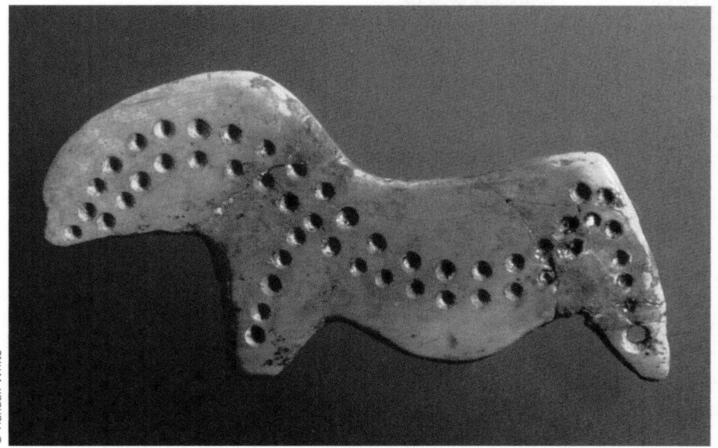

Dots are a common entopic form, and in art depicting visions seen in trance, lines of dots are not uncommon, as on this 24,000-year-old ivory pendant from Sungir, Russia.

Furthermore, the rock art of southern Africa shows the same painting of new images over older ones, as well as the same sort of fixation on large, powerful animals instead of the ones most often eaten. Thus, the cave art of Europe may well represent the same depictions of trance experiences, painted after the fact. Consistent with this interpretation, the isolation of the cave and the shimmering light on the cave walls themselves are conducive to the sort of sensory distortion that can induce trance.

© Claudio Vazquez

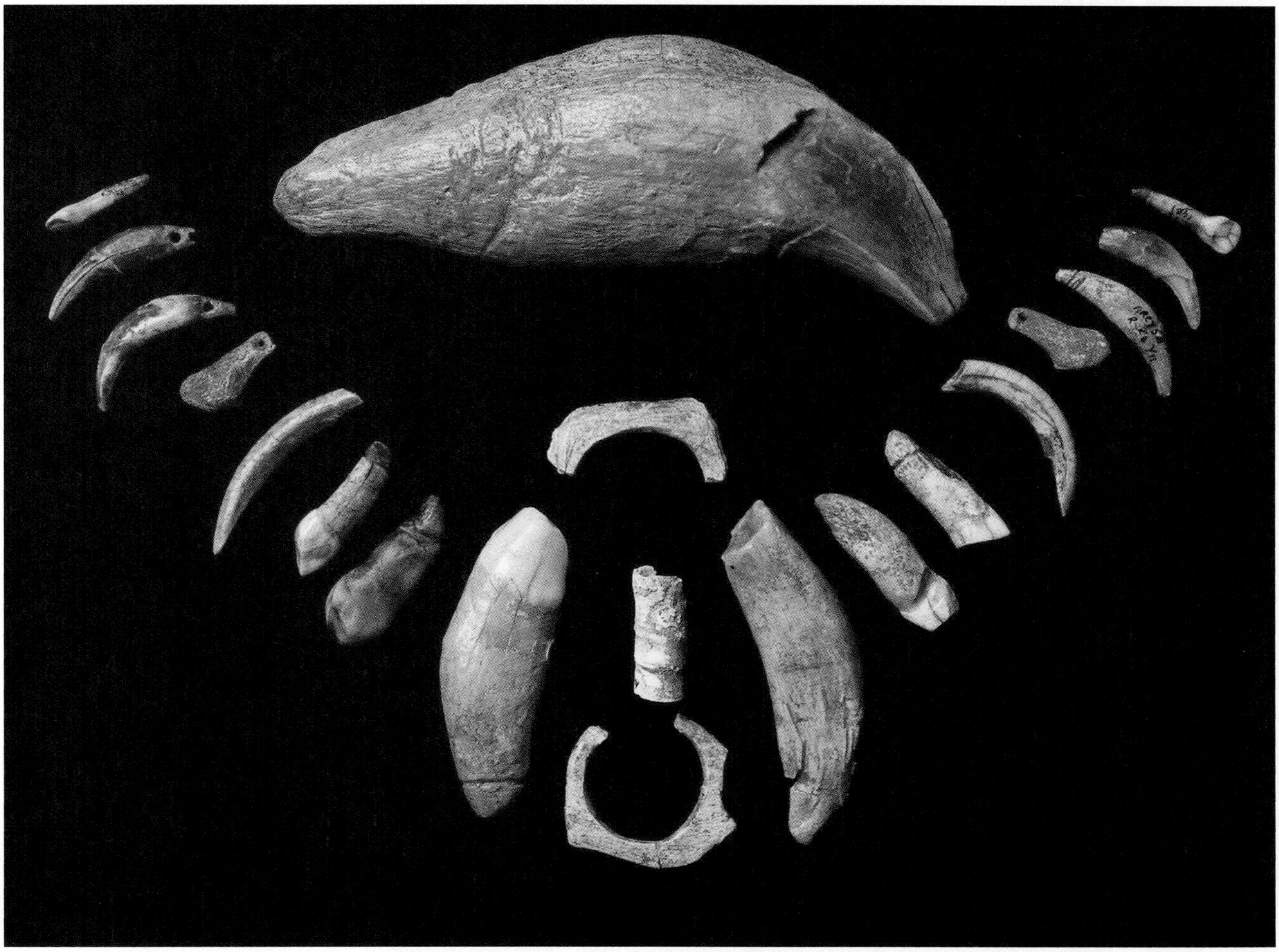

Pendants and beads for personal adornment became common in the Upper Paleolithic. In Europe, most were made by Cro-Magnons, but some—like these shown here—were made by Neandertals. The earliest undisputed items of personal adornment are some 40,000-year-old beads from Africa made from ostrich egg shell.

MEDIATREK

In order to protect the magnificent cave art at Lascaux cave, only six people per day can go inside the original while the French government has built an entire replica of the site to share this national treasure more widely. To take a virtual tour of Lascaux, go to MediaTrek 10.2 on the companion Web site or CD-ROM.

Artistic expression, whatever its purpose may have been, was not confined to rock surfaces and portable objects alone. Upper Paleolithic peoples also ornamented their bodies with necklaces of perforated animal teeth, shells, beads of bone, stone, and ivory; rings; bracelets; and anklets. Clothing, too, was adorned with beads. Quite a lot of art was probably also executed in perishable materials such as wood carving, paintings on bark, or animal skins, which have not been preserved. Thus, the rarity or absence of Upper Paleolithic art in some parts of the inhabited world may be more apparent than real, as people elsewhere worked with materials unlikely to survive so long in the archaeological record.

OTHER ASPECTS OF UPPER PALEOLITHIC CULTURE

Upper Paleolithic peoples lived not only in caves and rock shelters, but also in structures built out in the open. In Ukraine, for example, the remains have been found of sizable settlements, in which huts were built on frameworks of intricately stacked mammoth bones. Where the ground was frozen, cobblestones were heated and placed in the earth to sink in, thereby providing sturdy, dry floors. Their hearths, no longer shallow depressions or flat surfaces that radiated back little heat, were instead stone-lined pits that conserved heat for extended periods and made for more efficient cooking. For the outdoors, they had the same sort of tailored clothing worn in historic times by arctic and subarctic people. And they engaged in long-distance trade, as indicated, for example, by the presence of seashells and Baltic amber at sites several hundred kilometers from the sources of these materials. Although Middle Paleolithic peoples also made use of rare and distant materials, they did not do so with the regularity seen in the Upper Paleolithic.

THE SPREAD OF UPPER PALEOLITHIC PEOPLES

Upper Paleolithic peoples expanded into regions previously uninhabited by their archaic forebears. Colonization of Siberia began about 42,000 years ago, although it took something like 10,000 years before humans reached the northeastern part of that region. Much earlier, possibly by at least 60,000 years ago, people managed to get to Australia, Tasmania, and New Guinea, then connected to one another in a single land-

Reconstruction of an Upper Paleolithic hut with walls of interlocked mammoth mandibles.

mass called the **Sahul** (Figure 10.4).[10] To do this, they had to use some kind of watercraft because the Sahul was separated from the islands (which are geologically a part of the Asian landmass) of Java, Sumatra, Borneo, and Bali. At times of maximum glaciation and low sea levels, these islands were joined to one another in a single landmass called **Sunda,** but a deep ocean trench (called the Wallace trench, after Alfred Russel Wallace who, as described in Chapter 2, discovered natural selection at the same time as Charles Darwin) always separated Sunda and Sahul. Anthropologist Joseph Birdsell suggested several routes of island hopping and seafaring to make the cross between these landmasses.[11] Each of these routes still involves crossing open water without land visible on the horizon. The earliest known site in New Guinea dates to 40,000 years ago. Sites in Australia are dated to even earlier, but these dates are especially contentious because they relate back to the critical question about the relationship between anatomical modernity and the presence of humanlike culture discussed in Chapter 9. Early dates for the habitation of the Sahul indicate that archaic *Homo sapiens* rather than anatomically modern forms possessed the cultural capacity for navigation to the Sahul. Once in Australia, these people created some of the world's

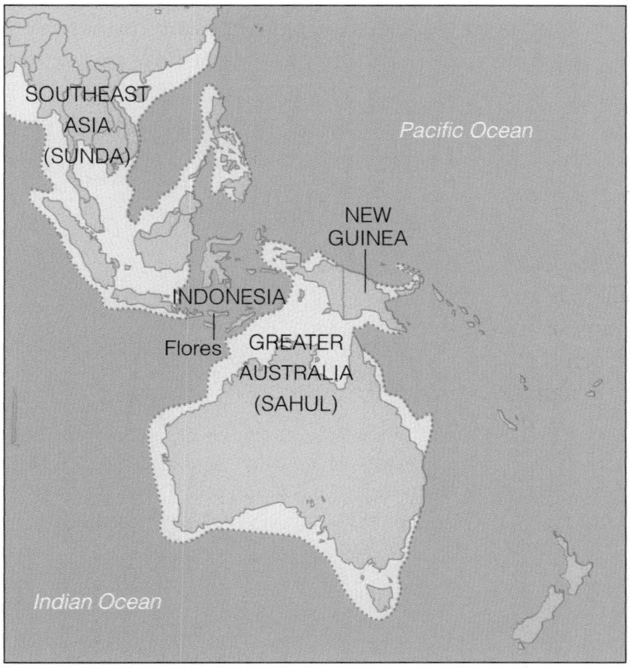

FIGURE 10.4
Habitation of Australia and New Guinea (joined together with Tasmania as a single landmass called Sahul) was dependent upon travel across the open ocean even at times of maximum glaciation when sea levels were low. This figure represents the coastlines of Australia New Guinea, and Tasmania—now and in the past. As in many other parts of the world, as sea levels rose with melting glaciers, sites of early human habitation were submerged under water.

Don Johanson, Institute of Human Origins

Willandra Lakes, a fossil lake region located in southeastern Australia, has provided some of the oldest evidence of human occupation of the continent and its symbolic activity. Some specimens from this region have a robust appearance reminiscent of earlier *Homo erectus* remains while others appear somewhat more anatomically modern.

[10] Rice, P. (2000). Paleoanthropology 2000—part 1. *General Anthropology, 7*(1), 11; Zimmer, C. (1999). New date for the dawn of dream time. *Science, 284,* 1,243.

[11] Birdsell, J. H. (1977). The recalibration of a paradigm for the first peopling of Greater Australia. In J. Allen, J. Golson, & R. Jones (Eds.), *Sunda and Sahul: Prehistoric studies in Southeast Asia, Melanesia, and Australia* (pp. 113–167). New York: Academic Press.

Sahul The greater Australian landmass including Australia, New Guinea, and Tasmania. At times of maximum glaciation and low sea levels, these areas were continuous.
Sunda The combined landmass of the contemporary islands of Java, Sumatra, Borneo, and Bali that was continuous with mainland Southeast Asia at times of low sea levels corresponding to maximum glaciation.

earliest sophisticated rock art, perhaps some 10,000 to 15,000 years earlier than the more famous European cave paintings.

Interestingly, considerable physical variation is seen in Australian fossil specimens from this period. Some specimens have the high forehead characteristic of anatomical modernity while others possess traits providing excellent evidence of continuity between living aboriginal people and the earlier *Homo erectus* and archaic *Homo sapiens* fossils from Indonesia. Willandra Lakes, the fossil lake region of southeastern Australia far from where the earliest archaeological evidence of human habitation of the continent was found, is particularly rich with fossils. The variation present in these fossils illustrates the problems inherent with making a one-to-one correspondence between the skull of a certain shape and cultural capabilities.

Other evidence for sophisticated ritual activity in early Australia is provided by the burial of a man at least 40,000 and possibly 60,000 years ago from the Willandra Lakes region. His body was positioned with his fingers intertwined around one another in the region of his penis, and red ocher had been scattered over the body. It may be that this pigment had more than symbolic value; for example, its iron salts have antiseptic and deodorizing properties, and there are recorded instances in which red ocher is associated with prolonging life and is used medicinally to treat particular conditions or infections. One historically known aboriginal Australian society is reported to have used ocher to heal wounds, scars, and burns. A person with internal pain was covered with the substance and placed in the sun to promote sweating.

As in many parts of the world, paleoanthropologists conducting research on human evolution in Australia are essentially constructing a view of the history of people and the world that conflicts with the beliefs of Australian aborigines. The story of human evolution is utterly dependent on Western conceptions of time, relationships established through genetics, and a definition of what it means to be human. While aboriginal creation stories account for human origins very differently, paleoanthropologists in Australia have worked closely with and advocated for Australian aboriginal peoples while conducting their research on evolution.

Just when people arrived in the Americas has been a matter of lively debate, but securely dated remains from Monte Verde, a site in south-central Chile, place people in southern South America by 12,500 years ago, if not earlier. Assuming the first populations spread from Siberia to Alaska, linguist Johanna Nichols suggests that the first people to arrive in North America did so by 20,000 years ago. She bases this estimate on the time it took various other languages to spread from their homelands—including Eskimo languages in the Arctic, and Athabaskan languages from interior western Canada to New Mexico and Arizona (Navajo). Her conclusion is that it would have taken at least 7,000 years for people to reach south-central Chile.[12]

The conventional wisdom has long been that the first people spread into North America over dry land that connected Siberia to Alaska. This so-called land bridge was a consequence of the buildup of great continental glaciers. As these ice masses grew, there was a worldwide lowering of sea levels, causing an emergence of land in places like the Bering Strait where seas today are shallow. Thus, Alaska became, in effect, an eastward extension of Siberia (Figure 10.5).

Although ancient Siberians did indeed spread eastward, it is now clear that their way south was blocked by massive glaciers until 13,000 years ago at the earliest.[13] By then, people were already living further south in the Americas. Thus the question of how people first

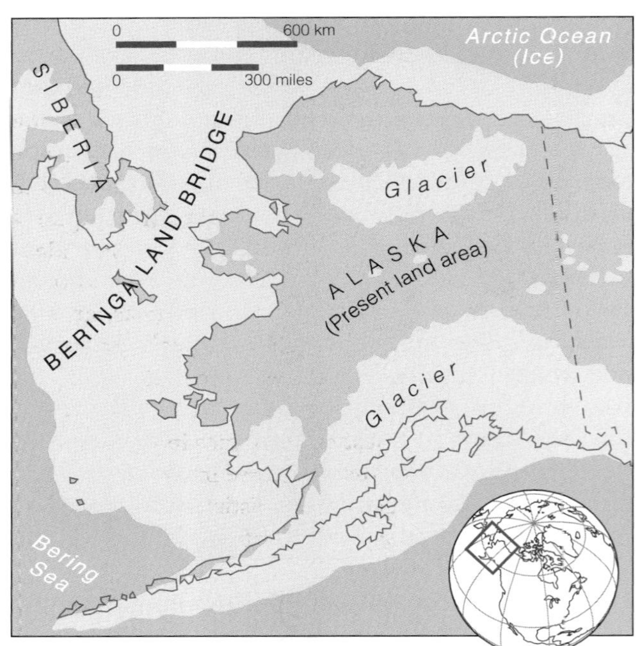

FIGURE 10.5

The Arctic conditions and glaciers in northeastern Asia and northwestern North America provided opportunity and challenges for ancient people spreading to the Americas. On the one hand, the Arctic conditions provided a land bridge (Beringa) between the continents, but on the other hand, these harsh environmental conditions pose considerable challenges to humans. Ancient people may have also come to the Americas by sea. Once in North America, glaciers spanning a good portion of the continent determined the areas open to habitation.

[12]The first Americans, ca. 20,000 B.C. (1998). *Discover, 19*(6), 24.

[13]Marshall, E. (2001). Preclovis sites fight for acceptance. *Science, 291*, 1,732.

came to this hemisphere has been reopened. One possibility is that, like the first Australians, the first Americans may have come by boat or rafts, perhaps traveling between islands or ice-free pockets of coastline, from as far away as the Japanese islands and down North America's northwest coast. Hints of such voyages are provided by a handful of North American skeletons that bear a closer resemblance to the aboriginal Ainu people of northern Japan and their forebears than they do to other Asians or contemporary Native Americans. Unfortunately, because sea levels were lower than they are today, coastal sites used by early voyagers would now be under water.

The picture currently emerging, then, is of people, who may not have looked like modern Native Americans, arriving by boats or rafts and spreading southward and eastward over time. In fact, contact back and forth between North America and Siberia never stopped. In all probability, it became more common as the glaciers melted away. As a consequence, through gene flow as well as later arrivals of people from Asia, people living in the Americas came to have the broad faces, prominent cheekbones, and round cranial vaults that tend to characterize the skulls of many Native Americans today. Still, Native Americans, like all human populations, are physically variable. The "Kennewick Man" controversy described in Chapter 4 illustrates the complexities of establishing ethnic identity based on the shape of the skull. In order to trace the history of the peopling of the Americas, anthropologists must combine archaeological, linguistic, and cultural evidence with evidence of biological variation.

Although the earliest technologies in the Americas remain poorly known, they gave rise in North America, about 12,000 years ago, to the distinctive fluted spear points of **Paleoindian** hunters of big game, such as mammoths, mastodons, caribou, and now extinct forms of bison. Fluted points are finely made, with large channel flakes removed from one or both surfaces. This thinned section was inserted into the notched end of a spear shaft for a sturdy haft. Fluted points are found from the Atlantic seaboard to the Pacific coast, and from Alaska down into Panama. So efficient were the hunters who made these points that they may have hastened the extinction of the mammoth and other large Pleistocene mammals. By driving large numbers of animals over cliffs, they killed many more than they could possibly use, thus wasting huge amounts of meat.

Joe Ben Wheat Photo

Paleoindians, like their Upper Paleolithic contemporaries in Eurasia, were such accomplished hunters that they, too, could kill more animals than could possibly be used at one time. These bones are the remains of some 200 bison that Paleoindian hunters stampeded over a cliff 8,500 years ago.

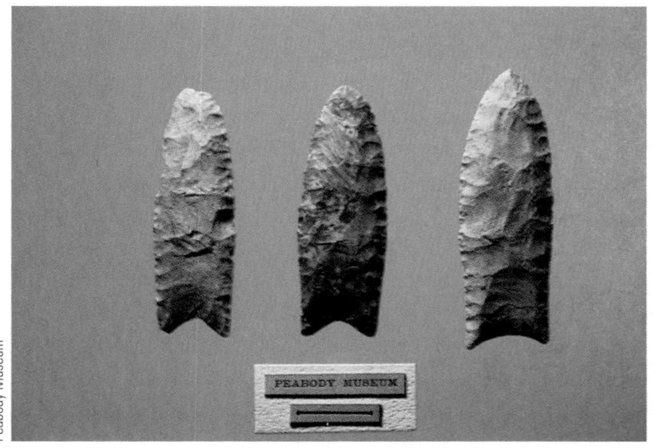

Peabody Museum

Fluted points, such as these, tipped the spears of Paleoindian hunters in North America about 12,000 years ago.

WHERE DID UPPER PALEOLITHIC PEOPLES COME FROM?

As noted in Chapter 9, scholars still debate whether the transition from archaic to anatomically modern *H. sapiens* took place in one specific population or was the result of populations living in Africa, Asia, and even Europe between 100,000 and 40,000 years ago evolving together. The argument for replacement of archaic by modern *Homo sapiens* has been most strongly made in Europe. Nevertheless, the most recent Neandertals display modern

Paleoindian The earliest inhabitants of North America.

In 1998, this skeleton of a 4-year-old child was found in a Portuguese rock shelter, where it had been ritually buried. It displays a mix of Neandertal and Cro-Magnon traits, but its 28,000-year-old date makes it too recent to be the product of a chance encounter between two populations (by then, "classic" Neandertals were long gone). Instead, it bespeaks earlier extensive interbreeding or is one more example of an Upper Paleolithic European showing evidence of Neandertal ancestry. In either case, the idea of Neandertals and Cro-Magnons as separate species is challenged.

features, whereas the most ancient moderns show what appear to be Neandertal holdovers. For example, a late Neandertal from Vindija, northern Croatia, shows a thinning of brow ridges toward their outer margins. Conversely, early Upper Paleolithic skulls from Brno, Mladec, and Predmosti, in the Czech Republic, retain heavy brow ridges and Neandertal-like muscle attachments on their backs.[14] As noted early in this chapter, some of the skulls from the Cro-Magnon rock shelter look Neandertal-like from the back. Of course, these features could all be the result of interbreeding between two populations that overlapped in time, rather than simple evolution from one into the other. Or, they could represent a single varied population whose average characters were shifting in a more "modern" direction. In either case, they do not fit with the idea of the complete extinction of the older population.

Looking at the larger picture, since the time of *Homo erectus,* evolving humans came to rely increasingly on cultural, as opposed to biological, adaptation. To handle environmental challenges, evolving humans developed appropriate tools, clothes, shelter, use of fire, and so forth rather than relying upon biological adaptation of the human organism. This was true whether human populations lived in hot or cold, wet or dry, forest or grassland areas. Though culture is ultimately based on what might loosely be called "brain power" or, more formally, **cognitive capacity,** it is learned and not carried by genes. Therefore, cultural innovations may occur rapidly and can easily be transferred between individuals and groups.

In the 2.5 million years since the genus *Homo* appeared, a trend toward improved cognitive capacity through the evolution of the brain occurred regardless of the environmental and climatic differences among

[14]Bednarik, R. G. (1995). Concept-mediated marking in the Lower Paleolithic. *Current Anthropology, 36,* 627; Minugh-Purvis, N. (1992). The inhabitants of Ice Age Europe. *Expedition, 34*(3), 33–34.

cognitive capacity A broad concept including intelligence, educability, concept formation, self-awareness, self-evaluation, attention span, sensitivity in discrimination, and creativity.

the regions in which populations of the genus lived. Increased cranial capacity was equally advantageous in all regions inhabited by evolving humans. This trend continued until the appearance of archaic *Homo sapiens.* At the same time, gene flow among populations would have spread whatever genes happen to relate to cognitive capacity. In an evolving species, in the absence of isolating mechanisms, genes having survival value anywhere tend to spread from one population to another. As a case in point, wolves, like humans, have a wide distribution, ranging all the way from the Atlantic coast of Europe eastward across Eurasia and North America to Greenland. Yet, wolves constitute a single species—*Canis lupus*—and never in its 5- to 7-million-year evolutionary history has more than a single species existed.[15] That wolves never split into multiple species relates to the size of territories occupied by successful packs and exchange of mates between packs. Both promoted gene flow across the species' entire range.

It is impossible to know just how much gene flow took place among ancient human populations, but that some took place is consistent with the sudden appearance of novel traits in one region later than their appearance elsewhere. For example, some Upper Paleolithic remains from North Africa exhibit the kind of mid-facial flatness previously seen only in East Asian fossils; similarly, various Cro-Magnon fossils from Europe show the short upper jaws, horizontally oriented cheek bones, and rectangular eye orbits previously seen in East Asians. Conversely, the round orbits, large frontal sinuses, and thin cranial bones seen in some archaic *H. sapiens* skulls from China represent the first appearance there of traits that have greater antiquity in Europe.[16] What appears to be happening, then, is that genetic variants from the East are being introduced into Western gene pools and vice versa. Support for this comes from studies of the Y chromosome in humans (found only in males). These studies indicate that some DNA carried by this chromosome originated in Asia at least 200,000 years ago and spread from there to Africa.[17] Not only is such gene flow consistent with the remarkable tendency historically known humans have to "swap genes" between populations, even in the face of cultural barriers to gene flow, it is also consistent with the tendency of other primates to produce hybrids when two subspecies (and sometimes even species) come into contact.[18] Moreover, without such gene flow, multiregional evolution inevitably would have resulted in the appearance of multiple species of modern humans, something that clearly has not happened. In fact, the low level of genetic differentiation among modern human populations can be explained easily as a consequence of high levels of gene flow.[19]

MAJOR PALEOLITHIC TRENDS

Certain trends stand out from the information anthropologists have gathered about the Old Stone Age, in most parts of the world. One was toward increasingly more sophisticated, varied, and specialized tool kits. Tools became progressively lighter and smaller, resulting in the conservation of raw materials and a better ratio between length of cutting edge and weight of stone. Tools became specialized according to region and function. Instead of crude all-purpose tools, more effective particularized devices were made to deal with the differing conditions of savannah, forest, and shore.

As humans came to rely increasingly on culture as a means to meet the challenges of existence, they were able to inhabit new environments. With more efficient tool technology, human population size could increase allowing humans to spill over into more diverse environments. Improved cultural abilities may also have played a role in the reduction of heavy physical features, favoring instead decreased size and weight of face and teeth, the development of larger and more complex brains, and ultimately a reduction in body size and robustness. This dependence on intelligence rather than bulk provided the key for humans' increased reliance on cultural rather than physical adaptation. The development of conceptual thought can be seen in symbolic artifacts and signs of ritual activity.

Through Paleolithic times, at least in the colder parts of the world, there appeared a trend toward the importance of and proficiency in hunting. Humans' intelligence enabled them to develop composite tools as well as the social organization and cooperation so important for survival and population growth. As discussed in the next chapter, this trend was reversed during the Mesolithic, when hunting lost its preeminence, and the gathering of wild plants and seafood became increasingly important.

---

[15]Brace, C. L. (2000). *Evolution in an anthropological view* (p. 341). Walnut Creek, CA: Altamira.

[16]Pope, G. C. (1992). Craniofacial evidence for the origin of modern humans in China. *Yearbook of Physical Anthropology, 35,* 287–288.

[17]Gibbons, A. (1997). Ideas on human origins evolve at anthropology gathering. *Science, 276,* 535–536.

[18]Simons, E. L. (1989). Human origins. *Science, 245,* 1,349.

[19]Relethford, J. H., & Harpending, H. C. (1994). Craniometric variation, genetic theory, and modern human origins. *American Journal of Physical Anthropology, 95,* 265.

As human populations grew and spread, cultural differences between regions also became more marked. While some indications of cultural contact and intercommunication are evident in the development of long distance trade networks, tool assemblages developed in response to the specific challenges and resources of specific environments. As Paleolithic peoples eventually spread over all the continents of the world, including Australia and the Americas, changes in climate and environment called for new kinds of adaptations. In forest environments, people needed tools for working wood; on the open savannah and plains, they came to use the bow and arrow to hunt the game they could not stalk closely; the people in settlements that grew up around lakes and along rivers and coasts developed harpoons and hooks; in the sub-Arctic regions they needed tools to work the heavy skins of seals and caribou. The fact that culture is first and foremost a mechanism by which humans adapt means that as humans faced new challenges in the Paleolithic throughout the globe, their cultures differentiated regionally.

Chapter Summary

- The Cro-Magnons and the other Upper Paleolithic peoples of the world, like archaic *Homo sapiens,* possessed a full-sized brain, but unlike them their skulls and bodies tended to be less robust than the earlier archaic forms like the Neandertals. Some have suggested that the modernization of the face of Upper Paleolithic peoples is a result of a reduction in the size of the teeth and the muscles involved in chewing and relates to the fact that teeth were no longer being used as tools. Similarly, bodies became somewhat less massive and robust as improved technology reduced the need for brute strength.
- Upper Paleolithic cultures evolved out of the Middle Paleolithic cultures of Africa, Asia, and Europe. The typical Upper Paleolithic tool was the blade. The blade technique of tool making was less wasteful of flint than Middle Paleolithic methods. Other efficient Upper Paleolithic tool-making techniques were pressure flaking of stone and the use of chisel-like tools called burins to fashion bone, antler, horn, and ivory into tools. The cultural adaptation of Upper Paleolithic peoples became specific; they developed different tools in different regions. Northern Upper Paleolithic cultures supported themselves by the hunting of large herd animals and catching smaller animals in nets. Small blades suitable for arrows developed in Africa during this time period, spreading later to Europe and other regions. Upper Paleolithic cultures are the earliest in which artistic expression is common.
- Humans spread to greater Australia and the Americas during the Upper Paleolithic. Some of the earliest evidence of symbolic expression is preserved in early cave engravings from Australia. In addition the ability to spread to greater Australia and the Americas provides evidence of humans' ability to cross the open water and live in Arctic regions.
- The emphasis in evolution of the genus *Homo* in all parts of the world was toward increasing cognitive capacity through development of the brain. This took place regardless of environmental or climatic conditions under which the genus lived. In addition, evolution of the genus *Homo* undoubtedly involved gene flow among populations. Lack of much genetic differentiation among human populations today bespeaks high levels of gene flow among populations in the past.
- Three trends are evident in the Paleolithic period. First was a trend toward more sophisticated, varied, and specialized tool kits. This trend enabled people to increase their population size and spread to new environments. It also had an impact on human anatomy, favoring decreased size and weight of face and teeth, the development of larger, more complex brains, and ultimately a reduction in body size and mass. Second was a trend toward the importance of and proficiency in hunting. Third was a trend toward regionalism, as people's technology and life habits increasingly reflected their association with a particular environment.

Questions for Reflection

1. A major challenge in the examination of human origins is determining the extent to which biological change is responsible for cultural change. What evidence from the Upper Paleolithic supports a one-to-one relationship between these two kinds of human change? What evidence from the Upper Paleolithic indicates that cultural change in that era is not connected to an underlying biological change? Which approach do you think is correct?
2. Why do you think that most of the studies of prehistoric art have tended to focus on Europe? Is it ethnocentrism or biases about the definition of art in Western cultures?
3. Why do people make art today and in the past?
4. Many animals without culture have spread to new environments. What is it about the spread of humans to Australia and the Americas that tells us about the cultural capabilities of past people?
5. Do you think that gender has played a role in anthropological interpretations of the behavior of our ancestors and the way that paleoanthropologists and archaeologists conduct their research? Do you believe that feminism has a role to play in the interpretation of the past?

Key Terms

Upper Paleolithic
Cro-Magnons
Blade technique
Pressure flaking
Burins
Entoptic phenomena
Sahul
Sunda
Paleoindian
Cognitive capacity

Multimedia Review Tools

Companion Web Site

Visit **http://www.wadsworth.com/anthropology_d/** and click on the companion Web site for this textbook to access a wide range of material to aid your study of anthropology. Among the options for self-study in each chapter are learning objectives, flash cards, Internet activities, Web links, InfoTrac College Edition exercises, and practice tests that can be scored and emailed to your instructor.

CD-ROM

The *Doing Anthropology Today* CD-ROM supplied with your textbook provides unique and valuable information designed to enhance your learning experience. This interactive multimedia resource includes video clips, interviews with renowned anthropologists, map and timeline exercises, chapter study quizzes, and much more. *Doing Anthropology Today* will not only help you in achieving your grade goals, but it will also make your learning experience fun and exciting!

Suggested Readings

Clottes, J., & Bennett, G. (2002). *World rock art* (conservation and cultural heritage series). San Francisco: Getty Trust Publication.

Written by Jean Clottes, a leading authority on rock art (and discoverer of the Upper Paleolithic cave art site Grotte de Cahuvet), this book provides excellent descriptions and beautiful images of rock art from throughout the world, beginning with the earliest rock art from Australia to rock art from the 20th century.

Dillehay, T. D. (2001). *The settlement of the Americas.* New York: Basic Books.

In an engaging clear style, this book provides a detailed account of the evidence from South America that has recently challenged theories about the peopling of the Americas with particular emphasis on the author's work in Chile.

Klein R. (2002). *The dawn of human culture.* New York: Wiley.

While this book covers the entire history of human evolution, it provides a particular focus on the theory of recent African origins of the species *Homo sapiens* and associated cultural abilities.

White, R. (2003). *Prehistoric art: The symbolic journey of humankind.* New York: Harry N. Abrams.

This sumptuously illustrated volume demonstrates the power of prehistoric imagery as well as providing a comprehensive overview of the theoretical approaches to studying prehistoric art. White presents a global survey of prehistoric art and demonstrates that Western notions of art have interfered with interpretations of art made in the past.

Wolpoff, M., & Caspari, R. (1997). *Race and human evolution.* New York: Simon & Schuster.

This book is a detailed but readable presentation of the multiregional hypothesis of modern human origins. Among its strengths is a discussion of the problem of defining what "anatomically modern" means.

PART 4

Erich Lessing/Art Resource, NY

Human Biocultural Evolution

The Challenge of Technology and Human Diversity

Introduction

Up until the Middle Paleolithic, the story of the evolution of genus *Homo* focuses on the origins of human culture and its underlying biological bases. The critical importance of adaptation through culture appears to have imposed selective pressures favoring a bigger, more elaborate brain, with greater cognitive power. Larger brains and a life-cycle pattern that includes a long period of childhood dependency, in which the young learn the social patterns of the group, in turn expanded possibilities for human adaptation through culture. Indeed, we could say that human biology today was shaped by cultural adaptation playing a vital role in the survival of our ancient ancestors, just as human biology made adaptation through culture possible.

By 200,000 years ago, the human brain had become as big as it would get, and there has been no subsequent increase in overall size, but some changes in the shape of the skull are evident since then. At some point in the course of human evolutionary history, macroevolution came to a halt, although just when and how this occurred is hotly debated by paleoanthropologists. It is also clear that a kind of "disconnect" occurred between cultural and biological change and their respective rates of change in human evolution. Although macroevolution has stopped, microevolution—changes in allele frequency—continues to this day at rates that are relatively slow. Human culture, by contrast, freed from the transmission of innovations through the biological process of reproduction, changes at a faster pace. These changes need not be technological innovations but rather changes in beliefs, practices, or worldview that occur as humans interact with their world. In other words, all cultures are changing through time at rates generally more rapid than biological rates of change.

In the Upper Paleolithic some of the major cultural changes evident in the archaeological record consist of new tool technologies, modes of expression, and the spread of humans over the entire globe by land and sea, illustrating the efficiency of cultural adaptation gained by the Upper Paleolithic.

© Staffan Widstrand/CORBIS

More or less simultaneously, around 10,000 years ago in several parts of the world, a second major cultural transition began. Called the Neolithic revolution, it consisted of a gradual shift from a food-foraging lifestyle to one based on food production, the subject of Chapter 11. These new cultural abilities were also incorporated into the art from this and later periods as seen in this cave painting of cattle herding from North Africa. Eventually, most of the world's peoples became food producers, even though food foraging remained a satisfactory way of life for some.

Today small populations of food foragers inhabit some of the most challenging environments on the earth. Inuit provide for themselves and preserve their cultural traditions through hunting and fishing in the Arctic regions of North America. Meanwhile food producers and their descendants in today's postindustrial cities and states have taken over the vast majority of the earth's surface. Chapter 12 discusses the emergence of cities and states, which form the basis of today's world.

Despite the increasing effectiveness of culture as the primary mechanism by which humans adapt to diverse environments, and the lack of macroevolutionary change since the emergence of the modern human species, human biology has not remained static. Microevolutionary change continued in the course of human movement into a variety of environments. On top of this, populations of food producers were exposed to selective pressures of a different sort than those affecting food foragers, thereby inducing further changes in human gene pools. Such changes continue to affect humans today, even though we remain the same species now as at the end of the Paleolithic. Chapter 13 discusses how the variation seen in *Homo sapiens* today came into existence as the result of forces altering the frequencies of alleles in human gene pools. It also focuses on the fallacy of using race as a category for explaining human biological variation. The chapter concludes with a look at forces apparently active today to produce further biological change.

CHAPTER 11

The Neolithic Revolution: The Domestication of Plants and Animals

© Keystone/The Image Works

CHALLENGE ISSUE

Beginning some time around 10,000 years ago, some of the world's people embarked on a new way of life solving the challenges of existence through the domestication of animals and plants and the formation of fixed settlements. With this cultural change, called the Neolithic revolution, humans used technological innovations to solve problems as they had done in the past, but the pace of technological innovation accelerated. Frequently such cultural innovations create new challenges for humans on biological and cultural levels. Today farmers in the mountains of Yemen, along the southwestern side of the Arabian Peninsula, grow two popular stimulants: coffee, primarily for export, and qat, primarily for daily local use by many Yemeni men. Although the practice of using terraced beds to capture small amounts of rain-water for farming is quite ancient in this region, the cultural and biological effects of this innovation are embedded in Yemeni life today.

When and Where Did the Change from Food Foraging to Food Production Begin?

Independent centers of early plant and animal domestication exist in Africa, China, Mesoamerica, North and South America, as well as Southwest and Southeast Asia. From these places, food production spread to most other parts of the world. Food production began independently at more or less the same time around 10,000 years ago in these different places—perhaps a bit earlier in Southwest Asia than other places. Though farming has changed dramatically over the millennia, crops people rely on today such as rice, wheat, and maize originated with those earliest farmers.

Why Did the Change Take Place?

Though the Neolithic revolution can appear to be a cultural advancement because later cities and states developed from Neolithic villages, food production is not necessarily a more secure means of subsistence than food foraging. In the Neolithic, farming often limited the diversity of the human diet and required more work than hunting, gathering, and fishing. In addition, being sedentary created new opportunity for disease. We can assume that people probably did not become food producers due to clear-cut advantages of this way of life. Of various theories that have been proposed, the most likely is that food production came about as a consequence of a chance convergence of separate natural events and cultural developments.

What Were the Consequences of the Neolithic Revolution?

Although food production generally leaves less leisure time than food foraging, it does permit some reallocation of the workload. Some people can produce enough food to support those who undertake other tasks, and so a number of technological developments, such as weaving and pottery making, generally accompany food production. In addition, a sedentary lifestyle in villages allows for the construction of more substantial housing. Finally, the new modes of work and resource allocation require new ways of organizing people, generally into lineages, clans, and common-interest associations.

Throughout the Paleolithic, people depended exclusively on wild sources of food for their survival. In cold northern regions, they came to rely on the hunting of large animals such as the mammoth, bison, and horse, but especially reindeer, as well as smaller animals such as hares, foxes, and birds. Elsewhere, they hunted, fished, or gathered whatever nature provided. There is no evidence in Paleolithic remains to indicate that livestock was kept or plants cultivated. Paleolithic peoples followed wild herds and gathered wild plant foods, relying on their wits and muscles to acquire what nature provided. Whenever favored sources of food became scarce, as sometimes happened, people adjusted by increasing the variety of food eaten and incorporating less favored food into their diets.

Over time, the subsistence practices of some people began to change in ways that radically transformed their way of life as they became food producers rather than food foragers.[1] This change in the means of obtaining food had important implications for human development, for it meant that people could lead a more sedentary existence. Moreover, by reorganizing the workload, some individuals could be freed from the food quest to devote their energies to other tasks. This was not a deliberate change undertaken to create a new lifestyle but rather one that came about gradually as humans incorporated new practices into their daily lives. Over the course of thousands of years, these changes brought about an unforeseen way of life. With good reason, the **Neolithic,** when this change took place, has been called a revolutionary one in human history. This period, and the changes that took place within it, are the subjects of this chapter.

THE MESOLITHIC ROOTS OF FARMING AND PASTORALISM

By 12,000 years ago, glacial conditions in the world were moderating, causing changes in human habitats. Throughout the world, climates warmed and sea levels were on the rise, ultimately flooding many areas that had been above sea level during periods of glaciation, such as the Bering Strait, parts of the North Sea, and an extensive area that had joined the eastern islands of Indonesia to mainland Asia. In some northern regions, milder climates brought about particularly marked changes, allowing the replacement of tundra with hardwood forests. In the process, the herd animals upon which northern Paleolithic peoples had depended for much of their food, clothing, and shelter disappeared from many areas. Some, like the reindeer and musk ox, moved to colder climates; others, like the mammoths, died out completely. In the new forests, animals were more solitary in their habits. As a result, large, cooperative hunts were less productive than before. However, plant food was more abundant, as was fish and other foods around lakeshores, bays, and rivers. At different times in different places, human populations developed new and ingenious ways to catch and kill a variety of smaller birds and animals, while at the same time they devoted more energy to fishing and the collection of a broad spectrum of wild plant foods. In Europe, Asia, and Africa this marked the end of the Paleolithic and the start of the **Mesolithic,** or Middle Stone Age. In the Americas the comparable period is known as the Archaic.

Mesolithic Tools and Weapons

New technologies were developed for the changed postglacial environment. Manufacture of ground stone tools, shaped and sharpened by grinding the tool against sandstone (often using sand as an additional abrasive), provided effective axes and adzes. Though such implements take longer to make, they are less prone to breakage under heavy-duty usage than those made of chipped stone. Thus, they were helpful in clearing forest areas and in the woodwork needed for the creation of dugout canoes and skin-covered boats. Evidence for the presence of seaworthy watercraft at Mesolithic sites indi-

Mesolithic tools such as these consisted of microliths set into handles made of wood, bone, or antler.

[1]Rindos, D. (1984). *The origins of agriculture: An evolutionary perspective* (p. 99). Orlando: Academic Press.

Neolithic The New Stone Age; characterized by plant and animal domestication and settlement in fixed villages.
Mesolithic The Middle Stone Age of Europe and Southwest Asia; began about 12,000 years ago.

cates that human foraging for food frequently took place on the water as well as the land. Thus, it was possible to make use of deep-water resources as well as those of coastal areas, rivers, and lakes.

The **microlith,** a small but hard, sharp blade, was the characteristic tool of the "Old World" Mesolithic. Although a microlithic tradition existed in Central Africa by about 40,000 years ago,[2] such tools did not become common elsewhere until the Mesolithic. Microliths could be mass produced because they were small, easy to make, and could be fashioned from materials other than flint. Also, they could be attached to arrow shafts by using melted resin (from pine trees) as a binder.

Microliths provided Mesolithic people with an important advantage over their Upper Paleolithic forebears: The small size of the microlith enabled them to devise a wider array of composite tools made out of stone and wood or bone. Thus, they could make sickles, harpoons, arrows, and daggers by fitting microliths into slots in wood, bone, or antler handles. Later experimentation with these forms led to more sophisticated tools and weapons.

It appears that a sedentary lifestyle was beginning to a certain degree during the Mesolithic. Dwellings from this period seem more substantial, an indication of some degree of permanency. By contrast, most hunting peoples, and especially those depending on herd animals, are nomadic: To be successful, hunters must follow migratory game. For people subsisting on diets of seafood and plants in the now milder forested environments of the north, frequent movement over large areas was not required.

Cultural Diversity in the Mesolithic

In the warmer parts of the world, the collection of wild plant foods complemented hunting in the Upper Paleolithic more than had been the case in the colder northern regions. Hence, in areas like Southwest Asia, the Mesolithic represents less of a changed way of life than was true in Europe. Here, the important **Natufian culture** flourished.

The Natufians lived between 12,500 and 10,200 years ago at the eastern end of the Mediterranean Sea in caves, rock shelters, and small villages with stone- and mud-walled houses. They are named after the Wadi en-Natuf, a ravine near Jerusalem, Israel, where the remains of this culture were first found. They buried their dead in communal cemeteries, usually in shallow pits without grave goods or decorations. A small shrine is known from one of their villages, a 10,500-year-old settlement at Jericho in the Jordan River Valley. Basin-shaped depressions in the rocks found outside homes and plastered storage pits beneath the floors of the houses indicate that the Natufians were the earliest Mesolithic people known to have stored plant foods. Certain tools found among Natufian remains bear evidence of their use to cut grain. These Mesolithic sickles consisted of small stone blades set in straight handles of wood or bone.

The Natufians from Southwest Asia were the earliest Mesolithic people known to have stored plant foods. Basin-shaped depressions are preserved in the rocks outside of their homes.

In the Americas, cultures comparable to Mesolithic cultures of the Old World developed, but here they are referred to as **Archaic cultures.** Outside of the Arctic, microlithic tools are not prominent as they are in the rest of the world, but ground stone tools such as axes, adzes, gouges, plummets, and spear-thrower weights are common. Archaic cultures were widespread in the Americas. One of the better documented was the **Maritime Archaic culture,** which began to develop about 7,000 years ago around the Gulf of St. Lawrence. Maritime Archaic people developed an elaborate assortment of bone and ground slate tools with which they hunted a wide variety of sea mammals, including whales; fish, including swordfish; and sea birds. To get some of these, they regularly paddled their dugout canoes far offshore.

microlith A small blade of flint or similar stone, several of which were hafted together in wooden handles to make tools; widespread in the Mesolithic.
Natufian culture A Mesolithic culture of Israel, Lebanon, and western Syria, between about 12,500 and 10,200 years ago.
Archaic cultures Term used to refer to Mesolithic cultures in the Americas.
Maritime Archaic culture An Archaic culture of northeastern North America, centered on the Gulf of St. Lawrence, that emphasized the utilization of marine resources.

[2] Bednarik, R. G. (1995). Concept-mediated marking in the Lower Paleolithic. *Current Anthropology, 36,* 606.

To appreciate the skills this required, one need only recognize the difficulty of landing a 500-pound swordfish, as these are extremely aggressive fish. They are known historically to have driven their swords through the hulls of substantial wooden vessels. The Maritime Archaic people also developed the first known elaborate burial ceremonialism in North America, involving the use of red ocher ("red paint") and the placement of finely made grave goods with the deceased.

Varied though Mesolithic and Archaic cultures were, this new way of life generally provided supplies of food sufficiently abundant to permit people in some parts of the world to live in larger and more sedentary groups. They became village dwellers, and some of these settlements went on to expand into the first farming villages, towns, and ultimately cities.

THE NEOLITHIC REVOLUTION

The Neolithic, or New Stone Age, was characterized by the transition from foraging for food to dependence upon domesticated plants and animals. It was by no means a smooth or rapid transition; in fact, the switch to food production spread over many centuries—even millennia—and was a direct outgrowth of the preceding Mesolithic. Where to draw the line between the two periods is not always clear.

The *New Stone Age* derives its name from the polished stone tools that are characteristic of this period. But more important than the presence of these tools is the transition from a hunting, gathering, and fishing economy to one based on food production, representing a major change in the subsistence practices of early peoples. One of the first regions to undergo this transition, and certainly the most intensively studied, was Southwest Asia. The remains of domesticated plants and animals are known from parts of Israel, Jordan, Syria, Turkey, Iraq, and Iran, from well before 10,000 years ago. The transition to relatively complete reliance on domesticates took several thousand years. Some of the evidence of the transition to food production in other parts of the world is as old (China) and other places a few thousand years younger (the Americas). The critical point is not differences in timing among distinct regions but rather the independent but more or less simultaneous transition to food production throughout the globe.

domestication An evolutionary process whereby humans modify, either intentionally or unintentionally, the genetic makeup of a population of plants or animals, sometimes to the extent that members of the population are unable to survive and/or reproduce without human assistance.

Worker ants have made a path as they go out to cut pieces of leaf that they bring back to their nest to make the soil in which they plant their fungus gardens.

Domestication: What Is It?

Domestication is an evolutionary process whereby humans modify, either intentionally or unintentionally, the genetic makeup of a population of plants or animals, sometimes to the extent that members of the population are unable to survive and/or reproduce without human assistance. Domestication is essentially a special case of interdependence between different species frequently seen in the natural world, where one species depends on another (that feeds upon it) for its protection and reproductive success. For example, certain ants native to the American tropics grow fungi in their nests, providing the ants with most of their nutrition. Like human farmers, the ants add manure to stimulate fungal growth and eliminate competing weeds both mechanically and through use of antibiotic herbicides.[3] The

[3]Diamond, J. (1998). Ants, crops, and history. *Science, 281,* 1,974–1,975.

VISUAL COUNTERPOINT Wild wheat kernels from a site in Syria (left) are compared with those of a domestic variety grown in Greece 2,000 to 3,000 years later (right). Increased size of edible parts is a common feature of domestication.

fungi are protected and ensured reproductive success while providing the ants with a steady food supply.

Numerous other examples of such cooperation between species exist, all characterized by mutual benefit. In plant–human interactions, domestication ensures the plants' reproductive success while providing the humans with food. As plant species were freed from biological mechanisms such as thorns, toxins, and bad-tasting chemical compounds that had served to ensure their survival and reproductive success, larger and tastier edible parts attractive to humans cemented the relationship between the protected and protector.

Evidence of Early Plant Domestication

Although the remains of the early domesticates may survive in dry climates, they do not where conditions are humid. Even so, evidence may exist in the form of **phytoliths.** These are microscopic silica bodies formed as plants take up silica from the groundwater. As the silica gradually fills the plant cells, it assumes their distinctive shape.

The characteristics of plants under human domestication that set them apart from their wild ancestors and have made them attractive to those who eat them include increased size, at least of edible parts; reduction or loss of natural means of seed dispersal; reduction or loss of protective devices such as husks or distasteful chemical compounds; loss of delayed seed germination (important to wild plants for survival in times of drought or other adverse conditions of temporary duration); and development of simultaneous ripening of the seed or fruit. Many of these characteristics can be seen in plant remains from archaeological sites. Paleobotanists can often tell the fossil of a wild plant species from a domesticated one, for example, by studying the seed of cereal grasses, such as barley, wheat, and maize (corn). Wild cereals have a very fragile stem, whereas domesticated ones have a tough stem. Under natural conditions, plants with fragile stems scatter their seed for themselves, whereas those with tough stems do not.

The structural change from a soft to a tough stem in early domesticated plants involves a genetic change, undoubtedly the result of what Darwin referred to as **unconscious selection:** the preservation of valued individuals and the destruction of less valued ones, with no thought as to long-range consequences.[4] When the grain stalks were harvested, their soft stem would shatter at the touch of sickle or flail, and many of their seeds would be lost. Inevitably, most of the seeds that people harvested would have been taken from the tough plants. Early domesticators probably also tended to select seed from plants having few husks or none at all—eventually breeding them out—because husking prior to pounding the grains into meal or flour was too time-consuming. Size of plants is another good indicator of the presence of domestication. For example, the large ear of corn (maize) we know today is a far cry from the tiny ears (about an inch long) characteristic of early maize. In fact, the ear of maize may have arisen as a simple gene

[4]Rindos, p. 86.

phytoliths Microscopic silica bodies preserving the structures of plants that are formed as plants take up silica from groundwater.
unconscious selection The preservation of valued variants of a plant or animal species and the destruction of less valued ones, with no thought as to the long-range consequences.

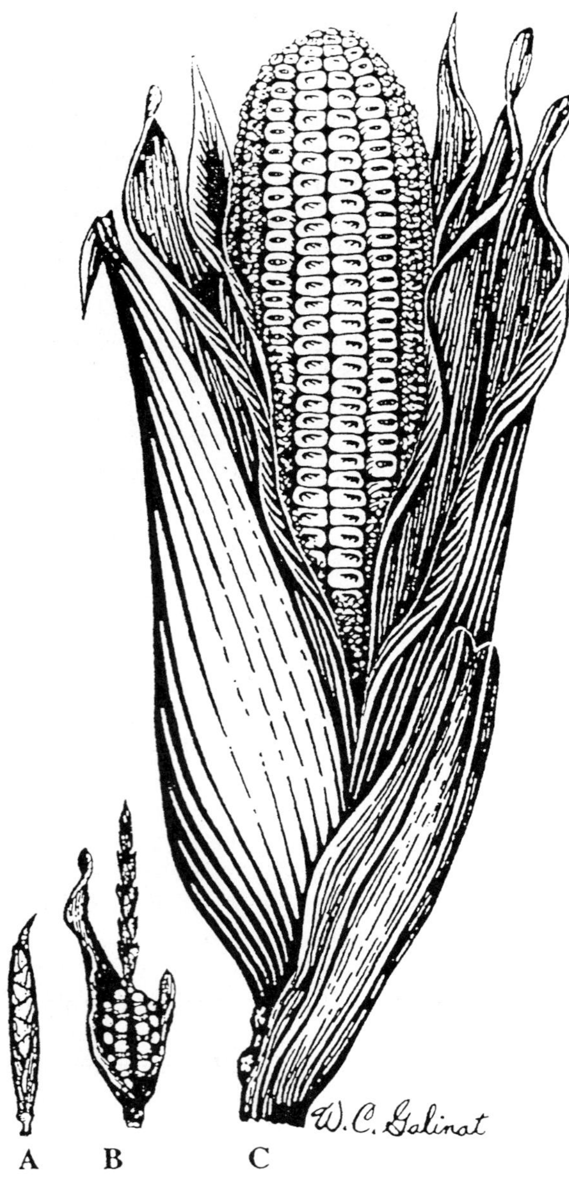

Teosinte (A), compared to 5,500-year-old maize (B) and modern maize (C). The wild grass from highland Mexico, teosinte, from which maize originated is far less productive and doesn't taste very good. Like most plants that were domesticated, it was not a favored food for foraging people. Domestication transformed it into something highly desirable.

mutation transformed male tassel spikes of the wild grass called teosinte into small earliest versions of the female maize ear.[5] Small though these were (an entire ear contained less nourishment than a single kernel of modern maize), they were radically different in structure from the ears of teosinte.

[5]Gould, S. J. (1991). *The flamingo's smile: Reflections in natural history* (p. 368). New York: Norton.

Evidence of Early Animal Domestication

Domestication also produced changes in the skeletal structure of some animals. For example, the horns of wild goats and sheep differ from those of their domesticated counterparts (most domesticated female sheep have none). Another structural change that occurred in domestication involves the size of the animal or its parts. For example, certain teeth of domesticated pigs are smaller than those of wild ones.

A study of age and sex ratios of butchered animals at an archaeological site may indicate whether or not animal domestication was practiced. Investigators have assumed that if the age and/or sex ratios at the site differ from those in wild herds, the imbalances are due to domestication. For example, at 10,000-year-old sites in the Zagros Mountains of Iran, there was a sharp rise in the numbers of young male goats killed. Evidently, people were slaughtering the young males for food and saving the females for breeding. Although such herd management does not prove that the goats were fully domesticated, it does indicate a step in that direction.[6]

In Peru, the high frequency of bones of newborn llama at archaeological sites (up to 72 percent at some), dating to around 6,300 years ago, is probably indicative of at least incipient domestication. Such high mortality rates for newborn animals are uncommon in wild herds but are common where animals are penned up. Under confined conditions, the inevitable buildup of mud and filth harbors bacteria that cause diarrhea and enterotoxemia, both of which are fatal to newborn animals.

Beginnings of Domestication

Over the past 30 years, a good deal of information has accumulated about the beginnings of domestication, primarily in Southwest Asia, Mexico, and Peru. We still do not have all the answers about how and why it took place. Nonetheless, some observations of general validity can be made that help us to understand how the switch to food production may have taken place.

The first of these observations is that the switch to food production was not the result of such discoveries that seeds, if planted, grow into plants. Contemporary food foragers are far from ignorant about the forces of nature and are perfectly aware of the role of seeds in plant growth, that plants grow better under certain conditions than others, and so forth. Physiologist Jared Diamond aptly describes contemporary food foragers as "walking encyclopedias of natural history with individual names for

[6]Zeder, M. A., & Hesse, B. (2000). The initial domestication of goats (*Capra hircus*) in the Zagros Mountains 10,000 years ago. *Science, 287,* 2,254–2,257.

as many as a thousand or more plant and animal species, and with detailed knowledge of those species' biological characteristics, distribution and potential uses."[7] What's more, they frequently apply their knowledge so as to manage actively the resources on which they depend. For example, indigenous people living in the northern part of Canada's Alberta Province put to use a sophisticated knowledge of the effects of fire to create local environments of their own design. Similarly, Indians of California used fire to perpetuate oak woodland savannah, to promote hunting and the collection of acorns. In northern Australia, runoff channels of creeks were deliberately altered so as to flood extensive tracts of land, converting them into fields of wild grain. People do not remain food foragers through ignorance, but through choice.

A second observation is that a switch from food foraging to food production does not free people from hard work. The available ethnographic data indicate just the opposite—that farmers, by and large, work far longer hours than do most food foragers. Furthermore, it is clear that early farming required people not only to work longer hours but also to eat more of the less desirable foods. In Southwest Asia and Mexico, the plants that were brought under domestication were clearly less desirable in their original wild forms.

A final observation is that food production is not necessarily a more secure means of subsistence than food foraging. Seed crops in particular—of the sort originally domesticated in Southwest Asia, Mexico, and Peru—are highly productive but very unstable on account of low species diversity. Without constant human attention, their productivity suffers.

From all of this, it is little wonder that food foragers do not necessarily regard farming and animal husbandry as superior to hunting, gathering, or fishing. Thus, there are some people in the world who have remained food foragers into the present, although it has become increasingly difficult for them, as food-producing peoples (including postindustrial societies) have deprived them of more and more of the land base necessary for their way of life. But as long as existing practices worked well, there was no need to abandon them. After all, their traditional way of life provided an eminently satisfactory way of living in small, intimate groups. American anthropologist Marshall Sahlins, noting that in fact hunter–gatherers have more leisure time than farmers, has called them the original affluent society.[8] Farming brings with it a whole new system of human relationships that offers no easily understood advantages and disturbs an age-old balance between humans and nature as well as the people who live together.

WHY HUMANS BECAME FOOD PRODUCERS

In view of what has been said so far, we may well ask: Why did any human group abandon food foraging in favor of food production?

Several theories have been proposed to account for this change in human subsistence practices. One

[7]Diamond, J. (1997). *Guns, germs, and steel* (p. 143). New York: Norton.

[8]Sahlins, M. (1972). *Stone age economics.* Chicago: Aldine.

Many of the domesticates from the Neolithic revolution play a major role in today's global economy. Sorghum, originally domesticated in Africa, is now grown throughout the world. In addition to its use as a food, work on a sorghum-based clean burning fuel for automobiles and biodegradable packaging are under development.

older theory, championed by Australian archaeologist V. Gordon Childe (see Anthropologist of Note), is the desiccation, or oasis, theory based on climatic determinism. Its proponents advanced the idea that the glacial cover over Europe and Asia caused a southern shift in rain patterns from Europe to northern Africa and Southwest Asia. When the glaciers retreated northward, so did the rain patterns. As a result, northern Africa and Southwest Asia became dryer, and people were forced to congregate at oases for water. Because of the scarcity of wild animals in such an environment, people were driven by necessity to collect the wild grasses and seeds growing around the oases, congregating in a part of Southwest Asia known as the Fertile Crescent (Figure 11.1). Eventually they had to cultivate the grasses to provide enough food for the community. According to this theory, animal domestication began because the oases attracted hungry animals, such as wild goats, sheep, and also cattle, which came to graze on the stubble of the grain fields. People, finding these animals too thin to kill for food, began to fatten them up.

Despite its initial popularity, evidence in support of the oasis theory was not immediately forthcoming. Moreover, as systematic fieldwork into the origins of domestication began in the late 1940s, other theories gained favor. One of the pioneers in this work was archaeologist Robert Braidwood, who proposed what is sometimes called the "hilly flanks" theory. Contrary to Childe, Braidwood argued that settlement by people living in the hill country surrounding the Fertile Crescent led to the other aspects of the Neolithic revolution. As people began to "settle in"—that is, become more sedentary—they became intimately familiar with the plants and animals around their settlements. According to Braidwood, the human capacity and enthusiasm for experimentation would have led inevitably to experimentation with grasses and animals, bringing them under domestication. Problems with this theory include the ethnocentric notion that nonsedentary food foragers are not intimately familiar with the plants and animals on which they rely for survival; in addition, this theory projects onto all human cultures the great value Western culture places on experimentation and innovation for its own sake. In short, the theory was culture-bound, strongly reflecting the notions of progress in which people in the Western world had such faith in the period following World War II.

Yet another theory that became popular in the 1960s suggests that population growth led to domestica-

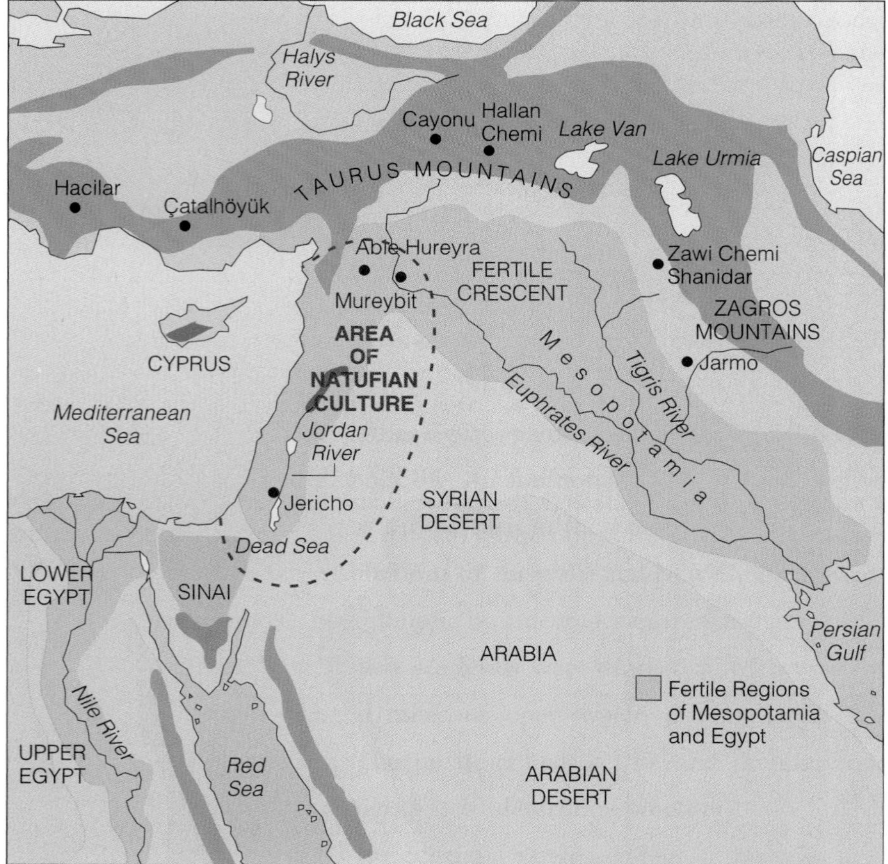

FIGURE 11.1
The Fertile Crescent of Southwest Asia and the area of Natufian culture.

Anthropologists of Note

V. Gordon Childe (1892–1957)

This distinguished Australian, once the private secretary to the premier of New South Wales, became one of the most eminent British archaeologists of his time. His knowledge of the archaeological sequences of Europe and the Middle East was unsurpassed, and he wrote two of the most popular and influential descriptions of prehistory ever written: *Man Makes Himself* and *What Happened in History.* He describes two great "revolutions" that added measurably to the capacity of humans to survive: the Neolithic and urban revolutions. The first of these transformed food foragers into farmers and brought with it a drastic reordering of society; populations increased, a cooperative group spirit arose, trade began on a large scale, and new religions arose to ensure the success of crops. This set the stage for the urban revolution, which transformed society from one of egalitarianism with a simple age-sex division of labor into one of social classes and organized political bodies. His ideas resulted in a new interest in the evolution of human culture in general.

tion. In Southwest Asia, so this theory goes, people successfully adapted to the cool, dry conditions of the last glacial period by hunting such animals as were available, harvesting wild cereal grasses, gathering nuts, and collecting a wide variety of birds, turtles, snails, crabs, and mussels. They did so well that their populations grew, requiring the development of new ways of providing sufficient food through the domestication of plants and animals.

Just as problems exist with Braidwood's theory, so do problems with this one. The most serious is that it requires an intentional decision on the part of the people involved to become producers of crops, whereas, as we have already seen, domestication (as illustrated by ant farmers) does not require conscious design. Furthermore, prior to domestication, people could have had no way of knowing that plants and animals could be so radically transformed as to permit a food-producing way of life. Even today, the long-term outcome of plant breeding cannot be predicted. Finally, even if people had wanted to become producers of their own food, there is no way such a decision could have had an immediate and perceptible effect. The transition to effective food production took thousands of years to accomplish, and even today farmers still gather, fish, and hunt. Although this may seem a relatively short period of time compared to the several million years since the appearance of the genus *Homo,* it was still too long to have made any difference to people faced with immediate food shortages. Under such conditions, the usual response among food foragers is to make use of a wider variety of foods than before.

Another theory—in accord with the evidence as we now know it but also more in accord with the role played by chance both in evolution (Chapters 2 and 5) and in cultural innovation—takes us back to some of the ideas of Childe, who, as it turns out, guessed what the environmental circumstances were, even though he did not fully understand the process. The present evidence indicates that the earliest plant domestication took place in the Fertile Crescent, the lands just east of the Mediterranean Sea, in a gradual fashion. As early as 13,000 years ago evidence exists for domestication of rye by people living at a site (Abu Hureyra) east of Aleppo, Syria, although they otherwise continued to rely heavily on wild plants and animals for food. Over the next several millennia they became full-fledged farmers domesticating rye and wheat.[9] By 10,300 years ago, others in the region were also domesticating plants.

Evidently, the process was a consequence of a chance convergence of independent natural events and cultural developments.[10] The process is exemplified by the Natufians, whose culture we looked at earlier in this chapter. These people lived at a time of dramatically changing climates in Southwest Asia. With the end of the last glaciation, climates not only became significantly warmer but markedly seasonal as well. Between 12,000 and 6,000 years ago, the region experienced the most extreme seasonality in its history, with dry summers significantly longer and more pronounced than today. As a consequence of increased evaporation, many shallow lakes dried up, leaving just three in the Jordan River Valley. At the same time, the region's plant cover changed dramatically. Those plants best adapted to environmental instability and seasonal dryness were annuals,

[9]Pringle, H. (1998). The slow birth of agriculture. *Science, 282,* 1,449.

[10]McCorriston, J., & Hole, F. (1991). The ecology of seasonal stress and the origins of agriculture in the Near East. *American Anthropologist, 93,* 46–69.

including wild cereal grains and legumes (such as peas, lentils, and chickpeas). Annuals can evolve very quickly under unstable conditions, because they complete their life cycle in a single year. Moreover, they store their reproductive abilities for the next wet season in abundant seeds, which can remain dormant for prolonged periods.

The Natufians, who lived where these conditions were especially severe, adapted by modifying their subsistence practices in two ways: First, they probably burned the landscape regularly to promote browsing by red deer and grazing by gazelles, the main focus of their hunting activities. Second, they placed greater emphasis on the collection of wild seeds from the annual plants that could be effectively stored to see people through the dry season. The importance of stored foods, coupled with the scarcity of reliable water sources, promoted more sedentary living patterns, reflected in the substantial villages of late Natufian times. The reliance upon seeds in Natufian subsistence was made possible by the fact that they already possessed sickles for harvesting grain and grinding stones for processing seeds. The grinding stones were used originally to process a variety of wild foods, whereas the sickles may originally have served to procure nonfood plants such as the sedges or reeds used to make baskets and mats. Natufian sites yielding large numbers of sickles tend to be located near coastal marshes and swamps.[11] Thus, these implements were not invented to enable people to become farmers, even though they turned out to be useful for that purpose.

[11]Olszewki, D. I. (1991). Comment. *Current Anthropology, 32,* 43.

The use of sickles to harvest grain turned out to have important consequences, again unexpected, for the Natufians. In the course of harvesting, it was inevitable that many easily dispersed seeds would be lost at the harvest site, whereas those from plants that did not readily scatter their seeds would mostly be carried back to where people processed and stored them.[12] The periodic burning of vegetation carried out to promote the deer and gazelle herds may have also affected the development of new genetic variation, for heat is known to be an effective mutagenic agent, and fire can drastically and quickly change allele frequencies. With seeds for nondispersing variants being carried back to settlements, it was inevitable that some lost seeds would germinate and grow there on dump heaps and other disturbed sites (latrines, areas cleared of trees, or burned-over terrain).

As it turns out, many of the plants that became domesticated were "colonizers," variants that do particularly well in disturbed habitats. Moreover, with people becoming increasingly sedentary, disturbed habitats became more extensive as resources in proximity to settlements were depleted over time. Thus, variants of plants particularly susceptible to human manipulation had more and more opportunity to flourish where people were living. Under such circumstances, it was inevitable that people sooner or later would begin to actively promote their growth, even by deliberately sowing them, especially as people other-

[12]Blumer, M. A., & Byrne, R. (1991). The ecological genetics and domestication and the origins of agriculture. *Current Anthropology, 32,* 30.

Courtesy of the Oriental Institute of the University of Chicago

Stands of wild wheat are still found in some parts of the Middle East.

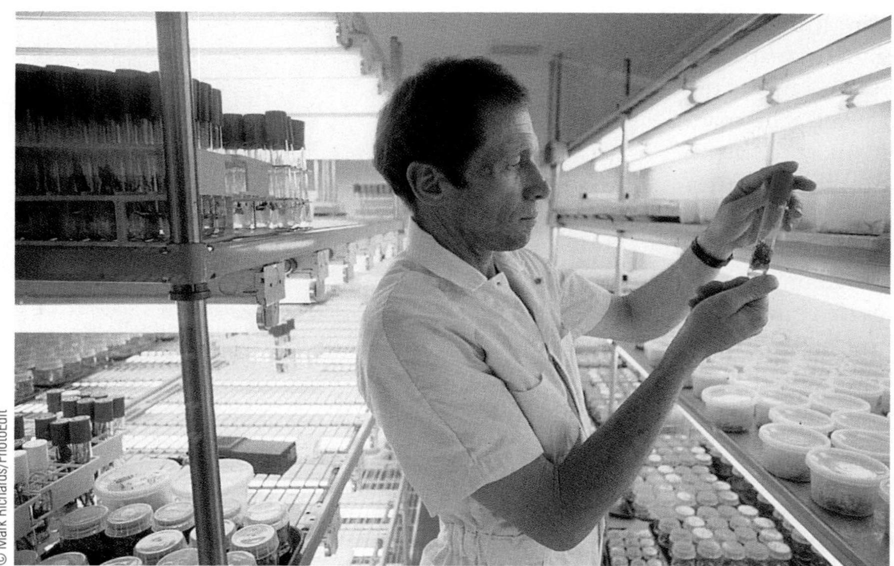

© Mark Richards/PhotoEdit

Today, deliberate attempts to create new varieties of plants take place in many a greenhouse, experiment station, or lab. But when first begun, the creation of domestic plants was not deliberate; rather, it was the unforeseen outcome of traditional food-foraging activities.

wise had to travel further to procure the resources that were depleted near their villages. Increased human manipulation in turn led to the appearance of other mutant strains of particular benefit. For example, barley, which in its wild state can be tremendously productive but difficult to harvest and process, had developed the tougher stems that make it easier to harvest by 9,000 years ago. By 8,000 years ago "naked" barley, which is easier to process, was common, and by 7,500 years ago six-row barley, which is more productive than the original two-row, was widespread. Sooner or later, people realized that they could play a more active role in the process by deliberately trying to breed more useful strains. With this, domestication may be said to have shifted from a process that was unintentional to one that was intentional.

The development of animal domestication in Southwest Asia seems to have proceeded along somewhat similar lines in the hilly country of southeastern Turkey, northern Iraq, and the Zagros Mountains of Iran. Large herds of wild sheep and goats, as well as much environmental diversity, characterized these regions. From the low alluvial plains of the valley of the Tigris and Euphrates rivers, for example, travel to the north or east takes one into the high country through three other zones: first steppe; then oak and pistachio woodlands; and, finally, high plateau country with grass, scrub, or desert vegetation. Valleys that run at right angles to the mountain ranges afford relatively easy access across these zones. Today, a number of pastoral peoples in the region practice a pattern of **transhumance,** in which they graze their herds of sheep and goats on the low steppe in the winter and move to high pastures on the plateaus in the summer.

Moving back in time to the Mesolithic, we find the region inhabited by peoples whose subsistence pattern, like that of the Natufians, was one of food foraging. Different plants were found in different ecological zones, and because of the difference in altitude, plant foods matured at different times in different zones. The animals hunted for meat and hides by these people included several species, among them bear, fox, boar, and wolf. Most notable, though, were the hoofed animals: deer, gazelles, wild goats, and wild sheep. Their bones are far more common in human refuse piles than those of other animals. This is significant, for most of these animals are naturally transhumant in the region, moving back and forth from low winter pastures to high summer pastures. People followed these animals in their seasonal migrations, making use along the way of other wild foods in the zones through which they passed: palm dates in the lowlands; acorns, almonds, and pistachios higher up; apples and pears higher still; wild grains maturing at different times in different zones; woodland animals in the forested zone between summer and winter grazing lands. All in all, it was a rich, varied fare.

Hunting of hoofed animals, including wild sheep and goats, provided meat and hides. At first, animals of all ages and sexes were hunted. But, beginning about 11,000 years ago, the percentage of immature sheep eaten, for example, increased to about 50 percent of the total. At the same time, the percentage of females among animals

transhumance Among pastoralists, the grazing of animals in low steppe lands in the winter and then moving to high pastures on the plateaus in the summer.

eaten decreased. Apparently, people were learning that they could increase yields by sparing the females for breeding, while feasting on male lambs. This marks the beginning of human management of sheep. As this management of flocks became more and more efficient, sheep were increasingly shielded from the effects of natural selection, allowing variants preferred by humans to have increased reproductive success. Variants attractive to humans did not arise out of need but at random, as mutations do. In such a way did those features characteristic of domestic sheep—such as greater fat and meat production, excess wool (Figure 11.2), and so on—begin to develop. By 9,000 years ago, the bones of domestic sheep had become distinguishable from those of wild sheep.

Eventually, sheep were introduced into areas outside their natural habitat. Farmers who kept sheep, and goats inhabited ancient Jericho, in the Jordan River Valley, 8,000 years ago (by which time farming, too, had spread widely, into Turkey to the north and into the Zagros Mountains in the east). At about the same time that these events were happening, similar developments were taking place in southeastern Turkey and the lower Jordan River Valley, where pigs were the focus of attention.[13]

To sum up, the domesticators of plants and animals sought only to maximize the food sources available to them. They were not aware of the revolutionary consequences of their actions. But as the process continued, the productivity of the domestic species increased relative to wild species. Thus they became increasingly more important to subsistence, resulting in further intensification of interest in, and management of the domesticates. Inevitably, the result would be further increases in productivity.

Although sheep and goats were first valued for their meat, hides, and sinew, the changes wrought by domestication made them useful for other purposes such as dairying. Today artisan-farmers make gourmet goat cheeses from milk of wild-ranging goats for export to cities.

OTHER CENTERS OF DOMESTICATION

In addition to Southwest Asia, the domestication of plants and, in some cases, animals took place independently in Southeast Asia, parts of the Americas (southern Mexico, Peru, the tropical forests of South America, and eastern North America), northern China, and Africa (Figure 11.3). In China, domestication of rice was underway along the middle Yangtze River by about 11,000 years ago.[14] It was not until 4,000 years later, however, that domestic rice dominated wild rice to become the dietary staple.

In Southeast Asia the oldest domestic plant so far identified is rice, in pottery dated to some time between 8,800 and 5,000 years ago. This region is primarily

[13]Pringle, p. 1,448.

[14]Pringle, p. 1,449.

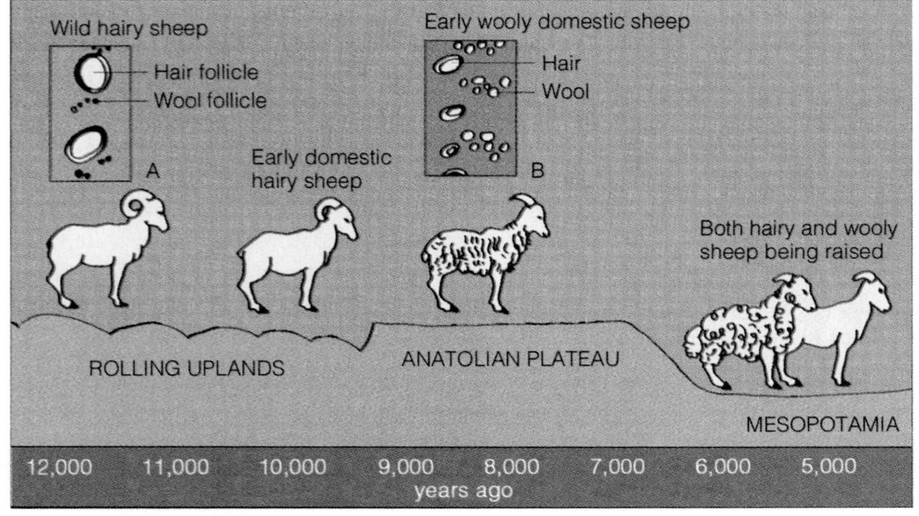

FIGURE 11.2
Domestication of sheep resulted in evolutionary changes that created more wool. Inset A shows a section, as seen through a microscope, of skin of wild sheep, showing the arrangement of primary (hair) and secondary (wool) follicles. Inset B shows a section of similarly enlarged skin of domestic sheep, showing the changed relationship and the change in size of follicles that accompanied the development of wool.

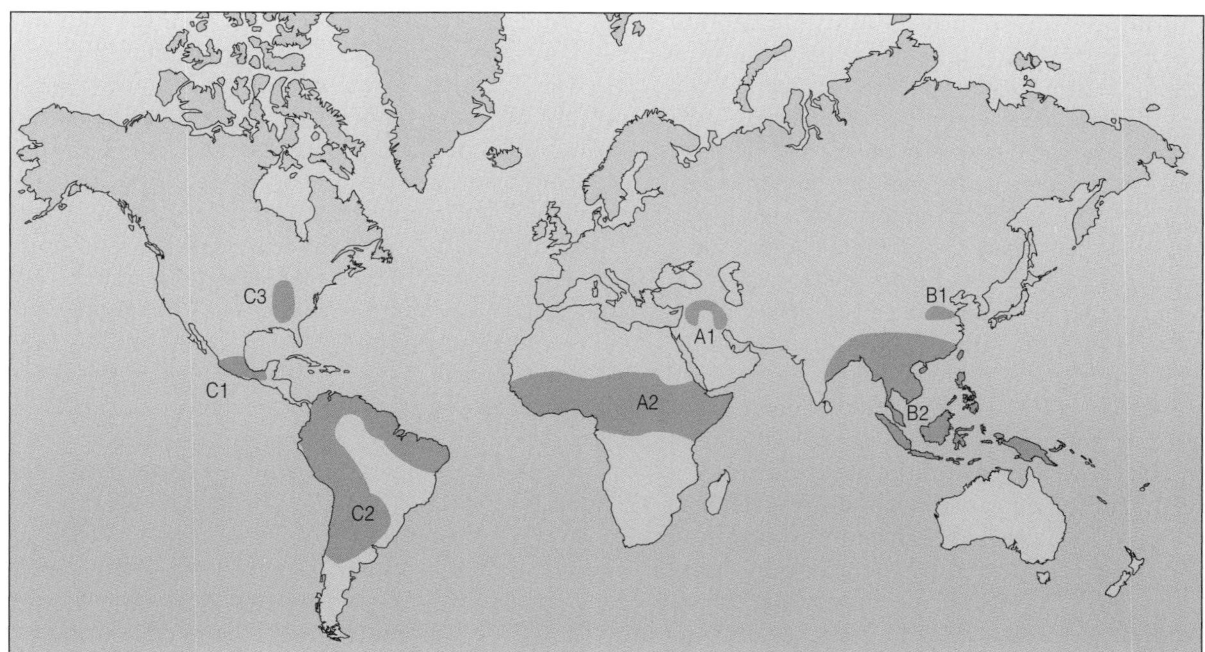

FIGURE 11.3

Early plant and animal domestication took place in such widely scattered areas as Southwest Asia (A1), Central Africa (A2), China (B1), Southeast Asia (B2), Mesoamerica (C1), South America (C2), and North America (C3).

known for the domestication of root crops, most notably yams and taro. Root crop farming, or **vegeculture,** typically involves the growing of many different species together in a single field. Because this approximates the complexity of the natural vegetation, vegeculture tends to be more stable than seed crop cultivation. Propagation or breeding of new plants typically occurs through vegetative means—the planting of cuttings—rather than the planting of seeds.

© Anders Ryman/Corbis

The Dani people of New Guinea specialize in growing sweet potatoes, a crop introduced in the 16th century into a region with a long history of vegeculture. Today villagers grow more than seventy species of sweet potato and have incorporated this root crop into many important rituals.

MEDIATREK

To consider the global origins of agriculture and civilization as well as the ability of countries to feed their populations in the future, visit MediaTrek 11.1 on the companion Web site or CD-ROM.

In the Americas, the domestication of plants began about as early as it did in these other regions. One species of domestic squash may have been grown as early as 10,000 years ago in the coastal forests of Ecuador; at the same time another species was being grown in an arid region of highland Mexico.[15] Evidently, these developments were independent of each other. Other crops were eventually added later; the earliest occurrence of maize (corn), for example, is from a site on the Gulf Coast of the Mexican state of Tabasco dated 7,700 years ago.[16] Because genetic evidence puts its place of origin somewhere in the highlands of western Mexico, it must have appeared

[15] Pringle, p. 1,447.

[16] Piperno, D. R. (2001). On maize and the sunflower. *Science, 292,* 2,260.

vegeculture The cultivation of domesticated root crops, such as yams and taro.

somewhat earlier there. Ultimately, American Indians domesticated over 300 food crops, including two of the four most important ones in the world today: potatoes and maize (the other two are wheat and rice). In fact, 60 percent of the crops grown in the world today were invented by America's indigenous peoples, who not only remain the developers of the world's largest array of nutritious foods but are also the primary contributors to the world's varied cuisines.[17] After all, where would Italian cuisine be without tomatoes? Thai cooking without peanuts? Northern European cooking without potatoes? Or Chinese cooking without sweet potatoes (the daily food of peasants, but also used to make noodles rivaling in popularity those made of wheat)? Small wonder American Indians have been called the world's greatest farmers.[18]

In addition, new evidence from the Amazon rainforest indicates that American Indians had developed sophisticated methods of enriching the rainforest soil to improve crop yields.[19] Generally the quality of soil in the rainforest soil is poor. However, an international team of archaeologists have discovered a mosaic of sites of ancient human habitation coinciding with patches of rich black soil known locally as *terra preta de Indio* (black Indian soil). The black color of the soil is due to the carbonized plant remains incorporated into the soil through ancient cultivation practices. Archaeologist James Petersen describes this black earth as "a gift from the past" because understanding its origins may provide contemporary people with a means of improving agriculture in this region today.

Archaeological evidence for the beginning of farming in Mexico comes from the highland valleys of Oaxaca, Puebla, and Tamaulipas. In the Tehuacan Valley of Puebla, for example, crops such as maize, beans, and squash very gradually came to make up a greater percentage of the food eaten (Figure 11.4). Like the hill country of Southwest Asia, the Tehuacan Valley is environmentally diverse, and the people living there had a cyclical pattern of hunting and gathering that made use of the resources of different environmental zones. In the course of their seasonal movements, people carried the wild precursors of future domesticates out of their native habitat, exposing them to different selective pres-

In coastal Peru, the earliest domesticates were the nonedible bottle gourd (like the one shown here) and cotton. They were used to make nets and floats to catch fish, which was an important source of food.

CULTIGENS		PERCENTAGE Hunting	Horticulture	Wild plant use	Years ago
Squash, Chili, Amaranth, Avocado	Cotton, Maize, Beans, Gourd, Sapote	29%		31%	3,000 – 4,000
Squash, Chili, Amaranth, Avocado	Maize, Beans, Gourd, Sapote	25%		50%	4,500 – 5,000
Squash, Chili, Amaranth, Avocado	Maize, Beans, Gourd, Sapote	34%		52%	5,500 – 6,500
Squash, Chili, Amaranth, Avocado		54%		40%	7,000 – 8,500

Years ago: 3,000; 3,500; 4,000; 4,500; 5,000; 5,500; 6,000; 6,500; 7,000; 7,500; 8,000; 8,500

FIGURE 11.4

Subsistence trends in Mexico's Tehuacan Valley show that here, as elsewhere, dependence of horticulture came about gradually, over a prolonged period of time.

[17]Weatherford, J. (1988). *Indian givers: How the Indians of the Americas transformed the world* (pp. 71, 115). New York: Fawcett Columbine.

[18]Weatherford, p. 95.

[19] Petersen, J. B., Neves, E., & Heckenberger, M. J. (2001). Gift from the past: *Terra preta* and prehistoric American occupation in Amazonia. In C. McEwan, C. Barreto, & E. Neves (Eds.), *Unknown Amazon* (pp. 86–105). London: British Museum Press; Mann, C. C. (2002). The real dirt on rainforest fertility. *Science, 297,* 920–923.

sures. Under such circumstances, potentially useful (to humans) variants that did not do well in the native habitat would, by chance, do well in novel settings.

The change to food production also took place in South America, including the Andean highlands of Peru—again, an environmentally diverse region. Although a number of crops first grown in Mexico eventually came to be grown here, there was greater emphasis on root crops, the best known being potatoes (of which about 3,000 varieties were grown, versus the mere 250 grown today in North America), sweet potatoes, and manioc (originally developed in the tropics). South Americans domesticated guinea pigs, llamas, alpacas, and ducks, whereas the Mexicans never did much with domestic livestock. They limited themselves to dogs, turkeys, and bees.

Although the American Indians living north of Mexico ultimately adopted several crops, such as maize and beans, from their southern neighbors, this occurred after they developed some of their own indigenous domesticates. These included local varieties of squash and sunflower (today, grown widely in Russia as a reliable source of edible oil).

Considering all of the separate innovations of domestic plants, it is interesting to note that in all cases people developed the same categories of foods. Everywhere, starchy grains (or root crops) are accompanied by one or more legumes: wheat and barley with peas, chickpeas, and lentils in Southwest Asia; maize with various kinds of beans in Mexico, for example. Together the amino acids (building blocks of proteins) in these starch and legume combinations provide humans with sufficient protein. The starchy grains are the core of the diet and are eaten at every meal in the form of bread, some sort of food wrapper (like a tortilla) or a gruel or thickening agent in a stew along with one or more legumes. Being rather bland, these sources of carbohydrates and proteins are invariably combined with flavor-giving substances that help the food go down. In Mexico, for example, the flavor enhancer par excellence is the chili pepper; in other cuisines it may be a bit of meat, a dairy product, mushrooms, or whatever. Anthropologist Sidney Mintz refers to this as the core-fringe-legume pattern (CFLP), noting that only recently has it been upset by the worldwide spread of processed sugars and high-fat foods.[20]

THE SPREAD OF FOOD PRODUCTION

Although population growth and the need to feed more people cannot explain the origin of the food-producing way of life, food production has affected population size. As already noted, domestication inevitably leads to higher yields, and higher yields make it possible to feed more people. While increased dependence on farming is associated with increased fertility across human populations,[21] the reasons behind this illustrate the complex interplay between human biology and culture in all human activity. The availability of soft foods for infants

[20]Mintz, S. (1996). A taste of history. In W. A. Haviland & R. J. Gordon (Eds.), *Talking about people* (2nd ed., pp. 81–82). Mountain View, CA: Mayfield.

[21]Sellen, D. W., & Mace, R. (1997). Fertility and mode of subsistence: A phylogenetic analysis. *Current Anthropology, 38,* 886.

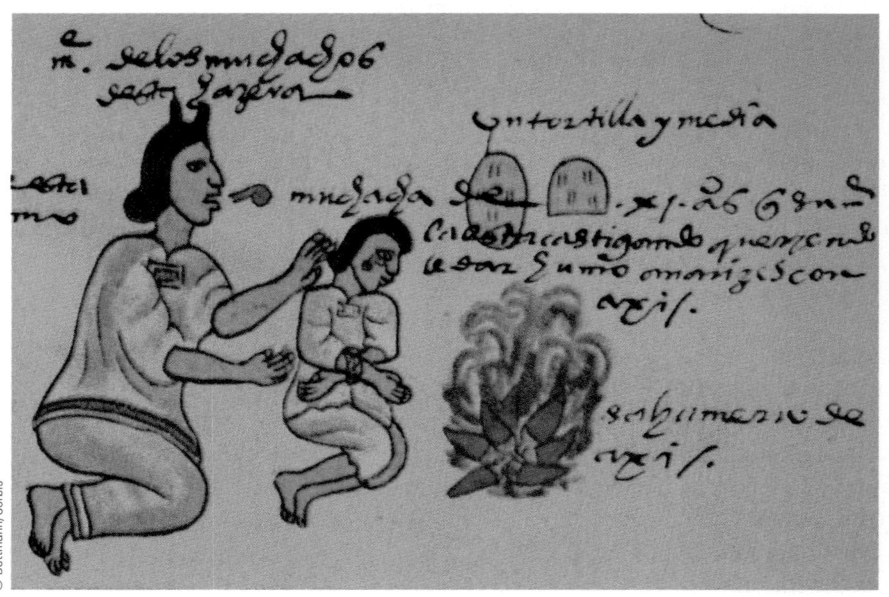

In Mexico, chili peppers have been a part of the diet for millennia. Chili peppers enhance the flavor of foods and aid digestion by helping with the breakdown of cellulose in diets heavy in plant foods. They had other uses as well: This illustration from a 16th-century Aztec manuscript shows a woman threatening her child with punishment by being exposed to smoke from chili peppers. Chili smoke was also used as a kind of chemical weapon in warfare.

Biocultural Connection

Breastfeeding, Fertility, and Beliefs

Cross-cultural studies indicate that farming populations tend to have higher rates of fertility than hunter-gatherers. These differences in fertility were calculated in terms of the average number of children born per woman and through the average number of years between pregnancies or birth spacing. Hunter-gatherer mothers have their children about 4 to 5 years apart while some contemporary farming populations not practicing any form of birth control have another baby every year and a half. For many years this difference was interpreted as a consequence of nutritional stress among the hunter-gatherers. This theory was based in part on the observation that humans and many other mammals require a certain percentage of body fat in order to reproduce successfully. The theory was also grounded in the mistaken cultural belief that the hunter-gatherer lifestyle, supposedly inferior to that of "civilized" people, could not provide adequate nutrition for closer birth spacing. Detailed studies by anthropologists Melvin Konner and Carol Worthman, among the !Kung or Ju/'hoansi people of the Kalahari Desert in southern Africa, disproved this theory, revealing instead a remarkable interplay between cultural and biological processes in human infant feeding.

Konner and Worthman combined detailed observations of Ju/'hoansi infant-feeding practices with studies of hormonal levels in nursing Ju/'hoansi mothers. Ju/'hoansi mothers do not believe that babies should be fed on schedules, as recommended by some North American child-care experts, nor do they believe that crying is "good" for babies. Instead, they respond rapidly to their infants and breastfeed them whenever the infant shows any signs of fussing both during the day and night. The resulting pattern is breastfeeding in short very frequent bouts. As Konner and Worthman document, this pattern of breastfeeding stimulates the body to suppress ovulation, or the release of a new egg into the womb for fertilization. They documented that hormonal signals from nipple stimulation through breastfeeding controls the process of ovulation. Thus, the average number of years between children among the Ju/'hoansi is not a consequence of nutritional stress. Instead, Ju/'hoansi infant feeding practices and beliefs directly affect the biology of fertility. ■ ■ ■

that farming brings about has been suggested as the causal agent in population growth. In humans, frequent breastfeeding has a dampening effect on mothers' ovulation, inhibiting pregnancy in nursing mothers who breastfeed exclusively. Because breastfeeding frequency declines when soft foods are introduced, fertility will tend to increase. However, it would be overly simplistic to limit the explanation for changes in fertility to the introduction of soft foods. Many other pathways can also lead to changes in fertility. For example, among farmers, numerous children are frequently seen as assets, to help out with the many household chores. Further, it is now known that sedentary lifestyles and diets emphasizing a narrow range of resources characteristic of the Neolithic led to high rates of infectious disease and mortality. High human infant mortality with sedentary lifeways parallels the high mortality rates seen among young domesticated animals such as the llamas described earlier in the chapter. High infant mortality may well have led to a cultural value placed on increased fertility. In other words, the relationship between farming and fertility is far from simple, as explored in this chapter's Biocultural Connection.

Paradoxically, although domestication increases productivity, it also increases instability. This is so because those varieties with the highest yields become the focus of human attention, while other varieties are less valued and ultimately ignored. As a result, farmers become dependent on a rather narrow range of resources, compared to the wide range utilized by food foragers. Modern agriculturists, for example, rely on a mere dozen species for about 80 percent of the world's annual tonnage of all crops.[22] This dependence upon fewer varieties means that when a crop fails, for whatever reason, farmers have less to fall back on than do food foragers. Furthermore, the likelihood of failure is increased by the common farming practice of planting crops together in one locality, so that a disease contracted by one plant can easily spread to others. Moreover, by relying on seeds from the most productive plants of a species to establish next year's crop, farmers favor genetic uniformity over diversity. The result is that if some virus, bacterium, or fungus is able to destroy one plant, it will likely destroy them all. This is what happened in the famous Irish potato famine of 1845–1850, which caused the death of about 1 million people due to hunger and disease, and forced another 1.5 million to abandon their homes and emigrate. The population of Ireland dropped from 8 million people before the famine to only 5 million after the famine was over.

The Irish potato famine illustrates how the combination of increased productivity and vulnerability may contribute to the geographic spread of farming. Time

[22]Diamond, p. 132.

VISUAL COUNTERPOINT The higher fertility of the Hutterites, a religious farming culture in North America, compared to that of the !Kung hunter-gatherers, from the Kalahari Desert, was originally attributed to differences in nutrition. It is now known to be related to differences in childrearing beliefs and practices.

and time again in the past, population growth followed by crop failures has triggered movements of people from one place to another, where they have reestablished the subsistence practices with which they were familiar. Thus, once farming came into existence, it was more or less guaranteed that it would spread to neighboring regions. From Southwest Asia, for instance, it spread to southeastern Europe by 8,000 years ago, reaching Central Europe and the Netherlands by about 6,000 years ago and England between 4,000 and 3,000 years ago. Those who brought crops to Europe brought other things as well, including new alleles for human gene pools. Some researchers suggest that as a consequence, those modern Europeans who most resemble their Upper Paleolithic predecessors are to be found around the northern fringes of the region.[23] Early farmers likely introduced languages ancestral to most of today's European languages as well, leaving Basque (spoken today on the Atlantic coast where France and Spain meet) as the sole survivor of languages once spoken by earlier Mesolithic people.

From Southwest Asia, farming also spread westward in North Africa and eastward to India. Here, crops domesticated in the west met those spreading from Southeast Asia, some of which spread further west. Facilitating this east–west exchange was the fact that localities shared the same seasonal variations in day length and more or less the same diseases, temperature, and rainfall.

In sub-Saharan Africa, a similar spread occurred creating the modern distribution of speakers of Bantu languages. Crops including sorghum (so valuable today it is grown in hot, dry areas on all continents), pearl millet, watermelon, black-eyed peas, African yams, oil palms, and kola nuts (source of modern cola drinks) were first domesticated in West Africa but began spreading east by 5,000 years ago.

Between 3,000 and 2,000 years ago, Bantu speakers with their crops reached the continent's east coast, and a few centuries later, reached the Great Fish River, 500 miles northeast of Cape Town, South Africa. Being well adapted to summer rains, African crops spread no farther, for the Cape of South Africa has a Mediterranean climate with winter rains.

In some instances, farming appears to have been adopted by food foragers from food-producing neighbors. By way of illustration, a crisis developed on the coast of Peru some 4,500 years ago as continental uplift caused lowering of the water table and destruction of marine habitats at a time of growing population; the result was an increasing shortage of the wild food resources on which people depended. Their response was to begin growing many of the domestic plants that their highland neighbors to the east had begun to cultivate a few thousand years earlier along the edges of rivers. Here, then, farming appears to have been a subsistence practice of last resort, which a food-foraging people took up only because they had no real alternative.

CULTURE OF NEOLITHIC SETTLEMENTS

A number of Neolithic settlements have been excavated, particularly in Southwest Asia. The structures, artifacts, and food debris found at these sites have revealed much about the daily activities of their former inhabitants as they pursued the business of making a living. Perhaps

[23] Brace, C. L. (1997). Cro-Magnons "R" us? *Anthropology Newsletter, 38* (8), 2.

the best known of these sites is Jericho, an early farming community in the Jordan River Valley of Palestine.

Jericho: An Early Farming Community

At the Neolithic settlement that later grew to become the biblical city of Jericho, excavation has revealed the remains of a sizable farming community inhabited as early as 10,350 years ago. This location had the benefits of the presence of a bounteous spring and the rich soils of an Ice Age lake that had dried up some 3,000 years earlier. Here, crops could be grown almost continuously, because the fertility of the soil was regularly renewed by flood-borne deposits originating in the Judean Highlands, to the west. To protect their settlement against these floods and associated mudflows, the people of Jericho built massive walls of stone around it.[24] Within these walls, an estimated 400 to 900 people lived in houses of mud brick with plastered floors arranged around courtyards. In addition to these houses, a stone tower that would have taken 100 people 104 days to build was located inside one corner of the wall, near the spring. A staircase inside it probably led to a mud-brick building on top. Nearby were mud-brick storage facilities as well as peculiar structures of possible ceremonial significance. A village cemetery also reflects the sedentary life of these early people; nomadic groups, with few exceptions, rarely buried their dead in a single central location.

Close contact between other people of the region and the farmers of Jericho and other villages are indicated by common features in art, ritual, use of prestige goods, and burial practices. Other evidence of trade consists of obsidian and turquoise from Sinai as well as marine shells from the coast, all discovered inside the walls of Jericho.

[24]Bar-Yosef, O. (1986) The walls of Jericho: An alternative interpretation. *Current Anthropology, 27,* 160.

MEDIATREK

To see the ruins and get a sense of what the ancient city of Jericho is like today, visit MediaTrek 11.2 on the companion Web site or CD-ROM.

Neolithic Technology

Early harvesting tools were made of wood or bone into which serrated flints were inserted. Later tools continued to be made by chipping and flaking stone, but during the Neolithic period, stone that was too hard to be chipped was ground and polished for tools. People developed scythes, forks, hoes, and plows to replace their simple digging sticks. Pestles and mortars were used for preparation of grain. Plows were later redesigned when, after 8,000 years ago, domesticated cattle became available for use as draft animals. Along with the development of diverse technologies, individuals acquired specialized skills for creating a variety of implements.

Pottery

Hard work on the part of those producing the food may also support other members of the society who devote their energies to various craft specialties such as pottery. In the Neolithic, different forms of pottery were created for transporting and storing food, artifacts, and other material possessions. Because pottery vessels are imper-

British School of Archaeology in Jerusalem

British School of Archaeology in Jerusalem

The Neolithic farming community of Jericho in the Jordan River Valley was surrounded by a stone wall (6½ feet wide and 12 feet high), as well as a large rock-cut ditch (27 feet wide and 9 feet deep), which served as protection against floods and invaders. The wall included a defense tower (left), which still survives to a height of 30 feet. The people of Jericho lived in substantial houses (right).

Ankara Archaeological Museum/Ara Guler, Istanbul

This pottery vessel from Turkey was made around 7,600 years ago. Pigs were under domestication as early as 10,500 to 11,000 years ago in southeastern Turkey.

vious to damage by insects, rodents, and dampness, they could be used for storing small grain, seeds, and other materials. Moreover, food can be boiled in pottery vessels directly over the fire rather than by such ancient techniques as dropping stones heated directly in the fire into the food being cooked. Pottery is also used for pipes, ladles, lamps, and other objects, and some cultures used large vessels for disposal of the dead. Significantly, pottery containers remain important for much of humanity today.

Widespread use of pottery, which is manufactured of clay and fired in very hot ovens, is a good, though not foolproof, indication of a sedentary community. It is found in abundance in all but a few of the earliest Neolithic settlements. Its fragility and weight make it less practical for use by nomads and hunters, who use baskets and hide containers. Nevertheless, there are some modern nomads who make and use pottery, just as there are farmers who lack it. In fact, food foragers in Japan were making pottery by 13,000 years ago, long before it was being made in Southwest Asia.

The manufacture of pottery is a difficult art and requires a high degree of technological sophistication. To make a useful vessel requires knowledge of clay, how to remove impurities from it, how to shape it into desired forms, and how to dry it without cracking. Proper firing is tricky as well; it must be heated sufficiently so that the clay will harden and resist future disintegration from moisture, but care must be taken to prevent the object from cracking or even exploding as it heats and later cools down. Coloration of the pot, too, is affected by the way it is fired; the presence of oxygen produces a reddish color, whereas absence of oxygen produces a darker color.

Pottery is decorated in various ways. For example, designs can be engraved on the vessel before firing, or special rims, legs, bases, and other details may be made separately and fastened to the finished pot. Painting is the most common form of pottery decoration, and there are literally thousands of painted designs found among the pottery remains of ancient cultures.

Housing

Food production and the new sedentary lifestyle brought about another technological development—house building. Permanent housing is of limited interest to most food foragers who frequently are on the move. Cave shelters, pits dug in the earth, and simple lean-tos made of hides and tree limbs serve the purpose of keeping the weather out. In the Neolithic, however, dwellings became more complex in design and more diverse in type. Some, like the Swiss lake dwellings, were constructed of wood, housed several families per building, had doors, and contained beds, tables, and other furniture. In other places, more elaborate shelters were made of stone, sun-dried brick, or branches plastered together with mud or clay.

Although permanent housing frequently goes along with food production, there is evidence that substantial housing could exist without food production. For example, on the northwestern coast of North America, people lived in substantial houses made of heavy planks hewn from cedar logs, yet their food consisted entirely of wild plants and animals, especially fish.

Clothing

During the Neolithic, for the first time in human history, clothing was made of woven textiles. The raw materials and technology necessary for the production of clothing came from several sources: flax and cotton from farming; wool from domesticated sheep, llamas, or goats; silk from silk worms; and the spindle for spinning and the loom for weaving from human invention.

Social Structure

Evidence of all the economic and technological developments listed thus far have enabled archaeologists to draw certain inferences concerning the organization of Neolithic societies. The general absence of elaborate buildings in all but a few settlements may suggest that neither religion nor government was yet a formally established institution able to wield real social power. Although evidence of ceremonial activity exists, little evidence of a centrally organized and directed religious life has been found. Burials, for example, show a marked absence social differentiation. Early Neolithic graves were rarely constructed of or covered by stone slabs and rarely included elaborate grave goods. Evidently, no person had attained the kind of exalted status that would

© John Kegan/Getty Images

Sometimes Neolithic villages got together to carry out impressive communal works. Shown here is Stonehenge, the famous ceremonial and astronomical center in England, which dates back to about 4500 years ago. Its construction relates to the new attitudes toward the earth and forces of nature associated with food production.

have required an elaborate funeral. The smallness of most villages suggests that the inhabitants knew one another very well, so that most of their relationships were probably highly personal ones, with equal emotional significance.

The general picture that emerges is one of a relatively egalitarian society with minimal division of labor and probably little development of new and more specialized social roles. Villages seem to have been made up of several households, each providing for most of its own needs. The organizational needs of society beyond the household level were probably met by kinship groups and common-interest associations.

NEOLITHIC CULTURE IN THE AMERICAS

In the Americas the shape and timing of the Neolithic revolution also differed compared to other parts of the world. For example, Neolithic agricultural villages were common in Southwest Asia between 9,000 and 8,000 years ago, but similar villages did not appear in the Americas until about 4,500 years ago, in **Mesoamerica** (southern Mexico and northern Central America) and Peru. Moreover, pottery, which arose in Southwest Asia shortly after plant and animal domestication, did not develop in the Americas until about 4,500 years ago. Neither the potter's wheel nor the loom and spindle were used by early Neolithic people in the Americas. Both pottery and textiles were manufactured by hand; evidence of the loom and spindle does not appear in the Americas until 3,000 years ago. None of these absences indicate any backwardness on the part of Native American peoples, who, as we have already seen, were highly sophisticated farmers and plant breeders. Rather, the effectiveness of existing practices was such that they continued to be satisfactory. When food production developed in Meosamerica and Peru, it did so wholly independently of Europe and Asia, with different crops, animals, and technologies.

Mesoamerica The region encompassing southern Mexico and northern Central America.

Outside Mesoamerica and Peru, hunting, fishing, and the gathering of wild plant foods remained important elements in the economy of Neolithic peoples in the Americas. Apparently, most American Indians chose not to make as complete a change from a food-foraging to a food-producing mode of life, even though maize and other domestic crops came to be cultivated just about everywhere that climate permitted.

THE NEOLITHIC AND HUMAN BIOLOGY

Although we tend to think of the invention of food production in terms of its cultural impact, it obviously had a biological impact as well. From studies of human skeletons from Neolithic burials, physical anthropologists have found evidence for a somewhat lessened mechanical stress on peoples' bodies and teeth. Although there are exceptions, the teeth of Neolithic peoples show less wear, their bones are less robust, and osteoarthritis (the result of stressed joint surfaces) is not as marked as in the skeletons of Paleolithic and Mesolithic peoples. On the other hand, there is clear evidence for a marked deterioration in health and mortality. Anthropologist Anna Roosevelt sums up our knowledge of this in the following Original Study.

Original Study

History of Mortality and Physiological Stress

Although there is a relative lack of evidence for the Paleolithic stage, enough skeletons have been studied that it seems clear that seasonal and periodic physiological stress regularly affected most prehistoric hunting-gathering populations, as evidenced by the presence of enamel hypoplasias [horizontal linear defects in tooth enamel] and Harris lines [horizontal lines near the ends of long bones]. What also seems clear is that severe and chronic stress, with high frequency of hypoplasias, infectious disease lesions, pathologies related to iron-deficiency anemia, and high mortality rates, is not characteristic of these early populations. There is no evidence of frequent, severe malnutrition, and so the diet must have been adequate in calories and other nutrients most of the time. During the Mesolithic, the proportion of starch in the diet rose, to judge from the increased occurrence of certain dental diseases, but not enough to create an impoverished diet. At this time, diets seem to have been made up of a rather large number of foods, so that the failure of one food source would not be catastrophic. There is a possible slight tendency for Paleolithic people to be healthier and taller than Mesolithic people, but there is no apparent trend toward increasing physiological stress during the Mesolithic. Thus, it seems that both hunter-gatherers and incipient agriculturalists regularly underwent population pressure, but only to a moderate degree.

During the periods when effective agriculture first comes into use, there seems to be a temporary upturn in health and survival rates in a few regions: Europe, North America, and the eastern Mediterranean. At this stage, wild foods are still consumed periodically, and a variety of plants are cultivated, suggesting the availability of adequate amounts of different nutrients. Based on the increasing frequency of tooth disease related to high carbohydrate consumption, it seems that cultivated plants probably increased the storable calorie supply, removing for a time any seasonal or periodic problems in food supply. In most regions, however, the development of agriculture seems not to have had this effect, and there seems to have been a slight increase in physiological stress.

Stress, however, does not seem to have become common and widespread until after the development of high degrees of sedentism, population density, and reliance on intensive agriculture. At this stage in all regions the incidence of physiological stress increases greatly, and average mortality rates increase appreciably. Most of these agricultural populations have high frequencies of porotic hyperostosis and cribra orbitalia [bone deformities indicative of chronic iron-deficiency anemia], and there is a substantial increase in the number and severity of enamel hypoplasias and pathologies associated with infectious disease. Stature in many populations appears to have been considerably lower than would be expected if genetically determined height maxima had been reached, which suggests that the growth arrests documented by pathologies were causing stunting. Accompanying these indicators of poor health and nourishment, there is a universal drop in the occurrence of Harris lines, suggesting a poor rate of full recovery from the stress. Incidence of carbohydrate-related tooth disease increases, apparently because subsistence by this time is characterized by a heavy emphasis on a few starchy food crops. Populations seem to have grown beyond the point at which wild food resources could be a meaningful dietary supplement, and even domestic animal

Alan H. Goodman, Hampshire College

Harris lines near the ends of these youthful thigh bones, found in a prehistoric farming community in Arizona, are indicative of recovery after growth arrest, caused by famine or disease.

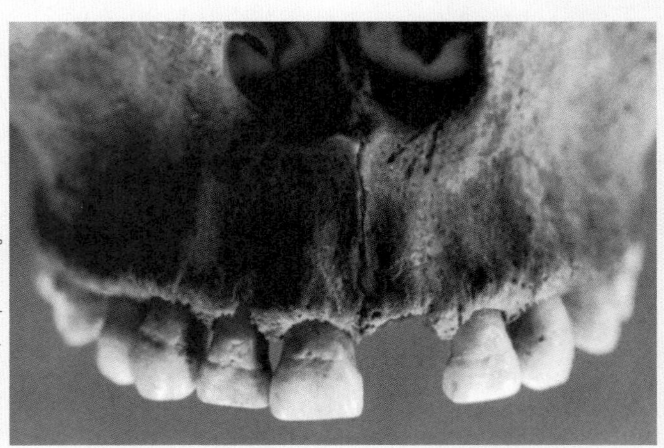

Alan H. Goodman, Hampshire College

Enamel hypoplasias, such as those shown on these teeth, are indicative of arrested growth caused by famine or disease. These teeth are from an adult who lived in an ancient farming community in Arizona.

[CONTINUED]

[CONTINUED]

resources were commonly reserved for farm labor and transport rather than for diet supplementation.

It seems that a large proportion of most sedentary prehistoric populations under intensive agriculture underwent chronic and life-threatening malnutrition and disease, especially during infancy and childhood. The causes of the nutritional stress are likely to have been the poverty of the staple crops in most nutrients except calories, periodic famines caused by the instability of the agricultural system, and chronic lack of food due to both population growth and economic expropriation by elites. The increases in infectious disease probably reflect both a poorer diet and increased interpersonal contact in crowded settlements, and it is, in turn, likely to have aggravated nutritional problems. *(By A. C. Roosevelt. (1984). Population, health, and the evolution of subsistence: Conclusions from the conference. In M. N. Cohen & G. J. Armelagos (Eds.),* Paleopathology at the origins of agriculture *(pp. 572–574). Orlando: Academic Press.)*

For the most part, the crops on which Neolithic peoples came to depend were selected for their higher productivity and storability rather than their nutritional value. Moreover, as already noted, their nutritional shortcomings would have been exacerbated by their susceptibility to periodic failure, particularly as populations grew in size. Thus, the worsened health and mortality of Neolithic peoples is not surprising. Some have gone so far as to assert that the switch from food foraging to food production was the worst mistake that humans ever made!

Another key contributor to the increased incidence of disease and mortality was probably the new mode of life in Neolithic communities. Sedentary life in fixed villages brings with it sanitation problems as garbage and human waste accumulate. These are not a problem for small groups of people who move about from one campsite to another. Moreover, airborne diseases are more easily transmitted where people are gathered into villages. Another factor, too, was the close association between humans and their domestic animals, a situation conducive to the transmission of some animal diseases to humans. A host of life-threatening diseases—including smallpox, chicken pox, and in fact all of the infectious diseases of childhood that were not overcome by medical science until the latter half of the 20th century—were transmitted to humans through their close association with domestic animals (Table 11.1).

Another example of the impact of food production on human biology is that of the abnormal hemoglobin responsible for sickle-cell anemia, discussed in Chapter 2. Other abnormal hemoglobin is associated with the spread of farming from Southwest Asia westward around the Mediterranean as well as eastward to India, and also with the spread of farming in Southeast Asia. In all these regions, changes in human gene pools took place as a biological response to malaria, which had become a problem as a result of farming practices.

Higher mortality rates in Neolithic villages were offset by increased fertility, for population growth accelerated dramatically at precisely the moment that health and mortality worsened. The factors responsible for higher birthrates have already been discussed in this chapter.

Like many infectious diseases, mad cow disease is a result of domestication and human manipulation of animal diets. In this case the infectious particle is not a virus or bacteria, but rather a prion—a newly discovered infectious protein particle. Prions were introduced to cows through their feed, which included ground remains of other animals with the infected prions. By eating infected beef, the disease may be transmitted to humans.

TABLE 11.1 DISEASES ACQUIRED FROM DOMESTICATED ANIMALS

Human Disease	Animal with Most Closely Related Pathogen
Measles	Cattle (rinderpest)
Tuberculosis	Cattle
Smallpox	Cattle (cowpox) or other livestock with related pox viruses
Influenza	Pigs, ducks
Pertussis ("whooping cough")	Pigs, dogs

Some of the diseases that humans have acquired from domestic animals. Close contact with animals provides a situation in which variants of animal pathogens may establish themselves in humans.

SOURCE: Diamond, J. (1997). *Guns, germs, and steel* (p. 207). New York: Norton.

THE NEOLITHIC AND THE IDEA OF PROGRESS

One of the more widely held beliefs of Western culture is that human history is basically a record of steady progress over time. The transition from food foraging to food production is generally viewed as a great step upward on a supposed ladder of progress. To be sure, farming allowed people to increase the size of their populations, to live together in substantial sedentary communities, and to reorganize the workload in ways that permitted craft specialization. This is not progress in a universal sense but, rather, a set of cultural beliefs about the nature of progress. Each culture, after all, defines progress (if it does so at all) in its own terms.

Whatever the benefits of food production, however, a substantial price was paid. As anthropologists Mark Cohen and George Armelagos put it,

> Taken as a whole, indicators fairly clearly suggest an overall decline in the quality—and probably in the length—of human life associated with the adoption of agriculture. This decline was offset in some regions, but not in others, by a decline in physical demands on the body. The studies support recent ethnographic statements and theoretical arguments about the relatively good health and nutrition of hunter–gatherers. They also suggest that hunter–gatherers were relatively well buffered against episodic stress. These data call in question simplistic popular ideas about human progress. They also call in question models of human population growth that are based on assumed progressive increases in life expectancy. The data suggest that the well-documented expansion of early farming populations was accomplished in spite of general diminution of both child and adult life expectancy rather than being fueled by increased survivorship.[25]

Rather than imposing ethnocentric notions of progress on the archaeological record, it is best to view the advent of food production as but one more factor contributing to the diversification of cultures, something that had begun in the Paleolithic. Although some societies continued to practice various forms of hunting, gathering, and fishing, others became **horticultural**—small communities of gardeners working with simple hand tools and using neither irrigation nor the plow. Horticulturists typically cultivate a variety of crops in small gardens they have cleared by hand. Some horticultural societies, however, developed **intensive agriculture.** Technologically more complex than horticultural societies, intensive agriculturalists employ such techniques as irrigation, fertilizers, and the wooden or metal plow pulled by two harnessed draft animals, such as oxen or water buffalo, to produce food on larger plots of land. The distinction between horticulturalist and intensive agriculturalist is not always an easy one to make. For example, the Hopi Indians of the North

Crops bred for higher productivity and storability, rather than nutritional value, contributed to the poor health of Neolithic people. Even today, plants are still bred for non-nutritional characteristics: long shelf life, appearance, and the like. This is true, too, of genetically engineered crops, which are altered to survive massive applications of herbicides and pesticides and not to produce viable seed (the latter solidifies corporate control of the food system). One may only wonder what the long-term consequences of such practices will be.

horticulture Cultivation of crops carried out with hand tools such as digging sticks or hoes.
intensive agriculture Intensive farming of large plots of land, employing fertilizers, plows, and/or extensive irrigation.

---

[25]Cohen, M. N., & Armelagos, G. J. (1984). Paleopathology at the origins of agriculture: Editors' summation. In *Paleopathology at the origins of agriculture* (p. 594). Orlando: Academic Press.

American Southwest traditionally employed irrigation in their farming while at the same time using simple hand tools.

Some societies became specialized **pastoralists** in environments that were too dry, too grassy, too steep, or too cold for effective horticulture or intensive agriculture. For example, the Russian steppes, with their heavy grass cover, were not suitable to farming without a plow, but they were ideal for herding. Thus, a number of peoples living in the arid grasslands and deserts that stretch from northwestern Africa into Central Asia kept large herds of domestic animals, relying on their neighbors for plant foods. A comparable development took place in the high, intermountain basins of South America. Finally, some societies went on to develop civilizations—the subject of the next chapter.

pastoralists People who rely on herds of domestic animals for their subsistence.

Chapter Summary

■ The end of the glacial period saw great physical changes in human habitats. Sea levels rose, vegetation changed, and herd animals disappeared from many areas. The European Mesolithic period marked a shift from big game hunting to the hunting of smaller game and gathering a broad spectrum of plants and aquatic resources. Increased reliance on seafood and plants made the Mesolithic a more sedentary period for many peoples. Ground stone tools, including axes and adzes, met the needs for new technologies in the postglacial world. Many Mesolithic tools in the Old World were made with microliths—small, hard, sharp blades of flint or similar stone that could be mass produced and hafted with others to produce implements like sickles.

■ The change to food production, took place independently and more or less simultaneously in various regions of the world. Along with food production, people became more sedentary allowing for a reorganization of the workload, so that some people could pursue other tasks. From the end of the Mesolithic, human groups became larger and more permanent as people domesticated plants and animals.

■ A domesticated plant or animal is one that has become genetically modified as an intended or unintended consequence of human manipulation. Analysis of plant and animal remains at a site will usually indicate whether or not its occupants were food producers. Wild cereal grasses, for example, usually have fragile stems, whereas cultivated ones have tough stems. Domesticated plants can also be identified because their edible parts are usually larger than those of their wild counterparts. Domestication produces skeletal changes in some animals. The horns of wild goats and sheep, for example, differ from those of domesticated ones. Age and sex imbalances in herd animals may also indicate manipulation by human domesticators.

■ The most probable theory to account for the Neolithic revolution is that domestication came about as a consequence of a chance convergence of separate natural events and cultural developments. This happened independently even if at more or less similar times in Southwest and Southeast Asia, highland Mexico and Peru, South America's Amazon forest, eastern North America, China, and Africa. In all cases, however, people developed food complexes based on starchy grains and/or roots that were consumed with protein-containing legumes plus some other flavor enhancers.

■ Two major consequences of domestication are that crops become more productive but also more vulnerable. This combination periodically causes population size to outstrip food supplies, whereupon people are apt to move into new regions. In this way, farming has often spread from one region to another, as into Europe from Southwest Asia. Sometimes, food foragers will adopt the cultivation of crops from neighboring peoples, in response to a shortage of wild foods, as happened in ancient coastal Peru.

■ Among the earliest known sites containing domesticated plants and animals, about 10,300 to 9,000 years old, are those of Southwest Asia. These sites were mostly small villages of mud huts with individual storage pits and clay ovens. There is evidence not only of cultivation and domestication but also of trade. At ancient Jericho, remains of tools, houses, and clothing indicate the oasis was occupied by Neolithic people as early as 10,350 years ago. At its height, Neolithic Jericho had a population of 400 to 900 people. Comparable villages developed independently in Mexico and Peru by about 4,500 years ago.

■ During the Neolithic, stone that was too hard to be chipped was ground and polished for tools. People developed scythes, forks, hoes, and plows to replace simple digging sticks. The Neolithic was also characterized by the extensive manufacture and use of pottery. The widespread use of pottery is a good indicator of a sedentary community; it is found in all but a few of the earliest Neolithic settlements. The manufacture of pottery requires knowledge of clay and the techniques of firing or baking. Other technological developments that accompanied food production and the sedentary life were the building of permanent houses and the weaving of textiles.

■ Archaeologists have been able to draw some inferences concerning the social structure of Neolithic societies. No evidence has been found indicating that religion or government was yet a centrally organized institution. Social organization was probably relatively egalitarian, with minimal division of labor and little development of specialized social roles.

- The development of food production had biological, as well as cultural, consequences. New diets, living arrangements, and farming practices led to increased incidence of disease and higher mortality rates. Increased fertility, however, more than offset mortality, and globally human population size appears to have increased since the Neolithic.

Questions for Reflection

1. The changed lifeways of the Neolithic included the domestication of plants and animals as well as settlement into villages. How did these cultural transformations both solve the challenges of existence while creating new challenges for humans of the past?
2. Why do you think some people of the past chose not to make the change from food foragers to food producers? What problems existing in today's world have their origins in the lifeways of the Neolithic?
3. Though human biology and culture are always interacting, the rates of biological change and culture change uncoupled at some point in the history of our development. Think of examples of how the differences in these rates had consequences for humans in the Neolithic and in the present.
4. Why are the changes of the Neolithic sometimes mistakenly associated with progress? Why have the social forms that originated in the Neolithic come to dominate the earth?
5. Although the archaeological record indicates some differences in the timing of domestication of plants and animals in different parts of the world, why is it wrong to say that one region was more advanced than another?

Key Terms

Neolithic
Mesolithic
Microlith
Natufian culture
Archaic cultures
Maritime Archaic culture
Domestication
Phytoliths
Unconscious selection
Transhumance
Vegeculture
Mesoamerica
Horticultural
Intensive agriculture
Pastoralists

Multimedia Review Tools

Companion Web Site

Visit **http://www.wadsworth.com/anthropology_d/** and click on the companion Web site for this textbook to access a wide range of material to aid your study of anthropology. Among the options for self-study in each chapter are learning objectives, flash cards, Internet activities, Web links, InfoTrac College Edition exercises, and practice tests that can be scored and emailed to your instructor.

CD-ROM

The *Doing Anthropology Today* CD-ROM supplied with your textbook provides unique and valuable information designed to enhance your learning experience. This interactive multimedia resource includes video clips, interviews with renowned anthropologists, map and timeline exercises, chapter study quizzes, and much more. *Doing Anthropology Today* will not only help you in achieving your grade goals, but it will also make your learning experience fun and exciting!

Suggested Readings

Childe, V. G. (1951). *Man makes himself.* New York: New American Library.

In this classic, originally published in 1936, Childe presented his concept of the Neolithic revolution. He places special emphasis on the technological inventions that helped transform humans from food gatherers to food producers.

Coe, S. D. (1994). *America's first cuisines.* Austin: University of Texas Press.

Writing in an accessible style, Coe discusses some of the more important crops grown by Native Americans and explores their early history and domestication. Following this she describes how these foods were prepared, served, and preserved by the Aztec, Maya, and Incas.

Diamond, J. (1997). *Guns, germs, and steel.* New York: Norton.

This book, which won a Pulitzer Prize and became a best-seller, tries to answer the question: Why are wealth and power distributed as they are in the world today? For Diamond, the answer requires an understanding of events associated with the origin and spread of food production. Although Diamond is a bit of an environmental determinist and falls into various ethnocentric traps, there is a great deal of solid information on the domestication and spread of crops and the biological consequences for humans. It is a lively book that can be read with pleasure.

MacNeish, R. S. (1992). *The origins of agriculture and settled life.* Norman: University of Oklahoma Press.

MacNeish was a pioneer in the study of the start of food production in the New World. In this book, he reviews the evidence from around the world in order to develop general laws about the development of agriculture and evolution of settled life.

Rindos, D. (1984). *The origins of agriculture: An evolutionary perspective.* Orlando: Academic Press.

This is one of the most important books on agricultural origins. After identifying the weaknesses of existing theories, Rindos presents his own evolutionary theory of agricultural origins.

Zohary, D., & Hopf, M. (1993). *Domestication of plants in the Old World* (2nd ed.). Oxford: Clarenden Press.

This book deals with the origin and spread of domestic plants in western Asia, Europe, and the Nile Valley. Included is a species-by-species discussion of the various crops, an inventory of remains from archaeological sites, and a conclusion summarizing present knowledge.

CHAPTER 12

The Emergence of Cities and States

© David Agee/Anthro-Photo

CHALLENGE ISSUE

WITH THE EMERGENCE OF CITIES AND STATES, HUMAN POPULATIONS DIVERSIFIED ECONOMICALLY AND SOCIALLY AS POPULATION SIZE INCREASED. Technological innovations continually led to further population expansion, creating new biological and social challenges and a feedback cycle between these challenges, technology, and population size. As old challenges were met through technological innovations, population size increased, posing new challenges with their own technological solutions. For example, the development of technology for flood control and protection was a vital part of the development of the great ancient cities of the Indus River Valley, located in today's India and Pakistan. Pictured here is Mohenjo-Daro, an Indus valley city at its peak as an urban center around 4,500 years ago. Note that this city was built on an artificial mound, safe from floodwaters. This densely populated city possessed streets laid out in a grid pattern and individual homes with sophisticated drainage systems.

1 When and Where Did the World's First Cities Develop?

Cities—urban settlements with well-defined centers, populations that are large, dense, and diversified both economically and socially—are characteristic of civilizations that developed independently in Eurasia, Africa, and the Americas. Between 6,000 and 4,500 years ago cities began to develop in China, the Indus and Nile valleys, Mesopotamia, Mesoamerica, and the central Andes. The world's oldest cities were those of Mesopotamia, but one of the largest was located in Mesoamerica.

2 What Changes in Culture Accompanied the Rise of Cities?

Four basic cultural changes mark the transition from Neolithic village existence to life in urban centers: agricultural innovation, as new farming methods were developed; diversification of labor, as more people were freed from food production to pursue a variety of full-time craft specialties; the emergence of centralized governments to deal with the new problems of urban life; and the emergence of social classes, as people were ranked according to the work they did or the position of the families into which they were born.

3 Why Did Cities Develop into States?

Ancient cities developed into what anthropologists call civilizations: societies in which large numbers of people live in cities, are socially stratified, and are governed by centrally organized political systems called states. A number of theories have been proposed to explain why civilizations develop. For example, population growth led to competition for space and scarce resources. This competition favored the development of centralized authority to control resources and, incidentally, organized warfare. Some civilizations, though, appear to have developed as a result of unifying beliefs and values. In some cases, the self-promoting actions of powerful individuals may have played a role. Thus, it may be that civilizations arose in different places for different reasons.

A walk down a busy street of a North American city brings us in contact with numerous activities essential to the well-being of North American society. Sidewalks are crowded with people going to and from offices and stores. Heavy traffic of cars, taxis, and trucks almost comes to a standstill. A brief two-block stretch may contain a department store; shops selling clothing, appliances, or books; a restaurant; a newsstand; a gasoline station; and a movie theater. Other features such as a museum, a police station, a school, a hospital, or a church distinguish some neighborhoods.

Each of these varied services or places of business is dependent on others from outside this two block radius. A butcher shop, for instance, depends on slaughterhouses and beef ranches. A clothing store depends on designers, farmers who produce cotton and wool, and workers who manufacture synthetic fibers. Restaurants depend on refrigerated trucking and vegetable and dairy farmers. Hospitals depend on insurance companies, pharmaceutical and medical equipment industries to meet their needs. All institutions, finally, depend on the public utilities—the telephone, gas, water, and electric companies. Although interdependence is not immediately apparent to the passerby, it is an important aspect of modern cities.

The interdependence of goods and services in a big city makes a variety of products readily available to people. For example, refrigerated air transport delivers fresh Maine lobsters to customers in California. But interdependence also creates vulnerability. If strikes, bad weather, or acts of violence cause one service to stop functioning, other services can deteriorate. Thus, major cities have had to do without vital services such as electricity (as in the blackout in summer 2003 spanning central Canada and the north-central and northeastern regions of the United States), newspapers, subways, schools, and trash removal.

The question is not "Why does this happen?" but rather "Why doesn't it happen more often, and why does the city continue to function as well as it does when one of its services stops?" The answer is that although their services are interdependent, cities are resilient in their response to stresses. When one service breaks down, others take over its functions. During a long newspaper strike in New York City in the 1960s, for example, several new magazines were launched, and television expanded its coverage of news and events. In many parts of the world the violence of war has caused extensive damage to basic facilities leading to the development of alternative systems to cope with everything from the most basic tasks such as procuring food to communication within global political systems.

On the surface, city life seems so orderly that we take it for granted; but a moment's reflection reminds us that the intricate fabric of city life did not always exist, and the availability of diverse goods is a very recent development in human history.

DEFINING CIVILIZATION

The word *civilization* comes from the Latin *civis,* which refers to one who is an inhabitant of a city, and *civitas,* which refers to the urban community in which one dwells. The concept of civilization therefore contains the idea of "citification," or "the coming-to-be of cities." The availability of goods and services in a small space is a mark of civilization itself. This does not mean that civilization is equivalent to modern industrial cities or with present-day Asian, European, or North American societies. People as diverse as the ancient preindustrial

AP/Wide World Photos

The violence of war destroys the basic facilities of cities, as seen in Kabul, Afghanistan, the site of years of constant war.

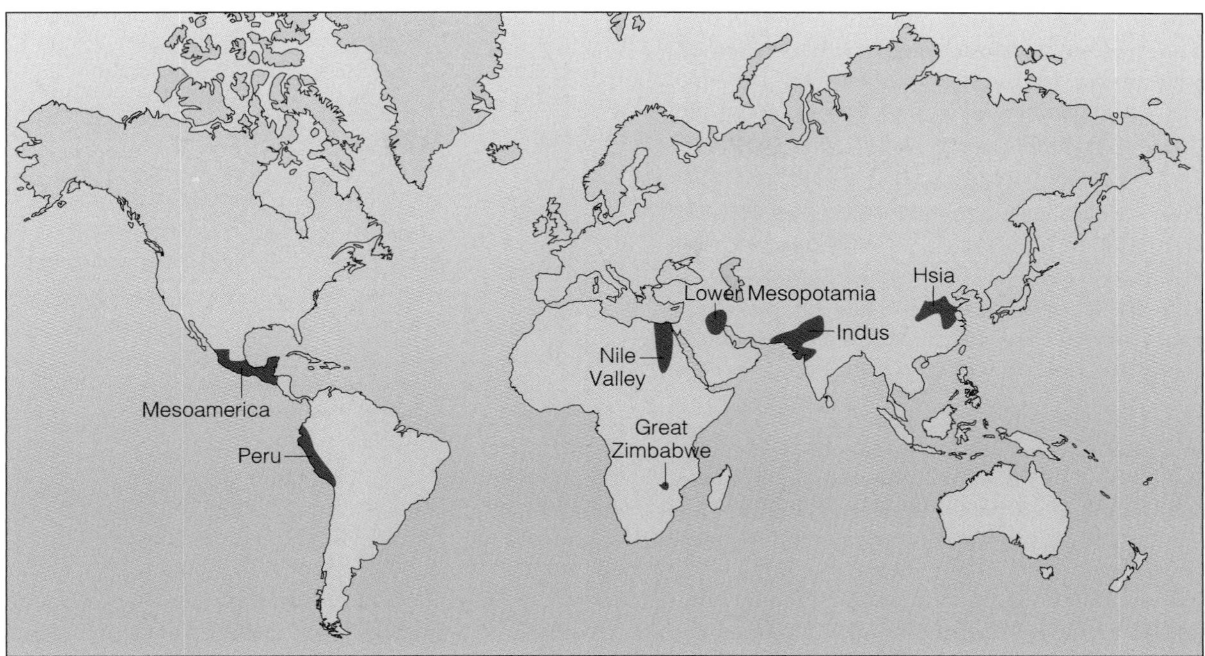

FIGURE 12.1

The major early civilizations sprang from Neolithic villages in various parts of the world. Those of the Americas developed wholly independently of those in Africa and Eurasia; Chinese civilization seems to have developed independently of Southwest Asia (including the Nile and Indus) civilizations.

Aztecs of Mexico and the industrial North Americans of today are included in the term *civilization,* but each represents a very different kind of society. The history of civilization is intimately bound to the history of the earliest preindustrial cities (Figure 12.1).

Civilization is one of those words that is used in different ways by different people. In everyday usage, it carries the notion of refinement and progress, and the term may imply judgments about cultures according to an ethnocentric standard. In anthropology, by contrast, the term has a more precise meaning that avoids culture-bound notions. As used by anthropologists, **civilization** refers to societies in which large numbers of people live in cities, are socially stratified, and are governed by a ruling elite working through centrally organized political systems called states. We shall elaborate on all of these points in the course of this chapter.

As Neolithic villages (discussed in Chapter 11) grew into towns, human culture gave birth to some of the world's first cities. This happened first in Mesopotamia (in modern-day Iraq), then in Egypt's Nile Valley and the Indus Valley (in today's India and Pakistan), between 6,000 and 4,500 years ago. The inhabitants of Sumer, in southern Mesopotamia, developed the world's first civilization about 5,500 years ago. In China, civilization was underway by 5,000 years ago. Independent of these developments in Eurasia and Africa, the first American Indian cities appeared in Peru around 4,000 years ago and in Mesoamerica about 2,000 years ago.

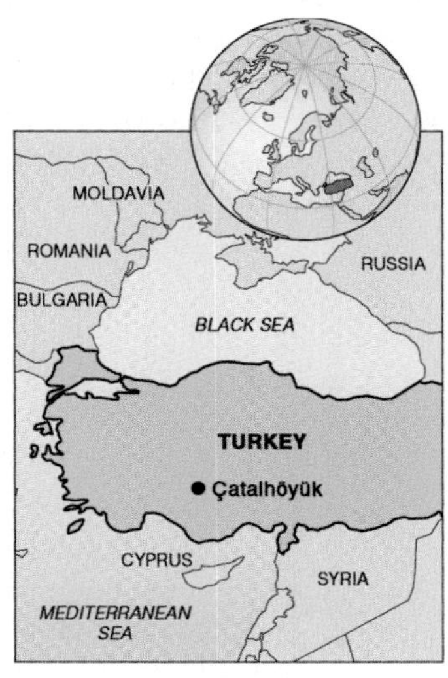

What characterized these first cities? Why are they called the birthplaces of civilization? The first characteristic of cities—and of civilization—is their large size and population. Consider the case of Çatalhöyük, a 9,500-year-old settlement in south-central Turkey.[1] Home to 5,000 or more people, its houses were so tightly packed together, leaving no room for streets, that people dropped through a hole in the roof to get into their houses, after

[1]Material on Çatalhöyük is drawn from Balter, M. (1998). Why settle down? The mystery of communities. *Science, 282,* 1,442–1,444; Balter, M. (1999). A long season puts Çatalhöyük in context. *Science, 286,* 890–891; Balter, M. (2001). Did plaster hold Neolithic society together? *Science, 294,* 2,278–2,281; Kunzig, R. (1999). A tale of two obsessed archaeologists, one ancient city and nagging doubts about whether science can ever hope to reveal the past. *Discover, 20*(5), 84–92.

civilization In anthropology a type of society marked by the presence of cities, social classes, and the state.

Çatalhöyük in Turkey was a compact village, as suggested by this photo, but it was not a true city.

traversing the roofs of neighboring houses. People grew some crops and tended livestock, but also collected significant amounts of food from wild plants and animals, never intensifying their agricultural practices. Because the village was located in the middle of a swamp, these activities were carried out at locations at least 12 kilometers away.

Presumably, Çatalhöyük was located in the middle of a swamp to take advantage of lime-rich clay that people used to plaster their walls, floors, and ovens. The walls were covered with all sorts of paintings, often of small men confronting large beasts, as well as bas-reliefs of leopards, bulls, and women's breasts. Evidence of a division of labor or of a centralized authority is minimal or nonexistent. The houses were structurally similar to one another, and no known public architecture existed. It was as if several Neolithic villages were crammed together in one place at Çatalhöyük.

By contrast, Teotihuacan, like other early urban centers in the Americas (Figure 12.2), illustrates organ-

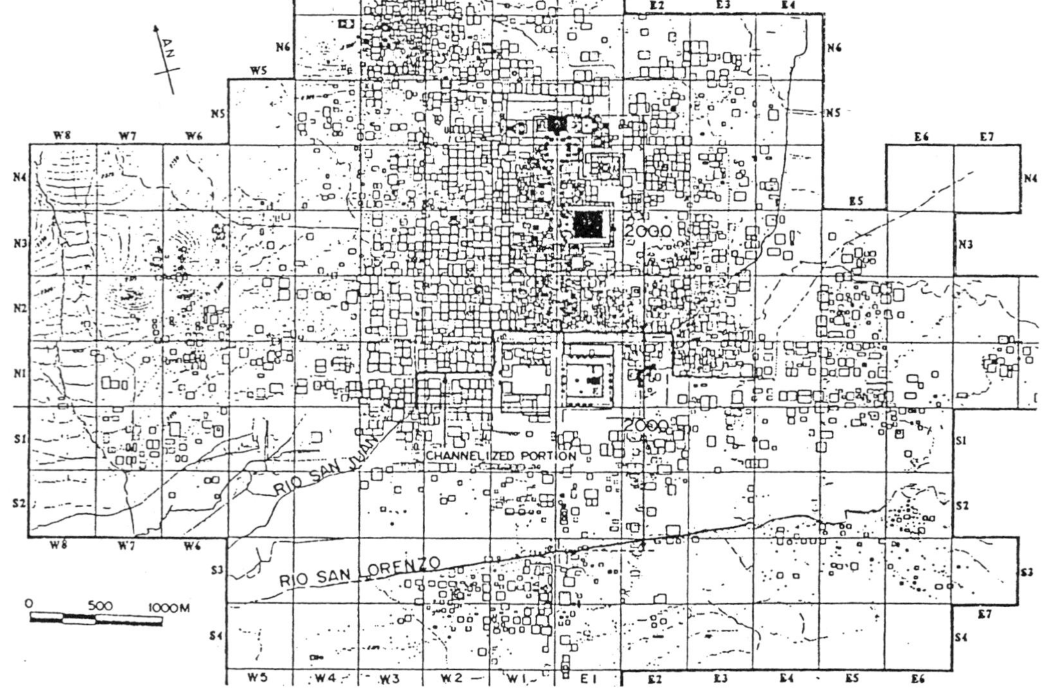

FIGURE 12.2

The founders of Teotihuacan imposed an audacious plan on several square kilometers of landscape in central Mexico. At the center is the Avenue of the Dead, running from the Temple of the Moon (near top), past the Temple of the Sun and, south of the San Juan River (Rio), the palace compound. Note the gridded layout of surrounding apartment compounds and the channeled San Juan River.

ized planning by a central authority, technological intensification, and the social stratification characteristic of cities. Located in the central Mexican highlands, in the first 400 years after its founding 2,200 years ago, its population grew rapidly, until it reached perhaps 80,000 people. Slower growth thereafter brought this figure to around 100,000, all within an area of about 20 square kilometers. Archaeological surveys reveal that over just a few hundred years, the population of the entire Basin of Mexico (5,000 km^2 in the area surrounding modern Mexico City) was relocated to Teotihuacan. The layout of the city was planned from the very start. At its center the Street of the Dead was a grand north-south axis bordered by the huge Sun and Moon pyramids as well as a royal palace compound. The Sun Pyramid was built above a cave, seen as a portal to the underworld, home of deities associated with death. The street itself was deliberately oriented to an astronomical marker, east of true north. Surrounding this core were thousands of apartment compounds, separated from one another by a grid of narrow streets, maintaining the east-of-north orientation throughout the city.

MEDIATREK

To learn about the incredible pre-Aztec city of Teotihuacan, stroll down the Avenue of the Dead, and visit the pyramids of the Sun and the Moon, go to MediaTrek 12.1 on the companion Web site or CD-ROM.

The arrangement of compounds seems to have translated the solar calendar into a unified spatial pattern. So rigid was this layout that the San Juan River was channeled to conform to the grid where it runs through the city. Finally, clear evidence for both social and economic diversity exists. Some six levels of society can be recognized by variation in size and quality of apartment rooms. Those at and near the top of the social scale lived on or near the Street of the Dead. Exotic goods and raw materials were imported from afar to be worked by Teotihuacan artisans, and at least two neighborhoods housed people with foreign affiliations—one with Oaxaca, the other ("merchant's barrio") with the Gulf and Maya lowlands. Also resident in the city were farmers, whose labor in fields (some of them irrigated) supplied the food to fellow city dwellers.[2]

As this comparison shows, early cities were far more than expanded Neolithic villages. The changes that took place in the transition from village to city were so great that the emergence of urban living is considered by some to be one of the great revolutions in human culture. The following case study gives us a glimpse of another of the world's ancient cities, how archaeologists studied it, and how it may have grown from a smaller farming community.

TIKAL: A CASE STUDY

The ancient city of Tikal, one of the largest lowland Maya centers in existence, is situated in Central America about 300 kilometers north of Guatemala City. Tikal was built on a broad limestone terrace in a rainforest. Here the Maya settled 3,000 years ago. Because the Maya calendar can be precisely correlated with our own, it is known that their civilization flourished until 1,100 years ago.

At its height, Tikal covered about 120 km^2, and its center or nucleus was the Great Plaza, a large, paved area surrounded by about 300 major structures and thousands of houses. Starting from a small, dispersed population, Tikal's population swelled to large proportions. By 1,550 years ago, the population density of Tikal

[2]Cowgill, G. L. (1997). State and society at Teotihuacan, Mexico. *Annual Review of Anthropology, 26,* 129–161.

William A. Haviland

© Tom Ives/Corbis

VISUAL COUNTERPOINT Looking south down Teotihuacan's principal avenue, the Street of the Dead, an urban axis unequaled in its scale until the construction of such modern-day avenues as the Champs Elysées in Paris.

William A. Haviland

William A. Haviland

VISUAL COUNTERPOINT The archaeological exploration of the World Heritage Site of Tikal provided considerable knowledge about the life of the ancient Maya and makes the site accessible for tourists and contemporary Maya people today. Note how the ruins were hidden and inaccessible before excavation compared to the site today.

was on the order of 600 to 700 persons per square kilometer, which was three times that of the surrounding region.

From 1956 through the 1960s, Tikal and the surrounding region were intensively explored under the joint auspices of the University of Pennsylvania Museum and the Guatemalan government. Until 1959, the Tikal Project had investigated only major temple and palace structures found in the vicinity of the Great Plaza, at the site's epicenter. It became evident, however, that in order to gain a balanced view of Tikal's development and composition, considerable attention would have to be devoted to hundreds of small mounds, thought to be the remains of dwellings, which surround the larger buildings. In some senses, this represented a shift in the practice of archaeology toward studying the complexities of everyday life. Imagine how difficult it would be to get a realistic view of life in a major city such as Washington, D.C., or Moscow by looking only at their monumental public buildings. Similarly, one cannot obtain a realistic view of Tikal without examining the full range of ruins in the area.

This long-range program of excavation of small structures, most of which were probably houses, was necessary at Tikal to provide an estimate of the city's population size and density. This information was critical for testing hypotheses regarding conventional assumptions about the Maya. One such idea was that the Maya could not have sustained large concentrations of population because their subsistence practices were not adequate. Extensive excavation would also provide a sound basis for a reconstruction of the everyday life and social organization of the Maya, a people then known almost entirely through a study of ceremonial remains. For example, differences in house construction and in the quality and quantity of associated remains might suggest social class differences; or features of house distribution might reflect the existence of extended families or other types of kin groups. The excavation of both large and small structures could reveal the variations in architecture and associated artifacts and burials; such variations might reflect the social structure of the total population of Tikal.[3]

Surveying the Site

Mapping crews extensively surveyed 6 km^2 of forested earth surrounding the Great Plaza, providing a preliminary map to guide the initial small structure excavation process.[4] For this mapping, aerial photography could not be used, because the tree canopy in this area is often 30 meters (about 100 feet) above the ground, obscuring all but the tallest temples. Many of the small ruins are practically invisible even to observers on the ground. Four years of mapping revealed that ancient Tikal was far larger than the originally 6 km^2 surveyed. More time and money were required to continue surveying the area in order to fully define the city's boundaries. To simplify the surveying problem, straight trails oriented toward north, south, east, and west, with the Great Plaza as the center point, were cut through the forest, measured, and staked by government surveyors. The distribution of ruins was plotted, in strips 500 meters wide, using the

[3]Haviland, W. A. (2002). Settlement, society and demography at Tikal. In J. Sabloff (Ed.), *Tikal*. Santa Fe: School of American Research.

[4]Haviland, W. A., et al. (1985). *Excavations in small residential groups of Tikal: Groups 4F-1 and 4F-2*. Philadelphia: University Museum.

© William A. Haviland

At Tikal only the tallest temples are visible above the forest canopy. The two farthest temples are at either end of the Great Plaza, the civic and ceremonial heart of the city. (Those familiar with the original *Star Wars* movie will recognize this view.)

trails as reference points, and the overall size of Tikal was calculated.[5]

Excavation

To begin, six structures, two plazas, and a platform were investigated. The original plan was to strip each of the structures to bedrock in order to obtain every bit of information possible. Three obstacles prevented this procedure, however. First was the discovery of new structures not visible before excavation; second, the structures turned out to be far more complex architecturally than anyone had expected; and, finally, the enormous quantity of artifacts found then had to be washed and catalogued, a time-consuming process. Consequently, not every structure was completely excavated, and some remained uninvestigated.

Following this initial work, over 100 additional small structures were excavated in different parts of the site in order to ensure that a representative sample was investigated. Numerous test pits were sunk in various other small structure groups to supplement the information gained from more extensive excavations.

Evidence from the Excavation

Excavation at Tikal revealed considerable evidence about the social organization, technology, and diversity in this ancient city, as well as the relationship between people in Tikal and other regions. For example, the site provides evidence of trade in nonperishable items. Granite, quartzite, hematite, pyrite, jade, slate, and obsidian all were imported, either as raw materials or finished products. Marine materials came from Caribbean and Pacific coastal areas. Tikal is located on top of an abundant source of flint, which may have been exported in the form of raw material and finished objects. The site is located between two river systems to the east and west, and so may have been on a major

© Enrico Ferorelli

This painting from Cacaxtla in southern Mexico shows a deity with the typical backpack of a Maya merchant. Imported raw materials and finished objects made from exotic materials provide abundant evidence of the presence of merchants and trade at Tikal.

[5]Puleston, D. E. (1983). *The settlement survey of Tikal.* Philadelphia: University Museum.

overland trade route between the two. Also, indirect evidence for trade in perishable goods such as textiles, feathers, salt, and cacao exists. We can safely conclude that there were full-time traders among the Tikal Maya.

In the realm of technology, specialized woodworking, pottery, obsidian, and shell workshops have been found. The skillful stone carving displayed on stone monuments suggests that occupational specialists did this work. The same is true of the fine artwork exhibited on ceramic vessels. Those who painted these had to envision what their work would look like after their pale, relatively colorless ceramics had been fired. To control the large population, estimated to have been at least 45,000 people, some form of bureaucratic organization must have existed. From Maya written records (glyphs) we know that the government was headed by a hereditary ruling dynasty with sufficient power to organize massive construction and maintenance. This included a system of defensive ditches and embankments on the northern and southern edges of the city. The longest of these ran for a distance of perhaps 19 to 28 km. Although we do not have direct evidence, there are clues to the existence of textile workers, dental workers, makers of bark cloth "paper," scribes, masons, astronomers, and other occupational specialists.

MEDIATREK

To take a 360-degree virtual tour of the ancient Maya ruins of Tikal and learn about the cultural practices of this great ancient civilization through the artifacts and ruins, go to MediaTrek 12.2 on the companion Web site or CD-ROM.

The religion of the Tikal Maya may have developed initially as a means to cope with the uncertainties of agriculture. Soils at Tikal are thin, and the only available water comes from rain that has been collected in ponds. Rain is abundant in season, but its onset tends to be unreliable. Once the wet season arrives, dry spells of varying duration can seriously affect crop productivity. Some years, too much rain rots crops in the fields. Other risks include storm damage, locust plagues, and incursions of wild animals. To this day, the inhabitants of the region display great concern about these very real risks involved in agriculture over which they have no direct control.

The Maya priests tried not only to win over and please the deities in times of drought but also to honor them in times of plenty. Priests, the experts on the Maya calendar, determined the most favorable time to plant crops and were concerned with other agricultural matters. The population in and around Tikal depended upon their priesthood to influence supernatural beings and forces on their behalf, so that their crops would not fail. This tended to keep people in or near the city, although a slash-and-burn method of agriculture, which was probably the prevailing method early in Tikal's history, required the constant shifting of plots and consequently would tend to disperse the population over large areas.

As the population increased, land for agriculture became scarce, and the Maya were forced to find new methods of food production that could sustain the dense population concentrated at Tikal. They added the planting and tending of fruit trees and other crops that could be grown around their houses in soils enriched by human waste (unlike houses at Teotihuacan, those at Tikal were not built close to one another). Along with increased reliance on household gardening, the Maya constructed artificially raised fields in areas that were flooded each rainy season. In these fields, crops could be intensively cultivated year after year, as long as they were carefully maintained. Measures also were taken to maximize collection of water for the dry season, by converting low areas into reservoirs and constructing channels to carry runoff from plazas and other architecture into these reservoirs. As these changes were taking place, a class of artisans, craftspeople, and other occupational specialists emerged to serve the needs of an elite consisting of the priesthood and a ruling dynasty. Numerous temples, public buildings, and houses were built.

Carved monuments like this were commissioned by Tikal's rulers to commemorate important events in their reigns. Portrayed on this one is a king who ruled about 1,220 years ago. Such skilled stone carving could only have been accomplished by a specialist. (For a translation of the inscription on the monument's left side, see Figure 12.4.)

For several hundred years, Tikal was able to sustain its ever-growing population. When the pressure for food and land reached a critical point, population growth stopped. At the same time, warfare with other cities was becoming increasingly destructive. All of this is marked archaeologically by abandonment of houses on prime land in rural areas, by the advent of nutritional problems visible in skeletons recovered from burials, and by the construction of the previously mentioned defensive ditches and embankments. In other words, a period of readjustment set in, which must have been directed by an already strong central authority. Activities then continued as before, but without further population growth for another 250 years or so.

The University Museum, University of Pennsylvania

This clay tablet map of farmland outside of the Mesopotamian city of Nippur dates to 3,300 years ago. Shown are irrigation canals separating the various fields, each of which is identified with the name of the owner.

CITIES AND CULTURAL CHANGE

If someone who grew up in a rural North American village today were to move to Chicago, Montreal, or Los Angeles, that person would experience a number of marked changes in his or her way of life. Similarly, changes in daily life would have been felt 5,500 years ago by a Neolithic village dweller upon moving into one of the world's first cities in Mesopotamia. Four basic changes mark the transition from Neolithic village life to life in the first urban centers: agricultural innovation, diversification of labor, central government, and social stratification.

Agricultural Innovation

The first culture change characteristic of life in civilization occurred in farming methods. The ancient Sumerians, for example, built an extensive system of dikes, canals, and reservoirs to irrigate their farmlands. With such a system, they could control water resources at will; water could be held and then run off into the fields as necessary. Irrigation was an important factor affecting an increase of crop yields. Because farming could now be carried on independently of seasons, more crops could be harvested in one year. On the other hand, this intensification of agriculture did not necessarily mean that people ate better than before. Under centralized governments, agricultural intensification was generally carried out with less regard for individual human health than when such governments did not exist.[6]

As described in the case study, the ancient Maya who lived at Tikal developed systems of tree cultivation and constructed raised fields in seasonally flooded swamplands to supplement slash-and-burn farming. The resultant increase in crop yields permitted a higher population density. Increased crop yields, resulting from agricultural innovations such as those of the ancient Maya and Sumerians, were undoubtedly a factor contributing to the high population densities of ancient civilizations.

Diversification of Labor

The second culture change characteristic of civilization is diversification of labor. In a Neolithic village without irrigation or plow farming, every family member participated in the raising of crops. The high crop yields made possible by new farming methods and the increased population permitted a sizable number of people to pursue nonagricultural activities on a full-time basis. In the early cities, some people still farmed (as at Tikal and Teotihuacan), but a substantial number of the inhabitants were skilled craftspeople, merchants, or were engaged in other tasks.

Ancient public records indicate a considerable variety of such specialized workers. For example, an early Mesopotamian document from the old Babylonian city of Lagash lists the artisans, craftspeople, and others paid from crop surpluses stored in the temple granaries.

[6]Roosevelt, A. C. (1984). Population, health, and the evolution of subsistence: Conclusions from the conference. In M. N. Cohen & G. J. Armelagos (Eds.), *Paleopathology at the origins of agriculture* (p. 568). Orlando: Academic Press.

Ban Chiang Project, University of Pennsylvania Museum

The earliest objects of bronze, such as this one, come from Ban Chiang, Thailand.

Among them were coppersmiths, silversmiths, sculptors, merchants, potters, tanners, engravers, butchers, carpenters, spinners, barbers, cabinetmakers, bakers, clerks, and brewers. At the ancient Maya city of Tikal we have evidence for traders, potters, shell workers, woodworkers, obsidian workers, painters, scribes, and sculptors, and perhaps textile workers, dental workers, and paper makers.

With specialization came the expertise that led to the invention of new ways of making and doing things. In Eurasia and Africa, civilization ushered in what archaeologists often refer to as the **Bronze Age,** a period marked by the production of tools and ornaments made of this metal. Metals were in great demand for the manufacture of farmers' and artisans' tools, as well as for weapons. Copper and tin (the raw materials from which bronze is made) were smelted, or separated from their ores, then purified, and cast to make plows, swords, axes, and shields. Later, such tools were made from smelted iron. In wars over border disputes or to extend a state's territory, stone knives, spears, and slings could not stand up against metal spears, arrowheads, swords, helmets, or armor.

The indigenous civilizations of the Americas also used metals. In South America, copper, silver, and gold were used for tools as well as ceremonial and ornamental objects. The Aztecs and Maya used the same soft metals for ceremonial and ornamental objects while continuing to rely on stone for their everyday tools. To those who assume that metal is inherently superior, this seems puzzling. However, the ready availability of obsidian (a glass formed by volcanic activity), its extreme sharpness (many times sharper than the finest steel), and the ease with which it could be worked made it perfectly suited to their needs. Moreover, unlike bronze and especially iron, copper, silver, and gold are soft metals and have limited practical use. As described in Chapter 10's Anthropology Applied feature, obsidian tools provide some of the sharpest cutting edges ever made.

Early civilizations developed extensive trade systems to procure the raw materials needed for their technologies. The city of Teotihuacan, for example, controlled most of the obsidian trade in central Mexico.

Bronze Age In the Old World, the period marked by the production of tools and ornaments of bronze; began about 5,000 years ago in China and Southwest Asia and about 500 years earlier in Southeast Asia.

American Museum of Natural History

Aztec spears tipped and edged with obsidian blades are shown in this 16th-century drawing of a battle with the Aztecs' Spanish conquerors. Though superior to steel for piercing, cutting, and slashing, the brittleness of obsidian placed the Aztecs at a disadvantage when faced with Spanish swords.

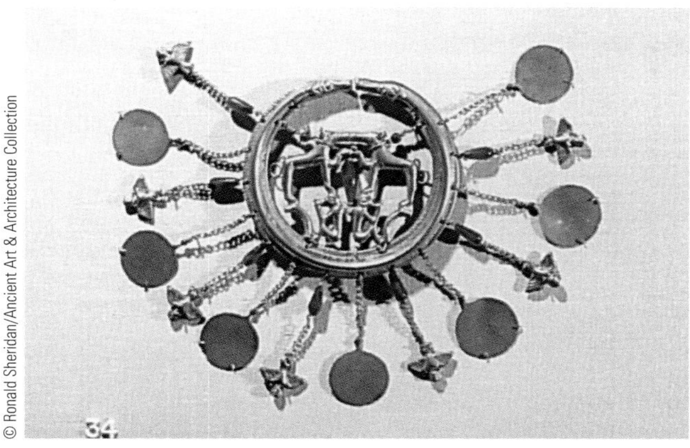

This ear pendant from Mycaenae, Greece, dating to about 3,200 years ago, is a fine example of the artistry that became possible with the introduction of bronze.

Trade agreements were maintained with distant peoples, not only to secure basic raw materials, but to provide luxury items as well. As newly discovered Maya sites such as El Pilar (see Anthropology Applied) are excavated, more will become clear about these trade networks.

MEDIATREK

To learn more about El Pilar and the ongoing work to develop this newly discovered Maya site responsibly, go to MediaTrek 12.3 on the companion Web site or CD-ROM.

In many parts of the world, boats gave greater access to trade centers for transporting large loads of imports and exports between cities at less cost than if they had been transported overland. A one-way trip from the ancient Egyptian cities along the Nile River to the Mediterranean port city of Byblos in Phoenicia (not far from the present city of Beirut, Lebanon) took far less time by rowboat compared to the overland route. With a sailboat, it took even less time.

Egyptian kings, or pharaohs, sent expeditions south to Nubia (northern Sudan) for gold; east to the Sinai Peninsula for copper; to Arabia for spices and perfumes; to Asia for lapis lazuli (a blue semiprecious stone) and other jewels; north to Lebanon for cedar, wine, and funerary oils; and southwest to central Africa for ivory, ebony, ostrich feathers, leopard skins, cattle, and the captives they enslaved. Evidence of trading from Great Zimbabwe in southern Africa indicates that these trading networks extended throughout the "Old World."

Increased contact with foreign peoples through trade brought new knowledge into trading economies, furthering the spread of innovations and even bodies of knowledge such as geometry and astronomy. For example, ancient Egyptians used geometry for such purposes as measuring the area of a field or staking off an accurate right angle at the corner of a building, and this knowledge spread to trading partners along with goods.

Astronomy grew out of the need to know when to plant and harvest crops or when to hold religious observances and to find exact bearings on voyages. Astronomy and mathematics were used to devise calendars. The Maya calculated that the solar year was 365 days (actually, it is 365$^{1}/_{4}$ days), accurately predicted the appearances over time of the planet Venus as morning and evening "star," predicted eclipses, and tracked other astronomical events. As one scholar comments, "Maya science, in its representation of numbers, and its empirical base, is in many respects superior to the science of their European contemporaries."[7]

[7] Frake, C. O. (1992). Lessons of the Mayan sky: A perspective from medieval Europe. In A. F. Aveni (Ed.), *The sky in Mayan literature* (p. 287). New York: Oxford University Press.

The construction of elliptical granite walls held together without any mortar at Great Zimbabwe in southern Zimbabwe, Africa, attest to the skill of the people who built these structures. When European explorers unwilling to accept the notion of "civilization" in sub-Saharan Africa discovered these magnificent ruins, they wrongly attributed them to white non-Africans. This false notion persisted until archaeologists demonstrated that these structures were part of a city with 12,000 to 20,000 inhabitants that served as the center of a medieval Bantu state.

Anthropology Applied

Action Archaeology and the Community at El Pilar

Resource management and conservation are palpable themes of the day. Nowhere is this more keenly felt than the Maya forest, one of the world's most biodiverse areas and among the last terrestrial frontiers. Over the next two decades this area's population will double, threatening the integrity of the tropical ecosystems with contemporary development strategies. Curiously, in the past the Maya forest was home to a major civilization with at least three to nine times the current population of the region.

I began my work as an archaeologist in the Maya forest in 1972. I was interested in the everyday life of the Maya through the study of their cultural ecology—the multifaceted relationships of humans and their environment—rather than monumental buildings. Despite my interest in daily life in the forest, monumental buildings became a part of my work. While conducting a settlement survey in the forest, I discovered El Pilar, a Maya urban center with temples and plazas covering more than 50 hectares. The observation that the ancient Maya evolved a sustainable economy in the tropics of Mesoamerica led my approach to developing El Pilar.

Astride the contemporary border separating Belize from Guatemala, El Pilar has been the focus of a bold conservation design for an international friendship park on a troubled border. My vision for El Pilar is founded on the preservation of cultural heritage in the context of the natural environment. With a collaborative and interdisciplinary team of local villagers, government administrators, and scientists, we have established the El Pilar Archaeological Reserve for Maya Flora and Fauna. Since 1993, the innovations of the El Pilar program have forged new ground in testing novel strategies for community participation in the conservation development of the El Pilar. This program touches major administrative themes of global importance: tourism, natural resources, foreign affairs, and rural development and education. Yet the program's impacts go further. Working with traditional forest gardeners impacts agriculture, rural enterprise, and capacity building. There are few areas untouched by the program's inclusive sweep, and more arenas can contribute to its evolution.

At El Pilar, I practice what I call "action archaeology," a pioneering conservation model that draws on lessons learned from the recent and distant past to benefit contemporary populations. For example, the co-evolution of Maya society and the environment provide clues about sustainability in this region today. At El Pilar we have advanced programs that will simulate "Maya forest gardens" as an alternative to resource-diminishing, plow and pasture farming methods. The forest survives and demonstrates resilience to impacts brought on by human expansion. The ancient Maya lived with this forest for millennia, and the El Pilar program argues there are lessons to be learned from our past.

Rolex Awards for Enterprise, Susan Gray

The El Pilar Program recognizes the privilege it has enjoyed in forging an innovative community participatory process, in creating a unique management planning design, and in developing a new tourism destination. The success of local outreach at El Pilar can best be seen in the growth of the community organization Amigos de El Pilar (Friends of El Pilar). With groups based in both Belize and Guatemala, the Amigos de El Pilar have worked together with the El Pilar program to build an inclusive relationship between the community and the reserve that is mutually beneficial. The development of this dynamic relationship lies at the heart of the El Pilar philosophy—resilient and with the potential to educate communities, reform local-level resource management, and inform conservation designs for the Maya Forest. *(By Anabel Ford, Director of Mesoamerican Research Center, University of California, Santa Barbara.)* ■ ■ ■

Central Government

The third culture change characteristic of civilization is the emergence of a governing elite, a strong central authority required to deal with the challenges new cities face because of their size and complexity. The new governing elite saw to it that different interest groups, such as farmers or craft specialists, provided their respective services and did not infringe on one another's rights (to the extent that they had rights). It ensured that the city was safe from its enemies by constructing fortifications (such as those at Tikal) and raising an army. It levied taxes and appointed tax collectors so that construction workers, the army, and other public expenses could be paid. It saw to it that merchants, carpenters, or farmers who made legal claims received justice according to standards of the legal system. It guaranteed safety for the lives and property of ordinary people and assured them that any harm done one person by another would be justly handled. In addition, surplus food had to be stored for times of scarcity, and public works such as extensive irrigation systems or fortifications had to be

Construction of large-scale public works such as the Great Wall of China reflects the power of a centralized government to mobilize and supervise the labor necessary to carry out such monumental undertakings.

supervised by competent, fair individuals. The mechanisms of government served all these functions.

Evidence of Centralized Authority

Evidence of centralized authority in ancient civilizations comes from such sources as law codes, temple records, and royal chronicles. Excavation of the city structures themselves provides further evidence. For example, archaeologists believe that the cities of Mohenjo-Daro and Harappa in the Indus Valley (see chapter opener) were governed by a centralized authority because they show definite signs of city planning. Both cities stretch out over a 3 mile distance, their main streets are laid out in a rectangular grid pattern, and both contain citywide drainage systems. Similar evidence for centralized planning from Teotihuacan described earlier, also attests to strong, centralized control.

Monumental buildings and temples, palaces, and large sculptures are usually found in civilizations. The Maya city of Tikal contained over 300 major structures, including temples, ball courts, and palaces. The Pyramid of the Sun in the city of Teotihuacan is 700 feet long and more than 200 feet high. Its interior is filled by more than 1 million cubic yards of sun-dried bricks. The tomb of the Egyptian pharaoh Khufu, known as the Great Pyramid, is 755 feet long and 481 feet high. It contains about 2,300,000 stone blocks, each with an average weight of 2.5 tons. The Greek historian Herodotus reports that it took 100,000 men 20 years to build this tomb. Such gigantic structures could be built only because a powerful central authority could harness the considerable labor force, engineering skills, and raw materials necessary for their construction.

Another indicator of the existence of centralized authority is writing, or some form of recorded information (Figure 12.3). With writing, central authorities could disseminate information and store, systematize, and deploy memory for political, religious, and economic purposes.

Like many other "firsts" in human experience, controversy surrounds the question of the earliest evidence of writing. Traditionally the earliest writing was linked to Mesopotamia. However, in 2003 archaeologists working in the Henan Province of western China discovered signs carved into 8,600-year-old tortoise shells resembling later written characters that pre-date the Mesopotamian evidence by about 2,000 years.[8] For symbols to be interpreted as writing they must either be linked with later writing systems or constitute a coherent complex system. The use of abstract symbols evident in the expressive art of the Upper Paleolithic may represent a precursor of writing.

The initial motive for the development of writing in Mesopotamia has been attributed to record keeping of state affairs, allowing early governments to track accounts of their food surplus, tribute records, and other business receipts. Some of the earliest documents appear to be just such records—lists of vegetables and animals bought and sold, tax lists, and storehouse inventories. Being able to record information was an extremely important invention, because governments could keep records of their assets instead of simply relying upon the memory of administrators.

Before 5,500 years ago, records consisted initially of "tokens," ceramic pieces with different shapes indicative of different commercial objects. Thus, a cone shape

[8]Li, X., Harbottle, G., Zhang, J., & Wang, C. (2003). The earliest writing? Sign use in the seventh millennium BC at Jiahu, Henan Province, China. *Antiquity, 77,* 31–44.

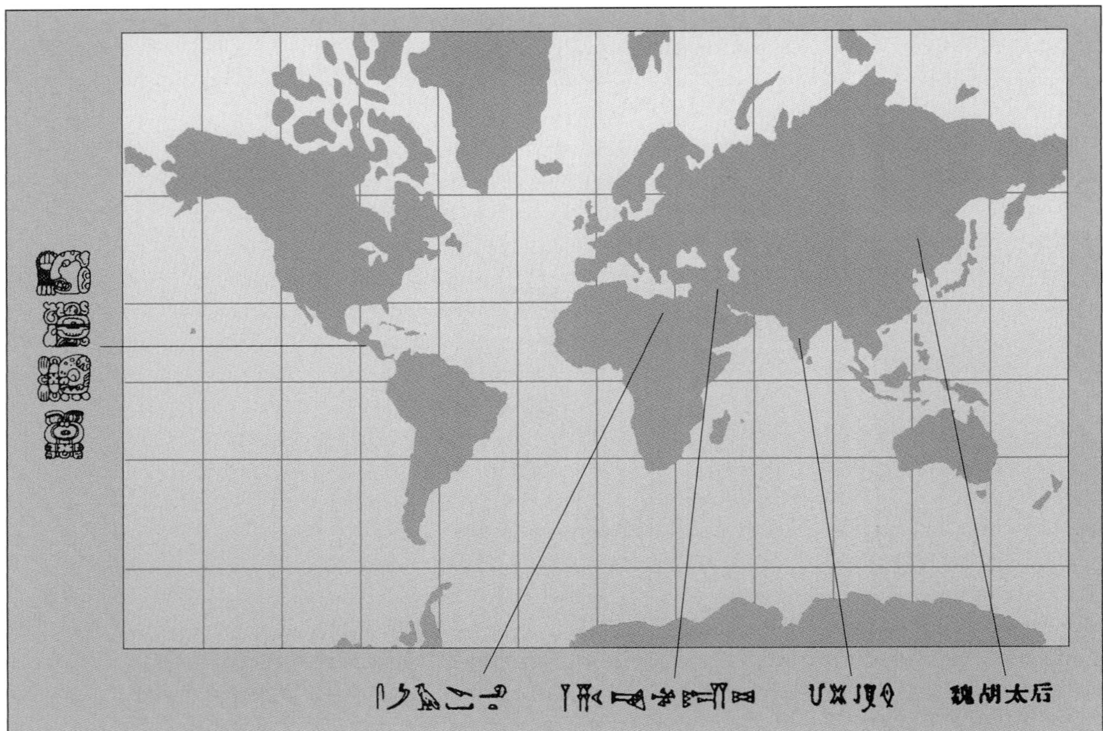

FIGURE 12.3
The impermanence of spoken words contrasts with the relative permanence of written records. In all of human history, writing has been independently invented at least five times.

could represent a measure of grain, or a cylinder could be an animal. As the system developed, tokens represented different animals; processed foods such as oil, trussed ducks, or bread; and manufactured or imported goods such as textiles and metal.[9] Ultimately, clay tablets with impressed marks representing objects replaced these tokens.

In the Mesopotamian city of Uruk, by 5,100 years ago, a new writing technique emerged, which used a reed stylus to make wedge-shaped markings on a tablet of damp clay. Originally, each marking stood for a word. Because most words in this language were monosyllabic, the markings came, in time, to stand for syllables. There were about 600 signs, half of them ideograms, the others functioning either as ideograms or as syllables.

In the Americas, writing systems came into use among various Mesoamerican peoples, but the Maya system is particularly sophisticated. The Maya writing system, like other aspects of Maya culture, appears to have roots in the earlier writing system of the Olmec civilization.[10] The Maya hieroglyphic system had less to do with keeping track of state properties than with extravagant celebrations of the accomplishments of their rulers. Maya lords glorified themselves by recording their dynastic genealogies, important conquests, and royal marriages; by using grandiose titles to refer to themselves; and by associating their actions with important astronomical events (Figure 12.4). Often, the latter involved complicated mathematical calculations. So important was the written word in reinforcing the power and authority of Maya kings that scribes were high-ranking members of royal courts. If their king was defeated in warfare, the scribe would be captured, tortured, or killed. The torture was highly symbolic, involving finger mutilation thus destroying a scribe's ability to produce politically persuasive written texts for any rival of the victor.

The Earliest Governments

A king and his advisors typically headed the earliest city governments. Of the many ancient kings known, one stands out as truly remarkable for the efficient government organization and highly developed legal system characterizing his reign. This is Hammurabi, the Babylonian king who lived in Mesopotamia sometime between 3,950 and 3,700 years ago. He issued a set of laws for his kingdom, now known as the Code of

[9]Lawler, A. (2001). Writing gets a rewrite. *Science, 292,* 2,419.

[10]Pohl, M. E. D., Pope, K. O., & von Nagy, C. (2002). *Science, 298,* 1,984–1,987.

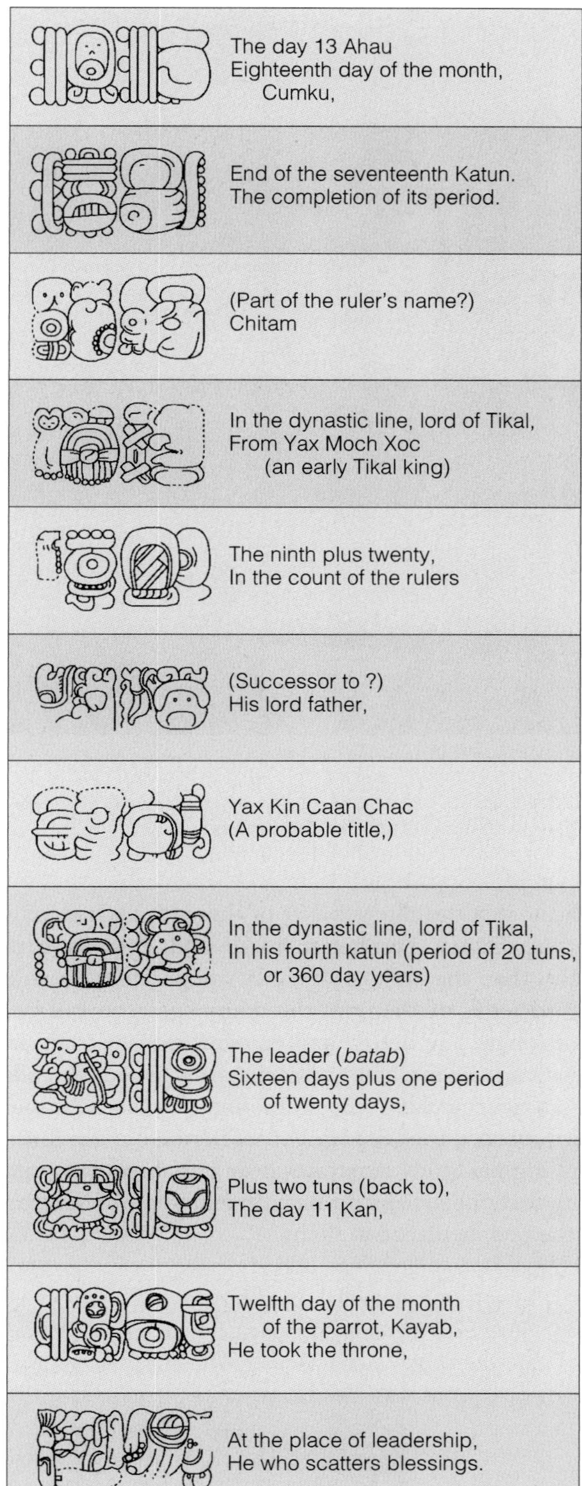

FIGURE 12.4

The translation of the text on the monument shown on page 298 gives some indication of the importance of dynastic genealogy to Maya rulers. The "scattering" mentioned may refer to bloodletting as part of the ceremonies associated with the end of one 20-year period, or Katun, and the beginning of the next.

Hammurabi, which is notable for its thorough detail and standardization. It prescribes the correct form for legal procedures and determines penalties for perjury, false accusation, and injustice done by judges. It contains laws applying to property rights, loans and debts, family rights, and even damages paid for malpractice by a physician. It defines fixed rates to be charged in various trades and branches of commerce and mechanisms to protect the poor, women, children, and slaves against injustice. The code was publicly displayed on huge stone slabs so that no one accused could plead ignorance. Even the poorest citizen was supposed to know his or her rights and responsibilities.

While some civilizations flourished under a ruler (such as Hammurabi) with extraordinary governing abilities, other civilizations possessed a widespread governing bureaucracy that was very efficient at every level. The government of the Inca empire is one such example. The Inca civilization of Peru and its surrounding territories reached its peak 500 years ago, just before the arrival of the Spanish invaders. By 1525, it stretched 2,500 miles from north to south and 500 miles from east to west, making it at the time one of the largest empires on the face of the earth. Its population, which numbered in the millions, was composed of people of many different ethnic groups. In the achievements of its governmental and political system, Inca civilization surpassed every other civilization of the Americas and most of those of Eurasia. An emperor, regarded as the divine son of the Sun God, headed the government, followed by the royal family, the aristocracy, imperial administrators, the lower nobility, and the masses of artisans, craftspeople, and farmers.

The empire was divided into four administrative regions, further subdivided into provinces, and so on down to villages and families. Government agricultural and tax officials closely supervised farming activities such as planting, irrigation, and harvesting. Teams of professional relay runners could carry messages up to 250 miles in a single day over a network of roads and bridges that remains impressive even today. The Inca are unusual in that they had no known form of conventional writing. Instead public records and historical chronicles were kept in the form of an ingenious system of colored beads, knots, and ropes.

Social Stratification

The rise of large, economically diversified populations presided over by centralized governing authorities brought with it the fourth culture change characteristic of civilization: social stratification, or the emergence of social classes. For example, symbols of special status and privilege appeared in the ancient cities of Mesopotamia, and people were ranked according to the kind of work they did or the family into which they were born.

People who stood at or near the head of government were the earliest holders of high status. Although specialists of one sort or another—metal workers, tanners, traders, or the like—generally outranked farmers, such specialization did not necessarily bring with it high status. Rather, people engaged in these kinds of economic activities were either members of the lower classes or outcasts.[11] The merchants who were in a position to buy their way into a higher class were the exception. With time, the possession of wealth and the influence it could buy became in itself a requisite for high status, as it is in some cultures today.

Evidence of Social Stratification

How do archaeologists know that different social classes existed in ancient civilizations? One way they are revealed is by burial customs. Graves excavated at early Neolithic sites are mostly simple pits dug in the ground, containing few, if any, grave goods. Grave goods consist of things such as utensils, figurines, and personal possessions, symbolically placed in the grave for the dead person's use in the afterlife. The lack of much variation between burials in terms of the wealth implied by grave goods in Neolithic sites indicates an essentially classless society. Graves excavated in civilizations, by contrast, vary widely in size, mode of burial, and the number and variety of grave goods. This indicates a stratified society, divided into social classes. The graves of important persons contain not only a great variety of artifacts made from precious materials, but sometimes, as in some early Egyptian burials, even the remains of servants evidently killed to serve their master in the afterlife. The skeletons from the burials may also provide evidence of stratification. At Tikal, skeletons from elaborate tombs indicate that the elite subjects of these tombs had longer life expectancy, ate better food, and enjoyed better health than the bulk of that city's population. In stratified societies of the past, the dominant groups usually lived longer, ate better, and enjoyed an easier life than lower-ranking members of society, just as they do today.

A spectacular tomb from one of the civilizations that preceded the Incas in Peru described in the following Original Study illustrates how burials provide information about social stratification and the other customs of the people placed in them.

[11] Sjoberg, G. (1960). *The preindustrial city* (p. 325). New York: Free Press.

Cultural Relics Bureau, Beijing

Grave goods frequently indicate the status of deceased individuals in stratified societies. For example, China's first emperor was buried with 7,000 life-size terra cotta figures of warriors.

Original Study

Finding the Tomb of a Moche Priestess

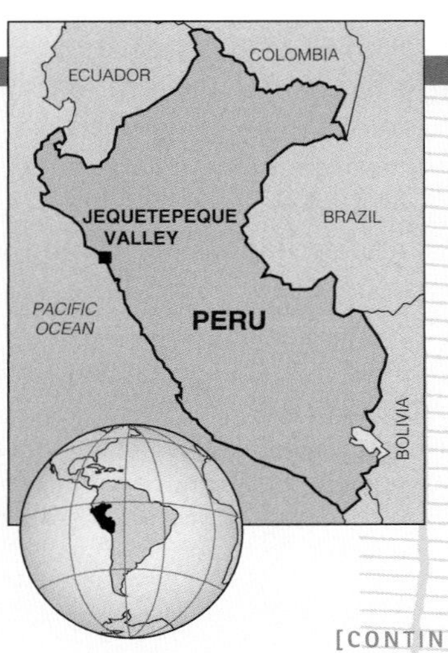

The Moche kingdom flourished on the north coast of Peru between A.D. 100 and 800. Although the Moche had no writing system, they left a vivid artistic record of their beliefs and activities on beautifully modeled and painted ceramic vessels. Because of the realism and detail of these depictions, we are able to reconstruct various aspects of Moche society such as religious

[CONTINUED]

ceremonies and mythology, as well as activities like hunting, weaving, and combat rarely preserved in the archaeological record.

During the past 20 years we have developed a major photographic archive of Moche art at the University of California, Los Angeles, which serves as an important resource for the study of their culture. Our goal has been to reconstruct aspects of Moche culture by combining systematic studies of their art with archaeological fieldwork in Peru. Our analyses of sites, including residential compounds, palaces, temples, and cemeteries, and the artifacts associated with them have allowed us to document archaeologically some of the complex scenes illustrated in Moche art, and to understand aspects of their culture that are not portrayed in the art.

During the past 10 years our research has focused on the Jequetepeque Valley, located in the northern portion of the territory occupied by the Moche. In this region we have undertaken several lines of research, concentrating our efforts on the relationship between Moche ceremonial activities and socio-economic organization. In June 1991, UCLA began excavations at San José de Moro, a major ceremonial center in the lower Jequetepeque Valley. It was clear from its various ceramic styles that the site had a long history of occupation and thus would be ideal for answering questions about the cultural sequence of the region. Moreover, the quantity and variation in monumental construction at the site strongly suggested that it had served as a major ceremonial center through most of its occupation and thus could provide us with good insights about the nature of Moche ceremonial activity.

During our first field season we excavated three complex late-Moche tombs—each consisting of a room-sized burial chamber made of mud bricks. The tomb chambers had originally been roofed with large wooden beams. The principal occupant of each tomb was lying face up in an extended position, with the remains of complete llamas, humans, or both, at their feet. In two of the tombs the principal occupants were flanked by other individuals. Hundreds of ceramic vessels and metal objects, including ceremonial knives, lance points, sandals, cups, masks, and jewelry, had been placed in the tombs as offerings.

The most elaborate of the three tombs was that of a high-status adult female. It is the richest Moche female burial ever scientifically excavated and clearly demonstrates that in Moche society extraordinary wealth and power were not the exclusive domain of males. The tomb chamber was approximately $7\frac{1}{2}$ by 14 feet. The walls, which were made of mud brick, had niches-six on each side and four at the head of the tomb—in which ceramic vessels and parts of llamas had been placed. Additional ceramic vessels had been stacked on the floor of the tomb chamber.

Some of the artifacts associated with this burial provide clear evidence that the Moche were involved in long-distance trade and that their elite expended a great deal of effort to obtain precious materials. Included among the offerings were three imported ceramic vessels—a plate of Cajamarca style, which must have been brought to San José de Moro from the highland area located more than 70 miles to the east, and two exotic ceramic bottles of Nieveria style, a type of pottery that was made in the area of Lima, more than 350 miles to the south. Two other kinds of materials associated with the tomb provide further evidence of long-distance trade. Over the woman's chest and hands were *Spondylus princeps* shells that had been brought from Ecuador to the north and around her neck were cylindrical beads of lapis lazuli that had been brought from Chile to the south.

The most remarkable aspect of this woman's tomb, however, was that the objects buried with her allow us to identify her as a specific priestess who is depicted in Moche art. This priestess was first identified in the Moche Archive at UCLA in 1975, at which time she was given the name "Figure C." Five years later, Anne Marie Hocquenghem and Patricia Lyon convincingly demonstrated that this individual was female. She was one of the principal participants in the "Sacrifice Ceremony," an event depicted in Moche art where prisoners of war were sacrificed and their blood ritually consumed in tall ceremonial goblets.

Figure C is always depicted with her hair in wrapped braids that hang across her chest, and wearing a long dresslike garment. Also characteristic of Figure C is

Dr. Christopher B. Donnan

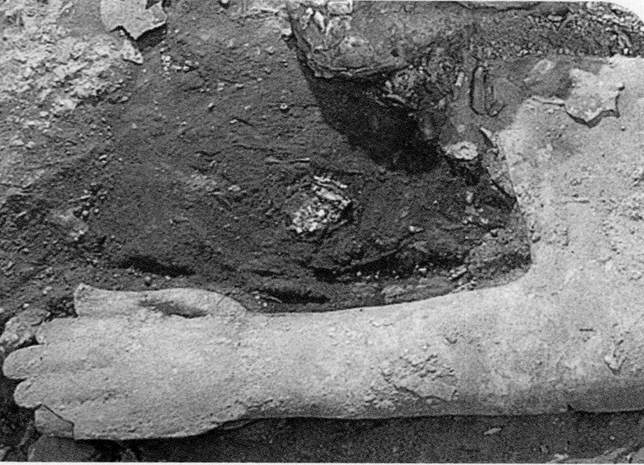

Dr. Christopher B. Donnan

VISUAL COUNTERPOINT A silver-copper alloy mask (left) was found near the priestess' skull. Her body (right) was covered with hammered metal.

[CONTINUED]

The Moche Sacrifice Ceremony

The Sacrifice Ceremony, an event at which prisoners of war are sacrificed and their blood ritually consumed, is a common iconographic theme in Moche art. One of the better-known representations of this ceremony appears on a stirrup spout bottle. The scene, center, shows four principal figures and attendants. Below them are bound captives having their throats slashed. During recent excavations at San José de Moro and at Sipán, the remains of several people who participated in this ceremony have been identified. Figure C, a priestess, was discovered at San José de Moro, while Figure A, a warrior-priest, and Figure B, a bird-warrior, were excavated at Sipán.

A goblet, recovered during the excavation of the priestess' tomb at San José de Moro, is decorated with a scene of anthropomorphic war clubs and shields drinking the blood of captives from tall goblets. A similar goblet is being passed between Figure A and Figure B in the drawing below.

Silver-copper alloy tassels worn by the principal occupant of the tomb allowed her to be identified as the priestess depicted in the Sacrifice Ceremony. The tassels are identical to those worn by Figure C in both the drawing and the Pañamarca mural, bottom.

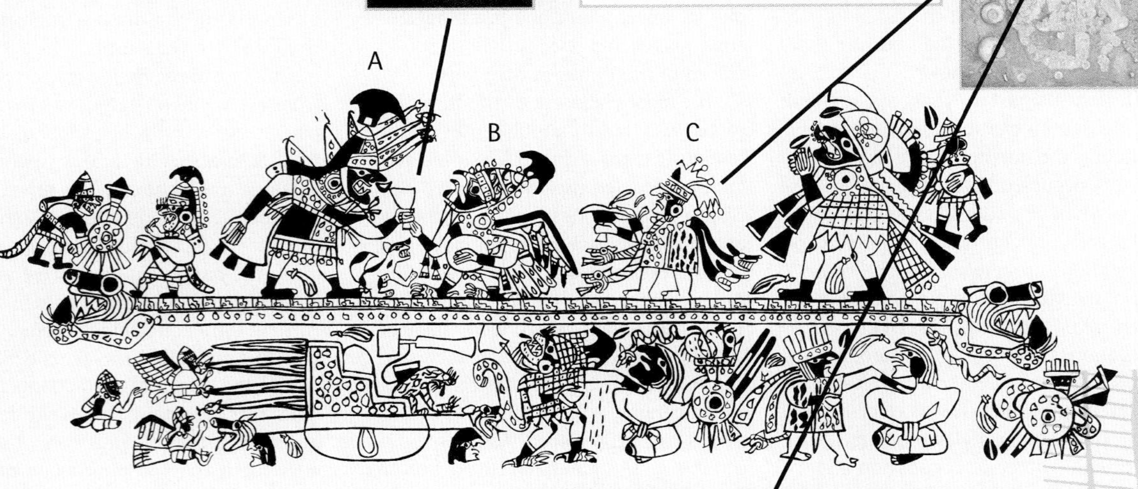

The Pañamarca mural, right, painted on an adobe wall at a Moche ceremonial center in the Nepeña Valley, shows Figure C accompanied by several attendants bearing goblets. Pictured too are three bound captives with their throats slashed and a ceramic basin containing cups. A similar basin, below, was found in the priestess' tomb.

her headdress, which is unique in having two prominent tassels. The tomb of the woman at San José de Moro contained an identical headdress with two huge tassels made of a silver copper alloy.

In one corner of the tomb was a large blackware ceramic basin containing cups and a tall goblet. An identical blackware basin with cups in it is shown associated with Figure C in a famous mural at the site of Pañamarca, a ceremonial center located in the Nepeña Valley. Furthermore, the tall goblet contained in the ceramic basin was of the type used in the Sacrifice Ceremony. It is

[CONTINUED]

decorated with a scene of anthropomorphized clubs and shields drinking blood from similar goblets. The tall goblet is a prominent feature in all depictions of the Sacrifice Ceremony, and it is often seen being presented by Figure C. Finding the tall goblet in her grave thus supports her identification as Figure C.

The tomb of Figure C at San José de Moro has profound implications for Moche studies. Excavations by Walter Alva at Sipán, located in a valley to the north of San José de Moro, have revealed the tombs of two other participants, Figure A and Figure B, in the Sacrifice Ceremony. The richest of these tombs is that of the Lord of Sipán, Figure A. He was buried with his characteristic crescent-shaped headdress, crescent-shaped nose ornament, large circular ear ornaments, and warrior's backflap, and was holding a rattle like that shown in representations of Figure A. The occupant of another tomb appears to be Figure B, a bird-warrior who is frequently shown as companion to Figure A. He was found wearing a headdress adorned with an owl. Although no grave of Figure C has yet been excavated at Sipán, it seems likely that someone who performed this role was also buried at that site.

How do the tombs at Sipán relate to the tomb of Figure C at San José de Moro? First, it should be noted that the two tombs at Sipán date to approximately A.D. 300 and those at San José de Moro at least 250 years later—sometime after A.D. 550. Clearly, the Sacrifice Ceremony had a long duration in Moche culture, with individuals consistently dressing in traditional garments and headdresses to perform the roles of specific members of the priesthood.

The Sacrifice Ceremony was also widespread geographically. The Pañamarca mural, which clearly depicts this ceremony, was found in the Nepeña Valley, in the southern part of the Moche kingdom. San José de Moro is more than 150 miles to the north of Pañamarca, and Sipán is another 40 miles further north. Moreover, in the 1960s rich tombs containing artifacts with Sacrifice Ceremony iconography were looted from the site of Loma Negra in the Piura Valley, more than 300 miles north of Pañamarca.

The four sites where evidence of the Sacrifice Ceremony has been found have certain characteristics in common. Each is located on an elevated area that rises naturally above the intensively cultivated valley floor and is near, but not immediately adjacent to, a river. Each was a major ceremonial complex, with multiple pyramids that for centuries served as staging areas for religious activities. Perhaps each of the other river valleys that made up the Moche kingdom also had a central ceremonial precinct where the Sacrifice Ceremony was enacted.

The fact that the Sacrifice Ceremony was so widespread in both time and space strongly implies that it was part of a state religion, with a priesthood in each part of the kingdom comprised of individuals who dressed in prescribed ritual attire. When members of the priesthood died, they were buried at the temple where the Sacrifice Ceremony took place, wearing their ceremonial paraphernalia and accompanied by the objects they had used to perform the ritual. Subsequently, other men and women were chosen to replace them, to dress like them, and to perform the same ceremonial role.

The careful excavation of the tomb of Figure C at San José de Moro has provided important new insights into the nature of Moche religious practices. As our excavations continue at this remarkable site, we expect to find additional archaeological evidence that will refine and improve upon these insights. *(By C. B. Donnan & L. J. Castillo (1992). Finding the tomb of a Moche priestess.* Archaeology, 48*(6), 38–42.)* Reprinted with the permission of Archaeology Magazine.

In addition to burials, there are three other ways by which archaeologists may recognize the stratified nature of ancient civilizations:

1. THE SIZE OF DWELLINGS In early Neolithic sites, dwellings tended to be uniformly small in size. In the oldest excavated cities, however, some dwellings were notably larger than others, well spaced, and located together in one district, whereas dwellings in other parts of the city were much smaller, sometimes little more than hovels. In the Mesopotamian city of Eshnunna, archaeologists excavated spacious houses on main thoroughfares and huts located along narrow back alleys. The rooms in the larger houses often contained impressive artwork, such as friezes or murals. At Tikal, and other Maya cities, the elite lived in large, multiroomed masonry houses, mostly in the city's center, whereas lower class people lived in small, peripherally scattered houses of one or two rooms, built partly or wholly of pole and thatch materials.

2. WRITTEN DOCUMENTS Preserved records of business transactions, royal chronicles, or law codes of a civilization reveal much about the social status of its inhabitants. Babylonian and Assyrian texts reveal three main social classes—nobles, commoners, and slaves. The members of each class had different rights and privileges. This stratification was clearly reflected by the law. If an aristocrat put out another's eye, then that person's eye was to be put out too; hence, the saying "an eye for an eye." If the aristocrat put out the eye of a commoner, however, the punishment was to pay a *mina* of silver.[12]

Even in the absence of written information, people may record much about their society in other ways. As the Original Study demonstrates, the Moche recorded much information about their society in their art. The

[12]Moseati, S. (1962). *The face of the ancient orient* (p. 90). New York: Doubleday.

William A. Haviland | © Anita de Laguna Haviland

VISUAL COUNTERPOINT Tikal's ruling dynasty lived in palaces such as this one while lower class residents lived in the same sort of houses in which most Maya live today.

stratified nature of this ancient society is clearly revealed by the scenes painted on ceramic vessels.

3. CORRESPONDENCE European documents describing the indigenous cultures of the Americas as seen by early European explorers and adventurers also offer evidence of social stratification. Letters written by the Spanish armed invaders about the Aztec empire indicate that they found a social order divided into three main classes: nobles, commoners, and serfs. Rulers allotted lands (from conquered peoples) and serfs to the nobles. The commoners were divided into lineages, on which they were dependent for land. Within each of these, individual status depended on the degree of descent from the founder; those more closely related to the lineage founder had higher status than those whose kinship was more distant. The third class in Aztec society consisted of serfs bound to the land or porters employed as carriers by merchants. Lowest of this class were the slaves. Some had sold themselves into bondage; others were captives taken in war.

Informative though accounts of other civilizations by Europeans may be, they are not without their problems. For example, explorers, missionaries, and others did not always understand what they saw; moreover, they had their own interests (or those of their sponsors) to look out for and were not above falsifying information to further those interests. These points are of major importance, given the tendency of Western peoples, with their tradition of literacy, to assume that written documents are reliable. In fact, they are not always reliable and must be checked for accuracy against other sources of information. The same is true of documents written by indigenous people about themselves, for they, too, had their particular agendas. Ancient Maya inscrip-

© Heather Angel/Biofotos

Paper making, invented in China 2,000 years ago, is an example of technological innovation by which farming societies evolved into civilizations.

tions, for example, were essentially propagandistic in their intent, which was to impress people with particular rulers' importance.

THE MAKING OF STATES

From northeastern Africa to China to the South American Andes, ancient civilizations are almost always associated with magnificent palaces built high above ground; sculptures so perfect as to be unrivaled by those of today's artists; and engineering projects so vast and daring as to awaken in us a sense of wonder. These impressive accomplishments could indicate to some that progress is embedded in the notion of civilization, particularly when civilizations have come to dominate people with other social systems due to differences in scale. It is important to bear in mind that not all cultures chose this route and that domination relates more to attitude and size rather than cultural superiority. In other words, the changes that have allowed cultures to dominate one another and for civilizations to flourish are both tied to the emergence of centralized governments. Anthropologists have proposed several theories to account for the transition from small, egalitarian farming villages to large urban centers in which population density, social inequality, and diversity of labor required a centralized government.

Irrigation Systems

One theory for the emergence of states was given its most forceful statement by German cultural historian Karl Wittfogel.[13] Simply put, the irrigation, or **hydraulic theory,** holds that Neolithic farmers in ancient Mesopotamia, China, and Egypt, and later in the Americas, noticed that the river valleys that were periodically flooded contained better soils than those that were not; but they also noted that violent floods destroyed their planted fields and turned them into swamps. At first farmers built simple dikes and reservoirs to collect the floodwater for future release into canals and fields. The success of the dikes and canals built by small groups of neighboring farmers led to larger, more complex irrigation systems. The growth of these water systems eventually necessitated the emergence of a group of "specialists"—people whose sole responsibility was managing the irrigation system. The centralized effort to control the irrigation process blossomed into the first governing body and elite social class, and civilization was born.

Several problems exist with this theory. One of them is that some of the earliest large-scale irrigation systems we know about anywhere in the world developed in highland New Guinea, where strong centralized governments never emerged. Conversely, actual field studies of ancient Mesopotamian irrigation systems reveal that by the time cities of this region were already flourishing, (4,000 years ago) irrigation was still carried out on a small scale, consisting of small canals and diversions of natural waterways. If state-managed irrigation existed already, it is argued, such a system would have been far more extensive than that seen through archaeological investigation. Moreover, documents indicate that irrigation was regulated by officials of local temples and not by centralized government. Similarly, in the Americas large-scale irrigation works were a consequence of civilization's development, rather than a cause.

Trade Networks

Some anthropologists argue that trade was a decisive factor in the development of states. In regions of ecological diversity, so the argument goes, trade is necessary to procure scarce resources. In Mexico, for example, maize was grown just about everywhere, but chilies were grown in the highlands, cotton and beans were planted at intermediate elevations, certain animals were found only in the river valleys, and salt was obtained along the coasts. Therefore, some form of centralized authority was necessary in order to organize trade for the procurement of these and other commodities. Once procured, a centralized authority was necessary to redistribute commodities throughout the population. Redistribution and procurement thus promoted the growth of a centralized government.

Although trade may have played an important role in the development of some states, it did not invariably do so. For example, the indigenous peoples of northeastern North America traded widely with one another for at least 6,000 years without developing civilizations comparable to those of Mexico or Peru. In the course of this trade, copper from deposits around Lake Superior wound up in such faraway places as New England, as did chert (a type of stone) from Labrador in northeast Canada and marine shells from the Gulf of Mexico. Wampum, made on the shores of Long Island Sound on

hydraulic theory The theory that explains civilization's emergence as the result of the construction of elaborate irrigation systems, the functioning of which required full-time managers whose control blossomed into the first governing body and elite social class.

[13]Wittfogel, K. A. (1957). *Oriental despotism, a comparative study of total power.* New Haven, CT: Yale University Press.

This mosaic death mask of greenstone, pyrite, and shell was worn by a king of the Maya city of Tikal who died about 1,500 years ago. Obviously the product of skilled craft work, such specialization developed first to serve the needs of religion, but soon served the needs of an emerging elite as well.

the Atlantic coast, was carried westward, and obsidian from the Yellowstone region of the Rocky Mountains has been found in mounds in Ohio.[14]

Environmental and Social Circumscription

In a series of papers, Robert Carneiro of the American Museum of Natural History in New York City advanced the theory that states develop where populations are hemmed in by such environmental barriers as mountains, deserts, seas, or other human populations.[15] As these populations grow, they have no space in which to expand, and so they begin to compete for increasingly scarce resources. Internally, this results in the development of social stratification, in which an elite controls important resources to which lower classes have limited access. Externally, this leads to warfare and conquest, which, to be successful, require elaborate organization under a centralized authority.

Religion

The three theories just summarized exemplify ecological approaches to the development of states. Such theories emphasize the interrelation between people and the environment in which they live. Theories of the emergence of civilization have commonly taken this kind of approach. Although few anthropologists would deny the importance of the human-environment interrelationship, a growing number of them are dissatisfied with theories that do not take into account the beliefs and values that regulate the interaction between people and their environment.[16]

The Tikal case study from earlier in the chapter suggests a balance of beliefs and environmental constraints in a theory accounting for the emergence of the Maya state.[17] This theory holds that Maya civilization was the result of a process of urbanization at places like Tikal. In its early days, Tikal seems to have been an important religious center, perhaps due to the role ritual played in resolving agricultural uncertainty. Because Tikal was seen as a place where supernatural power was especially strong, making it an effective spot for people to interact with cosmic forces and beings, people were drawn there, and its population grew in size and density. The concentration of a growing population, however, was incompatible with the prevailing slash-and-burn agriculture, which tends to promote dispersed settlement. Therefore, new subsistence techniques, such as raised fields, were developed. These were sufficiently productive to permit further population growth, and, by 1,500 years ago, Tikal had become an urban settlement of at least 45,000 people. By then, craft specialization had developed, at first in the service of religion but soon to meet the practical needs of an emerging social elite. This social elite was concerned at first with calendrical and other rituals, but through the control of ritual it developed into the centralized governing elite that could control a population that was growing more diversified in its interests.

Developing craft specialization also drew people into Tikal, where their products were in demand. Trade networks developed to provide exotic raw materials.

[14]Haviland, W. A., & Power, M. W. (1994). *The original Vermonters* (2nd ed., chs. 3 & 4). Hanover, NH: University Press of New England.

[15]Carneiro, R. L. (1970). A theory of the origin of the state. *Science, 169,* 733–738.

[16]Adams, R. M. (2001). Scale and complexity in archaic states. *Latin American Antiquity, 11,* 188.

[17]Haviland, W. A. (2003). *Tikal, Guatemala: A Maya way to urbanism.* Paper prepared for 3rd INAH/Penn State Conference on Mesoamerican Urbanism.

More long-distance trade contacts, of course, brought more contact with outside ideas, including some from distant Teotihuacan. In summary, several factors—religious, economic, and political—interacted in complex ways, with religion playing a central role, in establishing Tikal as an urban center.

Action Theory

One criticism of the above theories is that they fail to recognize the capacity of aggressive, charismatic leaders to shape the course of human history. Accordingly, anthropologists Joyce Marcus and Kent Flannery have developed what they call **action theory.**[18] This theory acknowledges the relationship of society to the environment in shaping social and cultural behavior, but it also recognizes that forceful leaders strive to advance their positions through self-serving actions. In so doing, they may create change. In the case of Maya history, for example, local leaders, who once relied on personal charisma for the economic and political support needed to sustain them in their positions, may have seized upon religion to solidify their power. They did this by developing an ideology endowing them and their descendants with supernatural ancestry. Only they were seen as having the kind of access to the gods on which their followers depended. In this case, certain individuals could monopolize power and emerge as divine kings, using their power to subjugate any rivals.

As the above example makes clear, the context in which a forceful leader operates is critical. In the case of the Maya, it was the combination of existing cultural and ecological factors that opened the way to the emergence of political dynasties. Thus, explanations of civilization's emergence are likely to involve multiple causes, rather than just one. Furthermore, we may also have the cultural equivalent of what biologists call *convergence,* where similar societies come about in different ways. Consequently, a theory that accounts for the rise of civilization in one place may not account for its rise in another.

CIVILIZATION AND ITS DISCONTENTS

Living in the context of civilization ourselves, we are inclined to view its development as a great step upward on a figurative ladder of progress. Whatever benefits civilization has brought, the cultural changes it represents has produced new problems. Among them is the problem of waste disposal. In fact, waste disposal probably began to be a problem in settled, farming communities even before the emergence of civilization. But as villages grew into towns and towns grew into cities, the problem became far more serious, as the buildup of garbage and sewage created optimum environments for such diseases as bubonic plague and typhoid. The latter is an intestinal disease caused by a *Salmonella* bacterium.

Genetically based adaptation to this threat of disease may also have influenced the course of civilization. In northern Europeans, for example, the mutation of a gene on Chromosome 7 that deletes three DNA bases (out of the gene's total of 250,000) makes carriers resistant to cholera, typhoid, and other bacterial diarrheas.[19] Because of the mortality caused by these diseases, selection favored spread of this allele among northern Europeans. But as with sickle-cell anemia, protection comes at a price. That price is cystic fibrosis, a usually fatal disease of the lungs and intestines contracted by those who are homozygous for the altered gene.

In addition to sanitation problems and their attendant gastrointestinal diseases, the rise of towns and cities brought with it other acute, infectious diseases. In a small population, such diseases as chicken pox, influenza, measles, mumps, pertussis, polio, rubella, and smallpox will kill or immunize so high a proportion of the population that the virus cannot continue to propagate. Measles, for example, is likely to die out in any human population with fewer than half a million people.[20] Hence, such diseases, when introduced into small communities, spread immediately to the whole population and then die out. Their continued existence depends upon the presence of large population aggregates, such as provided by towns and cities.

Early cities therefore tended to be disease-ridden places, with relatively high death rates. At Teotihuacan, for instance, very high infant and child mortality rates set a limit to the city's growth. Not until relatively recent times did public health measures reduce the risk of living in cities, and had it not been for a constant influx of rural peoples, areas of high population density might not have persisted. Europe's urban population, for example, did not become self-sustaining until early in the

[18] Marcus, J., & Flannery, K. V. (1996). *Zapotec civilization: How urban society evolved in Mexico's Oaxaca Valley.* New York: Thames & Hudson.

[19] Ridley, M. (1999). *Genome, the autobiography of a species in 23 chapters* (p. 142). New York: HarperCollins.

[20] Diamond, J. (1997). *Guns, germs, and steel* (p. 203). New York: Norton.

action theory The theory that self-serving actions by forceful leaders play a role in civilization's emergence.

Biocultural Connection

Social Stratification and Diseases of Civilization: Tuberculosis

Before the discovery of antibiotics in the early 20th century, individuals infected with the bacteria causing the disease tuberculosis (TB) would invariably waste away and die. But before the invention of cities, the disease TB in humans was rare. The bacteria that cause TB cannot survive in the presence of sunlight and fresh air. Therefore, TB, like many other sicknesses, can be called a disease of civilization. Before humans lived in dark, crowded urban centers, if an infected individual coughed and released the TB bacteria into the air, sunlight would prevent the spread of infection. But civilization affects disease in another powerful way. The social distribution of TB indicates that social stratification is as much a determinant of disease as any bacterium both in the past and in the present.

For example, Ashkenazi Jews of eastern Europe were forced into urban ghettos over several centuries, becoming especially vulnerable to the TB thriving in crowded, dark, confined neighborhoods. As we have seen with the genetic response to malaria (sickle cell and other abnormal hemoglobins) and bacterial diarrheas (the cystic fibrosis gene), TB triggered a genetic response in the form of the Tay-Sachs allele. Individuals heterozygous for the Tay-Sachs allele, were protected from this disease.[a]

Unfortunately, homozygotes for Tay-Sachs allele develop a lethal, degenerative condition that remains common in Ashkenazi Jews. Without the selective pressure of TB, the frequency of the Tay-Sachs allele would never have increased. Similarly, without the strict social rules confining poor Jews to the ghettos (compounded by rules about marriage), the frequency of the Tay-Sachs allele would never have increased.

© Paul Almasy/Corbis

The difficult living conditions in urban slums promote the spread of infectious disease. For example, the rates of tuberculosis, AIDS, hepatitis, and other infectious diseases are very high in this favella, or bustling slum neighborhood in postindustrial cities of Brazil as in many other parts of the world.

While antibiotics have reduced deaths from TB, resistant forms of the bacteria require an expensive regime of multiple drugs. Not only are poor individuals more likely to become infected with TB, they are also less likely to be able to afford expensive medicines required to treat this disease. For people in poor countries and for disadvantaged people in wealthier countries TB is like AIDS—an incurable, fatal, infectious disease. As Holger Sawert from the World Health Organization has said, "Both TB and HIV thrive on poverty." Before the social stratification accompanying the emergence of cities and states, as far as infectious microbes were concerned, all humans were the same. ■ ■ ■

[a]Ridley, M. (1999). *Genome, the autobiography of a species in 23 chapters* (p. 191). New York: HarperCollins.

20th century.[21] What led people to go live in such unhealthy places? Most likely, people were attracted by the same things that lure people to cities today: They are vibrant, exciting places that provide people with new opportunities. Of course, people's experience in the cities did not always live up to advance expectations, any more than they do today, particularly for the poor as described in the Biocultural Connection.

In addition to health problems, early cities faced social problems strikingly similar to those found in many cities all over the world today. Dense population, class systems, and a strong centralized government created internal stress. The poor (including slaves) saw that the wealthy had all the things that they themselves lacked. It was not just a question of luxury items; the poor did not have enough food or space in which to live with comfort and dignity.

Evidence of warfare in early civilizations is common. Cities were fortified; documents list many battles, raids, and wars between groups. Cylinder seals, paintings, and sculptures depict battle scenes, victorious kings, and captured prisoners of war. Increasing population and the accompanying scarcity of good farming land often led to boundary disputes and quarrels over land between civilized states or between so-called tribal peoples and a state. When war broke out, people crowded into walled cities for protection and to be near irrigation systems.

The class system also caused internal stress. As time went on, the rich became richer and the poor poorer. In

[21]Diamond, p. 205.

© Photo Researchers, Inc. © Lester Lefkowitz/Corbis

VISUAL COUNTERPOINT In the Maya city of Copan as in suburban North America, much of the best farmland, such as river valley bottoms, is taken over by buildings serving other functions. In Copan, loss of prime farmland contributed to the demise of the Maya as it became impossible to produce food for city residents. The lifestyle and land use in the United States is similarly unsustainable.

early civilizations one's place in society was relatively fixed. Wealth was based on free labor from slaves. For this reason there was little or no impetus for social reform. Records from the Mesopotamian city of Lagash indicate that social unrest due to exploitation of the poor by the rich grew during this period. Members of the upper class received tracts of farmland some twenty times larger than those granted to the lower class. Urukaginal, an upper-class reformer, saw the danger and introduced changes to protect the poor from exploitation by the wealthy, thus preserving the stability of the city.

It is discouraging to note that many of the problems associated with the first civilizations are still with us. Waste disposal, pollution-related health problems, crowding, social inequities, and warfare continue to be serious problems. Through the study of past civilizations, and through comparison of contemporary societies, we now stand a chance of understanding such problems. Such understanding represents a central part of the anthropologist's mission. In this sense, then, anthropology represents an effort to adapt, so that the next cultural revolution may see our species transcend these problems.

Chapter Summary

- The world's first cities grew out of Neolithic villages between 6,000 and 4,500 years ago—first in Mesopotamia, then in Egypt and the Indus Valley. In China, the process was underway by 5,000 years ago. Somewhat later, and completely independently, similar changes took place in Mesoamerica and the central Andes. Four basic culture changes mark the transition from Neolithic village life to life in civilized urban centers: agricultural innovation, diversification of labor, emergence of centralized government, and social stratification.
- The first culture change, agricultural innovation, involved the development of new farming methods. For example, the ancient Sumerians built an irrigation system that enabled them to control their water resources and thus increase crop yields. Agricultural innovations, in turn, brought about other changes such as increased population size.
- The second culture change, diversification of labor, occurred as part of population growth in cities. Some people could provide sufficient food for others who devoted themselves fully to specialization as artisans and craftspeople. With specialization came the development of new technologies, leading to the beginnings of extensive trade systems. An outgrowth of technological innovation and increased contact with foreign people through trade was new knowledge; within the early civilizations sciences such as geometry and astronomy were first developed.
- The third culture change that characterized urban life, the emergence of central government, provided an authority to deal with the complex problems associated with cities. Evidence of a central governing authority comes from such sources as law codes, temple records, and royal chronicles. With the invention of writing, governments could keep records of their transactions and/or boast of their own power and glory. Further evidence of centralized government comes from monumental public structures and signs of centralized planning. Typically, the first cities were headed by a king and his special advisors. The reign of the Babylonian King Hammurabi, sometime between 3,950 and 3,700 years ago, is well known for its efficient government organization and the standardization of its legal system. In the Americas, the Inca empire in Peru reached its culmination 500 years ago. With a population of several million people, the Inca state, headed by an emperor, possessed a widespread governing bureaucracy that functioned with great efficiency at every level.

- The fourth culture change characteristic of cities and states is social stratification, or the emergence of social classes. In the early cities of Mesopotamia, symbols of status and privilege appeared for the first time, and individuals were ranked according to the work they did or the position of their families. Archaeologists have been able to verify the existence of social classes in ancient civilizations in four ways: by studying burial customs, as well as skeletons, through grave excavations; by noting the size of dwellings in excavated cities; by examining preserved records in writing and art; and by studying the correspondence of Europeans who described the great civilizations that they destroyed in the Americas.
- A number of theories have been proposed to explain why cities and states developed emphasizing the interrelation of the actions of ancient people and their environment. The hydraulic theory holds that the effort to build and control an irrigation system required a degree of social organization that eventually led to the formation of states. Another theory suggests that in the multicrop economies of both the Old and New Worlds, some kind of system was needed to distribute the various food products throughout the population. A third theory holds that states developed where populations were circumscribed by environmental barriers or other societies. As such populations grew, competition for space and scarce resources led to the development of centralized authority to control resources and organize warfare. While these factors coincide with the emergence of states it is difficult to establish whether the environmental condition caused the cultural changes. Further, these theories omit the importance of the beliefs and values of the cultures of the past as well as the actions of forceful, dynamic leaders, whose efforts to promote their own interests may play a role in social change.
- A theory that lays greater stress on the beliefs and values that regulate the interaction between people and their environment seeks to explain the emergence of Maya civilization in terms of the role religion may have played in keeping the Maya in and about cities like Tikal. Probably, several factors acted together, rather than singly, to bring about the emergence of cities and states.
- Sanitation problems in early cities, coupled with large numbers of people living in close proximity, created environments in which infectious diseases were rampant. Early urban centers also faced social problems strikingly similar to those persisting in the world today. Dense population, class systems, and a strong centralized government created internal stress. Warfare was common; cities were fortified, and armies served to protect the state.

Questions for Reflection

1. Technological innovations are a double-edged sword. They both solve biological and cultural challenges while creating new challenges. How was this true in the earliest cities and states? How is this true now?

2. In previous chapters it was emphasized that human evolutionary history should not be thought of as progress. Why is it similarly incorrect to think of the shift from village to city to state as progress?

3. What are some of the ways that differences in social stratification are expressed in your community? Does your community have any traditions surrounding death that serve to restate the social differentiation of individuals?

4. With today's global communication and economic networks, will it be possible to shift away from social systems involving centralized governments or will a centralized authority have to control the entire world?

5. With many archaeological discoveries there is a value placed on "firsts" such as the earliest writing, the first city, or the earliest government. Given the history of the independent emergence of cities and states throughout the world, do you think that scientists should place more value on some of these events just because they are older?

Key Terms

Civilization
Bronze Age
City
Hydraulic theory
Action theory

Multimedia Review Tools

Companion Web Site

Visit **http://www.wadsworth.com/anthropology_d/** and click on the companion Web site for this textbook to access a wide range of material to aid your study of anthropology. Among the options for self-study in each chapter are learning objectives, flash cards, Internet activities, Web links, InfoTrac College Edition exercises, and practice tests that can be scored and emailed to your instructor.

CD-ROM

The *Doing Anthropology Today* CD-ROM supplied with your textbook provides unique and valuable information designed to enhance your learning experience. This interactive multimedia resource includes video clips, interviews with renowned anthropologists, map and timeline exercises, chapter study quizzes, and much more. *Doing Anthropology Today* will not only help you in achieving your grade goals, but it will also make your learning experience fun and exciting!

Suggested Readings

Diamond, J. (1997). *Guns, germs, and steel.* New York: Norton.

Also recommended in the last chapter, this book has an excellent discussion of the relation among diseases, social complexity, and social change.

Fagan, B. (2001). *The seventy great mysteries of the ancient world.* New York: Thames & Hudson.

Archaeologist Brian Fagan edited contributions from twenty-eight other archaeologists and historians about some of the great controversies in the field in this readable book.

Marcus, J., & Flannery, K. V. (1996). *Zapote civilization: How urban society evolved in Mexico's Oaxaca Valley.* New York: Thames & Hudson.

With its lavish illustrations, this looks like a book for coffee table adornment, but it is in fact a thoughtful and serious work on the rise of a pristine civilization. In it, the authors present their action theory.

McNeill W. (1992). *Plagues and people.* New York: Anchor Books.

This book offers an interpretation of world history through the impact of infectious disease. It documents the role disease played in the colonization of the Americas as well as continuing the investigation into the present with a social history of AIDS.

Sabloff, J. A. (1997). *The cities of ancient Mexico* (Rev. ed.). New York: Thames & Hudson.

This well-written and lavishly illustrated book describes the major cities of the Olmecs, Zapotecs, Maya, Teotihuacans, Toltecs, and Aztecs. Following the descriptions, Sabloff discusses the question of origins, the problems of archaeological reconstruction, and the basis on which he provides vignettes of life in the ancient cities. The book concludes with a gazetteer of fifty sites in Mesoamerica.

CHAPTER 13

Modern Human Diversity

© Peter Turnley/CORBIS

CHALLENGE ISSUE

ALTHOUGH OUR BIOLOGICAL DIVERSITY AS A SPECIES IS KEY TO OUR ADAPTIVE ABILITY, HUMANS ARE CHALLENGED TO FIND WAYS TO EMBRACE AND COMPREHEND THE RANGE OF THIS DIVERSITY WITHOUT SUCCUMBING TO OVERSIMPLIFICATION, DISCRIMINATION, AND EVEN BLOODSHED. For example, racism—the categorization of humans into inferior and superior "types," according to physical features such as head shape, hair, eye, and skin color—contributes to discrimination today, leading even to violence such as the 1992 Los Angeles riots. Biological evidence has demonstrated that separate races do not exist. Human biological variation is not distributed into discrete types of people. Race is a cultural construct without objective scientific merits.

1. What Are the Causes of Physical Variability?

Physical variability is a product of underlying genetic variation and the effects of the environment on the expression of genetic variation. Some physical traits are controlled by single genes, with variation present in alternate forms of the gene (alleles). Many physical characteristics like height, weight, or skin color are controlled by multiple genes and are thus expressed continuously, meaning this variation cannot be divided into discrete categories. Evolutionary forces such as natural selection and random drift may cause genetic variability to be unevenly expressed among geographically dispersed populations for a given allele or physical trait. Because evolutionary forces act on each physical trait independently, human biological variation can be studied only "one trait at a time."

2. Is the Biological Concept of Race Useful for Studying Physical Variation in the Human Species?

No. Because races are arbitrarily defined, the division of humans into discrete types does not represent the true nature of human variation. Allele frequencies and variation of phenotypic traits tend to occur in gradations from one population to another without sharp breaks. Furthermore, individual genes are inherited independently from one another so that the expression of variation for any given trait is not linked to other traits. For these and other reasons, anthropologists today actively work to expose the fallacy of race as a biological category that applies to humans while recognizing the significance of race as a cultural category in societies such as in the United States, Brazil, and South Africa.

3. Is Studying Differences in Intelligence from One Population to Another Valid?

These studies are flawed in many ways. First, studies attempting to document biological differences generally involve comparisons among races—a category that for humans is biologically false. Second, there are problems with defining intelligence cross-culturally, as intelligence involves different skills and abilities; each culture places different emphasis on specific aspects of intelligence it values. Third, most instruments (tests) used to measure intelligence are biased toward the dominant culture of the people who created the test. Finally, as a complex set of traits, intelligence cannot be linked to discrete evolutionary forces acting in a particular environment. Whatever genes affect aspects of intelligence, like other genes, most variation exists *within* populations rather than *among* populations.

From male to female, short to tall, light to dark, biological variation can be categorized in a number of ways, but in the end, we are all human. Minute variations of our DNA give each of us a unique genetic fingerprint, yet this variation remains within the bounds of being genetically human. Visible differences among modern humans are expressed within the framework of biological features shared throughout the species, as a species, humans are highly variable.

Human genetic variation generally is distributed across the globe in a continuous fashion with populations expressing variation in the frequency of biological traits. Sometimes this variation follows a pattern imposed by interaction with the environment. For example, alleles for dark skin are found in high frequency in human populations native to regions of heavy ultraviolet radiation (sunshine), whereas alleles for light skin have a high frequency in populations native to regions further from the equator where ultraviolet radiation is reduced. Though this explanation for variation in skin color presents a pattern that may be related to natural selection, other variation among populations or between individuals is fully random. However, the significance we give our variations is always patterned because the way we perceive variation—in fact, whether we perceive it at all—is determined by culture. For example, in many Polynesian cultures, where skin color is not a determinant of social status, people really pay little attention to this physical characteristic. By contrast, in countries such as the United States, Brazil, and South Africa, where skin color is a significant social and political category, it is one of the first things people notice.

Biological diversity, therefore, cannot be studied without an awareness of cultural dimensions that shape the questions asked about diversity as well as the history of how this body of knowledge has been used. When physical anthropologists first began their study of human variation in the 18th and 19th centuries, they were concerned with documenting differences among human groups in order to divide them into a hierarchy of progressively better "types" of humans. Today, this typological approach has been abandoned in the study of biological variation. It has been replaced by the evolutionary study of individual characteristics, combined with an awareness of the effects of the physical environment on the expression of these characteristics as well as the effects of culture on the interpretation of biological variation.

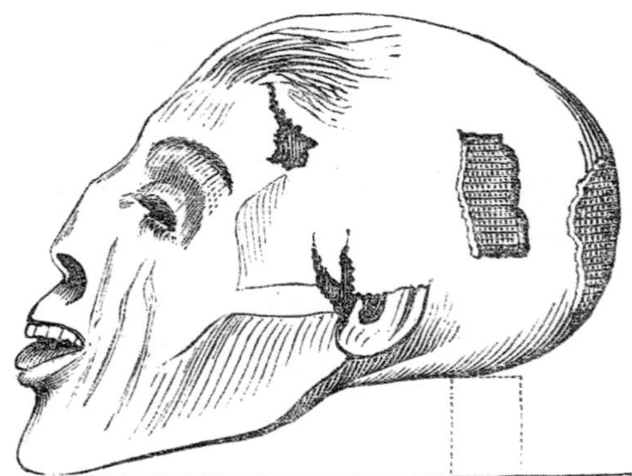

Head of an embalmed idiot, from Thebes

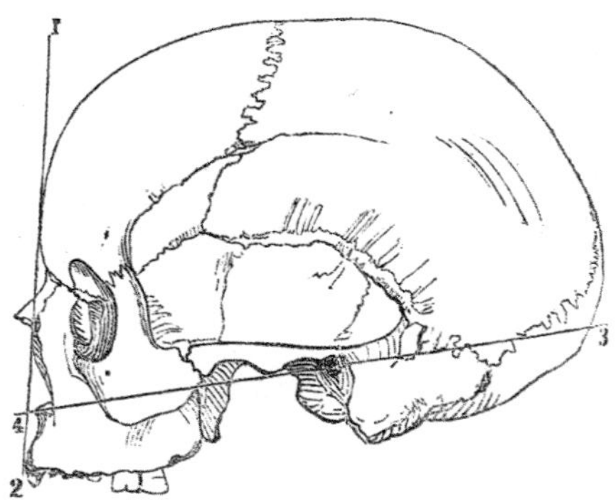

The facial angle measured on an ancient Egyptian head

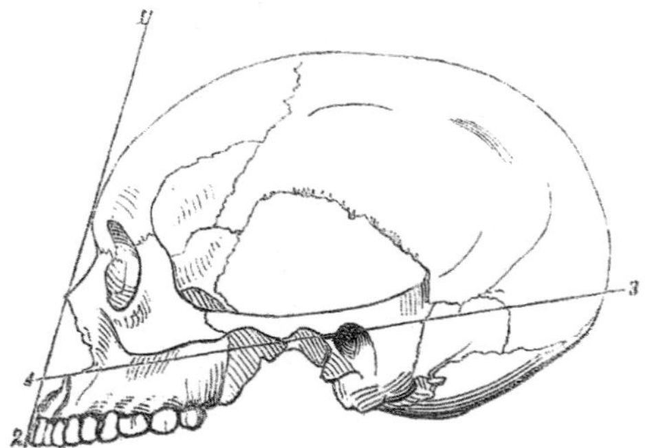

The facial angle measured on a Shoshonee Indian

The work of nineteenth century Philadelphia physician Samuel Morton epitomized the pseudoscientific work conducted to justify cultural beliefs about racial difference. He measured a series of skulls in an attempt to demonstrate the supposed biological superiority of certain people through features of skull shape and size.

BIOLOGICAL VARIATION

The physical characteristics of both populations and individuals, as we saw in Chapter 2, are a product of the interaction between genes and environments. Thus, genes predispose individuals to a particular skin color, for example, but the skin color one actually has, at any given moment, is strongly affected by cultural and environmental factors. The skin of sailors, for example, is darkened or burned after many hours of exposure to the sun and wind, depending not only on genetic predisposition but cultural practices regarding exposure to the sun. In other cases, such as A-B-O blood type, phenotypic expression closely reflects genotype.

For characteristics controlled by single genes, variation occurs through the presence of alternate forms of the genes, known as alleles. Such traits are called

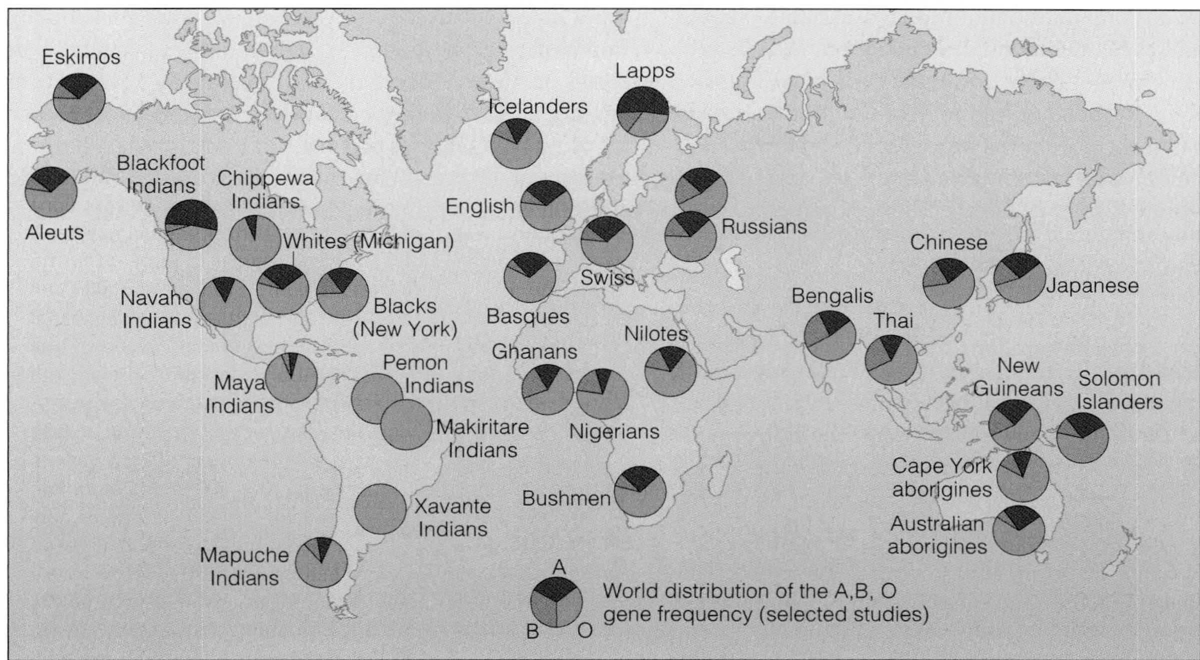

FIGURE 13.1

Frequencies of the three alleles for the A, B, and O blood groups for selected populations around the world illustrate the polytypic nature of *Homo sapiens*. The frequency of the alleles differs among populations.

polymorphic (meaning "many shapes"). Our blood types, determined by the alleles for types A, B, and O blood, are an example of a polymorphism, which in this case may appear in any of four distinct phenotypic forms (A, B, O, and AB). A species can also be considered polymorphic, meaning that variations among individuals exist in addition to differences between males and females in sexually reproducing species. Here "polymorphic" refers to continuous phenotypic variation that may be genetically controlled by many genes as well as the allelic variation described above. When a polymorphic species faces changing environmental conditions, the variation it has within its gene pool allows the species to survive through those individuals possessing traits appropriate to the altered environment. Individuals whose physical characteristics enable them to do well in the new environment will usually reproduce more successfully, so that their genes will become more common in subsequent generations. Thus, humankind, being polymorphic, has been able to occupy a variety of environments

When polymorphisms of a species are distributed into geographically dispersed populations, biologists describe this species as **polytypic** ("many types"); that is, genetic variability is unevenly distributed among groups. For example, in the distribution of the polymorphism for blood type (four distinct phenotypic groups: A, B, O, or AB), the human species is polytypic. The frequency of the O allele is highest in American Indians, especially among some populations native to South America; the highest frequencies of the allele for type A blood tend to be found among certain European populations (although the highest frequency of all is found among the Blackfoot Indians of North America); the highest frequencies of the B allele are found in some Asian populations (Figure 13.1). Though the distribution of human variation for a single trait reflects our species' polytypism, the concept is faulty when more than a single trait is involved.

THE MEANING OF RACE

Early anthropologists tried to explore the polytypic nature of the human species by systematically classifying *Homo sapiens* into subspecies, or races, based on geographic location and phenotypic features such as skin color, body size, head shape, and hair texture. Though the 18th-century Swedish taxonomist Carolus Linnaeus (Chapter 2) originally divided humans into varieties based on geographical location, the German medical doctor Johann Blumenbach (1752–1840) was responsible for creating a hierarchy of human types. Blumenbach first defined three major races—Caucasians (Europeans), Mongolians (Asians), and Negros (Africans)—according to his perceptions about the social relationships among

polymorphic A term to describe species with alternative forms (alleles) of particular genes.
polytypic The expression of genetic variants in different frequencies in different populations of a species.

human groups. He considered the Caucasians the superior original race: righteous descendants of Adam, created in God's image, direct descendants of Noah, surviving after the ark landed on Mount Ararat in the Caucasus mountains on the border between Turkey and Armenia. He considered other human groups to have degenerated from this perfect state of being. Blumenbach characterized the "Negroid" as having dark skin, thick lips, a broad nose, and tightly curled hair; the "Mongoloid," straight hair, a flat face, a flat nose, and spread nostrils; and the "Caucasoid," pale skin, a narrow nose, and varied eye color and hair form. To this system, Blumenbach later added two more categories of people—the American Indian and the Malay—crosses between the humans he considered the closest to God and the two varieties he considered inferior extremes. These mistaken hierarchical notions pervaded much of the work done by physical anthropologists in the late 19th and early 20th centuries.

Such classifications were continually being challenged by the presence of individuals who did not fit the categories, such as light-skinned "Negroids" or dark-skinned "Caucasoids." While these individuals were considered hybrids or the product of racial mixtures, the hybrid category also had negative social connotations. Lack of association among traits—such as the fact that long prominent noses are not only common among Europeans but have a high frequency in various East African populations—was usually explained away in a similar manner.

In an attempt to encompass such variations, physical anthropologists from Europe and North America proposed a variety of schemes of racial classification in the early 20th century. In 1926, J. Deniker classified twenty-nine races according to texture of hair, presumably improving upon Roland B. Dixon's 1923 classification based on three indexes of body measures. Hair texture and body build were the characteristics used for another set of racial categories proposed in 1930. By 1947, Earnest Hooton of Harvard University had proposed three new composite races resulting from the interbreeding of "primary" races. Despite these classificatory attempts on the part of Western physical anthropologists, no definitive grouping of distinct, discontinuous biological groups (subspecies) was found for modern humanity.

MEDIATREK

To read the American Anthropological Association's statement on race and see how professional anthropologists work to bring their intellectual framework into the realm of public policy, go to MediaTrek 13.1 on the companion Web site or CD-ROM.

During this same time period, while many anthropologists struggled with the problem of defining human races, others began to question the whole exercise. Franz Boas (1858–1942), the father of four-field American anthropology, gave an important speech criticizing hierarchical notions of race titled "Race and Progress" when he was president of the American Association for the Advancement of Science. His speech was published in the prestigious journal *Science* in 1909. Similarly, Ashley Montagu, one of the best-known anthropologists of his time, devoted his career to a thorough critique of the race concept (see Anthropologist of Note). Both of these scholars were Jewish, a group classified as inferior in the false racial hierarchies they worked to debunk.

Photo by R. R. Grinker

In this photograph, taken in Africa's Democratic Republic of Congo, we see full-grown men of noticeably different heights. The short man is an Efe (pygmy) whose people traditionally inhabit the Ituri rain forest. The tall man is a member of the Lese ethnic group who traditionally live and cultivate open land at the edge of the forest. Standing side by side, these neighbors illustrate the wide range of variation seen within a single so-called "racial" category.

Anthropologists of Note

Ashley Montagu (1905–1999)

AP/Wide World Photos

Born Israel Ehrenberg to a working-class immigrant Jewish family living in London's East End, Ashley Montagu (a name he adopted in the 1920s) went on to become a pioneering critic of the race concept and one of the best-known anthropologists of his time. In 1922 he attended University College of London, where he studied anthropology and psychology. Among his professors were founders of the eugenics movement—a proposal to improve humanity by identifying those with supposedly undesirable hereditary characteristics and removing them from the breeding population. It was also at this time that he changed his name in response to the strong anti-Semitism and class prejudice he experienced.

Also, in the 1920s, Montagu studied under the founders of British social anthropology at the London School of Economics. In 1927, however, he left for the United States, where he considered the society to be more congenial to social justice. At Columbia University, he studied under Franz Boas and other pioneers of North American anthropology, earning his doctorate in 1937 with a dissertation on knowledge of paternity among Australian aborigines.

Having felt the sting of prejudice himself, it is not surprising that Montagu became a strong critic of eugenics and other racist doctrines. As early as 1926, he focused on the mistake of viewing races as typological, bounded categories. This put him at odds with many of his old professors and colleagues (though not Boas), but, as he put it, he learned early on "not to let the shadows of great men block out the light."[a] All his life, Montagu fought racism in his writing, in academic and public lectures, and in the courts.

Ashley Montagu wrote over sixty books and hundreds of articles, including a series in *Ladies Home Journal.* These ranged over subjects from primate anatomy to the importance of nurturance in human development, and even the history of human swearing. Of all his works, none is more important than his book *Man's Most Dangerous Myth: The Fallacy of Race.* Published in 1942, it took the lead in exposing, on purely scientific grounds, the fallacy of human races as biological entities. Although Montagu's once controversial ideas have since become mainstream, the book remains the most comprehensive treatment of its subject.

[a]Sperling, S. (2000). Ashley Montagu (1905–1999). *American Anthropologist, 102,* 584.

The fact is, generalized references to human types such as "Asiatic" or "Mongoloid," "European" or "Caucasoid," and "African" or "Negroid" were at best mere statistical abstractions about populations in which certain physical features appeared in higher frequencies than in other populations; no example of "pure" racial types could be found. These categories turned out to be neither definitive nor particularly helpful. The visible traits were generally found to occur not in abrupt shifts from population to population but in a continuum that changed gradually, with few sharp breaks. To compound the problem, one trait might change gradually over a north-south gradient, whereas another might show a similar change from east to west. Human skin color, for instance, becomes progressively darker as one moves from northern Europe to central Africa, whereas blood type B becomes progressively more common as one moves from western to eastern Europe.

Finally, there are many variations within each group, and those within groups were often greater than those between groups. In Africa, the light-brown skin color of someone from the Kalahari Desert might more closely resemble that of a person from Southeast Asia than the darkly pigmented person from southern Sudan who was supposed to be of the same race.

RACE AS A BIOLOGICAL CONCEPT

To understand why the racial approach to human variation has been so unproductive and even damaging, we must first understand the race concept in strictly biological terms. In biology, a **race** is defined as a subspecies, or a population of a species differing in the frequency of some alleles or traits from other populations of the same species. Simple and straightforward though such a definition may seem, there are three very important things to note about it. First, it is arbitrary; there is no agreement on how many differences it takes to make a race. For example, if one researcher emphasizes skin color while another emphasizes blood group differences, they will not classify people in the same way. Ultimately, it proved impossible to reach agreement on the number of genes and precisely which ones are the most important for defining races. The arbitrariness of racial classification is well illustrated by the following Original Study.

race In biology, the taxonomic category of subspecies that is not applicable to humans because the division of humans into discrete types does not represent the true nature of human biological variation. In some societies race is an important cultural category.

Original Study

Race without Color

Science often violates simple common sense. Our eyes tell us that the Earth is flat, that the sun revolves around the Earth, and that we humans are not animals. But we now ignore that evidence of our senses. We have learned that our planet is in fact round and revolves around the sun, and that humans are slightly modified chimpanzees. The reality of human races is another commonsense "truth" destined to follow the flat Earth into oblivion.

What Could Be More Objective?

The commonsense view of races goes somewhat as follows. All native Swedes differ from all native Nigerians in appearance: There is no Swede whom you would mistake for a Nigerian, and vice versa. Swedes have lighter skin than Nigerians do. They also generally have blond or light brown hair, while Nigerians have very dark hair. Nigerians usually have more tightly coiled hair than Swedes do, dark eyes as opposed to eyes that are blue or gray, and fuller lips and broader noses.

In addition, other Europeans look much more like Swedes than like Nigerians, while other peoples of sub-Saharan Africa—except perhaps the Khoisan peoples of southern Africa—look much more like Nigerians than like Swedes. Yes, skin color does get darker in Europe toward the Mediterranean, but it is still lighter than the skin of sub-Saharan Africans. In Europe, very dark or curly hair becomes more common outside Scandinavia, but European hair is still not as tightly coiled as in Africa. Since it's easy then to distinguish almost any native European from any native sub-Saharan African, we recognize Europeans and sub-Saharan Africans as distinct races, which we name for their skin colors: whites and blacks, respectively.

As it turns out, this seemingly unassailable reasoning is not objective. There are many different, equally valid procedures for defining races, and those different procedures yield very different classifications. One such procedure would group Italians and Greeks with most African blacks. It would classify Xhosas—the South African 'black' group to which President Nelson Mandela belongs—with Swedes rather than Nigerians. Another equally valid procedure would place Swedes with Fulani (a Nigerian "black" group) and not with Italians, who would again be grouped with most other African blacks. Still another procedure would keep Swedes and Italians separate from all African blacks but would throw the Swedes and Italians into the same race as New Guineans and American Indians. Faced with such differing classifications, many anthropologists today conclude that one cannot recognize any human races at all.

If we were just arguing about races of nonhuman animals, essentially the same uncertainties of classification would arise. But the debates would remain polite and would never attract attention outside the halls of academia. Classification of humans is different "only" in that it shapes our views of other peoples, fosters our subconscious differentiation between "us" and "them," and is invoked to justify political and socioeconomic discrimination. On this basis, many anthropologists therefore argue that even if one could classify humans into races, one should not.

To understand how such uncertainties in classification arise, let's steer clear of humans for a moment and instead focus on warblers and lions, about which we can easily remain dispassionate. Biologists begin by classifying living creatures into species. A species is a group of populations whose individual members would, if given the opportunity, interbreed with individuals of other populations of that group. But they would not interbreed with individuals of other species that are similarly defined. Thus all human populations, no matter how different they look, belong to the same species because they do interbreed and have interbred whenever they have encountered each other. Gorillas and humans, however, belong to two different species because—to the best of our knowledge—they have never interbred despite their coexisting in close proximity for millions of years.

We know that different populations classified together in the human species are visibly different. The same proves true for most other animal and plant species as well, whenever biologists look carefully. For example, consider one of the most familiar species of bird in North America, the yellow-rumped warbler. Breeding males of eastern and western North America can be distinguished at a glance by their throat color: white in the east, yellow in the west. Hence they are classified into two different races, or subspecies (alternative words with identical meanings), termed the myrtle and Audubon races, respectively. The white-throated eastern birds differ from the yellow-throated western birds in other characteristics as well, such as in voice and habitat preference. But where the two races meet, in western Canada, white-throated birds do indeed interbreed with yellow-throated birds. That's why we consider myrtle warblers and Audubon warblers as races of the same species rather than different species.

Racial classification of these birds is easy. Throat color, voice, and habitat preference all vary geographically in yellow-rumped warblers, but the variation of those three traits is "concordant"—that is, voice differences or habitat differences lead to the same racial classification as differences in throat color because the same populations that differ in throat color also differ in voice and habitat.

Racial classification of many other species, though, presents problems of concordance. For instance, a Pacific island bird species called the golden whistler varies from one island to the next. Some populations consist of big birds, some of small birds; some have black-winged males, others green-winged males; some have yellow-

[CONTINUED]

breasted females, others gray-breasted females; many other characteristics vary as well. But, unfortunately for humans like me who study these birds, those characteristics don't vary concordantly. Islands with green-winged males can have either yellow-breasted or gray-breasted females, and green-winged males are big on some islands but small on other islands. As a result, if you classified golden whistlers into races based on single traits, you would get entirely different classifications depending on which trait you chose.

Classification of these birds also presents problems of "hierarchy." Some of the golden whistler races recognized by ornithologists are wildly different from all the other races, but some are very similar to one another. They can therefore be grouped into a hierarchy of distinctness. You start by establishing the most distinct population as a race separate from all other populations. You then separate the most distinct of the remaining populations. You continue by grouping similar populations, and separating distinct populations or groups of populations as races or groups of races. The problem is that the extent to which you continue the racial classification is arbitrary, and it's a decision about which taxonomists disagree passionately. Some taxonomists, the "splitters," like to recognize many different races, partly for the egotistical motive of getting credit for having named a race. Other taxonomists, the "lumpers," prefer to recognize few races. Which type of taxonomist you are is a matter of personal preference.

How does that variability of traits by which we classify races come about in the first place? Some traits vary because of natural selection: That is, one form of the trait is advantageous for survival in one area, another form in a different area. For example, northern hares and weasels develop white fur in the winter, but southern ones retain brown fur year-round. The white winter fur is selected in the north for camouflage against the snow, while any animal unfortunate enough to turn white in the snowless southern states would stand out from afar against the brown ground and would be picked off by predators.

Other traits vary geographically because of sexual selection, meaning that those traits serve as arbitrary signals by which individuals of one sex attract mates of the opposite sex while intimidating rivals. Adult male lions, for instance, have a mane, but lionesses and young males don't. The adult male's mane signals to lionesses that he is sexually mature, and signals to young male rivals that he is a dangerous and experienced adversary. The length and color of a lion's mane vary among populations, being shorter and blacker in Indian lions than in African lions. Indian lions and lionesses evidently find short black manes sexy or intimidating; African lions don't.

Finally, some geographically variable traits have no known effect on survival and are invisible to rivals and to prospective sex partners. They merely reflect mutations that happened to arise and spread in one area. They could equally well have arisen and spread elsewhere—they just didn't.

Nothing that I've said about geographic variation in animals is likely to get me branded a racist. We don't attribute higher IQ or social status to black-winged whistlers than to green-winged whistlers. But now let's consider geographic variation in humans. We'll start with invisible traits, about which it's easy to remain dispassionate.

Many geographically variable human traits evolved by natural selection to adapt humans to particular climates or environments—just as the winter color of a hare or weasel did. Good examples are the mutations that people in tropical parts of the Old World evolved to help them survive malaria, the leading infectious disease of the Old World tropics. One such mutation is the sickle-cell gene, so-called because the red blood cells of people with that mutation tend to assume a sickle shape. People bearing the gene are more resistant to malaria than people without it. Not surprisingly, the gene is absent from northern Europe, where malaria is nonexistent, but it's common in tropical Africa, where malaria is widespread. Up to 40 percent of Africans in such areas carry the sickle-cell gene. It's also common in the malaria-ridden Arabian Peninsula and southern India, and rare or absent in the southernmost parts of South Africa, among the Xhosas, who live mostly beyond the tropical geographic range of malaria.

The geographic range of human malaria is much wider than the range of the sickle-cell gene. As it happens, other antimalarial genes take over the protective function of the sickle-cell gene in malarial Southeast Asia and New Guinea and in Italy, Greece, and other warm parts of the Mediterranean basin. Thus human races, if defined by antimalarial genes, would be very different from human races as traditionally defined by traits such as skin color. As classified by antimalarial genes (or their absence), Swedes are grouped with Xhosas but not with Italians or Greeks. Most other peoples usually viewed as African blacks are grouped with Arabia's "whites" and are kept separate from the "black" Xhosas.

Antimalarial genes exemplify the many features of our body chemistry that vary geographically under the influence of natural selection. Another such feature is the enzyme lactase, which enables us to digest the milk sugar lactose. Infant humans, like infants of almost all other mammal species, possess lactase and drink milk. Until about 6,000 years ago most humans, like all other mammal species, lost the lactase enzyme on reaching the age of weaning. The obvious reason is that it was unnecessary—no human or other mammal drank milk as an adult. Beginning around 4000 B.C., however, fresh milk obtained from domestic mammals became a major food for adults of a few human populations. Natural selection caused individuals in these populations to retain lactase into adulthood. Among such peoples are northern and central Europeans, Arabians, northern Indians, and several milk-drinking black African peoples, such as the Fulani of West Africa. Adult lactase is much less common in southern European populations and in most other African black populations, as well as in all populations of East Asians, aboriginal Australians, and American Indians.

Once again races defined by body chemistry don't match races defined by skin color. Swedes belong with Fulani in the "lactase-positive race," while most African "blacks," Japanese, and American Indians belong in the "lactase-negative race."

Not all the effects of natural selection are as invisible as lactase and sickle cells. Environmental pressures have also

[CONTINUED]

[CONTINUED]

produced more noticeable differences among peoples, particularly in body shapes. Among the tallest and most long-limbed peoples in the world are the Nilotic peoples, such as the Dinkas, who live in the hot, dry areas of East Africa. At the opposite extreme in body shape are the Inuit, or Eskimo, who have compact bodies and relatively short arms and legs. The reasons have to do with heat loss. The greater the surface area of a warm body, the more body heat that's lost, since heat loss is directly proportional to surface area. For people of a given weight, a long-limbed, tall shape maximizes surface area, while a compact, short-limbed shape minimizes it. Dinkas and Inuit have opposite problems of heat balance: The former usually need desperately to get rid of body heat, while the latter need desperately to conserve it. Thus natural selection molded their body shapes oppositely, based on their contrasting climates.

Other visible traits that vary geographically among humans evolved by means of sexual selection. We all know that we find some individuals of the opposite sex more attractive than other individuals. We also know that in sizing up sex appeal, we pay more attention to certain parts of a prospective sex partner's body than to other parts. Men tend to be inordinately interested in women's breasts and much less concerned with women's toenails. Women, in turn, tend to be turned on by the shape of a man's buttocks or the details of a man's beard and body hair, if any, but not by the size of his feet.

But all those determinants of sex appeal vary geographically. Khoisan and Andaman Island women tend to have much larger buttocks than most other women. Nipple color and breast shape and size also vary geographically among women. European men are rather hairy by world standards, while Southeast Asian men tend to have very sparse beards and body hair.

What's the function of these traits that differ so markedly between men and women? They certainly don't aid survival: It's not the case that orange nipples help Khoisan women escape lions, while darker nipples help European women survive cold winters. Instead, these varying traits play a crucial role in sexual selection. Women with very large buttocks are a turn-on, or at least acceptable, to Khoisan and Andaman men but look freakish to many men from other parts of the world. Bearded and hairy men readily find mates in Europe but fare worse in Southeast Asia. The geographic variation of these traits, however, is as arbitrary as the geographic variation in the color of a lion's mane.

Fingerprints' patterns of loops, whorls, and arches are genetically determined. Grouping people on this basis would place most Europeans, sub-Saharan Africans, and East Asians together as "loops," Australian aborigines and the people of Mongolia together as "whorls," and central Europeans and the Bushmen of southern Africa together as "arches."

There is a third possible explanation for the function of geographically variable human traits, besides survival or sexual selection—namely, no function at all. A good example is provided by fingerprints, whose complex pattern of arches, loops, and whorls is determined genetically. Fingerprints also vary geographically: For example, Europeans' fingerprints tend to have many loops, while aboriginal Australians' fingerprints tend to have many whorls.

If we classify human populations by their fingerprints, most Europeans and black Africans would sort out together in one race, Jews and some Indonesians in another, and aboriginal Australians in still another. But those geographic variations in fingerprint patterns possess no known function whatsoever. They play no role in survival: Whorls aren't especially suitable for grabbing kangaroos, nor do loops help bar mitzvah candidates hold on to the pointer for the Torah. They also play no role in sexual selection: While you've undoubtedly noticed whether your mate is bearded or has brown nipples, you surely haven't the faintest idea whether his or her fingerprints have more loops than whorls. Instead it's purely a matter of chance that whorls became common in aboriginal Australians, and loops among Jews. Our rhesus factor blood groups and numerous other human traits fall into the same category of genetic characteristics whose geographic variation serves no function. *(By Jared Diamond. (1994). Race without color.* Discover, 15*(11), 83–88.)* Reprinted with permission of Dr. Jared Diamond.

After arbitrariness, the second thing to note about the biological definition of race is that it does not mean that any one race has exclusive possession of any particular variant of any gene or genes. In human terms, the frequency of a trait like the type O blood group, for example, may be high in one population and low in another, but it is present in both. In other words populations are genetically "open," meaning that genes flow between them. Because populations are genetically open, no fixed racial groups can exist.

The third thing to note about the biological definition of race with respect to humans is the differences among individuals and within a population are generally greater than the differences among populations. Evolutionary biologist Richard Lewontin demonstrated this through genetic analyses in the 1970s. He compared the amount of genetic variation within populations and among so-called racial types, finding a mere 7 percent of human variation existing among groups.[1] Instead the vast majority of genetic variation exists within groups.

[1]Lewontin R. C. (1972). The apportionment of human diversity. In T. Dobzhansky, et al. (Eds.), *Evolutionary biology* (pp. 381–398). New York: Plenum Press.

Among humans no barriers exist to gene flow except for those erected by cultures, as this couple and their children illustrate.

As the science writer James Shreeve puts it, "most of what separates me genetically from a typical African or Eskimo also separates me from another average American of European ancestry."[2] This follows from the genetic "openness" of races; no one race has an exclusive claim to any particular form of a gene or trait.

THE CONCEPT OF HUMAN RACES

As a device for understanding polytypic variation in humans, the biological race concept is false. At the same time, however, race exists as a significant cultural category, and human groups frequently insert a false notion of biological difference into the cultural category of race to make it appear more objective. In various different ways, cultures define religious, linguistic, and ethnic groups as races, thereby confusing linguistic and cultural traits with physical traits. For example, in many Central and South American countries, people are commonly classified as Indian, Mestizo (mixed), or Ladino (of Spanish descent). But despite the biological connotations of these terms, the criteria used for assigning individuals to these categories consist of things such as whether they wear shoes, sandals, or go barefoot; speak Spanish or some Indian language; live in a thatched hut or a European-style house; and so forth. Thus, an Indian—by speaking Spanish, wearing Western-style clothes, and living in a house in a non-Indian neighborhood—ceases to be an Indian, no matter how many "Indian genes" he or she may possess.

MEDIATREK
To explore the history of the scientific study of race and explore the new issues emerging as the science of genetics is merged with social beliefs about racial difference, go to MediaTrek 13.2 on the companion Web site or CD-ROM.

This sort of confusion of nonbiological characteristics with the biological notion of heredity is by no means limited to Central and South American societies. To one degree or another, such confusion is found in most societies of Europe and North America. Take, for example, the racial categories used by the U.S. Census Bureau; white, black, American Indian, Asian, and Pacific Islander are large catchall categories that include diverse people. Asian, for example, includes such different people as Chinese and East Indians (to which Indians, at least, take exception), whereas native Hawaiian and Aleut are far more restrictive. Hispanic is another problematic category, as it includes people who, in their countries of origin, might be classified as Indian, Mestizo, or Ladino. The addition of categories for native Hawaiians, Middle Easterners, and people who consider themselves multiracial does nothing to improve the situation. To compound the confusion, inclusion in one or another of these categories is usually based on self-identification. In short, what we are dealing with here are not biological categories at all, but rather cultural constructs.

In the United States, the Census Bureau statistics are applied in a variety of ways that exacerbate the confusion between biological and social categories. For example, health statistics are gathered using the same Census Bureau categories for the purposes of correcting health disparities among groups. Unfortunately, the false biological concept of race is frequently inferred in these analyses. For example, the increased risk of dying from a heart attack for African Americans compared to whites is attributed to biological difference rather than health-care disparities or other social factors contributing to the development of

[2]Shreeve, J. (1994). Terms of estrangement. *Discover, 15*(11), 60.

heart attacks. Similarly medical genetics research is regularly oversimplified into the three geographical areas as in the racial types defined by Blumenbach. Whether this genetic research will avoid the trap of recreating false genetic types that do not reflect the true nature of human variation remains to be seen. The recent claims made for race-specific drugs and vaccines based on limited scientific data indicate that the social category of race may again be limiting our ability to grasp the true nature of human genetic diversity.

To make matters even worse, the confusion of social with biological factors is frequently combined with attitudes that then serve to exclude whole categories of people from certain roles or positions in society. For example, the hierarchical notion of racial difference among European settlers, American Indians, and Africans imported as slaves that characterized colonial North America had antecedents in the unequal power relations between the English or Saxon race and the Irish or Celtic "race" in Europe. These "racial" worldviews assigned some groups to perpetual low status on the basis of their supposedly biological inferiority, whereas access to privilege, power, and wealth was reserved for favored groups of European descent.[3]

Because of the association of lighter skin with power and social status, people whose history includes domination by lighter-skinned Europeans have sometimes valued this phenotype. For example, in the Hindu caste system of India, the higher the caste, the lighter the skin color. This skin-color gradient is maintained by strict in-group marriage rules. In the United States, studies indicated a similar trend among African Americans until the Black Pride movement of the 1960s and 1970s led to reversal of this cultural selection factor.

A particularly evil consequence of the widely held racialized worldview occurred when the Nazis in Germany declared the superiority of the "Aryan race" and the inferiority of the Gypsy and Jewish "races," an official state doctrine using supposedly biological arguments to justify political repression and extermination. In all, 11 million people (Jews, Gypsies, homosexuals, and other supposedly inferior people as well as political opponents of the Nazi regime) were deliberately put to death.

[3]American Anthropological Association. (1998). Statement on "race." Available: *www.ameranthassn.org*.

clines Gradual changes in the frequency of an allele or trait over space.

Far from being a thing of the past, genocide continues to occur in the world today, as illustrated by this picture taken in 2003 at the site of a mass grave in Hilla, Iraq.

Tragically, the Jewish Holocaust (from the Greek word for "wholly burnt" or "sacrificed by fire") is not unique in human history. Such a program of extermination of one group by another or genocide has a long history that predates World War II and continues today. Recent and ongoing genocide in parts of South America, Africa, Europe, and Asia, like previous genocides, are accompanied by a rhetoric of dehumanization and a depiction of the people being exterminated as a lesser type of human.

Considering all the problems, confusion, and horrendous consequences, it is small wonder that most biological anthropologists have abandoned the race concept as being of no particular utility in understanding human biological variation. Instead, they have found it more productive to study the distribution and significance of single, specific, genetically based characteristics, or the characteristics of small breeding populations that are, after all, the smallest units in which evolutionary change occurs.

Some Physical Variables

Today anthropologists study biological diversity in terms of **clines,** or the continuous gradation over space in the form or frequency of a trait. As mentioned in Chapter 1 the spatial distribution or cline for the sickle-cell allele allowed anthropologists to identify the adaptive function of this gene in a malarial environment. Clinal analysis of a continuous trait such as body shape, which is controlled by a series of genes, allows anthropologists to interpret human global variation in body build as an adaptation to climate. Generally, people long native to regions with cold climates tend to have greater body bulk (not to be equated with fat) relative to their extremities (arms and legs) than do people native to regions with hot climates, who tend to be relatively long and slender. Interestingly, these differences show up as early as the time of *Homo erectus,* as described in Chapter 8. A person with larger body bulk and relatively shorter extremities may suffer more from summer heat than someone whose extremities are relatively long and whose body is slender. But they will conserve needed body heat under cold conditions. A bulky body tends to conserve more heat than a less bulky one, because it has less surface area relative to volume. In hot, open country, by contrast, people benefit from a long slender body that can get rid of excess heat quickly. A small slender body can also promote heat loss due to a high surface area to volume ratio.

AP/Wide World Photos

African Americans are disproportionately represented among professional basketball players in part because of the prevalence of tall, linear body shapes among them. This does not mean, however, that "whites can't jump" or that the anatomy of blacks necessarily makes them better basketball players. In fact, one reason there are so many African American basketball players has nothing to do with biology; rather, it is due to the socioeconomic opportunities available to them in a society that still discriminates on the basis of skin color.

In addition to these sorts of very long-term effects that climate may have imposed on human variation, climate can also contribute to human variation through its impact on the process of growth and development (developmental adaptation). For example, some of the physiological mechanisms for withstanding cold or dissipating heat have been shown to vary depending upon the climate an individual experiences as a child. Individuals spending their youths in very cold climates develop circulatory system modifications that allow them to remain comfortable at temperatures people from warmer climates cannot tolerate. Similarly, hot climate promotes the development of a higher density of sweat glands, creating a more efficient system for sweating to keep the body cool.

Cultural processes complicate studies of body build and climatic adaptation. For example, dietary differences particularly during childhood will cause variation in body shape through their effect on the growth process. Another complicating factor is clothing. Much of the way people adapt to cold is cultural, rather than biological. For example, Inuit peoples of northern Canada live in a region where much of the year is very cold. To cope with this, they long ago developed efficient clothing to keep the body warm. Because of this, the Inuit are provided with what amount to artificial tropical environments inside their clothing. Such cultural adaptations allow humans to inhabit the entire globe.

Some anthropologists have also suggested that variation in such features as face and eye shape relate to climate. For example, biological anthropologist Carleton Coon and colleagues once proposed that the "Mongoloid face," common in populations native to East and Central Asia, as well as Arctic North America, exhibits features adapted to life in very cold environments. The **epicanthic eye fold,** which minimizes eye exposure to the cold, a flat facial profile, and extensive fatty deposits may help to protect the face against frostbite. Although experimental studies have failed to sustain the frostbite hypothesis, it is true that a flat facial profile generally goes with a round head. A significant percentage of body heat may be lost from the head. A round head, having less surface area relative to volume, loses less heat than a longer, more elliptical head. As one would predict from this, long-headed populations are generally found

epicanthic eye fold A fold of skin at the inner corner of the eye that covers the true corner of the eye; common in Asiatic populations.

© Steve Elmore

The epicanthic eye fold is common among people native to East Asia. Still, a comparison of this individual with those shown on page 333 shows the absurdity of lumping all Asians in a single category.

in hotter climates; round-headed ones are more common in cold climates. However, these same features could be also present in populations due to genetic drift.

Skin Color: A Case Study in Adaptation

Generally, the idea of race is most commonly equated with skin color. Skin color is subject to great variation, and there are at least four main factors associated with it: transparency or thickness of the skin, a copper-colored pigment called carotene, reflected color from the blood vessels (responsible for the rosy color of lightly pigmented people), and the amount of **melanin** found in a given area of skin. Exposure to sunlight increases the amount of melanin, a dark pigment, causing skin color to deepen. Melanin is known to protect skin against damaging ultraviolet solar radiation;[4] consequently, darkly pigmented peoples are less susceptible to skin cancers and sunburn than are those whose skin has less melanin. They also seem to be less susceptible to photo-destruction of certain vitamins. Because the highest concentration of dark-skinned people tends to be found in the tropical regions of the world, it appears that natural selection has favored heavily pigmented skin as a protection against the strong solar radiation of equatorial latitudes, where ultraviolet radiation is most intense.

melanin The chemical responsible for dark skin pigmentation that helps protect against damage from ultraviolet radiation.

The inheritance of skin color involves several genes (rather than variants of a single gene), each with several alleles, thus creating a continuous range of phenotypic expression for this trait. In addition, the geographical distribution or cline of skin color, with few exceptions, tends to be continuous (Figure 13.2). The exceptions have to do with the recent movement of certain populations from their original homelands to other regions, or the practice of selective mating, or both.

Because skin cancers generally do not develop until later in life, they are less likely to have interfered with the reproductive success of lightly pigmented individuals in the tropics, and so are unlikely to have been the agent of selection. On the other hand, severe sunburn, which is especially dangerous to infants, causes the body to overheat and interferes with its ability to sweat, by which it might rid itself of excess heat. Furthermore, it makes one susceptible to other kinds of infection. In addition to all this, decomposition of folate, an essential vitamin sensitive to heavy doses of ultraviolet radiation, can cause anemia, spontaneous abortion, and infertility.[5]

The adaptive advantage of light skin in northern latitudes relates to the skin's important biological function as the manufacturer of vitamin D through a chemical reaction dependent upon sunlight. Vitamin D is vital for maintaining the balance of calcium in the body. In northern climates with little sunshine, light skin allows enough sunlight to penetrate the skin and stimulate the formation of vitamin D. Dark pigmentation interferes with this process. Individuals incapable of synthesizing enough of vitamin D in their own bodies were selected against, for they contracted rickets, a disease that seriously deforms children's bones. At its worst, rickets prevents children from reaching reproductive age; at the least, it interferes with a woman's ability to give birth due to malformation of the bones surrounding the birth canal. The severe consequences of vitamin D deficiency can be avoided through culture. Milk is often fortified with vitamin D. In the past, children in dark northern places were given a spoon of cod liver oil every week.

[4]Neer, R. M. (1975). The evolutionary significance of vitamin D, skin pigment, and ultraviolet light. *American Journal of Physical Anthropology, 43,* 409–416.

[5]Branda, R. F., & Eatoil, J. W. (1978). Skin color and photolysis: An evolutionary hypothesis. *Science, 201,* 625–626.

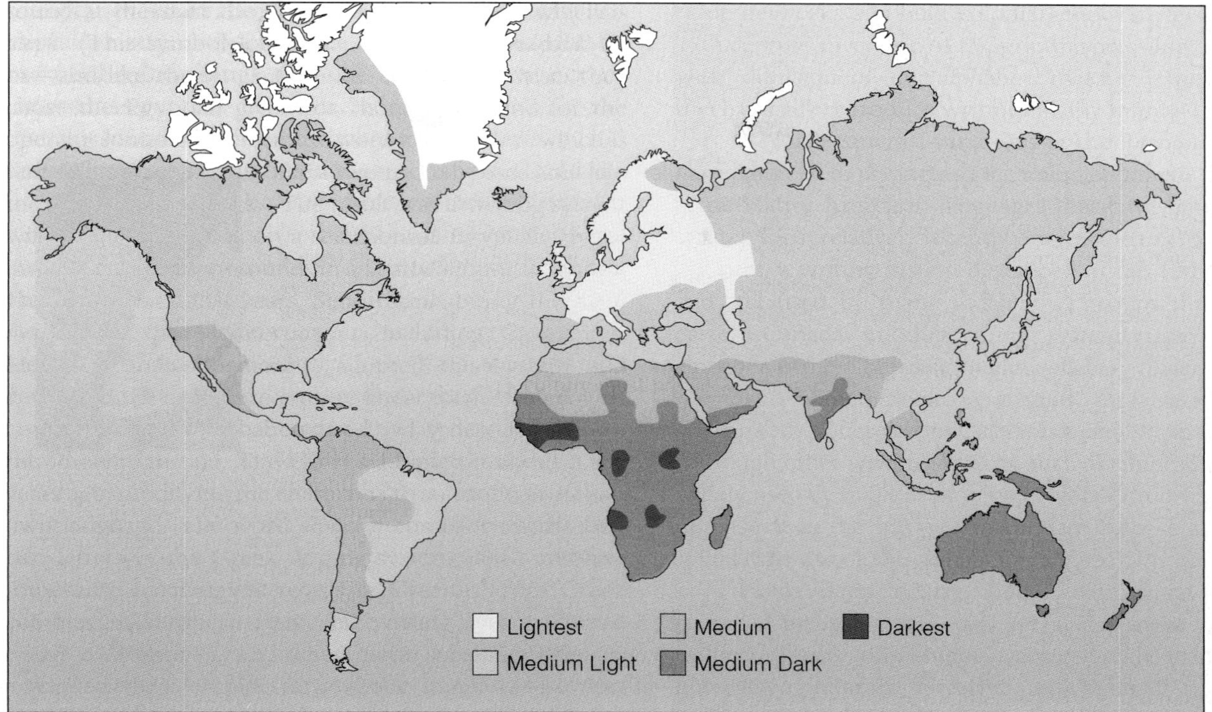

FIGURE 13.2
This map illustrates the distribution of dark and light human skin pigmentation before 1492. Medium-light skin color in Southeast Asia reflects the spread into that region of people from southern China, whereas the medium darkness of people native to southern Australia is a consequence of their tropical Southeast Asian ancestry. Lack of dark skin pigmentation among tropical populations of Native Americans reflects their ancestry in Northeast Asia a mere 20,000 years ago.

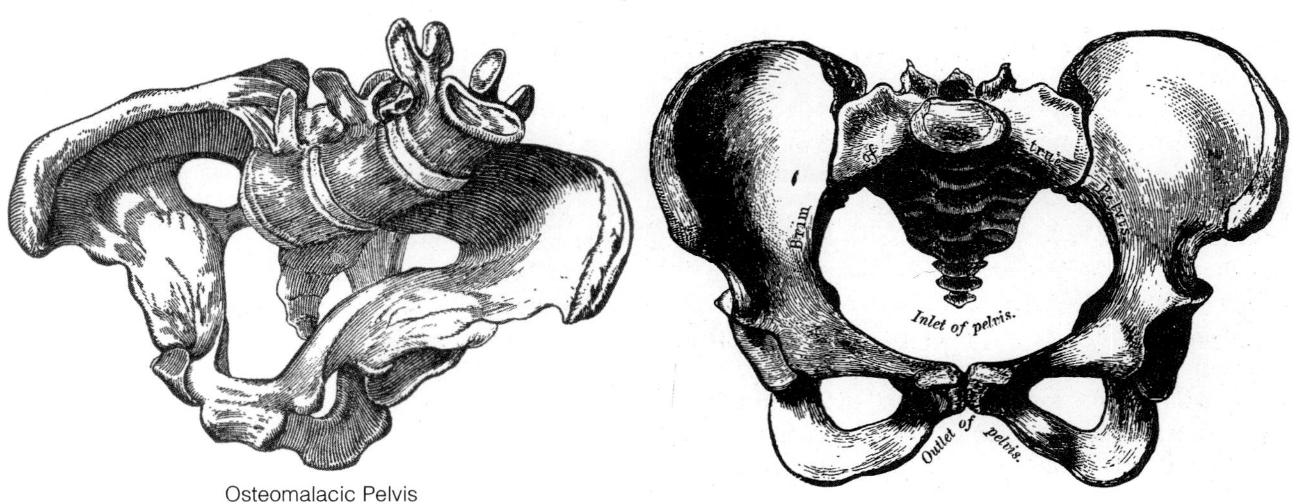

Osteomalacic Pelvis

VISUAL COUNTERPOINT Bone diseases caused by vitamin D deficiency can deform the birth canal of the pelvis to the degree that it can interfere with successful childbirth. Because sunshine is the source of the body's vitamin D, this disease was very common among the poor in northern industrial cities in the past whose exposure to sunlight was limited. Though food supplements have reduced the impact of rickets today, it continues to be a problem where social conventions such as complete veiling limit access to sunlight by women and girls.

RACE AND HUMAN EVOLUTION REVISTED

Given what we know about the adaptive significance of human skin color and the fact that, until 800,000 years ago, the genus *Homo* exclusively inhabited the tropics, it is likely that lightly pigmented skins are a recent development in human history. Darkly pigmented skins likely are quite ancient. Consistent with humanity's African origins, the enzyme tyrosinase, which converts the amino acid tyrosine into the compound that forms melanin, is present in lightly pigmented peoples in sufficient quantity to make them very "black." The reason it does not is that they have genes that inactivate or inhibit it.[6] Human skin, more liberally endowed with sweat glands and lacking heavy body hair compared to other primates, effectively eliminates excess body heat in a hot climate as described in Chapter 6. This would have been especially advantageous to our ancestors on the savannah, who could have avoided confrontations with carnivorous animals by carrying out most of their activities in the heat of the day. For the most part, carnivores rest during this period, being active from dusk until early morning. Without much hair to cover their bodies, selection would have favored dark skins in our ancestors. All humans appear to have had a "black" ancestry, no matter how "white" some of them may appear to be today.

An interesting question is how long it took for light pigmentation to develop in populations living outside the tropics. Whether or not one subscribes to the multiregional continuity model or the recent African origins hypothesis (Chapters 9 and 10), the settling of Greater Australia can be used to examine this question, as we know that the first people to reach Australia did so about 60,000 or so years ago. These people came there from tropical Southeast Asia, spreading throughout Australia eventually to what is now the island of Tasmania with a latitude and levels of ultraviolet radiation similar to New York City, Rome, or Beijing. As aboriginal Australians originally came from the tropics, we would expect them to have had darkly pigmented skin. In Australia, those populations that spread south of the tropics (where, as in northern latitudes, ultraviolet radiation is less intense) underwent some reduction of pigmentation. But for all that, their skin color is still far darker than that of Europeans or East Asians. Most of today's Southeast Asian population spread there from southern China following the invention of farming—hence their relatively light pigmentation. This expansion effectively "swamped" the original populations of this region, except in a few out-of-the-way places like the Andaman Islands, in the Bay of Bengal between India and Thailand.[7] The obvious conclusion is that 60,000 years is not enough to produce significant depigmentation.[8] These observations also suggest that Europeans and East Asians may have lived outside the tropics for far longer

[6]Wills, C. (1994). The skin we're in. *Discover, 15*(11), 79.

[7]Diamond, J. (1996). Empire of uniformity. *Discover, 17*(3), 83–84.

[8]Ferrie, H. (1997). An interview with C. Loring Brace. *Current Anthropology, 38*, 864.

Royal Anthropological Institute Photographic Collection

© Vittoriano Rastelli/CORBIS

VISUAL COUNTERPOINT
Although Tasmania is as far south of the equator as Italy is north of it, native Tasmanians were more darkly pigmented. The ancestors of both Europeans and Tasmanians lived in tropical regions, but populations did not arrive in Tasmania until a good deal later than they reached Europe. Consequently, Tasmanians have not been subject to selection for light pigmentation for as long as Europeans have.

© Dinodia Photo Library

© A. Ramey/PhotoEdit

VISUAL COUNTERPOINT The Andaman Islanders (left) represent the original inhabitants of Southeast Asia; the Vietnamese (right) are descendants of people from southern China who spread into the region after the invention of agriculture. In the process there was mixing of gene pools.

than the people of Tasmania or that settlement in latitudes even more distant from the equator were required for depigmentation to occur.

One should not conclude that, because it is newer, lightly pigmented skin is better, or more highly evolved, than heavily pigmented skin. The latter is clearly better adapted to the conditions of life in the tropics, although with cultural adaptations like protective clothing, hats, and sunscreen lotions, very lightly pigmented peoples can survive there. Conversely, the availability of supplementary sources of vitamin D allows heavily pigmented peoples to do quite well away from the tropics. In both cases, culture has rendered skin color differences largely irrelevant from a biological perspective. With time, skin color may lose its social significance as well.

THE SOCIAL SIGNIFICANCE OF RACE: RACISM

Scientific facts, unfortunately, have been slow to change what people think about race. **Racism** can be viewed solely as a social problem, although at times politicians have used it as a purportedly scientific tool. It is an emotional phenomenon best explained in terms of collective psychology. Racial conflicts result from social stereotypes, not known scientific facts.

Race and Behavior

The assumption that behavioral differences exist among human races remains an issue to which many people in contemporary society tenaciously cling. A critical part of this belief is the false notion of biological difference. Throughout history, certain "races" have been attributed certain characteristics under a variety of names—national character, spirit, temperament—all of them vague and standing for a number of concepts totally unrelated to any biological phenomena. Common myths involve the coldness of Scandinavians or the warlike character of Germans or the lazy nature of Africans. These generalizations serve to characterize a people unjustly.

To date, no in-born behavioral characteristic can be attributed to any group of people that the nonscientist would most probably term a "race" that cannot be explained in terms of cultural practices. If the Chinese happen to exhibit exceptional visuo-spatial skills, it is probably because the business of learning to read Chinese characters requires a visuo-spatial kind of learning that is not needed to master Western alphabets.[9] Similarly, the exclusion of African Americans from the sport of golf (until Tiger Woods) had more to do with the social rules of country clubs and the sport's expense. All such differences or characteristics can be explained in terms of culture.

Similarly, high crime rates, alcoholism, and drug use among certain groups can be explained with reference to

[9]Chan, J. W. C., & Vernon, P. E. (1988). Individual differences among the peoples of China. In J. W. Berry (Ed.), *Human abilities in cultural context* (pp. 340–357). Cambridge, England: Cambridge University Press.

racism A doctrine of racial superiority by which one group asserts its superiority over another.

culture rather than biology. Individuals alienated and demoralized by poverty, injustice, and unequal opportunity tend to display what the dominant members of society regard as antisocial behavior more frequently than those who are integrated into the dominant culture. In a racialized society, poverty and all its ill consequences disproportionately affect some groups of people more than others.

RACE AND INTELLIGENCE

A question frequently asked by those unfamiliar with the fallacy of biological race in humans is whether some races are inherently more intelligent than others. In the United States systematic comparisons of intelligence between "whites" and "blacks" began in the early 20th century and were frequently combined with data gathered by physical anthropologists about skull shape and size. During World War I, for example, a series of IQ tests known as Alpha and Beta were regularly given to draftees. The results showed that the average score attained by European Americans was higher than that obtained by African Americans. Even though many African Americans scored higher than some European Americans, and some African Americans scored higher than most European Americans, many people took this as proof of the intellectual superiority of "white" people. But all the tests really showed was that, on the average, European Americans outperformed African Americans in the social situation of IQ testing. The tests did not measure intelligence per se, but the ability, conditioned by culture, of certain individuals to respond appropriately to certain questions conceived by European Americans for comparable middle-class European Americans. These tests frequently require knowledge of European American middle-class values and linguistic behavior.

For these reasons, intelligence tests continue to be the subject of controversy. Many psychologists as well as anthropologists are convinced that they are of limited use, because they are applicable only to particular cultural circumstances. Only when these circumstances are carefully met can any meaningful generalizations be derived from the use of tests. When cultural and environmental factors are held constant, African and European Americans tend to score equally well.[10]

Nevertheless some researchers still insist that significant differences in intelligence among human populations exist. Recent proponents of this view are the psychologist Richard Herrnstein and Charles Murray, a social scientist who at the time was a fellow of the American Enterprise Institute, a conservative think tank in the United States. Their argument, in a lengthy (and highly publicized) book entitled *The Bell Curve,* is that a well-documented 15-point difference in IQ exists between African and European Americans, with the latter scoring higher, though not quite as high as Asian Americans. Furthermore, they assert that these differences are primarily determined by genetic factors and are therefore immutable.

MEDIATREK

To learn more about the problems and biases built into race-based intelligence testing and read leading scientists' critiques of Herrnstein and Murray's book, *The Bell Curve,* go to MediaTrek 13.3 on the companion Web site or CD-ROM.

Herrnstein and Murray's book has been justly criticized on many grounds, including violation of basic rules of statistics and their practice of utilizing studies, no matter how flawed, that appear to support their thesis while ignoring or barely mentioning those that contradict it. In addition, on purely theoretical grounds, they are also wrong. Because genes are inherited independently of one another, alleles that may be associated with intelligence bear no relationship with the ones for skin pigmentation or with any other aspect of human variation such as blood type.

Herrnstein and Murray support their claims with studies indicating an appreciable degree of hereditary control of intelligence. First, there is a general tendency for those pairs of individuals who are most genetically similar (identical twins) to be most similar in intelligence, even when reared in different environments. Furthermore, the scores on IQ tests of biological parents and their children are correlated and tend to be similar, whereas foster parents and their foster children show less of this tendency. There are, however, enormous problems in attempting to separate genetic components from environmental contributors.[11] As biologists Richard Lewontin and Steven Rose with psychologist Leon Kamin observe, twin studies are plagued by a host of problems: inadequate sample sizes, biased subjective judgments, failure to make sure that "separated twins" really were raised separately, unrepresentative samples of adoptees to serve as controls, untested assumptions about similarity of environments. In fact, children reared by the same mother resemble her

[10]Sanday, P. R. (1975). On the causes of IQ differences between groups and implications for social policy. In M. F. A. Montagu (Ed.), *Race and IQ* (pp. 232–238). New York: Oxford.

[11]Andrews, L. B., & Nelkin, D. (1996). The bell curve: A statement. *Science, 271,* 13.

© Bettman/CORBIS

The effects of the environment on the expression of genetic traits are well illustrated in the families of immigrants to North America. Typically, children born in North America, such as the ones in this photo, will attain greater height than their relatives who were born in the "old country." Presumably environmental differences account for the phenotypic differences because parents and children resemble one another genetically.

in IQ to the same degree, whether or not they share her genes.[12] Clearly, we do not know what the heritability of intelligence really is.[13]

Whatever the degree of heritability may be, clearly the effects of environment are important for intelligence. This should not surprise us, as even traits of high heritability are strongly influenced by environmental factors. Height in humans, for example, has a genetic basis while also being dependent both upon nutrition and health status (severe illness in childhood arrests growth and renewed growth never makes up for this loss). Several factors point to the importance of the environment in the expression of intelligence. For example, IQ scores of all groups in the United States, as in most industrial countries, have risen some 15 points since World War II. In addition, the gap between Americans of African and European descent, for example, is narrower today than in the past. Other studies show impressive IQ scores for African American children from poor backgrounds who have been adopted into affluent and intellectual homes. It is now known that disadvantaged children adopted into affluent and stable families can boost their IQs by 20 points. It is also well known that IQ scores rise in proportion to the test-takers' amount of schooling. More such cases could be cited, but these suffice to make the point: The assertion that IQ is biologically fixed and immutable is clearly false. The association of human intelligence with the nonexistent biological category of race is doubly false.

[12]Lewontin, R. C., Rose, S., & Kamin, L. J. (1984). *Not in our genes* (pp. 100, 113, 116). New York: Pantheon.

[13]Lewontin, Rose, & Kamin, pp. 9, 121.

Intelligence: What Is It?

What do we mean by the term *intelligence*? Unfortunately, there is no general agreement as to what abilities or talents actually make up what we call intelligence, even though some psychologists insist that it is a single quantifiable thing measured by IQ tests. Many more psychologists consider intelligence as the product of the interaction of different sorts of cognitive abilities: verbal, mathematical-logical, spatial, linguistic, musical, bodily kinesthetic, social, and personal.[14] Each may be thought of as a particular kind of intelligence, unrelated to the others. This being so, they must be independently inherited (to the degree they are inherited), just as height, blood type, skin color, and so forth are independently inherited. Thus, the various abilities that constitute intelligence are independently distributed like other phenotypic traits such as skin color and blood type (compare Figures 13.2 and 13.3).

The next question is: Are IQ tests a valid measure of inborn intelligence? Unfortunately, an IQ test measures performance (something that one does) rather than genetic disposition (something that the individual was born with). Performance reflects past experiences and present motivational state, as well as innate ability. In sum, it is fair to say that an IQ test is not a reliable measure of inborn intelligence.

Attempts to prove the existence of significant differences in intelligence among human populations have been going on for at least a century. But despite these efforts, the hypothesis that differences in intelligence exist

[14]Jacoby, R., & Glauberman, N. (Eds.). (1995). *The Bell Curve debate* (pp. 7, 55–56, 59). New York: Random House.

VISUAL COUNTERPOINT On one IQ test designed to be fair to both black and white American students, they are asked to identify either of two famous scientists, Albert Einstein or George Washington Carver. Unfortunately, Carver is mostly a white person's black hero, so a white person is more likely to identify either than is a black person (see Mark Cohen, 1995, "Anthropology and Race: The Bell Curve Phenomenon," *General Anthropology, 2*(1), 3).

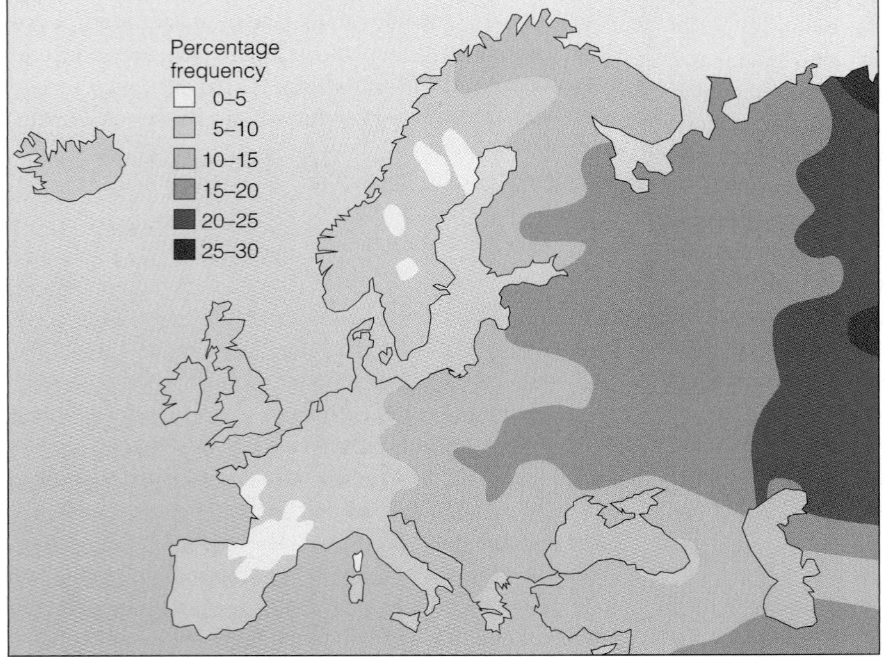

FIGURE 13.3
The east-west gradient in the frequency of the type B blood in Europe contrasts with the north-south gradient in skin color shown in Figure 13.2. Whatever genes are involved in the various abilities lumped together as "intelligence" must be independently assorted as well.

among populations remains unproved. Nor is it ever likely to be proved, in view of the major thrust in the evolution of the genus *Homo*. Over the past 2.5 million years, all populations of this genus have adapted through culture—actively inventing solutions to the problems of existence, rather than relying only on biological adaptation. Thus, we would expect a comparable degree of intelligence in all present-day human populations. But even if this were not the case, it would mean only that dull and bright people exist in all human populations, though in different frequencies. Remember: Within-group variation is greater than between-group variation. Thus, geniuses can and do appear in any population, regardless of what that population's average intelligence may be. The fact of the matter is that the only way to be sure that individual human beings develop their innate abilities and skills to the fullest is to make sure they have access to the necessary resources and the opportunity to do so. This certainly cannot be accomplished if whole populations are assumed at the outset to be inferior.

CONTINUING HUMAN BIOLOGICAL EVOLUTION

In the course of their evolution, humans in all parts of the world came to rely primarily on cultural rather than biological adaptation for their survival. Although intelligence and culture are part of human adaptation across the globe, humans have developed considerable physical variation from one population to another as they spread beyond their tropical homeland into other parts of the world. The forces responsible for this include genetic drift—especially at the margins of their range where small populations were easily isolated for varying amounts of time—and biological adaptation to differing environments.

The increasing effectiveness of cultural adaptation has often reduced the importance of physical variation thought to be due to adaptation. For instance, the consumption of cod liver oil or vitamin D-fortified milk has modified the selective advantage of lightly pigmented skin in northern peoples. At the same time, cultural forces have imposed their own selective pressures, as we have seen in preceding chapters. Just as the transition to food production was followed by poor health and high mortality rates, so are cultural practices today affecting the human organism in important, often surprising, ways.

The probability of alterations in human biology induced by culture raises a number of important questions. By trying to eliminate genetic variants for polymorphic traits, are we also removing alleles that have survival value? Are we weakening the gene pool by allowing people with hereditary diseases and defects to reproduce? What are the long-term consequences of medically assisted reproduction? Are we reducing chances for genetic variation by trying to control population size?

We do not have answers to these kinds of questions in part because they involve a complex interplay between culture and biology. For example, take the reproductive fitness of individuals with diabetes—a disease with a known genetic predisposition. In North America and Europe today, where medication is relatively available, people with diabetes are as biologically fit as anyone else. However, if diabetics are denied access to the needed medication, as they are in many parts of the world, their biological fitness is lost and they die out. In fact, one's financial status affects one's access to medication, and so, however unintentional it may be, one's biological fitness may be decided by one's financial status.

Cultural factors can also contribute directly to the development of disease. For example, one type of diabetes is very common among overweight individuals who get little exercise—a combination that describes 61 percent of people from the United States today who are increasingly beset by this condition. As people from traditional cultures throughout the world adopt a Western high sugar diet and activity pattern, the frequency of diabetes increases.

At times even specific cultural practices designed to promote health can have adverse consequences. One example can be seen in South Africa. About 1 percent of South Africans of Dutch descent (Afrikaners) has a gene that causes porphyria, a disorder that causes light sensitivity and the accumulation of toxins with exposure to some substances. If these Afrikaners remain in a rural environment, they suffer only minor skin abrasions as a result of their condition. However, the porphyria allele renders them very sensitive to modern medical treatment, such as they might receive in a large urban center like Johannesburg. If they are treated for some problem unrelated to porphyria, with barbiturates or similar drugs, they suffer acute attacks and very often die. In a relatively quiet rural environment where medical services are less readily accessible, the Afrikaners with this peculiar condition are able to live normal lives. By contrast, they can suffer physical impairment or loss of life in an urban context, where they are more likely to receive medical attention.

Another example of culture acting as an agent of biological selection has to do with lactose tolerance: the ability to digest **lactose,** the primary constituent of fresh milk. This ability depends on the capacity to make a particular enzyme, **lactase.** Failure to retain lactase production into adulthood causes gas pains and diarrhea for individuals who consume milk. Most mammals as well as most human populations—especially Asian, Native Australian, Native American, and many (but not all) African populations—do not continue to produce lactase into adulthood. Hence, only 10 to 30 percent of Americans of African descent and 0 to 30 percent of adult Asians are lactose tolerant.[15] By contrast, lactase retention and lactose tolerance are normal for over 80 percent of adults of northern European descent. Eastern Europeans, Arabs, and some East Africans are closer to northern Europeans in lactase retention than they are to Asians and other Africans. Generally speaking, a high retention of lactase is found in populations with a long tradition of fresh milk as an important dietary item. In such populations, selection in the past favored those individuals with the allele that confers the ability to assimilate lactose, selecting out those without this allele.

[15]Harrison, G. G. (1975). Primary adult lactase deficiency: A problem in anthropological genetics. *American Anthropologist, 77,* 815–819.

lactose A sugar that is the primary constituent of fresh milk.
lactase An enzyme in the small intestine that enables humans to assimilate lactose.

The "Got Milk?" ad campaign emphasizes that milk is good for all people's health, yet the vast majority of adults globally are unable to digest milk. Only populations with long traditions of dairying have high frequencies of the alleles for this biological capacity.

Because milk is associated with health in North American and European countries, powdered milk has long been a staple of economic aid to other countries. Such practices in fact work against the members of populations in which lactase is not commonly retained into adulthood. Those individuals who are not lactose tolerant will be unable to utilize the nutritive value of milk. Frequently they will also suffer diarrhea, abdominal cramping, and even bone degeneration, with serious results. In fact, the shipping of powdered milk to victims of South American earthquakes in the 1960s caused many deaths among them.

Among Europeans, the evolution of lactose tolerance is linked with the evolution of a nonthrifty genotype as opposed to the **thrifty genotype** that characterized humans until about 6,000 years ago.[16] The thrifty genotype permits efficient storage of fat to draw on in times of food shortage; and in times of scarcity it conserves glucose (a simple sugar) for use in brain and red blood cells (as opposed to other tissues such as muscle), as well as nitrogen (vital for growth and health) through the body's diminished exertion. Regular access to lactose, a source of glucose, led to selection for the nonthrifty genotype as protection against adult-onset diabetes, or at least its onset relatively late in life (at a nonreproductive age). By contrast, populations that are lactose intolerant retain the thrifty genotype. As a consequence, when they are introduced to Western-style diets (characterized by abundance, particularly of foods high in sugar content), the incidence of diabetes skyrockets.

In recent years human activities have extended to damaging human health through effects on the earth's ozone layer. The use of chlorofluorocarbons in aerosol sprays, refrigeration, and air conditioning and the manufacture of Styrofoam contribute substantially to the ozone layer's deterioration. Because the ozone layer screens out some of the sun's ultraviolet rays, its continued deterioration will expose humans to increased ultraviolet radiation. As we saw earlier in this chapter, some ultraviolet radiation is necessary for the production of vitamin D, but excessive amounts lead, among other things, to an increased incidence of skin cancers. Hence a rising incidence of skin cancers—particularly melanoma, a fatal cancer if not caught quickly—is not surprising, as the ozone layer continues to deteriorate despite international treaties limiting the use of chlorofluorocarbons. In many places such as Australia and the United States, melanoma is becoming one of the leading causes of death.

Global warming represents another challenge humans face as a consequence of their industrial activity. Rates of deadly infectious diseases such as malaria may increase as the carbon emissions from the combustion of petroleum warm the climate globally. Annually it is estimated that 1.5 million to 2.7 million deaths worldwide are caused by malaria, making it the fifth largest infectious killer in the world. Children account for about 1 million of these deaths, and more than 80 percent of these cases are in tropical Africa. It is at least possible that over the next century, an average temperature increase of 3°C could result in 50 million to 80 million new malaria cases per year.[17]

Ozone depletion and global warming are merely two of a host of problems confronting humans today that ultimately have an impact on human gene pools. In view of the consequences for human biology of such seemingly benign innovations as dairying or farming (as discussed in Chapter 11), we may wonder about many recent practices—for example, the effects of increased exposure to radiation from increased use of x-rays, nuclear accidents, increased production of radioactive wastes, and the like. In addition to exposure to radiation, humans also face increased exposure to other known mutagenic agents, including a wide variety of chemicals, such as pesticides. Despite repeated assurances about their safety, there have been tens of thousands of cases of poisonings in the United States alone (probably more in so-called underdeveloped countries, where controls are even less effective than in the United States and where substances banned in the United States are routinely used) and thousands of cases of cancer related to the manufacture and use of pes-

---

[16]Allen, J. S., & Cheer, S. M. (1996). The non-thrifty genotype. *Current Anthropology, 37,* 831–842.

[17]Stone, R. (1995). If the mercury soars, so may health hazards. *Science, 267,* 958.

thrifty genotype Human genotype that permits efficient storage of fat to draw on in times of food shortage and conservation of glucose and nitrogen.

Picturing Pesticides

The toxic effects of pesticides have long been known. After all, these compounds are designed to kill bugs. However, documenting the toxic effects of pesticides on humans has been more difficult, as they are subtle—sometimes taking years to become apparent. Anthropologist Elizabeth Guillette, working in a Yaqui Indian community in Mexico, combined ethnographic observation, biological monitoring of pesticide levels in the blood, and neurobehavioral testing to document the impairment of child development by pesticides.[a] Working with colleagues from the Technological Institute of Sonora in Obregón, Mexico, Guillette compared children and families from two Yaqui communities: one living in farm valleys who were exposed to large doses of pesticides and one living in ranching villages in the foothills nearby.

Guillette documented the frequency of pesticide use among the farming Yaqui to be forty-five times per crop cycle with two crop cycles per year. In the farming valleys she also noted that families tended to use household bug sprays on a daily basis, thus increasing their exposure to toxic pesticides. In the foothill ranches, she found that the only pesticides that the Yaqui were exposed to consisted of DDT sprayed by the government to control malaria. In these communities, indoor bugs were swatted or tolerated.

Pesticide exposure was linked to child health and development through two sets of measures. First, levels of pesticides in the blood of valley children at birth and throughout their childhood were examined and found to be far higher than in the children from the foothills. Further, the presence of pesticides in breast milk of nursing mothers from the valley farms was also documented. Second, children from the two communities were asked to perform a variety of normal childhood activities, such as jumping, memory games, playing catch, and drawing pictures. The children exposed to high doses of pesticides had significantly less stamina, eye-hand coordination, large motor coordination, and drawing ability compared to the Yaqui children from the foothills. These children exhibited no overt symptoms of pesticide poisoning—instead exhibiting delays and impairment in their neurobehavioral abilities that may be irreversible. Though Guillette's study was thoroughly embedded in one ethnographic community, she emphasizes that the exposure to pesticides among the Yaqui farmers is typical of agricultural communities globally and has significance for changing human practices regarding the use of pesticides everywhere. ■ ■ ■

[a] Guillette, E. A., et al. (1998). An anthropological approach to the evaluation of preschool children exposed to pesticides in Mexico. *Environmental Health Perspectives, 106* (June), 347.

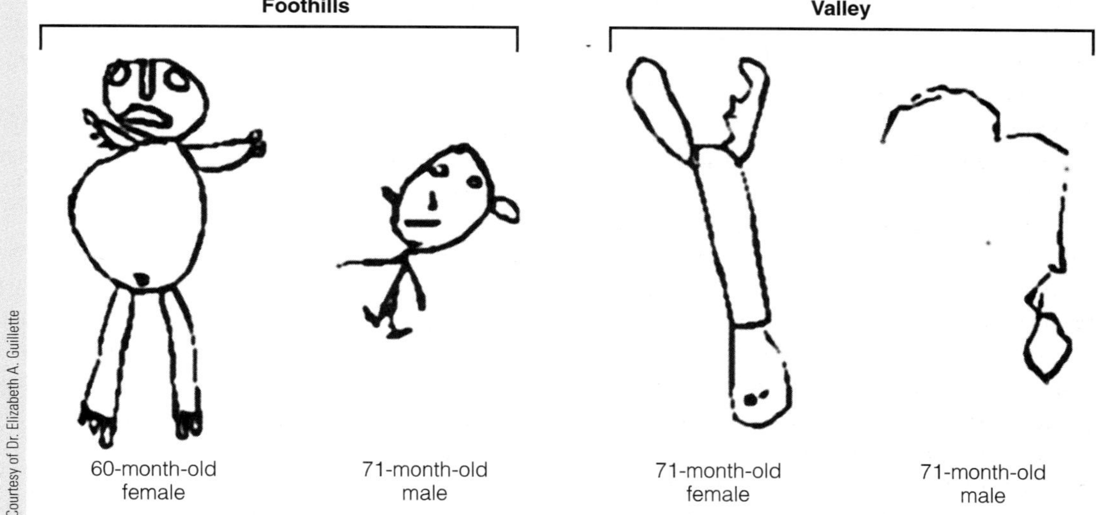

Compare the drawings typically done by Yaqui children heavily exposed to pesticides (valley) to those made by Yaqui children living in nearby areas who were relatively unexposed (foothills).

ticides. All this on top of the several million birds killed each year (many of which would otherwise have been happily gobbling down bugs and other pests), serious fish kills, honey bee kills (bees are needed for the efficient pollination of many crops), and the like. In all, pesticides alone (never mind other agricultural chemicals) are responsible for billions of dollars of environmental and public health damage in the United States each year.[18] Anthropologists are documenting the effects on individuals as described in the Anthropology Applied feature.

[18] Pimentel, D. (1991). Response. *Science, 252,* 358.

AP/Wide World Photos

The routine use of antibiotics to prevent disease and reduce the amount of feed needed to fatten animals has produced lethal strains of bacteria (previously harmless to humans) that resist antibiotic treatment. One example is the emergence of enterococci as a threat to public health. These bacteria usually dwell peacefully in the human gut, but new strains have emerged that poison organs and cause the immune system to go haywire. Because of the bacteria's resistance to antibiotics, thousands of people die each year.

Aside from pesticides, other dangerous substances exist such as hormone disrupting chemicals. For example, in 1938 a synthetic estrogen known as DES (diethylstilbestrol) was developed and subsequently prescribed for a variety of ailments ranging from acne to prostate cancer. Moreover, DES is routinely added to animal feeds. It was not until 1971, however, that the first indication that DES causes vaginal cancer in young women came to light. Subsequent research has shown that DES causes problems with the male reproductive system and causes deformities of the female reproductive tract. DES mimics the natural hormone, binding with appropriate receptors in and on cells, and thereby turns on biological activity associated with the hormone.[19]

DES is not alone in its effects: At least fifty-one chemicals—many of them in common use—are now known to disrupt hormones, and even this could be the tip of the iceberg. Some of these chemicals mimic hormones in the manner of DES, whereas others interfere with other parts of the endocrine system, such as thyroid and testosterone metabolism. Included are such supposedly benign and inert substances as plastics widely used in laboratories and chemicals added to polystyrene and polyvinyl chloride (PVCs) to make them more stable and less breakable. These plastics are widely used in plumbing, food processing, and food packaging. Hormone-disrupting chemicals are also found in many detergents and personal care products, contraceptive creams, the giant jugs used to bottle drinking water, and plastic linings in cans (about 85 percent of food cans in the United States are so lined).

The implications of all these developments are sobering. We know that pathologies result from extremely low levels of exposure to harmful chemicals. Yet, besides those used domestically, the United States exports millions of pounds of these chemicals to the rest of the world.[20] It is possible that hormone disruptions

[19]Colburn, T., Dumanoski, D., & Myers, J. P. (1996). Hormonal sabotage. *Natural History,* (3), 45–46.

[20]Colburn, Dumanoski, & Myers, p. 47.

are at least partially responsible for certain trends that have recently become causes for concern among scientists. These range from increasingly early onset of puberty in human females to dramatic declines in human sperm counts. With respect to the latter, some sixty-one separate studies confirm that sperm counts have dropped almost 50 percent from 1938 to 1990 (Figure 13.4). Most of these studies were carried out in the United States and Europe, but some from Africa, Asia, and South America show that this is essentially a worldwide phenomenon. If this trend continues, it will have profound results.

One of the difficulties with predicting future trends is that serious health consequences of new cultural practices are often not apparent until years or even decades later. By then, of course, these practices are fully embedded in the cultural system. Today, cultural practices, probably as never before, are currently having an impact on human gene pools. Unquestionably, this impact is deleterious to those individuals suffering the effects of negative selection, whose misery and death are the price paid for many of the material benefits of civilization we enjoy today. It remains to be seen just what the long-term effects on the human species as a whole will be. If the promise of genetic engineering offers hope of alleviating some of the misery and death that result from our own practices, it also raises the specter of removing genetic variants that might turn out to be of future adaptive value, or that might turn out to make us immediately susceptible to new problems that we do not even know about today.

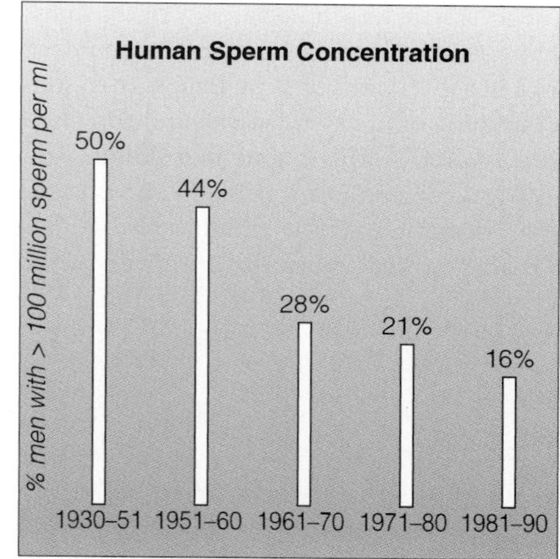

FIGURE 13.4

A documented decline in human male sperm counts worldwide may be related to widespread exposure to hormone-disrupting chemicals.

Chapter Summary

- Present-day humans are a single, highly variable species inhabiting the entire globe. Though biological processes are responsible for human variation, the biological concept of race or subspecies cannot be applied to human diversity. Contemporary human variation is not divided into discrete racial types. Instead, individual traits appear in continuous gradations from one population to another without sharp breaks. In addition, because of the independent inheritance of individual traits and the genetic openness of human populations, the vast majority of human variation exists within populations rather than among populations. While anthropologists work actively to show that the biological concept of race is false when applied to human diversity, they recognize the significance of race as a socio-political category in many countries such as the United States, Brazil, and South Africa.
- Today anthropologists study biological variation among humans without separating humans into nonexistent races or types. They focus on the gene pools of populations containing various alternative alleles also known as polymorphisms. Globally, anthropologists examine clines or the distribution of the frequency of an allele or trait across space. Traits and alleles must be examined one at a time because they are inherited independently.
- Due to its inherent variation, the human species can also be described as polymorphic. Some of the human variation observable globally can be attributed to the effects of natural selection while other variation is due to the random effects of genetic drift. Variation is a key component of our species' survival as variation fosters adaptation to a variety of environmental challenges. When the environment changes, a varied gene pool confers the possibility for the species' survival through the individuals possessing alleles well adapted to the new conditions.
- When the variation of a polymorphic species is unevenly distributed geographically, biologists describe the species as polytypic—that is, populations differ in the frequency with which genetic variability is expressed. Though polytypism is evident among humans for single traits or alleles, all of human variation cannot be subdivided into types.
- Physical anthropologists have determined that some human physical variation appears related to climatic adaptation. People native to cold climates tend to have greater body bulk relative to their extremities than individuals from hot climates; the latter tend to be relatively long and slender. Studies involving body build and climate are complicated by such other factors as the effects on physique of diet and of clothing.
- In many parts of the world, race is commonly thought of in terms of skin color. Subject to tremendous variation, skin

color is a function of several factors: transparency or thickness of the skin, distribution of blood vessels, and amount of carotene and melanin in a given area of skin. Exposure to sunlight increases the amount of melanin, darkening the skin. Natural selection has favored heavily pigmented skin as protection against the strong solar radiation of equatorial latitudes. In northern latitudes, natural selection has favored relatively depigmented skins, which can utilize relatively weak solar radiation in the production of vitamin D. Cultural factors such as selective mating, as well as geographic location, play a part in skin color distribution globally.

- Racism can be viewed solely as a social problem. It is an emotional phenomenon best explained in terms of collective psychology. Racial conflicts result from social stereotypes and not known scientific facts. Racists of the past and present frequently invoke the notion of biological difference to support unjust social practices.
- Notwithstanding the impossibility of defining biologically valid human races, many people have assumed that there are behavioral differences among human races. The innate behavioral characteristics attributed by these people to race can be explained in terms of experience as well as a hierarchical social order affecting the opportunities and challenges faced by different groups of people, rather than biology. In the United States, intelligence or IQ testing was used in the 20th century to try to establish racial differences in intelligence. In addition to problems relating to the cultural and environmental specificity of these tests, comparisons among people divided according to the false biological category of race are unwarranted. Furthermore, at present, it is not possible to separate the inherited components of intelligence from those that are culturally acquired. There is still no consensus on what intelligence really is, but it is generally agreed that intelligence is made up of several different talents and abilities.
- Although the human species has come to rely on cultural rather than biological adaptation for survival, human gene pools still change in response to external factors. Many of these changes are brought about by cultural practices; for example, the shipment of powdered milk to human populations that are low in the frequency of the allele for lactase retention into adulthood may contribute to the death of large numbers of people. Those who survive are most likely to be those with the allele for lactase retention. Unquestionably, this kind of selection is deleterious to those individuals who are "selected out" in this way. Just what the long-term effects will be on the human species as a whole remains to be seen.

Questions for Reflection

1. Humans are challenged to find ways to embrace and comprehend the range of biological diversity without succumbing to oversimplification, discrimination, and even bloodshed. How do anthropological approaches to race contribute to meeting this challenge?
2. From an evolutionary perspective, why is human biological diversity a key component of our collective identity as a species?
3. Why do biological anthropologists and evolutionary biologists use clines to study human variation rather than the biological concept of subspecies? Can you imagine another species of animal, plant, or microorganism for which the subspecies concept makes sense?
4. Globally, health statistics are gathered by country. In addition, some countries such as the United States gather health statistics by race. How are these two endeavors different and similar? Should health statistics be gathered by group?
5. How do you define the concept of intelligence? Do you think scientists will ever be able to discover the genetic basis of intelligence?
6. Environmental effects of human action contribute to ongoing microevolutionary changes in the human species. As the world becomes increasingly interconnected, how should humans regulate these kinds of actions globally?

Key Terms

Polymorphic	Melanin
Polytypic	Racism
Race	Lactose
Clines	Lactase
Epicanthic eye fold	Thrifty genotype

Multimedia Review Tools

Companion Web Site

Visit **http://www.wadsworth.com/anthropology_d/** and click on the companion Web site for this textbook to access a wide range of material to aid your study of anthropology. Among the options for self-study in each chapter are learning objectives, flash cards, Internet activities, Web links, InfoTrac College Edition exercises, and practice tests that can be scored and emailed to your instructor.

CD-ROM

The *Doing Anthropology Today* CD-ROM supplied with your textbook provides unique and valuable information designed to enhance your learning experience. This interactive multimedia resource includes video clips, interviews with renowned anthropologists, map and timeline exercises, chapter study quizzes, and much more. *Doing Anthropology Today* will not only help you in achieving your grade goals, but it will also make your learning experience fun and exciting!

Suggested Readings

Cohen, M. N. (1998). *Culture of intolerance: Chauvinism, class, and racism in the United States.* New Haven, CT: Yale University Press.

This very readable book was written to counter political propaganda claiming that science affirms the need to shape the political order on the basis of inherent inequality and mutual disdain. In it, Cohen summarizes what scientific data *really* say about biological differences among humans; explores the depth, power, beauty, and potential value of cultural differences; shows how the cultural blinders of U.S. culture cause people in this country to misunderstand others as well as themselves; and looks at questionable assumptions in U.S. culture that promote intolerance and generate problems where none need exist.

Gould, S. J. (1996). *The mismeasure of man* (2nd ed.). New York: Norton.

This is an updating of a classic critique of supposedly scientific studies that attempt to rank all people on a linear scale of intrinsic and unalterable mental worth. The revision was prompted by what Gould refers to as the "latest cyclic episode of biodeterminism" represented by the publication of the widely discussed book, *The Bell Curve.*

Graves, J. L. (2001). *The emperor's new clothes: Biological theories of race at the millennium.* New Brunswick, NJ: Rutgers University Press.

Graves, a laboratory geneticist as well as an African American intellectual, aims to show the reader that there is no biological basis for separation of human beings into races and that the idea of race is a relatively recent social and political construction. His grasp of science is solid and up-to-date, and readers can benefit from the case he presents.

Jacoby, R., & Glauberman, N. (Eds.). (1995). *The Bell Curve debate.* New York: Random House.

This is a collection of articles by a wide variety of authors including biologists, anthropologists, psychologists, mathematicians, essayists, and others critically examining the claims and issues raised in the widely read and much discussed book, *The Bell Curve.* Included are pieces written to address many of the same issues as they were raised by earlier writers. For anyone who hopes to understand the race and intelligence debate, this book is a must.

Marks, J. (1995). *Human biodiversity: Genes, race, and history.* Hawthorne, NY: Aldine de Gruyter.

In this book, Marks shows how genetics has undermined the fundamental assumptions of racial taxonomy. In addition to its presentation of the nature of human biodiversity, the book also deals with the history of cultural attitudes toward race and diversity.

Smedley, A. (1998). *Race in North America: Origin and evolution of a world view.* Boulder, CO: Westview Press.

Audrey Smedley traces the cultural invention of the idea of race and how this false biological category has been used to rationalize inequality in North America.

EPILOGUE

Culture, Disease, and Globalization

© Sean Spraguel/The Image Works

CHALLENGE ISSUE

DISEASE HAS CHALLENGED HUMANS ON INDIVIDUAL AND COMMUNITY LEVELS THROUGHOUT OUR EVOLUTIONARY HISTORY. Today, it is vital to add a global perspective to the anthropological examination of human health and disease. Global processes affect the distribution of disease and the means available to promote health. The smoking habits of these young children from Cambodia reflect local cultural processes combined with global forces ranging from the tobacco industry to the World Health Organization. Many times these global forces oppose one another when it comes to promoting health.

1

What Is the Anthropological Approach to Understanding Disease?

Although anthropologists, like health-care workers, think of disease in terms of biological processes, they also consider disease from social and cultural perspectives. Anthropologists examine the cultural meanings given to disease states as well as the cultural practices that promote both health and disease. In addition, they look at the contributions of the political economy to the promotion of health and the distribution of disease. Anthropologists employ a unified biocultural perspective to examine human health and disease.

2

What Is Evolutionary Medicine?

Evolutionary medicine, a branch of medical anthropology, uses the principles of evolutionary theory to contribute to human health. Basic to this approach is framing health issues in terms of the relationship between biological change and cultural change. Biological evolution shaped humans slowly over millions of years while cultural change occurs relatively quickly. The resulting disconnect between human biology and current cultural practices may lead to disease. Also, because culture shapes even scientific interpretations of the human body, evolutionary medicine acknowledges that some physiological phenomena conventionally regarded as symptoms of disease can be better understood as naturally evolving defense mechanisms.

3

What Is the Impact of Globalization on World Health?

The interconnectedness of humans to one another and to the environment is critical for understanding disease. Because local human environments are shaped by culture—including global political and economic systems—these features must all be included in a comprehensive examination of human disease. Simply describing disease in terms of biological processes involved in the problem at hand, such as infection or malnutrition, leaves out the deeper ultimate reasons that some individuals are more likely to become sick than others. By examining the political ecology of disease, we can reveal its social causes, bringing us closer to finding long-lasting cures.

Throughout millions of years of human evolutionary history, biology and culture interacted to make humans the species we are today. A look at the archaeological record and contemporary human variation also reveal that biology and culture continue to shape all areas of human experience, particularly health and disease. Indeed, an inside joke among anthropologists is that if you do not know the answer to an exam question about biology and culture, the answer is always "both" or "malaria." As explained in previous chapters, answering "malaria" is just like answering "both"' because it illustrates the relationship between two disease states—malaria and sickle-cell disease—and the cultural practices affecting the distribution or frequency of these diseases in groups of humans. Farming practices (culture) of the past created the perfect environment for the malarial parasite. The genetic response to this environmental change (biology) was increased frequencies of the sickle-cell allele.

To add a few more layers, think about how contemporary global inequalities (culture) contribute to the continued devastating effects of malaria (biology) in poorer countries today. If malaria were a problem plaguing North America or Europe today, would most citizens of the countries with rampant malaria still be without adequate treatment or cure? Similarly, public health initiatives for genetic counseling (culture) to reduce frequencies of sickle-cell anemia (biology) in the United States have been met with distrust by African Americans who have experienced racism rooted in a false message of biological difference (culture).[1] Would white citizens of the United States feel as comfortable with genetic testing to eliminate a disease gene if they had experienced some of the wrongs underprivileged ethnic minorities had experienced in the name of science?

Consider for example, the Tuskegee Syphilis Study, carried out by the United States Public Health Service in Macon County, Alabama, from 1932 to 1972. This study involved withholding adequate treatment for syphilis to a group of poor African American men without their knowledge to learn more about the biology of syphilis in the "Negro." These methods are now widely recognized as a moral breach that caused unnecessary pain and suffering to the men and their families. The unethical practices of the study caused the U.S. government to change its research policies involving the biological study of human subjects. In short, when examining a seemingly biological phenomenon such as disease, cultural factors must be considered at every level—from how biology is represented by each culture (reflected in this case in the false notion that the biology of syphilis would differ between people of different skin colors) to how biological research is conducted.

An integrated biocultural approach is one of the hallmarks of anthropology. In examples ranging from

MEDIA TREK

To learn more about the history of the Tuskegee study and how this has shaped the ethical conduct of research today, go to MediaTrek Epilogue.1 on the companion Web site or CD-ROM.

[1]Tapper, M. (1999). *In the blood: sickle-cell anemia and the politics of race.* Philadelphia: University of Pennsylvania Press.

The Tuskegee Syphilis Study wrongly justified denying African American men adequate treatment for the disease in order to study the supposed differences in the biology of the disease by race. This human experimentation was not only false from a biological perspective but represents a moral breach in research conduct. Public outcry about this experiment led to regulations that protect all human subjects in biomedical research.

infant feeding and sleeping practices to the relationship between poverty and tuberculosis, biocultural connections have been emphasized throughout this book. In this epilogue, we will focus on these issues in greater detail and examine some of the theoretical approaches biological and medical anthropologists use to examine the interaction of biology and culture. This integrated anthropological perspective is vital for the improvement of health on the individual, community, and global levels.

THE DEVELOPMENT OF MEDICAL ANTHROPOLOGY

During the course of its development as a distinct specialty within anthropology, the theoretical relationship between biological and cultural knowledge has seen a transformation in medical anthropology. The earliest research on **medical systems,** or patterned sets of ideas and practices relating to illness, was carried out by physician-anthropologists—individuals trained as medical doctors and as anthropologists who participated in the international public health movement emerging early in the 20th century. While delivering the medical care developed in Europe and North America, they simultaneously studied the health beliefs and practices of the cultures they were sent to help. Local cultural categories about sickness were translated into biomedical terms. At this time, human biology was considered universal, while the cultural meanings given to biological states varied. Western biomedical approaches were thought to be culture-free depictions of human biology and were therefore used as an interpretive framework for examining the medical beliefs and practices of other cultures. Implicit in this work was a notion that the Western approach, with its supposed objectivity, was superior.

MEDIATREK
To learn more about medical anthropology and its links with biological and cultural anthropology, go to MediaTrek Epilogue.2 on the companion Web site or CD-ROM.

Science, Illness, and Disease

Gradually the superiority of biomedicine eroded as a consequence of fieldwork conducted by cultural anthropologists who began to examine health beliefs outside of traditional public health interventions. For example, French cultural anthropologist Claude Lévi-Strauss described the healing powers of **shamans** (the name for indigenous healers, originally from Siberia, and now applied to many traditional healers) in terms that could also apply to medical practices in Europe and North America.[2] In both cases, the healer has access to a world of restricted knowledge (spiritual or scientific) from

[2]Lévi-Strauss, C. (1963). The sorcerer and his magic. In *Structural anthropology*. New York: Basic Books.

medical systems Patterned sets of ideas and practices relating to illness.
shamans The name for indigenous healers originally from Siberia now applied to many traditional healers.

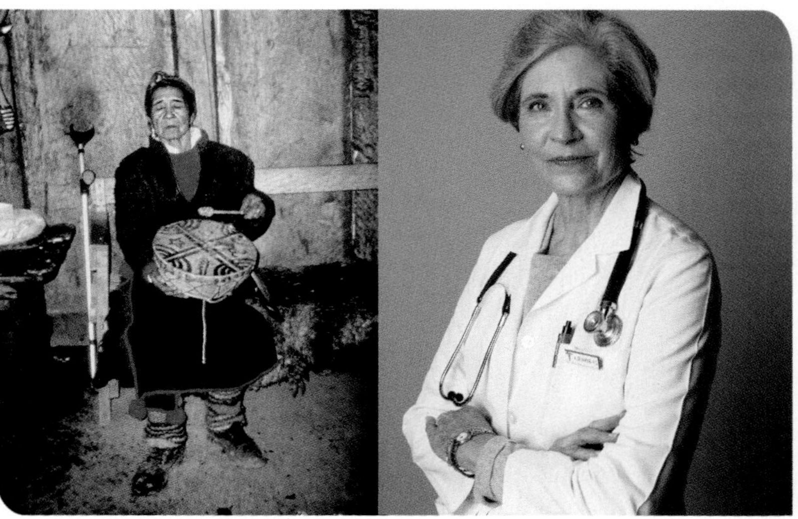
© Topham/The Image Works
© Ronnie Kaufman/Corbis

VISUAL COUNTERPOINT Shamans and biomedical doctors both rely upon manipulation of symbols to heal their patients. The physician's white coat is a powerful symbol of medical knowledge and authority that communicates to patients just as does the shaman's drum. Interestingly, medical schools in the United States are increasingly incorporating a "white coat" ceremony into medical education, conferring the power of the white coat onto new doctors.

which the average community member is excluded. Similarly, other studies revealed how medical categories, like other aspects of a people's unique worldview, reflect the value system of their particular culture. For example, the Subinam people of Mindinao, one of the large islands of the Philippines, give different names to fungal infections of the skin depending on whether the infection is openly visible or hidden under clothes. The biomedical and scientific categorization of fungal infections refer only to genus and species names.[3]

In the 1970s the place of biological and cultural knowledge in medical anthropology was dramatically reorganized. The admission of mainland China to the United Nations in 1971, and the subsequent improvement of diplomatic and other relationships between that communist country and Western powers, played a role in this theoretical shift.[4] Cultural exchanges revealed a professional medical system in the East rivaling that of Western biomedicine in its scientific basis and technical feats. For example, the practice of open heart surgery in China, using only acupuncture needles as an anesthetic, challenged the assumption of biomedical superiority within anthropological thought. At this time scholars proposed that biomedicine was a cultural system, just like the medical systems in other cultures, and that it, too, was worthy of anthropological study.[5]

To effectively compare medical systems and health cross-culturally, a theoretical distinction is made between disease and illness. **Disease** refers to a specific pathology: a physical or biological abnormality. **Illness** refers to the meanings and elaborations given to particular physical states. Disease and illness do not necessarily overlap. An individual may experience illness without having a disease, or a disease may occur in the absence of illness.

In cultures with scientific medical systems, a key component of the social process of illness involves delineating human suffering in terms of biology. At times this even extends to labeling an illness as a disease even though the biology is poorly understood. Think about alcoholism in the United States, for example. A person who is thought of as a drunk, partier, barfly, or boozer tends not to get sympathy from the rest of society. By contrast, a person struggling with the disease alcoholism receives cultural help from physicians, support from groups such as Alcoholics Anonymous, and financial aid from health insurance covering medical treatment for this disease. It matters little that the biology of this disease is still poorly understood and that alcoholism is treated through social support rather than expert manipulation of biology. By calling alcoholism a disease, it becomes a socially sanctioned and recognized illness within the dominant medical system of the United States.

Disease can also exist without illness. Schistosomiasis, infection with a kind of parasitic flatworm called a blood fluke, is an excellent case in point. Scientists have

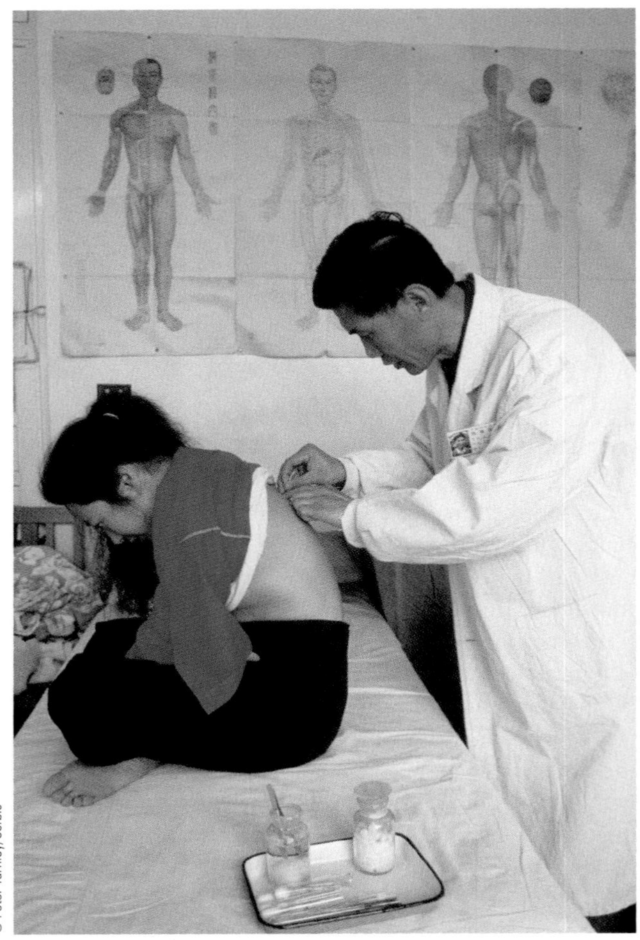

After diplomatic relationships were restored between the United States and China, and Western scientists learned of the effectiveness and scientific nature of acupuncture, it was no longer possible to think of Western biomedicine as the only scientific medical system.

[3] Frake, C. (1961). The diagnosis of disease among the Subinam of Mindinao. *American Anthropologist, 63*,113–132.

[4] Young, A. (1981). The creation of medical knowledge: Some problems in interpretation. *Social Science and Medicine, 17*, 1,205–1,211.

[5] Kleinman, A. (1976). Concepts and a model for the comparison of medical systems as cultural systems. *Social Science and Medicine, 12*(2B), 85–95.

disease Refers to a specific pathology;-a physical or biological abnormality.
illness Refers to the meanings and elaborations given to particular physical states.

© Lloyd Cluff/Corbis

Building the Aswan Dam in Egypt was a vital part of "modernization" for that country. Unfortunately, the dam dramatically increased the rates of schistosomiasis in the Nile River by creating a massive artificial lake upstream from the dam. This still water provides the ideal environment for snail hosts.

fully documented the life cycle of this parasite that alternates between water snail and human hosts. The adult worms live for many years inside the human intestines or urinary tract. Human waste then spreads the mobile phase of the parasite to freshwater snails. Inside the snails, the parasite develops further to a second mobile phase of the flatworm life cycle, releasing thousands of tiny creatures into freshwater. If humans swim, wade, or do household chores such as laundry in this infested water, the parasite can bore its way through the skin, traveling to the intestine or bladder where the life cycle continues.

The idea of parasites boring through the skin and living permanently inside the bladder or intestine may well be revolting. Ingesting poisons to rid the body of these parasites may be acceptable for people due to social and economic factors. But to people living in parts of the world where schistosomiasis is **endemic** (the public health term for a disease that is widespread in the population), this disease state is treated as normal, and no treatment is sought. In other words schistosomiasis is not an illness. Individuals may know about expensive effective biomedical treatments but given the likelihood of reinfection and the inaccessibility of the drugs, treatment with pharmaceutical agents is not the social norm. Over time, the forces of evolution have led to a tolerance between parasite and host so that infected individuals can live normal lives. So normal is the parasitic infection in some societies that the appearance of bloody urine at the time of adolescence (due to a high enough parasite load to cause this symptom) is regarded as a male version of menstruation.[6]

Cultural perspectives can thus be at odds with international public health goals that are based on a strictly Western biomedical understanding of disease. In the following Original Study, biological anthropologist Katherine Dettwyler shows that each perspective brings with it particular challenges and benefits.

[6]Desowitz, R. S. (1987). *New Guinea tapeworms and Jewish grandmothers.* New York: Norton.

endemic The public health term for a disease that is widespread in the population.

Original Study

Dancing Skeletons: Life and Death in West Africa

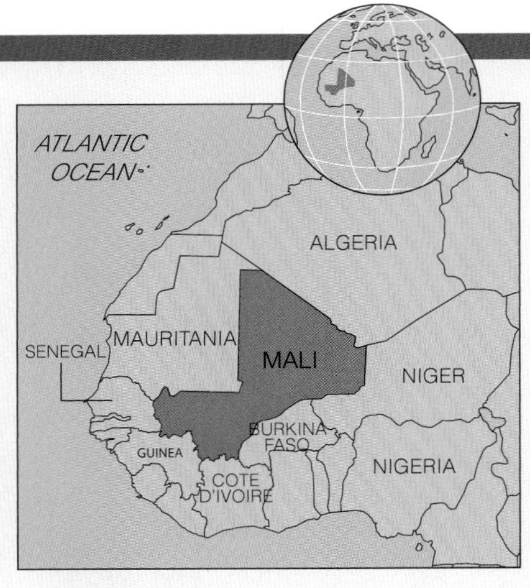

I stood in the doorway, gasping for air, propping my arms against the door frame on either side to hold me up. I sucked in great breaths of cool, clean air and rested my gaze on the distant hills, trying to compose myself. Ominous black thunderclouds were massed on the horizon and moved rapidly toward the schoolhouse. . . .

The morning had begun pleasantly enough, with villagers waiting patiently under the huge mango tree in the center of the village. But before long, the approaching storm made it clear that we would have to move inside. The only building large enough to hold the crowd was the one-room schoolhouse, located on the outskirts of the village. . . .

Inside the schoolhouse, chaos reigned. It was 20 degrees hotter, ten times as noisy, and as dark as gloom. What little light there was from outside entered through the open doorway and two small windows. The entire population of the village crowded onto the rows of benches, or stood three deep around the periphery of the room. Babies cried until their mothers pulled them around front where they could nurse, children chattered, and adults seized the opportunity to converse with friends and neighbors. It was one big party, a day off from working in the fields, with a cooling rain thrown in for good measure. I had to shout the measurements out to Heather, to make myself heard over the cacophony of noise. . . .

A middle-aged man dressed in a threadbare pair of Levis shoved a crying child forward. I knelt down to encourage the little boy to step up onto the scales and saw that his leg was wrapped in dirty bandages. He hesitated before lifting his foot and whimpered as he put his weight onto it. . . .

"What's the matter with his leg?" I asked his father.

"He hurt it in a bicycle accident," he said. . . .

The festering wound encompassed the boy's ankle and part of his foot, deep enough to see bone at the bottom. His entire lower leg and foot were swollen and putrid; it was obvious that gangrene had a firm hold. . . .

"You have to take him to the hospital in Sikasso immediately," I explained.

"But we can't afford to," he balked.

"You can't afford not to," I cried in exasperation, turning to Moussa. "He doesn't understand," I said to Moussa. "Please explain to him that the boy is certain to die of gangrene poisoning if he doesn't get to a doctor right away. It may be too late already, but I don't think so. He may just lose his leg." Moussa's eyes widened with alarm. Even he hadn't realized how serious the boy's wounds were. As the father took in what Moussa was saying, his face crumpled. . . . Father and son were last seen leaving Merediela, the boy perched precariously on the back of a worn-out donkey hastily borrowed from a neighbor, while the father trotted alongside, shoulders drooping, urging the donkey to greater speed. . . .

Lunch back at the animatrice's compound provided another opportunity for learning about infant feeding beliefs in rural Mali, through criticism of my own child feeding practices. This time it was a chicken that had given its life for our culinary benefit. As we ate, without even thinking, I reached into the center pile of chicken meat and pulled pieces of meat off the bone. Then I placed them over in Miranda's section of the communal food bowl and encouraged her to eat.

"Why are you giving her chicken?" Bakary asked.

"I want to make sure she gets enough to eat," I replied. "She didn't eat very much porridge for breakfast, because she doesn't like millet."

"But she's just a child. She doesn't need good food. You've been working hard all morning, and she's just been lying around. Besides, if she wanted to eat, she would," he argued.

"It's true that I've been working hard," I admitted, "but she's still growing. Growing children need much more food, proportionately, than adults. And if I didn't encourage her to eat, she might not eat until we get back to Bamako."

Bakary shook his head. "In Dogo," he explained, "people believe that good food is wasted on children. They don't appreciate its good taste or the way it makes you feel. Also, they haven't worked hard to produce the food. They have their whole lives to work for good food for themselves, when they get older. Old people deserve the best food, because they're going to die soon." . . .

. . . In rural southern Mali, "good food" (which included all the high protein/high calorie foods) was reserved for elders and other adults. Children subsisted almost entirely on the carbohydrate staples, flavored with a little sauce. My actions in giving Miranda my share of the chicken were viewed as bizarre and misguided—I was wasting good food on a mere child, and depriving myself. . . .

In N'tenkoni the next morning, we were given use of the men's sacred meeting hut for our measuring session. A round hut about 20 feet in diameter, it had a huge center pole made from the trunk of a tree that held up the thatched roof. Because it had two large doorways, it was light and airy and would provide protection in the event of another thunderstorm. . . .

There was some initial confusion caused by the fact that people outside

[CONTINUED]

couldn't really see what we were doing, and everyone tried to crowd in at once. That was straightened out by the chief, however, and measuring proceeded apace, men, women, children, men, women, children. One family at a time filed into the hut through one door, had their measurements taken, and departed through the other door. It was cool and pleasant inside the hut, in contrast to the hot sun and glare outside. Miranda sat off to one side, reading a book, glancing up from time to time, but generally bored by the whole thing.

Permission of Waveland Press from *Dancing Skeletons*

"Mommy, look!" she exclaimed in mid-morning. "Isn't that an *angel*?" she asked, using our family's code word for a child with Down syndrome. Down syndrome children are often (though not always!) sweet, happy, and affectionate kids, and many families of children with Down syndrome consider them to be special gifts from God, and refer to them as angels. I turned and followed the direction of Miranda's gaze. A little girl had just entered the hut, part of a large family with many children. She had a small round head, and all the facial characteristics of a child with Down syndrome—Oriental-shaped eyes with epicanthic folds, a small flat nose, and small ears. There was no mistaking the diagnosis. Her name was Abi, and she was about 4 years old, the same age as Peter.

I knelt in front of the little girl. "Hi there, sweetie," I said in English. "Can I have a hug?" I held out my arms, and she willingly stepped forward and gave me a big hug.

I looked up at her mother. "Do you know that there's something 'different' about this child?" I asked, choosing my words carefully.

"Well, she doesn't talk," said her mother, hesitantly, looking at her husband for confirmation. "That's right," he said. "She's never said a word."

"But she's been healthy?" I asked.

"Yes," the father replied. "She's like the other kids, except she doesn't talk. She's always happy. She never cries. We know she can hear, because she does what we tell her to. Why are you so interested in her?"

"Because I know what's the matter with her. I have a son like this." Excitedly, I pulled a picture of Peter out of my bag and showed it to them. They couldn't see any resemblance, though. The difference in skin color swamped the similarities in facial features. But then, Malians think all white people look alike. And it's not true that all kids with Down syndrome look the same. They're "different in the same way," but they look most like their parents and siblings.

"Have you ever met any other children like this?" I inquired, bursting with curiosity about how rural Malian culture dealt with a condition as infrequent as Down syndrome. Children with Down syndrome are rare to begin with, occurring about once in every 700 births. In a community where 30 or 40 children are born each year at the most, a child with Down syndrome might be born only once in 20 years. And many of them would not survive long enough for anyone to be able to tell that they were different. Physical defects along the midline of the body (heart, trachea, intestines) are common among kids with Down syndrome; without immediate surgery and neonatal intensive care, many would not survive. Such surgery is routine in American children's hospitals, but nonexistent in rural Mali. For the child without any major physical defects, there are still the perils of rural Malian life to survive: malaria, measles, diarrhea, diphtheria, and polio. Some, like Peter, have poor immune systems, making them even more susceptible to childhood diseases. The odds against finding a child with Down syndrome, surviving and healthy in a rural Malian village, are overwhelming.

Not surprisingly, the parents knew of no other children like Abi. They asked if I knew of any medicine that could cure her. "No," I explained, "this condition can't be cured. But she will learn to talk, just give her time. Talk to her a lot. Try to get her to repeat things you say. And give her lots of love and attention. It may take her longer to learn some things, but keep trying. In my country, some people say these children are special gifts from God." There was no way I could explain cells and chromosomes and nondisjunction to them, even with Moussa's help. And how, I thought to myself, would that have helped them anyway? They just accepted her as she was.

We chatted for a few more minutes, and I measured the whole family, including Abi, who was, of course, short for her age. I gave her one last hug and

[CONTINUED]

[CONTINUED]

a balloon and sent her out the door after her siblings. . . .

I walked out of the hut, . . . trying to get my emotions under control. Finally I gave in, hugged my knees close to my chest, and sobbed. I cried for Abi—what a courageous heart she must have; just think what she might have achieved given all the modern infant stimulation programs available in the West. I cried for Peter—another courageous heart; just think of what he might achieve given the chance to live in a culture that simply accepted him, rather than stereotyping and pigeonholing him, constraining him because people didn't think he was capable of more. I cried for myself—not very courageous at all; my heart felt as though it would burst with longing for Peter, my own sweet angel.

There was clearly some truth to the old adage that ignorance is bliss. Maybe pregnant women in Mali had to worry about evil spirits lurking in the latrine at night, but they didn't spend their pregnancies worrying about chromosomal abnormalities, the moral implications of amniocentesis, or the heart-wrenching exercise of trying to evaluate handicaps, deciding which ones made life not worth living. Women in the United States might have the freedom to choose not to give birth to children with handicaps, but women in Mali had freedom from worrying about it. Children in the United States had the freedom to attend special programs to help them overcome their handicaps, but children in Mali had freedom from the biggest handicap of all—other people's prejudice.

I had cried myself dry. I splashed my face with cool water from the bucket inside the kitchen and returned to the task at hand. *(Reprinted with permission from Katherine A. Dettwyler. (1994).* Dancing skeletons: Life and death in West Africa *(ch. 8). Long Grove, IL: Waveland Press.)*

While diseases are generally described in biological terms as understood through scientific investigation, the medical anthropological framework allows that the experience of disease is not universal. Whether these are based in the scientific study of biological processes, each culture's medical system provides individuals with a "map" of how to think about themselves in sickness and health. All cultures define specific terms and mechanisms for thinking about, preventing, and managing illness. In this way, medical systems define whether a particular biological state such as malnutrition, Down's syndrome, or schistosomiasis is recognized as an illness. Each cultural system delineates the choices and constraints available to individuals afflicted by particular disease states.

EVOLUTIONARY MEDICINE

One of the interesting recent developments within scientific medicine with roots in anthropology has been the development of **evolutionary medicine.** This is an approach to human sickness and health combining principles of evolutionary theory and human evolutionary history. While it may seem at first to concentrate on human biological mechanisms, evolutionary medicine's emphasis is true to the biocultural integration that figures so prominently in anthropological approaches. Biological processes are given cultural meanings, and cultural practices affect human biology. These two insights provide alternative approaches to promoting human health.

As with evolutionary theory in general, it is difficult to prove conclusively that some of the specific ideas and theories from evolutionary medicine are indeed beneficial to human health. Instead, scientists work to amass a sufficient body of knowledge that supports their theories. Where appropriate, the theories can lead to hypotheses that can be tested experimentally. Frequently "treatments" derived from evolutionary medicine lead to altering cultural practices and to a return to a more "natural" state in terms of human biology. As described in the Biocultural Connection of Chapter 8, evolutionary medicine contributes a variety of Paleolithic prescriptions for the diseases of civilization.

The work of biological anthropologist James McKenna is an excellent example of evolutionary medicine. McKenna has suggested that the human infant, immature compared to some other mammals, has evolved to co-sleep with adults who provide breathing cues to the sleeping infant, protecting the child from sudden infant death syndrome (SIDS).[7] He uses cross-cultural data of sleeping patterns and rates of SIDS to support his claim. McKenna conducted a series of experiments documenting differences between the brain-wave patterns of mother-infant pairs who co-sleep compared to mother-infant pairs who sleep in separate rooms. These data fit McKenna's theory, challenging North America's predominant cultural practice of soli-

evolutionary medicine An approach to human sickness and health combining principles of evolutionary theory and human evolutionary history.

[7]McKenna, J. (1999). Co-sleeping and SIDS. In W. Trevathan, E. O. Smith, & J. J. McKenna (Eds.), *Evolutionary medicine.* London: Oxford University Press.

Notre Dame Media Group

James McKenna used biological data from a variety of sources to encourage North Americans to change their infant sleeping practices to prevent sudden infant death syndrome. Together, these data make a convincing case that human mothers and infants evolved to co-sleep.

tary sleeping. Further, McKenna shows how the cultural pattern of sleeping directly impacts infant feeding practices such that co-sleeping and breastfeeding are mutually reinforcing behaviors. Evolutionary medicine suggests that cultural practices in industrial and postindustrial societies are responsible for a variety of other biomedically defined diseases, ranging from psychological disorders to jaundice (a yellow discoloration of the newborn).

Growth and Development as Mechanisms for Adaptation

Evolutionary medicine takes the perspective that human biology is the product of a series of interactions between the developing organism and the environment, as is evident in the co-sleeping study just described. While the growth process can be used across cultures as a marker of health status (as described in this chapter's Original Study), each culture defines the appropriate and acceptable trajectory of growth.

For example, in North America, visits to the doctor for growing children include measurement of height and weight. Individual children are compared to population-wide standards. When a given individual's height falls at the edges of the population's range, should this be considered normal variation or a sign of a problem? Very short, otherwise healthy adolescent males may receive a diagnosis of human growth hormone insufficiency and undergo treatment with synthetic growth hormones while adolescent girls do not. This diagnosis and treatment may therefore stem directly from the cultural value placed on larger male size in North America.

The inclusion of growth and development in biological anthropology has a long history dating back to the work of Franz Boas, one of the founders of four-field anthropology. Boas is credited with discovering the

© Barry Lewis/Corbis

These adolescent boys playing soccer illustrate the normal variation in the pattern of human growth at adolescence. Depending upon where they are in their adolescent growth spurt, heights can vary dramatically at this age.

The Smithsonian Institution

Although widely known for his contributions to cultural anthropology, Franz Boas not only shaped the whole notion of four-field anthropology but he also made major contributions to biological anthropology. He discovered the features of the human growth curve, demonstrated the effects of the environment on the growth process, and challenged the biological concept of race as described in Chapter 13. This photo shows Boas posing as a Kwakiutl *hanatsa* dancer from Canada's Pacific coast for a National Museum diorama in 1895.

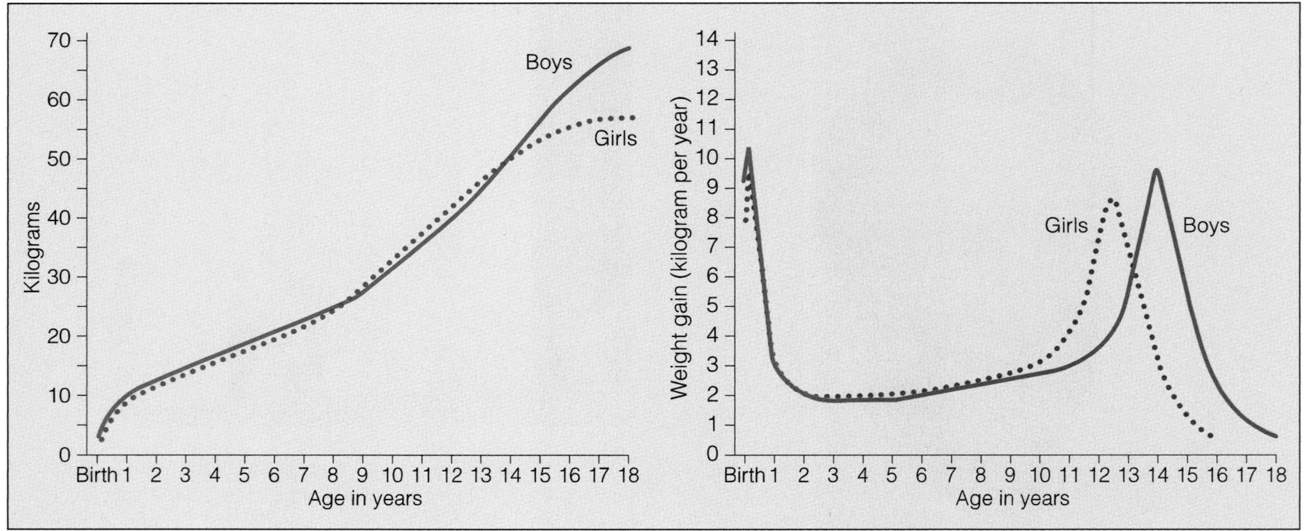

FIGURE EPILOGUE.1

Franz Boas defined the features of the human growth curve. The graph on the left depicts distance, or the amount of growth attained over time, while the graph on the right shows the velocity, or rate of growth over time. Growth charts are widely used throughout the globe to determine the health status of children.

features of the human growth curve (Figure Epilogue.1). He demonstrated that the rate of human growth varies in typical patterns until adulthood, when physical growth ceases. Humans experience a period of very rapid growth after birth through infancy, followed by a gradually slower rate of growth during childhood. At adolescence, the rate of growth increases again during the adolescent growth spurt. In addition to describing the long-term pattern of human growth, anthropologists have also demonstrated that within periods of growth, the actual growth process proceeds as a series of alternating bursts and relative quiet.[8] When challenged by malnutrition, physical growth slows to permit immediate survival at the expense of height in adulthood. This adaptive mechanism may have negative consequences for subsequent generations as individuals who were malnourished as children have been shown to experience reduced reproductive success as adults.[9] As described in this chapter's Original Study, cultural processes provide guidelines for infant and childhood food consumption, directly determining the trajectory of growth and lifetime health status.

Boas also demonstrated differences in the growth of immigrant children in the United States compared to their parents. This work was the earliest documentation of the variable effects of different environments on the growth process. Presumably, immigrant children resemble their parents genetically; therefore, size differences between immigrant children and their parents could be attributed to the environment alone. These physical differences among groups of related people from distinct time periods, known as **secular trends,** allow anthropologists to make inferences about environmental effects on growth and development.

For example, across the globe tremendous variation is seen in the age at menarche or first menstruation. Some of this variation can be attributed to genetically based population differences, while the remainder is due to environmental effects. The Bundi of New Guinea have the oldest average age at menarche (18). An important theory accounting for the timing of sexual maturation ties age at menarche to the percentage of body fat possessed by growing individuals as a regulator of hormonal production. Over the past 40 years a secular trend has become evident in North America toward a lower age at menarche. Whether this trend is attributable to healthy or problematic environmental stimuli (such as childhood obesity or hormones in the environment) has yet to be determined. Biological anthropologist Peter Ellison works extensively on the connections between hormones and the environment—a subspecialty defined as reproductive ecology (see Anthropologists of Note).

[8]Lampl, M., Velhuis, J. D., & Johnson, M. L. (1992). Saltation and stasis: A model of human growth. *Science, 258*(5083),801–803.

[9]Martorell, R. (1988). Body size, adaptation, and function. *GDP,* 335–347.

secular trends Physical differences among groups of related people from distinct time periods that allow anthropologists to make inferences about environmental effects on growth and development.

Symptoms as a Defense Mechanism

Scientists have documented that when faced with infection from a bacteria or virus, the human body mounts a series of physiological responses. For example, as a young individual learns his or her culture's medical system, the person might learn to recognize an illness as a "cold" or "flu" by responses of the body, such as fever, aches, runny nose, sore throat, vomiting, or diarrhea.

Think of how you may have learned about sickness as a young child. A caregiver or parent might have touched your forehead or neck with the back of the hand or lips to gauge your temperature. They may have placed a thermometer under your arm, in your mouth, or some other place to see if you had an elevated temperature or fever. (In the past, children's temperatures were usually taken rectally in North America.) If any of these methods revealed a temperature above the value defined as normal, the result might be giving a medicine to lower the fever.

Evolutionary medicine proposes that many of the symptoms that biomedicine treats are instead nature's treatments developed over millennia that should be tolerated rather than suppressed, so the body can heal itself. An elevated temperature is part of the human body's response to infectious particles, whereas eliminating the fever provides favorable temperatures for bacteria or viruses. Similarly within some physiological limits, vomiting, coughing, and diarrhea may be adaptive as they remove harmful substances or organisms from the body. In other words, the cultural prescription to lower a fever or suppress a cough might actually prolong the disease.

Evolutionary biologist Margie Profet proposed a particular benefit for the symptoms of nausea and vomiting during early pregnancy.[10] She suggests that many plants, particularly those in the broccoli and cabbage family, naturally contain toxins developed through the process of evolution by plants to prevent them from being eaten by animals. Profet suggests that eating these plants during the first weeks of pregnancy when the developing embryo is rapidly making new cells through mitosis and differentiating into specific body parts makes the embryo vulnerable to mutation. Therefore, a heightened sense of smell and lowered nausea threshold serves as the body's natural defense. It causes women to avoid these foods, thus protecting the developing embryo. Similarly, biological anthropologist Fatimah Jackson has studied a wide variety of human–plant interactions and the relationship between diet and disease (see Anthropologists of Note).

[10]Profet, M. (1991). The function of allergy: Immunological defense against toxins. *Quarterly Review of Biology, 66*(1),23–62; Profet, M. (1995). *Protecting your baby to be.* New York: Addison Wesley.

Evolution and Infectious Disease

In addition to a focus on symptoms as defense mechanisms, evolutionary medicine provides two key insights with regard to infectious disease. First, if infectious disease is viewed as competition between microorganisms and humans—as it is in biomedicine where patients fight infectious disease—microorganisms possess one very clear advantage. Viruses, bacteria, fungi, and parasites all have very short life cycles compared to humans. Therefore, when competing on an evolutionary level, they will always win because any new genetic variants appearing through a random mutation will become incorporated in the population's genome more quickly. This is of particular importance with regard to the use of antibiotics to fight infectious disease.

While antibiotics will kill many bacteria, increasingly resistant strains of bacteria are becoming more common. Resistant strains refer to genetic variants of a specific bacterium that are not killed by antibiotics. If a resistant strain appears in an infected individual who is

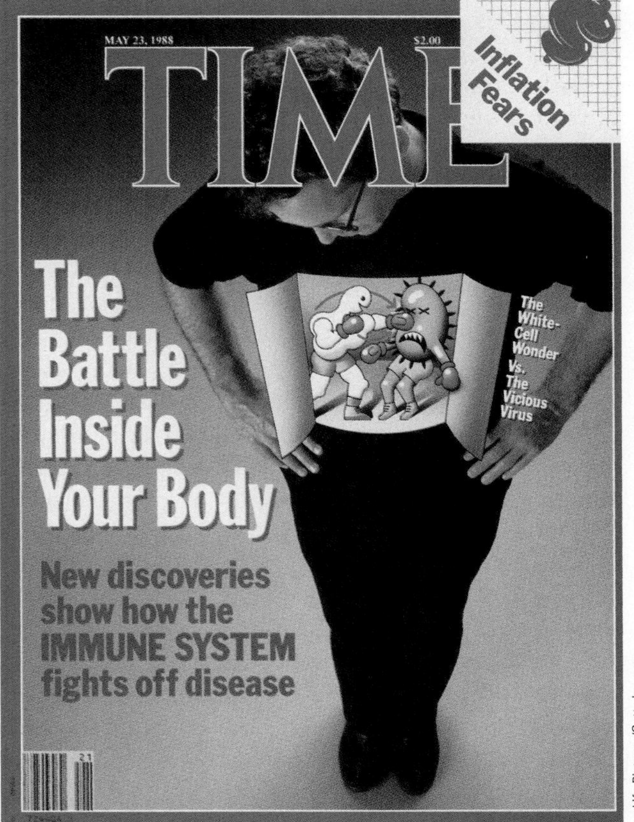

North American medical anthropologist Emily Martin has shown that scientific depictions of infectious disease draw upon military imagery common to the culture of the United States. Biomedical treatments involve taking antibiotics to kill "invading" organisms. An evolutionary perspective suggests that the quick life cycle of microorganisms makes this "battle" a losing proposition for humans.

Anthropologists of Note

Peter Ellison (1951–) ▪ Fatimah Jackson (1950–)

© Martha Stewart

Reproductive biology and human health across cultures have been the focus of the work of biological anthropologist Peter Ellison. In the 1970s, Ellison first read Darwin's *Origin of Species* as a college student at St. John's College in Annapolis, Maryland. He found Darwin's text transformative, and went to the University of Vermont to study biology; later he earned a Ph.D. in biological anthropology from Harvard, where he now runs a comprehensive program in reproductive ecology.

Ellison has pioneered techniques for hormonal analysis from saliva, and uses this technique to monitor individuals' hormonal response to a variety of environmental stressors. This noninvasive technique has allowed Ellison to conduct hormonal studies throughout the world and to correlate hormonal levels with social events. People from long-term field sites in the Congo, Poland, Japan, Nepal, and Paraguay have participated in this research, allowing Ellison to document the hormonal variation around biological events, such as egg implantation and breastfeeding, as well as cultural factors such as farm work or foraging. He is especially interested in how behavior and social stimuli affect reproductive physiology. In Western societies, he has explored hormonal levels of males and females in response to stimuli, such as winning a championship or taking a stressful exam. He has also studied the relationship between exercise, stress, and cancer development. In his recent book *On Fertile Ground,* Ellison illustrates how evolutionary forces have shaped human reproductive physiology into a system capable of precise responses to environmental stimuli.

Courtesy of Fatima Jackson

While at first glance Fatimah Jackson's research areas seem diverse, they are unified by consistent representation of African American perspectives in biological anthropology. With a keen awareness of how culture determines the content of scientific questions, Jackson chooses hers carefully. One of her earliest areas of research concerned the use of common African plants as foods and medicines. She has examined the co-evolution of plants and humans and the ways plant compounds serve to attract and repel humans at various stages of ripeness. Through laboratory and field research, she has documented that cassava, a New World root crop providing the major source of dietary energy for over 500 million people, also guards against malaria. This crop has become a major food throughout Africa in areas where malaria is common.

Jackson is also the genetics group leader for the African Burial Ground Project (mentioned in Chapter 1), a site uncovered during a New York City construction project. Jackson is recovering DNA from skeletal remains and attempting to match the dead with specific regions of Africa through the analysis of genetic markers in living African people. Jackson, one of the early advocates for ethical treatment of minorities in the human genome project, is concerned that the genetic work for the African Burial Project is conducted with sensitivity to African people. She is therefore working to establish genetic laboratories and repositories in Africa. For Jackson, these laboratories are symbolic of the fact of human commonality and that all humans today have roots in Africa.

being treated with antibiotics, the removal of all the nonresistant strains essentially opens up an entire ecological niche for that resistant strain inside the infected human. Here, without competition from the original form of the bacterium wiped out by the antibiotic, this mutant can proliferate easily and then spread to other individuals. The practice of taking antibiotics artificially alters the environment inside the human body.

Thus, antibiotic resistance illustrates the second key evolutionary medicine contributes to the understanding of infectious disease: Infectious disease and the human efforts to stop infectious disease always occur in the context of the human-made environment. Humans have been altering their external environments in increasingly major ways since the Neolithic transition (see Anthropology Applied), resulting in an increase in a variety of infectious diseases. In this regard, evolutionary medicine shares much with political ecology—a branch of medical anthropology described next.

POLITICAL ECOLOGY OF DISEASE

An ecological perspective considers organisms in the context of their environment. Because local human environments are shaped not only by local culture but by global political and economic systems, these features must all be included in a comprehensive examination of human disease from an ecological perspective. Simply describing disease in terms of biological processes leaves out the deeper, ultimate reasons that some individuals are more likely to become sick than others. A strictly biological approach also leaves out differences in the resources available to individuals, communities, and states to cope with and heal from disease and illness.

Kuru and Other Prion Diseases

Kuru is the name given in the local language to the fatal disease that afflicted the Fore (pronounced "foray") people of Papua New Guinea at high rates during the 20th

Anthropology Applied

Studying the Emergence of New Diseases

Ever since the Neolithic, humans have had to cope with a host of new diseases that got their start as a consequence of changes in human behavior. This has become a renewed source of concern following a recent resurgence of infectious diseases and appearance and spread of a host of new and lethal diseases. All told, more than thirty diseases new to medicine have emerged in the past 25 years, of which perhaps the best known is AIDS. This has now become number 4 among infectious killers of humans, with 5.8 million people infected in 1998 alone.[a] But there are others—like Ebola, which causes victims to hemorrhage to death, blood pouring from every orifice; hemorrhagic fevers like Dengue fever, Lassa fever, and Hantavirus; Invasive Streptococcus A, which consumes the victims' flesh; Legionnaire's disease; and Lyme disease. What has sparked the appearance and spread of these and other new diseases has been a considerable mystery, but one theory is that some are the result of human activities. In particular, the intrusion of people into new ecological settings, such as rainforests, along with construction of roads allows viruses and other infectious microbes to spread rapidly to large numbers of people. It is now generally accepted that the HIV virus responsible for AIDS transferred to humans from chimpanzees in the forests of the Democratic Republic of Congo as a consequence of hunting and butchering these animals for food. For the first 30 years, few people were affected; it was not until people began congregating in cities like Kinshasa that conditions were ripe for an epidemic.

To gain a better understanding of the interplay between ecological disturbance and the emergence of new diseases, anthropologist Carol Jenkins, whose specialty is medical anthropology, obtained a grant from the MacArthur Foundation in 1993. From her base at the Papua New Guinea Institute of Medical Research, she is following the health of local people in the wake of a massive logging operation, begun in 1993. From this should come a better understanding of how disease organisms spread from animal hosts to humans. Since most of the "new" viruses that have suddenly afflicted humans are in fact old ones that have been present in animals like monkeys (monkey pox), rodents (Hantavirus), deer (Lyme disease), and insects (West Nile virus), it appears that something new has enabled them to jump from their animal hosts to humans.

Travis Jenkins

Carol Jenkins at work with Hagahai people in Papua New Guinea.

A recent example comes from the Democratic Republic of Congo. Here civil war created a situation where villagers in the central part of the country were faced with starvation. Their response was to increase the hunting of animals, including monkeys, squirrels, and rats that carry a disease called monkey pox. Related to smallpox, the disease transfers easily to humans, resulting in the largest outbreak of this disease ever seen among humans. What makes this outbreak even more serious is an apparently new strain of the infection, enabling it to spread from person to person, instead of only from an animal host.[b]

Large-scale habitat disturbance is an obvious candidate for such disease transfers, but this needs to be confirmed and the process understood. So far, it is hard to make more than a circumstantial case, by looking back after a disease outbreak. The work of Jenkins and her team is unique in that she was able to get baseline health data on local people before their environment was disturbed. Thus, she is in a position to follow events as they unfold.

It will be some time before conclusions can be drawn from Jenkins' study. Its importance is obvious; in an era of globalization, as air travel and climatic warming allows tropical disease to spread beyond the tropics, we need a fuller understanding of how viruses interact with their hosts if we are to devise effective preventive and therapeutic strategies to deal with them. *(Adapted from A. Gibbons. (1993). Where are new diseases born?* Science, 261, 680–681.) ■ ■ ■

[a] Balter, M. (1998). On world AIDS day, a shadow looms over southern Africa. *Science, 282,* 1,790.

[b] Cohen, J. (1997). Is an old virus up to new tricks? *Science, 277,* 312–313.

century. This sickness was claiming the lives of the majority of women and children from Fore communities, so they welcomed assistance provided by an international team of health workers led by a physician from the United States, Carleton Gajdusek.

Kuru did not fit neatly into any known biomedical categories. Because the disease seemed to be limited to families of related individuals, cultural anthropologists Shirley Lindenbaum from Australia and Robert Glasse from the United States, who were doing fieldwork in the region, were recruited to contribute documentation of Fore kinship relationships. It was hoped this knowledge would reveal an underlying genetic mechanism for this disease.[11] When documentation of the kin relationships did not reveal a pattern of genetic transmission, the

[11] Lindenbaum, S. (1978). *Kuru sorcery: Disease and danger in the New Guinea highlands.* New York: McGraw-Hill.

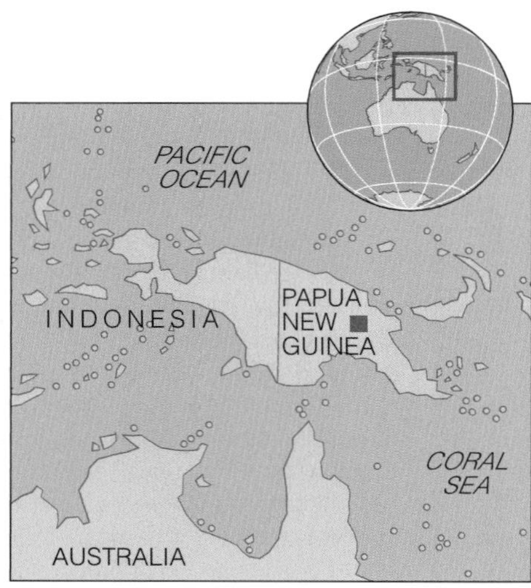

medical team turned instead to the notion of infectious disease, even though the slow progression of kuru seemed to weigh against an infectious cause. Material derived from infected individuals was injected into chimpanzees (see Chapter 5's Biocultural Connection for a discussion about the ethics of this practice) to see whether they developed the disease. After 18 months, injected chimpanzees succumbed to the classic symptoms of kuru, and their autopsied brains indicated the same pathologies as seen in humans with kuru. At this point, the disease was defined as infectious (garnering Gajdusek a Nobel Prize).

While at that time the infectious agent was described as an unidentified "slow virus," it was later determined that a **prion**—a completely new kind of infectious particle lacking any genetic material—was responsible. Prions are a kind of protein that can cause the reorganization and destruction of other proteins. While the important discovery and delineation of the mechanics of prion disease led to a Nobel Prize in medicine for the North American physician scientist Stanley Prusiner, the story of kuru is not complete without an examination of why some individuals were infected and not others. For this, one has to return to the local cultural and larger global perspectives of anthropology, as Lindenbaum explains in her book *Kuru Sorcery*. Lindenbaum demonstrates that kuru is related to cultural practices regarding the bodies of individuals who had died from kuru and the way global factors impacted these local practices.

prion An infectious protein lacking any genetic material but capable of causing the reorganization and destruction of other proteins.
medical pluralism The presence of multiple medical systems, each with its own practices and beliefs in a society.

Courtesy of Shirley Lindenbaum

The mystery of the disease kuru could not have been unraveled without the work of anthropologist Shirley Lindenbaum, pictured here with Fore women and children.

Culturally, Fore women are responsible for preparing the bodies of their loved ones for the afterlife. This practice alone put women at a greater risk for exposure to kuru. Lindenbaum also discovered that women and children were at risk due to a combination of these local practices with more global forces. In Fore society, men were responsible for raising pigs and slaughtering and distributing meat. The middle of the 20th century was a time of hardship and transition for the Fore people. Colonial rule by Australia had changed the fabric of society, threatening traditional subsistence patterns and resulting in a shortage of protein in the form of pigs. The limited amount of pig meat available was distributed by men preferentially to other men. Fore women told Lindenbaum that, as a practical solution to their hunger, they preferred eating their loved ones who had died in a relatively "meaty" state from kuru compared to eating individuals wasted from malnutrition. This temporary practice was abandoned as the Fore subsistence pattern recovered, and the biological mechanisms of kuru transmission were communicated to the Fore. The Fore medical system had its own explanations for the causes of kuru (primarily involving sorcery) that were compatible with biomedical explanations for the mechanisms of disease. Such blending of medical systems is common throughout the globe today.

Medical pluralism refers to the presence of multiple medical systems, each with its own practices and beliefs, in a society. As illustrated with the Fore, individuals generally can reconcile conflicting medical systems and incorporate diverse elements from a variety of medical systems to ease their suffering. While Western biomedicine has contributed some spectacular treatments and cures for a variety of diseases, many of its practices and values are singularly associated with the Euroamerican societies in which it developed. The interna-

AP/Wide World Photos

AP/Wide World Photos

VISUAL COUNTERPOINT A global economy in which animals are fed human-made products and in which meat is shipped abroad rather than consumed locally increases the scale of possible transmission of prion disease.

tional public health movement attempts to bring many of the successes of biomedicine based on the scientific understanding of human biology to the rest of the world. But to do so successfully, cultural practices and beliefs must be taken into account.

Today postindustrial societies are beset by prion diseases far more than the Fore. Prion diseases are nearly always transmitted through infected foods, although sometimes they are transmitted through the cultural practice of transplant surgery. The beef supply of several countries in Europe and North America has been tainted by prions resulting in mad cow disease. As with the Fore, cultural practices led to the disease, but this time on a much larger scale. When the biology of kuru was being unraveled, a similar neurodegenerative disease in sheep called scrapie was also identified. Prion disease jumped from sheep to cows through the cultural practice of grinding up sheep carcasses and adding them to the commercial feed of beef cattle. Thus, through the wide distribution of tainted feed, prion disease was spread. Today countries without confirmed mad cow disease ban the importation of beef from neighboring countries with documented prion disease. Such bans have tremendous effects on the local economies. Prion disease illustrates that no sickness in the 21st century can be considered in isolation; an understanding of these diseases must take into account political and economic forces as well as how these forces affect the ability to treat or cure.

GLOBALIZATION, HEALTH, AND STRUCTURAL VIOLENCE

One generalization that can be made across the globe is that with regard to most diseases, wealth means health. The World Health Organization defines health as "a complete state of physical, psychological, and social well-being, not the mere absence of disease or infirmity."[12] While the international public health community works to improve human health throughout the globe, heavily armed states, megacorporations, and very wealthy elites are using their powers to structure or rearrange the emerging world system and direct global processes to their own competitive advantage. When impersonal structural power undermines the well-being of others, we may speak of **structural violence**—physical and/or psychological harm (including repression, environmental destruction, poverty, hunger, illness, and premature death) caused by exploitative and unjust social, political, and economic systems. Clearly, the current structures are positioned in a way that leads to more wealth, power, comfort, and health for the happy few and little more than poverty, subservience, suffering, and death for multitudes. Every day millions of people around the world face famine, ecological disasters, health problems, political instability, and violence rooted in development programs or profit-making maneuvers directed by powerful states or global corporations.

As we saw in Chapter 12, **health disparities,** or differences in the health status between the wealthy elite and the poor in stratified societies, are nothing new. Globalization has expanded and intensified structural violence, leading to enormous health disparities among

[12] World Health Organization. *http://www.who.int/about/definition/en/.*

structural violence Physical and/or psychological harm (including repression, environmental destruction, poverty, hunger, illness, and premature death) caused by exploitative and unjust social, political, and economic systems.
health disparities Differences in the health status between the wealthy elite and the poor in stratified societies.

individuals, communities, and even countries. Medical anthropologists have examined how structural violence leads not only to unequal access to treatments but also to the likelihood of contracting disease through exposure to malnutrition, crowded conditions, and toxins.

Hunger and Obesity

As frequently dramatized in media reports, hundreds of millions of people face hunger on a regular basis, leading to a variety of health problems, premature death, and other forms of suffering. Today, fifty-four of the world's 191 countries do not produce enough food to feed their populations and cannot afford to import an adequate supply. The majority of these countries are in sub-Saharan Africa. All told, about 1 billion people in the world are undernourished. Some 6 million children aged 5 and under die every year due to hunger, and those who survive often suffer from physical and mental impairment.[13]

[13]Hunger Project 2003; Swaminathan, M. S. (2000). Science in response to basic human needs. *Science, 287,* 425.

AP/Wide World Photos

Hunger stalks much of the world as a result of a global food system geared to satisfy an affluent minority in the world's developed nations.

For the victims of this situation, the effect is violent, even though it was not caused by the deliberate hostile act of a specific individual. The source of the violence may have been the unplanned yet devastatingly real impact of global political and economic forces such as the collapse of local markets due to subsidized foreign imports.

Ironically, while many millions of people in some parts of the world are starving, many millions of others are overeating—quite literally eating themselves to death. In fact, the number of overfed people now exceeds those who are underfed. According to the World Watch Institute in Washington, DC, more than 1.1 billion people worldwide are now overweight, and 300 million of these are obese. Seriously concerned about the sharp rise in associated health problems (including stroke, diabetes, cancer, and heart disease), the World Health Organization classifies obesity as a global epidemic. In some industrial and postindustrial societies where machines have eased the physical burdens of work and other human activities, more than half of the people are overweight. However, the obesity epidemic is not due solely to excessive eating and lack of physical activity. A key cause is the high sugar and fat content of mass-marketed foods. The problem is spreading and has become a serious concern even in some developing countries. In fact, the highest rates of obesity in the world now exist among Pacific Islanders living in places such as Samoa and Fiji. On the island of Nauru, up to 65 percent of the men and 70 percent of the women are now classified as obese. (That said, not all people who are overweight or obese are so because they eat too much junk food and do too little exercise. In addition to cultural factors, being overweight or obese can also be the result of genetic or other biological causes.)

As for hunger cases, about 10 percent of them can be traced to specific events—droughts or floods, as well as various social, economic, and political disruptions, including warfare. During the 20th century, 44 million people died due to human-made famine.[14] For example, in several sub-Saharan African countries plagued by chronic civil strife, it has been almost impossible to raise and harvest crops, for hoards of refugees and soldiers constantly raid fields, often at gunpoint. Another problem is that millions of acres in Africa, Asia, and Latin America once devoted to subsistence farming have been given over to the raising of cash crops for export. This has enriched members of elite social classes in these parts of the world, while satisfying the appetites of people in the developed countries for coffee, tea, chocolate, bananas, and beef. Those who used to farm the land for their own food needs have been relocated—either to

[14]Hunger Project 2003; White, M. (2001). *Historical atlas of the twentieth century. http://users.erols.com/mwhite28/20centry.htm.*

© Annebicque Bernard/Corbis Sygma

© Kilcullen/Trocaire/Corbis Sygma

VISUAL COUNTERPOINT While obesity and starvation represent very different kinds of health problems, in both cases global processes contribute to the disease. Diets are largely determined by what is available and affordable. Starvation makes individuals more vulnerable to infectious disease while obesity increases vulnerability for chronic diseases such as diabetes, heart disease, and stroke. The poor members of each society will be disproportionately in poorer health.

urban areas, where all too often there is no employment for them, or to areas ecologically unsuited for farming. In Africa such lands are often occupied seasonally by pastoral nomads, and turning them over to cultivation has reduced pasture available for livestock and led to overgrazing. The increase in cleared land, coupled with overgrazing, has depleted both soil and water, with disastrous consequences to nomad and farmer alike. So it is that more than 250 million people can no longer grow crops on their farms, and 1 billion people in 100 countries are in danger of losing their ability to grow crops.[15]

MEDIATREK

To find out how much you consume and see the size of your ecological footprint, go to MediaTrek Epilogue.3 on the companion Web site or CD-ROM.

One strategy urged upon so-called underdeveloped countries, especially by government officials and development advisors from the United States, has been to adopt practices that have made North American agriculture so incredibly productive. However, this strategy ignores the crucial fact that these large-scale, commercial farming practices require a financial investment that small farmers and poor countries cannot afford—a substantial outlay of cash for chemical fertilizers, pesticides, and herbicides, not to mention fossil fuels needed to run all the mechanized equipment.

U.S.-style farming has additional problems, including energy inefficiency. For every calorie produced, at least 8—some say as many as 20—calories go into its production and distribution.[16] By contrast, an Asian wet-rice farmer using traditional methods produces 300 calories for each 1 expended. North American agriculture is wasteful of other resources as well: About 30 pounds of fertile topsoil are ruined for every pound of food produced.[17] In the midwestern United States, about 50 percent of the topsoil has been lost over the past 100 years. Meanwhile, toxic substances from chemical nutrients and pesticides pile up in unexpected places, poisoning ground and surface waters; killing fish, birds, and other useful forms of life; upsetting natural ecological cycles; and causing major public health problems. Despite its spectacular short-term success, serious questions arise about whether such a profligate food production system can be sustained over the long run, even in North America.

Yet another problem with the idea of copying U.S. farming styles has to do with subsidies. Despite official rhetoric about free markets, governments of the wealthiest capitalist states in North America and western Europe spend between $100 billion and $300 billion annually on agriculture subsidies. In the United States,

[15]Godfrey, T. (2000, December 27). Biotech threatening biodiversity. *Burlington Free Press,* p. 10A.

[16]Bodley, J. H. (1985). *Anthropology and contemporary human problems* (2nd ed., p. 128). Palo Alto, CA: Mayfield.

[17]Chasin, B. H., & Franke, R. W. (1983). US farming: A world model? *Global Reporter, 1*(2), 10.

© Tony Freeman/PhotoEdit

Spraying chemicals on crops, as here in California's Central Valley, trades short-term benefits for long-term pollution and health problems.

the world's largest agricultural exporter, 75 percent of these go to the wealthiest 10 percent of the farmers and large agricultural corporations.

Confronted with such economic forces in the global arena, small farmers in poor countries find themselves in serious trouble when trying to sell their products on markets open to subsidized agricultural corporations dumping mass-produced and often genetically engineered crops and other farm products. Unable to compete under those structural conditions, many are forced to quit farming, leave their villages, and seek other livelihoods in cities or as migrant workers abroad. Such is the fate of many Maya Indians today. Since the early 1980s, when so many fled Guatemala's violence and poverty, thousands have made their way to places like southeastern Florida and taken low-paying jobs as illegal immigrants. Because of endemic poverty in their homeland where they would face starvation, these victims of structural violence have no choice but to remain where they are, condemned to an uncertain life in exile as cheap laborers without civil rights, Social Security, or health insurance.

Pollution

The effects of big agribusiness practices are part of larger problems of environmental degradation in which pollution is tolerated for the sake of higher profits that benefit select individuals and societies. Industrial activities are producing highly toxic waste at unprecedented rates, and factory emissions are poisoning the air. For example, smokestack gases are clearly implicated in acid rain, which is damaging lakes and forests all over northeastern North America. Air containing water vapor with a high acid content is, of course, harmful to the lungs, but the health hazard is greater than this. As ground and surface waters become more acidic, the solubility of lead, cadmium, mercury, and aluminum, all of them toxic, rises sharply. For instance, aluminum contamination is high enough on 17 percent of the world's farmland to be toxic to plants—and has been linked to senile dementia, Alzheimer's, and Parkinson's diseases, three major health problems in industrial countries. Indeed, development itself seems to be a health hazard. It is well known that indigenous peoples in Africa, the Pacific Islands, South America, and elsewhere are relatively free from diabetes, obesity, hypertension, and a variety of circulatory diseases until they adopt the ways of the so-called developed countries.

Finding their way into the world's oceans, toxic substances also create hazards for seafood consumers. For instance, Canadian Inuit face health problems related to eating fish and sea mammals that feed in waters contaminated by industrial chemical waste such as polychlorinated biphenyls (PCBs). Living thousands of miles from the industrial sources poisoning their environment, Inuit women have a right to be alarmed that their breast milk now contains levels of PCBs five to ten times higher than women in southern Canada.[18] Obviously, environmental poisoning affects peoples all across the globe (Figure Epilogue.2).

As described in the previous chapter, experts predict that global warming will lead to an expansion of

[18]Inuit Tapiirit Kanatami. *http://www.tapirisat.ca/english_text/itk/departments/enviro/ncp/*

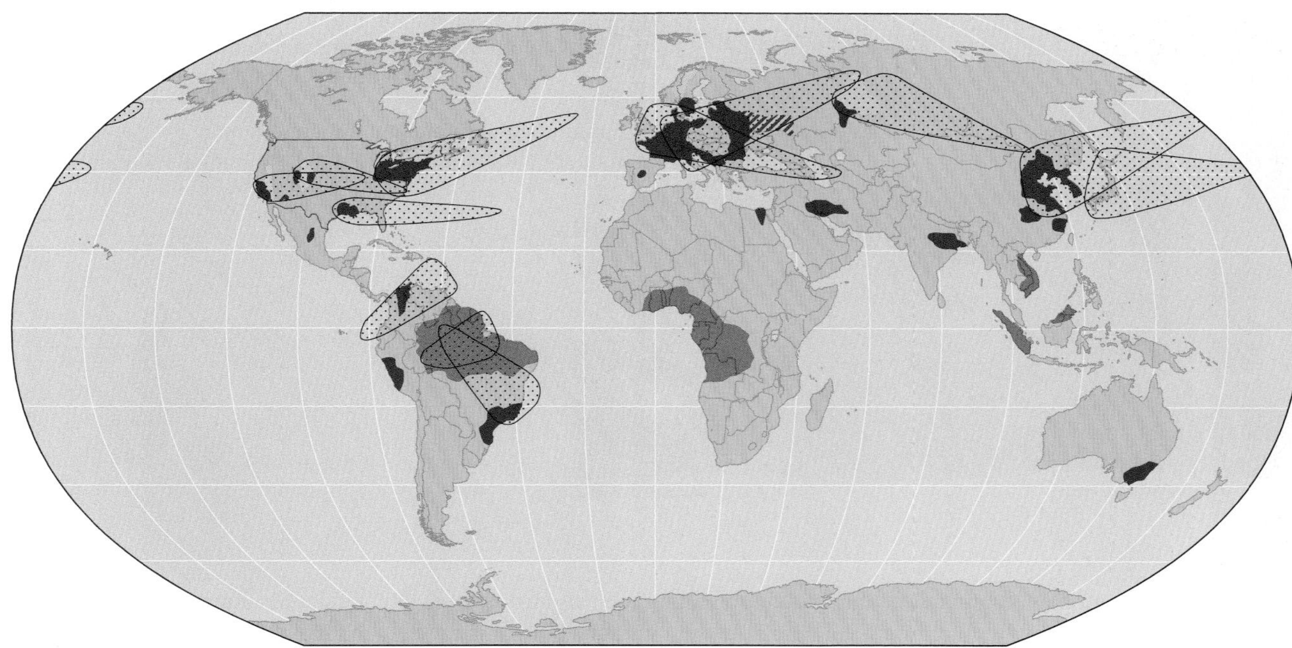

- Land areas with significant acid precipitation and atmospheric pollution
- Land areas with significant atmospheric pollution
- Land areas with significant acid precipitation
- Land areas of secondary atmospheric pollution
- Air pollution plume: average wind direction and force (Wind blows in the direction of the tapered end of the air pollution plume and the force of the wind is indicated by the size of the plume.)

FIGURE EPILOGUE.2

Almost all processes of physical geography begin and end with the flows of energy and matter among land, sea, and air. Because of the primacy of the atmosphere in this exchange system, air pollution is potentially one of the most dangerous human modifications in environmental systems. Pollutants such as various oxides of nitrogen or sulfur cause the development of acid precipitation, which damages soil, vegetation, and wildlife and fish. Air pollution in the form of smog is often dangerous for human health. There is a consensus among atmospheric scientists who believe that the efficiency of the atmosphere in retaining heat—the greenhouse effect—is being enhanced by increased carbon dioxide, methane, and other gases produced by industrial and agricultural activities. The result, they fear, will be a period of global warming that will dramatically alter climates in all parts of the world.

the geographical ranges of tropical diseases and increase the incidence of respiratory diseases due to additional smog caused by warmer temperatures. Also, they expect an increase in deaths due to heat waves, as witnessed in the 15,000 deaths attributed to the 2003 heat wave in France.[19] Unfortunately, public concern about this is minimal, in large part because energy interests sponsor public relations campaigns to convince people that global warming is not real—just as tobacco companies once ran campaigns claiming that smoking was not hazardous.

Structural violence also manifests itself in the shifting of manufacturing and hazardous waste disposal from developed to developing countries. This trend is encouraged by cheap labor and less stringent safety and environment regulations, which translate into lower production costs and larger profits for corporations.

AP/Wide World Photos

This picture of a flood in Bangladesh exemplifies the structural violence that will result from global warming. As sea levels rise, flooding of low-lying areas will become more extensive and frequent.

[19]World Meteorological Organization, quoted in "Increasing heat waves and other health hazards." Accessed December 2003 at *greenpeaceusa.org/climate/index.fpl/7096/article/907.html.*

The popularity of sports utility vehicles (SUVs) in North America illustrates how consumers in affluent countries contribute to environmental destruction in the world's poorer countries. In Brazil, chainsaws are used to destroy vast tracts of forest in order to procure wood for production of charcoal. This is required to make the pig iron used in the strongest steel to make SUVs. In addition to the environmental devastation, oppressed labor is used to burn the charcoal.

Typically, a few well-placed officials or businesspeople in the developing countries benefit financially from these overseas arrangements, while powerless workers are exploited and environmental pollution is expanded. For instance, not long ago the president of Benin in West Africa signed a contract with a European waste company enabling that company to dump toxic and low-grade radioactive waste on the lands of his political opposition.[20] In the United States, both government and industry have tried to persuade American Indians on reservations that the solution to their severe economic problems lies in allowing disposal of nuclear and other hazardous waste on their lands.

Given a general awareness of the causes and dangers of pollution, why is it that the human species as a whole is not committed to controlling practices that foul its own nest? At least part of the answer lies in philosophical and theological traditions. Western industrialized societies accept the Biblical assertion (found in the Koran as well) of human dominion over the earth, interpreting that to mean that it is their task to subdue and control the earth and all its inhabitants. These societies are the biggest contributors to global pollution. For example, on average, one North American consumes hundreds of times the resources of a single African, with all that implies with respect to waste disposal and environmental degradation. Moreover, each person in North America adds, on average, 20 tons of carbon dioxide (a greenhouse gas) a year to the atmosphere. In "underdeveloped" countries, less than 3 tons per person are emitted.[21] According to botanist Peter Raven, "if everyone lived like (North) Americans, you'd need three planet earths . . . to sustain that level of consumption."[22]

20 *Cultural Survival Quarterly* (1991), *15*(4), 5.

replacement reproduction When birthrates and death rates are in equilibrium; people produce only enough offspring to replace themselves when they die.

Structural Violence and Population Control

In 1750, 1 billion people lived on earth. Over the next two centuries our numbers climbed to nearly 2.5 billion. And between 1950 and 2000 it soared above 6 billion (Figure Epilogue.3). Today, India and China alone have more than 1 billion inhabitants each. Such increases are highly significant because population growth increases the scale of hunger and pollution—and the many problems tied to these two big issues. Although controlling population growth does not by itself make the other problems go away, it is unlikely those other problems can be solved unless population growth is stopped or even reversed.

For a population to hold steady, there must be a balance between birthrates and death rates. In other words, people must produce only enough offspring to replace themselves when they die. This is known as **replacement reproduction.** Prior to 1976, birthrates around the world generally exceeded death rates, with the exception of European and North American populations. Poor people, in particular, have tended to have large families

21 Broecker, W. S. (1992, April). Global warming on trial. *Natural History,* 14.

22 Quoted in Becker, J. (2004, March). *National Geographic,* 90.

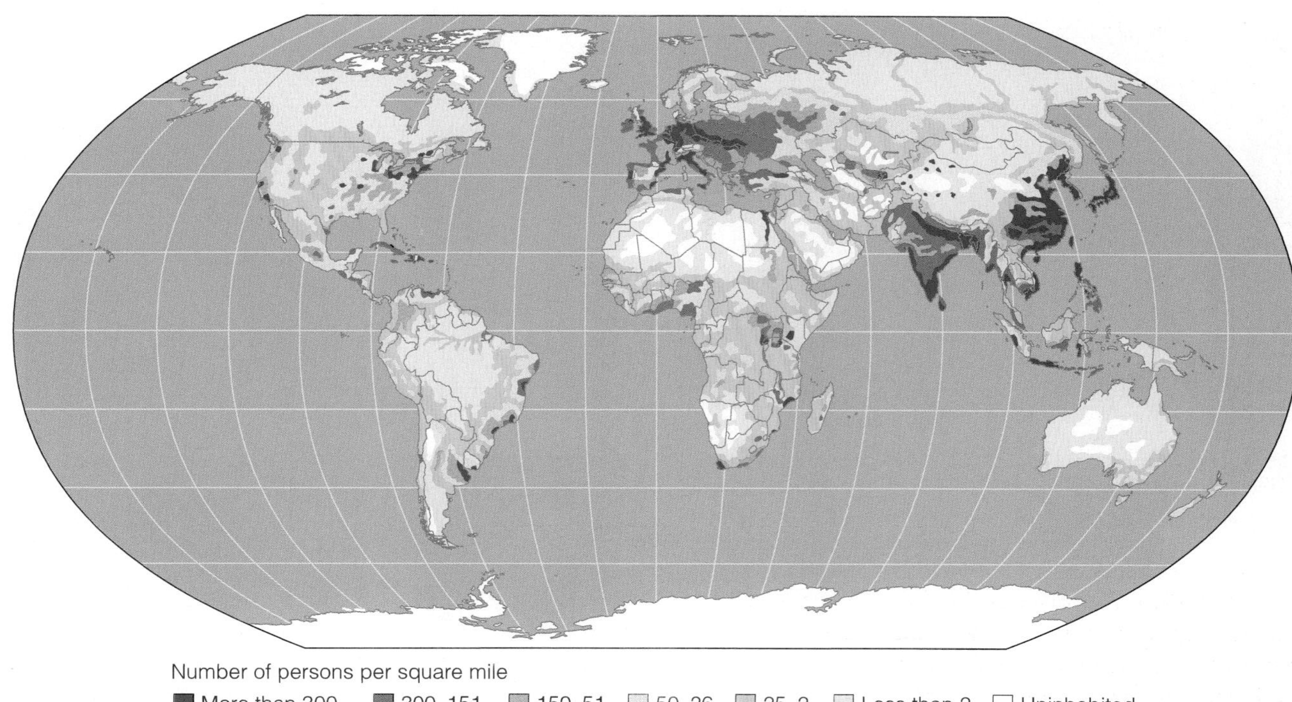

FIGURE EPILOGUE.3

Three great concentrations of human population appear on this map—East Asia, South Asia, and Europe—with a fourth, lesser concentration in eastern North America. Population growth is still rapid in South Asia, which is expected to become even more densely populated in the early 21st century. Density in the other three regions is expected to remain about as it now appears due to relatively stable population rates resulting from economic development. The areas of future high density population, in addition to those already existing, are likely to be Central Africa and Central and South America, where growth rates are well above the world average.

because children have been their main resource. Children can provide a needed labor pool to work farms, and they are the only source of security for the elderly. Historically, people were apt to limit the size of their families only when they became wealthy enough that their money replaced children as their main resource; at that point, children actually *cost* them money. Given this, we can see why birthrates remained high for so long in the world's poorer countries. To those who live in poverty, children are seen as the only hope.

Since the mid-1970s, birthrates have dropped below replacement level (which is about 2.1 children per woman) in virtually every industrialized country and also in nineteen "underdeveloped" countries—including China, the world's most populous country. In Africa, as well as much of South Asia and Central and South America (again, the world's poorer countries), birthrates have also declined but far less dramatically.[23]

Despite progress in population control, fertility rates on average remain above replacement, so the number of humans on earth continues to grow overall. Population projections are extremely tricky, given variables such as AIDS, but current projections suggest that global population will peak around 2050 at about 9.37 billion people.

Desirable though it may be to halt population growth, programs to do so, and their consequences, pose many new health problems. These are well illustrated by China's much publicized "one-child" policy, introduced in 1979 to control its soaring population growth. This policy led to a sharp upward trend in sex-selective abortions, as well as female infanticide and high female infant mortality due to abandonment and neglect. This trend has created an imbalance in China's male and female populations, often referred to as the "missing girl gap" of some 50 million. One study reported that China's male to female sex ratio had become so distorted that 111 million men would not be able to find a wife. Government regulations softened slightly in the 1990s, when it became legal for rural couples to have a second child if their first was a girl—

[23]Bongaarts, J. (1998). Demographic consequences of declining fertility. *Science, 282,* 419; Wattenberg, B. J. (1997, November 23). The population explosion is over. *New York Times Magazine,* 60.

© Reuters/Corbis

Amnesty International

"Never doubt that a small group of committed people can change the world; indeed it is the only thing that ever has." (Margaret Mead, anthropologist) Many anthropologists do fieldwork that results in information with practical value for the communities in which they do their studies. Not surprisingly, we find anthropologists working for international service organizations such as Oxfam, founded at Oxford University during World War II for famine relief in war-torn Europe. Today, Oxfam offers aid and advocacy worldwide for refugees and others in need. Anthropologists have also long been active in the United Nations Educational, Scientific and Cultural Organization (UNESCO), headquartered in Paris and with offices all over the globe. Founded in 1946, this international forum contributes to peace and security by promoting collaboration among the nations through education, science, and culture. Anthropologists are also likely participants in international human rights organizations such as Amnesty International, founded in London in 1961 to work on behalf of political prisoners. Active in more than 160 countries, Amnesty now has over 1 million members and is more broadly focused on exposing and ending all violations to the Universal Declaration of Human Rights. In 1977, it won the Nobel Peace Prize. Some anthropologists also work with Doctors Without Borders, another Nobel Peace Prize winner. Founded in Paris in 1971 by a group of medical doctors, it has some 2,000 volunteers serving in over eighty countries.

AP/Wide World Photos

and if they paid a fee. Millions of rural couples have circumvented regulations by not registering births—resulting in millions of young people who do not officially exist.[24]

The Culture of Discontent

For the past several decades, the world's poor countries have been sold on the idea they should and actually can enjoy a standard of living comparable to that of the rich countries. Yet, the resources necessary to maintain such a luxurious standard of living are not unlimited. This growing gap between expectations and realizations has led to the creation of a culture of discontent. The problem involves not just population growth outstripping

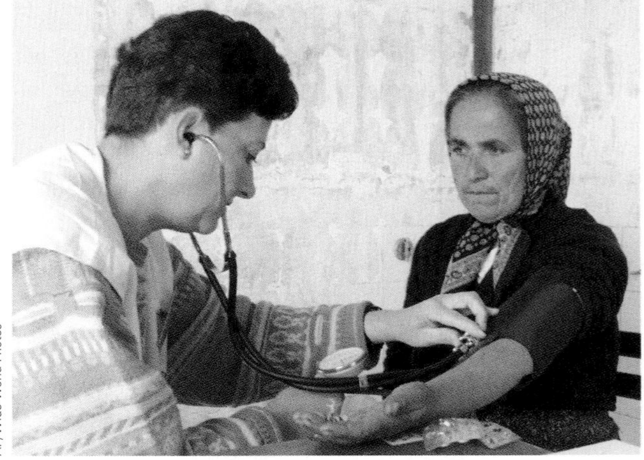

AP/Wide World Photos

[24]Bongaarts.

available natural resources, but also unequal access to decent jobs, housing, sanitation, health care, leisure, and adequate police and fire protection. It is one in which personal disappointments are echoed in a natural environment degraded by overcrowding, pollution, and soil erosion. This culture of discontent is not limited to people living in poor and overpopulated countries. Because capitalism thrives on growing demands, powerful advertising strategies target people with financial means to purchase more and more luxury goods and services. In the process, even those whose needs are more than met will be made to feel the pinch of discontent and spend their money in pursuit of material dreams.

Some dramatic changes in cultural values and motivations, as well as in social institutions and the types of technologies we employ, are required if humans are going to realize a sustainable future for generations to come. The short-sighted emphasis on consumerism and individual self-interest so characteristic of the world's affluent countries needs to be abandoned in favor of a more balanced social and environmental ethic. These can be created from values still found in many of the world's non-Western cultures. Such values include a worldview that sees humanity as part of the natural world rather than superior to it. Included, too, is a sense of social responsibility that recognizes that no individual, people, or state has the right to expropriate resources at the expense of others. Finally, an awareness is needed of how important supportive ties are for individuals, such as seen in kinship or other associations in the world's traditional societies. Is humanity up to the challenge? And will anthropology play a role in meeting that challenge?

As defined in this book's first chapter, anthropology is the comparative study of humankind everywhere and throughout time. Since the beginning of the discipline in the mid-1800s, generations of anthropologists have studied our species in all its cultural and biological varieties. In the process, they described in great detail an enormous number of different cultures and biological variations among humans in all parts of the world. Anthropologists' cross-cultural, biological, and evolutionary perspectives on local communities in the age of globalization enable them to make key contributions to the understanding of a variety of human health problems. They examine human biology and culture from an ecological perspective, considering human health in the context of human-made environments. Recognizing the value of anthropological knowledge and methods, international public health agencies and state governments now employ and contract professional anthropologists for projects all around the world.

Some anthropologists are reaching out to assist besieged groups struggling for survival in today's rapidly changing world. In so doing, they seek to put into practice their own knowledge about humankind—knowledge deepened through the biocultural perspective of anthropology. That anthropological research is fascinating in itself and has the potential to solve health problems on local and global levels continues to draw a unique group of people into the discipline. These individuals are inspired by the old but still valid idea that anthropology is the most liberating of the sciences.

Chapter Summary

- Although anthropologists, like health-care workers, think of disease in terms of biological processes, they also consider disease from social and cultural perspectives. Anthropologists examine the cultural meanings given to disease states as well as the cultural practices that promote both health and disease. In addition, they look at the contributions of the political economy to the promotion of health and the distribution of disease. Anthropologists employ a unified biocultural perspective to examine human health and disease, and they distinguish between disease and illness. Disease refers to a specific pathology, a physical or biological abnormality. Illness refers to the meanings given to particular physical states. Disease and illness do not necessarily overlap, as an individual may experience illness without having a disease, or a disease may occur in the absence of illness.
- Some anthropologists study medical systems, or patterned sets of ideas and practices relating to illness. In the early history of medical anthropology, Western biomedical approaches were thought to be culture-free depictions of human biology and were therefore used as an interpretive framework for examining the medical beliefs and practices of other cultures. Implicit in this work was the ethnocentric notion that Western approaches to health were superior in their supposed objectivity.
- Evolutionary medicine brings new theoretical perspectives to the understanding of human health and disease. Some diseases are caused by a disconnection between contemporary cultural practices and human biology. Evolutionary treatments consist of bringing cultural practices into accord with human biology. Evolutionary medicine also suggests that some of the body's physiological responses, which might

otherwise be regarded as symptoms, are better understood as natural defense mechanisms.

- The growth process is one of the primary means by which humans adapt biologically to their environment, as it fosters the adaptation of young humans to local conditions. At the same time, cultural factors determine local environments, and global political processes affect the distribution of resources available for growing humans. Other cultural factors also determine the pattern of growth that is deemed acceptable by a given society. Therefore, anthropologists make cross-cultural comparisons of the growth process to study both health and health beliefs globally.
- Anthropologists study local cultural processes and global political forces to determine who gets sick (the distribution of disease) and to assess resources available for recovery. For example, the prion diseases kuru and mad cow disease illustrate the effects of food economy on the distribution of disease.
- One result of globalization is worldwide and growing structural violence—physical and/or psychological harm (including repression, cultural and environmental destruction, poverty, hunger and obesity, illness, and premature death) caused by exploitative and unjust social, political, and economical systems. Uncontrolled population growth makes all of these problems worse. Due to rising expectations created by the media, coupled with limited opportunities, a culture of discontent is growing.
- A unified biocultural perspective that emphasizes the interconnectedness of humans throughout time and space will lead to better health globally. The World Health Organization's definition of health as a "complete state of physical, mental and social well-being, not the mere absence of disease or infirmity," requires a perspective that relates human biology to culture.

Questions for Reflection

1. Considering that disease has challenged humans throughout our evolutionary history, why is an understanding of global process so critical for promoting human health today?
2. The anthropological distinction between illness and disease provides a way to separate biological states from cultural elaborations given to those biological states. Can you think of some examples of illness without disease and disease without illness?
3. What do you think of the notion of letting a fever run its course instead of taking a medicine to lower it? Do these "Paleolithic prescriptions" suggested by evolutionary medicine run counter to your own medical beliefs and practices?
4. Are there any examples in your experience of how the growth process or human reproductive physiology served to help you adapt to environmental stressors? Does this ability help humans from an evolutionary perspective?
5. Do you see examples of structural violence in your community that make some individuals more vulnerable to disease than others?

Key Terms

Medical systems
Shamans
Disease
Illness
Endemic
Evolutionary medicine
Secular trends
Prion
Medical pluralism
Structural violence
Health disparities
Replacement reproduction

Multimedia Review Tools

Companion Web Site

Visit **http://www.wadsworth.com/anthropology_d/** and click on the companion Web site for this textbook to access a wide range of material to aid your study of anthropology. Among the options for self-study in each chapter are learning objectives, flash cards, Internet activities, Web links, InfoTrac College Edition exercises, and practice tests that can be scored and emailed to your instructor.

CD-ROM

The *Doing Anthropology Today* CD-ROM supplied with your textbook provides unique and valuable information designed to enhance your learning experience. This interactive multimedia resource includes video clips, interviews with renowned anthropologists, map and timeline exercises, chapter study quizzes, and much more. *Doing Anthropology Today* will not only help you in achieving your grade goals, but it will also make your learning experience fun and exciting!

Suggested Readings

Farmer, P. (2001). *Infections and inequalities: The modern plagues* (updated edition with a new preface). Berkeley: University of California Press.

Paul Farmer, continuing the tradition of the physician-anthropologist, traces the relationship between structural violence and infectious disease, demonstrating that the world's poor bear a disproportionate burden of disease.

Helman, C. B. (2003). *Culture, health and illness: An introduction for health professionals.* New York: Butterworth Heinemann Medical.

This well-referenced book provides a good overview and introduction to medical anthropology. Though written with health professionals in mind, it is very accessible for students who have fist-hand experience with biomedicine, the dominant medical system of North America, Europe, and International Public Health.

McElroy, A., & Townsend, P. K. (2003). *Medical anthropology in ecological perspective.* Boulder, CO: Westview Press.

Now in its fourth edition, this text lays out ecological approaches in medical anthropology including biocultural, environmental, and evolutionary perspectives. In addition to providing a clear theoretical perspective, it includes excellent examples of applied work by medical anthropologists to improve health globally.

Nesse, R. M., & Williams, G. C. (1996). *Why we get sick.* New York: Vintage.

The authors expanded on a scholarly article to bring health-promoting ideas from evolutionary medicine to the public.

Trevathan, W., Smith, E. O., &.McKenna, J. J. (Eds.). (1999). *Evolutionary medicine.* London: Oxford University Press.

This comprehensive edited volume collects primary research conducted by leaders in the field of evolutionary medicine. Examples from throughout the human life cycle range from sexually transmitted diseases to cancer.

Glossary

absolute or chronometric dating In archaeology and paleoanthropology, dates for archaeological materials based on solar years, centuries, or other units of absolute time.

Acheulean tradition The tool-making tradition of *Homo erectus* in Africa, Europe, and Southwest Asia in which hand-axes were developed from the earlier Oldowan chopper.

action theory The theory that self-serving actions by forceful leaders play a role in civilization's emergence.

adaptation A series of beneficial adjustments to the environment.

adaptive radiation Rapid diversification of evolving populations as they adapt to a variety of available niches

alleles Alternate forms of a single gene.

altruism Acts of selflessness or self-sacrificing behavior.

anagenesis A sustained directional shift in a population's average characteristics.

analogies In biology, structures possessed by different organisms that are superficially similar due to similar function; without sharing a common developmental pathway or structure.

ancestral Characteristics possessed by an organism or group of organisms due to shared ancestry.

Anthropoidea A suborder of the primates that includes New World monkeys, Old World monkeys, and apes (including humans).

arboreal Living in the trees

archaeology The study of material remains, usually from the past, to describe and explain human behavior.

Archaic cultures Term used to refer to Mesolithic cultures in the Americas.

Ardipithecus ramidus One of the earliest hominins that lived in eastern Africa about 5.8 to 4.4 million years ago.

artifact Any object fashioned or altered by humans.

Aurignacian tradition Tool-making tradition in Europe and western Asia at the beginning of the Upper Paleolithic.

Australopithecus The first well-known hominin; lived between 4.4 and 1 million years ago. Characterized by bipedal locomotion, but with an apelike brain; generally includes seven species: *A. afarensis, A. africanus, A. anamensis, A. boisei, A. robustus, A. aethiopicus,* and *A. gahri.*

binocular vision Vision with increased depth perception from two eyes set next to each other allowing their visual fields to overlap.

bioarchaeology The archaeological study of human remains emphasizing the preservation of cultural and social processes in the skeleton.

bipedalism A special form of locomotion on two feet found in humans and their ancestors. Also called bipedality.

blade technique A technique of stone tool manufacture by which long, parallel-sided flakes are struck off the edges of a specially prepared core.

brachiate To use the arms to move from branch to branch, with the body hanging suspended beneath the arms.

Bronze Age In the Old World, the period marked by the production of tools and ornaments of bronze; began about 5,000 years ago in China and Southwest Asia and about 500 years earlier in Southeast Asia.

burins Stone tools with chisel-like edges used for working bone and antler.

carrying capacity The number of people that the available resources can support at a given level of food-getting techniques.

Catarrhini An anthropoid infraorder that includes Old World monkeys, apes, and humans.

chromosomes In the cell nucleus, the structures visible during cellular division containing long strands of DNA combined with a protein.

civilization In anthropology a type of society marked by the presence of cities, social classes, and the state.

cladogenesis An evolutionary process in which an ancestral population gives rise to two or more descendant populations that differ from each other.

clavicle The collarbone connecting the sternum (breastbone) with the scapula (shoulder blades).

clines Gradual changes in the frequency of an allele or trait over space.

codon Three-base sequence of a gene that specifies a particular amino acid for inclusion in a protein.

cognitive capacity A broad concept including intelligence, educability, concept formation, self-awareness, self-evaluation, attention span, sensitivity in discrimination, and creativity.

community A unit of primate social organization composed of fifty or more individuals who inhabit a large geographical area together.

continental drift According to the theory of plate tectonics, the movement of continents embedded in underlying plates on the earth's surface in relation to one another over the course of the history of life on earth.

convergent evolution A process by which unrelated populations develop similarities to one another. In cultural evolution, the development of similar cultural adaptations to similar environmental conditions by different peoples with different ancestral cultures.

coprolites Preserved fecal material providing evidence of the diet and health of past organisms.

cranium The braincase of the skull.

Cro-Magnons Europeans of the Upper Paleolithic after about 36,000 years ago.

datum point The starting, or reference, point for a grid system.

dendrochronology In archaeology, a method of chronometric dating based on the number of rings of growth found in a tree trunk.

dental formula The number of each tooth type (incisors, canines, premolars, and molars) on one half of each jaw. Unlike other mammals, primates possess equal numbers on their upper and lower jaws so the dental formula for the species is a single series of numbers.

derived Characteristics that define a group of organisms that did not exist in ancestral populations.

diastema A space between the canines and other teeth allowing large projecting canines space within the jaw.

disease Refers to a specific pathology; a physical or biological abnormality.

diurnal Active during the day and at rest at night.

DNA Deoxyribonucleic acid. The genetic material consisting of a complex molecule whose base structure directs the synthesis of proteins.

domestication An evolutionary process whereby humans modify, either intentionally or unintentionally, the genetic makeup of a population of plants or animals, sometimes to the extent that members of the population are unable to survive and/or reproduce without human assistance.

dominance The ability of one allele for a trait to mask the presence of another allele.

dominance hierarchies An observed ranking system in primate societies ordering individuals from high (alpha) to low standing corresponding to predictable behavioral interactions including domination.

ecological niche A species' way of life considered in the full context of its environment, including other species found in that environment, geology, climate, and so on.

ecosystem A system, or a functioning whole, composed of both the physical environment and all the organisms living within it.

endemic The public health term for a disease that is widespread in the population.

endocast A cast of the inside of a skull; helps determine the size and shape of the brain.

entoptic phenomena Bright pulsating geometric forms that are generated by the central nervous system and seen in states of trance.

enzyme Proteins that speed the rate of chemical reactions.

epicanthic eye fold A fold of skin at the inner corner of the eye that covers the true corner of the eye; common in Asiatic populations.

estrus In some primate females, the time of sexual receptivity during which ovulation is visibly displayed.

evolution Genetic change over successive generations.

evolutionary medicine An approach to human sickness and health combining principles of evolutionary theory and human evolutionary history.

fact An observation verified by several observers skilled in the necessary techniques of observation.

flotation An archeological technique employed to recover very tiny objects by immersion of soil samples in water to separate heavy from light particles.

fluorine dating In archaeology or paleoanthropology, a technique for relative dating based on the fact that the amount of fluorine in bones is proportional to their age.

foramen magnum A large opening in the skull through which the spinal cord passes and connects to the brain.

forensic anthropology Field of applied physical anthropology that specializes in the identification of human skeletal remains for legal purposes.

fossil The mineralized preserved remains of plants and animals that lived in the past.

founder's effect A particular form of genetic drift deriving from a small founding population not possessing all the alleles present in the original population.

fovea centralis A shallow pit in the retina of the eye that enables an animal to focus on an object while maintaining visual contact with its surroundings.

gender The cultural elaborations and meanings assigned to the biological differentiation of the sexes.

gene flow The introduction of alleles from the gene pool of one population into that of another.

gene pool All the genetic variants possessed by members of a population.

genes Portions of DNA molecules that direct the synthesis of specific proteins.

genetic code The sequence of three bases (a codon) that specifies the sequence of amino acids in protein synthesis.

genetic drift Chance fluctuations of allele frequencies in the gene pool of a population.

genome The complete sequence of DNA for a species.

genotype The alleles possessed for a particular trait.

genus, genera (pl.) In the system of classification of living things, a group of like species.

gracile australopithecines Members of the genus *Australopithecus* possessing a more lightly built chewing apparatus.

grade A general level of biological organization seen among a group of species, useful for constructing evolutionary relationships.

grid system A system for recording data in three dimensions from an archaeological excavation.

Haplorhini In the alternate primate taxonomy, the suborder that includes tarsiers, monkeys, apes, and humans.

Hardy-Weinberg principle Demonstrates algebraically that the percentage of individuals that are homozygous for the dominant allele, homozygous for the recessive allele, and heterozygous should remain constant from one generation to the next, provided that certain specified conditions are met.

health disparities Differences in the health status between the wealthy elite and the poor in stratified societies.

hemoglobin The protein that carries oxygen in the red blood cells.

heterozygous Refers to a chromosome pair that bears different alleles for a single gene.

historical linguistics The branch of linguistics that studies the histories of and relationships between languages, both living and dead.

homeobox gene A gene containing a 180-base-pair segment (the "homeobox") that encodes a protein that regulates DNA expression. Homeobox genes are frequently responsible for major reorganization of body plans in organisms.

homeotherms Animals maintaining a relatively constant body temperature despite environmental fluctuations

home ranges The geographical areas within which groups of primates usually move.

hominid African hominoid family that includes two subfamilies: the Paninae (chimps, bonobos, and gorillas) and the Homininae (humans and their ancestors). Some scientists use "hominid" to mean only humans and their ancestors. Others, recognizing the close relationship of humans, chimps, bonobos, and gorillas, use this term to refer to all of the African hominoid groups.

hominin The taxonomic subfamily or tribe within the primates that includes humans and our ancestors.

hominoid The taxonomic division superfamily within the cattarrhine primates that includes gibbons, siamangs, orangutans, gorillas, chimpanzees, bonobos, and humans and their ancestors.

Homo erectus A species within the genus *Homo* first appearing in Africa and ultimately migrating through out the Old World.

Homo habilis Earliest representative of the genus *Homo;* lived between 2.4 and 1.6 million years ago. Characterized by tool use and expansion and reorganization of the brain, compared to *Australopithecus.*

homologies In biology, structures possessed by two different organisms that arise in similar fashion and pass through similar stages during embryonic development though they may possess different functions.

homozygous Refers to a chromosome pair that bears identical alleles for a single gene.

horticulture Cultivation of crops carried out with simple hand tools such as digging sticks or hoes.

hydraulic theory The theory that sees civilization's emergence as the result of the construction of elaborate irrigation systems, the functioning of which required full-time managers whose control blossomed into the first governing body and elite social class.

hypoglossal canal The opening in the skull through which the tongue-controlling hypoglossal nerve passes.

illness Refers to the meanings and elaborations given to particular physical states.

integrative mechanisms Cultural mechanisms that oppose forces for differentiation in a society; in modernizing societies, they include formal governmental structures, official state ideologies, political parties, legal codes, labor and trade unions, and other common-interest associations.

intensive agriculture Crop cultivation using technologies other than hand tools, such as irrigation, fertilizers, and machinery or the wooden or metal plow pulled by harnessed draft animals.

isolating mechanisms Factors that separate breeding populations, thereby preventing gene flow, creating divergent subspecies, and ultimately (if maintained) divergent species.

isotherms Animals whose body temperature rises or falls according to the temperature of the surrounding environment.

Kenyanthropus platyops A new proposed hominin contemporary with early australopithecines; may not be separate genus.

k-selected Reproduction involving the production of relatively few offspring with high parental investment.

lactase An enzyme in the small intestine that enables humans to assimilate lactose.

lactose A sugar that is the primary constituent of fresh milk.

law of competitive exclusion When two closely related species compete for the same niche, one will out-compete the other, bringing about the latter's extinction.

law of independent assortment The Mendelian principle that genes controlling different traits are inherited independently of one another.

law of segregation The Mendelian principle that variants of genes for a particular trait retain their separate identities through the generations.

Levalloisian technique Tool-making technique by which three or four long triangular flakes were detached from a specially prepared core. Developed by humans transitional from *Homo erectus* to *Homo sapiens*.

Lower Paleolithic The first part of the Old Stone Age; its beginning is marked by the appearance 2.6 million years ago of Oldowan tools.

macroevolution Evolution above the species level.

mammals The class of vertebrate animals distinguished by bodies covered with fur, self-regulating temperature, and in females milk-producing mammary glands.

Maritime Archaic culture An Archaic culture of northeastern North America, centered on the Gulf of St. Lawrence, that emphasized the utilization of marine resources.

marrow The tissue inside of long bones where blood cells are produced.

material culture The durable aspects of culture such as tools, structures, and art.

medical pluralism The presence of multiple medical systems, each with its own practices and beliefs in a society.

medical anthropology A specialization in anthropology that brings theoretical and applied approaches from cultural and biological anthropology to the study of human health and disease.

medical systems Patterned sets of ideas and practices relating to illness.

meiosis A kind of cell division that produces the sex cells, each of which has half the number of chromosomes found in other cells of the organisms.

melanin The chemical responsible for dark skin pigmentation that helps protect against damage from ultraviolet radiation.

Mesoamerica The region encompassing southern Mexico and northern Central America.

Mesolithic The Middle Stone Age of Europe and Southwest Asia; began about 12,000 years ago.

microlith A small blade of flint or similar stone, several of which were hafted together in wooden handles to make tools; widespread in the Mesolithic.

middens A refuse or garbage disposal area in an archaeological site.

Middle Paleolithic The middle part of the Old Stone Age characterized by the emergence of archaic *H. sapiens* and the development of the Levalloisian and Mousterian traditions of tool making.

mitosis A kind of cell division that produces new cells having exactly the same number of chromosome pairs, and hence copies of genes, as the parent cell.

molecular anthropology A branch of biological anthropology that uses genetic and biochemical techniques to test hypotheses about human evolution, adaptation, and variation.

molecular clock The hypothesis that dates of divergences among related species can be calculated through an examination of the genetic mutations that have accrued since the divergence.

monogamous Mating for life with a single individual.

Mousterian tradition Tool-making tradition of the Neandertals and their contemporaries of Europe, western Asia, and northern Africa, featuring flake tools that are lighter and smaller than earlier Levalloisian flake tools.

multiregional hypothesis The model for modern human origins through simultaneous local transition from *Homo erectus* to modern *Homo sapiens* with links among these populations through gene flow.

mutation Chance alteration of genetic material that produces new variation.

natal group The group or the community an animal has inhabited since birth.

Natufian culture A Mesolithic culture of Israel, Lebanon, and western Syria, between about 125,000 and 30,200 years ago.

natural selection The evolutionary process through which factors in the environment exert pressure, favoring some individuals over others to produce the next generation.

Neandertals Representatives of "archaic" *Homo sapiens* in Europe and western Asia, living from about 125,000 years ago to about 30,000 years ago.

Neolithic The New Stone Age; began about 10,000 years ago in Southwest Asia.

Neolithic revolution The profound culture change associated with the early domestication of plants and animals.

nocturnal Active at night and at rest during the day.

notochord A rodlike structure of cartilage that, in vertebrates, is replaced by the vertebral column.

Oldowan tool tradition The earliest identifiable stone tools.

opposable Able to bring the thumb or big toe in contact with the tips of the other digits on the same hand or foot in order to grasp objects.

ovulation Moment when an egg released from the ovaries into the womb is receptive for fertilization.

paleoanthropology The study of the origins and predecessors of the present human species.

Paleoindian The earliest inhabitants of North America.

palynology In archaeology and paleoanthropology, a method of relative dating based on changes in fossil pollen over time.

pastoralism Breeding and managing of herds of domesticated grazing animals, such as goats, sheep, cattle, llamas, or camels.

percussion method A technique of stone tool manufacture performed by striking the raw material with a hammerstone or by striking raw material against a stone anvil to remove flakes.

phenotype The observable or testable appearance of an organism that may or may not reflect a particular genotype due to the variable expression of dominant and recessive alleles.

physical anthropology Also known as biological anthropology. The systematic study of humans as biological organisms.

physiological adaptation Short-term physiological responses of the human body to the environment and the process by which these changes occur.

phytoliths Microscopic silica bodies preserving the structures of plants that are formed as plants take up silica from groundwater.

Platyrrhini An anthropoid infraorder that includes New World monkeys.

polygenetic inheritance When two or more genes contribute to the phenotypic expression of single character.

polymerase chain reaction (PCR) A technique for amplifying or creating multiple copies of fragments of DNA so that it can be studied in the laboratory.

polymorphism The presence of alternative forms (alleles) of genes. Species such as humans in whom polymorphisms are common are sometimes referred to as polymorphic.

polytypic The expression of genetic variants in different frequencies in different populations of a species.

population In biology, a group of similar individuals that can and do interbreed.

potassium-argon dating In archaeology and paleoanthropology, a technique for chronometric dating that measures the ratio of radioactive potassium to argon in volcanic debris associated with human remains.

preadapted Possessing characteristics that prove to be advantageous in future environmental conditions.

prehensile Having the ability to grasp.

prehistoric A conventional term used to refer to the period of time before the appearance of written records. Does not deny the existence of history, merely of *written* history.

pressure flaking A technique of stone tool manufacture in which a bone, antler, or wooden tool is used to press, rather than strike off, small flakes from a piece of flint or similar stone.

primates The group of mammals that includes lemurs, lorises, tarsiers, monkeys, apes, and humans.

primatology The study of living and fossil primates.

prion An infectious protein lacking any genetic material but capable of causing the reorganization and destruction of other proteins.

Prosimii A suborder of the primates that includes, lemurs, lorises, and tarsiers.

punctuated equilibria A model of macroevolutionary change that suggests evolution occurs via an alternation of long periods of stability or stasis punctuated by periods of rapid change.

race In biology, the taxonomic category of subspecies that is not applicable to humans because the division of humans into discrete types does not represent the true nature of human biological variation. In some societies race is an important cultural category.

racism A doctrine of racial superiority by which one group asserts its superiority over another.

radiocarbon dating In archaeology and paleoanthropology, a technique for chronometric dating based on measuring the amount of radioactive carbon (^{14}C) left in organic materials found in archaeological sites.

recent African origins The model for modern human origins in which anatomically modern humans arose in Africa approximately 200,000 years ago, replacing archaic forms in the rest of the world. Also called the "Eve" or "Out of Africa" hypothesis.

recessive An allele for a trait whose expression is masked by the presence of a dominant allele.

relative dating In archaeology and paleoanthropology, designating an event, object, or fossil as being older or younger than another.

replacement reproduction When birthrates and death rates are in equilibrium; people produce only enough offspring to replace themselves when they die.

ribosomes Structures in the cell where translation occurs.

RNA Ribonucleic acid; similar to DNA but with uracil substituted for the base thymine. Transcribes and carries instructions from DNA from the nucleus to the ribosomes where it directs protein synthesis.

robust australopithecines Slightly larger and more robust than gracile members of genus *Australopithecus,* with large, more powerful jaws and teeth.

r-selection Reproduction involving the production of large numbers of offspring with relatively low parental investment.

sagittal crest A crest running from front to back on the top of the skull along the midline to provide a surface of bone for the attachment of the large chewing muscles.

Sahul The greater Australian landmass including Australia, New Guinea, and Tasmania. At times of maximum glaciation and low sea levels, these areas were continuous.

savannah Arid plains environment of eastern Africa.

scapula The shoulder blade.

secular trends Physical differences among related people from distinct time periods that allow anthropologists to make inferences about environmental effects on growth and development.

seriation Technique for putting groups of objects into a relative sequence

sexual dimorphism Within a single species, differences in the shape or size of a feature for males and females in body features not directly related to reproduction such as body size or canine tooth shape and size.

shaman A person who enters an altered state of consciousness—at will—to contact and utilize an ordinarily hidden reality in order to acquire knowledge, power, and/or to help others.

sickle-cell anemia An inherited form of anemia caused by a mutation in the hemoglobin protein that causes the red blood cells to assume a sickle shape.

soil marks Stains that show up on the surface of recently plowed fields that reveal an archaeological site.

speciation The process of formation of new species.

species The smallest working unit in the system of classification. Among living organisms, species are populations or groups of populations capable of interbreeding and producing fertile viable offspring.

stabilizing selection Natural selection acting to promote stability, rather than change, in a population's gene pool.

stereoscopic vision Complete three-dimensional vision from binocular vision plus connections from each eye to both sides of the brain allowing nerve cells to integrate the images derived from each eye.

stratified Layered; said of archaeological sites where the remains lie in layers, one upon another.

stratified societies Societies in which people are divided or ranked into social tiers and do not share equally in the basic resources that support life, influence, and prestige.

stratigraphy In archaeology and paleoanthropology, the most reliable method of relative dating by means of strata.

Strepsirhini In the alternate primate taxonomy, the suborder that includes the lemurs and lorises without the tarsiers.

structural violence Physical and/or psychological harm (including repression, environmental destruction, poverty, hunger, illness, and premature death) caused by exploitative and unjust social, political, and economic systems.

Sunda The combined landmass of the contemporary islands of Java, Sumatra, Borneo, and Bali that was continuous with mainland Southeast Asia at times of low sea levels corresponding to maximum glaciation.

suspensory hanging apparatus The broad powerful shoulder joints and muscles found in all the hominoids allowing these large-bodied primates to hang suspended below the tree branches.

swidden farming Also known as slash-and-burn. An extensive form of horticulture in which the natural vegetation is cut, the slash is subsequently burned, and crops then planted among the ashes, which fertilize the soil.

taphonomy The study of how bones and other materials come to be preserved in the earth as fossils.

taxonomy The science of classification.

tertiary scavenger In a food chain, the third animal group (second to scavenge) to obtain meat from a kill made by a predator.

therapsids The mammal-like reptiles

thrifty genotype Human genotype that permits efficient storage of fat to draw on in times of food shortage and conservation of glucose and nitrogen.

tool An object used to facilitate some task or activity. Although tool making involves intentional modification of the material of which it is made, tool use may involve objects either modified for some particular purpose or completely unmodified.

transcription Process of conversion of instructions from DNA into RNA.

transhumance In pastoralism, the pattern of strict seasonal movement between highlands and lowlands.

translation Process of conversion of RNA instructions into proteins.

unconscious selection The preservation of valued variants of a plant or animal species and the destruction of less valued ones, with no thought as to the long-range consequences.

Upper Paleolithic The last part of the Old Stone Age, characterized by the emergence of more modern-looking hominins and an emphasis on the blade technique of tool making.

vegeculture The cultivation of domesticated root crops, such as yams and taro.

vertebrates Animals with a backbone including fish, amphibians, reptiles, birds, and mammals.

visual predation A hypothesis for the primate origins through adaptation to predation by sight in trees.

Bibliography

Abbot, E. (2001). *A history of celibacy.* Cambridge, MA: Da Capo Press.

Aberle, D. F., Bronfenbrenner, U., Hess, E. H., Miller, D. R., Schneider, D. H., & Spuhler, J. N. (1963). The incest taboo and the mating patterns of animals. *American Anthropologist, 65,* 253–265.

Abu-Lughod, L. (1986). *Veiled sentiments: Honor and poetry in a Bedouin society.* Berkeley: University of California Press.

Adams, R. E. W. (1977). *Prehistoric Mesoamerica.* Boston: Little, Brown.

Adams, R. M. (1966). *The evolution of urban society.* Chicago: Aldine.

Adams, R. M. (2001). Scale and complexity in archaic states. *Latin American Antiquity, 11,* 188.

Adbusters. *www.adbusters.org.* Accessed January 2003.

AIDS Monthly Surveillance Summary (through July 1997). (1997). San Francisco.

Al-Issa, I., & Dennis, W. (Eds.). (1970). *Cross-cultural studies of behavior.* New York: Holt, Rinehart & Winston.

Alland, A., Jr. (1970). *Adaptation in cultural evolution: An approach to medical anthropology.* New York: Columbia University Press.

Alland, A., Jr. (1971). *Human diversity.* New York: Columbia University Press.

Allen, J. L., & Shalinsky, A. C. (2004). *Student atlas of anthropology.* New York: McGraw-Hill/Dushkin.

Allen, J. S., & Cheer, S. M. (1996). The non-thrifty genotype. *Current Anthropology, 37,* 831–842.

Allen, S. L. (1984). Media anthropology: Building a public perspective. *Anthropology Newsletter, 25,* 6.

Amábile-Cuevas, C. F., & Chicurel, M. E. (1993). Horizontal gene transfer. *American Scientist, 81,* 332–341.

Ambrose, S. H. (2001). Paleolithic technology and human evolution. *Science, 291,* 1,748–1,753.

American Anthropological Association. (1998). Statement on "race." Available at *www.ameranthassn.org.*

Amiran, R. (1965). The beginnings of pottery-making in the Near East. In F. R. Matson (Ed.), *Ceramics and man* (pp. 240–247). Viking Fund Publications, in *Anthropology,* No. 41.

Anderson, C. M. (1989). Neanderthal pelvis and gestational length. *American Anthropologist, 91,* 327–340.

Andrews, L. B., & Nelkin, D. (1996). The bell curve: A statement. *Science, 271,* 13.

Ankel-Simons, F., Fleagle, J. G., & Chatrath, P. S. (1998). Femoral anatomy of *Aegyptopithecus zeuxis,* an early Oligocene anthropoid. *American Journal of Physical Anthropology, 106,* 413–424.

Appadurai, A. (1996). *Modernity at large: Cultural dimensions of globalization.* Minneapolis: University of Minnesota Press.

Appenzeller, T. (1998). Art: Evolution or revolution? *Science, 282,* 1,451–1,454.

Arensberg, C. M. (1961). The community as object and sample. *American Anthropologist, 63,* 241–264.

Armstrong, D. F., Stokoe, W. C., & Wilcox, S. E. (1993). Signs of the origin of syntax. *Current Anthropology, 34,* 349–368.

Ashmore, W. (Ed.). (1981). *Lowland Maya settlement patterns.* Albuquerque: University of New Mexico Press.

Bailey, R. C., & Aunger, R. (1989). Net hunters vs. archers: Variation in women's subsistence strategies in the Ituri Forest. *Human Ecology, 17,* 273–297.

Balandier, G. (1971). *Political anthropology.* New York: Pantheon.

Balikci, A. (1970). *The Netsilik Eskimo.* Garden City, NY: Natural History Press.

Balter, M. (1998). Why settle down? The mystery of communities. *Science, 282,* 1,442–1,444.

Balter, M. (2001). In search of the first Europeans. *Science, 291,* 1,724.

Balter, M. (1999). A long season puts Çatalhöyük in context. *Science, 286,* 890–891

Balter, M. (2001). Did plaster hold Neolithic society together? *Science, 294,* 2,278–2,281

Banton, M. (1968). Voluntary association: Anthropological aspects. In *International encyclopedia of the social sciences* (Vol. 16, pp. 357–362). New York: Macmillan.

Barber, B. (1957). *Social stratification.* New York: Harcourt.

Barfield, T. J. (1984). Introduction. *Cultural Survival Quarterly, 8,* 2.

Barham, L. S. (1998). Possible early pigment use in South-Central Africa. *Current Anthropology, 39,* 703–710.

Barnard, A. (1995). Monboddo's *Orang Outang* and the definition of man. In R. Corbey & B. Theunissen (Eds.), *Ape, man, apeman: Changing views since 1600* (pp. 71–85). Leiden: Department of Prehistory, Leiden University.

Barnett, H. (1953). *Innovation: The basis of cultural change.* New York: McGraw-Hill.

Barnouw, V. (1985). *Culture and personality* (4th ed.). Homewood, IL: Dorsey Press.

Barr, R. G. (1997, October). The crying game. *Natural History, 47.*

Barth, F. (1961). *Nomads of South Persia: The Basseri tribe of the Khamseh confederacy.* Boston: Little, Brown (series in anthropology).

Barth, F. (1962). Nomadism in the mountain and plateau areas of South West Asia. *The problems of the arid zone* (pp. 341–355). Paris: UNESCO.

Barton, R. F. (1919). Ifugao law. Berkeley: *University of California Publications in American Archaeology and Ethnology, XV.*

Bar-Yosef, O. (1986). The walls of Jericho: An alternative interpretation. *Current Anthropology, 27,* 157–162.

Bar-Yosef, O., Vandermeesch, B., Arensburg, B., Belfer-Cohen, A., Goldberg, P., Laville, H., Meignen, L., Rak, Y., Speth, J. D., Tchernov, E., Tillier, A-M., & Weiner, S. (1992). The excavations in Kebara Cave, Mt. Carmel. *Current Anthropology, 33,* 497–550.

Bascom, W. (1969). *The Yoruba of southwestern Nigeria.* New York: Holt, Rinehart & Winston.

Bates, D. G. (2001). *Human adaptive strategies: Ecology, culture, and politics* (2nd ed.). Boston: Allyn & Bacon.

Bates, D. G., & Plog, F. (1991). *Human adaptive strategies.* New York: McGraw-Hill.

Beals, A. R. (1972). Gopalpur: *A South Indian village.* New York: Holt, Rinehart & Winston.

Beattie, J. (1964). *Other cultures: Aims, methods and achievements.* New York: Free Press.

Becker, J. (2004), March). *National Geographic,* 90.

Bednarik, R. G. (1995). Concept-mediated marking in the Lower Paleolithic. *Current Anthropology, 36,* 605–634.

Behrensmeyer, A. K., Todd, N. E., Potts, R., & McBrinn, G. E. (1997). Late Pliocene faunal turnover in the Turkana basin, Kenya, and Ethiopia. *Science, 278,* 1,589–1,594.

Beidelman, T. O. (Ed.). (1971). *The transition of culture: Essays to E. E. Evans-Pritchard.* London: Tavistock.

Bell, D. (1997). Defining marriage and legitimacy. *Current Anthropology, 38,* 241.

Belshaw, C. S. (1958). The significance of modern cults in Melanesian development. In W. Lessa & E. Z. Vogt (Eds.), *Reader in comparative religion: An anthropological approach.* New York: Harper & Row.

Benedict, R. (1959). *Patterns of culture.* New York: New American Library.

Bennett, J. W. (1964). Myth, theory, and value in cultural anthropology. In E. W. Caint & G. T. Bowles (Eds.), *Fact and theory in social science.* Syracuse, NY: Syracuse University Press.

Berdan, F. F. (1982). *The Aztecs of Central Mexico.* New York: Holt, Rinehart & Winston.

Bermúdez de Castro, J. M., Arsuaga, J. L., Cabonell, E., Rosas, A., Martinez, I., & Mosquera, M. (1997). A hominid from the lower Pleistocene of Atapuerca, Spain: Possible ancestor to Neandertals and modern humans. *Science, 276,* 1,392–1,395.

Bernal, I. (1969). *The Olmec world.* Berkeley: University of California Press.

Bernard, H. R. (2002) *Research methods in anthropology: Qualitative and quantitative approaches* (3rd ed.). Walnut Creek, CA: Altamira Press.

Bernard, H. R., & Sibley, W. E. (1975). *Anthropology and jobs.* Washington, DC: American Anthropological Association.

Bernardi, B. (1985) *Age class systems: Social institutions and policies based on age.* New York: Cambridge University Press.

Berra, T. M. (1990). *Evolution and the myth of creationism.* Stanford, CA: Stanford University Press.

Berreman, G. D. (1962). *Behind many masks: Ethnography and impression management in a Himalayan village.* Ithaca, NY: Society for Applied Anthropology (Monograph No. 4).

Berreman, G. D. (1968). Caste: The concept of caste. *International Encyclopedia of the Social Sciences* (Vol. 2, pp. 333–338). New York: Macmillan.

Bicchieri, M. G. (Ed.). (1972). *Hunters and gatherers today: A socioeconomic study of eleven such cultures in the twentieth century.* New York: Holt, Rinehart & Winston.

Binford, L. R. (1972). *An archaeological perspective.* New York: Seminar Press.

Binford, L. R., & Chuan, K. H. (1985). Taphonomy at a distance: Zhoukoudian, the cave home of Beijing man? *Current Anthropology, 26,* 413–442.

Birdsell, J. H. (1977). The recalibration of a paradigm for the first peopling of Greater Australia. In J. Allen, J. Golson, & R. Jones (Eds.), *Sunda and Sahul: Prehistoric studies in Southeast Asia, Melanesia, and Australia* (pp. 113–167). New York: Academic Press.

Blumberg, R. L. (1991). *Gender, family, and the economy: The triple overlap.* Newbury Park, CA: Sage.

Blumer, M. A., & Byrne, R. (1991). The ecological genetics and domestication and the origins of agriculture. *Current Anthropology, 32,* 23–54.

Boas, F. (1962). *Primitive art.* Gloucester, MA: Peter Smith.

Boas, F. (1966). *Race, language and culture.* New York: Free Press.

Bodley, J. H. (2000). *Anthropology and contemporary human problems* (4th ed.). Palo Alto, CA: Mayfield.

Bodley, J. H. (1997). Comment. *Current Anthropology, 38,* 725.

Bodley, J. H. (1998). *Victims of progress* (4th ed.). San Francisco: McGraw-Hill.

Boehm, C. (2000). The evolution of moral communities. *School of American Research, 2000 Annual Report, 7.*

Bohannan, P. (Ed.). (1967). *Law and warfare: Studies in the anthropology of conflict.* Garden City, NY: Natural History Press.

Bohannan, P., & Dalton, G. (Eds.). (1962). *Markets in Africa.* Evanston, IL: Northwestern University Press.

Bohannan, P., & Middleton, J. (Eds.). (1968). *Kinship and social organization.* Garden City, NY: Natural History Press (American Museum Source Books in Anthropology).

Bohannan, P., & Middleton, J. (Eds.). (1968). *Marriage, family, and residence.* Garden City, NY: Natural History Press (American Museum Source Books in Anthropology).

Bolinger, D. (1968). *Aspects of language.* New York: Harcourt.

Bongaarts, J. (1998). Demographic consequences of declining fertility. *Science, 182,* 419.

Bonvillain, N. (2000). *Language, culture, and communication: The meaning of messages* (3rd ed.). Upper Saddle River, NJ: Prentice Hall.

Boone, E. S. (1987). Practicing sociomedicine: Redefining the problem of infant mortality in Washington, D.C. In R. M. Wulff & S. J. Fiske (Eds.), *Anthropological praxis: Translating knowledge into action* (p. 56). Boulder, CO: Westview Press.

Bordes, F. (1972). *A tale of two caves.* New York: Harper & Row.

Bornstein, M. H. (1975). The influence of visual perception on culture. *American Anthropologist, 77*(4), 774–798.

Brace, C. L. (1981). Tales of the phylogenetic woods: The evolution and significance of phylogenetic trees. *American Journal of Physical Anthropology, 56,* 411–429.

Brace, C. L. (1997). Cro-Magnons R us? *Anthropology Newsletter, 38*(8), 1, 4.

Brace, C. L., Nelson, H., & Korn, N. (1979). *Atlas of human evolution* (2nd ed.). New York: Holt, Rinehart & Winston.

Brace, C. L., Ryan, A. S., & Smith, B. (1981). Comment. *Current Anthropology, 22*(4), 426–430.

Brace, C. L. (2000). *Evolution in an anthropological view* (p. 341). Walnut Creek, CA: Altamira.

Bradfield, R. M. (1998). *A natural history of associations.* (2nd ed.). New York: International Universities Press.

Bradford, P. V., & Blume, H. (1992). *Ota Benga: The pygmy in the zoo.* New York: St. Martin's Press.

Braidwood, R. J. (1960). The agricultural revolution. *Scientific American, 203,* 130–141.

Braidwood, R. J. (1975). *Prehistoric men* (8th ed.). Glenview, IL: Scott, Foresman.

Brain, C. K. (1968). Who killed the Swartkrans ape-men? *South African Museums Association Bulletin, 9,* 127–139.

Brain, C. K. (1969). The contribution of Namib Desert Hottentots to an understanding of australopithecine bone accumulations. *Scientific Papers of the Namib Desert Research Station,* 13.

Branda, R. F. & Eatoil, J. W. (1978). Skin color and photolysis: An evolutionary hypothesis. *Science, 201,* 625–626.

Brettell, C. B., & Sargent, C. F. (Eds.). (2000). *Gender in cross-cultural perspective* (3rd ed.). Upper Saddle River, NJ: Prentice-Hall.

Brew, J. O. (1968). *One hundred years of anthropology.* Cambridge, MA: Harvard University Press.

Broecker, W. S. (1992, April). Global warming on trial. *Natural History, 14.*

Brothwell, D. R., & Higgs, E. (Eds.). (1969). *Science in archaeology* (Rev. ed.). London: Thames & Hudson.

Brown, B., Walker, A., Ward, C. V., & Leakey, R. E. (1993). New *Australopithecus boisei* calvaria from East Lake Turkana, Kenya. *American Journal of Physical Anthropology, 91,* 137–159.

Brown, D. E. (1991). *Human universals.* New York: McGraw-Hill.

Brues, A. M. (1977). *People and races.* New York: Macmillan.

Brunet, M., et al. (2002). A new hominid from the Upper Miocene of Chad, Central Africa. *Nature, 418,* 145–151.

Burling, R. (1969). Linguistics and ethnographic description. *American Anthropologist, 71,* 817–827.

Burling, R. (1970). *Man's many voices: Language in its cultural context.* New York: Holt, Rinehart & Winston.

Burling, R. (1993). Primate calls, human language, and nonverbal communication. *Current Anthropology, 34,* 25–53.

Butzer, K. (1971). *Environment and anthropology: An ecological approach to prehistory* (2nd ed.). Chicago: Aldine.

Byers, D. S. (Ed.). (1967). *The prehistory of the Tehuacan Valley: Vol. 1. Environment and Subsistence.* Austin: University of Texas Press.

Cachel, S. (1997). Dietary shifts and the European Upper Paleolithic transition. *Current Anthropology, 38,* 590.

Calloway, C. (1997). Introduction: Surviving the Dark Ages. In C. G. Calloway (Ed.), *After King Philip's War: Presence and persistence in Indian New England* (pp. 1–28). Hanover, NH: University Press of New England.

Campbell, B. G., & Loy, J. D. (1995). *Humankind emerging* (7th ed.). New York: HarperCollins.

Carmack, R. (1983). Indians and the Guatemalan revolution. *Cultural Survival Quarterly, 7*(3), 52–54.

Carneiro, R. L. (1970). A theory of the origin of the state. *Science, 169,* 733–738.

Caroulis, J. (1996). Food for thought. *Pennsylvania Gazette, 95*(3), 16.

Carpenter, E. (1973). *Eskimo realities.* New York: Holt, Rinehart & Winston.

Carroll, J. B. (Ed.). (1956). *Language, thought and reality: Selected writings of Benjamin Lee Whorf.* Cambridge, MA: MIT Press.

Cartmill, M. (1998). The gift of gab. *Discover 19*(11), 64.

Cashdan, E. (1989). Hunters and gatherers: Economic behavior in bands. In S. Plattner (Ed.), *Economic anthropology* (pp. 21–48). Stanford, CA: Stanford University Press.

Catford, J. C. (1988). *A practical introduction to phonetics.* Oxford: Clarendon Press.

Caton, S. C. (1999). *Laurence of Arabia: A film's anthropology.* Berkeley: University of California Press.

Cavalli-Sforza, L. L. (1977). *Elements of human genetics.* Menlo Park, CA: W. A. Benjamin.

Cavallo, J. A. (1990, February). Cat in the human cradle. *Natural History,* 54–60.

Centers for Disease Control. (1997). *Centers for Disease Control Semi-Annual AIDS Report* (through June 1996). Atlanta, GA.

Chagnon, N. A. (1988). *Yanomamo: The fierce people* (3rd ed.). New York: Holt, Rinehart & Winston.

Chagnon, N. A., & Irons, W. (Eds.). (1979). *Evolutionary biology and human social behavior.* North Scituate, MA: Duxbury Press.

Chambers, R. (1983). *Rural development: Putting the last first.* New York: Longman.

Chan, J. W. C., & Vernon, P. E. (1988). Individual differences among the peoples of China. In J. W. Berry (Ed.), *Human abilities in cultural context* (pp. 340–357). Cambridge, England: Cambridge University Press.

Chang, K. C. (Ed.). (1968). *Settlement archaeology.* Palo Alto, CA: National Press.

Chapple, E. D. (1970). *Cultural and biological man: Explorations in behavioral anthropology.* New York: Holt, Rinehart & Winston.

Chase, C. (1998). Hermaphrodites with attitude. *Gay and Lesbian Quarterly, 4*(2), 189–211.

Chasin, B. H., & Franke, R. W. (1983). U.S. farming: A world model? *Global Reporter, 1*(2), 10.

Chatty, D. (1996). *Mobile pastoralists: Development planning and social change in Oman.* New York: Columbia University Press.

Chicurel, M. (2001). Can organisms speed their own evolution? *Science, 292,* 1824–1827.

Childe, V. G. (1951). *Man makes himself. New York: New American Library.* (orig. 1936)

Childe, V. G. (1954). *What happened in history.* Baltimore: Penguin.

Cigno, A. (1994). *Economics of the family.* New York: Oxford University Press.

Ciochon, R. L., & Fleagle, J. G. (Eds.). (1987). *Primate evolution and human origins.* Hawthorne, NY: Aldine.

Ciochon, R. L., & Fleagle, J. G. (1993). *The human evolution source book.* Englewood Cliffs, NJ: Prentice-Hall.

Clark, E. E. (1966). *Indian legends of the Pacific Northwest* (p. 174). Berkeley: University of California Press.

Clark, G. (1967). *The Stone Age hunters.* New York: McGraw-Hill.

Clark, G. (1972). *Starr Carr: A case study in bioarchaeology.* Reading, MA: Addison-Wesley.

Clark, G. A. (1997). Neandertal genetics. *Science, 277,* 1,024.

Clark, G. A. (2002) Neandertal archaeology: Implications for our origins. *American Anthropologist 104*(1), 50–67.

Clark, J. G. D. (1962). *Prehistoric Europe: The economic basis.* Stanford, CA: Stanford University Press.

Clark, W. E. L. (1960). *The antecedents of man.* Chicago: Quadrangle Books.

Clark, W. E. L. (1966). *History of the primates* (5th ed.). Chicago: University of Chicago Press.

Clark, W. E. L. (1967). *Man-apes or ape-men? The story of discoveries in Africa.* New York: Holt, Rinehart & Winston.

Clarke, R. J. (1998). First ever discovery of a well preserved skull and associated skeleton of *Australopithecus. South African Journal of Science, 94,* 460–464.

Clarke, R. J., & Tobias, P. V. (1995). Sterkfontein member 2 foot bones of the oldest South African hominid. *Science, 269,* 521–524.

Clay, J. W. (1987). Genocide in the age of enlightenment. *Cultural Survival Quarterly 12*(3).

Clay, J. W. (1996). What's a nation? In W. A. Haviland & R. J. Gordon (Eds.), *Talking about people* (2nd ed., pp. 188–189). Mountain View, CA: Mayfield.

Clough, S. B., & Cole, C. W. (1952). *Economic history of Europe* (3rd ed.). Lexington, MA: Heath.

Codere, H. (1950). *Fighting with property.* Seattle: University of Washington Press (American Ethnological Society, Monograph 18).

Coe, S. D. (1994). *America's first cuisines.* Austin: University of Texas Press.

Coe, W. R. (1967). *Tikal: A handbook of the ancient Maya ruins.* Philadelphia: University of Pennsylvania Museum.

Coe, W. R., & Haviland, W. A. (1982). *Introduction to the archaeology of Tikal.* Philadelphia: University Museum.

Cohen, J. (1997). Is an old virus up to new tricks? *Science, 277,* 312–313.

Cohen, M., & Armelagos, G. (Eds.). (1984). *Paleopathology at the origins of agriculture.* Orlando, FL: Academic Press.

Cohen, M. L. (1967). Variations in complexity among Chinese family groups: The impact of modernization. *Transactions of the New York Academy of Sciences, 295,* 638–647.

Cohen, M. L. (1968). A case study of Chinese family economy and development. *Journal of Asian and African Studies, 3,* 161–180.

Cohen, M. N. (1977). *The food crisis in prehistory.* New Haven, CT: Yale University Press.

Cohen, M. N. (1995). Anthropology and race: The bell curve phenomenon. *General Anthropology, 2*(1), 1–4.

Cohen, M. N., & Armelagos, G. J. (1984). Paleopathology at the origins of agriculture: Editors' summation. In M. N. Cohen & G. J. Armelagos (Eds.), *Paleopathology at the origins of agriculture.* Orlando, FL: Academic Press.

Cohen, R., & Middleton, J. (Eds.). (1967). *Comparative political systems.* Garden City, NY: Natural History Press.

Cohen, Y. (1968). *Man in adaptation: The cultural present.* Chicago: Aldine.

Colburn, T., Dumanoski, D., & Myers, J. P. (1996, March). Hormonal sabotage. *Natural History,* 45–46.

Cole, S. (1975). *Leakey's luck: The life of Louis Seymour Bazett Leakey. 1903–1972.* New York: Harcourt Brace Jovanovich.

Collier, J., Rosaldo, M. Z., & Yanagisako, S. (1982). Is there a family? New anthropological views. In B. Thorne & M. Yalom (Eds.), *Rethinking the family: Some feminist questions* (pp. 25–39). New York: Longman.

Collier, J. F., & Yanagisako, S. J. (Eds.). (1987). *Gender and kinship: Essays toward a unified analysis.* Stanford, CA: Stanford University Press.

Connelly, J. C. (1979). Hopi social organization. In A. Ortiz (Ed.), *Handbook of North American Indians, Vol. 9, Southwest* (pp. 539–553). Washington, DC: Smithsonian Institution.

Connor, M. (1996). The archaeology of contemporary mass graves. *SAA Bulletin, 14*(4), 6, 31.

Conroy, G. C. (1997). *Reconstructing human origins: A modern synthesis* (p. 427). New York: Norton.

Constable, G., & the Editors of Time-Life. (1973). *The Neanderthals.* New York: Time-Life.

Cook, S. F. (1972). *Prehistoric demography.* Reading, MA: Addison-Wesley.

Coon, C. S. (1957). *The seven caves.* New York: Knopf.

Coon, C. S. (1958). *Caravan: The story of the Middle East* (2nd ed.). New York: Holt, Rinehart & Winston.

Coon, C. S. (1971). *The hunting peoples.* Boston: Little, Brown.

Coon, C. S., Garn, S. N., & Birdsell, J. (1950). *Races: A study of the problems of race formation in man.* Springfield, IL: Charles C Thomas.

Cooper, A., Poinar, H. N., Pääbo, S., Radovci, C. J., Debénath, A., Caparros, M., Barroso-Ruiz, C., Bertranpetit, J., Nielsen-March, C., Hedges, R. E. M., & Sykes, B. (1997). Neanderthal genetics. *Science, 277,* 1,021–1,024.

Coppens, Y., Howell, F. C., Isaac, G. L., & Leakey, R. E. F. (Eds.). (1976). *Earliest man and environments in the Lake Rudolf Basin: Stratigraphy, paleoecology, and evolution.* Chicago: University of Chicago Press.

Corbey, R. (1995). Introduction: Missing links, or the ape's place in nature. In R. Corbey & B. Theunissen (Eds.), *Ape, man, apeman: Changing views since 1600* (p.1). Leiden: Department of Prehistory, Leiden University.

Cornwell, T. (1995, November 10). Skeleton staff. *Times Higher Education,* p. 20.

Corruccini, R. S. (1992). Metrical reconsideration of the Skhul IV and IX and Border Cave I crania in the context of modern human origins. *American Journal of Physical Anthropology, 87,* 433–445.

Cottrell, F. (1965). *Energy and society: The relation between energy, social changes and economic development.* New York: McGraw–Hill.

Cottrell, L. (1963). *The lost pharaohs.* New York: Grosset & Dunlap.

Courlander, H. (1971). *The fourth world of the Hopis.* New York: Crown.

Cowgill, G. L. (1980). Letter. *Science, 210,* 1,305.

Cowgill, G. L. (1997). State and society at Teotihuacan, Mexico. *Annual Review of Anthropology, 26,* 129–161.

Cox, O. C. (1959). *Caste, class and race: A study in dynamics.* New York: Monthly Review Press.

Crane, L. B., Yeager, E., & Whitman, R. L. (1981). *An introduction to linguistics.* Boston: Little, Brown.

Crocker, W. A., & Crocker, J. (1994). *The canela, bonding through kinship, ritual and sex.* Fort Worth, TX: Harcourt Brace.

Culbert, T. P. (Ed.). (1973). *The Classic Maya collapse.* Albuquerque: University of New Mexico Press.

Culotta, E. (1992). A new take on anthropoid origins, *Science, 256,* 1,516–1,517.

Culotta, E. (1995). Asian hominids grow older. *Science, 270,* 1,116–1,117.

Culotta, E. (1995). New finds rekindle debate over anthropoid origins. *Science, 268,* 1,851.

Culotta, E. (1995). New hominid crowds the field. *Science, 269,* 918.

Culotta, E., & Koshland, D. E., Jr. (1994). DNA repair works its way to the top. *Science 266,* 1,926.

Cultural Survival Quarterly. (1991). 15(4), 5.

Cultural Survival Quarterly. (1991). 15(4), 38.

Dalton, G. (Ed.). (1967). *Tribal and peasant economics: Readings in economic anthropology.* Garden City, NY: Natural History Press.

Dalton, G. (1971). *Traditional tribal and peasant economics: An introductory survey of economic anthropology.* Reading, MA: Addison-Wesley.

Daniel, G. (1970). *The first civilizations: The archaeology of their origins.* New York: Apollo Editions.

Daniel, G. (1975). *A hundred and fifty years of archaeology.* (2nd ed.) London: Duckworth.

Darwin, C. (1936). *The descent of man and selection in relation to sex.* New York: Random House (Modern Library). (orig. 1871)

Darwin, C. (1967). *On the origin of species.* New York: Atheneum. (orig. 1859)

Davenport, W. (1959). Linear descent and descent groups. *American Anthropologist, 61,* 557–573.

Davis, S. H. (1982). *Victims of the miracle.* Cambridge: Cambridge University Press.

Day, G. M. (1972). Quoted in T. C. Vogelman (Director) and Department of Anthropology (Producer). *Prehistoric life in the Champlain Valley* [Film]. Burlington, VT: University of Vermont.

Dean, M. C., Beynon, A. D., Thackeray, J. F., & Macho, G. A. (1993). Histological reconstruction of dental development and age at death of a juvenile *Paranthropus robustus* specimen, SK 63, from Swartkrans, South Africa. *American Journal of Physical Anthropology, 91,* 401–419.

Death and disorder in Guatemala. (1983). *Cultural Survival Quarterly, 7*(1).

DeBeer, Sir G. R. (1964). *Atlas of evolution.* London: Nelson.

Deetz, J. (1967). *Invitation to archaeology.* New York: Doubleday.

Deevy, E. S., Jr. (1960). The human population. *Scientific American, 203,* 194–204.

de Laguna, F. (1977). *Voyage to Greenland: A personal initiation into anthropology.* New York: Norton.

de Laguna, G. A. (1966). *On existence and the human world.* New Haven, CT: Yale University Press.

DeMello, M. (2000). *Bodies of inscription: A cultural history of the modern tattoo community.* Durham, NC: Duke University Press.

De Mott, B. (1990). *The imperial middle: Why Americans can't think straight about class.* New York: Morrow.

de Pelliam, A., & Burton, F. D. (1976). More on predatory behavior in nonhuman primates. *Current Anthropology, 17*(3).

d'Errico, F., Zilhão, J., Julien, M., Baffier, D., & Pelegrin, J. (1998). Neandertal acculturation in Western Europe? *Current Anthropology, 39,* 521.

Desowitz, R. S. (1987). *New Guinea tapeworms and Jewish grandmothers.* New York: Norton.

Dettwyler, K. A. (1997, October). When to wean. *Natural History, 49.*

Devereux, G. (1963). Institutionalized homosexuality of the Mohave Indians. In H. M. Ruitenbeck (Ed.), *The problem of homosexuality in modern society.* New York: Dutton.

DeVore, I. (Ed.). (1965). *Primate behavior: Field studies of monkeys and apes.* New York: Holt, Rinehart & Winston.

de Waal, A. (1994). Genocide in Rwanda. *Anthropology Today, 10*(3), 1–2.

de Waal, F. (1996). *Good natured: The origins of right and wrong in humans and other animals.* Cambridge, MA: Harvard University Press.

de Waal, F., Kano, T., & Parish, A. R. (1998). Comments. *Current Anthropology 39,* 407–408, 410–411, 413–414.

de Waal, F. (2001). Sing the song of evolution. *Natural History, 110*(8), 77.

de Waal, F. (2001). *The ape and the sushi master.* New York: Basic Books.

Diamond, J. (1994). How Africa became black. *Discover, 15*(2), 72–81.

Diamond, J. (1994). Race without color. *Discover, 15*(11), 83–89.

Diamond, J. (1996). Empire of uniformity. *Discover, 17*(3), 78–85.

Diamond, J. (1997). The curse of QWERTY. *Discover, 18*(4), 34–42.

Diamond, J. (1997). *Guns, germs, and steel* (p. 203). New York: Norton.

Diamond, J. (1998). Ants, crops, and history. *Science, 281,* 1,974–1,975.

Dissanayake, E. (2000). Birth of the arts. *Natural History, 109*(10), 89.

Dixon, J. E., Cann, J. R., & Renfrew, C. (1968). Obsidian and the origins of trade, *Scientific American, 218,* 38–46.

Dobyns, H. F., Doughty, P. L., & Lasswell, H. D., (Eds.). (1971). *Peasants, power, and applied social change.* London: Sage.

Dobzhansky, T. (1962). *Mankind evolving.* New Haven, CT: Yale University Press.

Doist, R. (1997). Molecular evolution and scientific inquiry, misperceived. *American Scientist, 85,* 475.

Domestic violence against women and girls. (2000, June). *Innocenti Digest,* 6. p. 4. Florence: United Nations Children's Fund, Innocenti Research Center.

Donnan, C. B., & Castillo, L. J. (1992). Finding the tomb of a Moche priestess. *Archaeology, 45*(6), 38–42.

Douglas, M. (1958). Raffia cloth distribution in the Lele economy. *Africa, 28,* 109–122.

Dozier, E. (1970). *The Pueblo Indians of North America.* New York: Holt, Rinehart & Winston.

Draper, P. (1975). !Kung women: Contrasts in sexual egalitarianism in foraging and sedentary contexts. In R. Reiter (Ed.), *Toward an anthropology of women* (pp. 77–109). New York: Monthly Review Press.

Driver, H. (1964). *Indians of North America.* Chicago: University of Chicago Press.

Dubois, C. (1944). *The people of Alor.* Minneapolis: University of Minnesota Press.

Dubos, R. (1968). *So human an animal.* New York: Scribner.

Dumurat-Dreger, A. (1998, May/June). Ambiguous sex or ambivalent medicine? *The Hastings Center Report, 28*(3), 24–35. (Posted on the Intersex Society of North America Web site: *www.isna.org.*)

Duncan, A. S., Kappelman, J., & Shapiro, L. J. (1994). Metasophalangeal joint function and positional behavior in *Australopithecus afarensis. American Journal of Physical Anthropology, 93,* 67–81.

Dundes, A. (1980). *Interpreting folklore.* Bloomington: Indiana University Press.

Duranti, A. (2001). Linguistic anthropology: History, ideas, and issues. In A. Duranti (Ed.), *Linguistic anthropology: A reader* (pp. 1–38). Oxford: Blackwell.

Durant, J. C. (2000, April 23) Everybody Into the gene pool. New York Times Book Review, p. 11.

Durkheim, E. (1964). *The division of labor in society.* New York: Free Press.

Durkheim, E. (1965). *The elementary forms of the religious life.* New York: Free Press.

duToit, B. M. (1991). *Human sexuality: Cross-cultural readings.* New York: McGraw-Hill.

Eastman, C. M. (1990). *Aspects of language and culture* (2nd ed.). Novato, CA: Chandler & Sharp.

Edey, M., & the Editors of Time-Life. (1972). *The missing link.* New York: Time-Life.

Edey, M. A., & Johannson, D. (1989). *Blueprints: Solving the mystery of evolution.* Boston: Little, Brown.

Edmonson, M. S. (1971). *Lore: An introduction to the science of folklore.* New York: Holt, Rinehart & Winston.

Edwards, J. (Ed.). (1999). *Technologies of procreation: Kinship in the age of assisted conception.* New York: Routledge (distributed by St. Martin's Press).

Edwards, S. W. (1978). Nonutilitarian activities on the Lower Paleolithic: A look at the two kinds of evidence. *Current Anthropology. 19*(l), 135–137.

Eggan, F. (1954). Social anthropology and the method of controlled comparison. *American Anthropologist, 56,* 743–763.

Eiseley, L. (1958). *Darwin's century: Evolution and the men who discovered it.* New York: Doubleday.

Eisenstadt, S. N. (1956). *From generation to generation: Age groups and social structure.* New York: Free Press.

Elkin, A. P. (1964). *The Australian aborigines.* Garden City, NY: DoubleDay / Anchor Books.

Ellison, P. T. (1990). Human ovarian function and reproductive ecology: New hypotheses. *American Anthropologist, 92,* 933–952.

Ember, C. R., & Ember, M. (1985). *Cultural anthropology* (4th ed.). Englewood Cliffs, NJ: Prentice–Hall.

Ember, C. R., & Ember, M. (1996). What have we learned from cross-cultural research? *General Anthropology, 2*(2), 5.

Enard, W., et al. (2002). Molecular evolution of FOXP2, a gene involved in speech and language. *Nature, 418,* 869–872.

Epstein, A. (1968). *Sanctions. In International Encyclopedia of the Social Sciences* (Vol. 14, p. 3). New York: Macmillan.

Erasmus, C. J. (1950). Patolli, Pachisi, and the limitation of possibilities. *Southwestern Journal of Anthropology, 6,* 369–381.

Erasmus, C. J., & Smith, W. (1967). Cultural anthropology in the United States since 1900. *Southwestern Journal of Anthropology, 23,* 11–40.

Erickson, P. A. & Murphy, L. D. (2003). *A history of anthropological theory* (2nd ed.). Peterborough, Ontario: Broadview Press.

Errington, F. K., & Gewertz, D. B. (2001). *Cultural alternatives and a feminist anthropology: An analysis of culturally constructed gender interests in Papua New Guinea.* New York: Cambridge University Press.

Ervin-Tripp, S. (1973). *Language acquisition and communicative choice.* Stanford, CA: Stanford University Press.

Esber, G. S., Jr. (1987). Designing Apache houses with Apaches. In R. M. Wulff & S. J.Fiske (Eds.), *Anthropological praxis: Translating knowledge into action* (pp. 187–196). Boulder, CO: Westview Press.

Evans, W. (1968). *Communication in the animal world.* New York: Crowell.

Evans-Pritchard, E. E. (1937). *Witchcraft, oracles, and magic among the Azande.* London: Oxford University Press.

Evans-Pritchard, E. E. (1968). *The Nuer: A description of the modes of livelihood and political institutions of a Nilotic people.* London: Oxford University Press.

Fagan, B. M. (1995). The quest for the past. In L. L. Hasten (Ed.), *Annual Editions 95/96, Archaeology* (p. 10). Guilford, CT: Dushkin.

Fagan, B. M. (1998). *People of the earth* (9th ed.). New York: Longman.

Fagan, B. M. (1999). *Archaeology: A brief introduction* (7th ed.). New York: Longman.

Fagan, B. M. (2000). *Ancient lives: An introduction to archaeology.* (pp. 125–133). Englewood Cliffs, NJ: Prentice-Hall.

Falk, D. (1975). Comparative anatomy of the larynx in man and the chimpanzee: Implications for language in Neanderthal. *American Journal of Physical Anthropology, 43*(1), 123–132.

Falk, D. (1989). Ape-like endocast of "Ape Man Taung." *American Journal of Physical Anthropology, 80,* 335–339.

Falk, D. (1993). A good brain is hard to cool. *Natural History, 102*(8), 65.

Falk, D. (1993). Hominid paleoneurology. In R. L. Ciochon & J. G. Fleagle (Eds.), *The human evolution source book.* Englewood Cliffs, NJ: Prentice-Hall.

Farmer, P. (1992). *AIDS and accusation: Haiti and the geography of blame.* Berkeley: University of California Press.

Farnell, B. (1995). *Do you see what I mean? Plains Indian sign talk and the embodiment of action.* Austin: University of Texas Press.

Farsoun, S. K. (1970). Family structures and society in modern Lebanon. In L. E. Sweet (Ed.), *Peoples and cultures of the Middle East* (Vol. 2). Garden City, NY: Natural History Press.

Fausto-Sterling, A. (1993, March/April). The five sexes: Why male and female are not enough. *The Sciences, 33*(2), 20–24.

Fausto-Sterling, A. (2000, July/August). The five sexes revisited. *The Sciences. 40*(4),19–24.

Fausto-Sterling, A. (2003, August 2). Personal email communication.

Feder, K. L. (1999). *Frauds, myths, and mysteries* (3rd ed.). Mountain View, CA: Mayfield.

Federoff, N. E., & Nowak, R. M. (1997). Man and his dog. *Science, 278,* 305.

Fedigan, L. M. (1986).The changing role of women in models of human evolution. *Annual Review of Anthropology, 15,* 25–56.

Female genital mutilation. (2000). Fact sheet no. 241. World Health Organization.

Fernandez-Carriba, S., & Loeches, A. (2001). Fruit smearing by captive chimpanzees: A newly observed food-processing behavior. *Current Anthropology, 42,* 143–147.

Ferrie, H. (1997). An interview with C. Loring Brace. *Current Anthropology, 38,* 851–869.

Finkler, K. (2000). *Experiencing the new genetics: Family and kinship on the medical frontier.* Philadelphia: University of Pennsylvania Press.

The First Americans, ca. 20,000 b.c. (1998). *Discover, 19*(6), 24.

Firth, R. (1952). *Elements of social organization.* London: Watts.

Firth, R. (1957). *Man and culture: An evaluation of Bronislaw Malinowski.* London: Routledge.

Firth, R. (1963). *We the Tikopia.* Boston: Beacon Press.

Firth, R. (Ed.). (1967). *Themes in economic anthropology.* London: Tavistock.

Fisher, R., & Ury, W. L. (1991). *Getting to yes: Negotiating agreement without giving in* (2nd ed.). Boston: Houghton Mifflin.

Fishman, J. (1994). Putting a new spin on the human birth. *Science, 264,* 1,082–1,083.

Flannery, K. V. (1973). The origins of agriculture. In B. J. Siegel, A. R. Beals, & S. A. Tyler (Eds.), *Annual Review of Anthropology* (Vol. 2, pp. 271–310). Palo Alto, CA: Annual Reviews.

Flannery, K. V. (Ed.). (1976). *The Mesoamerican village.* New York: Seminar Press.

Fleagle, J. G. (1992, December). *Early anthropoid evolution.* Paper presented at the 91st annual meeting of the American Anthropological Association.

Folger, T. (1993). The naked and the bipedal. *Discover, 14*(11), 34–35.

Forbes, J. D. (1964). *The Indian in America's past.* Englewood Cliffs, NJ: Prentice-Hall.

Forbes International 500 List. (2003).

Forde, C. D. (1953). *Habitat, economy, and society.* New York: Dutton.

Forde, C. D. (1955). The Nupe. In D. Forde (Ed.), *Peoples of the Niger-Benue confluence.* London: International African Institute (Ethnographic Survey of Africa. Western Africa, part 10).

Forde, C. D. (1968). Double descent among the Yako. In P. Bohannan & J. Middleton (Eds.), *Kinship and social organization* (pp. 179–191). Garden City, NY: Natural History Press.

Fortes, M. (1950). Kinship and marriage among the Ashanti. In A. R. Radcliffe-Brown & C. D. Forde (Eds.), *African systems of kinship and marriage.* London: Oxford University Press.

Fortes, M. (1969). *Kinship and the social order: The legacy of Lewis Henry Morgan.* Chicago: Aldine.

Fortes, M., & Evans-Prichard, E. E. (Eds.). (1962). *African political systems.* London: Oxford University Press. (orig.1940)

Fossey, D. (1983). *Gorillas in the mist.* Burlington, MA: Houghton Mifflin.

Foster, G. M. (1955). Peasant society and the image of the limited good. *American Anthropologist, 67,* 293–315.

Fox, R. (1967). *Kinship and marriage in an anthropological perspective.* Baltimore: Penguin.

Fox, R. (1968). *Encounter with anthropology.* New York: Dell.

Frake, C. O. (1961). The diagnosis of disease among the Subinam of Mindinao. *American Anthropologist, 63,*113–132.

Frake, C. O. (1992). Lessons of the Mayan sky. In A. F. Aveni (Ed.), *The sky in Mayan literature* (pp. 274–291). New York: Oxford University Press.

France, D. L., & Horn, A. D. (1992). *Lab manual and workbook for physical anthropology* (2nd ed.). New York: West.

Frankfort, H. (1968). *The birth of civilization in the Near East.* New York: Barnes & Noble.

Fraser, D. (1962). *Primitive art.* New York: Doubleday.

Fraser, D. (Ed.). (1966). *The many faces of primitive art: A critical anthology.* Englewood Cliffs, NJ: Prentice-Hall.

Frayer, D. W. (1981). Body size, weapon use, and natural selection in the European Upper Paleolithic and Mesolithic. *American Anthropologist, 83,* 57–73.

Frazer, Sir J. G. (1961 reissue). *The new golden bough.* New York: Doubleday, Anchor Books.

Freeman, J. D. (1960). The Iban of western Borneo. In G. P. Murdock (Ed.), *Social structure in Southeast Asia.* Chicago: Quadrangle Books.

Freeman, L. G. (1992). *Ambrona and Torralba: New evidence and interpretation.* Paper presented at the 91st annual meeting of the American Anthropological Association, San Francisco.

Fried, M. (1960). On the evolution of social stratification and the state. In S. Diamond (Ed.), *Culture in history: Essays in honor of Paul Radin.* New York: Columbia University Press.

Fried, M. (1967). *The evolution of political society: An essay in political anthropology.* New York: Random House.

Fried, M. (1972). *The study of anthropology.* New York: Crowell.

Fried, M., Harris, M., & Murphy, R. (1968). *War: The anthropology of armed conflict and aggression.* Garden City, NY: Natural History Press.

Friedl, E. (1975). *Women and men: An anthropologist's view.* New York: Holt, Rinehart & Winston.

Friedman, J. (Ed.). (2003). *Globalization, the state, and violence.* Walnut Creek, CA: Altamira Press.

Fritz, G. J. (1994). Are the first American farmers getting younger? *Current Anthropology, 35,* 305–309.

Frye, M. (1983). *Sexism. In The politics of reality* (pp. 17–40). New York: Crossing Press.

Furst, P. T. (1976). *Hallucinogens and culture* (p. 7). Novato, CA: Chandler & Sharp.

Gamble, C. (1986). *The Paleolithic settlement of Europe.* Cambridge: Cambridge University Press.

Gardner, R. A., Gardner, B. T., & Van Cantfort, T. E. (Eds.). (1989). *Teaching sign language to chimpanzees.* Albany: State University of New York Press.

Gamst, F. C., & Norbeck, E. (1976). *Ideas of culture: Sources and uses.* New York: Holt, Rinehart& Winston.

Garn, S. M. (1970). *Human races* (3rd ed.). Springfield, IL: Charles C Thomas.

Gates, H. (1996). Buying brides in China—again. *Anthropology Today, 12*(4), 10.

Gebo, D. L., Dagosto, D., Beard, K. C., & Tao, Q. (2001). Middle Eocene primate tarsals from China: Implications for haplorhine evolution. *American Journal of Physical Anthropology, 116,* 83–107.

Geertz, C. (1963). *Agricultural involution: The process of ecological change in Indonesia.* Berkeley: University of California Press.

Geertz, C. (1965). The impact of the concept of culture on the concept of man. In J. R. Platt (Ed.), *New views of man.* Chicago: University of Chicago Press.

Geertz, C. (1984). Distinguished lecture: Anti-relativism. *American Anthropologist, 86,* 263–278.

Gelb, I. J. (1952). *A study of writing.* London: Routledge.

Gell, A. (1988). Technology and magic. *Anthropology Today, 4*(2), 6–9.

Gellner, E. (1969). *Saints of the atlas.* Chicago: University of Chicago Press (The Nature of Human Society Series).

Gennep, A. Van (1960). *The rites of passage.* Chicago: University of Chicago Press.

Gibbons, A. (1992). Mitochondrial Eve: Wounded, but not yet dead. *Science, 257,* 873–875.

Gibbons, A. (1996). Did Neandertals lose an evolutionary "arms" race? *Science, 272,* 1,586–1,587.

Gibbons, A. (1997). Ideas on human origins evolve at anthropology gathering. *Science, 276,* 535–536.

Gibbons, A. (1997). A new face for human ancestors. *Science, 276,* 1,331–1,333.

Gibbons, A. (1998). Ancient island tools suggest *Homo erectus* was a seafarer. *Science, 279,* 1,635.

Gibbons, A. (2001). Studying humans—and their cousins and parasites. *Science, 292,* 627.

Gibbons, A. (2001). The riddle of coexistence. *Science, 291,* 1,726.

Gibbons, A., & Culotta, E. (1997). Miocene primates go ape. *Science, 276,* 355–356.

Gibbs, J. L., Jr. (1965). The Kpelle of Liberia. In J. L. Gibbs (Ed.), *Peoples of Africa* (pp. 197–240). New York: Holt, Rinehart & Winston.

Giddens, A. (1990). *The consequences of modernity* (p. 64). Stanford, CA: Stanford University Press.

Ginsburg, F. D., Abu-Lughod, L., & Larkin, B. (Eds.). (2002). *Media worlds: Anthropology on new terrain.* Berkeley: University of California Press.

Gleason, H. A., Jr. (1966). *An introduction to descriptive linguistics* (Rev. ed.). New York: Holt, Rinehart & Winston.

Gledhill. J. (2000). *Power and its disguises: Anthropological perspectives on politics* (2nd ed.). Boulder, CO: Pluto Press.

Glob, P. (1969). *The bog people.* London: Faber & Faber.

Gluckman, M. (1955). *The judicial process among the Barotse of Northern Rhodesia.* New York: Free Press.

Goddard, V. (1993). Child labor in Naples. In W. A. Haviland & R. J. Gordon (Eds.), *Talking about people* (pp. 105–109). Mountain View, CA: Mayfield.

Godfrey, T. (2000, December 27). Biotech threatening biodiversity. *Burlington Free Press,* 10A.

Godlier, M. (1971). Salt currency and the circulation of commodities among the Baruya of New Guinea. In G. Dalton (Ed.), *Studies in economic anthropology.* Washington, DC: American Anthro-pological Association (Anthropological Studies No. 7).

Golden, M., Birns, B., Bridger, W., & Moss, A. (1971). Social–class differentiation in cognitive development among black preschool children. *Child Development, 42,* 37–45.

Goodall, J. (1986). *The chimpanzees of Gombe: Patterns of behavior.* Cambridge, MA: Belknap Press.

Goodall, J. (1990). *Through a window: My thirty years with the chimpanzees of Gombe.* Boston: Houghton Mifflin.

Goodall, J. (2000). *Reason for hope: A spiritual journey.* New York: Warner Books.

Goode, W. (1963). *World revolution and family patterns.* New York: Free Press.

Goodenough, W. (1956). Residence rules. *Southwestern Journal of Anthropology, 12,* 22–37.

Goodenough, W. (1961). Comment on cultural evolution. *Daedalus, 90,* 521–528.

Goodenough, W. (Ed.). (1964). *Explorations in cultural anthropology: Essays in honor of George Murdock.* New York: McGraw–Hill.

Goodenough, W. (1965). Rethinking status. and Role: Toward a general model of the cultural organization of social relationships. In M. Benton (Ed.), *The relevance of models for social anthropology.* New York: Praeger (ASA Monographs l).

Goodenough, W. (1970). *Description and comparison in cultural anthropology.* Chicago: Aldine.

Goodenough, W. H. (1990) Evolution of the human capacity for beliefs. *American Anthropologist* 92:601.

Goodman, M., Bailey, W. J., Hayasaka, K., Stanhope, M. J., Slightom, J., & Czelusniak, J. (1994). Molecular evidence on primate phylogeny from DNA sequences. *American Journal of Physical Anthropology, 94,* 3–24.

Goodman, M. E. (1967). *The individual and culture.* Homewood, IL: Dorsey Press.

Goody, J. (1969). *Comparative studies in kinship.* Stanford, CA: Stanford University Press.

Goody, J. (Ed.). (1972). *Developmental cycle in domestic groups.* New York: Cambridge University Press (Papers in Social Anthropology, No. 1).

Goody, J. (1976). *Production and reproduction: A comparative study of the domestic domain.* Cambridge: Cambridge University Press.

Goody, J. (1983). *The development of the family and marriage in Europe.* Cambridge, MA: Cambridge University Press.

Gordon, R. (1981, December). [Interview for Coast Telecourses, Inc.]. Los Angeles.

Gordon, R. (1990). The field researcher as a deviant: A Namibian case study. In P. Hugo (Ed.), *Truth be in the field: Social science research in southern Africa.* Pretoria: University of South Africa.

Gordon, R. J. (1992). *The Bushman myth: The making of a Namibian underclass.* Boulder, CO: Westview Press.

Gordon, R. J., & Megitt, M. J. (1985). *Law and order in the New Guinea highlands.* Hanover, NH: University Press of New England.

Gorer, G. (1943). Themes in Japanese culture. *Transactions of the New York Academy of Sciences,* series 11, 5.

Gorman, E. M. (1989). The AIDS epidemic in San Francisco: Epidemiological and anthropological perspectives. In A. Podolefsky & P. J. Brown (Eds.), *Applying anthropology, An introductory reader.* Mountain View, CA: Mayfield.

Gornick, V., & Moran, B. K. (Eds.). (1971). *Woman in sexist society.* New York: Basic Books.

Gottlieb, A., & DeLoache, J. S. (Eds.). (2000). *A world of babies: Imagined childcare guides for seven societies.* New York: Cambridge University Press.

Gould, S. J. (1983). *Hen's teeth and horses' toes.* New York: Norton.

Gould, S. J. (1985). *The flamingo's smile: Reflections in natural history.* New York: Norton.

Gould, S. J. (1986). Of kiwi eggs and the Liberty Bell. *Natural History, 95,* 20–29.

Gould, S. J. (1989). *Wonderful life.* New York: Norton.

Gould, S. J. (1991). *Bully for brontosaurus.* New York: Norton.

Gould, S. J. (1994). The geometer of race. *Discover, 15*(11), 65–69.

Gould, S. J. (1996). *Full house: The spread of excellence from Plato to Darwin* (pp. 176–195). New York: Harmony Books.

Gould, S. J. (1996). *The mismeasure of man* (Rev. ed.). New York: Norton.

Gould, S. J. (1997). *Questioning the millennium.* New York: Crown.

Gould, S. J. (2000). The narthex of San Marco and the pangenetic paradigm. *Natural History 109*(6), 29.

Gould, S. J. (2000). What does the dreaded "E" word mean anyway? *Natural History, 109*(1), 34–36.

Graburn, N. H. (1969). *Eskimos without igloos: Social and economic development in Sugluk.* Boston: Little, Brown.

Graburn, N. H. (1971). *Readings in kinship and social structure.* New York: Harper & Row.

Graham, S. B. (1979). Biology and human social behavior: A response to van den Berghe and Barash. *American Anthropologist, 81*(2), 357–360.

Graves, P. (1991). New models and metaphors for the Neanderthal debate. *Current Anthropology, 32*(5), 513–543.

Gray, P. M., et al. (2001). The music of nature and the nature of music. *Science, 291,* 52.

Green, E. C. (1987). The planning of health education strategies in Swaziland. In R. M. Wulff & S. J. Fiske (Eds.), *Anthropological praxis: Translating knowledge into action* (pp. 15–25). Boulder, CO: Westview Press.

Greenberg, J. H. (1968). *Anthropological linguistics: An introduction.* New York: Random House.

Greenfield, L. O. (1979). On the adaptive pattern of Ramapithecus. *American Journal of Physical Anthropology, 50,* 527–547.

Greenfield, L. O. (1980). A late divergence hypothesis. *American Journal of Physical Anthropology, 52,* 351–366.

Griffin, B. (1994). CHAGS7. *Anthropology Newsletter, 35*(1), 12–14.

Grine, F. E. (1993). Australopithecine taxonomy and phylogeny: Historical background and recent interpretation. In R. L. Ciochon & J. G. Fleagle (Eds.), *The human evolution source book,* Englewood Cliffs, NJ: Prentice-Hall.

Grün, R., & Thorne, A. (1997). Dating the Ngandong humans, *Science, 276,* 1,575.

Guillette, E. A., et al. (1998, June). An anthropological approach to the evaluation of preschool children exposed to pesticides in Mexico. *Environmental Health Perspectives 106,* 347.

Gulliver, P. (1968). *Age differentiation. In International encyclopedia of the social sciences* (Vol. 1, pp. 157–162). New York: Macmillan.

Guthrie, S. (1993). *Faces in the clouds: A new theory of religions.* New York: Oxford University Press.

Gutin, J. A. (1995). Do Kenya tools root birth of modern thought in Africa? *Science, 270,* 1,118–1,119.

Haeri, N. (1997). The reproduction of symbolic capital: Language, state and class in Egypt. *Current Anthropology, 38,* 795–816.

Hafkin, N., & Bay, E. (Eds.). (1976). *Women in Africa.* Stanford, CA: Stanford University Press.

Hall, E. T. (1959). *The silent language.* Garden City, NY: Anchor Press/Doubleday.

Hall, E. T., & Hall, M. R. (1986). The sounds of silence. In E. Angeloni (Ed.), *Anthro-pology 86/87* (pp. 65–70). Guilford, CT: Dushkin.

Hall, K. R. L., & DeVore, I. (1965). Baboon social behavior. In I. DeVore (Ed.), *Primate behavior.* New York: Holt, Rinehart & Winston.

Hallowell, A. I. (1955). *Culture and experience.* Philadelphia: University of Pennsylvania Press.

Halperin, R. H. (1994). *Cultural economies: Past and present.* Austin: University of Texas Press.

Halverson, J. (1989). Review of Altimira Revisited and other essays on early art. *American Antiquity, 54,* 883.

Hamblin, D. J., & the Editors of Time-Life. (1973). *The first cities.* New York: Time-Life.

Hamburg, D. A., & McGown, E. R. (Eds.). (1979). *The great apes.* Menlo Park, CA: Cummings.

Hammond, D. (1972). *Associations.* Reading, MA: Addison-Wesley.

Hannah, J. L. (1988). *Dance, sex and gender.* Chicago: University of Chicago Press.

Harlow, H. F. (1962). Social deprivation in monkeys. *Scientific American, 206,* 1–10.

Harner, M. (1980). *The way of the shaman: A guide to power and healing* (p. 20). San Francisco: Harper & Row.

Harpending, J. H., & Harpending, H. C. (1995). Ancient differences in population can mimic a recent African origin of modern humans. *Current Anthropology, 36,* 667–674.

Harris, M. (1965). The cultural ecology of India's sacred cattle. *Current Anthropology, 7,* 51–66.

Harris, M. (1968). *The rise of anthropological theory: A history of theories of culture.* New York: Crowell.

Harrison, G. G. (1975). Primary adult lactase deficiency: A problem in anthropological genetics. *American Anthropologist, 77,* 812–835.

Hart, C. W., Pilling, A. R., & Goodale, J. (1988). *Tiwi of North Australia* (3rd ed.). New York: Holt, Rinehart & Winston.

Hartwig, W. C., & Doneski, K. (1998). Evolution of the Hominid hand and toolmaking behavior. *American Journal of Physical Anthropology, 106,* 401–402.

Hatch, E. (1983). *Culture and morality: The relativity of values in anthropology.* New York: Columbia University Press.

Hatcher, E. P. (1985). *Art as culture, an introduction to the anthropology of art.* New York: University Press of America.

Haviland W. (1967). Stature at Tikal, Guatemala: Implications for ancient Maya, demography, and social organization. *American Antiquity, 32,* 316–325.

Haviland, W. (1970). Tikal, Guatemala and Mesoamerican urbanism. *World Archaeology, 2,* 186–198.

Haviland, W. A. (1972). A new look at Classic Maya social organization at Tikal. *Ceramica de Cultura Maya, 8,* 1–16.

Haviland, W. A. (1974). Farming, seafaring and bilocal residence on the coast of Maine. *Man in the Northeast, 6,* 31–44.

Haviland, W. A. (1975). The ancient Maya and the evolution of urban society. *University of Northern Colorado Museum of Anthropology, Miscellaneous Series, 37.*

Haviland, W. A. (1983). *Human evolution and prehistory* (5th ed.). Fort Worth, TX: Harcourt Brace.

Haviland, W. A. (1991). *Star wars at Tikal, or did Caracol do what the glyphs say they did?* Paper presented at the 90th annual meeting of the American Anthropological Association.

Haviland, W. A. (1997). Cleansing young minds, or what should we be doing in introductory anthropology? In C. P. Kottak, J. J. White, R. H. Furlow, & P. C. Rice (Eds.), *The teaching of anthropology: Problems, issues, and decisions* (p. 35). Mountain View, CA: Mayfield.

Haviland, W. A. (1997). The rise and fall of sexual inequality: Death and gender at Tikal, Guatemala. *Ancient Mesoamerica, 8,* 1–12.

Haviland, W. A., et al. (1985). *Excavations in small residential groups of Tikal: Groups 4F-1 and 4F-2.* Philadelphia: University Museum.

Haviland, W. A., & Moholy-Nagy, H. (1992). Distinguishing the high and mighty from the hoi polloi at Tikal, Guatemala. In A. F. Chase & D. Z. Chase (Eds.), *Mesoamerican elites: An archaeological assessment.* Norman: Oklahoma University Press.

Haviland, W. A., & Power, M. W. (1994). *The original Vermonters: Native inhabitants, past and present* (Rev. and exp. ed.). Hanover, NH: University Press of New England.

Haviland, W. A. (2003). Settlement, society and demography at Tikal. In J. Sabloff (Ed.), *Tikal.* Santa Fe: School of American Research.

Haviland, W. A. (2003). *Tikal, Guatemala: A Maya way to urbanism.* Paper prepared for 3rd INAH/Penn State Conference on Mesoamerican Urbanism.

Hawkes, K., O'Connell, J. F., & Blurton-Jones, N. G. (1997). Hadza women's time allocation, offspring, provisioning, and the evolution of long postmenopausal life spans. *Current Anthropology, 38,* 551–577.

Hawkins, G. S. (1965). *Stonehenge decoded.* New York: Doubleday.

Hays, H. R. (1965). *From ape to angel: An informal history of social anthropology.* New York: Knopf.

Heichel, G. (1976). Agricultural production and energy resources. *American Scientist, 64.*

Heilbroner, R. L. (1972). *The making of economic society* (4th ed.). Englewood Cliffs, NJ: Prentice-Hall.

Heilbroner, R. L., & Thurow, L. C. (1981). *The economic problem* (6th ed.). Englewood Cliffs, NJ: Prentice-Hall.

Helm, J. (1962). The ecological approach in anthropology. *American Journal of Sociology, 67,* 630–649.

Henry, D. O. et al. (2004). Human behavioral organization in the Middle Paleolithic: Were Neandertals different? *American Anthropologist, 107*(1), 17-31.

Henry, J. (1965). *Culture against man.* New York: Vintage Books.

Henry, J. (1966). The metaphysic of youth, beauty, and romantic love. In S. Farber & R. Wilson (Eds.), *The challenge of women.* New York: Basic Books.

Henry, J. (1974). A theory for an anthropological analysis of American culture. In J. G. Jorgensen & M. Truzzi (Eds.), *Anthropology and American life.* Englewood Cliffs, NJ: Prentice-Hall.

Herskovits, M. J. (1952). *Economic anthropology: A study in comparative economics* (2nd ed.). New York: Knopf.

Herskovits, M. J. 1964. *Cultural dynamics.* New York: Knopf.

Hertz, N. (2001). *The silent takeover: Global capitalism and the death of democracy.* New York: Arrow Books.

Hewes, G. W. (1973). Primate communication and the gestural origin of language. *Current Anthropology, 14,* 5–24.

Himmelfarb, E. J. (2000). First alphabet found in Egypt. *Archaeology, 53*(1).

Hodgen, M. (1964). *Early anthropology in the sixteenth and seventeenth centuries.* Philadelphia: University of Pennsylvania Press.

Hoebel, E. A. (1954). *The law of primitive man: A study in comparative legal dynamics.* Cambridge, MA: Harvard University Press.

Hoebel, E. A. (1958). *Man in the primitive world: An introduction to anthropology.* New York: McGraw-Hill.

Hoebel, E. A. (1960). *The Cheyennes: Indians of the Great Plains.* New York: Holt, Rinehart & Winston.

Hoebel, E. A. (1972). *Anthropology: The study of man* (4th ed.). New York: McGraw-Hill.

Hogbin, I. (1964). *A Guadalcanal society.* New York: Holt, Rinehart & Winston.

Holden, C. (1983). Simon and Kahn versus Global 2000. *Science, 221,* 342.

Holden, C. (1996). Missing link for Miocene apes. *Science, 271,* 151.

Holden, C. (1998). *No last word on language origins.* Science, 282, 1,455–1,458.

Holden, C. (1999). Ancient child burial uncovered in Portugal. *Science, 283,* 169.

Hole, F. (1966). Investigating the origins of Mesopotamian civilization. *Science, 153,* 605–611.

Hole, F. & Heizer, R. F. (1969). *An introduction to prehistoric archeology.* New York: Holt, Rinehart & Winston.

Holloway, R. L. (1980). The O. H. 7 (Olduvai Gorge, Tanzania) hominid partial brain endocast revisited. American Journal of *Physical Anthropology, 53,* 267–274.

Holloway, R. L. (1981). The Indonesian Homo erectus brain endocast revisited. *American Journal of Physical Anthropology, 55,* 503–521.

Holloway, R. L. (1981). Volumetric and asymmetry determinations on recent hominid endocasts: Spy I and II, Djebel Jhroud 1, and the Salb Homo erectus specimens, with some notes on Neanderthal brain size. *American Journal of Physical Anthropology, 55,* 385–393.

Holloway, R. L., & de LaCoste-Lareymondie, M. C. (1982). Brain endocast asymmetry in pongids and hominids: Some preliminary findings on the paleontology of cerebral dominance. *American Journal of Physical Anthropology, 58,* 101–110.

Holmes, L. D. (2000). Paradise Bent (film review). *American Anthropologist, 102*(3),604–605.

Hostetler, J., & Huntington, G. (1971). *Children in Amish society. New York:* Holt, Rinehart & Winston.

Houle, A. (1999). The origin of platyrrhines: An evaluation of the Antarctic scenario and the floating island model. *American Journal of Physical Anthropology, 109,* 554–556.

Howell, F. C. (1970). *Early man.* New York: Time-Life.

Hsiaotung, F. (1939). Peasant life in China. London: Kegan, Paul, Trench, & Truber.

Hsu, F. L. (1961). *Psychological anthropology: Approaches to culture and personality.* Homewood, IL: Dorsey Press.

Hsu, F. L. (1997). Role, affect, and anthropology. *American Anthropologist, 79,* 805–808.

Hsu, F. L. K. (1977). Role, affect, and anthropology. *American Anthropologist, 79,* 805–808.

Hsu, F. L. K. (1979). The cultural problems of the cultural anthropologist. *American Anthropologist, 81, 517–532.*

Hubert, H., & Mauss, M. (1964). *Sacrifice.* Chicago: University of Chicago Press.

Human development report 2000. *Deepening democracy in a fragmented world.* United Nations Development Program.

Hunger Project. (2003). www.thp.org.

Hunt, R. C. (Ed.). (1967). *Personalities and cultures: Readings in psychological anthropology.* Garden City, NY: Natural History Press.

Hymes, D. (1964). *Language in culture and Society: A reader in linguistics and anthropology.* New York: Harper & Row.

Hymes, D. (Ed.). (1972). *Reinventing anthropology.* New York: Pantheon.

Inda, J. X., & Rosaldo, R. (Eds). (2001). *The anthropology of globalization: A reader.* Malden, MA, and Oxford: Blackwell.

Ingmanson, E. J. (1998). Comment. *Current Anthropology, 39,* 409–410.

Inkeles, A., Hanfmann, E., & Beier, H. (1961). Modal personality and adjustment to the Soviet socio-political system. In B. Kaplan (Ed.), *Studying personality cross-culturally.* New York: Harper & Row.

Inkeles, A., & Levinson, D. J. (1954). *National character: The study of modal personality and socio-cultural systems. In G. Lindzey (Ed.), Handbook of social psychology.* Reading, MA: Addison-Wesley.

Inuit Tapiirit Kanatami. *http://www.tapirisat.ca/english_text/itk/departments/enviro/ncp/*

Interview with Laura Nader. *California Monthly.* November 2000.

Ireland, E. (1991). Neither warriors nor victims, the wauja peacefully organize to defend their land. *Cultural Survival Quarterly, 15*(1), 54–59.

Iroquois constitution. Available at *http://www.law.ou.edu/hist/iroquois.html.*

It's the law: Child labor protection. (1997, November/December). *Peace and Justice News,* 11.

Jacobs, S. E. (1994). Native American Two-spirits. *Anthropology Newsletter, 35*(8), 7.

Jacoby, R., & Glauberman, N. (Eds.). (1995). *The bell curve.* New York: Random House.

Jennings, F. (1976). *The invasion of America.* New York: Norton.

Jennings, J. D. (1974). *Prehistory of North America* (2nd ed.). New York: McGraw-Hill.

Johanson, D., & Shreeve, J. (1989). *Lucy's child: the discovery of a human ancestor.* New York: Avon.

Johanson, D. C., & Edey, M. (1981). *Lucy, the beginnings of humankind.* New York: Simon & Schuster.

Johanson, D. C., & White, T. D. (1979). A systematic assessment of early African hominids. *Science, 203,* 321–330.

John, V. (1971). Whose is the failure? In C. L. Brace, G. R. Gamble, & J. T. Bond (Eds.), *Race and intelligence.* Washington, DC: American Anthropological Association (Anthropological Studies No. 8).

Johnson, A. (1989). Horticulturalists: Economic behavior in tribes. In S. Plattner (Ed.), *Economic anthropology* (pp. 49–77). Stanford, CA: Stanford University Press.

Johnson, A. W., & Earle, T. (1987). *The evolution of human societies, from foraging group to agrarian state.* Stanford, CA: Stanford University Press.

Johnson, D. (1996). Polygamists emerge from secrecy, seeking not just peace but respect. In W. A. Haviland & R. J. Gordon (Eds.), *Talking about people* (2nd ed., pp. 129–131). Mountain View, CA: Mayfield.

Jolly, A. (1985). The evolution of primate behavior. *American Scientist 73*(3), 230–239.

Jolly, A. (1985). *The evolution of primate behavior* (2nd ed.). New York: Macmillan.

Jolly, A. (1985). Thinking like a Vervet. *Science, 251,* 574.

Jolly, C. J. (1970). The seed eaters: A new model of hominid differentiation based on a baboon analogy. *Man, 5,* 5–26.

Jolly, C. J., & Plog, F. (1986). *Physical anthropology and archaeology* (4th ed.). New York: Knopf.

Jones, S., Martin, R., & Pilbeam, D. (1992). *Cambridge encyclopedia of human evolution.* New York: Cambridge University Press.

Jopling, C. F. (1971). *Art and aesthetics in primitive societies: A critical anthology.* New York: Dutton.

Jorgensen, J. (1972). *The sun dance religion.* Chicago: University of Chicago Press.

Joukowsky, M. A. (1980). *A complete field manual of archeology: Tools and techniques of field work for archaeologists.* Englewood Cliffs, NJ: Prentice-Hall.

Joyce, C. (1991). *Witnesses from the grave: The stories bones tell.* Boston: Little, Brown.

Kahn, H., & Wiener, A. J. (1967). *The year 2000.* New York: Macmillan.

Kaiser, J. (1994). A new theory of insect wing origins takes off. *Science, 266, 363.*

Kalwet, H. (1988). *Dreamtime and inner space: The world of the shaman.* New York: Random House.

Kaplan, D. (1972). *Culture theory.* Englewood Cliffs, NJ: Prentice-Hall (Foundations of Modern Anthropology).

Kaplan, D. (2000). The darker side of the original affluent society. *Journal of Anthropological Research, 53*(3), 301–324.

Karavani, I., & Smith, F. H. (2000). More on the Neanderthal problem: The Vindija case. *Current Anthropology, 41,* 839.

Kardiner, A. (1939). *The individual and his society: The psycho-dynamics of primitive social organization.* New York: Columbia University Press.

Kardiner, A., & Preble, E. (1961). *They studied men.* New York: Mentor.

Kay, R. F., Fleagle, J. F., & Simons, E. L. (1981). A revision of the Oligocene apes of the Fayum Province, Egypt. *American Journal of Physical Anthropology, 55,* 293–322.

Kay, R. F., Ross, C., & Williams, B. A. (1997). Anthropoid origins. *Science, 275,* 797–804.

Kay, R. F., Theweissen, J. G. M., & Yoder, A. D. (1992). Cranial anatomy of Ignacius graybullianus and the affinities of the plesiadapiformes. *American Journal of Physical Anthropology, 89*(4), 477–498.

Keen, B. (1971). *The Aztec image in western thought* (p. 13). New Brunswick, NJ: Rutgers University Press.

Kehoe, A. (2000). *Shamans and religion: An anthropological exploration in critical thinking.* Prospect Heights, IL: Waveland Press.

Kendall, L. (1990, October). In the company of witches. *Natural History*, 92–95.

Kenyon, K. (1957). *Digging up Jericho.* London: Ben.

Kerri, J. N. (1976). Studying voluntary associations as adaptive mechanisms: A review of anthropological perspectives. *Current Anthropology, 17*(1).

Kessler, E. (1975). *Women.* New York: Holt, Rinehart & Winston.

Key, M. R. (1975). *Paralanguage and kinesics: Nonverbal communication.* Metuchen, NJ: Scarecrow Press.

Kirkpatrick R. C. (2000) The evolution of human homosexual behavior. *Current Anthropology* 41:384.

Klass, M. (1995). *Ordered universes: Approaches to the anthropology of religion.* Boulder, CO: Westview Press.

Klass, M., & Weisgrau, M. (Eds.). (1999). *Across the boundaries of belief: Contemporary issues in the anthropology of religion.* Boulder, CO: Westview Press.

Kleinman, A. (1976). Concepts and a model for the comparison of medical systems as cultural systems. *Social Science and Medicine, 12*(2B), 85–95.

Kleinman, A. (1982). The failure of western medicine. In D. Hunter & P. Whitten (Eds.), *Anthropology: Contemporary perspectives.* Boston: Little, Brown.

Kluckhohn, C. (1970). *Mirror for Man.* Greenwich, CT: Fawcett.

Kluckhohn, C. (1994). Navajo witchcraft. Papers of the Peabody Museum of American Archaeology and Ethnology, 22(2).

Knauft, B. (1991). Violence and sociality in human evolution. *Current Anthropology, 32,* 391–409.

Koch, G. (1997). Songs, land rights, and archives in Australia. *Cultural Survival Quarterly, 20*(4).

Konner, M., & Worthman, C. (1980). Nursing frequency, gonadal function, and birth spacing among !Kung hunter-gatherers. *Science, 207,* 788–791.

Koufos, G. (1993). Mandible of Ouranopithecus macedoniensis (hominidae: primates) from a new late Miocene locality in Macedonia (Greece). *American Journal of Physical Anthropology, 91,* 225–234.

Krader, L. (1968). *Formation of the state.* Englewood Cliffs, NJ: Prentice-Hall (Foundation of Modern Anthropology).

Krajick, K. (1998). Greenfarming by the Incas? *Science, 281, 323.*

Kramer, P. A. (1998). The costs of human locomotion: maternal investment in child transport. *American Journal of Physical Anthropology, 107,* 71–85.

Kroeber, A. (1958). Totem and taboo: An ethnologic psycho-analysis. In W. Lessa & E. Z. Vogt (Eds.), *Reader in comparative religion: An anthropological approach.* New York: Harper & Row.

Kroeber, A. L. (1939). Cultural and natural areas of native North America. *American Archaeology and Ethnology* (Vol. 38). Berkeley: University of California Press.

Kroeber, A. L. (1963). *Anthropology: Cultural processes and patterns.* New York: Harcourt.

Kroeber, A. L., & Kluckhohn, C. (1952). *Culture: A critical review of concepts and definitions.* Cambridge, MA: Harvard University Press (Papers of the Peabody Museum of American Archaeology and Ethnology, 47).

Kuhn, T. (1968). *The structure of scientific revolutions.* Chicago: University of Chicago Press (International Encyclopedia of Unified Science, 2[27].

Kummer, H. (1971). *Primate societies: Group techniques of ecological adaptation.* Chicago: Aldine.

Kunzig, R. (1999). A tale of two obsessed archaeologists, one ancient city and nagging doubts about whether science can ever hope to reveal the past. *Discover, 20*(5), 84–92.

Kuper, H. (1965). The Swazi of Swaziland. In J. L. Gibbs (Ed.), *Peoples of Africa* (pp. 479–511). New York: Holt, Rinehart & Winston.

Kurath, G. P. (1960). Panorama of dance ethnology. *Current Anthropology, 1,* 233–254.

Kurth, P. (1998, October 14). Capitol Crimes. *Seven Days, 7.*

Kurtz, D. V. (2001). *Political anthropology: Paradigms and power.* Boulder, CO: Westview Press.

Kushner, G. (1969). *Anthropology of complex societies.* Stanford, CA: Stanford University Press.

La Barre, W. (1945). Some observations of character structure in the Orient: The Japanese. *Psychiatry,* 8.

LaFont, S, (Ed.). (2003). *Constructing sexualities: Readings in sexuality, gender, and culture.* Upper Saddle River, NJ: Prentice-Hall.

Lai, C. S. L., et al. (2001). A forkhead-domain gene is mutated in severe speech and language disorder. *Nature, 413,* 519–523.

Lampl, M., Velhuis, J. D., & Johnson, M. L. (1992). Saltation and statsis: A model of human growth. *Science, 258*(5083), 801–803.

Lancaster, J. B. (1975). *Primate behavior and the emergence of human culture.* New York: Holt, Rinehart & Winston.

Landau, M. (1991). *Narratives of human evolution.* New Haven, CT: Yale University Press.

Landes, R. (1982). Comment. *Current Anthropology, 23,* 401.

Lanning, E. P. (1967). *Peru before the Incas.* Englewood Cliffs, NJ: Prentice-Hall.

Lanternari, V. (1963). *The religions of the oppressed.* New York: Mentor.

Lasker, G. W., & Tyzzer, R. (1982). *Physical anthropology* (3rd ed.) New York: Holt, Rinehart & Winston.

Laughlin, W. S., & Osborne, R. H. (Eds.). (1967). *Human variation and origins.* San Francisco: Freeman.

Laurel, K. (1990). In the company of witches. *Natural History,* 92.

Lawler, A. (2001) Writing gets a rewrite. *Science 292,* 2,419.

Layton, R. (1991). *The anthropology of art* (2nd ed.). Cambridge: Cambridge University Press.

Leach, E. (1961). *Rethinking anthropology.* London: Athione Press.

Leach, E. (1962). The determinants of differential cross-cousin marriage. *Man, 62,* 238.

Leach, E. (1962). On certain unconsidered aspects of double descent systems. *Man, 214,* 13–34.

Leach, E. (1965). *Political systems of highland* Burma. Boston: Beacon Press.

Leach, E. (1982). *Social anthropology.* Glasgow: Fontana Paperbacks.

Leacock, E. (1981). *Myths of male dominance: Collected articles on women cross culturally.* New York: Monthly Review Press.

Leacock, E. (1981). Women's status in egalitarian society: Implications for social evolution. In *Myths of male dominance: Collected articles on women cross culturally.* New York: Monthly Review Press.

Leakey, L. S. B. (1965). *Olduvai Gorge, 1951–1961* (Vol. 1). London: Cambridge University Press.

Leakey, L. S. B. (1967). Development of aggression as a factor in early man and prehuman evolution. In C. Clements &

D. Lundsley (Eds.), *Aggression and defense.* Los Angeles: University of California Press.

Leakey, M. D. (1971). *Olduvai Gorge: Excavations in Beds I and II. 1960–1963.* London and New York: Cambridge University Press.

Leakey, M. G., Spoor, F., Brown, F. H., Gathogo, P. N., Kiare, C., Leakey, L. N., & McDougal, I. (2001). New hominin genus from eastern Africa shows diverse middle Pliocene lineages. *Nature, 410,* 433–440.

Leap, W. L. (1987). Tribally controlled culture change: The Northern Ute language revival project. In R. M. Wulff & S. J. Fiske (Eds.), *Anthropological praxis: Translating knowledge into action* (pp. 197–211). Boulder, CO: Westview Press.

Leavitt, G. C. (1990). Sociobiological explanations of incest avoidance: A critical review of evidential claims. *American Anthropologist, 92,* 971–993.

Lee, R. (1993). *The Dobe Ju/hoansi. Ft.* Worth, TX: Harcourt Brace.

Lee, R. B., & Daly, R. H. (1999). *The Cambridge encyclopedia of hunters and gatherers.* New York: Cambridge University Press.

Lee, R. B., & DeVore, I. (Eds.). (1968). *Man the hunter.* Chicago: Aldine.

Leeds, A., & Vayda, A. P. (Eds.). (1965). *Man, culture and animals: The role of animals in human ecological adjustments.* Washington, DC: American Association for the Advancement of Science.

Lees, R. (1953). The basis of glottochronology. *Language, 29,* 113–127.

Legros, D. (1997). Comment. *Current Anthropology, 38,* 617.

Lehmann, A. C., & Myers, J. E. (Eds.). (1993). *Magic, witchcraft and religion: An anthropological study of the supernatural* (3rd ed.). Mountain View, CA: Mayfield.

Lehmann, W. P. (1973). *Historical linguistics, An introduction* (2nd ed.). New York: Holt, Rinehart & Winston.

Leigh, S. R., & Park, P. B. (1998). Evolution of human growth prolongation. *American Journal of Physical Anthropology, 107,* 331–350.

Leinhardt, G. (1964). *Social anthropology.* London: Oxford University Press.

Leinhardt, G. (1971). Religion. In H. Shapiro (Ed.), *Man, culture and society* (2nd ed.). London: Oxford University Press.

LeMay, M. (1975). The language capability of Neanderthal man. *American Journal of Physical Anthropology, 43*(1), 9–14.

Lenski, G. (1966). *Power and privilege: A theory of social stratification.* New York: McGraw-Hill.

Lerner, R. N. (1987). Preserving plants for Pomos. In R. M. Wulff & S. J. Fiske (Eds.), *Anthropological praxis: Translating knowledge into action* (pp. 212–222). Boulder, CO: Westview Press.

Leroi-Gourhan, A. (1968). The evolution of Paleolithic art. *Scientific American, 218,* 58ff.

Lestel, D. (1998). How chimpanzees have domesticated humans. *Anthropology Today, 12* (3); Miles, H. L. W. (1993). Language and the orangutan: The "old person" of the forest. In P. Cavalieri & P. Singer (Eds.), *The great ape project* (pp. 45–50). New York: St. Martin's Press.

Lett, J. (1987). *The human enterprise: A critical introduction to anthropological theory.* Boulder, CO: Westview Press.

Levanthes, L. E. (1987). The mysteries of the bog. *National Geographic, 171,* 397–420.

Levine, N. E., & Silk, J. B. (1997). Why polyandry fails. *Current Anthropology, 38,* 375–398.

Levine, R. (1973). *Culture, behavior and personality.* Chicago: Aldine.

Levine, R. P. (1968). *Genetics.* New York: Holt, Rinehart & Winston.

Lévi-Strauss, C. (1963). The sorcerer and his magic. In *Structural anthropology.* New York: Basic Books.

Lewellen, T. C. (2002). *The anthropology of globalization: Cultural anthropology enters the 21st century.* Westport, CT: Greenwood Publishing Group/Bergin & Garvey.

Lewin, R. (1983). Is the orangutan a living fossil? *Science, 222,* 1,223.

Lewin, R. (1985). Tooth enamel tells a complex story. *Science, 228,* 707.

Lewin, R. (1986). New fossil upsets human family" *Science, 233,* 720–721.

Lewin, R. (1987). Debate over emergence of human tooth pattern. *Science, 235,* 749.

Lewin, R. (1987). The earliest "humans" were more like apes. *Science, 236,* 1,062–1,063.

Lewin, R. (1987). Four legs bad, two legs good. *Science, 235,* 969.

Lewin, R. (1987). Why is ape tool use so confusing? *Science, 236,* 776–777.

Lewin, R. (1988). Molecular clocks turn a quarter century. *Science, 235,* 969–971.

Lewin, R. (1993). Paleolithic paint job. *Discover, 14*(7), 64–70.

Lewis, I. M. (1965). Problems in the comparative study of unilineal descent. In M. Banton (Ed.), *The relevance of models for social organization* (A.S.A. Monograph No. 1). London: Tavistock.

Lewis, I. M. (1976). *Social anthropology in perspective.* Harmondsworth, England: Penguin.

Lewis-Williams, J. D. (1990). *Discovering southern African rock art.* Cape Town and Johannesburg: David Philip.

Lewis-Williams, J. D., & Dowson, T. A. (1988). Signs of all times: Entoptic phenomena in Upper Paleolithic art. *Current Anthropology, 29,* 201–245.

Lewis-Williams, J. D., & Dowson, T. A. (1993). On vision and power in the Neolithic: Evidence from the decorated monuments. *Current Anthropology, 34,* 55–65.

Lewis-Williams, J. D., Dowson, T. A., & Deacon, J. (1993). Rock art and changing perceptions of Southern Africa's past: Ezeljagdspoort reviewed. *Antiquity, 67,* 273–291.

Lewontin, R. C. (1972). The apportionment of human diversity. In T. Dobzhansky et al. (Eds.), *Evolutionary biology* (pp. 381–398). New York: Plenum Press.

Lewontin, R. C., Rose, S., & Kamin, L. J. (1984). *Not in our genes.* New York: Pantheon.

Li, X., Harbottle, G., Zhang, J., & Wang, C. (2003).The earliest writing? Sign use in the seventh millennium BC at Jiahu, Henan Province, China. *Antiquity, 77,* 31–44. Ridley, M. (1999). *Genome: The autobiography of a species in 23 chapters* (p. 40). New York: HarperCollins.

Lindenbaum, S. (1978). *Kuru sorcery: Disease and danger in the New Guinea highlands.* New York: McGraw-Hill.

Little, K. (1964). The role of voluntary associations in West African urbanization. In P. van den Berghe (Ed.), *Africa: social problems of change and conflict.* San Francisco: Chandler.

Livingstone, F. B. (1973). The distribution of abnormal hemoglobin genes and their significance for human evolution. In C. Loring Brace & J. Metress (Eds.), *Man in evolutionary perspective.* New York: Wiley.

Lock, M. (2001). *Twice dead: Organ transplants and the reinvention of death.* Berkeley: University of California Press.

Louckey, J., & Carlsen, R. (1991). Massacre in Santiago Atitlán. *Cultural Survival Quarterly, 15*(3), 70.

Lorenzo, C., Carretero, J. M., Arsuaga, J. L., Gracia, A., & Martinez, I. (1998). Intrapopulational body size variation and cranial capacity variation in middle Pleistocene humans: The Sima de los Huesos sample (Sierra de Atapuerca, Spain). *American Journal of Physical Anthropology, 106,* 19–33.

Lounsbury, F. (1964). The structural analysis of kinship semantics. In H. G. Lunt (Ed.), *Proceedings of the Ninth International Congress of Linguists.* The Hague: Mouton.

Lovejoy, C. O. (1981). Origin of man. *Science, 211*(4480), 341–350.

Lowenstein, J. M. (1992, December). Genetic surprises. *Discover 13,* 82–88.

Lowie, R. H. (1948). *Social organization.* New York: Holt, Rinehart & Winston.

Lowie, R. H. (1956). *Crow Indians.* New York: Holt, Rinehart & Winston. (orig. 1935)

Lowie, R. H. (1966). *Culture and ethnology.* New York: Basic Books.

Lustig-Arecco, V. (1975). *Technology strategies for survival.* New York: Holt, Rinehart & Winston.

MacCormack, C. P. (1977). Biological events and cultural control. *Signs, 3,* 93–100.

MacLarnon, A. M., & Hewitt, G. P. (1999). The evolution of human speech: The role of enhanced breathing control. *American Journal of Physical Anthropology, 109,* 341–363.

MacNeish, R. S. (1992). *The origins of agriculture and settled life.* Norman: University of Oklahoma Press.

Mair, L. (1969). *Witchcraft.* New York: McGraw-Hill.

Mair, L. (1971). *Marriage.* Baltimore: Penguin.

Malefijt, A. de W. (1969). *Religion and culture: An introduction to anthropology of religion.* London: Macmillan.

Malefijt, A. de W. (1974). *Images of man.* New York: Knopf.

Malinowski, B. (1922). *Argonauts of the western Pacific.* New York: Dutton.

Malinowski, B. (1945). *The dynamics of culture change.* New Haven, CT: Yale University Press.

Malinowski, B. (1951). *Crime and custom in savage society.* London: Routledge.

Mann, A., Lampl, M, & Monge, J. (1990). Patterns of ontogeny in human evolution: Evidence from dental development. *Yearbook of Physical Anthropology, 33,* 111–150.

Mann, C. C. (2000). Misconduct alleged in Yanomamo studies. *Science, 289,* 2, 253.

Mann C. C. (2002) The real dirt on rainforest fertility. *Science 297,* 920–923.

Marano, L. (1982). Windigo psychosis: The anatomy of an emic-etic confusion. *Current Anthropology, 23,* 385–412.

Marcus, J., & Flannery, K. V. (1996). *Zapotec civilization: How urban society evolved in Mexico's Oaxaca Valley.* New York: Thames & Hudson.

Marks, J. (1995). *Human biodiversity: Genes, race and history.* Hawthorne, NY: Aldine.

Marks, J. (2000, May 12). 98% alike (what our similarity to apes tells us about our understanding of genetics). *Chronicle of Higher Education,* p. B7.

Marks, J. (2002). *What it means to be 98 percent chimpanzee: Apes, people, and their genes.* Berkeley: University of California Press.

Marsella, J. (1982). Pulling it together: Discussion and comments. In S. Pastner & W. A. Haviland (Eds.), *Confronting the creationists.* Northeastern Anthropological Association, Occasiona Proceedings, No. 1, 77–80.

Marshack, A. (1972). *The roots of civilization: A study in prehistoric cognition; the origins of art, symbol and notation.* New York: McGraw-Hill.

Marshack, A. (1976). Some implications of the Paleolithic symbolic evidence for the origin of language. *Current Anthropology, 17*(2), 274–282.

Marshack, A. (1989). Evolution of the human capacity: The symbolic evidence. Yearbook of physical anthropology (Vol. 32, pp. 1–34). New York: Alan R. Liss.

Marshall, L. (1961). Sharing, talking and giving: Relief of social tensions among !Kung bushmen. *Africa, 31,* 231–249.

Marshall, M. (1990). Two tales from the Trukese taproom. In P. R. DeVita (Ed.), *The humbled anthropologist* (pp. 12–17). Belmont, CA: Wadsworth.

Martin, E. (1994). *Flexible bodies: Tracking immunity in American culture-from the days of polio to the age of AIDS.* Boston: Beacon Press.

Martorell, R. (1988). Body size, adaptation, and function. *GDP,* 335–347.

Mascia-Lees, F. E., & Black, N. J. (2000). *Gender and anthropology.* Prospect Heights, IL: Waveland Press.

Mason, J. A. (1957). *The ancient civilizations of Peru.* Baltimore: Penguin.

Matson, F. R. (Ed.). (1965). *Ceramics and man.* New York: Viking Fund Publications in Anthropology, No. 41.

Maybury-Lewis, D. (1960). Parallel descent and the Apinaye anomaly. *Southwestern Journal of Anthropology, 16,* 191–216.

Maybury-Lewis, D. (1984). The prospects for plural societies. *1982 Proceedings of the American Ethnological Society.*

Maybury-Lewis, D. (1993, fall). A new world dilemma: The Indian question in the Americas. *Symbols,* 17–23.

Maybury-Lewis, D. (2001). *Indigenous peoples, ethnic groups, and the state.* (2nd ed.). Boston: Allyn & Bacon.

Maybury-Lewis, D. H. P. (1993). A special sort of pleading. In W. A. Haviland & R. J. Gordon (Eds.), *Talking about people* (pp. 16–24). Mountain View, CA: Mayfield.

McCorriston, J., & Hole, F. (1991). The ecology of seasonal stress and the origins of agriculture inthe Near East. *American Anthropologist, 93,* 46–69.

McDermott, L. (1996). Self-representation in Upper Paleolithic female figurines. *Current Anthropology, 37,* 227–276.

McFee, M. (1972). *Modern Blackfeet: Montanans on a reservation.* New York: Holt, Rinehart & Winston.

McGrew, W. C. (2000). Dental care in chimps. *Science, 288,* 1,747.

McHale, J. (1969). *The future of the future.* New York: Braziller.

McHenry, H. (1975). Fossils and the mosaic nature of human evolution. *Science, 190,* 524–431.

McHenry, H. M. (1992). Body size and proportions in early hominids. *American Journal of Physical Anthropology, 87,* 407–431.

McKenna, J. (1999). Co-sleeping and SIDS. In W. Trevathan, E. O. Smith, & J. J. McKenna (Eds.), *Evolutionary medicine.* London: Oxford University Press.

McKenna, J. J. (2002, September-October). Breastfeeding and bedsharing. *Mothering,* 28–37.

Mead, M. (1928). *Coming of age in Samoa.* New York: Morrow.

Mead, M. (1963). *Sex and temperament in three primitive societies* (3rd ed). New York: Morrow. (orig.1935)

Mead, M. (1970). *Culture and commitment.* Garden City, NY: Natural History Press, Universe Books.

Meadows, D. H., Meadows, D. L., Randers J., & Behrens, III, W. W. (1974). *The limits to growth* New York: Universe Books.

Medicine, B. (1994). Gender, In M. B. Davis (Ed.), *Native America in the twentieth century.* New York: Garland.

Melaart, J. (1967). *Catal Hüyük: A Neolithic town in Anatolia.* London: Thames & Hudson.

Mellars, P. (1989). Major issues in the emergence of modern humans. *Current Anthropology, 30* 356–357.

Meltzer, D., Fowler, D., & Sabloff, J. (Eds.). (1986). *American archaeology: Past & future.* Washington, DC: Smithsonian Institution Press.

Merin, Y. (2002). *Equality for same-sex couples: The legal recognition of gay partnerships Europe and the United States.* Chicago: University of Chicago Press.

Merrell, D. J. (1962). *Evolution and genetics: The modern theory of genetics.* New York: Holt, Rinehart & Winston.

Merriam, A. P. (1964). *The anthropology of music.* Chicago: Northwestern University Press.

Mesghinua, H. M. (1966). Salt mining in Enderta. *Journal of Ethiopian Studies, 4*(2).

Michaels, J. W. (1973). *Dating methods in archaeology.* New York: Seminar Press.

Middleton, J. (Ed.). (1970). *From child to adult: Studies in the anthropology of education.* Garden City, NY: Natural History Press (American Museum Source Books in Anthropology).

Miles, H. L. W. (1993). Language and the orangutan: The old person of the forest. In P. Singer (Ed.), *The great ape project* (p. 46). New York: St. Martin's.

Miller, J. M. A. (2000). Craniofacial variation in *Homo habilis:* An analysis of the evidence for multiple species. *American Journal of Physical Anthropology, 112,* 122.

Millon, R. (1973). *Urbanization of Teotihuacán, Mexico: Vol. 1, Part 1. The Teotihuacán map.* Austin: University of Texas Press.

Mintz, S. (1996). A taste of history. In W. A. Haviland & R. J. Gordon (Eds.), *Talking about people* (2nd ed., pp. 79–82). Mountain View, CA: Mayfield.

Minugh-Purvis, N. (1992). The inhabitants of Ice Age Europe. *Expedition, 34*(3), 23–36.

Mitchell, W. E. (1973, December). A new weapon stirs up old ghosts. *Natural History Magazine,* 77–84.

Mitchell, W. E. (1978). *Mishpokhe: A study of New York City Jewish family clubs.* The Hague: Mouton.

Molnar, S. (1992). *Human variation: Races, types and ethnic groups* (3rd ed.). Englewood Cliffs, NJ: Prentice-Hall.

Montagu, A. (1964). *The concept of race.* London: Macmillan.

Montagu, A. (1964). *Man's most dangerous myth: The fallacy of race* (4th ed.) New York: World Publishing.

Montagu, A. (1975). *Race and IQ.* New York: Oxford University Press.

Moore, J. (1998). Comment. *Current Anthropology, 39,* 412.

Morgan, L. H. (1877). *Ancient society.* New York: World Publishing.

Morse, D., et al. (1979). *Gestures: Their origins and distribution.* New York: Stein & Day.

Moscati, S. (1962). *The face of the ancient orient.* New York: Doubleday.

Mullings, L. (1989). Gender and the application of anthropological knowledge to public policy in the United States. In S. Morgan (Ed.), *Gender and anthropology* (pp. 360–381). Washington, DC: American Anthropological Association.

Murdock, G. (1960). Cognatic forms of social organization. In G. P. Murdock (Ed.), *Social structure in Southeast Asia* (pp. 1–14). Chicago: Quadrangle Books.

Murdock, G. P. (1965). *Social structure.* New York: Free Press.

Murdock, G. P. (1971). How culture changes. In H. L. Shapiro (Ed.), *Man, culture and society* (2nd ed.) New York: Oxford University Press.

Murphy, R. (1971). *The dialectics of social life: Alarms and excursions in anthropological theory.* New York: Basic Books.

Murphy, R., & Kasdan, L. (1959). The structure of parallel cousin marriage. *American Anthropologist, 61,* 17–29.

Murray, G. F. (1989). The domestication of wood in Haiti: A case study in applied evolution. In A. Podolefsky & P. J. Brown (Eds.), *Applying anthropology, an introductory reader.* Mountain View, CA: Mayfield.

Mydens, S. (2001, August 12). He's not hairy, he's my brother. *New York Times,* sec. 4, p. 5.

Myrdal, G. (1974). Challenge to affluence: The emergence of an "under-class." In J. G. Jorgensen & M. Truzzi (Eds.), *Anthropology and American life.* Englewood Cliffs, NJ: Prentice-Hall.

Nader, L. (Ed.). (1965). The ethnography of law, part II. *American Anthropologist, 67*(6).

Nader, L. (Ed.). (1969). *Law in culture and society.* Chicago: Aldine.

Nader, L. (1981, December). [Interview for Coast Telecourses, Inc.]. Los Angeles.

Nader, L. (1997). Controlling processes: Tracing the dynamic components of power. *Current Anthropology, 38,* 714–715.

Nader, L. (2002). *The life of the law: Anthropological projects.* Berkeley: University of California Press.

Nader, L. (Ed.). (1996). *Naked science: Anthropological inquiry into boundaries, power, and knowledge.* New York: Routledge.

Nader, L., & Todd, Jr., H. F. (1978). *The disputing process: Law in ten societies.* New York: Columbia University Press.

Nance, C. R. (1997). Review of Haviland's *Cultural anthropology* (p. 2). [Manuscript in author's possession].

Nanda, S. (1990). *Neither man nor woman: The hijras of India.* Belmont, CA, Wadsworth.

Nanda, S. (1992). Arranging a marriage in India. In P. R. De Vita (Ed.), *The naked anthropologist* (pp. 139–143). Belmont, CA: Wadsworth.

Naroll, R. (1973). Holocultural theory tests. In R. Naroll & F. Naroll (Eds.), *Main currents in cultural anthropology.* New York: Appleton.

Natadecha-Sponsal, P. (1993). The young, the rich and the famous: Individualism as an American cultural value. In P. R. DeVita & J. D. Armstrong (Eds.), *Distant mirrors: America as a foreign culture* (pp. 46–53). Belmont, CA: Wadsworth.

Needham, R. (Ed.). (1971). *Rethinking kinship and marriage.* London: Tavistock.

Needham, R. (1972). *Belief, language and experience.* Chicago: University of Chicago Press.

Neer, R. M. (1975). The evolutionary significance of vitamin D, skin pigment and ultraviolet light. *American Journal of Physical Anthropology, 43,* 409–416.

Nesbitt, L. M. (1935). *Hell-hole of creation.* New York: Knopf.

Netting, R. M., Wilk, R. R., & Arnould, E. J. (Eds.). (1984). *Households: Comparative and historical studies of the domestic group.* Berkeley: University of California Press.

Nettl, B. (1956). *Music in primitive culture.* Cambridge, MA: Harvard University Press.

Newman, P. L. (1965). *Knowing the Gururumba.* New York: Holt, Rinehart & Winston.

Nietschmann, B. (1987). The third world war. *Cultural Survival Quarterly, 11*(3), 1–16.

Norbeck, E., Price-Williams, D., & McCord, W. (Eds.). (1968). *The study of personality: An interdisciplinary appraisal.* New York: Holt, Rinehart & Winston.

Normile, D. (1998). Habitat seen as playing larger role in shaping behavior. *Science, 279,* 1,454.

Nunney, L. (1998). Are we selfish, are we nice, or are we nice because we are selfish? *Science, 281,* 1,619.

Nye, E. I., & Berardo, F. M. (1975). *The family: Its structure and interaction.* New York: Macmillan.

Nye, J. (2002). *The paradox of American power: Why the world's only superpower can't go it alone.* New York: Oxford University Press.

Oakley, K. P. (1964). *Man the tool-maker.* Chicago: University of Chicago Press.

O'Barr, W. M., & Conley, J. M. (1993). When a juror watches a lawyer. In W. A. Haviland & R. J. Gordon (Eds.), *Talking about people* (2nd ed., pp. 44–47). Mountain View, CA: Mayfield.

Oboler, R. S. (1980). Is the female husband a man? Woman/woman marriage among the Nandi of Kenya. *Ethnology, 19,* 69–88.

Offiong, D. (1985). Witchcraft among the Ibibio of Nigeria. In A. C. Lehmann & J. E. Myers (Eds.), *Magic, witchcraft, and religion* (pp. 152–165). Palo Alto, CA: Mayfield.

Okonjo, K. (1976). The dual-sex political system in operation: Igbo women and community politics in midwestern Nigeria. In N. Hafkin & E. Bay (Eds.), *Women in Africa* (pp. 45–58).Stanford, CA: Stanford University Press.

Olszewki, D. I. (1991). Comment. *Current Anthropology, 32,* 43.

O'Mahoney, K. (1970). The salt trade. *Journal of Ethiopian Studies, 8*(2).

Ong, A. (1999). *Flexible citizenship: The cultural logics of transnationality.* Durham, NC: Duke University Press.

Ortiz, A. (1969). *The Tewa world.* Chicago: The University of Chicago Press.

Oswalt, W. H. (1970). *Understanding our culture.* New York: Holt, Rinehart & Winston.

Oswalt, W. H. (1972). *Habitat and technology.* New York: Holt, Rinehart & Winston.

Oswalt, W. H. (1972). *Other peoples other customs: World ethnography and its history.* New York: Holt, Rinehart & Winston.

Otten, C. M. (1971). *Anthropology and art: Readings in cross-cultural aesthetics.* Garden City, NY: Natural History Press.

Otten, M. (2000). On the suggested bone flute from Slovenia. *Current Anthropology, 41,* 271.

Ottenberg, P. (1965). The Afikpo Ibo of eastern Nigeria. In J. L. Gibbs (Ed.), *Peoples of Africa.* New York: Holt, Rinehart & Winston.

Ottenheimer, Martin. (1996). *Forbidden relatives: The American myth of cousin marriage.* Chicago: University of Illinois Press.

Otterbein, K. F. (1971). *The evolution of war.* New Haven, CT: HRAF Press.

Pandian, J. (1991). *Culture, religion, and the sacred self: A critical introduction to the anthropological study of religion.* Englewood Cliffs, NJ: Prentice-Hall.

Parades, J. A., & Purdum, E. J. (1990). Bye bye Ted. . . . *Anthropology Today, 6*(2), 9–11.

Parés, J. M., Perez-Gonzalez, A., Weil, A. B., & Arsuaga, J. L. (2000). On the age of hominid fossils at the Sima de los Huesos, Sierra de Atapuerca, Spain: Paleomagnetic evidence. *American Journal of Physical Anthropology, 111,* 451–461.

Parish, A. R. (1998). Comment. *Current Anthropology, 39,* 413–414.

Parker, R. G. (1991). *Bodies, pleasures, and passions: Sexual culture in contemporary Brazil.* Boston: Beacon Press.

Parker, S., & Parker, H. (1979). The myth of male superiority: Rise and demise. *American Anthropologist, 81*(2), 289–309.

Parkin, R. (1997). *Kinship: An introduction to basic concepts.* Cambridge, MA: Blackwell.

Parnell, R. (1999). Gorilla exposé. *Natural History, 108*(8), 43

Partridge, W. (Ed.). (1984). *Training manual in development anthropology.* Washington, DC: American Anthropological Association.

Pastner, S., & Haviland, W. A. (Eds.). (1982). Confronting the creationists. *Northeastern Anthropological Association Occasional Proceedings, I.*

Patterson, F., & Linden, E. (1981). *The education of Koko.* New York: Holt, Rinehart & Winston.

Patterson, T. C. (1981). *Archeology: The evolution of ancient societies.* Englewood Cliffs, NJ: Prentice-Hall.

Peacock, J. L. (2002). *The anthropological lens: Harsh light, soft focus.* (2nd ed.). New York: Cambridge University Press.

Pease, T. (2000). Taking the third side. *Andover Bulletin,* spring.

Pelliam, A. de, & Burton, F. D. (1976). More on predatory behavior in nonhuman primates. *Current Anthropology, 17*(3), 512–513.

Pelto, G. H., Goodman, A. H., & Dufour, D. L. (Eds.). (2000). *Nutritional anthropology: Biocultural perspectives on food and nutrition.* Mountain View, CA: Mayfield,

Pelto, P. J. (1973). *The snowmobile revolution: Technology and social change in the Arctic.* Menlo Park, CA: Cummings.

Penniman, T. K. (1965). *A hundred years of anthropology.* London: Duckworth.

Peters, C. R. (1979). Toward an ecological model of African Plio-Pleistocene hominid adaptations. *American Anthropologist, 81*(2), 261–278.

Petersen J. B., Neuves, E., & Heckenberger, M. J. (2001). Gift from the past: *Terra preta* and prehistoric American occupation in Amazonia. In C. McEwan and C. Barreo (Eds.) *Unknown Amazon* (pp. 86–105). London: British Museum Press.

Peterson, F. L. (1962). *Ancient Mexico, An introduction to the pre-Hispanic cultures.* New York: Capricorn Books.

Pfeiffer, J. E. (1977). *The emergence of society.* New York: McGraw-Hill.

Pfeiffer, J. E. (1978). *The emergence of man.* New York: Harper & Row.

Pfeiffer, J. E. (1985). *The creative explosion.* Ithaca, NY: Cornell University Press.

Piddocke, S. (1965). The potlatch system of the southern Kwakiutl: A new perspective. *Southwestern Journal of Anthropology, 21,* 244–264.

Piggott, S. (1965). *Ancient Europe.* Chicago: Aldine.

Pilbeam, D. (1987). Rethinking human origins. In *Primate evolution and human origins.* Hawthorne, NY: Aldine.

Pilbeam, D., & Gould, S. J. (1974). Size and scaling in human evolution. *Science, 186,* 892–901.

Pimentel, D. (1991). Response. *Science, 252,* 358.

Pimentel, D., Hurd, L. E., Bellotti, A. C., Forster, M. J., Oka, I. N., Sholes, O. D., & Whitman, R. J. (1973). Food Production and the Energy Crisis. *Science,* 182.

Piperno, D. R., & Fritz, G. J. (1994). On the emergence of agriculture in the new world. *CurrentAnthropology, 35,* 637–643.

Pitt, D. (1977). Comment. *Current Anthropology, 18,* 628.

Pitts, V. (2003). *In the flesh: The cultural politics of body modification.* New York: Palgrave Macmillan.

Plane, A. M. (1996). Putting a face on colonization: Factionalism and gender politics in the life history of Awashunkes, the "Squaw Sachem" of Saconnet. In R. S. Grumet (Ed.), *Northeastern Indian Lives, 1632–1816* (pp.140–175). Amherst: University of Massachusetts Press.

Plattner, S. (1989). Markets and market places. In S. Plattner (Ed.), *Economic anthropology.* Stanford, CA: Stanford University Press.

Podolefsky, A., & Brown, P. J. (Eds.). (1989). *Applying anthropology, an introductory reader.* Mountain View, CA: Mayfield.

Pohl, M. E. D., Pope, K. O., & von Nagy, C. (2002). Olmec Origins of MesoAmerican writing. *Science, 298,* 1,984–1987.

Polanyi, K. (1968). The economy as instituted process. In E. E. LeClair, Jr. & H. K. Schneider (Eds.), *Economic anthropology: readings in theory and analysis* (pp. 122–167). New York: Holt, Rinehart & Winston.

Pope, G. (1989, October). Bamboo and human evolution. *Natural History, 98,* 48–57.

Pope, G. G. (1992). Craniofacial evidence for the origin of modern humans in China. *Yearbook of Physical Anthropology, 35,* 243–298.

Pospisil, L. (1971). *Anthropology of law: A comparative theory.* New York: Harper & Row.

Powdermaker, H. (1966). *Stranger and friend: The way of an anthropologist.* New York: Norton.

Power, M. G. (1995). Gombe revisited: Are chimpanzees violent and hierarchical in the free state? *General Anthropology, 2*(1), 5–9.

Premack, A. J., & Premack, D. (1972). Teaching language to an ape. *Scientific American, 277*(4), 92–99.

Price, T. D., & Feinman, G. M. (Eds.). (1995). *Foundations of social inequality.* New York: Plenam.

Price-Williams, D. R. (Ed.). (1970). *Cross-cultural studies: Selected readings.* Baltimore: Penguin (Penguin Modern Psychology Readings).

Prideaux, T., & the Editors of Time-Life. (1973). *Cro-Magnon man.* New York: Time-Life.

Pringle, H. (1997). Ice Age communities may be earliest known net hunters. *Science, 277,* 1,203 1,204.

Pringle, H. (1998). The slow birth of agriculture. *Science, 282,* 1,446–1,450.

Prins, A. H. J. (1953). *East African class systems.* Groningen, The Netherlands: J. B. Wolters.

Prins, H. E. L. (1996). *The Mi'kmaq: Resistance, accommodation, and cultural survival.* Belmont, CA: Wadsworth/Holt, Rinehart & Winston.

Prins, H. E. L. (1998). Book review of Schuster, C., and Carpenter, E. (1996). *American Anthropologist,100* (3), 841.

Prins, H. E. L. (2002). Visual media and the primitivist perplex: Colonial fantasies, indigenous imagination, and advocacy in North America. In F. D. Ginsburg et al. *Media worlds: Anthropology on new terrain* (pp. 58–74). Berkeley: University of California Press.

Prins, H.E. L., & Carter, K. (1986). *Our lives in our hands.* Video and 16mm. Color. 50 min. Distributed by Watertown, MA: Documentary Educational Resources and Bucksport, ME: Northeast Historic Film.

Profet, M. (1991). The function of allergy: Immunological defense against toxins. *Quarterly Review of Biology, 66*(1), 23–62.

Profet, M. (1995). *Protecting your baby to be.* New York: Addison Wesley.

Puleston, D. E. (1983). *The settlement survey of Tikal.* Philadelphia: University Museum.

Radcliffe-Brown, A. R. (1931). Social Organization of Australian tribes. *Oceania Monographs,* No. 1. Melbourne: Macmillan.

Radcliffe-Brown, A. R., & Forde, C. D. (Eds.). (1950). *African systems of kinship and marriage.* London: Oxford University Press.

Rappaport, R. A. (1969). Ritual regulation of environmental relations among a New Guinea people. In A. P Vayda (Ed.), *Environment and Cultural behavior* (pp. 181–201). Garden City, NY Natural History Press.

Rappaport, R. A. (1984). *Pigs for the ancestors* (Enl. ed.). New Haven, CT: Yale University Press.

Rappaport, R. A. (1994). Commentary. *Anthropology Newsletters, 35*(6), 76.

Rappaport, R. A. (1999). *Holiness and humanity: Ritual in the making of religious life.* New York: Cambridge University Press.

Rathje, W. L. (1974). The garbage project: A new way of looking at the problems of archaeology. *Archaeology, 27,* 236–241.

Rathje, W. L. (1993). Rubbish! In W. A. Haviland & R. J. Gordon (Eds.), *Talking about people: Readings in contemporary cultural anthropology,* Mountain View, CA: Mayfield.

Read, C. E. (1973). *The role of faunal analysis in reconstructing human behavior: A Mousterian example.* Paper presented at the meetings of the California Academy of Sciences, Long Beach.

Read-Martin, C. E., & Read, D. W. (1975). Australopithecine scavenging and human evolution: An approach from faunal analysis. *Current Anthropology, 16*(3), 359–368.

Recer, P. (1998, February 16). *Apes shown to communicate in the wild.* Burlington Free Press, p 12A.

Redfield, R., Linton, R., & Herskovits, M. J. (1936). Memorandum of the study of acculturation. *American Anthropologist, 38,* 149–152.

Redman, C. L. (1978). *The rise of civilization: From early farmers to urban society in the ancient Near East.* San Francisco: Freeman.

Reid, J. J., Schiffer, M. B., & Rathje, W. L. (1975). Behavioral archaeology: Four strategies. *American Anthropologist, 77,* 864–869.

Reina, R. (1966). *The law of the saints.* Indianapolis: Bobbs-Merrill.

Reiter, R. (Ed.). (1975). *Toward an anthropology of women.* New York: Monthly Review Press.

Relethford, J. H. (2001). Absence of regional affinities of Neandertal DNA with living humans does not reject multiregional evolution. *American Journal of Physical Anthropology, 115,* 95–98.

Relethford, J. H., & Harpending, H. C. (1994). Craniometric variation, genetic theory, and modern human origins. *American Journal of Physical Anthropology, 95,* 249–270.

Renfrew, C. (1973). *Before civilization: The radiocarbon revolution and prehistoric Europe.* London: Jonathan Cape.

Reynolds, V. (1994). Primates in the field, primates in the lab. *Anthropology Today, 10*(2), 3–5.

Rice, D. S. & Prudence, M. (1984). Lessons from the Maya. *Latin American Research Review, 19*(3), 7–34.

Rice, P. (2000). Paleoanthropology 2000—part 1. *General Anthropology, 7*(1), 11.

Richmond, B. G., Fleangle, J. K., & Swisher III, C. C. (1998). First Hominoid elbow from the Miocene of Ethiopia and the evolution of the Catarrhine elbow. *American Journal of Physical Anthropology, 105,* 257–277.

Ridley, M. (1999). *Genome, the autobiography of a species in 23 chapters* (p. 142). New York: HarperCollins.

Rightmire, G. P. (1990). *The evolution of Homo erectus: Comparative anatomical studies of an extinct human species.* Cambridge: Cambridge University Press.

Rightmire, G. P. (1998). Evidence from facial morphology for similarity of Asian and African representatives of Homo erectus. *American Journal of Physical Anthropology, 106,* 61–85.

Rindos, D. (1984). *The origins of agriculture: An evolutionary perspective.* Orlando, FL: Academic Press.

Rodman, H. (1968). *Class culture. International encyclopedia of the social sciences* (Vol. 15, pp. 332–337). New York:Macmillan.

Rogers, J. (1994). Levels of the genealogical hierarchy and the problem of hominoid phylogeny. *American Journal of Physical Anthropology, 94,* 81–88.

Romer, A. S. (1945). *Vertebrate paleontology.* Chicago: University of Chicago Press.

Roosevelt, A. C. (1984). Population, health, and the evolution of subsistence: Conclusions from the conference. In M. N. Cohen & G. J. Armelagos (Eds.), *Paleopathology at the origins of agriculture.* Orlando, FL: Academic Press.

Rosas, A., & Bermdez de Castro, J. M. (1998). On the taxonomic affinities of the Dmanisi mandible (Georgia). *American Journal of Physical Anthropology, 107,* 145–162.

Roscoe, P. B. (1995). The perils of "positivism" in cultural anthropology. *American Anthropologist, 97,* 497.

Rowe, T. (1988). New issues for phylogenetics. *Science, 239,* 1,183–1,184.

Ruhlen, M. (1994). *The origin of language: Tracing the evolution of the mother tongue.* New York: Wiley.

Ruvdo, M. (1994). Molecular evolutionary processes and conflicting gene trees: The hominoid case. *American Journal of Physical Anthropology, 94,* 89–113.

Sabloff, J., & Lambert-Karlovsky, C. C. (1973). *Ancient civilization and trade.* Albuquerque: University of New Mexico Press.

Sabloff, J. A. (1989). *The cities of ancient Mexico.* New York: Thomas & Hudson.

Sabloff, J. A., & Lambert-Karlovsky, C. C. (Eds.). (1974). *The rise and fall of civilizations, modern archaeological approaches to ancient cultures.* Menlo Park, CA: Cummings.

Sahlins, M. (1961). The segmentary lineage: An organization of predatory expansion. *American Anthropologist, 63,* 322–343.

Sahlins, M. (1968). *Tribesmen.* Englewood Cliffs, NJ: Prentice-Hall (Foundations of Modern Anthropology).

Sahlins, M. (1972). *Stone age economics.* Chicago: Aldine.

Salthe, S. N. (1972). *Evolutionary biology.* New York: Holt, Rinehart & Winston.

Salzman, P. C. (1967). Political organization among nomadic peoples. Proceedings of the *American Philosophical Society, 3,* 115–131.

Sanday, P. R. (1975). On the causes of IQ differences between groups and implications for social policy. In A. Montagu (Ed.), *Race and IQ.* London: Oxford.

Sanday, P. R. (1981). *Female power and male dominance: On the origins of sexual inequality.* Cambridge: Cambridge University Press.

Sangree, W. H. (1965). The Bantu Tiriki of western Kenya. In J. L. Gibbs (Ed.), *Peoples of Africa.* New York: Holt, Rinehart & Winston.

Sanjek R. (1990). On ethnographic validity. In R. Sanjek (Ed.) *Fieldnotes.* Ithica, New York: Cornell University Press.

Sapir, E. (1921). *Language.* New York: Harcourt.

Savage, J. M. (1969). *Evolution* (3rd ed.). New York: Holt, Rinehart & Winston.

Scaglion, R. (1987). Contemporary law development in Papua New Guinea. In R. M. Wulff & S. J. Fiske (Eds.), *Anthropological praxis: Translating knowledge into action.* Boulder, CO: Westview Press.

Scarr-Salapatek, S. (1971). Unknowns in the IQ equation. *Science, 174,* 1,223–1,228.

Schaller, G. B. (1971). *The year of the gorilla.* New York: Ballantine.

Scheflen, A. E. (1972). *Body language and the social order.* Englewood Cliffs, NJ: Prentice-Hall.

Schepartz, L.A. (1993). Language and human origins. *Yearbook of Physical Anthropology, 36,* 91–126.

Scheper-Hughes, N. (1979). *Saints, scholars and schizophrenics.* Berkeley: University of California Press.

Schlegel, A. (1977). Male and female in Hopi thought and action. In A. Schlegel (Ed.), *Sexual stratification* (pp. 245–269). New York: Columbia University Press.

Schrire, C. (Ed.). (1984). *Past and present in hunter-gatherer studies.* Orlando, FL: Academic Press.

Schurtz, H. (1902). *Alterklassen und Männerbünde.* Berlin: Reimer.

Schusky, E. L. (1975). *Variation in kinship.* New York: Holt, Rinehart & Winston.

Schusky, E. L. (1983). *Manual for kinship analysis* (2nd ed.). Lanham, MD: University Press of America.

Schuster, C., & Edmund Carpenter, E. (1996). *Patterns that connect: Social symbolism inancient & tribal art.* New York: Abrams.

Schwartz, J. H. (1984). Hominoid evolution: A review and a reassessment. *Current Anthropology, 25(5), 655–672.*

Scupin, R. (Ed.). (2000). *Religion and culture: An anthropological focus.* Upper Saddle River, NJ: Prentice-Hall.

Sellen, D.W., & Mace, R. (1997). Fertility and mode of substance: A phylogenetic analysis. *Current Anthropology, 38,* 878–889.

Semenov, S. A. (1964). *Prehistoric technology.* New York: Barnes & Noble.

Sen, G., & Grown, C. (1987). *Development, crisis, and alternative visions: Third World women's perspectives.* New York: Monthly Review Press.

Senut, B., et al. (2001). First hominid from the Miocene (Lukeino formation, Kenya). *C. R. Acad Sci. Paris, 33,*137–144.

Seyfarth, R. M. et al. (1980). Monkey responses to three different alarm calls: Evidence for predator classification and semantic communication. *Science, 210,* 801–803.

Seymour, D. Z. (1986). Black children, black speech. In P. Escholz, A. Rosa & V. Clark (Eds.), *Language Awareness* (4th ed.). New York: St. Martin's Press.

Shapiro, H. (Ed.). (1971). *Man, culture and society* (2nd. ed.). New York: Oxford University Press.

Sharer, R. J., & Ashmore, W. (1993). *Archaeology: Discovering our past* (2nd ed.). Palo Alto,CA: Mayfield.

Sharp, L. (1952). Steel axes for Stone Age Australians. In E. H. Spicer (Ed.), *Human problems in technological change.* New York: Russell Sage.

Shaw, D. G. (1984). A light at the end of the tunnel: Anthropological contributions toward global competence. *Anthropology Newsletter, 25,* 16.

Shearer, R. R. & Gould S. J. (1999) Of two minds and one nature. *Science 286,* 1093.

Sheets, P. (1993). Dawn of a new Stone Age in eye surgery. In R. J. Sharer & W. Ashmore, *Archaeology: Discovering our past* (2nd ed.). Palo Alto, CA: Mayfield.

Shimkin, D. B., Tax, S., & Morrison, J. W. (Eds.). (1978). *Anthropology for the future.* Urbana: Department of Anthropology, University of Illinois, Research Report No. 4.

Shinnie, M. (1970). *Ancient African kingdoms.* New York: New American Library.

Shipman, P. (1981). *Life history of a fossil: An introduction to taphonomy and paleoecology.* Cambridge, MA: Harvard University Press.

Shore, B. (1996). *Culture in mind: Meaning, construction, and cultural cognition.* New York: Oxford University Press.

Shostak, M. (1983). *Nisa: The life and worlds of a !Kung woman.* New York: Vintage.

Shreeve, J. (1994). "Lucy," crucial early human ancestor, finally gets a head. *Science, 264,* 34–35.

Shreeve, J. (1994). Terms of estrangement. *Discover, 15*(11), 56–63.

Shreeve, J. (1995). *The Neandertal enigma.* New York: Morrow.

Shuey, A. M. (1966). *The testing of Negro intelligence.* New York: Social Science Press.

Sillen, A., & Brain, C. K. (1990). Old flame. *Natural History, 4,* 6–10.

Simons, E. L. (1972). *Primate evolution.* New York: Macmillan.

Simons, E. L. (1989) Human origins. *Science 245,* 1,349.

Simons, E. L. (1995). Skulls and anterior teeth of Catopithecus (primates: anthropoidea) from the Eocene and anthropoid origins. *Science, 268,* 1,885–1,888.

Simons, E. L., Rasmussen, D. T., & Gebo, D. L. (1987). A new species of Propliopithecus from the Fayum, Egypt. *American Journal of Physical Anthropology, 73,* 139–147.

Simpson, G. G. (1949). *The meaning of evolution.* New Haven, CT: Yale University Press.

Sjoberg, G. (1960). *The preindustrial city.* New York: Free Press.

Skelton, R. R., McHenry, H. M., & Drawhorn, G. M. (1986). Phylogenetic analysis of early hominids. *Current Anthropology, 27,* 21–43.

Skolnick, A., & Skolnick, J. (Eds.). (2001). *Family in transition* (11th ed.). Boston: Allyn &Bacon.

Slobin, D. I. (1971). *Psycholinguistics.* Glenview, IL: Scott, Foresman.

Small, M. F. (1997). Making connections. *American Scientist, 85,* 503.

Smith, A. H., & Fisher, J. L. (1970). *Anthropology.* Englewood Cliffs, NJ: Prentice-Hall.

Smith, B. D. (1977). Archaeological inference and inductive confirmation. *American Anthropologist, 79*(3), 598–617.

Smith, B. H. (1994). Patterns of dental development in Homo, Australopithecus, Pan, and gorilla. *American Journal of Physical Anthropology, 94,* 307–325.

Smith, F. H., & Raynard, G. C.. (1980). Evolution of the supraorbital region in Upper Pleistocene fossil hominids from South-Central Europe. *American Journal of Physical Anthropology, 53,* 589–610.

Smith, P. E. L. (1976). *Food production and its consequences* (2nd ed.). Menlo Park, CA: Cummings.

Smith, R. (1970). Social stratification in the Caribbean. In L. Plotnicov & A. Tudin (Eds.), *Essays in comparative social stratification.* Pittsburgh: University of Pittsburgh Press.

Smuts, B. (1987). What are friends for? *Natural History. 96*(2), 36–44.

Snowden, C. T. (1990). Language capabilities of nonhuman animals. *Yearbook of Physical Anthropology, 33,* 215–243.

Solomon, R. (2001, February 20). Genome's riddle. *New York Times,* p. D3.

Sparks, J. (2003, December 22). The power game. *Newsweek, 142*(25).

Speck, F. G. (1920). Penobscot shamanism. *Memoirs of the American Anthropological Association, 6,* 239–288.

Speck, F. G. (1935). Penobscot tales and religious beliefs. *Journal of American Folk-Lore, 48*(187), 1–107.

Speck, F. G. (1970). *Penobscot man: The life history of a forest tribe in Maine.* New York: Octagon Books.

Spencer, F., & Smith, F. H. (1981). The significance of Ales Hrdlicka's "Neanderthal phase of man": A historical and current assessment. *American Journal of Physical Anthropology, 56,* 435–459.

Spencer, H. (1896). *Principles of sociology.* New York: Appleton.

Spiro, M. E. (1966). Religion: problems of definition and explanation. In M. Banton (Ed.), *Anthropological approaches to the study of religion* (A.S.A. Monographs). London: Tavistock.

Spitz, R. A. (1949). *Hospitalism. The psychoanalytic study of the child* (Vol. 1). New York: International Universities Press.

Spradley, J. P. (1979). *The ethnographic interview.* New York: Holt, Rinehart &Winston.

Spradley, J. P. (1980). *Participant observation.* New York: Holt, Rinehart & Winston.

Squires, S. (1997). The market research and product industry discovers anthropology. *Anthropology Newsletter, 38*(4), 31.

Stacey, J. (1990). *Brave new families.* New York: Basic Books.

Stahl, A. B. (1984). Hominid dietary selection before fire. *Current Anthropology, 25,* 151–168.

Stanford, C. B. (1998). The social behavior of chimpanzees and bonobos: Empirical evidence and shifting assumptions. *Current Anthropology, 39,* 399–420.

Stanford, C. B. (2001). *Chimpanzee and red colobus: The ecology of predator and prey.* Cambridge, MA: Harvard University Press.

Stanley, S. M. (1979). *Macroevolution.* San Francisco: Freeman.

Stannard, D. E. (1992). *American holocaust.* Oxford: Oxford University Press.

Stanner, W. E. (1968). *Radcliffe-Brown, A. R. International encyclopedia of the social sciences* (Vol. 13). New York: Macmillan.

Steward, J. H. (1972). *Theory of culture change: The methodology of multilinear evolution.* Urbana: University of Illinois Press.

Stewart, D. (1997). Expanding the pie before you divvy it up. *Smithsonian, 28,* 82.

Stiles, D. (1979). Early Acheulean and developed Oldowan. *Current Anthropology, 20*(l), 126–129.

Stiglitz, J.E. (2003). *Globalization and its discontents.* New York: Norton.

Stiles, D. (1992). The hunter-gatherer "revisionist" debate. *Anthropology Today, 8*(2), 13–17.

Stirton, R. A. (1967). *Time, life, and man.* New York: Wiley.

Stocker, T. (1987, spring). A technological mystery resolved. *Invention and Technology,* 64.

Stocking, G. W., Jr. (1968). *Race, culture and evolution: Essays in the history of anthropology.* New York: Free Press.

Stoler, M. (1982). *To tell the truth.* Vermont Visions, 82(3), 3.

Stone, R. (1995). If the mercury soars, so may health hazards. *Science, 267,* 958.

Strasser, B. J. (2003). Who cares about the double helix? Collective memory links the past to the future in science as well as history. *Nature, 422,* 803–804.

Straughan, B. (1996). The secrets of ancient Tiwanaku are benefiting today's Bolivia. In W. A. Haviland & R. J. Gordon (Eds.), *Talking about people* (2nd ed., pp. 76–78). Mountain View, CA: Mayfield.

Straus, W. L., & Cave, A. J. E. (1957). Pathology and the posture of Neanderthal man. *Quarterly Review of Biology, 32.*

Stringer, C. B., & McKie, R. (1996). *African exodus: The origins of modern humanity.* London: Jonathan Cape.

Stuart-MacAdam, P., & Dettwyler, K. A. (Eds.). (1995). *Breastfeeding: Biocultural perspectives.* New York: Aldine.

Suarez-Orozoco, M. M., Spindler, G., & Spindler, L. (1994). *The making of psychological anthropology, II.* Fort Worth, TX: Harcourt Brace.

Sullivan, M. (1999). Chimpanzee hunting habit yield clues about early ancestors. *Chronicle of Higher Education.*

Susman, R. L. (1988). Hand of Paranthropus robustus from Member 1, Swartkrans: Fossil evidence for tool behavior. *Science, 240,* 781–784.

Swadesh, M. (1959). Linguistics as an instrument of prehistory. Southwestern *Journal of Anthropology, 15,* 20–35.

Swaminathan, M. S. (2000). Science in response to basic human needs. *Science, 287,* 425.

Swartz, M. J., Turner, V. W., & Tuden, A. (1966). *Political Anthropology.* Chicago: Aldine.

Swisher III, C. C., Curtis, G. H., Jacob, T., Getty, A. G., Suprijo, A., & Widiasmoro. (1994). Age of the earliest known hominids in Java, Indonesia. *Science, 263,* 1,118–1,121.

Tague, R. G. (1992). Sexual dimorphism in the human bony pelvis, with a consideration of theNeanderthal pelvis from Kebara Cave, Israel. *American Journal of Physical Anthropology, 88,* 1–21.

Tannen, D. (1990). *You just don't understand: Women and men in conversation.* New York: Morrow.

Tapper, M. (1999). *In the blood: sickle-cell anemia and the politics of race.* Philadelphia: University of Pennsylvania Press.

Tax, S. (1953). *Penny capitalism: A Guatemalan Indian economy.* Washington, DC: Smithsonian Institution, Institute of Social Anthropology, Pub. No. 16.

Tax, S. (Ed.). (1962). *Anthropology today: Selections.* Chicago: University of Chicago Press.

Tax, S., Stanley, S., et al. (1975). In honor of Sol Tax. *Current Anthropology. 16,* 507–540.

Taylor, G. (2000). *Castration: Abbreviated history of western manhood* (pp. 38–44, 252–259). New York: Routledge.

Templeton, A. R. (1994). Eve: Hypothesis compatibility versus hypothesis testing. *American Anthropologist, 96*(1), 141–147.

Templeton, A. R. (1995). The "Eve" Hypothesis: A genetic critique and reanalysis. *American Anthropologist 95*(1), 51–72.

Templeton, A. R. (1996). Gene lineages and human evolution. *Science, 272,* 1,363–1,364.

Terashima, H. (1983). Mota and other hunting activities of the Mbuti archers: A socio-ecological study of subsistence technology. *African Studies Monograph* (Kyoto), 3, 71–85.

Thomas, D. H. (1974). *Predicting the past.* New York: Holt, Rinehart & Winston.

Thomas, D. H. (1998). *Archaeology* (3rd ed.). Fort Worth, TX: Harcourt Brace.

Thomas, E. M. (1994). *The tribe of the tiger.* New York: Simon & Schuster.

Thomas, W. L. (Ed.). (1956). *Man's role in changing the face of the earth.* Chicago: University of Chicago Press.

Thompson, S. (1960). *The folktale.* New York: Holt, Rinehart & Winston.

Thomson, K. S. (1997). Natural selection and evolution's smoking gun. *American Scientist, 85,* 516–518.

Thorne, A. G., & Wolpoff, M. D. H. (1981). Regional continuity in Australasian Pleistocene hominid evolution. American *Journal of Physical Anthropology, 55,* 337–349.

Thornhill, N. (1993). Quoted in W. A. Haviland & R. J. Gordon (Eds.), *Talking about people* (p. 127). Mountain View, CA: Mayfield.

Tiffany, S. (Ed.). (1979). *Women in Africa.* St. Albans, VT: Eden Press.

Tobias, P. V. (1980). The natural history of the heliocoidal occlusal plane and its evolution in early Homo. *American Journal of Physical Anthropology, 53,* 173–187.

Tobias, P. V., & von Konigswald, G. H. R. (1964). A comparison between the Olduvai hominines and those of Java and some implications for hominid phylogeny. *Nature, 204,* 515–518.

Togue, R. G. (1992). Sexual dimorphism in the human bony pelvis, with a consideration of the Neanderthal pelvis from Kebara Cave, Israel. *American Journal of Physical Anthropology, 88,* 1–21.

Trevor-Roper, H. (1992). Invention of tradition: The Highland tradition of Scotland. In E. Hobsbawm & T. Ranger (Eds.), *The invention of tradition* (Ch. 2). Cambridge: Cambridge University Press.

Trinkaus, E. (1986). The Neanderthals and modern human origins. *Annual Review of Anthropology, 15,* 197.

Trinkaus, E., & Shipman, P. (1992). *The Neandertals: Changing the image of mankind.* New York: Knopf.

Trouillot, M. R. (2003). *Global transformations: Anthropology and the modern world.* New York: Palgrave Macmillan.

Tuden, A. (1970). Slavery and stratification among the Ila of central Africa. In A. Tuden & L. Plotnicov (Eds.), *Social stratification in Africa.* New York: Free Press.

Tumin, M. M. (1967). *Social stratification: The forms and functions of inequality.* Englewood Cliffs, NJ: Prentice-Hall (Foundations of Modern Sociology).

Turnbull, C. (1983). *Mbuti Pygmies: Change and adaptation.* New York: Holt, Rinehart & Winston.

Turnbull, C. M. (1961). *The forest people.* New York: Simon & Schuster.

Turnbull, C. M. (1983). *The human cycle.* New York: Simon & Schuster.

Turner, T. (1991). Major shift in Brazilian Yanomami policy. *Anthropology Newsletter, 32*(5), 1, 46.

Turner, V. W. (1957). *Schism and continuity in an African society.* Manchester, England: University Press.

Turner, V. W. (1969). *The ritual process.* Chicago: Aldine.

Tylor, E. B. (1871). *Primitive culture: Researches into the development of mythology, philosophy, religion, language, art and customs.* London: Murray.

Tylor, Sir E. B. (1931). Animism. In V. F. Calverton (Ed.), *The making of man: An outline of anthropology.* New York: Modern Library.

Ucko, P. J., & Rosenfeld, A. (1967). *Paleolithic cave art.* New York: McGraw-Hill.

Ucko, P. J., Tringham, R., & Dimbleby, G. W. (Eds.). (1972). *Man, settlement, and urbanism.* London: Duckworth.

Ury, W. L. (1993). *Getting past no: Negotiating your way from confrontation.* New York: Bantum Books.

Ury, W. L. (1999). *Getting to peace: Transforming conflict at home, at work, and in the world.* New York: Viking.

Ury, W. L. (2002). A global immune system. *Andover Bulletin,* winter.

Ury, W. L. (Ed.). (2002). *Must we fight?: From the battlefield to the schoolyard—A new perspective on violent conflict and its prevention.* Hoboken, NJ: Jossey-Bass.

U.S. Department of Commerce, Census Bureau. (2000, January).

Valentine, C. A. (1968). *Culture and poverty.* Chicago: University of Chicago Press.

Van Allen, J. (1979). Sitting on a man: Colonialism and the lost political institutions of Igbo women. In S. Tiffany (Ed.), *Women in society* (pp. 163–187). St. Albans, VT: Eden Press.

Van Den Berghe, P. (1992). The modern state: Nation builder or nation killer? *International Journal of Group Tensions, 22*(3), 191–207.

Van Gennep, A. (1960). *The rites of passage.* Chicago: University of Chicago Press.

Vansina, J. (1965). *Oral tradition: A study in historical methodology* (H. M. Wright, Trans.). Chicago: Aldine.

Van Willigen, J. (1986). *Applied anthropology.* South Hadley, MA: Bergin & Garvey.

Vayda, A. (Ed.). (1969). *Environment and cultural behavior: Ecological studies in cultural anthropology.* Garden City: Natural History Press.

Vayda, A. P. (1961). Expansion and warfare among swidden agriculturalists. *American Anthropologist, 63,* 346–358.

Vincent, J. (1979). On the special division of labor, population, and the origins of agriculture. *Current Anthropology, 20*(2), 422–425.

Vogelman, T. C., et al. (1972). *Prehistoric life in the Champlain Valley* (Film). Burlington, VT: Department of Anthropology, University of Vermont.

Voget, F. W. (1960). Man and culture: An essay in changing anthropological interpretation. *American Anthropologist, 62,* 943–965.

Voget, F. W. (1975). *A history of ethnology.* New York, Holt, Rinehart & Winston.

Vogt, E. Z. (1990). *The Zinacantecos of Mexico, a modern way of life* (2nd ed.). New York: Holt, Rinehart & Winston.

Wagner, P. L. (1960). *A history of ethnology.* New York: Holt, Rinehart & Winston.

Wallace, A. F. C. (1956). Revitalization movements. *American Anthropologist, 58,* 264–281.

Wallace, A. F. C. (1965). The problem of the psychological validity of componential analysis. *American Anthropologist, Special Publication (Part 2), 67*(5), 229–248.

Wallace, A. F. C. (1966). *Religion: An anthropological view.* New York: Random House.

Wallace, A. F. C. (1970). *Culture and personality* (2nd ed.). New York: Random House.

Wallace, E., & Hoebel, E. A. (1952). *The Comanches.* Norman: University of Oklahoma Press.

Ward, C. V., Walker, A., Teaford, M. F., & Odhiambo, I. (1993). Partial skeleton of Proconsul nyanzae from Mfangano Island, Kenya. *American Journal of Physical Anthropology, 90,* 77–111.

Wardhaugh, R. (1972). *Introduction to linguistics.* New York: McGraw-Hill.

Wattenberg, B. J. (1997, November 23). The population explosion is over. New York *Times Magazine,* p. 60.

Washburn, S. L., & Moore, R. (1980). *Ape into human: A study of human evolution* (2nd ed.). Boston: Little, Brown.

Weatherford, J. (1988). *Indian givers: How the Indians of the Americas transformed the world.* New York: Fawcett Columbine.

Weaver, M. P. (1972). *The Aztecs, Maya and their predecessors.* New York: Seminar Press.

Weiner, A. B. (1977). Review of Trobriand cricket: An ingenious response to colonialism. *American Anthropologist, 79,* 506.

Weiner, A. B. (1988). *The Trobrianders of Papua New Guinea.* New York: Holt, Rinehart & Winston.

Weiner, J. S. (1955). *The Piltdown forgery.* Oxford: Oxford University Press.

Weiner, M. (1966). *Modernization: The dynamics of growth.* New York: Basic Books.

Weiss, M. L., & Mann, A. E. (1990). *Human biology and behavior* (5th ed.). Boston: Little, Brown.

Weitzman, L. J. (1985). *The divorce revolution: The unexpected social and economic consequences for women and children in America.* New York: Free Press.

Werner, D. (1990). *Amazon journey.* Englewood Cliffs, NJ: Prentice-Hall.

Wernick, R., & the Editors of Time-Life. (1973). *The Monument Builders.* New York: Time-Life.

Westermarck, E. A. (1926). *A short history of marriage.* New York: Macmillan.

Wheeler, P. (1993). Human ancestors walked tall, stayed cool. *Natural History, 102*(8), 65–66.

Whelehan, P. (1985). Review of Incest, A Biosocial View. *American Anthropologist, 87,* 677–678.

White, D. R. (1988). Rethinking polygyny: Co-wives, codes and cultural systems. *Current Anthropology, 29,* 529–572.

White, E., Brown, D., & the Editors of Time-Life. (1973). *The first men.* New York: Time-Life.

White, L. (1949). *The science of culture: A study of man and civilization.* New York: Farrar, Strauss.

White, L. (1959). *The evolution of culture: The development of civilization to the fall of Rome.* New York: McGraw-Hill.

White, M. (2001). *Historical atlas of the twentieth century. http://users.erols.com/mwhite28/20centry.htm*

White, M. (2001). Historical atlas of the twentieth century. *http://users.erols.com/mwhite28/20centry.htm.*

White, P. (1976). *The past is human* (2nd ed.). New York: Maplinger.

White, R. (1992). The earliest images: Ice Age "art" in Europe. *Expedition, 34*(3), 37–51.

White, T., Asfaw, B., Degusta, D., Gilbert, H., Richards, G., Suwa, G., Howell, F. C. (2003). Pleistocene Homo sapiens from the Middle Awash, Ethiopia. *Nature, 423,* 742–747.

White, T. D. (1979). Evolutionary implications of Pliocene hominid footprints. *Science, 208,* 175–176.

White, T. D. (2003). Early hominids—diversity or distortion? *Science, 299,* 1,994–1,997.

White, T. D., & Toth, N. (2000). Cutmarks on a Plio-Pleistocene hominid from Sterkfontein, South Africa. *American Journal of Physical Anthropology, 111,* 579–584.

Whitehead, N., & Ferguson, R. B. (Eds.). (1992). *War in the tribal zone.* Santa Fe: School of American Research Press.

Whitehead, N. L., & Ferguson, R. B. (1993, November 10). Deceptive stereotypes about tribal warfare. *Chronicle of Higher Education,* p. A48.

Whiting, B. B. (Ed.). (1963). *Six cultures: Studies of child rearing.* New York: Wiley.

Whiting, J. W. M., & Child, I. L. (1953). *Child training and personality: A cross-cultural study.* New Haven, CT: Yale University Press.

Whiting, J. W. M., Sodergem, J. A., & Stigler, S. M. (1982). Winter temperature as a constraint to the migration of preindustrial peoples. *American Anthropologist, 84,* 289.

Wilk, R. R. (1996). *Economics and cultures: An introduction to economic anthropology.* Boulder, CO: Westview Press.

Willey, G. R. (1966). *An introduction to American archaeology: Vol. 1. North America.* Englewood Cliffs, NJ: Prentice-Hall.

Willey, G. R. (1971). *An introduction to American archaeology, Vol. 2: South America.* Englewood Cliffs, NJ: Prentice-Hall.

Williams, A. M. (1996). *Sex, drugs and HIV: A sociocultural analysis of two groups of gay and bisexual male substance users who practice unprotected sex.* Unpublished manuscript.

Williamson, R. K. (1995). The blessed curse: Spirituality and sexual difference as viewed by Euro-American and Native American cultures. *The College News, 17*(4).

Willigan, J. V. (1986). *Applied anthropology* (pp. 128–129, 133–139). South Hadley, MA: Bergin & Garvey.

Wills, C. (1994). The skin we're in. *Discover, 15*(11), 77–81.

Wilson, A. K., & Sarich, V. M. (1969). A molecular time scale for human evolution. *Proceedings of the National Academy of Science, 63,* 1,089–1,093.

Wingert, P. (1965). *Primitive art: Its tradition and styles.* New York: World.

Winick, C, (Ed.). (1970). *Dictionary of anthropology* (p. 202). Totowa, NJ: Littlefield, Adams.

Wirsing, R. L. (1985). The health of traditional societies and the effects of acculturation. *Current Anthropology 26*(3), 303–322.

Wittfogel, K. A. (1957). *Oriental despotism, a comparative study of total power.* New Haven, CT: Yale University Press.

Wolf, E. R. (1959). *Sons of the shaking earth.* Chicago: University of Chicago Press.

Wolf, E. R. (1966). *Peasants.* Englewood Cliffs, NJ: Prentice-Hall.

Wolf, E. R. (1982). *Europe and the people without history.* Berkeley: University of California Press.

Wolf, E. R. (1999). *Envisioning power: Ideologies of dominance and crisis* (p. 263). Berkeley: University of California Press.

Wolf, M. (1972). *Women and the family in rural Taiwan.* Stanford, CA: Stanford University Press.

Wolf, M. (1985). *Revolution postponed: Women in contemporary China.* Stanford, CA: Stanford University Press.

Wolpoff, M. H. (1971). Interstitial wear. *American Journal of Physical Anthropology, 34,* 205–227.

Wolpoff, M. H. (1977). Review of earliest man in the Lake Rudolf Basin. *American Anthropologist, 79,* 708-711.

Wolpoff, M. H. (1982). Ramapithecus and hominid origins. *Current Anthropology, 23,* 501–522.

Wolpoff, M.H. (1993). Evolution in Homo erectus: The question of stasis. In R. L. Ciochon & J. G. Fleagle (Eds.), *The human evolution source book.* Englewood Cliffs, NJ: Prentice-Hall.

Wolpoff, M. H. (1993). Multiregional evolution: The fossil alternative to Eden. In R. L. Ciochon & J. G. Fleagle (Eds.), *The human evolution source book.* Englewood Cliffs, NJ: Prentice-Hall.

Wolpoff, M. (1996). Australopithecus: A new look at an old ancestor. *General Anthropology, 3*(1), 2.

Wolpoff, M. & Caspari, R. (1997). *Race and human evolution.* New York: Simon & Schuster.

Wolpoff, M. H., Wu, X. Z. & Thorne, A. G. (1984). Modern *Homo sapiens* origins: a general theory of hominid evolution involving fossil evidence from east Asia. In F. H. Smith and F. Spencer (Eds.), *The origins of modern humans.* New York: Alan R. Liss pp. 411–483.

Womack, M. (1994). Program 5: *Psychological anthropology. Faces of culture.* Fountain Valley, CA: Coast Telecourses, Inc.

Wong, K. (1998, January). Ancestral quandary: Neanderthals not our ancestors? Not so fast. *Scientific American, 30–32.*

Wood, B., & Aiello, L. C. (1998). Taxonomic and functional implications of mandibular scaling in early hominines. *American Journal of Physical Anthropology, 105,* 523–538.

Wood, B., Wood, C., & Konigsberg, L. (1994). Paranthropus boisei: An example of evolutionary stasis? *American Journal of Physical Anthropology, 95,* 117–136.

Woodward, V. (1992). *Human heredity and society.* St. Paul, MN: West.

Woolfson, P. (1972). Language, thought, and culture. In V. P. Clark, P. A. Escholz, & A. F. Rosa (Eds.), *Language.* New York: St. Martin's Press.

World Bank. (1982). *Tribal peoples and economic development.* Washington, DC: World Bank.

World Bank. (2003). *www.worldbank.org/poverty.* Accessed January 2003.

World Health Organization. *http://www.who.int/about/definition/en/.*

World Meterological Organization. (2003). Quoted in Increasing heatwaves and other health hazards. Accessed December, 10, 2003, at *greenpeaceusa.org/climatge/index.fpl/7096/article/907.html.*

Wright, R. (1984). Towards a new Indian policy in Brazil. *Cultural Survival Quarterly 8*(1).

Wright, R. M. (1997). Violence on Indian day in Brazil 1997: Symbol of the past and future. *Cultural Survival Quarterly, 21* (2), 47–49.

Wulff, R. M., & Fiske, S. J. (1987). *Anthropological praxis: Translating knowledge into action.* Boulder, CO: Westview Press.

Yip, M. (2002). *Tone.* New York: Cambridge University Press.

Young, A. (1981). The creation of medical knowledge: Some problems in interpretation. *Social Science and Medicine, 17,*1,205–1,211.

Zeder, M. A., & Hesse, B. (2000). The initial domestication of goats (*Capra hircus*) in the Zagros Mountains 10,000 years ago. *Science, 287,* 2,254–2,257.

Zilhão, J. (2000). Fate of the Neandertals. *Archaeology, 53*(4), 30.

Zimmer, C. (1999). New date for the dawn of dream time. *Science, 284,* 1,243.

Zohary, D., & Hopf, M. (1993). *Domestication of plants in the Old World* (2nd ed.). Oxford: Clarenden Press.

Zur, J. (1994). The psychological impact of impunity. *Anthropology Today, 10*(3), 12–17.

Photo Credits

2 © Sandi Fellman 1984; **3** Scala/Art Resource, NY; **4** (top left) © Anup and Manoj Shah; **4** (top) © Jodi Cobb/National Geographic Image Collection; **4** (middle) © James L. Stanfield/National Geographic Image Collection; **4** (bottom) © George H. H. Huey/Corbis; **7** Documentary Educational Resources; **8** (left) Smithsonian Institution Photo No. 56196; **8** (middle) AP/Wide World Photos; **9** (left) © Michael Newman/PhotoEdit; **9** (right) © Maria Stenzel/National Geographic Image Collection; **11** © 1998 Jim Leachman; **12** (left) © Susan Meiselas/Magnum Photos; **12** (right) © Rich Press; **13** U.S. General Services Administration; **15** (left) © Rhoda Sidney/PhotoEdit; **15** (middle) © Laura Dwight/PhotoEdit; **15** (right) © Bruce Broce; 16 Kerry Culllinan; **19** (left) © Mark Richards/PhotoEdit; **19** (right) © Sarah Wesch; **21** (top left) © Bettmann/Corbis; **21** (top middle) The Granger Collection, New York; **21** (top right) Culver Pictures; **21** (bottom right) © Anita Haviland; **25** (right) © Henry S. Hamlin; **25** (left) © Joyce Choo/Corbis; **26** (left) © Gordon Gahan/National Geographic Image Collection; **26** (right) Wartenberg/Picture Press/Corbis; **27** © Alden Pellett/The Image Works; **28** © Patrick Barth/Getty Images; **30** © Andrew Syred/Photo Researchers, Inc.; **33** Art Resource, NY; **34** (left) © Michael J. Doolittle/The Image Works; **34** (right) © Morgan/Anthro-Photo; **35** (top left) © Cleo Freelana Photos/PhotoEdit; **35** (top right) © Colin Milkins, Oxford Scientific Films/Animals, Animals; **35** (bottom left) AP/Wide World Photos; **37** © Karel Havlicek/National Geographic Image Collection; **39** © Biophoto Associates/Photo Researchers; **40** © Miriam Chua, 2000; **43** Courtesy of Rayna Rapp; **44** © Meckes/Ottawa/Photo Researchers, Inc.; **45** Richard H. Marks; **47** 'X-MEN' © 2000 Twentieth Century Fox. All rights reserved.; **48** AP/Wide World Photos; **49** (top left) © Corbis Sygma; **49** (top right) American Museum of Natural History; **49** (bottom) © Bob Daemmrich/The Image Works; **51** © Camille Tokerud/Getty Images; **52** (left) © George D. Lepp/Corbis; **52** (right) © Terry W. Eggers/Corbis; **54** Otorohanga Zoological Society; **58** © Austin J. Stevens/Animals Animals; **61** © McGuire/Anthro-Photo; **62** (left) © Dani/Jeske/Animals Animals; **62** (right) © David Harring/OSF/Animals Animals; **63** © James Moore/Anthro-Photo; **65** © A. Walker/Anthro-Photo; **66** (left) © Irven DeVore/Anthro-Photo; **66** (right) Columbia/The Kobal Collection; **69** (top left) © Jeff Greenberg/Photo Researchers, Inc.; **69** (top right) © D. Chivers/Anthro-Photo **69** (bottom left) © Reuters/Getty Images; **70** (left) © Michael K. Nichols/National Geographic Image Collection; **70** (right) © Bromhall/Animals Animals; **71** (left) © Jean-Gerard Sidaner/Photo Researchers, Inc.; **71** (right) © Corbis. All Rights Reserved; **73** (top) © S. Blaffer Hrdy/Anthro-Photo; **73** (bottom) © Michael Dick/Animals Animals; **74** © J. Pickering/Anthro-Photo; **75** (left) © Mickey Gibson/Animals Animals; **75** (right) Illustration from Curious George by H. A. Rey. Copyright © 1941, and renewed 1969 by H. A. Rey. Copyright assigned to Houghton Mifflin Company in 1993. Reprinted by permission of Houghton Mifflin Company. All rights reserved; **76** (top left) © PA/Topham/The Image Works; **76** (top right) © Peter Drowne/Color-Pic, Inc.; **76** (bottom left) © Michael K. Nichols/National Geographic Image Collection; **77** © M. Colbeck/OSF/Animals Animals; **79** © Amy Parish/Anthro-Photo; **81** (top left) © Anita de Laguna Haviland; **81** (top right) © Anita de Laguna Haviland; **81** (bottom left) © Zig Leszczynski/Animals Animals; **82** left) © Irven DeVore/Anthro-Photo; **82** (middle) Courtesy Bunataro Imanishi; **85** Photo by Ulli Bonnekamp. Courtesy of Dr. Shirley Strum; **86** © Bromhall/Animals Animals; **90** University of Pennsylvania Museum; **91** © Bojan Brecelj/Corbis; **92** © Javier Trueba/Madrid Scientific Films; **95** AP/Wide World Photos; **97** Courtesy of Glenn Sheehan and Anne Jensen; **99** © 1985 David L. Brill; **100** (top) © G. Gorgoni/eStock Photo; **100** (bottom) © Mike Andrews/Ancient Art & Architecture Collection; **101** © James B. Petersen, Dept. of Anthropology, University of Vermont; **102** AP/Wide World Photos; **105** both © William A. Haviland; **106** Reprinted with permission from Kuttruff et al, Science 281, 73 (1998) fig. 1. Copyright 1998 American Association for the Advancement of Science; **107** From *Tikal, A Handbook of the Ancient Maya Ruins* by William R. Coe. University of Pennsylvania Museum, Philadelphia 1967; **108** (left) © Andrew Lawler/Science Magazine **108** (right) © Christophe Calais/In Visu/Corbis; **109** © 2001 David L. Brill\Brill Atlanta **110** © Kenneth Garrett/National Geographic Image Collection; **112** University of Pennsylvania Museum; **114** (left) © Macduff Everton/Corbis; **114** (right) © Royalty-Free/Corbis **115** © Kenneth Garrett/National Geographic Image Collection; **118** Russel L. Ciochon, University of Iowa; **121** (top) © 1999 Don Couch Photography; **121** (bottom) © Oliver Meckes/Photo Researchers; **122** (top left) © David Bygott/Kibuyu Partners; **122** (top right) © Donna Day/Corbis; **122** (bottom) © Gianni Dagli Orti/Corbis; **125** (left) © Wolfgang Kaehler/Corbis; **125** (right) © Pete Saloutos/Corbis; **127** The Kobal Collection/Hammer; **128** © Anita de Laguna Haviland; **129** © Martin Harvey; **130** Illustration by Nancy J. Perkins, Carnegie Museum of Natural History; **131** (left) © E. L. Simons/Duke Primate Center; **131** (right) © Sergio Pitzmitz/Corbis; **132** (left) © Ollie Ellison/Duke University; **133** (top) Courtesy of PETA; **133** (bottom) © 1985 David L. Brill; **135** Art Resource, NY; **136** (top left) Courtesy of Mrs. Leona Wilson, photo by Jan Sheer; **136** (bottom right) © 1985 David L. Brill; artifact credit, Peabody Museum, Harvard University; **137** © Anup and Manoj Shah; **139** (left) © Michel Brunet; **139** (right) © Marc Deville/GAMMA; **142** © Andrew Hill/Anthro-Photo; **144** AP/Wide World Photos; **145** (left) Mary Evans Picture Library; **145** (right) © The Geological Society/NHMPL; **146** © Kenneth Garrett/National Geographic Image Collection; **147** © Dr. Fred Spoor/National Museums of Kenya; **151** (top) © George F. Mobley/National Georgrahic Image Collection; **151** (bottom left) © Gregory Manchess, 2004; **151** (bottom right) © 1994 Tim O. White/David L. Brill, Atlanta; **152** © Melville Bell Grosvenor/National Geographic Image Collection; **153** 1985 David L. Brill by permission of Owen Lovejoy; **156** (left) © 1985 David L. Brill; **156** (right) © 1985 David L. Brill; **157** (top) © 1998 David L. Brill/Brill Atlanta; **157** (bottom) © National Museums of Kenya; **160** Photo by Dr. Rose Sevcik. Courtesy of The Language Research Center, Georgia State University; **161** © John Giustina; **162** (left) © Dennis MacDonald/PhotoEdit; **162** (right) © Suzanne Arms/The Image Works; **163** © Michael Nichols/National Geographic Image Collection; **165** © James Cotier/Getty Images; **168** AP/Wide World Photos; **169** © John-Marshall Mantel/Corbis; **170** © 1999 David L. Brill; **175** both © 1985 David L. Brill; **178** Artifact credit: National Museum of Ethiopia. Photo credit: © 1999 David L. Brill; **179** all David L. Brill, copyright © The National Geographic Society; **180** © r. r. jones; **181** The Field Museum, negative number A102513c; **182** Fossil Credit: National Museum of Ethiopia, Addis Ababa. Photo credit: © 1999 David L. Brill; **183** © Tom Brown; **184** (top) © 1993 Mary Ann Fittipaldi; **184** (bottom) © William A. Haviland; **185** © J & B Photo/Animals, Animals; **186** © E. R. Degginger/Color-Pic, Inc.; **190** © Russell L. Ciochon, University of Iowa; **192** Negative No. A11. Courtesy Department of Library Sciences, American Museum of Natural History; **194** © Russell Ciochon, University of Iowa; **196** (left) Transparency No. 626. Courtesy Department of Library Sciences, American Museum of Natural History; **196** (right) © 1985 David L. Brill; artifact credit, National Museum of Kenya, Niarobi;

197 (top) National Museums of Kenya; **197** (bottom) © Antoine Devouard/REA/Corbis SABA; **198** Courtesy of Dr. Phillip V. Tobias, South Africa; **199** (top) © John Reader/Photo Researchers; **200** (top) Negative No. 335658. Courtesy Department of Library Sciences, American Museum of Natural History; **200** (middle) Courtesy of Dr. Xinzhi Wu; **201** © Kenneth Garrett/National Geographic Image Collection; **202** (left) © R. Potts, Smithsonian Institution; **202** (right) © 1988 David L. Brill/Brill Atlanta; **204** © Michael S. Yamashita/Corbis; **206** Geoffrey G. Pope, Anthropology Department, The William Paterson College of New Jersey; **208** © Gusto/Photo Researchers; **209** © Kenneth Garrett/National Geographic Image Collection; **210** © Alexander Marshack; **214** © Gianni Dagli Orti/Corbis; **217** (top) © Javier Trueba/Madrid Scientific Films; **217** (bottom right) Zhou Guoxing, Beijing Natural History Museum; **217** (bottom left) AP/Wide World Photos; **218** © PhotoDisc/Getty Images ; **219** (left) © Bettmann/Corbis; **219** (right) The Field Museum, negative number A111668c, Photographer John Weinstein; **221** ©1985 David L. Brill; **222** Paul Jaronski, UM Photo Services. Karen Diane Harvey, Sculptor; **223** © 1995 David L. Brill; **224** © Photo Researchers; **225** (left) © Erik Trinkaus; **225** (right) © Kenneth Garrett/National Geographic Image Collection; **226** (top) © Brian Concannon; **226** (bottom) Courtesy Professor Ralph Solecki; **227** (top) © Alexander Marshack, New York University; **227** (bottom) Neandertal flute/University of Liege. Courtesy of Marcel Otte; **230** (top) © Milford H. Wolpoff; **230** (bottom) © SPL/Photo Researchers; **231** (top) Photo © 1998 David L. Brill/Brill Atlanta; **231** (bottom) © 2001 David L. Brill /Brill Atlanta; **232** From Newsweek 1/11/1988 © 1988 Newsweek Inc. Reprinted by permission. Artwork © 1988 Braldt Bralds; **234** Courtesy of Dana Walrath; **236** Qafzeh archives & and Dr. B. Vandermeersch. Courtesy of Dr. Ofer Bar-Yosef; **237** © Michael Coyne/Getty Images; **240** © John Van Hasselt/Corbis Sygma; **243** (top left) © 1985 David L. Brill; artifact credit, Musee De L'Homme, Paris; **243** (top right) Artifact Credit: Original housed in Musee De L'Homme, Paris © David L. Brill; **243** (bottom) Jonesfilm/Warner Bros/The Kobal Collection; **245** (top left) © Gianni Dagli Orti/Corbis; **245** (top right) Artifact credit: Musee National de Prehistoire, Les Eyzies de Tayac. © 1985 David L. Brill; **245** (bottom) Courtesy Andrew Majorsky; **246** Negative No. K15806. Courtesy Department of Library Services, American Museum of Natural History; **247** (both) © William A. Haviland/UVM Photo Service; **248** (left) © Alexander Marshack, 1997; **248** (right Erich Lessing/Art Resource, NY; **249** (top) © Anthony Bannister; Gallo Images/Corbis; **249** (bottom) Image of Venus Figurine and human female figure in "Self-Representation in Upper Paleolithic Female Figurines" in Current Anthropology, Vol. 37(s), April 1996. Courtesy of Dr. LeRoy McDermott; **250** (top) Courtesy of Theresa Babineau; **250** (bottom) Negative No. K15823. Courtesy Department of Library Services, American Museum of Natural History; **251** © Jean Vertut; **252** Musée National de Préhistoire, Les Eyzie-de-Tayac, Dordogne, France; **253** (top) © Randall White; **253** (bottom) © Claudio Vazquez; **254** © Göran Burenhult; **255** Don Johanson, Institute Of Human Origins; **257** (top) Joe Ben Wheat Photo, University of Colorado Museum, Boulder; **257** (bottom) Peabody Museum; **258** Jose Zilhao © Instituto Portugues Arqueologia; **262** Erich Lessing/Art Resource, NY; **263** © Staffan Widstrand/Corbis; **264** © Keystone/The Image Works; **266** © Photo Researchers, Inc.; **267** © Daniel Lieberman/Anthro-Photo; **268** William A. Haviland; **269** (both) Dr. W. van Zeist, Biologisch-Archaeologisch Institut, Rijksuniversiteit Gronigen; **270** Illustration by W. C. Galinat. Reprinted with permission from W. C. Galinat, "The origin of maize: grain of humanity," Economic Botany Vol. 49, pp. 3–12, fig. 2A-C, copyright 1995, The New York Botanical Garden; **271** © Liba Taylor/Corbis; **273** AP/Wide World Photos; **274** Courtesy of the Oriental Institute of the University of Chicago; **275** © Mark Richards/PhotoEdit; **276** © Craig Lovell/Corbis; **277** © Anders Ryman/Corbis; **278** © Harvey Finkle; **279** © Bettmann/Corbis; **281** (left) © Irvin DeVore/Anthro-Photo; **281** (right) © Visum/Timm Rautert/The Image Works; **282** (both) British School of Archaeology in Jerusalem; **283** Ankara Archaeological Museum /Ara Guler, Istanbul; **284** © John Kegan/Getty Images; **285** (both) Alan H. Goodman, Hampshire College; **286** © Polak Matt/Corbis Sygma; **287** © Sepp Seitz/Woodfin Camp & Associates; **290** © David Agee/Anthro-Photo; **292** AP/Wide World Photos; **294** © Arlette Mellaart; **295** (left) William A. Haviland; **295** (right) © Tom Ives/Corbis; **296** (both) William A. Haviland; **297** (top) William A. Haviland; **297** (bottom) © Enrico Ferorelli; **298** © Anita de Laguna Haviland; **299** The University Museum, University of Pennsylvania (neg. #T4-398); **300** (top) Ban Chiang Project, Courtesy of The University of Pennsylvania Museum; **300** (bottom) Negative No. 330878. Courtesy Department of Library Sciences, American Museum of Natural History; **301** (top) © Ronald Sheridan/Ancient Art & Architecture Collection; **301** (bottom) © Robert Holmes/Corbis; **302** Rolex Awards for Enterprise, Susan Gray; **303** © Getty Images; **306** Cultural Relics Bureau, Beijing; **307** (both) Dr. Christopher B. Donnan/UCLA Fowler Museum of Cultural History; **308** (top, middle, bottom left) Dr. Christopher B. Donnan/UCLA Fowler Museum of Cultural History; **308** (bottom right) Studied by Duccio Bonavia, reproduction by Gonzalo de Reparaz, Painting by Felix Caycho; **310** (top left) © Anita de Laguna Haviland; **310** (top right) William A. Haviland **310** (bottom) © Heather Angel/Natural Visions; **312** © Victor R. Boswell/National Geographic Image Collection; **314** © Paul Almasy/Corbis; **315** (left) © Wesley Bocxe/Photo Researchers, Inc.; **315** (right) © Lester Lefkowitz/Corbis; **318** © Peter Turnley/Corbis; **322** photo by R. R. Grinker; **323** AP/Wide World Photos; **326** (left) Wadsworth Publishing; **326** (middle) © Laurence Dutton/Getty Images; **326** (right) Wadsworth Publishing; **327** © Kit Kittle/Corbis; **328** © Jehad Nga/Corbis; **329** AP/Wide World Photos; 330 © Steve Elmore; **331** (left) T. L. and S. T. Garber. 1940. Stedman's Practical Medical Dictionary. 14th Ed. Baltimore, MD: Williams and Wilkins Company. Page 827; **332** (left) Royal Anthropological Institute Photographic Collection; **332** (right) © Vittoriano Rastelli/Corbis; **333** (left) Photo © Dinodia Photo Library; **333** (right) © A. Ramey/PhotoEdit; **335** © Bettmann/Corbis; **336** (both) AP/Wide World Photos; **338** © Susan Van Etten/PhotoEdit; **339** From E. A. Guillette, et. al., "An Anthropological Approach to the Evaluation of Preschool Children Exposed to Pesticides in Mexico," Environmental Perspectives, 106 (6), 347–53. Courtesy of Dr. Elizabeth A. Guillette; **340** AP/Wide World Photos; **344** © Sean Sprague/The Image Works; **346** © Sygma/Corbis; **347** © (left) Troham/The Image Works; **347** (right) © Ronnie Kaufman/Corbis; **348** © Peter Turney/Corbis; **349** © Barry Lewis/Corbis; **351** Permission of Waveland Press from *Dancing Skeletons;* **353** (top left) Notre Dame Media Group; **353** (top right) © Barry Lewis/Corbis; **353** (bottom) The Smithsonian Institution Photo No.8304; **355** Time Life Pictures/Getty Images; **356** (top left) © Martha Stewart; **356** (middle) Courtesy Robert T. Jackson; **357** Travis Jenkins; **358** Courtesy of Shirley Lindenbaum; **359** (left) © AP/Wide World Photos; **359** (right) © AP/Wide World Photos; **360** AP/Wide World Photos; **361** (left) © Annebicque Bernard/Corbis Sygma; **361** (right) © Kilcullen/Trocaire/Corbis Sygma; **362** © Tony Freeman/PhotoEdit; **363** AP/Wide World Photos; **364** © Chuck Nacke/Woodfin Camp & Associates; **366** (top left) © Reuters/Corbis; **366** (top right) Amnesty International; **366** (middle) AP/Wide World Photos; **366** (bottom) AP/Wide World Photos.

Index